Mark Whittaker worked for many years as a crime and investigative reporter and feature writer at News Limited and *The Australian Magazine*. He has authored and co-authored numerous books and now works as a freelance writer based in Berry, NSW.

In a career spanning 35 years, Les Kennedy covered some of Australia's most infamous cases for the *Daily Telegraph*, *Sydney Morning Herald* and *Sun Herald*. Les died in 2011 aged 53. The Kennedy Awards for excellence in NSW journalism live on in his honour.

SINS OF THE BROTHER

The definitive story of Ivan Milat
and the backpacker murders

MARK WHITTAKER
& LES KENNEDY

PAN
Pan Macmillan Australia

First published 1998 in Macmillan by Pan Macmillan Australia Pty Ltd
First published in Pan 2001 by Pan Macmillan Australia Pty Ltd
This Pan edition published in 2015 by Pan Macmillan Australia Pty Ltd
1 Market Street, Sydney, New South Wales, Australia, 2000

Copyright © Mark Whittaker and Les Kennedy 1998
The moral right of the author has been asserted.

All rights reserved. No part of this book may be reproduced or transmitted by any person or entity (including Google, Amazon or similar organisations), in any form or by any means, electronic or mechanical, including photocopying, recording, scanning or by any information storage and retrieval system, without prior permission in writing from the publisher.

Cataloguing-in-Publication entry is available
from the National Library of Australia
http://catalogue.nla.gov.au

Typeset by Post Pre-press Group
Printed in Australia by McPherson's Printing Group

Please note, to preserve vernacular accuracy currency changes to decimal from chapter 9 onwards and imperial measure to metric from chapter 16 onwards. This is consistent with changes to the Australian system.

Far from being the basis of the good society, the family, with its narrow privacy and tawdry secrets, is the source of all our discontents.

Sir Edmund Leach, social anthropologist

AUTHORS' NOTE

Between 1989 and 1992 Ivan Milat murdered seven hitchhikers, and tried to kill at least one other. Six of those eight were foreign to these shores, but on the whole the comfortable Australia they saw didn't differ so very greatly from the worlds they left at home. Until they met Milat.

This is a story from the places that don't make the brochures and postcards. It's a story about Milat's narrow little world and what happened when he let his delusions and fantasies become reality. It is also about the efforts to stop him and find out if he acted alone. It is a story about murder, but there is no murder in it. That can only be told when Milat confesses to what went on in the forest, and who, if anybody, was with him. It is a peculiarly Australian story.

Much of it is told in a novelistic style, but at all times the events and details are, to the best of our knowledge, true. The language may at times sound rather crude, but the story is told in the manner in which it was told to us. In a few instances, names have been changed. People have continually surprised us with their willingness to tell the story. We thank them all wholeheartedly for their co-operation and note that, apart from an occasional beer or coffee, no payment has been made to any person for any information. Where there are conflicting versions of the same event, we have often steered a line of best fit. At other times, we have stuck to one person's version and marked it with an endnote.

MW & LK

CONTENTS

PROLOGUE 1

PART ONE

ONE (1902–1944) Margaret and Steve 9
TWO (1944–1950) Rossmore 14
THREE (1950s) Moorebank 19
FOUR (1950s) Boys Town 27
FIVE (1960–1962) The Vendetta 33
SIX (1963) The Buzz 44
SEVEN (1964) 'Thou Shalt . . .' 49
EIGHT (1965) The Hurtin' 54
NINE (1966–1967) Family Affair 63
TEN (1968–1970) Maureen 72
ELEVEN (Early 1971) Death, Love, Rape and Marriage 82
TWELVE (Mid 1971) Stick'm Up 90
THIRTEEN (July 1971) Gangsters 98
FOURTEEN (1971) The Collar 104
FIFTEEN (Late 1971–1973) The Gap 109
SIXTEEN (Early 1974) Mr Brown 120
SEVENTEEN (Late 1974) Marsden 126
EIGHTEEN (1975–1976) Karen 137
NINETEEN (1977–1978) Novak 146
TWENTY (1979–1982) Blackett 152
TWENTY-ONE (1983–1987) Breakdown 160
TWENTY-TWO (1988–1989) Old Flames 172

PART TWO

TWENTY-THREE The Highway 181
TWENTY-FOUR (1990) The Void 189

TWENTY-FIVE (Early 1991) Hornets and Wasps	**203**
TWENTY-SIX (Mid 1991) The Unloader	**212**
TWENTY-SEVEN (Late 1991) Bondi Beach Party	**220**
TWENTY-EIGHT (Early 1992) Worlds Apart	**232**
TWENTY-NINE (April 1992) Dope Talk	**242**
THIRTY (Mid 1992) Limbo	**248**
THIRTY-ONE (September 1992) The Forest	**267**
THIRTY-TWO (Late 1992) Which Way South?	**285**
THIRTY-THREE (Late 1992) Offender 2	**293**
THIRTY-FOUR (January–October 1993) The Potter	**301**
THIRTY-FIVE (October 1993) Executioners Drop	**311**
THIRTY-SIX (October 1993) Task Force Eyre?	**327**
THIRTY-SEVEN (November 1993) Area A	**339**
THIRTY-EIGHT (November 1993) Fifty Metres	**352**
THIRTY-NINE (Dec 1993–Jan 1994) Deliverance	**362**
FORTY (Feb–Mar 1994) The Highway Revisited	**374**
FORTY-ONE (April 1994) Out of the Bag	**384**
FORTY-TWO (Early May 1994) Onions	**394**
FORTY-THREE (22 May 1994) Air I	**405**
PART THREE	
FORTY-FOUR (May–June 1994) Revelations	**431**
FORTY-FIVE (Mid to late 1994) Father Dearest	**439**
FORTY-SIX (Mid to late 1994) The Gun	**444**
FORTY-SEVEN (Late 1994) Wired	**453**
FORTY-EIGHT (1995) Jenolan State Forest	**472**
FORTY-NINE (1996) Trial	**476**
FIFTY (1996) The Pack	**494**
EPILOGUE	**505**
END NOTES	**523**
INDEX	**527**

PROLOGUE

It should be a solemn family occasion. Margaret Milat is in a pretty bad way in hospital with a crook heart, shot hips, a hernia, and Lord knows what other complications a woman gets after bearing fourteen children. There is a chance she might not make it. Most of her brood are coming all the way to the city to see her. Except Mick, of course, being in jail for those armed robberies he and Ivan did. And Margaret who died in a car accident three years ago.

There is no reason, though, why Ivan can't get there, even if he is on the run. He's been hiding from the cops for two and a half years now, since October '71, but he isn't hard to find. So long as you call him by one of his aliases, Bill, Bill Harris to be sure, or Joe Spanner, there are no dramas. He's pretty certain the police have lost interest in him, and he feels safe enough to visit family most weekends. He doesn't know that he is a possible suspect in a murder six months old that police are now investigating.

Ivan's brother Wally and Wally's wife Maureen are going in to Royal Prince Alfred Hospital to visit Mum. They got word to him she was crook.

'I'll come with you, if that's okay,' he volunteers. 'I'll take yas in the new car.' He has traded in the maroon Holden for a brand new, lime green 1974 Charger, VJ, despite his flatmate's '72 Charger being a dog.

Ivan seems pretty relaxed when he picks up his brother and sister-in-law at their Moorebank home. It's obvious he's looking after himself. His muscles cut sharper than ever through the T-shirt. He's with-it. Hair cut in a Prince Valiant almost down to the shoulders, supported by thick sideburns. The new car suits the image. If it worries him that he is free while Mick is doing time for those robberies, it doesn't show.

The tension that had earlier veiled the relationship between Ivan and Wally is no longer evident as they drive the 27 kilometres to the hospital at Camperdown, in Sydney's inner-west. Maureen's affair with Ivan is well behind them all now. Maureen got back with Wally again right after Ivan jumped bail and bolted for New Zealand. She was pregnant straightaway and married to Wally and soon Rob, a beautiful dark-haired boy, was born. Rob is in the cramped back seat of the two-door Charger with her now. He is almost two. Wally's unfounded suspicions about his fatherhood have apparently gone.

Behind the wheel, Ivan cruises. The engine purrs with potential grunt. Kids on the street give the peace sign, singing out, 'Hey, Charger,' following him through the sights of the V in their fingers. Just like the TV ads tell them to. For a man wanted on rape and armed robbery charges, Ivan doesn't seem to mind the attention that much. Besides, if the cops ever pull him up, he's got a licence in the name of William Milat. His brother Bill is one of the few Milat boys who's hardly been in any trouble, so it won't have any outstanding warrants on it.

Mum's room is way upstairs in the Royal Prince Alfred tower block. They all pile into one of those large smelly hospital elevators and go up. It takes them a bit to find her ward but, once they do, they know the instant they go through the big swinging doors that there is going to be trouble. Oh my goodness, they're here, thinks Maureen. Right in front, just off to the left, Ivan's brother Boris and his wife Marilyn are sitting on the end of Mum's bed with their little girl Lynise running around the place. Boris and Marilyn look just as shocked as the three walking in the door. Ivan is behind the other two, but there is no doubt Boris has seen him.

'I'll be back later,' says Ivan, turning, leaving Wally and Maureen there to make the small talk. 'Hello, how are you?'

'Good,' says Marilyn, as she and Boris gather their things and round up Lynise. They can't stay, she says. 'Gotta go.' They make their goodbyes and walk out.

'So, how are you, Mum?' The sudden exit doesn't need explaining. Everyone there thinks it ended remarkably peacefully. They think that the two brothers are respecting their mother's condition.

For Lynise, almost nine, hundreds of incidents like this will blur in her childhood memories, but this day will stand out. This day, the huge concrete pillars, and the great big hospital doors in the late afternoon light will stay with her. What will really remain, though, is this uncle of hers, Ivan. She is thinking his name is Michael, thinking there is something special about him. She picked the face right. Mick and Ivan share the same sharp, dark features, but all the brothers – her uncles – are hazy to her. There are so many of them. A mythical blur from whom Dad has hidden his family and about whom he tells her only tales of badness.

This uncle might not even look at her, but she can feel something coming from herself, some kind of intensity, sort of wanting to get his attention. But Dad is storming out the door. Gran is saying to Dad that if she'd known the uncle was coming she'd have told him.

Dad takes them all down to the gift shop. They are waiting for something but she can't figure out what. Mum tells her: 'Pick yourself a present.' She doesn't really want anything because of the fight she can sense is coming between her parents, but she chooses this hard plastic Pluto dog that pops out of its yellow kennel at the press of a button. She'll cart that thing around with her every time she moves house for the next twenty years. And that is often. It is the only toy she'll ever keep. She'll always feel it is important, never knowing why. Sometimes she'll feel like smashing it, but isn't quite ready to. Twenty years later, Lynise will realise this day is the last she'd see her real father a free man. However, even after learning the truth, she'll always call Boris 'Dad'. By that time her real father will be infamous.

The sense of looming tension between Mum and Dad this day in the gift shop will stay with her, too. A blue can start with the mere mention of this uncle. She's heard the fights about Mum having an affair with him; sleeping with him. You know about that stuff when you're nearly nine. She'll remember a lot of violence, but won't be able to say if it happened all the time, or whether it's just that the violence is all she remembers. Certainly, in her mind, she is the one always trying to pull Dad off Mum. She can't help feeling she is responsible for starting it, and so it is her responsibility to stop it. Of course, she knows nothing of the background, but there is enough for her child's eye in the foreground.

Despite the history, no one up in the ward with Mrs Milat really expects what comes next – except maybe those nurses who file into the room and sit on the bed opposite making small talk: Hello, how are you? Nice day, isn't it? 'Mac' (Ivan) returns in the wake of Boris and Marilyn, grinning that broad grin of his. Seats are few, and he settles on the edge of his mum's bed. The talk is stilted. The baby, Rob, is crying in Maureen's arms as she walks him around the room, rocking him. Looking out the square pane of glass as she passes the swinging door, she sees blue uniforms and brown suits all down the hallway. 'Oh my God,' she calls, inhaling. 'There's police everywhere,' her voice rising. Wally jumps up quickly to check. Ivan bolts over to the big windows to make good his escape, throwing his wallet and car keys at Maureen. 'Don't give 'em to anybody.'

'Oh my goodness. What's he doing? It's too high!' They are about ten storeys up. There are bars on the windows. There is no way out. It's all happening in seconds. There are shouts. The room is full of police; all very polite really, asking 'Mac' and Wally to go with them. The boys don't struggle and suddenly they are gone. The two women are left there in shock. Why have they taken both boys? Maureen goes to the door. The hallway is as suddenly empty as it had been full.

'Oh no, how am I going to get home?' She is a nervous wreck. Wally will look after himself, but she's only just got her licence and she's got this great big Charger to get home. She doesn't even know where she is. She's in a panic, but Mrs Milat knows what to do. She rolls her round figure out of bed and goes directly to the phone. Maureen is staggered. Mrs Milat isn't even meant to be able to walk. But, of course, two of her boys are in trouble. She's been getting her boys out of strife for twenty years. It's just about taken her to her death bed before this and it will do so again, but while there's breath in her body she's going to believe in her sons and protest their innocence. She rings the family home at Guildford.

'Mac and Wally have been arrested.' Wally is actually released minutes later, once the police figure out which brother they want. No one in the family has any doubt that Boris has dobbed Mac in (although Boris says it was Marilyn). They are angry with Boris, but not so angry as to be planning to do anything to him. It is more a matter of helping their brother, getting a lawyer and getting him out of the police cells – doin' what you're supposed to.

And get a lawyer they do. After Ivan spends eight months at Long Bay awaiting trial, a rising young solicitor from out of the south-western suburbs, John Marsden, will win two separate trials in four days and be leading his client from court a free man. Like their mum, Marsden's been getting the Milats out of trouble for years already and he'll continue doing it for twenty years more, plus their insurance claims, divorces and conveyancing.

It will be the last time Ivan Milat will sit in a dock without the glare of the world's media upon him. He will learn from this experience.

Firstly, it's amazing what a good lawyer can do. These charges that he thought so insurmountable that he faked his own death to avoid them were not so watertight after all. Secondly, from now on, no victim survives.

He's there in the very same court twenty-two years later; sitting in the very same dock. The jury has been out for days, behind the doors they came back through last time to set him free. He's so damn confident that he will walk on these seven murder charges that the family has a plan to bring him back to Bill and Carol's place for a victory dinner, then they'll whisk him off to the house of a family friend, to keep him away from the media. From there, he will be moved to a string of safe houses already mapped out until the storm passes.

With those incredible piercing pale blue eyes, he carries an air of detachment, at ease throughout the trial. Same as he did in 1974. That stupid half grin – a natural setting of his face, accentuated around company when he is uneasy – leaves him looking cocky. For those who want to believe him, it's a sign of his innocence. Others have different interpretations, but those who believe him, really do.

Never mind the ballistic evidence, or the evidence of the English guy that got away, or the gear found in Ivan's house. Never mind that his defence is based on blaming two of his brothers, Richard and Wally. The family haven't seen any of the trial – only from the witness stand – so none of this evidence or argument has weight to them. Some even reckon Ivan's explanation is believable – that it wasn't him, but someone either in the family or very closely linked to it . . . They don't say if it is palatable.

Meanwhile, Richard and Wally – who were never warned that they were about to be ambushed by their brother's lawyers – continue to stick by him even if they were pissed off about it. They are Milats – staunch no matter what. It's been them against the world for a long time.

PART ONE

ONE

1902–1944

MARGARET AND STEVE

Stijphan Marko Milat was born on 26 December 1902 in the Croatian town of Blato, on the Adriatic island of Korcula. He was one of twenty-two children carried by his mother. Only four survived infancy: two boys, two girls. Toughness would always be his defining quality. Korcula was then part of the crumbling Austro-Hungarian Empire. It was reputed to be the birthplace of Marco Polo in the days when it was part of the Venetian Empire. Stijphan's father, so the story went, was descended from a French nobleman,[1] banished to the east some six generations previously for daring to marry an Asian woman. There was something in the eyes of their descendants which bore witness to that forbidden love, that dubious story.

The house of Milat had crumbled, figuratively and literally. Stijphan's father was a humble stonemason, who owned a little property. Stijphan, a hard man of few words, would later tell his sons cryptic and at times conflicting tales of his past. He told them he served in the army of the British Empire in the latter days of World War I, but he never mentioned this to his wife. The war ended a month short of his sixteenth birthday.

'Senseless, senseless,' he would grumble at the slaughter. 'Not good enough to be sitting there with a machine-gun shooting people. It is silly. I am on one side and my brother on the other,' he said of his sibling's service in the German merchant navy. Cousins were lost on both sides.[2]

With no prospects in the fledgling Yugoslavia, their father encouraged Stijphan and his brother 'Jack' to seek their fortunes elsewhere. They visited Australia and New Zealand as crewmen on a sailing ship in the early 1920s. When they later decided to emigrate, Jack went to New Zealand and Stijphan chose Australia because they had a cousin there and he liked the climate. He arrived with no discernible politics other than a love of law, order and the British Monarch. The country was well established but without too many restrictions on freedoms – like gun ownership.[3] His arrival in 1926 coincided with an influx of Croatian miners and the lure of money in the silver and lead mines of Queensland drew him away from Sydney. In Mount Isa, he lived beside a creek in a crude tent of hessian bags slung over branches, alongside the many other immigrants and itinerant Australians working the mines. Lead poisoning cut short his life as a miner, however, so he returned to Sydney, to a small tenement in Argyle Street, The Rocks, then regarded as the worst address in Sydney. The rat plagues and the flu epidemic of 1919 which killed hundreds of locals were a recent memory. His neighbours still called it the black plague.

He had a cousin with a small market garden at St Johns Park in Sydney's south-western backblocks. His sister Pelly had also migrated and settled in the dairy country of South Granville, 15 miles west of Sydney. They were Stijphan's only family in the new world, and he saw them regularly, travelling by train and walking miles along roads which were variously dusty or muddy.

Stanley Gordon Piddlesden migrated to Australia from England in 1912 at the behest of his father. At the outbreak of war with Germany two years later, he promptly enlisted and found himself at Gallipoli. He survived that to be sent to France where he took a bullet in the shoulder on the Somme. He was shipped to England for convalescence, then back to Australia, but eleven days into the voyage was struck by a mystery illness, the effects of which he carried for years. He'd have his good days and bad, but it never stopped him working, and neither did the bullet hole blasted in the back of his shoulder so big you could put your fist into it.

He met and married Lillian. Their first daughter, Margaret Elizabeth Piddlesden, was born on 13 September 1920. She grew up in the rolling green hills at Granville. The Depression came and, while their neighbours were subject to the tyranny of falling commodity prices and the collapse of employment, the Piddlesdens were relatively comfortable because Stanley was fortunate to have a plum position as caretaker of Granville Tech.[4]

Stijphan Milat also managed to stay in work while almost a third of all men lost their jobs. He was the sort of worker a boss held onto till the end, such was his capacity for hard yakka in an era when there was no shortage of young men like him: sinewy, tanned and hungry.

One dull, rainy afternoon in 1934, he was all dressed up, walking to visit his sister Pelly. Near Granville Park, a young girl riding her bike home from the Holy Trinity Catholic School, with a cattle dog running behind, lost her chain and ran square into him. The girl, Margaret Piddlesden, thought she hit the man pretty bad. But as they dusted themselves off he seemed more concerned for her than any injury to himself. She asked him home for a cuppa. They walked the last 500 yards from the old Dog Trap Gates (the opening in an early dingo fence that ran down Woodville Road) to the Piddlesden home at 25 Excelsior Street, with the cattle dog at their heels. Margaret was fourteen. The stranger who introduced himself as Steven, with a thick accent and a soft voice, was thirty-two. The migrant tradesman began to court the schoolgirl. He visited almost every day. Her parents' acceptance of the older European caller was cause for tongue wagging, but that didn't worry them.

He was tall, thin and good looking with fair, wispy hair. He called her 'Capelli' which meant 'little one'. Together at her home they would read or listen to the wireless. Sometimes they went to the pictures at Granville. They never rowed.

Margaret left school and found a job in a shop making milkshakes. It wasn't like any girl expected to stay in school much after turning fifteen. Stijphan proposed just before her sixteenth birthday, causing a stir among her relatives. Never mind the age gap, these mixed marriages didn't work. But at least he was Catholic.

They were married after a short engagement on Armistice Day, 11 November 1936 in the Catholic church at Guildford. She was sixteen and two months. He was almost thirty-four. Margaret's parents held a small reception at their home. There was no honeymoon because the couple decided to save for a house. They moved to a small flat with harbour views in the still working-class suburb of Milsons Point, on the north side of the new Harbour Bridge.

Stijphan had become a wharf labourer in an era when the Sydney waterfront from The Rocks to Darling Harbour was known as the Hungry Mile; where the 'bull' system saw men turn up to work each day unsure if they'd get a start. A few of the bosses' favourites, the bulls, got first pick, leaving the rest to fight for the remaining tickets. If flour was being loaded, you lifted huge sacks and came home covered in the stuff. The union had no power because there were too many men prepared to work for nothing, but left-wing radicals were constantly agitating for the revolution, and being countered by gangs of thugs employed by the bosses. There were many violent battles.

Stijphan didn't worry about any of that. So long as he could work, he was happy. There's every probability, given his immense capacity for toil, that he was a 'bull'. This was an era when wharfies weren't on good money, but Stijphan was apparently making enough to want to take his young bride to Europe to show her his homeland. Margaret was afraid of travel. Subsequently, the war in Europe took the decision out of her hands and ensured she would never leave Australia. Around late 1937, the couple moved to Canley Vale, very much out in the sticks with no electricity and no sewerage. Stijphan was still a wharfie, commuting 19 miles into the city on the new electric train system which had just been extended to Liverpool.

Margaret became pregnant as Europe prepared to tear itself apart. As soon as war was declared in September 1939, the authorities began rounding up aliens. Many local Italian men were carted off to the new internment camp at Holsworthy but, fortunately, Croatians didn't qualify.

The birth of Olga, a month later, on 17 October, was terribly painful and Margaret vowed to a nursing sister that the baby would be her last. The sister smiled. 'See you next year.' She was right. A year and three days after Olga, Margaret gave birth to a son, Alexander.

It was a time of great uncertainty and high expectations. Stijphan was having a go at market gardening. He and his father-in-law, Stanley Piddlesden, had leased a block near Canley Vale. Stijphan was lured to it by the boasts of his relatives making good money on a nearby plot. The first year was hard and money was scarce, so Stijphan left his father-in-law to work the garden while he returned to the docks. There was plenty of demand for labour with so many men enlisting in the services.

Stijphan moved his family to The Old Homestead, on Prairie Vale Road, Bossley Park, a run-down nineteenth century settlers' home. The family was 23 miles from the city and about four miles from the nearest railway station, but still Stijphan trudged to work in town.

Margaret gave birth to her third child, Boris Stanley, at home on 23 February 1942. Shortly after, Stijphan, who had now legally anglicised his name to 'Steven', was sent to the wharves of the steelworks at Newcastle, about 100 miles north of Sydney. The industrial town, with its coal production and its belching steel furnaces, was deemed a key Japanese target. The Milats kept a pram full of tinned food in case a raid forced them into the bomb shelter in the grounds of a nearby coalmine – sandbags piled along an open ditch, often filled with puddles of smelly water. Margaret prayed she'd never have to use it.

It was a happy time, and the Milats contemplated settling there permanently. Margaret liked the picture theatre, near the Newcastle Railway Station, because it had a crying room for babies. Mothers could take their screaming kids and watch the film without disturbing others. That's how she saw *Gone With the Wind*. Sometimes, other women would mind the kids so she could actually go into the main theatre.

Steven Milat's time on the Novocastrian waterfront was short-lived, but there was no shortage of jobs. He worked in a factory making clay pipes then, for almost a year, underground at the Belmont Colliery, walking three miles to the pit carrying his own shovel.

Margaret needed a rest, but she wasn't going to get one because she was again heavy with child. Her fourth, Mary, was born in Newcastle in 1943. The baby reacted badly to the thick pollution from Newcastle's smokestacks so, at the end of the year, Steven moved the whole brood back to Bossley Park, behind Margaret's parents' market garden.

Margaret still loved Steven. They still never argued and if they got cross with one another they didn't go to bed till they made up. She was twenty-three years old with four children under the age of five.

The next was already on the way.

TWO

1944–1950

ROSSMORE

Christmas 1944 came with the Allied armies advancing irresistibly towards Germany and Japan. Margaret Milat was, inevitably, swollen with her fifth child due any moment. She stayed at home Boxing Day for Steven's birthday, until her waters broke and the contractions began in earnest that evening. Steven walked to a neighbour's home to use their telephone to call a cab. Grandma Piddlesden looked after the children while the couple travelled all the way to the inner-city Crown Street Women's Hospital. Steven left Margaret there because he had to go back to look after the kids.

Ivan Robert Marko, an eight-pounder, was born in the early hours of Wednesday, 27 December. He looked like all her other kids, except they were all special to Margaret. Steven registered the baby's birth in early 1945, listing his own age as thirty-nine – perhaps embarrassed that his wife was twenty-four and he was actually forty-two.

Around this time, Steven bought Alex, five, a slug gun and set up a small range for him. Alex, too small to even hold it himself, learned to shoot under Steven's strict supervision.[5] Alex was the first to come under his father's old-world adherence to obedience, and the first to absorb his work ethic. He'd always have an image in his mind of Dad carrying a bag of manure on each shoulder; a tough old bastard who seemed taller than his 5'7" frame. When not working alongside his father-in-law in the market garden, Steven was back on the wharves. He'd work six or seven days a week for three decades to feed his family.

Life returned to normal after the war. Margaret had child number six, Shirley, on 21 February 1946. The family was living at Quarry Road, Bossley Park, in a big shed divided down the middle by a curtain, then the bedroom side was divided by another curtain – mum and dad one side, the kids the other. The 'living area' had a wooden floor, but you stepped down onto dirt in the kitchen. The legs of the kitchen cupboard, meat safe and ice chest all rested in containers of water to stop ants getting in. The family's only luxury was a wireless. They were struggling, but they never went hungry.

Olga and Alex attended their first school in nearby Fairfield. Alex became the subject of playground taunts about his slightly Asiatic features. 'Jap eyes, slanty eyes,' the older boys called. It was a hard introduction to school for a small boy at a time when Changi and the Burma Railway could not be forgiven. He learned to fight and not to go crying to his dad.[6]

Steven was working shifts on the wharves. Sometimes he worked all night, other times he came home between 11.30 p.m. and midnight, after walking five miles from Fairfield Station. On his return, he'd call out to Margaret by her pet name, 'Capelli', and whistle a distinct call as part of a security signal in the isolated house. He made sure she locked all the doors and under no circumstances opened them to strangers at night. Then one night she heard the call 'Capelli', followed by a whistle. It wasn't right. She felt fear.

The caller persisted. She knew it wasn't Steven. She held her tongue. Five foot two, no phone, no help within earshot, and with the children fast asleep, she had no option. She climbed from her bed and searched in the darkness for the axe. The window rattled, then slowly began to rise.

'Who's there?'

Silence. She saw one hand on the sill, another lifting the window.

'Get out or I'll hit you with it,' she screamed.

The hand didn't move. She lifted the axe and without thinking swung it down hard. There was a dull thud as it hit flesh, bone and wood. A man screamed, then she heard whimpers abating into the darkness. Four fingers lay on the blood-splattered sill. Blood dripped to the floor, testament to a mother's protective instinct – something she would show time and again in future years. Margaret Milat was not a woman to be taken lightly.

Steven arrived home an hour later. 'Capelli. Capelli!' He had to call her name sternly before she let him in. He found his petrified wife still clutching the axe. She scolded him for being late. A neighbour took him to Fairfield Police Station with the fingers while Margaret was comforted by the neighbour's wife. Nobody claimed the missing digits, nor did anyone apparently seek treatment for such wounds.[7]

Margaret couldn't understand what the intruder might have wanted. 'He must have thought we had money,' she said to Steven, but the wireless was about their only possession of value. Steven gave up work on the wharves that night. 'I'm not going back. It's not worth it.'

He thought it was a good time to move, to once again become his own boss in a market garden. He had saved enough to lease 35 acres in the Liverpool district.

Rossmore – on the south-western outskirts of Liverpool, itself on the outer south-western fringe of Sydney – was in the sticks. The region was once the frontier of colonial Sydney, where the early colonials went to establish their pastoral empires. Rossmore was on the edge of the district's first great subdivision of three-acre residential lots, the Hoxton Park Estate, during the real-estate boom of the 1880s. It was billed then as a place where a working man could raise his family along with a few pigs and some chooks and, of course, it was a failure and, of course, it turned into Shitkickerville West. Too small to be viable for agriculture, too far from transport to commute. By the 1940s, it may as well have still been on the frontier as far as basic services like sewerage and electricity went. But Steven's acreage on Kelly Street was at least viable. The soil was loamy and rich. He had a dam, and nearby Kemps Creek gave him the water needed for the garden.

He set to work getting the place fit to live on. He purchased a war surplus hut from the nearby Ingleburn army camp and carted it to the property for conversion into a home. He built a concrete shed for his gear. He felled the trees which covered half the property, blowing up the stumps. Margaret's parents followed them out there and set up house in a garage on the property. Stanley Piddlesden this time answered to Steven's orders as they laboured on the new garden beds, growing tomatoes and cabbages for the Sydney market. Margaret, pregnant again, walked Olga and Alex a mile to Bringelly Road to get them on the school bus safely each morning and repeated the journey in the afternoon.

On 9 July 1947, with their first harvest in, the clan Milat expanded once more with the birth of child number seven, William Allan. Though only seven, Alex was old enough to help with the gardens and his reward was independence with the air gun. Dad once again built him a small target range in a corner of the block. He also had guardianship of the crop. He'd sit there after school shooting any bird that came within cooee of the garden or the chook feed. By the time he was eight, he was using a shotgun. Steven thought he made sure Alex handled it with respect, but at that age, how good can you be?

One afternoon Alex saw a flock of birds on the roof. They were an easy shot. He ran inside and got the shotgun, aimed and fired, peppering bird shot through the fibro wall of the living room. Loud Croatian swear words boomed out of the house followed by the sound of heavy feet on a wooden floor. Steven had not insisted his children learn his native tongue but Alex knew what the words meant: he was in big strife.

By the time Steven reached the door, Alex had covered the hundred or so yards to the back fence like a champion athlete and disappeared into the bushes. He stayed there for hours until Mum came looking at dusk to give him the all-clear.

That wasn't the first time Alex was in strife with guns. He and his little brother Boris were running around with their air guns playing cowboys and Indians, popping shots off at each other, oblivious to the potential danger until, bullseye, a slug hit Boris right between the eyes, leaving a nasty red welt and causing a flood of tears. They never played like that again.[8] Over the years, Alex would instil his knowledge of weaponry and safety in all his younger brothers.

Life continued. The tomatoes did well. Mum gave birth to child number eight, Michael Gordon, on 29 July 1949. There was no time for outings like picnics, just the occasional trip into the city when Steven wanted to see a friend on the docks, or on an incoming vessel. He was still known among the wharfies, who'd call out his name. There was, however, a marked change in Dad's temperament. He had taken to drinking heavily too often. It upset Margaret and his explosive outbursts scared the children, especially when he struck her. Boris might run to his mum's defence, but was too small to do anything.

Margaret nagged Steven about his drinking, and making ends meet. He gave her just as much lip back, about dinner not being ready when he wanted it, little things like that. Then she'd say something like, 'you drunken bastard', and he'd snap, get up, grab her by the hair, and give her a whack across the back of the head while the little ones cowered. She'd threaten to leave him; Steven couldn't understand why, and would talk her out of it. It happened at least once a week. Mum could be quite savage, too, with her hidings, though they were far between and few. She hit Boris once with a knife for an indiscretion which disappeared from his memory, but the wound never did. 'Nearly cut me bloody arm off.' Once, he was whacked so hard with a tomato stake it broke his arm. He never felt frightened because it was over in a flash and, besides, it was normal.[9] Ivan copped it, too. They all did. Before leaving Rossmore, Boris and Alex copped one justified flogging. Playing around the sheds, they had come across Dad's stash of a couple of a hundred pounds hard-earned, hidden in an old biscuit tin. Boris found some matches and, having no concept of money, set fire to some of it. Though only about seven, he never forgot that hiding.

Although the market garden was operating well, and Margaret had both her mother and eldest daughter, Olga, eleven, to help with the seven children, there had been talk of easing her burden by placing some of them temporarily in a church home. It was only idle talk. By his second year of primary school, Boris was regarded as a sickly child. His face would swell inexplicably into a giant ball. The doctors didn't seem to have an answer. It wasn't happening to any of the other children. His health became Margaret's preoccupation. The ailment came and went like the seasons; he'd get a rash, complain of breathing problems and then this extraordinary swelling of the glands. He went to hospital and the swelling subsided. He came home, and his face ballooned again. After a battery of tests, the doctor concluded that it was an allergy caused by a patch of messy scrub down the back of the place. Little did they know Boris' swollen glands had been a sham, with his little fingers stabbing into the glands when backs were turned. He didn't want to be sent away but, equally, he came to enjoy all the attention in hospital, especially the food.[10]

Boris' health would be better elsewhere, Margaret thought. After four years of building the Rossmore place up, Steven finally had enough cash to purchase a plot of his own. He had inspected a site at Moorebank on the eastern side of the Georges River at Liverpool. There, the Milat culture would be shaped.

THREE

1950s

MOOREBANK

Moorebank was bequeathed to the Church of England by Thomas Moore in 1840. A mere ship's carpenter when he arrived in the colony in 1792, Moore built his 375-acre free grant to an influential 7000 acres by the time it went to the Church. The C of E subdivided the land into small farms during the 1888 boom and its agents made outrageous claims about the land's potential. The scrubby sandstone country to the south became 'verdure-clad hilltops', with unlimited potential.[11] It was soon to be a fashionable suburb with a rail line and a tramway running through it, said the Church's copywriters, ill with the fever of speculation. Of course, it became just another area too small for viable farms, too remote for people with money, perfect for breaking the hearts of hard-working people. On the wrong side of the river from Liverpool, only seventy of the 500 lots were occupied by the time the next boom came in 1900. Again, all that was left were the ordinary folk battling with their vines and chooks and tomatoes. It would have stayed that way longer, had Lord Kitchener not needed somewhere to inspect the colonial troops during a visit in 1910. Moorebank was chosen and, subsequently, 17,000 acres on the south side of the district and Holsworthy was set aside to be a military remount depot and veterinary hospital. War came and the Liverpool Camp saw 47,000 horses and many more men pass through it on their way to the distant front. War was good for Moorebank.

The vineyards, orchards and the moonshine for which the area gained a reputation had changed little by the time Steven Milat moved his thirty-year-old wife and their eight children there around the end of 1950. It was a time when large families were still common, though the arrival of a woman with eight children under the age of eleven didn't go unnoticed. Moorebank after World War II was a backwater of battlers making ends meet: returned soldiers, migrants, eccentrics, drunks. Poverty was common. People accepted others as they found them.

Margaret's figure was long gone and people just presumed she was older than her years, given what she had in tow. Mrs Enid Card was the first to greet the new Junction Road neighbours as they unloaded their belongings from a truck. She lived opposite. Her husband Chris, an invalid World War II veteran, was trying to make a go of a poultry business. Mrs Card went straight over with some vegetables and eggs, because that was the sort of thing you did in those days. Moving was such a horrendous thing before the motor vehicle became common, she wanted to make them welcome. Her twelve-year-old daughter Betty couldn't understand the lack of emotion shown by Mrs Milat and her husband towards her mother's gifts. The only feeling seemed to be surprise that anyone would do such a thing, but they took the food anyway.

The Milats weren't as neighbourly as others. Mind you, it wasn't a neighbourhood where women did a lot of talking. There were no backyard fences to have a leisurely natter over. If you spoke to your neighbour, you had to yell. But nobody yelled. Conversation was expected of you, though, if you bumped into someone on the street. There was room enough to mind your own business. But the urban planners who in 1948 set aside large chunks of outer Sydney as a green belt gave Moorebank the short straw and zoned it industrial. Two factories had already opened, both giants: Cable Makers and Leyland. The future was bright. Factories meant jobs. Robert Menzies was newly in power. Steven loved the Liberal Party leader who was on his way to becoming Australia's longest-serving prime minister.

The Milats' shed at 24 Junction Road, Moorebank, was on 11.8 acres atop a hill, looking down over similar places towards Heathcote Road. The lack of new building during the Depression and war had left the country ripe for an acute housing shortage when the soldiers came home. Just a mile away on the other side of the Georges River at Warwick Farm there was a shanty town made from ex-navy Nissen huts – 5000 people in 200 huts and the overflow were issued tents by the Housing Commission.

No one, therefore, was going to think the Milats odd in their two-roomed shack, packed-dirt floor and two poky windows facing the road.

It had a skillion roof with a chimney at one end for the fuel stove. Everyone slept on bed rolls on the ground. Before breakfast, they rolled them up and packed them away, then assembled the large table. They were strong, healthy, good-looking kids. No one wore shoes, except to school, and the Milats always had shoes. To young Betty Card, they were no grubbier or shabbier than other children because clothes weren't washed then like they are now. Monday was washing day and it was common for children to have one or two shirts to last the week.

Steven began work on the place to turn it into a market garden, and Margaret had a brief respite from making babies. Betty tried to become friends with Olga who was the same age, but she was never allowed out to play. Betty watched the backbreaking work Steven put the older boys through. They worked like Trojans. Alex, the oldest, bore most of it. Boris and Ivan did a little alongside Dad cutting at the wattle and ti-tree scrub and a few large gums. Beds were dug and levelled by hand. Huge piles of manure were delivered and the boys shovelled it onto the beds. The seedlings were planted and watered by a hose, the nozzle covered with hessian so that the roots would not be damaged. There was no watering system so, dawn and dusk, the children were beholden to the garden. All the while, an extreme work ethic was being absorbed. It would stay with them all and set them apart from their contemporaries.

Steven built the crop up to 5000 tomato plants with some cabbages and occasional other crops. Margaret kept ducks and chickens. Her couple of geese grew to a gaggle, like her children. All the while, the Milats kept their distance from the neighbours who continued to pronounce the name as 'millet'. There was an insularity about them. The house only had one door and neighbours regularly saw kids spilling out of it, all arms and legs, yelling or fighting. Sometimes, Steven would be right behind them, bellowing, with his face ground into hard lines, swinging a strap or something more solid. The children's faces marked with desperation as they scrambled silently from the doorway to disappear helter-skelter into the scrub behind, or up the road out front. Other times, the place was full of shouting, laughing children at play. Or, just sometimes, they might see them walking to the nearby Cocos store in Nuwarra Road or trooping down Junction Road to catch the bus for Sunday services in the army's tiny weatherboard Catholic church.

As the children came to an age where they could understand such things, they grew to respect and fear their father. Steven Milat was a brute. Fair-haired, tall and solid, all muscle and bone. When the brood was out of hand, they'd see Margaret mutter that their father would sort them out, striking fear into their souls. One 'sorting' terrified Betty Card leaving an indelible memory. It was so public. Two boys, lying face down in the dirt out in front of the shack, their father standing on them with a boot in the small of each back, while he walloped their legs and behinds with a piece of four-by-two. The plank seemed wildly inefficient for its task. Steven's position seemed all wrong, but he was inflicting great pain on the two screaming boys and that seemed to be the object. When he stepped down, they shot off like rabbits into the bushes.

Going by their ages, the two boys were probably Ivan and Boris, or Ivan and Bill, but with so many running around, they became an anonymous blur to Betty. It certainly wasn't the oldest, Alex. He and Olga always stood out because they were never children, always serious and responsible. They seemed sombre and guarded. They knew hard work and harder discipline.

Ivan, at seven or eight, worked long hours with his brothers and father. Tomato growing was hard work. A glut season sent prices down and meant a year of poverty, but there was no competition from interstate so if you had a good year and others didn't, the crop was a bonanza. Steven Milat used the profits from one good season to build a house. Neighbours watched it going up with a sense of wonder. It was a square, utilitarian and ugly building of unpainted fibro with one door at the back and none at the front – a perfect symbol of the family's insularity. There was no hallway. Each room led into the next. And after it was finished, the neighbours never saw the inside again.

The old shack remained at the front, with no pretence of an ornamental garden. The dirt out front was pulverised into dust in the dry season, mud when it rained. There was a sense of fear about the place. A strange atmosphere, totally different from any other.

After a three-year respite, Margaret gave birth to her ninth child Walter Francis, on 3 March 1952. Such was her figure by this time, there was no telling when she was pregnant. She was thirty-two and losing her teeth. Her tenth child, George Peter, was on the way almost immediately.

Olga was being kept home from school to look after the babies long before she was legally old enough to leave. Steven was adamant she would have an old-world European girl's upbringing. The girls could have no social life. The moment they were out of school, they had to work.

Any socialising was done on the school bus. Olga certainly got stares from the local boys. They would remember her for her womanly figure walking down the aisle. When the buses weren't running for whatever reason, the army used to get the children from the base to school in the back of their trucks, picking up other children as well. That's how Olga met a nice teenage boy by the name of Henry Shipsey whose father was in the army. She'd marry him and get out of home as soon as she could.

Margaret gave birth to her eleventh child, Margaret Maria, in 1955. Family life was still dominated by the tomatoes. With his regime of fear, Steven kept the older boys bound to those plants as tightly as Margaret was bound to her children. They would cover the plants with bags in the evening to guard against frost, then uncover them each morning. At harvest time, they picked only in the cool of the night while the little kids slept on mattresses nearby so Mum could keep an eye on them while she worked.

During the summer of perhaps early 1956, they worked as ever into the early morning hours, watering the crop by hand, falling into bed around 2 a.m. Waking at dawn, they found every single one of the great reddy-green balls hanging from thousands of plants gone. Stolen. Maybe 10,000 tomatoes, they would claim. Even the little unripe ones. They needed that crop to get them through to the next season. The thieves – who had worked silently through the five available hours – had an unforeseen, but profound, effect on the Milat family.

'Right, you're going to get a proper job. I'm having no more to do with this,' Margaret told Steven, but he needed no more convincing that market gardening was a mug's game. Too much work for too little reward. Aged fifty-two, he began labouring for Normie Smee, a concrete manufacturer at Punchbowl. He'd lecture his boys on the importance of working hard. To Alex, Dad's idea of a solid day's work was to rise early, walk six or so miles to Punchbowl, work from seven to seven and then walk home. Steven was paid more than other labourers. He was stronger than the young men and able to go twice as long.

When he finished, he liked a drink at one of the pubs near Liverpool Station. They were tough places to have a beer, but he would remain a cleanskin with the law. Neighbours would see him in the dusk, after work, lurching up Junction Road, covered in cement dust, snarling and ranting to himself in his guttural way, smelling thickly of sour spirits.[12] The other men who had been on the same bus all walked back together, in this era when people still walked and talked . . . but they kept their distance from Milat. He seemed to refuse to acknowledge anybody. Nobody else existed. Young Betty Card always crossed the street when she saw him. She'd seen what he did to his own children and had a great fear of him lunging at her. Of course he never did.

Many neighbours didn't know about the tomato robbery. They just saw the well-tended garden go to ruin. Within months, everything was overgrown, but the beds were still there, visible for years after, testifying to better days.

Suddenly, these disciplined and well-behaved kids had nothing to do. Suddenly, Steven's iron fist wasn't hanging over them twenty-four hours a day. Like the weeds in the garden, they exploited the opportunity. But there were battles still to be fought. Their father would come home tired and dusty, in no mood for a report card from Mum on any unruly behaviour. The 'old man' sometimes arrived home with a whacking stick in case it was needed.[13] If they were good, he might reach into his pocket and take out what loose change he had and ceremoniously place it on the kitchen table for them to divide up.

Margaret's mother, Lillian Piddlesden, was a frequent visitor. She'd help around the place and loved being among the grandchildren. She and Margaret would get on the bus to go shopping in Liverpool, amazing the local children. How did two such fat ladies squeeze onto the tiny seats?

Margaret's younger sister Shirley – who the children called 'Big Shirl', so as not to confuse her with their own sister – was a complete contrast, representing, perhaps, what Margaret would have been like with eight or nine less children. She was petite and slim, a woman who turned heads.

By the mid-fifties, Alex was old enough to go to work. Like most boys in the district he bought old cars and motorbikes even before he was old enough for a licence. He'd take his mates and the younger boys paddock bashing and rabbit shooting. Rabbits provided meat for the family and cash from the pelts.

While Ivan took charge of the little brothers, Alex and Boris sought out older kids. Boris, fourteen, had learned to drive and had a knack for tinkering with cars. One night, Boris and Alex went for a ride with some mechanic bloke in an old Ford. Boris was driving. The mechanic told them to stop the car. Boris and Alex later told the cops they had no inkling what he was about to do.

They're sitting in the car outside this place in the dark and next thing an alarm's gone off. Struth! Then they've watched their mate come running from the property and scarper up a tree as fast as he could. Out of the house came a bloke with a .303 rifle.

'Let's get out of here,' Boris said starting the car up in a panic.

'No, we can't leave him. We've got to go back,' said Alex.

'Don't be stupid. He'll get away. He's on foot. We're in a car.' Next thing they knew some feller with a gun had blocked them off, and was ordering them from the car. All the while Boris was telling Alex to have nothing to do with it.

'I'm taking youse to the police station,' the bloke said, fumbling with the rifle, as spare .303 shells dropped on the ground from his hand, making both boys laugh.

'Nah, mate. Shoot me if you bloody like. I'm not going with ya,' said Boris, cockily. But Alex forced him to follow the man's orders. It was too late to run, anyway. The bloke already had the number of the car.

Boris and Alex spent the night in a special juvenile holding cell made of rubber to stop them from hurting themselves. They copped a bond.[14]

Life at home for the younger Milat boys was spent in paddocks or around the rusting corrugated-iron sheds that had once been used for storing tools and packing tomatoes. There was no sports gear or pets. Loneliness was unknown; but so was privacy and solitude for reflection. Because of their chores, they had never been allowed to play with other children. Now that there was no work to do, they showed little inclination to join in the swimming, football or games that the others enjoyed. It was a brilliant place for kids to grow up with the bush on hand, the meeting place around the willows of Clinches Pond, and the river to make their own – but what the Milats did make their own was guns. There was nothing unusual in that. Just about every house had a .22.

Even the Italians had guns. No one minded rabbits being shot, they were vermin. But birds, unless they were a problem to a crop, were a no-go. If there was one complaint neighbours had about the young Milat boys, it was shooting birds. Their dad had no objections to it. He encouraged it. He also encouraged them to join the Chipping Norton Scouts, believing steadfastly in all the values of loyalty to Queen and country. When a passing news photographer, amazed at the size of the clan, offered to take a family portrait one day, the sweetly smiling Milat children posed in their Sunday best. Ivan had centre place proudly sporting his scout belt. Their white clothes in the photo are far whiter than anyone ever saw them in real life.

Margaret's washing was quite notorious. She had more than enough worries managing the copper. She'd have to make the fire underneath it, then boil the clothes up for thirty minutes – whites first – swirling them with the copper stick. Then she'd drag them across to the tubs, rinsing them three times with cold water, before topping up the copper and doing the next load, and the next, until she was down to the work gear in the now murky waters. Whereas most women washed on Mondays, Margaret would do it a couple of times a week. There were also the constant loads of nappies. With no end in sight. On 7 May 1956, her twelfth child, Richard James, was born.

FOUR

1950s

BOYS TOWN

The older Milat kids had gone to local state schools until an order came from the Bishop that Catholic children should go to the new secondary Catholic schools opening in the west. So, from the start, Ivan's schooling was in the hands of the Church – St Mary's Convent School. He wore its grey jacket, shorts and little English prep-school hat – but nobody wore that out the gate. They were meant to have their socks up and their ties on, but Ivan and the other kids up the back of the classroom, with names like Suplat and Wysinskis, never did.

He teamed up with the other children of migrants. The boys all left the sisters after fourth class, going over the road to the newly opened Liverpool Patrician Brothers, which only went up to second form at that time. There were about 400 kids at the school, ninety-three in fifth class.

While the Milat girls were quiet and retiring, their brothers were known because they travelled as a unit. You couldn't take just one of them on, so most kept their distance. Billy had a reputation as a pretty tough kind of kid. Very aggressive. The sort of kid who, if there was a dispute over whose turn it was to bat, he would, or else.

Ivan, too, was tough, but so were a lot of others. Like all the Milat boys, he straddled the divide between 'wogs' and 'Aussies' in the classroom apartheid of the day, but he came down on the side of the outcasts who'd cop a belting if they were caught speaking their own language. None of the Milat kids knew any Croatian anyway.

Ivan made little impression. The sort of kid whose friends wouldn't notice much about him. He wasn't scholarly, but compared to other members of his family he was a bookworm. The thing that people remembered most about young Ivan Milat was his huge mother always coming to the school. She looked so old with hardly any teeth that the legend grew: Old Mother Milat, she had twenty-two kids and they lived in half a shed. While her children presented as neat and tidy, she exuded poverty to the children who saw her.[15] They'd never see the father.

Mrs Milat, just in her early thirties, valiantly supported her brood through thick and thin. Her round figure on the school bus escorting the kids to school was an image that would be etched in many people's minds. She felt she had to prevent other children from picking on her sons. Whenever there was trouble, it was because they were being singled out. The bus driver might have refused to let one on, or a teacher had beaten one. She was a very strong-willed woman and it didn't matter what other people said, her kids had done nothing. She had to go along to make sure they were given a fair go. And she'd often have to visit the headmaster while she was there to sort out some problem one of them would inevitably be facing. Then she would catch the bus home, only to be there waiting at the gates to bring them home when the final bell rang.

A schoolmate of Ivan's who bore the nickname 'Collar' because his Polish name was hard on young Anglo tongues, saw the Milats' rustic charm as something like a Ma and Pa Kettle movie. The only thing that ruined the picture was the father yelled a lot more than Pa Kettle.

When at home, it was rare that Mrs Milat would come outside, but when she did, all the other kids stared – she was that big. The arrival of the milkman or baker was an event. Their deliveries were huge – five times more bread than anybody else.

Collar, who lived around the corner, never felt at ease playing at the Milat place. Kids thought of Steven as the 'Gestapo'. When he said something, you could hear a pin drop. Collar could see how scared the Milat kids were. When he yelled, everyone scattered like chooks across the yard. Collar always asked: 'Is your father home?' before venturing in to play.

He was playing marbles there one day while the little ones were mucking up. Steven opened the door and said one word in Croatian. Everyone went silent and Collar was petrified by the way he said it. Mr Milat was like his own parents: steeped in old European ways and isolated by the language barrier. Collar's Polish dad spoke some Croatian and sometimes drank with Steven Milat at the Golden Fleece Hotel in Liverpool.

It was easy to think of all the Milats as roughnecks, but those who knew Margaret could see that she was not like that. They sensed that, given the opportunity of an easier life, she could have been quite refined. For all that, she never let on that she felt trapped. If she ever had misgivings, she gave a damn good show of coping with them.

Ivan wasn't bad at sport, but didn't like it. He was forced to play cricket and rugby. The Brothers were as liberal as Steven in dishing out sadistic punishment for slight indiscretions. If you were sent to see Brother Ignatius, you knew you were in for it. You didn't stand up to him. You told him it didn't hurt – whack – 'How was that?' The consensus was that you pretended to be more hurt than you were. They didn't worry about child psychology.

Mrs Milat always thought Ivan had a good memory and an aptitude for maths, but he couldn't handle niggling from one teacher who called him the 'Sleeping Professor'. He'd have his eyes closed but he was taking it all in. He had the answers, she'd say. When his mates like Collar and Suplat began wagging school regularly, he was always willing to join them. Collar justified his jigging 'because of what some of the Brothers did'. He only went on sports days: Monday and Thursday. The Brothers gave him letters to give his dad, but his father couldn't read English.

Collar would pretend to go to school and wait for his mother to leave, then shoot back and wait for the other kids to come over. There'd be seven or eight of them sitting out the front, maybe taking pot shots at beer bottles with Collar's shotgun. They'd go to milk bars. They'd steal balls from the fairways at New Brighton Golf Club. They swam in the Georges River under the old Bailey Bridge at Chipping Norton until one day some kid yelled 'shark' and that was it for there. Ivan was often around. He was the type of kid who wasn't afraid of anything and would jump off the bridge to prove it.

They were still only young when a mob of about fifteen of them started roaming the streets at night. Boris and Ivan would sneak out when their parents were in bed, with a shilling hidden in a shoe in case they got into strife with the cops: you could prove you had more than the bus fare home and it'd buy your way out of a good kick up the bum for loitering with intent.

They'd meet down the bottom of Junction Road. There was one

old bloke down there whose roof would cop a few stones before they ran like mad through the bush and up through the brickworks. They'd pull out billycarts with ball-bearing wheels and go screeching down the hills, piercing the late night tranquillity. Ivan was usually along, but it was funny how there was nothing really to remember about him. He was just there. Wouldn't say much.

Ivan's truanting got worse. His mother caught him jigging once and took him straight to school, but he was back home before she was. This went on for months. She knew about it but couldn't stop it. Sometimes, the police brought him home, 'like a taxi service', after finding him wandering about Liverpool. This was the start of a long line of police visits that would always distinguish the family from its neighbours.

Steven wasn't any help with the truanting. Margaret was loath to tell him any of the boys' indiscretions because of the increasingly fierce hidings he was dishing out. She was at her wits' end about what to do with Ivan. With no one else to turn to, she asked a Brother's advice and he recommended Boys Town, a home for wayward boys. Some were delinquents sent by the courts, others were more like Ivan, from poor families who could no longer manage. Margaret Milat applied to have him put there in late 1957. He began in February 1958, aged thirteen. He was allowed home during school holidays and, after the May holiday, his brother Bill, who was also getting into strife at school, joined him. It was as much to do with taking the pressure off Margaret as anything. She would tell people Bill wanted to go because of the glowing reports Ivan gave. It was a holiday camp, he said.

The two boys stayed at the home, run by the Salesian Order, until December. They were both altar boys there. Ivan was the champion boxer in his weight division and even got the best and fairest player award for Aussie Rules football, a sport he never pursued.[16] There were no records kept of his academic achievements or conduct. He was a model student, his mother would say. Ivan was only just going fourteen years old when he got out and already considered himself beyond schooling. He'd learnt a bit about pastry cooking at Boys Town and wanted to do that, but he couldn't get an apprenticeship. When he did apply he was ridiculed. 'Go home, sonny, you're too little. You'll get minced up in the flour bin.'

His return from Boys Town coincided with their mother being about to give birth to her thirteenth child in nineteen years – David John.

Ivan never went back to school. Mum pushed him on Dad and Alex and he joined them at Normie Smee's concrete works at Punchbowl for a while. He and Boris then worked making new American-style chicken cages in great metal frames, as the Australian public turned into chicken eaters. They were working out the back of Bringelly for 'Black Billy' Ryan, a future mayor of Liverpool. Ivan was only there two weeks when he knocked off the tea money. Another young bloke was suspected, so Ivan got away with it. Then a workmate brought in his recently acquired, single-barrelled shotgun to show around work one day. Antique-looking, it was a pretty gun. It dazzled Ivan. The guy didn't even notice it missing at first. Ivan smuggled it home and cut the stock and barrel down to nine inches. The next morning, driving to work with Boris, he took the sawn-off shotty from a bag. 'Hey, look at this, Boris,' he said proudly.

'What. You've got a bloody gun now? Yer mad! You'll up'n kill somebody with it. Ruin your life. Give it here.' Boris wrenched it off him and threw it out the window, into a creek near Hoxton Park. Ivan was shitty with him for the rest of the day, but it was done.[17]

Although television had been introduced to Australians in 1956 the Milats were slow to catch on. The kids would go around to Grandma Piddlesden's house at Cabramatta to watch it. Steven was dead against having that cancer in his house, but Margaret thought she'd go and get one anyway. When the man came to deliver it, Steven chased him out of the house. 'We don't want one. We don't need that garbage.'

So Margaret arranged for the fellow to come back while Steven was at work. He was angry when he came home and saw the picture glowing in the corner with all the kids circled around, but he sat on the edge of a chair and started to watch it. He stayed there then, after a long period without a word, said: 'Can I have my tea in front of it ... I didn't know it would be like this. Why didn't we get one earlier?'

After that, the old man was hooked. He'd be up at 5 a.m. on a Sunday, his one day off, complaining that it didn't come on until 8 a.m. He'd watch it until it closed at 10 p.m., getting the boys to change the channel for him. The children always shut up when he was watching it. He went deaf in later years. Still didn't turn it up. Ivan never watched much TV. He was more into reading his comics or drawing things: houses, cars, motorbikes.

Margaret gave Ivan his first nickname, 'McCackie', after comedian Roy Rene's character Mo McCackie, because, as a little boy, he did good impersonations of him. It was later reduced to 'Mac'. But with TV now in the house, they saw the teen idol cop 'Kookie' in '77 Sunset Strip' and the way he was always combing his hair. It was Ivan all over so his mother started calling him Kookie. It became her special name for him, but to the brothers and sisters he'd always be Mac.

Alex had, meanwhile, met Joan, a local girl who didn't think the Milats so poor. They were the first family she'd met with an automatic washing machine. Like his older sister, Alex couldn't wait to leave home. At nineteen he was out the door and married to Joan. He'd had his one small brush with the law and was determined to go straight.

Like so many kids growing up round there at the time, Collar came to a crossroads. Two really. He got caught by police stealing cars in his early teens and was stopped by his parents from going out for two years. Then, when he was seventeen, he got involved in what they knew as a gang bang near the Liverpool Bridge. There were meant to be about eight boys and one girl who was agreeable to it. 'Youse want it, youse go for it.' Twenty-five turned up. Collar was one of the extras. The station master from the nearby Liverpool Station saw it. Eight of them were charged and that's when he made up his mind to pull his head in and go straight. It was a simple fork in the road.

Over the coming decade, all the Milat boys would have the same choice. They went both ways.

FIVE

1960–1962

THE VENDETTA

Peter Cantarella had the tight black waves, rich brows and dark eyes of a Sicilian. He made his money cutting sugarcane up in north Queensland. He knew about work, and he judged a man by his ability to do it. His trick for working through the stinking wet heat of the tropics was to drink only tea or hot water. If you drank cold water, it poured straight out of you, he'd tell his co-workers. Cantarella was good enough at cutting cane to beat the north Queensland champion, 'some Russian block'. He had to cut 27 ton with a machete in four hours, and he did it three years running – '49, '50, '51. He came south to Moorebank in 1955, and married a local girl, Carmel.

In 1960, he used the money he saved up north to buy a fruit shop. The former owner, Eric Pember, had employed most of the older Milat children as spud boys and general hands at some time or other. Mary, an attractive, full-figured blonde, worked there full-time and stayed on after the sale.

Cantarella liked Mary. She was 'tops'. She was seventeen or eighteen and she never ever stopped working. Cantarella got to know all the family, and his opinions of each were always prefaced by 'good worker' or something similar. And he had never seen anyone work so hard as their father, which was a mighty big concession for him.

The shop, with ample space in front for parking, was on Newbridge Road which had become a major thoroughfare after the bridge across the Georges River to Bankstown replaced the ferry in the 1950s. Fruit and vegie stores sprang up all around. Business was good. Mary recommended her sister Shirley, so Cantarella put her on too. Then

Shirley said her big brother 'Mac' was looking for a job too. 'He work like you?' asked Cantarella. Of course he did.

Ivan stacked boxes, lugged fruit and veg, and he helped at the markets. Cantarella took an instant shine to the sixteen-year-old who became his sidekick. The Sicilian picked him up before dawn most mornings in his old International truck to go to the Haymarket in central Sydney. On the rare occasions when he wasn't ready, Cantarella had to carefully negotiate all the junk in the Milat yard to knock on the door. He'd crash about everywhere in the darkness, waking the whole family.

But Ivan was usually punctual. Cantarella liked him even though he never looked him in the eye. He was always smiling at the ground. Cantarella would buy him breakfast. Once, he told Ivan: 'If you run out of clothes, I give you some. Just come to me if you need anything.'

After six, eight months of good work, Ivan took him up on the offer. He'd found a car he wanted, but his mother wouldn't guarantee the loan with the finance company. So he turned to his boss.

'C'mon, Peter. It's a great car. C'mon, Peter.'

'What's ya money like?'

'Me brother Billy'll give me the rest of the money soon. He's got some coming in.'

Cantarella relented and guaranteed his young employee's loan. Ivan went straight out and bought the white '55 Ford from Parramatta. A day or two later, Cantarella came around in the International to pick him up for work and Mrs Milat came to the door. 'He didn't come back home last night.'

The same thing happened for the next few mornings. He wasn't there, or he was too tired to work. Cantarella cursed having signed for the car. He went around to see Ivan one afternoon.

'Why you not come back to work?'

'I'm running round with me mates now.' That was all the explanation he got. Ivan was driving his brothers and their damn mates all over the place all night. The Sicilian walked out, disgusted. Cantarella had lost him. Couldn't help feeling he would have been a really good bloke if someone had've been there guiding him. He was too easily led. It was plain that his mother couldn't handle them all. His father might have been a good worker, but Cantarella thought maybe he was having a few too many drinks, finding a corner and quietly going to sleep while chaos reigned.

Pretty soon Cantarella was getting letters from the finance company demanding payment of the £300 loan. He wrote the money off.

Ivan knew where Cantarella lived and he knew where he kept a .38 Smith and Wesson pistol plus a shotgun, a .22 rifle and another long-barrelled weapon. When they all went missing, along with Carmel Cantarella's jewellery, Ivan was the logical suspect. Then Carmel's brother, Jim Casata, told Cantarella that one of the Milat boys had told him they'd knocked all this gear off; said Ivan knew the dog, a labrador cross, and that's why it never barked when they snuck in the back.

'Jimmy,' Cantarella said to his brother-in-law, 'talk to them and getta me guns back, will ya.' Jimmy was the sort of bloke to convince them, he knew.

Jimmy spoke to Ivan: 'You better give them guns back to Peter because Peter not muck about.' Anyway, a day or two later, Jimmy came back to Cantarella with the booty. 'Here's bloody all the guns.'

'Where's that pistol?'

'He said he shoved it in the river.'[18] They never saw the wife's jewellery again, yet Cantarella was happy with Jimmy's deal and was going to leave it at that. Somehow, though, the police found out that Cantarella had got his guns back. He had reported them stolen and, suddenly, the police got nasty because he hadn't reported how he got them back. He wanted to keep everything quiet. Then the Milats started going silly because the police were knocking on their door and they thought Cantarella had put them in.

A couple of weeks later, Cantarella – who had copped a fine for failing to keep his weapons secure[19] – was coming home from the shop at dusk, driving the International along Nuwarra Road, when he saw his wife's car angled off the road, near their home. Another car was wedged in front of it. As he got closer, he saw in the twilight that it was Ivan's Ford. A group of four or five blokes jumped in it and shot off.

Cantarella pulled up next to Carmel. She was screaming and shaking.

'Watsamatta?' he shouted, trying to make sense of the situation.

'Aagghh. They force me off the road.'

'Who?'

'The Milat boy forced me off the road. Ivan.' She wailed some more.

All Cantarella's boxes had swayed loose when the truck lurched to a halt in the gravel. They were teetering to one side, making a chase after the louts impossible. He went for his big American '44 Ford Ranch Wagon parked at home, but Carmel grabbed the key and threw it in the bushes. He was armed. He was always armed. She knew her husband was going to try and kill the lot of them. And she feared they would do the same to him.[20]

He cooled down and in the following weeks went looking for Ivan to try to talk sense into the young bastard. Get him to leave his family in peace. Then Cantarella began to hear stories about people having their houses knocked off. He heard something about Ivan bashing a bloke for money in the streets of Liverpool. The local milko was having problems with money going from bottles placed on home doorsteps overnight. A contact told him Ivan and some mates had taken the till from a service station after filling up and hitting the attendant over the head. They were doing this sort of thing all over the place: Parramatta, Villawood and as far as Mascot, 18 miles east. He heard police were after them for a long time.

So, knowing that the boys were out of control, it was a bit of a worry when Ivan turned up on his doorstep one night with some younger kids on pushbikes, riding up and down outside Cantarella's house shouting abuse.

'Come out, ya bloody wog!' They only threw a couple of stones on the roof that first night, but the campaign went on – sometimes on bikes, sometimes on foot. And there were threats against his five-year-old son: 'We're gunna kidnap Maurice ... We're gunna kidnap Maurice,' they yelled from a distance. It was always Ivan and at least three other younger boys disappearing into nearby scrub by the time Cantarella stepped onto his porch.[21] The threat against his son was upping the ante, even if it was only a childish taunt.

Ivan was still only sixteen. Maybe he'd tire of it. Cantarella didn't want to provoke him by reporting the problem to police. Then one morning he came out to his Ranch Wagon and found the tyres slashed, the aerial broken, and all the wiring messed up. The windscreen wipers on the truck were bent backwards. All that didn't matter so much, but the rear brakelight cables had been cut and that made him blow up.[22] He didn't need much explaining who done it, but that was the silly part – they were telling everybody around Liverpool. One bloke who was apparently fencing stolen car parts for Ivan came up to Cantarella: 'That Ivan Milat, he tell me, "I slashed Peter tyre in there".'

Cantarella decided he'd ring Boris and try to talk to him. Boris said he understood. But they kept coming back to the street at night, crying out. 'Ya bloody wog! Bloody wog!' Up and down. Throwing stones. 'We're gunna kidnap Maurice.'

It had to stop.

At twenty-nine, Cantarella still considered himself pretty tough. When he was up cutting cane he'd get up and fight at the tent boxing shows coming through and reckons he fought bush legend Bronco Johnson. He wasn't going to let some kids mess him around. A day or two after their last visit, Cantarella came across Ivan and Bill. Cantarella's story was that he saw a car full of Milats and their friends. Cantarella was with some other blokes and they cut the other car off. He pulled one boy out of the car and some others fled. He went berserk – the money, the gun, the tyres, the threats, they all came to a head – smashing whoever he could get his hands on. He didn't know who. Ivan got away with a few thumps in the head while Cantarella, in a blind rage, hammered the first kid he could get his hands on until the boy's face was a bloody mess. He later learned it was fourteen-year-old Billy.

They left the boy lying there on the edge of Heathcote Road. Clobbered.

Billy's telling of the story lacks the car being run off the road and has two grown men bashing him all alone, after dragging him off his pushbike while looking for his brother. Ivan just happened to come along and find him with a bloodied face after the bashers had left. Whatever, the boys had chosen to play with men. They were seeing how hard you had to be.

Boris, nineteen, was driving home in his ute when he came across Ivan supporting Billy, covered in blood, staggering along Heathcote Road towards home, trying to wheel his bike. As Boris came closer he saw Bill's eye hanging out of its socket and his usually prominent Milat cheekbone pushed in. Boris got him in the ute and took them home to Mum, then on to Liverpool Hospital.

Margaret Milat was sick with a hernia and all sorts of complications. Thirteen children had taken their toll. She'd been in to see the doctor about it all, but had refused the doctor's urgings to stay in hospital. After she got Bill into casualty, Dr Steven Dobell-Brown went with her to the police station where she reported the assault. She didn't believe her boys had ever stolen any guns. She just thought Cantarella was a cruel man who exploited his workers.[23] That was Mum for you.

They went back to the hospital and a nursing sister grabbed her: 'Now I've got you, you won't go anywhere.'

'You aren't taking me anywhere. I'm stopping here with Billy.' And she did.

That wasn't the end of the feud, neither. Bill was in danger of losing an eye. It couldn't stop there. Boris left Mum at the hospital and returned home to find the boys gathered. Ivan, Michael, twelve, even Alex, twenty-two, newly married, and expecting his first child, when he got the call to get over to the house.

Boris was fuming. The boys were all fired up. No matter what Ivan had done, Cantarella was a mongrel, they said, geeing each other up. 'Billy done nothing to them.'

Originally, in Boris' eyes, it had been 'a hurting . . . just a hate thing between Cantarella and Ivan'. But now it was the family's vendetta, a blood feud. Moorebank wasn't big enough for Cantarella to hide. The brothers went hunting that night. They were really gunna let fly; really gunna do harm to Cantarella and the blokes with him. They knew he was armed so they piled into cars and headed for the fruit shop equipped with anything which could inflict pain: axes, tomahawks and a shotgun.[24] The only one missing was Dad. He was at work. He'd threatened to belt them if they ever got in trouble, but they all thought that this time he wouldn't mind. Not that they cared much what the old man thought any more.

Cantarella wasn't at the shop when they got there, so they went after some employees in a truck. Their terrified faces stared out from the cab as the boys rocked it about and hit it with sticks before letting them go unscathed.

Late that afternoon, Cantarella came back from delivering a large order of fruit to the Holsworthy army camp. He noticed two cars parked outside the shop. Each was full of silhouetted heads but, fortunately, Newbridge Road was busy enough for them not to notice him. He reckoned there was a dozen of them. He had a 44/40, but he wasn't going near this mob. He thought they'd shoot him for sure. He called the cops and as soon as they arrived, the Milats shot through.

*

Watching the Milat boys prepare to blue that day was Marilyn Childs. Boris was taking a strong interest in girls and they were taking an interest in him. It was partly having wheels, but he had a bit of the gab, too. This Marilyn from Chipping Norton was a beauty. She had it all. She was spirited, friendly, knew how to handle a gun and she didn't shy away from hard work. She grew up in the backblocks on the same side of the river as the Milats in a family of eight. Her father, Archie, worked for the council. He was a tough, stout man whose trousers were held up with string. They called him Doggie. He had carted soil to the Milats' when they had the garden operating.

Marilyn's family lived in a terrace with a front yard so small her mother Eileen cut the lawn with a pair of scissors. Her grandfather had been in charge of the 47,000 horses that went through the Moorebank remount depot on their way to World War I. His property faced her parents' place in Childs Road, named after the family – such was their pioneering status. Marilyn was twelve and going to school at Liverpool Primary when she met Shirley Milat who caught the same bus to St Mary's. When she was fourteen, with green eyes and jet black hair in a ponytail down her backside, she was among a group of girls who hung about Boris' mate Donny's place at the end of Childs Road, admiring the '32 Ford he was always working on, turning it into a mean street-racing machine.

Boris was nearing the end of a mechanic's apprenticeship and was busy hotting up his own car. He'd drop in and see Donny for advice or go with him and a few of the boys down the sand-dredged lakes at the back of Chipping Norton to shoot carp with shotguns. That's how Boris remembered meeting Marilyn.

Then one day, Marilyn sent him a note saying that she was through with her boyfriend who had almost killed her in a motorbike accident. She said she fancied Boris. He dropped around to her place and was having a 'pash' with her in the front seat when her old boyfriend turned up and went berserk. Boris chased the bloke in his car and challenged him to come and have a go, but the guy told Boris he could have her.

He took to seeing Marilyn more and more, her face still scarred from the bike accident. Pretty soon he was sleeping overnight in the front bedroom at her parents' place. The parents didn't mind. He thought it funny that he was going out with old-man Childs' daughter because years earlier, aged fourteen, he and Ivan and some mates regularly crept into Doggie's yard at night to milk petrol from his trucks.

Boris took her and her girlfriends cruisin' in his car to get hamburgers or to the Star picture theatre in Liverpool. Marilyn was among the few girls Mrs Milat allowed into the house. Mum even gave her a nickname. 'Rare'. Rare by name, rare by nature.

She needed rare tolerance going out with this mob. She never shied away, even after Alex accidentally knocked her sister over with a car[25]. Her relationship with Boris had got too serious too quickly. She was pregnant.

She reflected this day, amid the madness, with Billy in hospital and war breaking out, that Ivan – taller than Boris – was a bit of a loner, different. Interesting.[26]

The feud fizzled once the police became involved. Billy was lucky to keep his sight. Mrs Milat instituted civil proceedings against Cantarella, who also faced police charges. The magistrate put him on twelve months good-behaviour and ordered him to pay Billy's medical costs, legal fees, court costs and £140 compensation. When Billy was old enough to drive, he used £45 of the compo to buy his first car. A 1939 Chevy. He carried a dent in his head for years.

Cantarella regretted hurting Billy, but couldn't help wondering what had gone wrong with them. They used to be such nice boys. Good blokes. Good workers. All of a sudden they were mad, especially Ivan.

Some time later, Cantarella received a letter from Alex in Cairns apologising and saying he wanted nothing more to do with fighting his little brothers' fights. 'I don't want any more trouble with anybody.'[27]

Cantarella never got his .38 back. It reappeared one day in Ivan's hands and seemed to hang around for some time, developing a bit of history of its own.[28] Then it disappeared in a hurry. Those who knew its role in Ivan's teen years would never say.

As soon as Bill was better, the doctors grabbed Margaret and put her in the Royal Women's Hospital, in the inner-eastern suburb of Paddington, where she stayed for a while. Her return home was brief. She soon found herself back in Liverpool Hospital, sick and pregnant with child number fourteen. It was January 1962. Hot as hell. One of the kids came running into the ward and told her Ivan was in trouble. This time it was serious. He'd been arrested and was at Liverpool cop shop.

She rolled herself out of bed, deeply upset by his betrayal. She dressed and walked the two blocks from the hospital across Bigge Park to the station in Moore Street. At forty-one, she was a two-months pregnant grandmother. The station sergeant told her Ivan had been caught burglarising a house. They let her in to see him. The moment she walked into the cell she struck out, slapping him about the head. She wanted to kill him. How could he do this to her? The bemused cops pulled her off. He told her years later how much the flogging hurt. She had hit him for the first time only the year before: a stiff backhander for answering back. That shocked him too. But it was all so late.

Her condition deteriorated after the police station incident, and she spent the next six months in hospital waiting out her pregnancy. She wanted one more girl. The nine boys were giving her so much grief. She had already thought of a name. Rebecca.

On 11 June 1962, Ivan, aged seventeen, went before Liverpool Children's Court to answer the charge of stealing in a dwelling. The magistrate was very understanding. It was his first known offence, he was contrite and his mother was ill. Of course he had to be shown leniency. He was given a good-behaviour bond and told to keep his nose clean until the age of eighteen, only a few months away.

But it didn't help. He was back before the same court on 27 August, charged with break and enter on a garage. He was in breach of his bond and the magistrate felt he needed to be taught a lesson. He was sent to Mount Penang Juvenile Institution near Gosford on the Central Coast for six months hard labour.

Set in bushland overlooking the little fishing town of Woy Woy, the Mount Penang centre was no holiday camp. It was a time when beltings were routine for minor offences, like answering back. Some of the hardest kids in the state went there. If it didn't scare them on to the straight and narrow first time, they were lost. Bad kids came out worse.

Three days after she heard that 'Kookie' had become her first son jailed, and still very sick, Margaret gave birth to boy number ten, Paul Thomas. The doctors wouldn't let her go home because they knew she'd get no rest, but she'd been in hospital since January and was desperate to get back to the family.

After pleading for months, the doctors relented and let her go two days before Christmas, 1962. She got home and everybody was tiptoeing around. It nearly drove her stupid. It was a long time before she was active again. A neighbour saw her at the clothes line sitting down, having a break. It was the first time she'd ever seen Margaret rest. She always had so much energy and strength, but she stayed like this for a long time.

One place where young people would gather in the days when you had to be twenty-one to get a beer was a straight stretch of Heathcote Road they called the Mad Mile – about five miles out of Liverpool in the bush past Deadmans Creek. It was where you went if you fancied your car could run a bit. There'd probably be five or six cars racing on a Saturday night – two at a time, side by side. Plenty more would come to watch, cheering and yahooing, checking out the cars and each other. There was a rise in the course, so a car load would go down one end and sound an all-clear with a foghorn to signal that nothing was coming the other way.

Boris was racing a hotted-up American Ford and he and Ivan hooked up with an old mate, John Parsons, who they'd known while welding chook cages. Parsons was starting to race his car too. The old engines were a delicate balancing act of air and petrol, and you'd have to tune them by feel. Boris was brilliant at it and he used to help Parsons with his motor, so Parsons, though four years older than Boris, started hanging out with the Milat boys again. Amazingly, there was room for him to regularly stay over at their place.

A month after Mum gave birth to Paul, Marilyn went into labour. She was living with Boris in the dilapidated old shed the Milats first lived in when they came to Moorebank. She gave birth to a girl, Charlene, but there were no wedding bells, just the guarantee of a roof over her head in the shack. She became a witness to the changes in the family. She saw the cops always knocking on the door and heard Mrs Milat telling them about all the other kids in the area who they should be looking at – the real troublemakers. Through Marilyn's teenage eyes, though, they were just boys having fun. They still lived in dread of their father, especially the little ones. He was still powerful but he was getting slower on his feet. They knew, however, that no matter how old he was getting, if he caught them it'd hurt bad.

The neighbour Betty Card had moved away to marry, but when she returned two years later, in 1961, she could tell there'd been big changes at the Milat place. The boys had gone wild. The police were there all the time. With Margaret in hospital throughout 1962, and Steven at work most days, the brakes had come off completely.

SIX

1963

THE BUZZ

In Margaret's eyes Ivan came out of Mount Penang in early 1963 as good as gold. He turned eighteen inside the juvenile correctional institution, and had learned to smoke, but had no inclination to drink. 'I'll never go back,' he promised his mother and, with the little things he was doing, it was easy to believe. He told her to go out and leave the Sunday roast to him one day. When the family came home, dinner was ready and he'd even baked some cup cakes and made a dessert. He was such a good boy.

It was inevitable, though, that Ivan and some of his brothers gravitated back to the richer life of the Liverpool streets and the pickings from petty crime. When it happened, Margaret blamed his mates. He was in with the wrong crowd. He was easily led. Unfortunately, some of the Milat boys were the wrong crowd. They became wilder as time went on; visits from police more frequent. And all the while Margaret Milat retained the firm public stance that her innocent sons were subject to harassment and persecution.

Saturday night in Liverpool was, at times, a small riot and, once a fortnight, army payday wasn't bad either. Compulsory national service was in full swing, bringing a new batch of fresh-faced youths to town each year, and payday meant they were cashed up, looking for a place to spend. Police wagons cruised the streets around the railway station waiting for the fight to start. Right behind them were the military police.

But the old Liverpool was giving way to the new. The population of the district increased by 5000 a year through the sixties. The Green Belt restrictions had been busted up and the housing minister had turned the first sod on the Green Valley Garden Housing Project in

1961. What the first arrivals got was fibro houses on dirt and clay with no footpaths, no shops, no transport. Plenty of babies, though. They called it Pram City. Same thing was happening in Moorebank on a smaller scale. A social crisis in waiting.

Cruising was entertainment. It might only go as far as lairising or yelling abuse, but if anyone ever wanted to take it further, the Milats were always ready with a small arsenal. Always.

One early morning, Boris, Ivan and some mates did a smash-and-grab on a George Street gun shop between Haymarket and Town Hall. With Central Police Station not far away, they had to be quick. The alarm went off when they went through the front window, and some garbos came running around the corner, armed with brooms. When the garbos saw guns levelled at them, they turned and bolted. The boys pissed themselves laughing as they piled back into Boris' hotted-up Ford. He gunned it down Broadway, running lights all the way to the safety of the Hume Highway at Ashfield. All they had to show for it was a pair of binoculars.[29]

One time there was a gang of them in the Ford. They had just done a smash-and-grab on a shop in St Marys, about 18 miles north-west of Moorebank, in Sydney's outer-west. Lots of people had seen them and now they were running scared out in the open, full throttle back towards home. Nought to a hundred in no time flat. No one could catch Boris' Ford. But sure enough, a car swung in behind them, and was closing in. Boris pushed it up to maybe 115 mph with a red light staring at them as they hit the Great Western Highway. There was no time to do anything. They shut their eyes and shot straight across the busy intersection. Fuck it was a buzz.

They hammered down Mamre Road, sure they had got away clean, but then the other car appeared through the intersection, closing in. They started throwing all the stolen gear out: tape recorders, cameras, watches. All the evidence. The pursuit car was bearing down quickly.

'What the fuck are the cops driving?'

They'd never shot at anyone before this, but they were ready, all yelling, panicking over the throaty engine. 'We're not going to jail. No way. We can get out of this. As soon as the bastard comes alongside, we'll get him.'

They all agreed. All except Ivan. He just wasn't going to do it.

As the car drew up with them, everyone's guns came up. All except Ivan's. He was sitting behind Boris in the prime shooting position. The only thing that saved the guy was that the others weren't in as good a spot. Before anybody could get a shot off, the guy saw all the guns, shit himself, and hit the brakes.[30]

'Struth, he's not a bloody cop.'

He was just another petrolhead in for a drag. Back then, Ivan and Boris were more like mates than brothers. When they were out cruising, trying to chat up girls, they adopted a strategy of never using their real names. Their mates did it too. Ivan was 'Kookie' to Mum, 'Mac' to his siblings and his few friends, but out on the prowl he'd be 'Joe Spanner' or 'Sid Chrome'. Boris was called 'Bull', with its good and bad connotations – as in bull at a gate, or bullshit.

One day, they stopped to pick up a young sheila thumbing a ride to a caravan park. Ivan fancied her from the start. She was friendly, nice looking, even if she was sporting a big black eye from where someone had punched her. She didn't talk much about that specifically, just about her family problems. She was obliging, too. Boris took them to a caravan where the three shacked up for a couple of hours. She was 'willin' to have a root' when Ivan put it on her. Never complained. Only about the hassle she was having with her own life. He never displayed any violence to her. They were only kids.[31]

The brothers left her and continued to cruise about, with no particular purpose. It was dark, all the shops had shut, when Boris' car battery began to play up. They were on the Hume Highway near The Crossroads on Liverpool's outer boundary. They came to a stop outside a Shell Service Station. It was closed, but Ivan was out of the car heading towards it.

'What are you doin'?' asked Boris.

'Just stay there. I'll be back in a minute.'

Boris had his suspicions but didn't want to know. Before he could do anything about it the alarm was ringing. Boris didn't have time to get out of the car before the police were suddenly on top of him. God only knows how they got there so quick – uniformed cops, detectives and all. One said something about a man running around with a sawn-off shotgun. As far as Boris was concerned he had nothing to do with whatever was going on. His car had broken down and he wasn't breaking the law. Just sitting there minding his own business. 'Just nick off . . . just leave me alone. I have nothin' to do with that.'

As police surrounded the garage the sound of shattering glass came from the rear of the building. Inside, Ivan had seen them, and reacted like a cornered animal, hurling the battery he'd planned to nick through a side window, then jumping out. He ran for his life down the hill at the back, through paddocks towards the Georges River, blood flowing from a deep gash on his leg. Kept running straight into the river and swam across to the Moorebank side, then covered at least four miles cross-country. It was only when he reached home that he saw how deep the cut was. He'd carry that scar for life, telling mates that he'd run through a window holding the battery out in front of him.[32]

Boris was in deep trouble back at Liverpool Police Station, copping a few clips around the ear. He was still denying he had anything to do with the break-in. He genuinely believed he'd done nothing wrong, and he expected them to believe it. But with a flat battery in his car, him sitting outside a garage with the burglar alarm ringing while someone inside steals a battery – come on. He stuck to his guns, though.

All they wanted to know was the identity of his accomplice.

'I've had nothing to do with that. Really . . . I just broke down.'

'This is what we found in your car,' said an officer, displaying one little round seed in the palm of his hand. Boris didn't know what the hell it was.

'This is marijuana. A very serious offence.' They could have shown him asparagus. He had never seen a cannabis plant in his life, let alone a seed, nor had any of his brothers then. He didn't even know if it was something you ate or drank, but he knew that drugs were a bloody serious criminal matter. They gave him a clip around the ear.

'You're not proving anything,' Boris protested, petrified.

'Oh well, that's what you're going to be charged with.'

The threat forced him to agree to admit his part in the burglary. He refused to give Mac up, though. It enraged one officer, a red-headed bloke, who come running at him. Whhamm, as hard as he could. Literally flung Boris across the room. Boris knew it looked bad, but didn't hurt much, so he bunged on the screams and groans. 'Me back. Me back.' They panicked and the red-headed officer was taken from the room. Boris made a statement without mentioning Mac, and signed it.

At court the following morning he said nothing about any of this. A cop said they'd say he had no priors and was a good young bloke, overall, so long as he didn't mention the bashing.[33] He was charged with accessory to break and enter and later fined and placed on a good-behaviour bond. Mum came and collected him from the police cells and took him home where Ivan had his leg all bandaged up. Boris decided that day that crime wasn't his calling.

Boris had been staunch. He hadn't given his brother up to the cops. They were still mates, but the first cracks were appearing. Mac seemed too friendly with Marilyn. He should have shown more respect. Maybe it was Bull's imagination, but Ivan was always coming to their old shack and chatting away real cosy. It gnawed away.

The family had acquired an old scrap metal truck. No windows in it. Nothing. Between normal working days, the boys would go around in it collecting scrap metal to sell. This day, Marilyn was sitting in the front beside Boris with Ivan standing on the tray at the back, smiling at her. Boris was fuming with an irrational pain in his belly. As they approached a sharp bend, he couldn't help but turn hard into it. 'I'll kill this bastard.'

Ivan came rolling off, landing hard on the road. Boris stopped and Marilyn ran over to Mac. She picked him up and helped him into the cabin. He was concussed and she cuddled him all the way home.

SEVEN

1964

'THOU SHALT...'

Ivan, nineteen, was doing some casual labouring for the Water Board on twenty quid a week. Then, for almost two months, nothing. For a bloke who wasn't bludging cash, he managed to have a good time. Most of the family seemed to think he was responsible for a theft that cost Billy his job with the local milko, though there was no way the poor bloke could prove who done it.

Then, one night, Ivan and his mate Johnny Parsons got talking about Johnny's money problems, trying to bring up two girls on compo. Ivan seemed genuinely concerned and thought he could do Parsons a good turn, but he had to be game.[34]

'The army camp's down the road there. It's bloody got no guards or anything. You can just walk in, walk out,' Ivan told him. Parsons was up for it. He was desperate.

'Let's go and have a look. We'll take my ute.' So they jumped in and drove the mile down to the Holsworthy Village where soldiers with families lived. No guards, just like Ivan said. The Partridge Club boozer – wet canteen – was all shut up, and there was this beautiful great lock on the door called an Impregnable or something. It was hanging on a tiny bit of tin. They had cutting gear, but hardly needed it because one of them grabbed the Impregnable lock with his hands, and just twisted the tin off the door. They could see a safe bolted to the wall. One of them got a blanket to lessen the racket when they crowbarred it off. It came away without a problem and they wheeled it out to the ute on a trolley.

They drove 18 miles to isolated bushland out the back of Bringelly and set to the steel safe with an axe and a sledgehammer. It was a long noisy slog, but they eventually got a little hole in one corner, then put the axe in the opening and used it like a chisel. A few hours more and they had it open like a tin of baked beans. Bingo. They pulled out somewhere between £200 and £400 – ten to twenty weeks' pay. Ivan put £36 towards repayments on his Ford Zephyr, but he wrecked it within weeks hooning around the back of the army camp. Still flush, he bought an old Dodge for £45.

Almost two months after they hit the jackpot at the army club, Parsons and Ivan decided to do the same place again. This time, on 12 July, two others went along for the ride. They were like kids amok in a lolly shop. One of them got some dye and threw it over the racks of drycleaning hanging there. One of them shat in an ice cream tin. It was that thrill of vandalism. It was the buzz.[35] They got the safe and a treasure trove of other goodies sold at the club.

They cut the safe open the same way, but didn't do so well this time. Got between £15 and £45 total. They put the safe back in the ute and drove to the bridge over the Nepean River at Wallacia where they threw it in. Parsons dropped Ivan home at about six o'clock in the morning. Mum went crook so he told her he was driving around in John's ute and it broke down. Next day was Sunday, anyway.

Shirley had married a German, Gerhard Soire, and they settled at Hillview where the Housing Commission was in the process of knocking up 1764 new houses. Gerry was a builder's labourer who shared her brothers' interest in guns, so they all got on fine, despite some ingrained anti-German prejudice. No sooner had they married and settled than she was pregnant.

Four of the older Milat children had left the fold now, leaving Boris, twenty-two, and Ivan, nineteen, as the senior offspring, helping keep the remaining eight kids – aged between seventeen and almost two – in check. So long as they lived at home they were expected to help Dad put bread on the table. Nine-year-old Margaret – a sweet, quiet child whom they all adored and protected – was the only girl left at home and was learning to look after the baby, Paul. Then there was Marilyn, ensconced in the old house at the front, who also lent a hand with the young ones.

Ivan became the leader. He was around more than Boris who was holding down a regular day job and two part-timers at night trying to get the cash to move his young family out and start a business of his own. His relationship with Ivan was starting to splinter, as Mac always seemed to be in his home with Marilyn.

Once, Boris came home and found them in the bedroom, wrestling on the bed like two kids, giggling away. He blew his stack over it. 'Keep your bloody mitts off her.' They had a blue in the front yard and he beat Ivan, but everyone told him he was being stupid. Another time he found Ivan behind the lounge, but that was dismissed as a game of hide-and-seek.

Marilyn knew Ivan had been up to no good, but there was a certain cheekiness to it all. He was exciting to be around, more daring than Boris. He wasn't so much a loner as an individual. Her liking for him grew as she saw him mature physically: his dark hair, incredible blue eyes and physique; that smiling yet distant air that made her think he was shy. He was kinder, more caring and gentle towards her than Boris, who was sometimes rough and explosive like his dad.

Ivan would stick up for her during their rows. Then Boris, driven by jealousy, hit her a few times after Charlene come along. Mac went off at him and was told to mind his own business. At first, she just liked to flirt with Mac – girl stuff – but the way she saw it Boris' suspicions were pushing them closer together.

Boris had cooled towards her. Bed became just a place for sleeping. He was punishing her, he thought. She was bound to Bull by a child, but whenever she saw Mac her heart went 'Ooooh Yeeaah'. Other family members could see what was going on, but they never interfered. It wasn't their business.

Ivan had started talking about Marilyn to his mates, like Johnny Parsons. Never anything about fancying her, just about what a top bird she was. They'd be yacking about something else and Ivan would bring her name up completely out of context. Parsons thought it strange, Ivan talking about his sister-in-law all the time.[36]

Parsons was never too clear on how the cops got onto him. He thought an in-law might have dobbed him in to curry favour with the cops.

Ivan may well have had warning of what was going on. His records at the Water Board show that he didn't turn up 24 July, a Wednesday. He saw Marilyn and they had it off. She wasn't on the pill. He didn't use a condom. They were living out on the edge.

Next day, just after the winter dawn, the police knocked on the Milats' door at Junction Road. Detectives Brennan, Newall and Campbell had a conversation with Mrs Milat. They pushed their way through and found Ivan under his bed.

Their version: 'We are from the Liverpool detectives. Get up off the floor.'

He got up.

'What were you doing on the floor?'

'I was looking for my shoes.'

'We are making enquiries into a robbery committed on the Partridge Club . . .' they said, launching into the copybook arrest routine that made it to court. '. . . I want you to understand you are not obliged to answer any questions . . .'

Bail was set at £250. Milat didn't have it, his mother couldn't afford it, so he landed in Parramatta Jail. About a fortnight later, Mrs Milat turned up at the Liverpool detectives office and handed Brennan some of the booty: a lady's Sunbeam hair drier, one pair of Fairview binoculars, one Ronson Varaflame cigarette lighter, and one Philips transistor radio.

On 24 August, Ivan and Parsons stood in the dock at Liverpool Court of Petty Sessions and agreed with the prosecutor that they would plead guilty, except they weren't happy with the amount of loot the cops said they got. 'There wasn't that much money there,' said Ivan. It was his first conviction as an adult.

Not long afterwards, police were again knocking on 24 Junction Road, this time to tell Margaret that they'd arrested Billy, seventeen, and Mick, fifteen, the two brothers immediately younger than Ivan. In his absence, or perhaps excited by stories about the safe job, they'd followed him off the rails. On 7 September, they faced Liverpool Children's Court on three counts of stealing batteries. Because it was their first offence, they were released on twelve months' probation.

Both Ivan and Parsons were committed to the Campbelltown Court of Quarter Sessions for separate sentencing. On 29 October, the judge gave Ivan eighteen months. On 2 December, he went from remand at Parramatta Jail, to Long Bay, then a month later to the fenceless, minimum-security Emu Plains Prison Farm at the foot of the Blue

Mountains, west of Sydney, where he worked in the gardens. Parsons got no such luxury. He copped twenty-seven months in maximum security at Parramatta.

Mrs Milat visited Mac regularly, taking him small luxuries. His sentence and the arrest of the two younger boys convinced her more than ever that the police had it in for the boys. For the second time in his life, thirteen-year-old George Milat found himself being dragged along with the younger kids to see Ivan in jail. Those visits were George's most vivid schoolboy images of Mac. Marilyn joined them. She was pregnant.

Steven Milat could only vent his anger at the remaining children, lecturing them to obey the law and to fear what he'd do to them after the police had dealt with them. Yet, there was still part of him that chose to believe his sons – that the persecution of his family was somehow the work of the Yugoslavian secret police. Dad was kept in the dark for years about just how often the police did come knocking while he was at work. It was in everyone's interest, Mum's included, that he didn't know because he'd go right off. The boys helped lead the old man along with the secret police story. Whenever they'd see a police car cruise past, checking them out, they'd shout, 'It's the secret police,' and run for cover, laughing. All one big joke.

EIGHT

1965

THE HURTIN'

Marilyn's waters broke just before midnight while she and Boris were asleep. Amniotic fluid was everywhere and Boris started carrying on about her having done it on purpose.[37]

She had been told by her doctor during a check-up two weeks before that if the baby wasn't born within a week they would induce her. She never went back to that doctor, just let the baby come when it was good and ready – the pre-dawn of 5 May.

Boris wasn't there for the birth of his second daughter who Marilyn named Lynise, but it broke his heart when he saw her next morning, almost devoid of hair, squinting at the harsh light through blue eyes. It should have been a happy time, but he wasn't feeling right. Other family had gathered, admiring the baby through the glass of the nursery ward, pointing at the little bundle, making all the appropriate cooing noises.

Boris studied the child. He felt she was completely different to his first, Charlene.

'That's not my child,' he said, under his breath. His stomach knotted. All the suspicion of Ivan came to the fore when he looked at that child. Marilyn – black hair, green eyes. Boris – dark hair, brown eyes. Baby – wisp of light blonde hair and blue eyes.

He did something crazy. He telephoned his old flame Lyn for revenge. He'd been seeing her during the pregnancy. He knew he was a bit of a bad bastard cheating on his missus, but reasoned fair was fair. It was payback for the cheating he couldn't prove.

Boris had at first tried psychology on Marilyn. Tried to win her back by refusing to sleep with her. That's when she got pregnant.[38] Ivan had been in custody for nine months and eleven days – not that Boris knew the exact dates. He'd recall that the baby might have come early, perhaps two weeks early, but Marilyn knew she was a few days over full term.

He drove to Lyn's place. She was waiting with a friend. He took both of them to a movie. Later he bawled his eyes out to her, telling her his problems: how he still loved Marilyn; how could she do this? They cuddled in the back seat of his car, then cried together in each other's arms, knowing that they could never have a relationship – she was Marilyn's best friend. It was wrong. It had to end. They cried some more.[39]

Boris calmed down next day and went to see Marilyn and the baby as if nothing had happened. Later, he brought them back to the shack at Junction Road, back to all their old arguments. The hostility was rising with his growing certainty she had betrayed him. Marilyn had denied his accusations right through the pregnancy, not out of fear, but because she didn't want to believe it herself. She was still denying it to Boris after Lynise's birth. Better to let things be that way, she supposed.[40] Then, one afternoon, after weeks of soul searching, Boris decided to accept the situation. He picked the child up and, as he rocked her in his arms, he decided she was his. 'I'll be the father,' he said, fondly. 'Look at her, Marilyn, isn't she lovely? My beautiful daughter.' Life seemed so good at that moment.

'What makes you think she's yours?' Marilyn sneered.

He went still, like nothing he'd felt in his life. As if he was dead, brain dead. Then a quickly rising rage went through him, out beyond any rage he'd ever felt before – and he'd had some beauties. He wanted to smash Lynise into the wall. He nearly killed a baby that day, and he'd never forget it as long as he lived. He was so close. If Marilyn knew what was in his mind at that instant, she would have been terrified. He went all shaky inside. If he had his gun on, he probably would have shot them all.

But he handed Marilyn the baby and walked out – totally off his head.[41] For someone who didn't drink, he had an incredible well of anger.

A few days later Ivan was paroled. Everyone in the family was looking forward to his homecoming; except Boris who'd been told by Mum to bite his tongue. Marilyn was especially bubbly.[42]

Mac came out of Emu Plains Prison Farm bronzed and fitter than ever, despite smoking a fag every thirty minutes. He had served barely eleven months of his eighteen-month lag. The day he came home, 18 June 1965, Boris wasn't among those to greet him. Marilyn was sitting in the lounge room. Mac walked in and went straight to the baby in the pram, beaming his broad smile. His chest puffed up when he saw her. Proud as Punch. He knew she was his. Marilyn told him so.[43]

Despite all the drama, Boris had been trying to make a go of his own business. In the two years since he copped the bond over the petrol station break and enter, he held down at least five jobs and figured he'd be better off being his own boss. With all the Housing Commission work around Liverpool there were fortunes to be made. He tried site preparation work, digging foundation ditches. The old man came out to show him how and to give a hand from time to time. Then he worked at clearing rubbish and waste material from building sites. Then he and Alex cottoned on to a more lucrative scheme – scrubbing off the excess cement from finished brickwork. It was hard yakka, but good money.

Work wasn't that easy to get for someone like Ivan, unskilled and straight out of the can, so Alex, who was still great mates with Mac, offered to help him out with a few days labouring. Boris agreed. Their relationship was a strange one. And it wasn't helped when Mum started calling Lynise 'Kookie', the name she had given Ivan as a boy. The rest of the family called her 'Nanook'.

Thursday, 15 July. Army provost sergeant Andrew 'Andy' Anderson was patrolling the vast bushland perimeter of the Holsworthy army base with a corporal when he saw a small civvy van barrelling along the dirt track towards them. Barely minutes earlier, a wireless message from Liverpool police had come over the military police mobile radio to keep an eye out for a stolen 1960 Holden panel van. Description: cream in colour, registration Charlie-Echo-Zulu-four-six-one, stolen this date from Macquarie Street, Liverpool. Owner . . .

The military police, 'provos', liaised well with the New South Wales coppers in the area. They had to if they were going to break up all the fights. Roads surrounding the bases were deemed to be joint jurisdiction. Anderson took note of the oncoming panel van with two people inside, tearing along towards Liverpool from the direction of Deadmans Creek. He saw the numberplate CEZ 461 as it shot past. The MPs turned around and gave chase with their siren blaring. The rough track gave the military vehicle an edge and they bore down on the van quickly, but it wouldn't stop. They drew level and Anderson shouted at the wide-eyed teenager at the wheel: 'Military Police, pull over, driver.'

The van raced on so they rammed it into the scrub. The MPs pulled over in front and scrambled out to make the arrest, but the van came at them, colliding with their driver's-side door and front mudguard. The occupants bolted into the bush with the provos chasing. The corporal tackled the young driver, as the older bloke disappeared into the scrub. They handcuffed the one they had and took him to Liverpool Police Station.[44] It was Billy Milat. Six days earlier, he turned eighteen. Now he was in deep trouble – again. The night before, he was caught stealing an axe from the Railways Department and was only just out on bail.

Now, detectives hammered him about who his accomplice in the car was, but Billy wasn't saying. They asked the provos if they got a look at the passenger. They reckoned they did. Young bloke in his early twenties with dark wavy hair. Anderson was given a small file of eleven mug shots. 'That one,' he said, pointing to a photo of a handsome, unshaven rocker with a messed-up, teddy-boy quiff – curling right to left over the brow. Detective Sergeant Burnie looked at the name on the mug shot which had been concealed from Anderson. 'Ivan Robert Marko Milat.' The height, 5'11", seemed wrong. Perhaps he was wearing high heels when the shot was taken.

Twenty-seven days out of jail and he was back in trouble.

The panel van Ivan and Billy stole belonged to Ernie Tomasello, a contract electrician from Cabramatta. He had parked it in Macquarie Street, Liverpool, just before 2 p.m., opposite McGraths Holden where he had business to do. He threw the keys onto the seat and covered them with his leather jacket, leaving the door unlocked. He didn't plan to be there long and could see it from the yard. He got yaking to a salesman, occasionally glancing over at the van. He was distracted briefly, then looked up to see another motorist parking in his spot. 'Mama mia.' Tomasello's livelihood – £150 worth of electrical goods and tools – was in the van. The driver of the car now parked in the spot said he saw two men drive off in the van.

As the driver gave the despondent Tomasello a lift to the police station, Billy and Ivan had already crossed the Georges River bridge, heading towards Deadmans Creek. About two and a half miles past the creek, near Menai, they turned off Heathcote Road and down a dirt track, stopping 100 yards along it.

Tomasello was still in reporting the loss to police when they heard of the van's recovery. He got his tools back but never saw the leather jacket again.

Billy Milat knew he was in real trouble this time. The cops had identified Ivan as being with him. He had no choice but to save his own neck. He was headed for the big house if he didn't.

The night before Billy stole the panel van with Ivan, he had breached his latest bond for stealing the batteries by stealing the axe. So he confessed to the panel van job, and put Ivan in. Billy scrawled the confession in running writing and block letters.

Ivan wasn't home when detectives raided the house at Moorebank that night. He'd done a bolt. The next day, Friday, 16 July, Billy fronted Liverpool Court and pleaded guilty to stealing the axe. He copped a £20 fine, but was still in deep shit over the car. He fronted court for that on Friday, 24 September, with Ivan still at large. Boris was the only family member who came to plead for leniency; that Billy was a young kid who had been led astray by a bad influence – Ivan. He offered to put up a bond. He told Judge McKillop that he too had been bad, but had reformed. Billy's solicitor, Mr Hall, established that Boris had his own successful business, then asked him about Billy being rehabilitated.

Boris: *I've known Billy Milat, my brother ever since he was born and it's very hard to explain, but he's one of my few brothers that's very considerate to my mother, myself and the rest of the family and I have been talking to him since about this and he himself has said to me he would like another chance and that if he could he is quite willing to go to work and behave himself in future. It's very hard to explain, but my personal opinion is that he will behave himself in future.*

You committed a number of offences nearly all of which you were arrested for on the spot or shortly after?
That's quite true.
Criminally minded?
I was probably more criminally minded than my brother was.

What I want to put to you, is your own career in crime was not a successful one?

No, it wasn't. I've explained to him time and time again that you can do better going out and working honestly.

Do you think that if His Honour gave your brother the chance you would be able to help him, and he would be able to give up these associates?

He hasn't seen any of these associates for a great long time. Since the trouble, he has been under very strict surveillance at home. Dad realises the importance of keeping a better eye on him and so does Mum and I've taken an interest in helping him and that's what I want to do. If he can get a chance here today I want him to come to work under me and I can employ him.

He is at the moment working for the Water Board?

He is. He hasn't a very bright future there.

Billy was sent to prison for eighteen months, but he was out earlier than expected. His time in jail had two consolations – he escaped being drafted into the army for Vietnam, and he proved the court wrong by going straight when he got out. He had come to that fork in the road. Far from him not having a bright future at the Water Board, he would still be there thirty years later in a middle-management role.

The day Billy was caught, Ivan came home in the dark across the paddocks from Anzac Village and through the old weed-infested garden beds. He looked pretty ratshit. He didn't hang around long. Got some clothes and headed off to Grandma Piddlesden's place at Cabramatta. The cops came at least eight times looking for him over the following months. Every time, Mrs Milat told them: 'Haven't seen him, don't know where he is.' Despite all the problems he put them through, she shielded him, told a bold-faced lie. She couldn't put him in.

He was coming and going, skulking in late when he thought the police weren't likely to come knocking. He got so cocksure, he went back to work for the Water Board under a false name until the police arrived one day asking after an Ivan Milat. They were told there was no such employee. He later bragged about spotting them and scarpering before they eyeballed him. Didn't stop to give his notice or pick up his pay.

Steven Milat was always gruff but polite to the police, but when they left, he'd explode. He'd had a gutful of it, coming on top of Billy and Michael. He was quick to collar Mac and another brother after one such visit. He bounced them around the backyard while twelve-year-old George looked on at what the future might hold for him. 'Youse must obey the laws.' Belt and Bang. When they got away from him, he chased them, chucking anything he could pick up. Then he lectured the little ones with the same lecture he'd once given Ivan and the older boys: the only way to be good was to get up at 4 a.m., walk to work, work hard, then walk home. Earn a crust the right way. Work, work, work . . .[45]

When not working or shouting at the younger children, Steven Milat was glued to the television. His favourite show was the 'Alfred Hitchcock Mystery Hour'. He became such a fan of Hitchcock he wrote him a few letters. While watching the box, Steven would be deep in his own world playing a strange version of solitaire, muttering unintelligible words to himself, scooping his cup into a bucket of homemade wine under the table.

Ivan was caught napping. On Saturday, 6 November, at 8.15 a.m., the same four cops who put Billy away – Millington and Spicer, and two junior Ds, Bucton and Brennan – drove their unmarked car onto the front lawn of the ramshackle place and blocked the driveway. Mrs Milat heard them coming, but it was too late. Bucton went to the right of the house, Brennan stayed out near the car, while Spicer and Millington went around the back and banged on the kitchen door.

'I haven't seen him. Haven't seen him for a couple of weeks,' Mrs Milat said staunchly. George was in the house when the cops come busting in the back. He saw Ivan panic and jump out one of the house's few windows, then saw him chased. The cop grabbed him so hard George thought he almost pulled Ivan's arm and leg off. Detective Constable Keith Bucton wrote in his report that he merely went to the right side of the house and saw the accused disappearing under the house and grabbed him by the leg.

'I'm from the police. What's your name?'

'Ivan Milat.'

'Where are you going?'

'I was going up under the house to look for tennis balls.'

Millington and Spicer questioned Milat for thirty minutes back at

Liverpool Police Station. They accused him of stealing the van and the axe for another safe job.

Ivan denied it, then, when asked if he wanted to make a statement, said: 'No, I'll see Mum first.'

Ivan Milat appeared in Liverpool Magistrate's Court on Monday, 8 November, charged with larceny of a motor vehicle. His mum organised Liverpool solicitor Paul Winter to appear for him to try to get him bail. He had little to work with: 'The defendant has been at his mother's home or at his grandmother's home. He is in constant employment. The defendant has been available for a period of something like four months . . . Why he couldn't be found I am unable to say. He has been working regularly and resides regularly with his mother.'

Mrs Milat wanted to take the witness stand, but the Prosecutor, Sergeant Boland, objected. 'When police last visited the mother, [she] said she hadn't seen her son for three weeks and then the defendant jumped out of a window and tried to escape.' The magistrate allowed her to be called and she was sworn in.

I have been asked about three times over the last three months where my son was. The first time was 15 July 1965. This was at night. I said to the police that he wasn't at home. I said I didn't know where he was then. At the time I didn't know where he was. He came home later at about 8 p.m. I told him the police had come. He said he hadn't done nothing so they don't want him. They came a few days later, it was about 4.30 p.m. I said I don't know where Ivan was. I did not know where he was. He was at my mother's in Lyons Avenue. The third time I saw him [the policeman] was at about 5 p.m. a week after that. I said he wasn't there. He was at Lyons Avenue then . . . He was away for about a fortnight and then he came home and been there ever since . . .

Boland: 'On the Saturday morning you were asked, before your son was arrested, about his whereabouts and you told them you hadn't seen him for a fortnight.'

I said I hadn't seen him.

'You knew he was in the house?'

Yes.

'He ran out of the house?'

Yes.

'The police have been to your home on numerous occasions inquiring about your son's whereabouts?'

About three times.

'More like eight or nine times.'

No.

'You didn't tell the police your son was staying at his grandmother's?'

No. She's a sick woman.

'(Did you) know that he was working at the Water Board under an assumed name?'

Yes.

The magistrate was well aware of the dodgy testimony. 'Mrs Milat has obviously misled the inquiring officers.' He set bail at a whopping £500 – six months wages for a labourer. The Milats couldn't raise that sort of money and so Ivan bided his time in Parramatta Jail awaiting his committal two weeks later, on 22 November. On that day, his lawyer attacked the validity of the alleged records of interview what defence lawyers had come to know as 'verbals' – unsigned records of interview, backed up only by other police witnesses – but to no avail. Ivan was committed to stand trial the following year.

He spent Christmas and his twenty-first birthday on remand in Parramatta Jail.

NINE

1966–1967

FAMILY AFFAIR

In the old days, felons sentenced at Darlinghurst Court for crimes like murder and rape didn't have far to walk to the gallows in the jail out the back. But the Court of Quarter Sessions, with its sandstone walls now blackened by the Taylor Square exhaust fumes, was somewhat more benign by this Monday, 28 February 1966, when the matter of Regina v Ivan Robert Marko Milat came to it.

The one-day hearing before Judge Cameron Smith was short and to the point.

The jurors heard Milat plead his innocence from the dock instead of the witness stand – a legal move which prevented the Crown prosecutor from cross-examining him. Mac stood as the jury of twelve men returned after deliberating for just twenty-five minutes. Guilty. The judge wasted no time in passing sentence. Two years hard labour, backdated to 6 November 1965, the day of his arrest.

Despite the growing feud, Boris had taken the stand to give alibi evidence for his brother: that Mac couldn't have committed the theft, no way, because he was working with him that day. The cops were pretty well pissed off with Boris after the trial and threatened to charge him with perjury. Of course he had lied. He was sticking up for his brah despite the festering hatred.[46] Once Ivan was locked up, though, Boris figured it would help him and Marilyn get their life in some order. As a first step, he moved her and the girls out of the folks' place to a house nearby. She welcomed the move into a decent place.

Mealtimes at the Milat home were an unpredictable affair. There was always lots of food on the table – more food than elbow room. Squabbles were common and at times heated. Marilyn had more than once seen Steven Milat just pick the table up and flip it over – food, plates, cups flying through the air while everyone was in the middle of eating. She'd seen him lash out at Margaret in front of the children for the smallest reasons – food not ready, or not to his liking. 'What's this garbage!' Or too much noise. Then Mrs Milat would get cranky because she'd been working all day herself, looking after the kids.

In some ways it explained to Marilyn why Boris was so screwed up for such a young man. She feared him and found it hard to forgive him for the times he'd struck her. The peace she and Boris hoped the move away from Junction Road would bring never came, though it brought a brief ceasefire.

Boris still visited Ivan in prison, never raising the topic of Lynise's parentage. They had words over Marilyn, but not about the baby. Marilyn's denials had appeased him to a degree. He still harboured suspicions, but didn't know if it was Mac or someone else. Anyway, Ivan was out of the way for a long time, he figured. For once he knew exactly where he was every night.

Ivan was in Long Bay Jail for two months when the governor told him he was being moved to Grafton Maximum Security Prison in the hinterland of the New South Wales coast. A prisoner had to be bad to go to Grafton. It was where the 'tracs' went, the 'intractables'. You went there to be taught a lesson and Grafton had evil teachers. Its barbarity was unknown to the general public until a royal commission exposed it in the seventies, yet it was long a place genuinely feared by the criminal milieu. Hard bastards like Russell 'Mad Dog' Cox, and Whiskey au Go Go bomber John Stuart; ruthless stickup merchants and killers like Neddy Smith, or escape artists like Darcy Dugan all graduated from there – might have gone in soft, but come out scarred, harder and meaner. Grafton was the place to break a man. It was flogged into them from the moment they entered the gate. Break the spirit and they'll emerge reformed. But many came out with calloused hatred burning through them, and no respect for humanity. Treat a man like an animal, that's what he becomes. You had to watch the other crims in there too. Dog eat dog. Cop just as big a flogging from them as from the guards.

When Ivan was transferred from Long Bay on 27 April 1966 he felt like he was being given the VIP treatment. The cops took him to

Mascot Airport and put him on his first aeroplane ride, handcuffed to a detective. He felt like a real big shot. When he entered the Grafton reception wing, he knew different. Dressed in overalls and slippers, his wrists handcuffed to a security belt, he was taken into the yard and ordered to strip.

'Prisoner Milat. Turn and face the wall. Stand at aye-ten-shhunn! Look at the ground. Don't look at us, mongrel.'

His buttocks were parted and searched. Then, smash! A king hit out of the blue. Right in the back of the head with such force his face cracked into the wall. Welcome to Grafton. Do as you're told and you'll be sweet. Whack! Look the wrong way. Whack! Step out of line. Whack! Open ya mouth without permission. Whack! You're history. Whack! Whack! The 'reception biff' was on. Got that? Three or four guards going at him with large rubber batons, beating around the ribs, kidneys and the back of the legs.

He was thrown into a cell, thinking it was over, lying naked on the floor. Whimpering. Then the big metal door clanged open. 'Get on your fucking feet, cunt, and face the back wall . . .' It was on again. New prisoners pissed blood for days after the reception.

Each prisoner occupied a separate cell for more than seventeen hours a day. The cell had one small, two-shelf cupboard which was an almost immovable block of wood doubling as a chair and table. The bed was two coir (coconut fibre) mats on the concrete floor. There was no sewerage. Prisoners were issued with buckets. There were no televisions, radios or newspapers.

The beatings did not end with the reception biff. Mindless beatings came from trivial offences such as failure to fold a blanket in an acceptable manner. Prisoners called the major beatings 'SNTs' (stark naked terror) and smaller ones 'JCs' after the Jimmy Cagney backhanded slap. They were exercised for twenty minutes a day, marching non-stop, in cell order, up and down a 12-foot-long yard, wearing their hats and coats with all buttons done up. Eyes were always to be kept on the ground. Prisoners who looked up or undid a button in the North Coast heat copped a beating.

Just about every night, and sometimes more than once a night, Milat was woken by the sound of keys jangling and a metal cell door opening. Then there'd be a jumble of noise, laughter, thuds, bangs and chilling screams. Sometimes it would go on for ages. No one ever escaped from Grafton except by suicide, which was common. But Mac's time there was brief, although he'd be back. After a week, he was taken in the back of a prison van, along a winding track they called a road, over the Great Dividing Range to the cooler mountain climes of Glen Innes on the Northern Tablelands and Her Majesty's remote Glen Innes Forestry Prison Camp. Described as a minimum security complex, there was very little in the way of walls to stop a prisoner from bolting. The dense bush and mountain climate – sweltering in summer, near freezing at night – were the true barriers. The town of Glen Innes was 30 miles away as the crow flew, but a hell of a slog through the rugged bush. It was common for escaped prisoners to be knocking on the gate within seventy-two hours, cold and hungry, begging to be taken back. They kept them skinny on a basic diet and hard work out in the pine plantations, ensuring there was little body fat to insulate a man on the run.

At Glen Innes, Milat developed a love of body building. He also broadened his knowledge of how to get cushy jobs in prison, especially in the kitchen, looking out for number one.

Ivan's absence from Moorebank did not bring peace to the neighbourhood. Police still came knocking on the door looking for – among other things – the phantom rock thrower, a teenage lad smashing the windows in Junction Road, who always seemed to disappear around the Milat home.[47] Young Georgie was quizzed, but never collared.

It was no joke when, on April Fools' Day 1967, prison guards told Mac he was being freed on parole after serving seventeen months of his two-year sentence. It was a Saturday and by Tuesday he was working on the roads around Liverpool for the Department of Main Roads. He came out of jail with a taste for alcohol, having tried prison brew. It wasn't long before he was having the odd beer or spirit in pubs, but he still preferred cruising. He was supposed to be keeping his nose clean, but one night he found himself out the back of Austral, creeping through an old cemetery to do a break and enter with some mates. Like a lot of his robberies, it didn't go to plan and an alarm was triggered. They were forced to toe it back through the cemetery, trying not to fall over the gravestones in the dark back to the car. In their absence, a trucker had pulled over for a break nearby. As they ran for the car, the truck started up and took off down Bringelly Road in the direction of Liverpool. They piled in the car, shit-scared he might have taken down their number plate. They followed the truck, making plans on what they'd do to him if he stopped at Liverpool Police Station. They relaxed when he kept on driving through to the city.[48]

The late sixties was a boom time in the car market – and the illicit spare-parts market. Moorebank was the centre of a flourishing car-theft ring which ranged widely over Sydney with few hassles from the law. Cars were fire-bombed after the parts were taken, usually in the backblocks of Heathcote and Menai.

Ivan got pretty good at torching cars. Sometimes he and his mates would steal a car just for the thrill of seeing it burn. Blowing things up was a highly skilled undertaking with just a little petrol. They took bets on how far they could lift the roof or boot off. It never ceased to amaze them what came flying out when a car went bang. They got cocky. Didn't give themselves time to get clear. One explosion blew them off their feet as the windscreen went sailing 40 yards through the air.

They tried homemade bombs made by filling a metal pipe with gunpowder, and squashing the ends over. They stopped making them when they planted one under an old vandalised car in the bush. The blast lifted the car a couple of feet and sent a chunk of shrapnel flying past their heads. Would have killed them.

The family legend was that they wore the blame for one another's crime if a brother stood to cop a heftier sentence because he'd been in trouble too many times. The brothers were blokes who'd do anything for each other and share anything they owned: cars, bikes, you name it. Boris drew the line at sharing girlfriends. Bull and Marilyn had been living away from Junction Road for almost a year, though only a few blocks away. Mac's return re-ignited Boris' paranoia – or was it exploiting his naivety? He'd come home of an evening and find Ivan's car parked around the corner, but no Ivan. He was seriously considering some form of psychotherapy, such was his state of suspicion and anxiety. He had even accused Marilyn of affairs with Ivan's mates. She'd tell him he was being stupid. Crazy.

One day, while taking a short cut from Warwick Farm through to Chipping Norton to get to a job, Boris thought he saw Marilyn's car parked near the old Bailey bridge across the Georges River. He asked her about it that night, but she said it must have been someone with a similar car. Boris had to cop it. Some time later he was travelling past the same spot in his truck with George Liestins, a family friend who he employed. 'That's your wife's car there. And isn't that Ivan's?' Liestins asked. Boris turned back. Both cars had moved off, but the one he could see disappearing in the distance looked like Ivan's. He felt ill. That was it. He had to have it out with his brother. He found Ivan in the driveway at Moorebank.

'What's going on, Mac? Are you having it off with Rare?' His temper rising with each word. Ivan looked shocked.

'No, I'm not,' Ivan said innocently. 'If you want her, take her! She's yours. I don't want to have nothin' to do with her.'

'Well are ya gunna leave us alone?'

'Guarantee it brah.'[49]

Boris wasn't happy when he left. But what else could he do? He had no proof, just a belly full of suspicion.

Boris' fears reached ludicrous proportions. One day, he took Marilyn's upper denture plate to work, so she wouldn't leave the house.[50] He began to suspect that she was taking off during the day leaving the girls alone to fend for themselves or dumping them with other people. Going off to secret rendezvous.

Then, one day Boris was at work and one of the blokes said he ought to go home and make sure his house was in order. Just that. Both Marilyn and Boris have long disputed the following events. In Boris' telling, he arrived home and caught Ivan semi-naked and quivering in his wardrobe. Boris pulled the knife from his boot.

Boris recounted: 'He was shaking and sweating. I was gunna kill 'im. I'd made up my mind to kill 'im and then I didn't think he or her was worth it. I really was gunna kill 'im. All I needed was for him to come back at me one little bit and he would've been a dead boy, I'm tellin' ya.' Ivan begged for mercy and became teary, saying they weren't up to no good. George would remember Boris throwing Ivan out of his house after belting him about, Ivan still denying that anything had happened.

Marilyn would claim that all they were doing was sitting at the table talking. Ivan was fully clothed eating a pickle sandwich she had made him.

Though smaller than Ivan, Boris' temper and bulldog physique made him a formidable punching machine. He didn't think Ivan could fight. If Mac hit you first you might know it, but he had to get in first. Mac's style of fighting was more putting his head down and just charging in with his arms flailing about.

For all his anger and distrust, Boris refused to give up Marilyn and he especially wasn't going to give up his daughters. They became a bargaining chip. She wouldn't leave the girls, as much as she loved Ivan. Ivan wouldn't take them. He just wanted Marilyn, he said, knowing full well she'd never leave the girls. She had no choice but to follow Boris wherever he took them. In the end, the police solved the problem.

About 1.45 a.m., 17 August, carpenter Bill Cooke was woken up by his wife Margaret telling him his '57 Ford was missing. Cooke dressed and scouted around. The odd abandoned car had been found near the old wool mills on the other side of the railway line, so he walked down into Speed Street and a short ways along turned right into Mill Road. There, under a railway viaduct, he saw his car lying on the ground. Two wheels were missing while the remaining two had been taken off and put under the car. Cooke checked the car in the poor light. It was a mess. It had been stripped of a tail-light, glass and bulb, all four hub caps, even the interior light. It looked like the thief had also tried to milk petrol from it. The rear seat had been pulled out by someone trying to get into the boot. Whoever had done it had been quick. The car couldn't have been gone for more than an hour. Cooke notified police, then he and a mate went for a drive around the district. Up on the highway, they saw some blokes in a car with one lovely white-wall tyre, just like his, and three standard black tyres. He noted the number plate and gave it to the police.

Shortly before 9 o'clock that morning, Cooke, went to Liverpool Police Station where detectives had already pulled in a young bloke called Alex Hemming, and the owner of the car with the suspicious white-wall tyre – Michael Milat. They were in the cells out the back being questioned. By lunchtime, Hemming had shopped both Mick and his brother Ivan.

Mick Milat, eighteen, was a revhead like his brothers and spent much of his spare time fixing up his car. He looked up to Ivan. Like his older brothers, he was educated by the nuns and then the Brothers. He also had a stint at a church school at Bangalow; then Liverpool Boys High, but he left at fifteen, same as the others. His hands and muscles were his only qualifications. Work was hard to get when you'd been in strife with the law, even though he'd been lucky to escape with good-behaviour bonds. Then Boris got his business up and running and he gave Mick some steady work. The pay was excellent for those days – $6 an hour.

Ivan was only earning $45 a week before penalties, far less money than Mick was getting through Boris, which makes it hard to understand why Mick did something so stupid.[51] The reports on the theft don't explain how the police got the tip that led them to Ivan's car. The Ford sedan, BFL 268, was parked in Woodward Park, Liverpool, opposite a smash repair and car wreckers yard near the intersection of Copeland Street and Hoxton Park Road. Its owner was nowhere in sight. Cooke watched the detectives open the boot. Inside was a tyre and tube of his, the hub caps and a tail-light clasp.

At 2.10 that afternoon Mick Milat was taken to see Detective Senior Constable Leo Purcell for his second interview. The first time he'd fed them a load of bull about a mate giving him the tyres, but this time, according to Purcell, Mick came clean and implicated Ivan.

Purcell listed the property they'd just found in Ivan's car. 'Can you offer me any explanation as to how they got into your brother's car?'

'Yeah, I put them in there.'

Mick said he borrowed the keys off Ivan before stealing the car, but he didn't know where the other tyre was, or the other stolen gear, he said. The interview concluded with Mick being asked if he wanted to make a written statement.

'No, I don't want to make anything.' Nor did he sign anything. He was charged with larceny of a motor vehicle and the cops went searching for Ivan. George Milat saw them pull up in Junction Road. 'He's in trouble again. What's he done this time?' he wondered of his bullying big brother. They came in and said Mick was in shit: 'Where's Ivan?' George didn't know, but the police didn't have far to look.

Ivan knew he was badly in breach of his parole. At 5 p.m., he fronted on the doorstep of the cop shop. He was taken to see Detective Purcell and was shown Alex Hemming's statement implicating both him and Mick. Ivan did a 180 degree turn on his previous form and co-operated. He was charged with accessory after the fact of car theft.

On 31 August, the two brothers appeared together in Liverpool Court of Petty Sessions and indicated they would plead guilty. Mrs Milat went surety for both boys' bail: $200 for Mick and only $80 for Ivan, since he was being helpful.

*

Ivan and Mick appeared for sentencing before Judge N.D. Macintosh at the Sydney Court of Quarter Sessions, Darlinghurst – familiar ground to Mac. If he hoped for leniency for helping police, the scheduling of the appearance should have been an ominous sign. It was Friday the 13th of October.

Purcell furnished a presentencing report on both Mick and Ivan, running through their criminal form and work histories. On Ivan: 'The prisoner was known to me prior to his arrest. He is not an associate of the criminal class and consumes intoxicating liquor in moderation only.'

Purcell's kind words didn't help. Ivan had breached his parole, so he copped three years jail with eighteen months non-parole. Michael got two years hard, with twelve months non-parole. Ivan was sent to Long Bay to wait out an appeal on the severity of his sentence. On 8 December the Court of Criminal Appeal – Justices McClemens, Brereton and Taylor – knocked him back.

Mac just couldn't win. Four and a half months on the outside and busted again. Aged twenty-two, the greater part of his young adult life was slipping by behind prison walls – the rock'n'roll revolution and the social upheavals of the sixties were nothing to him. The sexual revolution, even less. In another world, they were experiencing what became known as the Summer of Love. He was never out long enough to have a steady girl of his own. No one saw him with a girlfriend in the sixties and there weren't any where he was going to see out the decade.

TEN

1968–1970

MAUREEN

Maureen Parsons – no relation to Johnny – a skinny-legged teenager with long, mousey-brown hair and blue eyes, was thirteen going on fourteen, and starting to get interested in boys when she met Lynn Lambert. Lynn had turned up in second form at Liverpool Girls High, and Maureen was told to show her around and get her on the right bus home. They couldn't have picked a better match. On the bus, Lynn told Maureen she'd struck gold moving to Junction Road a mile up the hill from Maureen. 'I've got all these boys living next door to me – all brothers too. Wow.' The clincher was the fact that they weren't just boys, they were boys with cars. This put a visit to Lynn's place top of the agenda.

The girls' high school then was segregated from Liverpool Boys High. The closest they got during school time was glimpses across the football oval buffer zone, and the once-a-year dance in the shared auditorium. Liverpool Boys was an industrial arts school, with metalwork and woodwork – turning out the next generation of workers. The girls did compulsory cooking and sewing – 'domestic science' – turning out their wives.

Lynn and Maureen's interests were pop stars, lesser males and horses. There was still enough acreage around to keep a pony, and the two girls had one each. They'd be riding their horses and see these brothers driving around in their cars, sometimes even stopping to talk.

Lynn, taller than Maureen, was a dark-haired beauty – despite the thick glasses. She hated the glasses, but they were all the better to look at boys with. At lunchtime, they'd go down to the oval to perv, scattering when a teacher sprung them in the forbidden zone.

Over time, the girls became inseparable. They'd hang around Lynn's house hoping to see the boys. The best vantage point was Lynn's bathroom window. They'd peer out in anticipation. 'Oh, here come the cars, they're coming.' The girls would run out the front, then pretend to be doing nothing in particular and casually walk by, hoping for the thrill of a whistle or a 'g'day, what yas up to? . . .'

After a while, they got to know Wally and Billy and if ever Maureen was at Lynn's place after dark, one of the boys would inevitably give her a lift home. That's how they got to know them better.

Mick was released on parole in October 1968 after twelve months, but Maureen and Lynn didn't know that. In both girls' eyes, the family was just real friendly. There was talk of more brothers and sisters who had moved away, but no one mentioned Ivan. The household revolved around the remaining boys: Billy, Wally, Georgie, Richard, David and Paul. Margaret was the only daughter left. Lynn and Maureen knew her from school, but she was always in the background. She had to stay home with Mum. Maureen and Lynn made small talk with her. She was a year older and she didn't seem to have friends out of school.

The brothers were always working away on cars and motorbikes. The yard was full of them. George, fifteen, seemed to have a natural gift for mechanics. His whole world existed under a bonnet, and he made the fastest rods of all the Milat boys. They were low at the back and high at the front as was the hot rod fashion of the time. They roared. He was a real character, but the girls weren't interested in him. Being about the same age as them, he was way too young. Lynn had the hots for Billy, twenty-one, and Maureen went for sixteen-year-old Wally.

In Maureen's eyes Wally was a young rebel. He was always walking around in jeans, no shirt, no shoes. She was sure he kept the shirt off just for her and Lynn. Made him feel good, and she didn't mind either. He was tanned and it was a great body. He was a gyprocker. Fit as anything.

Billy had a blue Ford Falcon. Maureen knew all their car number plates on sight so she could pick them coming down the street. She'd remember Billy's for the rest of her life, BCV 242. Unlike Georgie's hotted up cars, Billy's was neat and, like Billy himself, didn't have so much growl. He was always polite and proper.

Soon, the two girls were off parking with Billy and Wally. Clinches

Pond, Deadmans Creek, Picnic Point and along Georges Hall. They'd get a hamburger or go to the drive-in at Casula, Bass Hill or Blacktown.

Maureen had been amazed at how the Milats managed to get so many people into their little house. Yet, when Mrs Milat invited her in for the first time, she found they were quite comfortable inside, but with nothing fancy or elaborate. She'd watch Mr Milat play cards by himself after dinner, sitting in a corner of the lounge room, slapping the cards down on a small table and muttering in 'Yugoslavian', no one game to interrupt him. He minded his own business. Maureen would say hello to him and that was about it. She spent most of her time talking to Mrs Milat who was always trying to force-feed her and Lynn, always giving them tea, coffee and cake.

Ivan had been in Long Bay Jail a year and nine months when they told him he was moving. A screw told him to pack his bags. He was moving to the maximum security hellhole at Grafton, only three months shy of being eligible for parole. Somewhere along the line, he'd stepped on someone's toes. Ivan knew what was in store. When he and other new arrivals were mustered at reception, they were ordered to stand to attention and face the wall, their heads a few inches from the concrete. Ivan placed his brow hard up against the wall to brace for the blow he knew was coming. It came. Hard to the back of the head. Still hurt, but not as badly as the first time he'd copped it. Grafton was as tough as expected, but Ivan knew enough to get by, sucking up to the guards, never raising his eyes, doing as he was told, always polite. Pretty soon he was made a sweeper, a trusted position, one step down from a job in the kitchen.

He was still writing to Marilyn from jail. Her relationship with Boris was still a rollercoaster, even though Ivan was out of the picture. Boris came home from work one afternoon and found the house empty. He didn't know what made him look, but he found himself moving the wardrobe in their bedroom. On the floor underneath it, he found the letter. Boris knew he shouldn't read it, knew it would hurt, but he couldn't help himself.

It was full of Ivan expressing his love for Marilyn. It shattered Boris. Confirmed that she lied when she said it was over. There was a hell of a row when she got home. Their fights reached the point where Marilyn's parents tried to intervene. One of her brothers come around to sort him out, but Boris gave him a hiding. Boris did lay off Marilyn, though, after her father threatened him. Archie Childs was someone you listened to.

The Milats didn't have many friends. One of the few outsiders in the little circle was a nineteen-year-old tough called Johnny Preston, a mate of Mick's. He was an up-and-coming street brawler. Trouble. He'd done all the petty crimes and been done for them too: receiving stolen cars, stealing cars, break and entering, carnal knowledge, indecent language, underage drinking, street fighting and more street fighting.

Mick was working for the Water Board, trying to keep his nose clean, but in the family's eyes, the cops wouldn't give him a chance. He was an easy mark, and hanging out with Preston didn't help any of them. Over the years, hanging out in the local pubs, Preston's older brother, Dave decided that the Milats were mad when they were full of piss. You could belt them all day and there was no pain. It was an opinion that had its origins from when he was at school with Billy. He'd get caned, then bash his head against a wall, turn around to the teacher and say 'you never hurt me'. The whole class thought he was dead-set crazy.

The Milats and the Prestons had two things in common at school, though, they were always getting in trouble and their mothers were always in the headmasters' office defending them. That's how their mums got to know each other. Mrs Preston said to Dave once: 'Every time I go to school over you, Dave, Mrs Milat's always there.' She had nothing but respect for the way Margaret Milat stuck up for her kids.

Johnny Preston didn't last too long at school. He went to Mount Penang Juvenile Detention Centre a few days after his sixteenth birthday, in 1966, for two charges of stealing a motor vehicle and one of carnal knowledge.

There were street fighting and offensive behaviour problems. Then on 27 September 1969 Preston and Mick walked into Curley's milk bar opposite Liverpool Station about 10.30 p.m. It was a Saturday night and Preston was pissed, talking loud and looking for trouble. A soldier, Graham Connell, who was sitting up the back of the milk bar waiting for a meal turned around to see who was making all the noise.

'Have a good look,' Preston told him. 'Go on. Had your sixpence worth?'

'Yes,' Connell answered, turning back around. Connell's mate, Paul Lennon, saw Preston walk out then come back in with some other youths who all stood along the counter. The soldiers' meals were served and some young bloke with a plaster cast on his leg walked up to Connell: 'Are you coming out?'

'I'm eating my meal.'

'You're wanted outside.'

Connell didn't reply and didn't look at them as they stood over him. Someone put two fingers under his plate and flicked it at the wall. They hauled Connell out of his seat, punching him, then dragging him to the street. Lennon got up and they were onto him too, dragging him into the games room out back. He fought off whoever had him and managed to get out the back door.

Mick and Preston had Connell out the front. He was punched again in the head as he came out the door, going down on the footpath. They kicked and punched him as he curled up with his hands over his head. Then it all stopped. He waited five or ten seconds and got up. There were people all around. His watch was missing. He went to his hip pocket and his wallet wasn't there. He searched around the gutter, but only found his leave pass. He wasn't badly hurt, just a few cuts in the mouth.

The cops suspected Preston and pulled him in for a line-up a few days later. Connell couldn't be sure but his mate, Paul Lennon, went straight to Preston and put his hand on his shoulder. They pulled Mick in a few days later.

Moorebank had changed much in the near-on two decades that the Milat family had been there. The pastures on the high ground had given way to new homes, and the low-lying areas were being swallowed by small factories. Developers had bought most of the land around the Milat property and secured its rezoning to residential.

Their next-door neighbour, Cosmo Lombardo, had given up his market garden to open a fruit and veg shop in 1966. The Lombardos moved to a block on the Hume Highway at Casula, which became their new home and business. Despite early run-ins with some of the younger Milat boys thieving their vegetables, the Lombardos had become friends with Mrs Milat who continued to keep in touch.

Now, a road was planned to run right through the Milat shack, to serve the new brick houses on the drawing board. Council rates suddenly went through the roof and the Milats were being offered a good price by Timber Crest Pty Ltd. Steven Milat sold up on 7 November 1969. Twenty days later, he bought a house in the area in which he first met and courted Margaret – South Granville/Guildford. The tribe was on the move. Maureen and Lynn had nothing to worry about, though, they'd become Wally and Billy's regular girls.

Before leaving, Mrs Milat confided to Betty Card that they had bought a house near a police station, 'to keep my boys in order'. It was a new start for the family, including Ivan who had written that he was due for release early in the new year.

The kids in the Guildford area soon knew there was a new mob living at 55 Campbell Hill Road. The younger Milats had the full summer holiday to stamp their mark on the virgin neighbourhood, making their presence felt on their bicycles, having the odd blue. Nothing unusual. They blended right in.

Down the street was the 'dunny depot' at Barbers Road, towards the giant waterpipes which cut under Campbell Hill Road. Over the road was the oldest cotton mill in the state, still going clackety-clack within earshot and, up in the other direction, where a golf course would later be built, was a tannery within easy smelling distance. But it wasn't really industrial. There were dairy cows behind the nearby Rothmans plant, and you could still bag a rabbit in waste ground down the road. It was said that cabbies took female passengers there for payment in kind.

The new home was an average, three-bedroom weatherboard house, though the rooms were quite large. Steven and Margaret had one bedroom while the eight remaining children seemed to fit comfortably into the other two and an enclosed veranda at the back. Dad planted grapevines around the house with a view to brewing up some grappa, and all the farmyard poultry – the chickens, ducks and quail – followed them from Moorebank.

Mac came out of jail and got back home to find that Mick and his mate Johnny Preston were in court that day for beating up the soldier in

Liverpool. Before the case began, Preston and Mick found their victim, Graham Connell, on the veranda of the old colonial courthouse: 'Are you going to drop the charges?' Preston wanted to know.

'No,' said Connell.

'I've just come out of jail and I'm not looking forward to a trip back. We've got a bloke up from Melbourne. I'm not going to muck around.' Preston and Mick turned and walked away.

The robbery charges were thrown out because no one could positively say who took the wallet and watch. They both admitted the assault. Mick claimed Connell called him a wog.

A young solicitor from Campbelltown, John Marsden, represented both boys. Of Mick he said: 'I appreciate his record is not good, but he has not been involved in an assault. They have all been allegations of dishonesty and a minor street offence. His mother informs me her son was getting into trouble and she felt he was mixing in bad company and as a result of this he has been led into trouble. She has taken the step to move out of the area, have sold their home, and she informs me that since moving out of the area the lad has kept a regular job.'

Mick copped a $50 fine and Preston $100.

Maureen Parsons had sensed the excitement among the brothers on the day that Ivan got out of jail.

'There's another one?' she inquired. 'I thought I'd met you all.'

'He's been in Grafton.' She could see that all the young Milats looked up to him. They cared for each other, except maybe Boris, who seemed to be out on his own. Ivan had been away for two years and three months. The last six months at Grafton where he turned twenty-six, ten days before his release. He had a string of tough-guy stories about his time in the nick. He reckoned he was the only prisoner ever to do time in Grafton without having a bone broken. He came home, still smoking, and with some advice for his brothers: keep ya trap shut. 'They'll never prove anything. If the cops arrest ya, just say nothin',' he preached. 'Don't even give 'em your name. Say nothin'.'[52]

Maureen was at Lynn's home next to the old Milat place when Billy pulled up in his Falcon. 'This is my brother, Ivan.' He didn't say much. Seemed really shy. She was looking in from the driver's side across Billy. Ivan was thin with a pale, jail complexion, and didn't make any impression.

The feud with Boris was simmering. Ivan didn't call him Bull any more. He was 'Warthog'. If they saw each other at their parents' home, they just walked past with no glimmer of recognition. It was inevitable that Ivan and Marilyn came to see each other – and that Boris would be back to thinking she was sneaking around behind his back.

Boris was determined to put some distance between them. He moved his family to a house in the remote pastures of Wallgrove Road, ten kilometres west of Liverpool, but his paranoia followed him. He saw Ivan in every shadow. He became so obsessed trying to catch Ivan and Marilyn out, he bugged the phone. He was always feeling sick and sad at work, couldn't concentrate on anything. He'd ring her at every opportunity to make sure she hadn't gone out. Ivan was everywhere. Boris would get in his car to drive to work of a morning and see Ivan in a car coming down the road with all his hoodlum mates, just waiting for him to leave. One night he thought he saw Ivan's car parked on a nearby hill with the headlights on, beaming down at the house. He ran inside and emerged with a shotgun and let off two blasts in its direction.[53] Another time, he dropped by the folks' place and Ivan was standing in the front yard. Ivan said something that he didn't quite hear, but he didn't like the tone. The dam broke. It was on. He started laying into Ivan. Billy and some of the boys come running to Ivan's defence, all of them punching into Boris.

For some reason, Boris moved his family and his paranoia back closer to Liverpool, to Mount Pritchard. He still saw Ivan and his mates prowling around his home, waiting for him to go out. One time, Marilyn came home with her dress torn and a cut lip. The police came calling soon after, looking for a girl called 'Rose' who'd been involved in some sort of fight. Marilyn wouldn't tell Boris what happened. She was afraid of him. Ivan was an angel by comparison.[54]

Everyone seemed to know what was still going on between Mac and Rare. Everyone except Boris, who guessed, but couldn't catch them. Maureen knew about it. Ivan told her. She knew that Lynise was Ivan's baby. Though the funny thing was she never saw Ivan and Marilyn together alone. They always met secretly.

Maureen had a personal interest. She was on-again-off-again with Wally and was starting to see Ivan herself. After a while out of jail, he regained his colour and seemed more confident. He started visiting her at her mother's place. Mrs Parsons really liked him. She thought he was a lovely person, even though he was ten years older than Maureen. She thought he was very honest because he'd always look you directly in the face. He was polite and he'd sit around having a coffee and a chat. He had a nice sense of humour, too, which set him apart from the other boys like Mick, who drank beer and used foul language.

Ivan was way above that. He was also handsome with those amazing blue eyes and a nice body, but Maureen noticed that he never had girlfriends around. Although he would pop over to visit a girl next door at Guildford. She was kind of plump and plain and maybe a bit of a loon.

She thought he must have found it hard to find women. Maybe it was his shyness, or maybe because the Milats didn't have a real social life. They had an inside sort of family life but, externally, nothing. She could see what had happened with Marilyn, her being vulnerable, and Ivan being so understanding and gentle – and available. One day Ivan picked Maureen and Lynn up at Moorebank after he finished work and drove them to Guildford.

Maureen's relationship with Ivan and Wally became a strange one, viewed from the outside, but she was just a fickle fifteen-year-old dealing with a strange, moody family. There'd be a dispute with Wally – I-don't-like-you-any-more sort of thing – then she'd be back with Ivan. Then he'd go all funny and be off chasing Marilyn, then Wally would come back in the picture. This continued for the next eighteen months – more Wally than Ivan – until events eventually forced the issue.

Ivan needed wheels, and the vehicle of the moment was Ford's new line of muscle cars, the five-litre Falcon GTs. They won the team prize in the 1968 London–Sydney marathon. Then the new Falcon GTHO took first and second in the 1970 Bathurst 500, Australia's most prestigious car race. Five hundred miles of continuous endurance driving up and around Mount Panorama in central New South Wales.

So when Ivan walked into the yard at Jack Brabham Ford, Bankstown, in December 1970, the choice was obvious. Ivan, however, bought the more refined version, a gold XY Fairmont. At 5.75 litres, it had the same size engine as the winning Falcons, but cost $3582 – $1000 more than the base model. The brakes, lowered suspension and handling were twenty years behind the grunt in the mighty engine. Cartridge players were an optional extra.

Sometimes, Ivan took Maureen and Lynn to the drive-in or for a cruise into Kings Cross. It was a big 'wow', all those lights and people, and the big rumbling engine. One time, Ivan was giving Maureen a lift. She was just making conversation and asked him: 'Have you ever killed someone?' She was so naive, she thought people only went to jail because they had murdered.

'Oh, I killed a man,' he said, laughing. 'Killed him with a knife and buried him in the bush.' She took it as a joke, but still told her mum who, of course, told her not to worry about it.

Another time she was around at the Milat home when Ivan was talking to the boys about dead bodies. Being hypothetical. 'Yeah, you'd bury a body, like, down in the bush,' he said, referring to the scrub around Heathcote Road. 'Bury a body out there and put a bag of lime on them and no one would ever know.' She never really knew what to make of it all, but it was easier to dismiss than take seriously.

They were all into that sort of thing and could talk a lot of crap on their weekends away. Maureen had never been camping in her life. They said it was great fun and took her one weekend somewhere west, past the mountains. It was a cold, miserable experience. No sleeping bags. No tent. They slept in the back of the car where she spent most of the trip while the brothers wandered around the scrub blasting away at makeshift targets.

Despite his Mum and Dad's urging to leave Marilyn alone, Ivan persisted with the affair. It drove Boris to the brink. He bought himself a pistol and thought long and hard about what he was going to do with it. Kill Ivan? Kill himself? He chose Ivan. It was the only way.

He drove to Campbell Hill Road. 'Fucking cunt . . . I'll get 'im out of me hair.'

Dad saw Boris coming down the drive, gun in hand; rage in his face. Steven knew what Boris intended to do and made him pause.

'Boris, you have got to kill him. I see this,' the old man said, sitting his son down and telling him about women and the stages they went through. 'He has dishonoured you. You have got to kill him. That is what I would say with any other man, but I do not want you to kill him because he is my son. He is my flesh too, your brother, you cannot do this.'

Boris left, despondent.

ELEVEN

Early 1971

DEATH, LOVE, RAPE AND MARRIAGE

Summer in Sydney was muggy, wet and windy, and Alex Milat was dreaming of snakes again. He and his wife, Joan, had their own family of two kids to contend with, but he kept in regular contact with Mum and Dad. Mum always took an interest in his dreams. As children, when he or Olga dreamt of snakes, bad things followed. Never major dramas, just the odd broken bone or cut. He told his mother about this latest dream over a cuppa during a weekend visit in late January – there were three snakes: 'One's got a lump on the head. The second one has no teeth, and the third one's eyes are cut right down and crushed.'[55]

A week later, another wet morning dawned. Ivan was still crashed out after coming home from a nightshift, when Wally took off down Campbell Hill Road taking Georgie and Margaret to work in his new car, barely six weeks out of the saleyard. Despite the rain, he promised to get them there quick. But they'd gone less than half a mile, over the waterpipes and right into Gurney Road, when disaster struck: bumps on a slippery bend; a pothole; faulty steering; a car coming the wrong way. The reasons became blurred.

Mrs Milat was in the kitchen when Georgie came in, panting. She thought it odd. Had he missed Wally's lift?

'What's wrong?'

He couldn't talk. Just sat down on the lounge, dazed. Then she saw the bruises and the lump on his head.

'What's wrong? What's happened to ya?'

Minutes passed before she got it out of him . . . an accident down the road . . . Margaret and Wally hurt . . . It's bad.

With Dad having left for work hours earlier, Mum rushed to Ivan. 'Get out of bed, Mac. Come quickly.'

'I'm sleeping.'

'There's been an accident. Get up quick.'

A crowd, some still in pyjamas, was milling about the car when they reached it. No ambulance had arrived, nor police. Wally's face was all swollen and one of his legs was clearly busted up, but Margaret was a frightful sight, her face a bloody mess. She was unconscious after going headfirst through the windscreen.

'Don't move her,' said one of the crowd.

'Where's the ambulance?' Mum asked.

'It's all right. I rang them. One's on the way,' a woman said. No one came forward with a towel or cloth to help stem the bleeding. Ivan was trying to calm his mother, and look after both kids, but there was little he could do. He stayed by Margaret's side, holding her, while Mum ran around, frantic in the morning stillness. There were no sirens. She ran off, desperate to find out where the ambulance was. Three doorknocks later, she found a phone. The emergency operator knew nothing of the accident.

By the time an ambulance got there, twenty minutes had passed. A second arrived. Wally and George were taken in one and Margaret in the other to Fairfield District Hospital. The surgeons did all they could. Margaret was in a coma, her face a purple quilt of 160 stitches from her eyebrows across and down to her throat. Mrs Milat stayed there praying at her bedside and Ivan joined her. A week turned to two and the doctors lost hope. She was sixteen years and one month old when she died on Tuesday, 9 February without regaining consciousness.

Wally missed the funeral. He was in hospital sucking soup through a straw between the wires holding his broken jaw together. Boris and Ivan struck a truce for the funeral.

'We will hold peace for the day,' Mum told the pair. She always thought the feud was just a matter of Boris' jealous streak.

Mrs Milat never gave up grieving for her youngest daughter. None of Ivan's ill deeds or betrayals, no matter how bad, would ever compare to this pain. Ivan lost what little faith he had in God that day. He rarely spoke about his little sister again, and people knew not to raise the subject.

*

It was an ill decision of Boris' to move Marilyn and the two girls close to his parents' home. The rented house in Mona Street, South Granville, was about a mile from 55 Campbell Hill Road.

'Are you still seeing him?' he demanded of Marilyn one day.

She denied it, but not convincingly enough. Boris demanded proof. 'I can't sustain this relationship unless I know,' he said. 'We'll end this relationship now . . . You can have him but you can't have the girls.'

She had to break it off with Mac or lose the girls.[56] Only her telling Ivan to his face – in Boris' presence – could settle things. She got on the phone and rang Ivan while Boris watched. Mac wanted to see her one more time. Boris demanded to be present. They arranged to meet in a park that night. Boris drove her. Ivan was waiting in his Ford. Marilyn got out and walked to his car, leaving Boris alone, watching.

She sat in the front seat with Ivan, just talking. They weren't there long but, to Boris, watching their silhouettes, their chat just seemed too pally, like they were laughing. He imagined they were treating it as a big joke. He got out of his car and barged into the back seat behind them.

'We're out of it. Okay, we're finished,' he yelled at Marilyn, his temper about to explode.

'No, it's all right. He's not going to have nothin' more to do with me,' Marilyn said.

Ivan backed her up: 'We're just sitting having a chat.'

Then Ivan said something smart. Boris' right fist flashed over the bench seat into Ivan's head, and then again. Jab, jab, jab. Marilyn was screaming. Ivan couldn't fight backwards, so he picked up a torch from the seat and banged it into Boris as hard as he could. The torch shattered, but Boris didn't feel a thing through his anger. He kept on into Ivan until his rage was spent, then got out of the car. 'You can have her, but you're not taking the children.[57] If you want her . . . she's got to make up her mind what she's gunna do, but if she goes, she goes by herself. The girls stay.'[58]

Marilyn still loved Ivan, but he didn't want the girls, he just wanted her all to himself. He didn't want the commitment of kids. Or that's what he told her. She had to choose then and there, and she chose the kids. And as she drove off with Boris, arguing already, she couldn't help fearing what he'd do to her when they got home. Then Boris told her he was going to change; get her and the girls far away. Start a new life. Things were going to be better, he promised. 'We'll move to the Central Coast and get married. What do you think about that?'

'Okay,' she said.

They removed themselves to the sleepy bayside town of Umina north of Sydney. Marilyn never lost her feelings for Ivan, but she tried to believe she could grow to love Boris. Ivan took the news of the marriage hard. A few weeks later he saw two girls hitching near Liverpool Station and pulled the Fairmont in to the kerb.

It was Good Friday and Greta had decided she'd had it with Sydney and the psych hospital. She wanted to go back to live at her parents' place in Melbourne. She convinced her good friend, Margaret, to get leave from the hospital and come down with her for a holiday. Margaret was eighteen and had only been outside the Sydney metropolitan area twice in her life. Once to Newcastle. Once to Nowra.

Greta had a beautiful round face, her brows fashionably plucked to a pencil line. She was massively hung-over from spending last night at a discotheque where she met some guy who she went home with.[59]

It was Greta's idea to hitch. Margaret went along with it even though she was really nervous. Her mother had warned her about accepting lifts from strangers ever since she was a little girl. She knew some girls who'd had sexual advances made to them while hitching. They usually went along with it, but Margaret wasn't so much into that.

They didn't get out of the city until late in the day. The two women caught a train to Liverpool, arriving about 8 p.m. The streets were unusually quiet for a Friday, with all the pubs closed for the religious holiday. The girls didn't have much gear with them: jumpers, jeans, toothbrushes. They had hardly started walking towards the Hume Highway when a gold Ford purred up beside them.

'You want a ride?' the driver asked.

'Sure. We're going to Melbourne.' Greta thought she heard the guy say he was going to Canberra. 'The Canberra turn-off will be quite okay, thank you,' she said.

'No, Camden, not Canberra.'

'Well, that will be quite all right too.'

Greta got in the front, Margaret in the back with their little bit of luggage. The driver was slightly older than them, dressed in shorts and a singlet. He seemed really quiet. Maybe a bit strange, and not interested in making conversation. That was all right because the girls were tired. Margaret had taken three sleeping tablets. She was being treated for depression, and she didn't always take the tablets in the prescribed doses. She was dozing as Greta tried to make general conversation in the front, talking about her hangover while battling the effects of the Valium she'd taken. Greta was into the zodiac and asked the driver his sign.

'Gemini,' he lied.

She asked him his name and age. He lied about that, too. The trip went on. Greta dozed as well. They didn't know where they were; didn't know they'd passed Camden hours ago. Suddenly, the rhythm of the road changed. Greta was shaken from her sleep. There was gravel underneath. No oncoming headlights. 'We're not on the highway. What are you doing?'

The driver pulled over to the side of a dirt road. 'I'm going to have sex with both of you.'

'Oh no, you're not.' Greta didn't believe he was serious. Margaret was awake now. She watched from the back as her friend tried to talk him around. He was sweating a pungent body odour, but was calm in his demand.

'I'm going to have sex with both of you. If you don't, I'm going to kill you.'

'Well, you'll just have to kill us,' Greta retorted, getting angry. Then her tone changed. In the poor light she could see what Margaret couldn't from the back seat – two knives on the floor, partly covered by a street directory.

With fear hanging thickly in the blackness, Greta began to reason with the man. He seemed to like that. Margaret got the feeling he only wanted to have sex with her friend. And Greta sat there, it seemed like forever, telling him that they were both psychiatric patients. They both had sexual problems. That's why they were in hospital. Margaret thought her friend was doing well, at least confusing him with her psychiatric spiel. True as it was.

Sexual dysfunction was behind all her problems, Margaret thought. She still slept in the same bed as her mother, and had been camp for two years, but she didn't enjoy that so much. Her mother was devoutly religious and couldn't accept her sleeping with anybody. Margaret couldn't make a decision about her sexual identity, and she saw her stay in the hospital as an opportunity to make her mind up. Generally, she rejected the advances of men. The American Psychiatric Association was still two years away from removing homosexuality from its list of psychiatric disorders, and it was still common to admit someone to a psych hospital for confused sexuality.

Greta wasn't camp, she just hung around the scene. She was battling through the haze of the yellow Valium tablets she took three times a day. She had threatened to overdose on the stuff the previous night. Now she was saying she was going to take them all right here. They sat there for a long time with the lights off in the blackness of a country lane. Greta was trying to tell him why having sex wasn't a good idea. She said she would call the police. She asked him what value he placed on life . . . How would his mother feel?

He said something about knowing a girl in a psychiatric hospital in Parramatta. He didn't believe in God because his sixteen-year-old sister had been killed in a car accident. The only time Greta was able to spark a reaction from him was when she announced: 'I'm going to be sick.' The possibility of her dirtying his car made him angry.

The night was getting so cold, but the guy was getting more heated. Sweating more. He made a couple of gentle advances towards Greta, but she kept resisting and kept talking. Margaret, still in the back, was sure he was only interested in her beautiful friend, who seemed to her to be almost luring him in the way that Margaret herself found so seductive. At one point, though, Greta went for the door. She hardly reached the handle before he had her by the fashionable leather choker round her neck. He pulled it hard and she thought he was going to strangle her. Then he let her go, threatening to slap her face. After about an hour of this, he told her: 'If you don't give me sex, I'm going to kill you.' Two knives came out from under the street directory on the floor. One had a curved blade. Margaret still didn't see them. 'Oh, you're going to rape us.' Greta said.

'You could call it that.'

'Have you done it before?'

'Yeah. I'm always prepared,' he said, bringing out two lengths of pink nylon cord.

Margaret thought of a way out. 'We won't go to the police,' she promised. 'You can tie us up so you can get away. By the time we get ourselves free, you'll be well away.' He agreed and got them out of the car. Greta was tied hand and foot with one piece of cord. She felt trussed up like a chicken. He gave Margaret the choice of how she wanted to be tied, and he was just starting on her hands when headlights appeared in the distance. Both women tried to attract the driver's attention, but the guy grabbed Margaret and tried to stuff her in the boot. Then the lights disappeared. Margaret was waiting for him to let them go, like in the deal.

Standing at the boot, he turned and said, very quiet: 'You know what I am going to do? I am going to kill you. You won't scream when I cut your throats, will you?'

Greta didn't say anything. Margaret decided she just wanted to get the whole thing over with. 'If I have sex with you, will you . . . will you sort of drop us somewhere and we'll let the whole thing go?'

He softened. 'That's okay.'

He only tied Margaret's hands and walked her to the front seat. He picked up Greta, still tied hand and foot, and put her in the back. He took off his shorts, then Margaret's brown slacks. He got on top of her. Greta looked on in her Valium haze. She could see the top half of both their bodies. Margaret was still wearing the top of her slacksuit. Her bare knees stuck up above the seat.

'Don't watch,' he snarled at Greta. 'Look out in case other cars are coming.'

Greta sat there, acutely aware of the guy's eyes bearing down upon her, listening to her friend.

'You're hurting me . . . Don't climax inside me. I don't want to get pregnant.'

'Uhh.' It was over in a minute or two.

Margaret pulled her slacks up from around her ankles. 'We won't go to the police if you let us go. If you dropped us off at the corner of the dirt road on the highway, we won't go to the police. You'll have plenty of time to get away.'

'No. I think we'll sleep here in the car, and I'll let you go in the morning. You'll get a lift easily then.'

Greta was feeling quite sick. 'We have done you a favour. Now you could do me a favour. I would really like a drink or else I am going to be sick in your car,' she said. He decided that he wanted a can of lemonade, too. He drove them towards the nearest town. On the way, he suggested to Margaret that the two of them should have a week's holiday in Melbourne together.

'No, thank you.'

He drove a short distance north to a BP Service Station on the southern fringe of Goulburn's shopping centre, where the highway took a right-angle turn. He let Margaret go in to the cafe/restaurant to get the drinks, but kept Greta, untied now, in the back seat. Margaret saw a blonde woman working in the garage's cafe. It was 2.45 a.m., Saturday, 10 April, and Joan Eldridge was just about to close the cafe. She was sitting on the public side of the counter when she saw Margaret coming towards her, looking a bit strange.

'There's a chap in the car. He has a knife and he has raped me,' Margaret said.

'Just a moment.' Eldridge called her boss.

Margaret went on: 'He broke my glasses . . . Please help me. I am afraid. I can see the Wanda murders happening again.' (Fifteen-year-olds Marianne Schmidt and Christine Sharrock disappeared on 11 January 1965 at Sydney's Cronulla Beach. Their bodies were found next day buried in sand dunes at nearby Wanda Beach.)

'I'll call the police,' Eldridge said.

'No, my friend is still in the car.'

Suddenly, the man appeared in the cafe, his shirt undone. 'Have you got enough money?' he asked, quiet and polite.

'Yes.' She turned to Eldridge looking shaken. 'I want three cans of drink.' She was handed the drinks and paid for them. Eldridge noticed that she had gone quiet, but there was no sign of tears. The guy and the girl walked out and the boss and two Greek lads followed them.

Margaret got back in the car timidly, but was then emboldened by the sight of the three men coming towards them. 'You can't keep us in the car any longer,' she said. 'You can't do anything about it.' The men surrounded the car, and Margaret jumped out, grabbing her small bag. 'Come on, Greta, we're getting out of this.' Greta was still sitting there too scared to move. She grabbed her bag and bolted just before the car skidded off up the main street of Goulburn. The smell of burnt rubber was thick in their nostrils. The arsehole – whoever he was – was hammering north, back up the Hume Highway.

TWELVE
Mid 1971

STICK'M UP

Constable Allen Fielder took the call just before 3 a.m.: look out for a car wanted in connection with a suspected sexual assault. He and his partner, stationed at Marulan 18 miles north of Goulburn, drove two miles south, and waited.

About 3.30 a.m. they saw a Ford sedan coming out of the night. They skidded out of the gravel and turned on the blue revolving light, but their new Ford Falcon still hadn't been fitted with a damn siren. The other driver put his foot down when he saw them and moved effortlessly up to 105 miles per hour. They gave their six cylinders all they could, and stayed with him for a few minutes but, about three miles north of Marulan, the 351-cubic-inch Fairmont pulled away from the Falcon. Five miles north, they lost sight of the tail-lights altogether.

Fielder kept up the chase, though, because he knew what was up ahead at Paddy's River: a semi-trailer parked across the approach to the bridge. The gold Ford was trapped. Other police had the driver face down. Fielder got out and told the little turd he was to be arrested for speed dangerous to the public. 'I'm going to take you to Goulburn where some detectives want to talk to you.'

'What for?'

'I believe it is to do with an assault on a girl. I don't know the full particulars of it. I am not going to speak to you in relation to the matter.'

Detective Sergeant Dennis Rayner was in bed when he was called to the station. He was there by the time Fielder brought the handcuffed suspect, Ivan Milat, in at about 4 a.m. They took him into a side room. 'I have received a complaint from a woman named Margaret – that you raped her after having threatened her with a knife . . .'

'Raped her? Come off it... Can I see them? Let them tell me that.'

Rayner had the two girls brought to the room. Milat stared at them. 'You didn't keep your side of the bargain,' he said calmly to Margaret.

'What sort of bargain is that?' she sneered, her brown slacksuit all skewed. 'You used my body... You aren't so big and brave now, are you?'

'What are you talking about?' he said, calm as could be.

'You know darn well what we're talking about. I suppose you've got rid of all the evidence.'

'What evidence?'

'My, we are innocent aren't we.'

'Come off it.'

'You had your fun, you animal, but you're not so brave now.'

'I don't know what you're talking about. I think you're screwy.'

'What about tying us up?' Greta shot back.

'What with?'

'You know very well what with. Those pieces of rope. I suppose you've thrown those away.'

'That's all new to me. I don't know what I done to deserve this.'

Margaret was angry. 'What about tying us up while you made what you call love, and what we call sex? You are one of the lowest. You are not a man. You are a male.'

'Look at 'em,' he spat. 'They were willing. They're both lesbians anyway.'

The girls were taken from the station to see a doctor at Goulburn Base Hospital. The doctor, Keith Lyttle, found no evidence of brutality. No blood stains. There were no bruises on Margaret but Greta had red rings around her wrist consistent with having been tied up. He took a vaginal swab from Margaret and gave it to Detective Rayner. Rayner took Milat for a two-hour record of interview. He admitted having sex with Margaret, but denied rape.

Rayner: 'She also alleges that you took a knife that you had in your car, and threatened that you would kill them both if they didn't allow you to have intercourse with them. What do you say about that allegation?'

'She's a liar.'

The police found no knives, no ropes and no sign of a struggle.

When they told Milat he was going to be charged with rape, he kicked in a glass door in a rage. His demeanour changed in the cold hard reality of a prison cell, though. He tore up a blanket and they took it away from him so he wouldn't neck himself . . . and so he'd have a nice warm night. Welcome to sunny Goulburn, sonny.

Bail was a problem. Monday was a public holiday and every government building in rural Goulburn – a Southern Highlands town renowned for its bitter winters – was closed. Goulburn police nabbed 308 drivers during the Easter holiday rush. With the re-opening of the Magistrate's Court on Tuesday, the police blitz ensured a few yarns for the Goulburn *Evening Post*. Milat made the front page: MAN CHARGED ON 4 COUNTS.

Johnny Preston was starting to get involved with organised, heavy types. Dave Preston, still with slicked-back bodgie hair, fronted his brother. 'Brah, where ya getting all this money from? What are ya doin'?'

'Brah, don't get involved, I'm doing business,' said Johnny. 'There's a wog bloke settin' me up with the jobs.'

Later, Dave found a gun in Johnny's wardrobe in the bedroom they still shared at 108 Moore Street. 'Brah, what are you carrying a gun for at your age? Can't you handle your fists?'

Johnny told him he was heading his own gang now Mick Milat was involved.

The egg wars were in full swing. Big money was being made bringing cheap eggs down from Queensland, undercutting the New South Wales Egg Board monopoly. Eric Pember, who, eleven years earlier had employed a lot of the Milats in the fruit shop he sold to Peter Cantarella, was now in the egg trade, based part time in Toowoomba and part-time in Sydney.

This Thursday, 21 June, he was up in Queensland and his wife Eileen and son John were looking after the Sydney end. Thursday was a big day. John was out all day selling eggs across west and south-west Sydney. He did two loads in the little panel van full to the brim and took maybe $800.

That night, John and his mother were expecting a truckload from Toowoomba delivered to their small fibro house at the corner of Stacey

Street and Verbena Avenue, Punchbowl. It was due around 4 a.m., so they went to bed early.

John was sound asleep when his mother came into his room.

'The truck driver's here. He's a bit early.'

John got out of bed yawning, half asleep in his pyjamas. It was only 12.20 a.m. It didn't cross his mind to wonder why the driver was knocking on the front door when he knew to go to the back. So John opened the door without suspicion. 'What the . . . ?' Three masked men carrying sawn-off .22s were standing on the little front porch. The strange part was, they weren't even looking at him. They were watching a car in Stacey Street come over the bridge. But in an instant, they refocused, and a barrel was shoved into Pember's face. The first man pushed him backwards – the gun in his chest, a hand at his shoulder – and kept him going into the lounge room, straight onto the couch.

'Is there anyone else here?' one of them snarled. Pember didn't answer.

'Where's the money?'

Pember stayed quiet, but his mother, watching from the bedroom, piped up: 'Don't tell 'em anything.' He wasn't paying much attention, however. He was sitting there, hands on his head, trying to stay cool, trying to remember descriptions of the gunmen. 'White overalls, blue and white gym boots, black stockings and they've all got guns. Okay.' But the thoughts were flying out of his head as quick as they came to him.

Even if he wanted to tell where the money was, he and his father never knew how much money his mum kept. She had a lot of black money because they dealt in cash which neither they nor the tax man need know about. They'd see it go into her black handbag and that was it. John and his father were always trying to figure out how much she had and where she had it.

One of the men stood by the bedroom door with a gun pointed at Pember on the couch, while the others ransacked the place, pulling drawers out and throwing things out of wardrobes. They tipped his mother off the edge of her bed and pulled up all the sheets.

'If you're looking for money, we banked it today,' she told them coolly.

'There's money here,' one of them answered. 'We know you haven't banked it.'

John saw one of the two shorter guys find her handbag behind the bedroom door. It was stuffed full of letters and bills and the guy was tossing everything on the floor as he went through it. Pember saw a roll of money big enough to choke a horse drop to the floor, just as the big guy came into the lounge room looking agitated. 'Search the other room,' he ordered the one who had been doing the guarding.

Pember was thinking: 'They've got the money. It'll be over in a few minutes. They'll be out of here. Just stay calm.' He didn't think it possible that the guy had missed seeing the money fall to the floor. Surely they knew that brown cellophane rolls were money.

The big guy was getting aggro. He put his sawn-off against Pember's throat. 'Where's the money? We're not doing this for fun, you know. I'll give you a count,' he said, agitated. 'I'll give you to the count o' five . . .'

'One, two . . . Ya gunna tell us?'

Pember stayed quiet. It was all happening too quick for Pember to think.

'Fuck you. Five.'

Pember heard a loud bang. 'Don't kill him!' his mother screamed.

He was thinking: 'These guys are serious, better tell 'em anything they want to know.'

The other two men bolted into the room. The tall one who'd fired the gun took a step backwards. Even under the masks, they looked stunned. Pember felt something like hot tea running down his neck. He put a hand up to it. When he pulled the hand away, it was covered in blood. 'Hell! He shot me.'

'Where's the keys to the Fairlane?' one of them yelled at him.

He pointed at the table by the phone. 'They're there.'

Mrs Pember started saying she was going to call an ambulance but the tall one didn't want her calling no one. Everyone was yelling. Mrs Pember made a dash for the phone. One of them knocked the phone out of its socket as he swiped the car keys, then ran out to the car. He kicked the engine over. It was a great big purring American Galaxie. The other two followed him out to the car and they took off.

Pember was on auto pilot, but he was still standing. That was good. His hand was around his throat, a finger stuck in the bullet's entry hole. His mother had run outside screaming for help. John knew the keys to his Holden Premier were on his dressing table. He grabbed them . . .

focused . . . went to the car . . . jumped in . . . steadied, and headed for Bankstown Hospital.

The Premier was white, with white upholstery. Blood was running all over it. Damn. It was two hazy miles to the hospital. He came up outside casualty, his upholstery ruined. All he had to do was stop, but his foot slipped from the brake. The car lurched forward, banging into another.

He opened the door . . . Almost there . . . Have they seen me?

He was about to get an important lesson as he stepped out. His flannelette pyjamas fell to his knees. He didn't have a cord in them. He tried moving forward, holding the blood in. The pyjamas went to his ankles. He stumbled to the ground, his white bum sticking out, a finger still in his neck, blood everywhere. Pember vowed that if he lived, he would never go to bed without a cord in his pyjamas again. As he struggled to his feet, modesty demanded he bring his pants up above the yardarm on this cold winter's night. Breathing became his top priority over the final few yards to the white light of reception. He barrelled through the front door, a finger still in his neck. 'I've been shot,' he gargled at a startled nurse.

John's mum had woken some neighbours who rang the police. They started an immediate search, but it was some time before they rang the hospital.

'He's here. He's made it. We've got him on a bed,' a nurse said.

As he lay there, someone asked: 'Do you want a priest?'

'Yes please.' He wasn't taking any chances. He didn't know which way he was going. If there was a God, Pember wanted him on side. The priest turned up and found him holding on to the rails of the bed like grim death, telling himself that as long as he held on to those rails he was okay.

Then a cop came in: 'Do you know who did this?'

'No,' said Pember, honestly.

'Do you need to tell us anything?'

'Nothing . . . . Where are you from?' asked Pember.

'Homicide.'

Oh shit, he thought. I'm stuffed. A priest and homicide. The nurses had to pry his fingers off the bed one finger at a time. They made him be violently ill to bring up all the blood in his stomach. 'Okay, we're putting you to sleep now.'

*

Mick Milat had just pocketed the brown cellophane roll and was going over to the dressing table to look for more when he heard the shot. He ran out into the lounge room to see what was going on and the bloke was standing there holding his neck with blood pouring through his fingers. Fucking Preston! The lady come racing out screaming, so he grabbed the keys and bolted to the Yank tank in the garage. The others jumped in and they made for where he'd parked his Valiant, quick smart.

He got out and Preston and this other feller, Keith, pissed off in the Galaxie. Mick followed in roughly the same direction until he found them standing on a corner about a mile away. He picked them up and they drove hard, got lost and then found where they were: coming down The River Road at Revesby. It was Keith's idea to throw the gun off the bridge over Little Salt Pan Creek. It was a murder weapon, far as they knew. Mick turned the car around and they headed back to Liverpool on Henry Lawson Drive, changing clothes as they went. They counted and split the money – $800 tops.

'There was meant to be more fucking money. I'm telling you there was more in there,' Preston was saying.

'Why'd you go shoot the fucker for? Ya stupid fuckin' idiot.'

Preston went quiet.

He and Mick had discussed it the night before when they were driving back from a night in Sydney. Johnny had said how he'd been tipped into it by these Italian blokes he was doing business with. 'There's this bloke keeps a stack of money. We do him then retire for a while.' Yeah right. As for this Keith character, Mick only met him that night at the El Torro Hotel. He was a mate of Preston's. Meant to be some big copper's son. He brought his own .22 along.

Mick dropped the two near John's place in Moore Street, Liverpool. Keith took all the stockings and gloves and burnt them. Mick went home to Guildford. Preston went around to his brother Dave's place and told him what happened. Dave's missus didn't like it. 'John, get out. Get out of this house. Don't involve Dave.'

'Get fucked he's me bruvver,' Dave told her. 'What do you do now, Brah?'

'Mate, I'm panicking.'

'Well, mate, you make your own life. See you later.' John left. He saw Dave at the Railway Hotel, Liverpool, a few days later. John told him the details.

'Brah, if Mum and Dad finds out what you're doin', it's gunna kill 'em,' said Dave.

'They won't find out. It'll be right.'

The shooting made the Sydney *Daily Mirror*: MAN SHOT IN NECK, ROBBED. The story said it was one of two armed robberies early that morning.

Despite the apparently small profits, Mick was able to buy himself a new car, a plum-coloured Chrysler Hemi Pacer, for $2978. It had six big cylinders and no sound baffles in the split exhaust, so it had what the motoring writers called a 'virile rumble' to compete with the V8s. Fat tyres, stiff suspension, bright colours and three gears on the floor all came standard. It got 18 mile to the gallon.

There is a suggestion that they were paid a flat rate to do the Pember job and, even though they only got about $800 from the robbery itself, they were actually paid more in expectation of a much larger haul.[60]

Dr Ray Salama examined John Pember: it was a 'flesh wound'. The bullet went in the right side of the neck, skimmed the voice box, missed the arteries, clipped the spine at the C5 vertebra and came out on the back left side at the top of the shoulder. Some flesh wound.

The doctor told him you could put a bullet through there 200 times and you'd be lucky to come out once without permanent damage or death. 'Buy yourself a lottery ticket.' Police dug the bullet out of the wood at the back of the Pembers' divan.

Next morning in hospital, two detectives spoke to Pember. 'We tracked down every person we know who does armed hold-ups with violence,' the older cop told him. 'We've got about nine of them on our files who are into this sort of thing. We know where every one of them was last night. And they're all clear. This looks like someone new.' They were very interested to know who the new gang in town was.

THIRTEEN

July 1971

GANGSTERS

The Milats had a mate called John Powch. Powchie liked Chrysler Valiants. He had an ignition switch so he didn't have to worry about hot-wiring them. Like Victa mowers, they started first go every time. He pinched one from Leichhardt on 12 July 1971. Next day, Mick Milat was convicted of drink-driving, fined $250 and had his licence taken away for two years. But still, when he, Preston and Powch went to hold up the Mount Pritchard post office agency three days later, they made Mick getaway driver.

Mick lent Powch a .22 rifle which had been converted into a machine-gun. It could fire eight to nine rounds in a second, but after that it always jammed. Preston was unarmed and Mick was outside in the stolen Valiant on Hemphill Street. Powch forced the agency owner, Mrs Jean Douglas, to open the cash box and hand over $618 in cash and tax stamps.

They rated two paragraphs in the next day's *Sydney Morning Herald*: MASKED MEN GET $200.

The next week about 3 p.m., 21 July, Mrs Dora Fagan at the Bonnyrigg Post Office saw a white car come up the driveway. She thought her daughter had arrived, so she walked to the side of the tiny, garage-sized post office, but she couldn't see the car properly. She walked back to the counter as two men with stockings over their faces came in. A little feller had a sawn-off rifle. The tall one jumped the counter. Seven times he told her he would shoot her if she moved.

'Give me the keys,' he demanded.

'You won't let me move. How can I give them to you?'

'Give them to me,' he shouted, his finger on the trigger. She started to give them to him when he screamed, 'Keep your hands off the counter.'

They stole the cash box holding $90 cash and $156 in tax stamps. Again, it was Powch and Preston with Mick driving the Valiant Powch stole. Unfortunately for them, Mrs Fagan had done the mail early – against post office regulations. There was $1500 lying around in mail bags as they tramped all over them shouting for the money and the keys.

This time the gang rated three pars in the *Sydney Morning Herald*: TWO HOLD UP PO AGENCY TAKE $246.

The boys were too busy to read it. They were on their way to Greystanes in a Valiant sedan Powch stole that morning. About 2.50 p.m. they robbed a little mixed business on the corner of Cumberland and Merrylands roads. Same MO. Powch held the gun on the owner's wife, while Preston jumped the counter. Michael drove. They got $80 – slightly less than the average weekly wage back then. Again, they rated three paragraphs in the *Sydney Morning Herald*. Around this time the boys went into a gun shop in George Street, Sydney, with Ivan, who had finally been released on bail pending a committal hearing on the rape charge. All four chipped in to buy a $38 shotgun.

They went back to the Milat place at Campbell Hill Road and watched Powch cut off the barrel. They were on a roll, so that afternoon they went out in Ivan's gold Fairmont and Powch knocked off another Valiant sedan from nearby Granville and drove south to Revesby. About 7.40 p.m., they burst into a tiny suburban store, at 56 Bransgrove Road, run by a Peter Nicola. Powch had the sawn-off .22 automatic, Preston had one of the Milats' other .22s, and Ivan had a small Stitz .22.

Ivan filled his pockets from the cash register and Powch, standing in the middle of the little square shop, demanded: 'Where is the other money?'

'What other money?' Peter's wife, Katrina Nicola, pleaded, standing over the frozen-food cabinet.

'There must be more money.'

She grabbed an empty bag from under the counter and passed it over to him to have a look.

'There's no money,' said Nicola. 'What do you think I am? I am only a poor shopkeeper.'

Powch threw the money bag back at Katrina and quickly searched the place for more cash. Satisfied, the three of them walked backwards to the door, then just before they reached it, turned and bolted to the car. They piled into the Valiant. Mick drove about half a mile to the gold Fairmont. They switched cars, split the money and split up. Nicola claimed he lost $248, the boys claimed they got $10 each. Powch went to town, and the others went home.

Four days later, the gang got together again. Perhaps dissatisfied with their meagre pickings at Revesby, the gang were keen to go up a grade. Mick Milat and Powch had knocked off a white Valiant sedan, BDV 312, at Cabramatta, near Liverpool, the night before. That morning, Preston, Powch and Mick headed to Parramatta where they planned to do the Commercial Bank of Australia. Ivan followed in the Fairmont.

They dumped the Valiant about half a mile from the bank and drove past in the Fairmont. An armoured van was outside, guarded by two men with guns and a dog. They decided to give the bank a big miss.

They drove around aimlessly, figuring out what to do. Mick was leading in the Valiant, when, driving through Canley Heights, they saw a little bank sub-branch. They could only see two tellers and reasoned it was probably too small to have security cameras.

They left the Fairmont about 200 yards away in Cambridge Street and piled in the Valiant. They pulled their stockings and gloves on outside, then Preston with the shotgun, Powch with the .22 automatic, and an empty-handed Ivan ran into the bank. Mick kept the motor running with a .22 by his side.

'This is a hold-up. Up against the wall. Up against the wall,' yelled Preston. 'Where's the money?'

The teller, Pat Gooley, didn't answer.

'Where's the bloody money?' The voice wasn't loud, but the tone made the point well enough.

Powch and Ivan were shuffling through cupboards and the old safe. They were into the pigeon holes in the walls, throwing cash boxes about.

Preston, on the counter, was screaming now: 'Where's the bloody money?'

Gooley pointed at the teller's drawer. Ivan pulled it open. He saw only coins in the front section, then pulled it further, and saw notes. He scrunched them all up in his hand. 'Where's the rest of it? This is not enough. Where's the rest of it?'

'I haven't got any more,' said Gooley. They kept rummaging.

Preston had had enough. 'Come on,' he barked. The other two jumped back over the counter while he kept them covered. 'Are you all right?' he asked the staff, but they didn't answer. He turned and ran out.

The gang dumped the Valiant on Kiora Street, two small blocks behind the bank, then dashed around the corner to the Fairmont in Cambridge Street. They split the money evenly, $84 each – $360 was stolen, the even split should have been $90 – as they drove away, then they split up. Preston went to unload his gun and realised it wasn't loaded. They left all the stuff, including the stockings and gloves, at Campbell Hill Road. Mick went and had a drink.

They might have seen the afternoon tabloid, *The Sun*, which gave them their biggest write-up to date. Six pars in the last edition. $310 BANK HOLD-UP. But they didn't know that a local businessman had taken down Ivan's number plate: ALQ 485.

The gang's activities were to be curtailed somewhat by John Preston having to go to court to face unrelated assault charges. That day, 29 July, John Pember was back in Sydney. Two police officers took him to the Fairfield Court of Petty Sessions. He wasn't told much at first, but as they approached, one of them said: 'The guy who shot you is appearing in court on another charge this morning. He's standing on the steps outside court. Go up and see if you can identify him.'

'No worries.' Pember slowly approached the steps, looking closely into every male face. Next thing, the cops were gone and he was all alone. 'Oh beauty.' He stood on the stairs and quietly had a look at everybody coming in. He felt very alone and was trying to stay calm. The gunman had worn a mask, so Pember had no idea what he looked like, yet the guy would know exactly what *he* looked like. It wasn't a good set-up. He stayed for five minutes, nothing clicking, then walked back to the cops. 'Nah. I can't help you at all.'

'Okay. Never mind. Shame, though.'

'Who is he? What's he done?'

'He's been charged with something else and we'll know exactly where to find him for the next couple of weeks. He'll be in jail.'

This was some relief. While he was in Sydney, Pember got his car back from police. The blood had curdled and it smelt disgusting. He had to get rid of it, but found it very difficult to sell.

Preston was put away for two months hard labour, but that didn't stop his mates. Two days later, Powch stole another Valiant from Fairfield and, on Saturday, 31 July, he and Mick did over a little mixed business on the corner of Cromwell and Norton streets, Ashfield. It was the first time Mick had gone inside on a job. They got $120 from the till and the purse off a woman customer.

Three days later, on Tuesday, 3 August, the gang was reshaping itself.

Tina Roulis was behind the counter at the front of her shop in St Johns Road, Cabramatta. Her husband, George, was serving a customer. In came a masked man. 'Stand back!' He was pointing a sawn-off gun of some sort. She ducked below the counter which ran up the side of the store and, with her head down, made for the back, calling out in Greek to her mother upstairs, 'Get the shotgun! Get the shotgun!'

She got to the end of the counter and saw another masked man standing there, aiming down at her. 'Shut up!' He motioned her back to the front of the shop. The first man came behind the counter and pulled the money out of the wooden cash drawer.

Another gunman had Tina's mother covered in the kitchen.

One of them demanded more money. George was holding lollies in his hand. 'Help yourself with the lollies, I have got no other money.'

'Give us your wallet! Empty your pockets!'

George pulled a one dollar note from his pocket. That's all he ever carried. He handed it over and the three masked men bolted.

But that wasn't the end for the Roulises. George had fought off an intruder in their bedroom only months before, and they were in no mood for surrender. He ran upstairs for his gun, cursing that it wasn't downstairs where he usually left it. Tina ran outside, picked up a milk bottle and hurled it at the fleeing bandits. She picked up another bottle. Smash! Into the side of the car parked next to the shop. Then another. Smash! Powch shouldered the shotgun and let off a blast.

'Fuck off!'

Tina hit the ground.

'Are they shooting at us, John?' Mick wanted to know.

'No.'

George heard the bang before he made it to the top of the stairs, and ran straight back down. He saw Tina standing just out the entrance, screaming something about her leg. He grabbed the phone and dialled 000 for the police. Tina had a bleeding knee but didn't know if she'd been shot. The shotgun left a tight blast pattern ten feet above the street, so it is unlikely any fragment hit her knee.

They split the money at Mick's place – $45 each, even though the Roulises maintained they lost $300. Powch took the guns and stockings back to his place at Leichhardt for safekeeping.

Next day, 4 August, the gang made a bigger media splash. Nine pars in the *Sydney Morning Herald* – THIEVES SHOOT AT IRATE WOMAN – and thirteen in the *Daily Telegraph* – WOMAN SHOT BY BANDITS. That day, however, the media's attention turned to the biggest story of the year: the arrest of Peter Macari, better known as Mr Brown, who took $500,000 from Qantas in a bomb hoax extortion.

Another Milat was watching the story on the telly with a bit too much interest.

FOURTEEN

1971

THE COLLAR

Detective Sergeant Bob Bradbury arrived at work at the Criminal Investigation Branch Friday, 6 August, to be told by his boss, Chief Superintendent Dick Lendrum, to keep his hat on. 'There's been a spate of robberies in the south-west and I want you to go out and help the locals.' Bradbury rang the Liverpool detectives to see what the score was.

'Well, we've got something going at the moment,' they said. 'The fellow we suspect is probably going to make a phone call to his girlfriend ... So stay where you are. We'll be in touch.' Powch was madly obsessed by a woman, Eve, who was co-operating with the police in order to get him off her back. Bradbury waited in his little office in the Special Crime Squad, later renamed the Homicide Squad. All the squads had 'special' in their names then, just like they're all 'task forces' now. Back then, armed robbery wasn't nearly so prevalent. Those that did it were in professional gangs, although amateurs like the Milats were coming into the game.

At about 2.45 p.m., John Powch was brought in handcuffs to the 'Hat Factory' in Surry Hills – a dark brick warehouse that had been converted into the CIB headquarters. Bradbury looked at the small, young man. 'I am Detective Sergeant Bradbury and this is Detective Tunstall. I have every reason to believe that you have been concerned in armed hold-ups in the western suburbs.'[61]

'No, not me. I don't know anything about any hold-ups,' said Powch. They asked to search his premises and Powch said go right ahead. They searched the rooms. Tunstall pulled a navy blue overnight bag from a wardrobe. He threw it on the bed and opened it. The heavy black metal of three guns, mixed in with gloves and stockings, stared up at the coppers.

Powch looked shocked. They all looked shocked. Why would he lead them straight to his hold-up kit? Then the landlady explained that a woman had just dropped off the bag she was minding for Powch.

Powch was sitting on his bed with Tunstall guarding him. Tunstall saw a strip of black and white passport-type photos on the dressing table. The sort taken in a booth. It showed a man holding a sawn-off shotgun with his head turned away from the camera.

'Is that you?' growled Bradbury.

'Yeah. The gun's in the bag.'

'Why did you have this photograph taken?'

'Big-noting. That's all.'

They could see how each photo in the strip had a little section cut out of his left hand where the policemen could see he had a tattoo. The photo also showed a scar on the inside of his right wrist, the result of a suicide attempt.

They took Powch back to the Hat Factory where Powch proposed a deal: he'd tell them everything if they brought Eve in so he could talk to her.[62]

Tunstall was dispatched to find Eve. She didn't want to come in, but he went the heavy on her. Told her she had no choice and she relented. She was led into an unadorned room where Powch was handcuffed to a chair. Police were around the walls, but she felt very alone – just him and her, squared off.

'You shot me, Eve, didn't you.'

'Yes.' So it began, and continued for two or three hours. All Powch's obsessive energy was unleashed. He was calm, but intense. His greatest fear was that Preston and the Milats would find out Eve put them in, and they'd get her.

'I can hurt you. No one else can,' he told her.

Powch stuck to his word. He had his say, then Bradbury asked him: 'Who was involved with you in these robberies?'

'A fellow named Mick, but I do not know his address, but his phone number is [he gave the number] and he has got ten brothers . . . Mick's brother Ivan who owns the Falcon which we used as a getaway car lives with Mick. He was in the Canley Heights bank and the Revesby job.'

About 5.35 p.m., Bradbury put out the word to go pick up the

Milat boys, then began the formal interviews of Powch. Powch fessed up and kept on doing it for three hours. The four records of interview finished a bit after 9 p.m. Each neat, flowing signature at the bottom was signing Mick and Ivan away.

Police arrested Mick in his car early in the evening and left it till 3 a.m. to raid the Milat home. Detective Sergeant Doug Knight went into Ivan's bedroom, gun drawn, and pulled him out of bed and into a cop car.

Michael was still at the Hat Factory. They'd been interviewing him for six hours and he'd been signing his name at the bottom each time they asked. Mick later claimed he was forced to answer questions and sign the typed statements. When Mrs Milat saw her boy's face the next day, she was horrified. It was red and swollen. By the time the first interview got to court, it was a bizarre pastiche of cut-and-pasted questions and answers. By 4 a.m. they had him on his final interview, re the Pember shooting. Fortunately for Ivan, they didn't have him in the frame for that one. They only wanted him for the Canley Heights bank job and the Nicolas' mixed business.

Ivan's first formal interview began at about 4.45 a.m., with Knight asking the questions and another detective typing.

Knight asked about the mixed business.

'What makes you think it was us?' Ivan asked.

'Your brother Michael has already been interviewed and has admitted the offence and has nominated that you, Powch and Preston were with him,' said Knight

'If your brother puts you in, it's not much good trying to get out of it. I was in it but it wasn't my idea.'

After the interview finished, he was asked if he wanted to sign the interview.

'Not just now. I'd like to get some legal advice.'

The second interview, re the Canley Heights bank, went ahead at 6.15 a.m. despite Ivan's protest that he wasn't signing anything till he got legal advice.

'We told you the signing of the document is a matter for yourself,' said Knight, according to the record. 'Our information is that this robbery was committed by you, your brother Michael, John Powch, and John Preston. What do you have to say about that?'

'Have they told you that I was in this one with them too?'

'If you are referring to your brother Michael and John Powch, my answer to you is yes . . .'

'All right I was in on it. No one would ever believe that your brother had put you in cold for something you hadn't done.'

The young Campbelltown solicitor John Marsden set about trying to get them bail. They denied all the allegations. Marsden had met Ivan months earlier in the Goulburn police cells when he was charged with rape. He saw him just after the police claimed he tried to kill himself by banging his wrists against the cells. Marsden got Ivan bail for that one and the committal was due next month.

Mrs Milat had hired him because he'd helped get one of the boys out of trouble over an incident with a girl a few years earlier. He had a great deal of respect for Mrs Milat. Thought she was a wonderful old lady who had battled hard in difficult circumstances to bring up a lot of kids. She was a woman who stood by her children come hell or high water . . . and she always paid the bills.[63]

The barrister Marsden hired went into bat hard. His clients were living at home with their mother. Their father had recently deserted them and their sister had recently been killed in a car accident, he said. 'Their mother needs them badly.' (The authors could find no evidence that Steven ever left Margaret.)

The prosecutor said the offences carried maximum penalties of penal servitude for life. Ivan got bail of $1000. Mum put up the money.

She was having a bad trot. Wally was also facing charges over a stolen Triumph engine where Marsden had pleaded: 'This is a young man with a large family who was recently the driver of a motor vehicle in which his sister was killed. This has imposed a great stress upon him.'

Wally was fined $50.

Johnny Preston was already in jail so the police didn't have to rush to pick him up. He'd been there since the day John Pember had failed to identify him at Fairfield Court. On 19 August, almost a fortnight after Michael and Ivan had been shopped by Powchie, police took Preston from prison and charged him for his part in the robberies.

The Preston family knew Johnny was going to go down in a big way this time. Like the Milats, they were accustomed to the police knocking on their door.

So when the gang got busted for these armed robberies, the Preston family thought Johnny – being the shooter – would get life. His old man couldn't read or write but he knew his way around. He went to some police he knew. 'Youse come up with $50,000,' this copper told him, 'we'll get 'im bail.'[64]

Dave Preston didn't give two hoots about the money. He sold his house and paid the coppers, who saw to it that bail wasn't opposed. His wife left him because of it. After paying the cops, Dave had $3000 left over and he gave it to John. He told his brother to put at least 1000 miles between him and Sydney and never look back.

'Don't ring Mum, Dad or me, just go. Go to Perth. Go to the Northern Territory, just go,' Dave said, emphasising each point. 'You've cost me the house . . . the missus . . . Go!' Dave thought John took his advice, but the silly bastard went and got a flat behind the Stardust Hotel at Cabramatta. He was hung up on some young bird. Thinking with his balls.

At 5 a.m. on Sunday, 10 October, Preston and another guy went to the Lansvale Autoport on the Hume Highway. They tied the lube attendant, John William Brown, to a chair with electrical cord, then stole $323.87 from the office.

Like Preston, Ivan knew that with his record, he was going to get locked up for a long time. He'd already spent half the previous decade in the can. He didn't need the next one wiped out, too.

FIFTEEN

Late 1971–1973

THE GAP

Despair, heartbreak, depression, fear, insanity. Whatever drove people to the brink in Sydney, it drove them here. To The Gap, at the southern entrance to the harbour. Most came for the views, or the rock fishing, but The Gap was best known as the place to kiss off this life. So many people did it that newspapers adopted a policy of rarely reporting them because it encouraged copycats.

Ivan thought long and hard about it. It hadn't been his year as a villain. The rape case and the stick-ups were hanging over him, and his chances in court didn't look good. He told his mum the cops were out to get him, that the girl was willing and that the robbery charges were a get-square from the cops if the other case failed. Mum believed him.

In his eighteen months of freedom, Ivan had pretty well stuffed his life up again. Marilyn and Boris had tied the knot and taken off to the Central Coast. His sister had died. And now he was going back inside.

When the day came for the committal hearing on the armed robberies, Wednesday, 13 October, Preston had bolted and the dog Powch was crook in jail. He'd got hold of about forty tablets and downed them in a suicide attempt, then refused to tell the authorities what type of tablet they were, or how he got them. Now, he was lying in the prison hospital threatening to do it again.

Ivan turned up at the historic Central Court of Petty Sessions in Liverpool Street, Sydney, with a couple of relatives for support, including his sick mother. They got there early so he could discuss the defence with his solicitor, John Marsden. He was facing two counts each of assault and robbery whilst armed and carrying an unlicensed pistol. Mick was in the underground holding cells.

Ivan saw Marsden in a room upstairs. 'What do you think's going to happen?' he asked at the end of the meeting.

The lawyer didn't muck about. 'I think you're going to go to jail for a long time.'[65]

Ivan said he was going outside to have a coffee and a cigarette. When the case opened at 10 a.m., he was nowhere to be seen. Calls for his presence echoed around the tatty old stone foyer. Finally, a court attendant entered the courtroom and announced to Magistrate Anderson, and a stunned Marsden, 'No show, Your Worship'.

When Ivan failed to appear by the morning tea break, a bench warrant was issued for his arrest. His description and details of his car were circulated. That afternoon, they found the car parked at The Gap. A search of the cliff tops turned up a pair of shoes which were identified as the ones he wore that morning.

The news was conveyed to Marsden. Unless police could prove otherwise, misadventure had befallen his client. As far as he was concerned, Ivan was dead. Back in court, Mick was told that Mac had bolted and that Mum was going to lose her $1000. She could no longer afford the lawyer and so Mick was left without representation.

All alone and with no legal counsel, Mick sat there quietly as a string of victims and police were led through their evidence. It was only when they put the interrogating officer, Detective Sergeant Brian Thompson, in the stand that Mick got to his feet: 'At the time of these interviews I was forced to sign them. As far as they go, I did sign them, but I was forced to answer them. That is it. What goes in there, I was forced to sign them and I didn't make them of my own request.'

Magistrate Anderson: 'You say it was not voluntary?'

'That is right, sir. All the witnesses were other police around, that is what I have got to say. This girl that was with me, she has seen I was bashed and hit around the head and there were still red marks that my brother saw. They also bashed him.' And so it went on.

Mick continued objecting to the police version of events. Thompson continued his evidence with all the rigid language of an officer used to being in the stand and Mick kept jumping up with outrage. 'You may as well just give me life the way things are going right now.'

*

Ivan turned up at Maureen Parsons' place. She was barely sixteen-and-a-half, but he turned to her. They had connected. She had slept with him on occasion, even though she'd gotten serious with Wally. She felt she could relate to Ivan in a different way to Wally. They were on the same wavelength and seemed to have the same sense of humour. She found Ivan fascinating. Her girlfriend Lynn, who was dating Bill Milat, asked about going out with two brothers.

'Mac's totally different, you know what I mean,' answered Maureen. 'Like, Ivan would go out of his way to help you. Wally wouldn't care less.' Maureen never once had an argument with Ivan. He was a placid sort of person. 'He's gentle, Lynn.'

Maureen saw violence in Wally, not physical, but in his voice and manner. Anything could set him off. They were always fighting. What really upset her was the way they weren't able to resolve things through plain, calm talk. That was Wally.

Ivan, on the other hand, did things Wally never thought of. He came around to her place four days before his arrest to give her a lift to Grace Bros, Parramatta, where she worked. Sydney was in the grip of a three-day train strike so the drive was a nightmare. He did it three days running. That was Ivan. One day, he even bought her flowers for no reason. Then about a month later, when he was out on bail, he dropped by.

'I've come to say goodbye. I'm going away,' he said.
'Why?'
'I'm in some trouble.'

Maureen knew about the rape charge and the bank robbery jazz, but Ivan never spoke in any detail about them. He said his going away had something to do with that, but again he didn't want to talk about it. Maureen thought she'd never see him again. It upset her. He was such a nice person.

'Why don't you go and face it?' she said. 'And, you know, you'll still be here. If you have to go to jail, well you do your time and you come out, and everything's over and done with.'

Mac just said goodbye, gave her and her mother a kiss and drove off. Maureen was crying. She didn't want him to go. She didn't know if it was love. At that age, how do you know?[66] She fell back to Wally.

*

The next day, Thursday, 14 October, Powch had recovered sufficiently from his suicide bid to be bought to court. He and Mick were kept apart during their appearance. Mick didn't want anything to do with the filthy grub. Powch was charged with six counts of assault and robbery, as well as possession of a machine-gun, an unlicensed pistol and a sawn-off rifle.

They were both way out of their depth and both had long confused rants at the legal system and both were committed to stand trial. Powch had another rant, calling it a 'kangaroo court'.

About a week after the committal, Preston stole a 1969 Holden Monaro sedan from John William Hynes at Panania. It was worth about $2200. He was arrested in it the next day. The police figured he had something sinister planned. They allegedly found an unlicensed pistol and a sawn-off shotgun in the boot.

If Mrs Milat thought she was the victim of police harassment or that they were unsympathetic to her plight, she was wrong. A few detectives understood that she was the victim of betrayal by her son. Without her realising it, Detective Senior Constable Ian Worley, put in a favourable report to help her save the house.

The surety is a person of good character. The surety is a married woman with fourteen children whose ages range from nine years to thirty-two years and although her husband is employed, there is little doubt her financial position is not good and it is most unlikely that she is in a position to afford to lose the amount of $1000 which she lodged.

The surety has not given police any assistance to locate the offender. She has stated he has not made any contact with her since absconding. There is no reason to believe that before absconding the offender recompensed the surety. The offender has not been arrested.

Clearly too young to be married, Maureen, like so many kids of the love-and-liberation generation, wasn't going to be free either. She was sweet sixteen and preggers. This generation which grew up with the Beatles and the Pill, and who raced off and fucked as if no one had ever done it before, were actually practising love with all the strings attached. Teen pregnancies hit an all-time high in 1971, as did the road toll, coincidentally, and teenage marriages peaked in 1972. One in three women turning twenty that year was already married.

Maureen was facing the biggest drama of her life while the two men she cared for most weren't around to give her any support. Ivan had bolted, and Wally was behind bars. A week before Christmas '71, he'd been heading south on the Hume Highway in Billy's blue V8 Falcon around 5.55 p.m. when Constable Peter Moore of Tarcutta police saw him speed by. On went the siren. But Wally wasn't stopping. He floored it and was soon doing close to 100 miles an hour as they careened through the 35-mile-an-hour main street of Tarcutta – all done up for Christmas. Moore clocked him at 97 mph. The chase continued for another 41 miles until he lost control in the gravel. The overheating engine cut out. He got out. 'All right, you got me. I was trying to get away cause I got no licence,' he told Moore.

He faced Wagga Wagga Court of Petty Sessions and pleaded guilty to charges of speeding, driving in a manner dangerous to the public and unlicensed driving. He got four months in Goulburn Prison.

John Pember, with the hole in his neck healing remarkably well, was still on tenterhooks. When he had to talk about his experience, he'd sit on his hands to stop them from shaking. There was no counselling for victims or even a diagnosis of 'post-traumatic stress syndrome'. You just got on with life.

After he moved out of home, his friends were often bemused by his odd behaviour. One time some mates knocked at the door of his Cronulla flat, late at night. He could see different sets of feet under the door. He bolted straight over the balcony and out onto the southern Sydney beach.

During the trial at Darlinghurst Courthouse in March 1972, Pember often chatted with the police. During a break, one told him they'd heard the gang was going to try to bust out. Then the cop smiled: 'I hope they try.' Pember got the impression John Powch had been persuaded to dob in his mates after a chat down in the cells in which he got to study a phone book at close quarters.

The case was short and simple. Both Johnny Preston and Mick Milat pleaded guilty to four armed robbery charges and one of wounding Pember. Preston had his pregnant girlfriend in court. They were planning to marry, he told His Honour Judge Hicks. It did no good. On Friday, 4 March, Preston was sentenced to eighteen years with an eight and-a-half-year non-parole period. Mick got sixteen years with seven and a half, non-parole. Pember's only problem with the result was that police never got the third bandit, 'Keith'. Pember's father, Eric, had some good police connections and was later told that Keith was the son of a police sergeant who pulled some strings. Preston and Mick wouldn't dob him in.

The case earned the Milats their biggest write up to date: twenty paragraphs in the *Sydney Morning Herald*: ROBBERS JAILED EIGHTEEN AND SIXTEEN YEARS.

Having given his mates up, Powch went and pleaded not guilty and subsequently got an even bigger sentence than them – twenty years, reduced on appeal to eighteen. Shopping his mates had done him no good at all, and he wasn't even there when Pember was shot. Powchie was a born loser. Preston was waiting for him when he arrived at Parramatta Jail. The dog was going to pay his debt to a different society.

Somehow, Preston got hold of Powch's hand under a metal grille at the bottom of a cell door. Someone held it down while Preston jumped up and down on it, smashing his fingers and knuckles to bits.[67] Preston told his brother Dave that the Valiant around at the Milats' place was his. 'Go and get it. It's mine.'

'What if they won't hand it over?'

'Fuck them anyway and get the car.'

Dave Preston went around there, but Billy Milat wouldn't give it up, arguing it was half Mick's. Dave, not wanting any trouble and knowing from school days how you couldn't hurt the bastards, didn't press the point.

To some, Johnny Preston might have been a hard case before he went in. To Dave, he was still a kid, but he went real hard in the next few years. He 'didn't want to get fucked, so he fought every bastard in there. He belted every Tom, Dick and Harry.' He was crazy. They sent him straight to maximum.

Wally turned twenty behind bars. Maureen, almost seventeen, was seven months gone. The previous eight months had produced the biggest dramas of her short life: Ivan taking off; Wally going to jail; finding out she was pregnant; and her best friend Lynn had died of complications from a routine operation. She wrote to Wally in Goulburn and they picked a name for the baby. When he came out in April, the parents had brokered a marriage over lunch at the Milat home.

Maureen's mum liked old Mr Milat. It was Steven who put it to his son: 'Vally, you should marry de girl. You must do dis for your mothar.'

Mrs Parsons made sure the final say was Maureen's. Wally said: 'I suppose we better get married.' Or something like that. She said: 'Yeah.'

Ivan was out of the picture. She never knew where he was until her mum rang her at work one day just before her birthday on 7 May.

'You've got a letter here... You know who it's from. You know who.'

'Oh wow!' Her mother didn't say anything more over the phone. Maureen was excited. She couldn't wait to get home.

The letter was postmarked Auckland, New Zealand. Back then, citizens didn't need passports to cross the Tasman. All Ivan needed was a ticket in a bodgie name. Mac wrote that he was living in Mount Eden, near Auckland, and working as a rigger on some tall buildings. 'My room's great. It looks just like yours.' He always liked Maureen's bedroom. Her mother let her do what she wanted with it. She'd painted one wall bright green with black around it. Her girlfriend Lynn had drawn over the walls. She had one really big poster, black with an orange tree on it. The tree was actually all these bodies in a tree shape – tree of man – psychedelia and all that.

He gave her instructions to write to him as Joe Spanner. There was no 'I love you', or anything like that. She thought about him a lot, imagining him up on the tall buildings, short-haired and clean-shaven. That's the way he'd always be in her mind. There were more letters and she wrote back enthusiastically. It was a dreamy interlude for Maureen as harsh reality loomed. She didn't keep the letters because she was due to marry Wally and it wouldn't have been right.

Maureen gave birth to a son, Robert, on 22 July 1972. Wally was missing again. Two days earlier, he'd been sentenced to three months hard labour and sent to Parramatta Jail. He'd been fooling around on a motorbike in the dirt, down the end of Campbell Hill Road, and was done for riding whilst disqualified. That was on top of the lesser charges of unregistered motorcycle, uninsured motorcycle and no helmet. When Robert was born, Mrs Parsons rang the jail. 'Just tell him his wife's had a baby boy.' They weren't married yet, but the message had a better chance of getting through that way. Maureen took Robert to the jail a few days later: 'Here you are. Here's your son,' she said, showing him the boy.

'Aw, he looks like Ivan,' said Wally.

'Thank you!' she said, miffed. 'This is Robert, he's your son, Wally.' Wally got it in his head from then that the child might not be his. Maureen dismissed it. She knew whose kid it was. She felt Wally's suspicion came from his having seen what happened between Ivan and Marilyn.

Then, when Robert was just nine weeks old, Ivan turned up at the door out of the blue. 'Hi, how are you?' He came in and had a look at the baby lying on the floor. Mrs Parsons wasn't impressed even though she liked Ivan. 'Oh no, what's he doing back here?' She hoped he wouldn't complicate things. Wally was due out of jail any day and Maureen was to marry him in a month.

Ivan didn't cause any trouble. He finished his coffee – always black, no sugar and in a white mug – then disappeared again without saying where he was going. His unexpected return caught the family by surprise, too. His mum maintained she never knew he was in New Zealand until he wrote to her a week before he came back. She had been ill for most of '71 and well into '72. She thought a relative might have been harbouring him in Sydney, but no one would tell her.

Ivan didn't hang around. He took off again without telling his mum where he was headed.

Maureen and Wally had a registry wedding at Parramatta on 20 October. Wally had to change a flat tyre for his mother-in-law after the ceremony, before they went to the Milats' for lunch. It was no big deal or anything. They moved into a house at Taloma Avenue, Lurnea, almost the same day.

A week later, Billy married a local girl, Carol Pritchard, who he'd been seeing for a while, and they moved in with Wally and Maureen.

Ivan kept his distance from the family. He turned up at a bash at Shirley and Gerry Soire's place in Liverpool where all he would tell Alex about New Zealand was that he drove a Zephyr, and that the Kiwi girls were like cut snakes, mad as meat axes. He told Maureen how he was using Bill's name now because Billy was respectable and hadn't been in any trouble for years. He'd always have an alibi.

But he had another alias as well.

When Geoff Post moved into a boarding house around Summer Hill/Ashfield in Sydney's inner-west, in late 1972, the landlord introduced his new roommate as Bill Harris. The two of them got on pretty good. You'd want to, sharing a 20-foot-long room with a total stranger. Geoff was a tidy sort of person, but Bill left him in the shade. He was immaculate. Geoff brought his telly in and sat it on the chest of drawers between the two beds. They spent hours just watching the box.

Geoff was only in the boarding house temporarily. He owned a place and was waiting for the tenants to leave. 'Do you want to come and share my place out Blacktown?' Geoff asked Bill, after a couple of months. 'No rent, just five dollars a week to cover expenses.' Bill jumped at it.

Geoff had all his furniture locked up in the garage so they were pretty well set up when they moved out there, probably some time early 1973. A Swedish fellow, Stephan, moved in later on as well. Geoff had met him at the golf club. Bill didn't play golf. Come to mention it, Bill never seemed to go out much at all. He'd just sit at home and watch the telly or work on his car, a mid-sixties maroon Holden. He polished it so much it glittered. They joked that you could see it five miles away.

Bill got around in T-shirt and jeans, or a shirt like the one Hoges wore, with the sleeves cut off. He was pretty fit looking. You'd come into a room and he'd be doing push-ups or throwing a few dumbbells around.

Bill didn't talk much about himself. Said he was working for the Water Board digging sewerage tunnels up under the new suburbs around Carlingford, North Rocks. But, after they'd been at Blacktown a while, Bill opened up a bit and told Geoff he was wanted over a bank robbery which his brother was in jail for.

'Bullshit,' thought Geoff.

Bill said they didn't have the evidence to get him on it, but Geoff thought that if that was the case why didn't he front up to it. He never mentioned anything about rape. It was none of Geoff's business anyway.

Bill never had any visitors. After he finished polishing the car of a

Saturday morning, he'd say he was going to visit some brother, usually Alex, and they wouldn't see him till late Sunday arvo. He seemed close to his family, except for someone he called 'the Warthog'.

Bill took Geoff out to Alex's property at Yanderra one time. Alex's kids were hooning around in circles and through the trees in a beat up old Volkswagen, while the adults had a yak. Alex asked Geoff something like how he got along with Bill.

'He's all right. A reasonable sort of bloke,' said Geoff.

'He'd put a knife in you as quick as look at you,' said Alex. Geoff looked at him, wondering what he was on about, the comment was so totally out of the blue.

Wally, with the stolen bike parts and the mad car chases, was a bit of a hero to Richard. The younger brother used to talk about him all the time to his little group of mates who hung around the shops near South Granville High. Richard was a little older than most of the gang, and he seemed a world apart to Pat Casey, who was pretty low down the gang's hierarchy.

About late '73, he was the first one to have a bike. He always seemed a bit older and bit world weary – and he was, compared to the rest of them. And he had girls. All the little gang would be thinking 'how 'bout that?'

Casey got to know Richard through another one of the local kids, Phil Polglase, who was this tall skinny kid with long blond hair down over his shoulders. Phil was a bit older again, more level-headed. 'The elder statesman of the problem children.'

Phil was mischievous – who wasn't? – but not in the same league as Richard. Richard was a likeable, fun sort of kid, but you wouldn't want to get too close. If there was going to be a fight and anybody was going to pull a knife, he would have. Nobody else would have even had one, let alone pull one. Casey only saw him with a knife once, but was sure he carried it all the time. 'We were innocent. He wasn't.'

He used to tell them about stealing motorbikes and, certainly, when the kids went over to his place they saw a lot of bikes. It wasn't the place kids like Casey wanted to hang around. As he'd later put it, in nineties dialect, he was out of his comfort zone. There was a 'rough kind of atmosphere, scary personalities'. He knew they'd do things he'd never think of doing.

He wasn't mates with Richard by any means, and Casey would later not be able to remember how he came to be with him alone, but there was a bike, maybe a 250cc, in a car park at Granville that Richard said he wanted. They grabbed a handlebar each and started pushing. The owner – some other teenager – saw them and gave chase. They couldn't outrun him so they dropped it and bolted.

Casey couldn't believe he was so dumb to get himself involved with Richard. But it was only a year or so later that he realised he had to keep right away from him.

SIXTEEN

Early 1974

MR BROWN

'Mr Brown', the great plane robber of 1971, became an instant figure of folklore the moment his van pulled away from Qantas' Sydney headquarters with $500,000 on board. The stupid bastard might have got away with it too, only he got big-headed and went on a spending spree.

Real name Peter Macari, Mr Brown came by the idea for his extortion from a movie, *Doomsday Flight*. Within two months of seeing it, the illegal English immigrant had built an altitude bomb and placed it in a locker at Sydney Airport with his $500,000 ransom demand. He phoned a man who he thought was Captain Ritchie, the Qantas general manager, and said a similar bomb was on flight 755 en route to London via Hong Kong. It would explode if the plane descended below 20,000 feet. The plane circled above Brisbane as crew searched around the feet of terrified passengers. In Sydney, a staff member was dispatched to the Reserve Bank to pick up the cash. Macari drove past Qantas headquarters, and a man put the money in his van. Bungling by police and Qantas security meant that not a single car chased him into the peak-hour traffic. He was home free, but had the decency to ring Captain Ritchie to say there wasn't a bomb on the plane after all.

Three years later, someone was at it again. The voice on the other end of the blower was boyish, but the language ... phew! The switchboard operator at Qantas House had never heard such a foul young mouth. The caller seemed confused about exactly what he wanted, but the telephonist knew the drill. Ever since Mr Brown, they took all such calls seriously.

By 3.30 p.m., the extortionist had made twenty calls and upped the ante to $500,000. With each call he seemed more angry and abusive. At one stage he wanted the money in small denominations, to be left at the front counter of Qantas headquarters. That was done, but nothing happened. Perhaps he was bluffing. The police waited. They hadn't been able to get a successful phone trace nor had the extortionist been specific about whether a bomb had actually been planted. The police sweated all night on the next call, but it didn't come until 2 p.m. Friday. Now, he wanted the dosh delivered by a hostie – one of those sorts from the TV ads. He wanted her for the weekend, and was explicit about what he planned to do with her. His language appalled even hardened police. An hour later he phoned back and was told Qantas was agreeing to all the demands. Where did he want the money delivered?

The corner of Barbers Road and Campbell Hill Road, Guildford, and don't forget the hostie.

Kimbal Cook, a policeman who had watched the Milat house during the armed robberies of 1971, was still working for the Observation Squad – the 'dogs'. Cops and crims alike were still trying to find the bulk of Mr Brown's loot which had never been recovered . . . and now it was happening again.

Cook parked his police Valiant Charger in a Guildford back street. The problem with the Chargers was its advertising slogan 'Hey Charger' had become so popular with kids calling out and making the 'V' victory sign, it had rendered the car useless for surveillance. Crims couldn't help but notice the cops on their tail every time they passed a school with all these kids going silly.

Cook did a commando-style leopard crawl into bushes about 300 metres from the drop-off point. He was on his guts watching through a set of 'binos' with other cops scattered around in strategic positions. Detectives, armed to the teeth with automatic rifles, were spread through streets further away, ready for the signal to strike.

Constable Nerida Keeley got the job of playing air hostess. At that time, policewomen were a rarity in the CIB. She also had a degree in criminology from Sydney University law school, which was even rarer. At about 5 p.m., Keeley delivered a Gladstone bag full of cash to the designated point, near the 'dunny depot'.

Cook and his team watched her haul the bulging bag over a battered fence on the western side of the road and place it in long grass. Keeley waited and waited, but there was no show, so she left the bag and drove off. The dogs waited.

Eventually, a bus pulled up in the little dead-end section of Barbers Road. The driver swept the bus and then got out to stretch his legs. The driver saw the bag and picked it up. The police swooped on the driver – old Harry Rich – before he could pop it inside the bus.

One shoved a pistol in his back. Scared the bejesus out of him. Harry had to do some hard talking. He was going to hand it in to Granville police as lost property, he said. The police believed him and quickly returned the bag to its spot, but it looked like they'd blown the operation.

Cook was shaking his head in dismay at the thought of another fiasco. Then it struck him. 'Hang on, what about the kid?' There had been this kid hanging around on a dragster pushbike with high handlebars and a 'sissy bar' at the back. He was just riding up and down Campbell Hill Road. He'd been there from the start. Come to think of it, the kid had even ridden close to the fence, although he never went near the bag.

Cook had never forgotten sitting off the Milats' back in 1971 because his sister lived nearby at Chester Hill and he was reminded of them every time he visited her. He got on the two-way. 'Look, I think I might know who's behind this.' He arranged to meet a detective.

'This has got to be one of the fuckin' Milats,' he told the D. 'Their house's just up there and that kid on the bike's got to be responsible because he keeps coming back.'

'Who are the Milats? Why them?' asked the detective.

'Look, it's got to be them,' Cook said. 'I've followed this family before and some of them, they're a team of shits, and they've been doing stick-ups and that type of thing. The kid's got to be one of 'em.'

Cook figured that maybe the kid had been put up to it by one of his older brothers. 'I reckon they're smart enough to use the kid, and big brother's just telling him what to say.'

The detective in charge, Nelson Chad, held off at first. Wanted the dogs to watch where the kid went if he showed up again. Sure enough, he emerged from the Milat place only to disappear straight back inside.

'We've seen him go into the house, it's on,' Cook radioed.

'Well, we've got nothing else on, let's do it,' came the reply.[68]

The cops swarmed like locusts. They knocked at the next-door neighbours', the Carrolls, front door to ask if they could come through the house to jump the back fence. The Carrolls had seen the police come and go from the Milat place often enough, but this was the first time they'd ever asked to go through their house.[69]

'Stay inside,' warned the cops.

As the Milats prepared for dinner, just after 6 p.m., twenty detectives were in position nearby. Constable Keeley marched up to the small veranda with the bag of money and knocked on the door. It opened and she entered. Then twenty detectives with guns drawn, crashed in, shouting and pulling the whole family outside. Billy's pregnant wife Carol was up against the wall too. She'd never had anything to do with the police before this. 'Hands up above your head.' It was horrific. They frisked her. 'You get over in the corner.'[70]

Twenty-year-old George Milat arrived home from work with his cousin Mark Needham and saw a large crowd of men in suits pushing people around in the front yard. It was Needham's birthday and he and George were just going to wash up before heading off to get pissed at the Grand Villa Hotel down the road. The pair had only walked a couple of metres when a detective started shouting at them. Next thing, they were spun around and pushed up against their car.

The cops were shouting questions about Qantas. No one knew what they were talking about. They were on the verge of arresting the old man, Steven, when Bodge, fifteen-year-old David John, suddenly piped up: 'I did it.'

The cops looked at the fat kid.

'What do you know about it?' they demanded.

Bodge told them everything. It was all him. Nobody put him up to it. The calls, the demand for a hostie – all him. Some cops broke up laughing and called him 'Mr Brown'.[71] It was to be the only time Bodge ever got arrested. The story was front-page news in three of Sydney's five daily newspapers. The others ran it on page two. The *Daily Mirror* gave the police operation the biggest wrap. The story – GIRL COP TRAPS HALF A MILLION DOLLARS QANTAS HOAXER POLICE CHARGE BOY, FIFTEEN with a photograph of Nerida Keeley – was splashed over three-quarters of Saturday's page one. The Qantas people were over the moon. They put on a big spread for the cops, but the cops were disappointed they'd only pinned a kid, because they knew he'd get off lightly.

David John Milat appeared in Minda Children's Court at Lidcombe charged with demanding money with menaces. He said it was all a joke, a childish prank, and was let off with a bond and placed in the care of his oldest brother, Alex, and his sister-in-law, Joan, for two years. But Bodge was soon back at home. His mates like Scott Urquhart and Phil Polglase thought it was one of the funniest things they'd ever heard.

Margaret Milat became sick again and went back into hospital shortly after the Qantas hoax. As far as Ivan knew, the police had bought the suicide ploy. No worries. He had traded in his maroon Holden for a new lime green 1974 Charger VJ even though Geoff's '72 Charger was a dog. He said he'd take Wally and Maureen in to visit in the new car.

He didn't know his name recently came up as police sifted through all known sex offenders in their hunt for the killer of Bronwyn Richardson down at Albury six months earlier. Homicide detectives drew up a list of possible suspects. Ivan Robert Marko Milat, being on the run for a rape further north on the Hume Highway, was a natural suspect.

The way Boris would tell it years later, he saw Ivan come in with his hair dyed jet black. He knew his brother was coming, he'd say, and he'd asked the others to ask Ivan to behave. After all, they thought their mum was about to die. But Ivan and Marilyn started laughing and smiling and carrying on and Boris let it get to him. She was going, 'doesn't he look nice', sort of thing, they were acting like kids and Mum was dying.

'You friggin' bitch,' he said, being immature, as he would later freely admit. He walked out and Marilyn followed him down into the gift shop. They began to row. Marilyn tried to assure him that there was nothing left between her and Ivan.

'All right,' he said, 'if you're over him, darlin', there's the telephone . . . Dob him in.' (Marilyn's version has always been that Boris called the police and made Lynise and her wait in the gift shop until the cops arrived.)

*

At 8.15 p.m. Ivan was charged with breaching his bail. He listed his occupation as labourer, but lied about his address. He said he was living at 30 Rutherford Street, Blacktown, his next-door neighbour's place.

Bail was, naturally, refused.

Marilyn would deny Boris' version of events – and Maureen would never remember any giggling or goings-on between Marilyn and Ivan. They weren't there long enough.

Boris saved his invective for the cops: 'They were asked to take it easy and not go in the hospital. These bastards, there were thirteen of them, barged in and pulled him out. It almost killed her [Mum]. My father gave me a lecture.'

The first Geoff Post knew about the arrest was when the cops came knocking on the door, wanting to search the place.

'Can't see why not,' he said. They only went into 'Bill's' little bedroom and rummaged around in his cupboard for a bit. They didn't find anything, and soon left. About two years later, Geoff was fixing up an old '43 jeep out in the shed where Bill had pottered around, when he found 45 centimetres of a sawn-off barrel from a .22. It was under a bench, behind some tools and engine pieces. He thought it must have been Bill's but didn't think too much about it as he threw it in the bin. Twenty years later he'd wonder what the thing might have been used for.

SEVENTEEN

Late 1974

MARSDEN

Milat mostly kept to himself on remand at Long Bay Jail. He rarely spoke to his cellmate Noel Manning during the day except to talk about his body. Reckoned he built it up holding jackhammers above his head digging tunnels. The calluses on his hands were testimony to it as much as his biceps. Manning would later say he feared the nights when the two were locked in together. Milat's macabre bragging gave him the shivers. Ivan apparently talked about all the murders he'd done. The same stories over and over again.[72] The way he did them and dumped the bodies. In the month they shared a cell, Ivan tried once to put the hard word on him for sex, but he backed off when Manning refused.[73] (All Manning's later claims must be viewed in the light that he was a conman out to make money from his story.)

Milat's armed robbery case was decided within two days. He was acquitted due to lack of identification and the fact that, although Mick and Powch had lagged him, their evidence could not be used against a co-accused without corroboration. So, on 12 December 1974, the day after beating the robbery rap, he faced a jury of one woman and eleven men in the case of Regina v Ivan Robert Marko Milat, before His Honour Justice Jack O'Brien in the St James Square Supreme Court. Its heavy wood panelling had seen better days. It was dark and in need of a paint job, but it still bore down on the man in the dock with all the authority Victorian architecture could muster. The charge was read to the court: 'For that on the 10th of April 1971 at Goulburn in the state of New South Wales he did without her consent ravish and carnally know Margaret –' Asked by Justice O'Brien how he pleaded, Milat stood. 'Not guilty.'

Marsden knew he had quite a task ahead. He thought of Jack O'Brien as a 'hanging judge'. Marsden's mere presence in the court was impetuous. Solicitors then rarely appeared in the higher courts, let alone took on a Queen's Counsel – the most respected of barristers. The prosecutor, Leon Tanner QC, wore a wig and robes, like the judge. Marsden wore a wide-lapelled suit and a fat tie.

Margaret, the alleged victim, was the first witness. She gave her address as Cumberland House, Parramatta, where she said she was undergoing psychotherapy. She apologised for her voice. 'I've got tonsillitis.'

Margaret did not want to be in court. She was very nervous. This was a continuation of the nightmare. It had screwed her up but, over time, she had come to feel pity for her attacker. Maybe, she thought, she would have dropped the whole thing if he'd just said he was very sorry.

When Tanner asked if she could identify the man who picked her up that night, almost four years earlier, she pointed to Ivan Milat in the dock. As the lawyer took her through her evidence, she couldn't help giving more detail than Tanner wanted. 'I don't remember very much at the time because, as I said before, I was under the effect of three sleeping tablets. I had been having psychiatric treatment at the time and I was on tablets, only, you know, I used to take too many at times... I was taking medication about four times a day. I was pretty sleepy and that's why I don't remember very much about it.'

She described Milat stopping the car and demanding sex, and Tanner asked her: 'Did you in fact have some psychiatric problem in relation to sex?'

'Oh yes, that's what I'm at Cumberland House for.'

'What is the reaction to sex that worries you?'

'I slept with my mother until I was nineteen and I was camp for two years. I don't really enjoy being camp. I can't seem to make a decision about sexual identity, and that's why I'm at Cumberland House trying to figure that out.'

'What about your reaction to sex with a man?'

'Generally, I seem to sort of take off and say, "Oh, don't do it", and at the same time I sort of hope they will go on. He was put in a position where he made a decision for me about having sex. Because my mother is very religious and she never accepts the fact that I have sex with anyone.'

Tanner asked if Milat had caused her any concern.

'No,' she said.

'Did he produce anything?'

'Not that I remember. Greta said something about knives, but I don't actually remember it at all. At no time was I hurt in any way. I just don't remember.'

She did, though, remember the rope. 'So as I could get away from the situation, I suggested he tie us up and sort of leave us on the track and go away, just forget the whole thing.'

'How were you feeling at that stage?'

'Rather nauseated and pretty tired from the sleeping tablets ... extremely cold, it was a very cold night.'

'What was your emotional reaction to what had been said?'

'I wasn't really worried. I was just sort of hoping to get the whole thing over, that he would have sex with one of us and drop us off somewhere and that it would be over. That's what I was thinking at the time.'

'You suggested to him that he tie you up and leave you there?'

'Yes, so I could avoid having sex with him.'

'Did you notice anything about him and his emotional reaction at the time?'

'I guess he was pretty sort of sexually excited from sitting next to Greta and she was rather tantalising him, I think, with the idea of sex. She was sort of saying: "Oh you, you can't have it," but at the same time she was being rather seductive. That was the way I saw it.'

Margaret described being tied up, but said it didn't hurt.

Tanner tried to get her to remember the threats she'd talked about in her initial statement to police, but she didn't follow his leads.

'Did you give it [the sexual act] any description?' he then asked.

'Just ordinary sex. I asked him if he could withdraw before he climaxed because I didn't want to get pregnant.'

'I am going to ask you, was anything said about forced intercourse?'

'Not that I remember.'

Tanner asked if Milat made any promises.

'Just that he would let us go, just drop us off somewhere, a service station or something, and he would go on his way.'

'What was done after that?'

'Greta got in the back seat of the car on the right-hand side. She was looking out the window. I got in the front seat on the left-hand side. I think I removed my pants and that. I don't know. I just had sex with him.'

'What do you mean by that?'

'Put his penis in my vagina.'

'How long was he in that position?'

'Not very long; maybe a minute and a half, two minutes.'

'Did he remain still or did he move in any way?'

'He moved a bit.'

'Do you know whether or not he ejaculated?'

'Not inside me; I really don't think he did.'

Margaret then identified her brown slacksuit for the court.

Tanner was desperate to show the coercion which both women had initially alleged. 'Did you want this man to have sex with you, to have intercourse?' he asked.

'Yes, well, if I could explain a bit about the problems I was having at the time. My mother is very religious and my father was drinking a lot, and they have a grocery shop. I don't know, I was going to technical college and it just wasn't working out, and I was getting more and more depressed about it, life in general.'

'Why did you allow him to have sexual intercourse with you?'

'Well, he made the decision. I didn't have to make it.'

'Why did you accept his decision?'

'Because when it comes to sexuality, I don't really know whether I'm coming or going.'

What Margaret wasn't telling the court was that as part of the therapy she'd been undergoing since the attack, her psychiatrist tried to convince her to take responsibility for her sexual actions, and this had a huge impact on her testimony. Tanner asked more questions, trying to twig something in her mind about her fears that night, but she didn't respond.

Marsden got up for cross-examination. He asked her about being in the psychiatric hospital. '... And also about this time you were involved in the camp scene, I think you said?' (There were rumours in 1994 that Marsden saw the two women the night before the trial at a gay bar which he frequented in Bondi, and that he used the knowledge to discredit them before the jury. Marsden does not deny it is possible, but says he can't remember, adding that he only went to that bar on weekends. Margaret had already said she was 'camp' in her evidence in chief.)

'And was your friend Greta with you, going to homosexual places?'

'Yes.'

Tanner objected to the question and the judge asked Margaret for clarification about these places.

'We used to go to one particular bar and sit around and talk and that,' she said.

'All females?' the judge asked.

'Mostly females.'

'It was a homosexual bar?'

'Yes.'

'Was this lesbianism?' the judge inquired.

'I don't know. Greta often used to think about . . .'

'No, not what Greta did,' Marsden interrupted. 'What was the nature of this homosexual situation?'

'Yes, I have a number of female friends who were lesbians,' said Margaret.

Marsden was not yet openly gay, and even if he was out, it wouldn't have affected his decision to use the women's sexuality to discredit them before the jury. He reasoned that it would be remiss of him as a lawyer not to do everything legally possible to secure a not-guilty verdict for his client.

'Were you a lesbian yourself?' he asked, pushing the theme.

'Not at the time,' she said. 'My mother used to tell me how it was pretty bad, so I was pretty much in conflict about that and I was living with my mother at the time, because I was sort of forced to, being on medication and being very depressed. I couldn't be camp and I couldn't be straight, so what was there?'

'You were neither lesbian nor engaged in normal sexual enterprises?'

'No.'

'During this time, did you have lesbian relationships of some nature?'

'I did when I was about fourteen, but my mother found out about it and after that I just didn't do it.'

'Was there any type of relationship between you and Greta?'

'I used to sleep with her, but I got the feeling from her that if I touched her in any way sexually she would be very annoyed.'

'You slept in the same bed together. Is that right?'

'Yes.'

'You told the court that at the time you had sexual problems?'

'Yes.'

'I think you said that with a male you would give an indication that you didn't want it, but you hope he comes on. Is that right?'

'Yes.'

Marsden continued: 'In fact, what you are saying to the court is that you put him off as far as possible, but all the time you are hoping that he is going to have sex with you. Is that right?'

'Yes, that is so.'

O'Brien asked: 'Was that so at this time, four years ago?'

'Yes, I had a boyfriend and he was sort of involved in some sort of criminal activity – cat burglaries and that. I think about that time he went to jail and I was really sort of missing him, and he just ignored me at the time.'

'Would you say in the case of this accused that was probably your attitude . . . you wanted to put him off, but you were hoping he would come on?' Marsden asked.

'Ah huh, yes.'

'Did he in any way frighten you?'

'Not really. No. Not when I think back now, without any drama or anything. Not really. No.'

'Did he in any way threaten you to have sex?'

'No, not really.'

'Did he in any way force you to have sex?'

'No, it was my decision, more or less.'

'It was your decision?'

'Yes.'

'I think you told us that Greta was in the front seat with him and she was being rather seductive and tantalising him? Is that the word you used?'

'Yes.'

'Could you tell the court a little more about what she was doing to tantalise him?'

'I suppose she was sort of using a similar technique to what I was doing – the old smiling, and she has very large eyes, looking very seductive, and yet all the time backing away and at the same time threatening to take an overdose.'

Marsden came back: 'When you said to him: "If I have sex with you, we will drop the whole thing and let us go," do you remember that?'

'Yes.'

'He was not forcing you to have sex? He was not forcing you to stay there until he had sex was he?'

'Not really, no.'

'He had not said to you, "I won't let you go until you have sex with me"?'

'No, probably if I had been clear enough, if I hadn't taken the sleeping tablets, I would have been able to get out of it quite easily.'

The judge asked: 'Why would you have wanted to get out of it? You said if you had not had these tablets you would have been able to get out of it quite easily?'

'I suppose I did. I set the situation up. I am considerably clearer now than I was then.'

Marsden couldn't resist: 'You are on the road to recovery now, aren't you?' The question was rejected. He tried again. 'The reports you are receiving from the hospital are excellent aren't they?' Rejected.

'Put it this way, I try pretty hard,' said Margaret. She said she was not on any antidepressants, but she'd been back in the residential wing of the psych hospital for three months. Then Marsden came back to a point she hadn't quite answered before. When Tanner had asked, 'Did you want this man to have sex with you?' and she had answered, 'Yes, well if I could explain,' Tanner had veered the questioning away. But the young solicitor sensed victory. 'Would you agree with me that, in reality now, at the present stage, when you think back and think about it, you did want this man to have sex with you?'

'Yes.'

'Do you remember you told my friend, when you went to the shop – this is after he let you out at the shop – is it true that he freely let you out at the shop when he drove you to this garage?'

'Yes.'

'And there was no effort to hold you in the car when he got there?'

'No.'

'And Greta was in the back seat, was she not, at that stage?'

'Yes.'

'And her door was there beside her?'

'Yes, she could have got out.'

'And you went in and spoke to a lady and you said something about the word "rape". Do you remember using that word at the time?'

'Yes.'

'What do you say about the use of that word now?'

'Well, it definitely wasn't rape. The whole thing was very dramatised. Greta was saying it: "He raped you. Wasn't it terrible?" And all that sort of thing, you know.'

'Greta dramatising it, was she?'

'Yes.'

'Greta had threatened to take an overdose of Valium, hadn't she?'

'Yes.'

'And was this a highly dramatic type of scheme?'

'Yes.'

'Would you describe your friend Greta as a highly dramatic person?'

'Yes.'

'Tends to build things up and exaggerate them?' Tanner objected and the question was rejected, as were a string of Marsden's questions designed to make Greta look scatty. 'Was this man kind to you after the intercourse took place?' asked Marsden.

'Yes, he said quite truly . . .'

'He said what?'

'He said quite kindly that I could get a drink, and he even offered to drive us to Melbourne, you know, in case we still wanted to go there.'

'And you have now no bitterness towards this man?'

'None at all, no. I think I understand the situation reasonably well.'

The cross-examination fizzled, but Marsden knew the case was as good as won. Tanner had to try to save it in his re-examination. He tried to elicit some sense of the fear that Milat had instilled in the women.

'Did the accused frighten you at the time?' Tanner asked.

'Yes. I was frightened,' said Margaret.

The judge asked: 'What were you frightened of? Tell us the things that frightened you.'

'I really don't know. I withdraw that. Probably I was just dramatising and I wasn't generally frightened.'

'What do you mean by not generally frightened? You were frightened and you think you should not have been?' the judge continued.

'No, well, over dramatic and . . . my fear wasn't justified at all now, thinking back.'

'What was over dramatic?'

'Well, he didn't rape me. He didn't hurt me.'

'What was over dramatic?' the judge asked again.

'Saying that he raped me in the cafe bar, at the service station, that was over dramatic.'

Tanner resumed, but his case was slipping away: 'You also told my learned friend, Mr Marsden, that thinking back now, "I did want the man to have sex with me"?'

'Yes.'

'What was your reaction at the time?'

'Sex usually repulses me.'

'Did it then?' the judge asked.

'Not really, because, as I said, I was in a position where I didn't have to make a decision.'

'I want to know what your reaction at the time was,' Tanner asked.

'I don't know. I think I rather enjoyed it actually, underneath.'

Tanner's case was lost.

Justice O'Brien asked about the psychotherapy. 'Is it to try to get you to accept the male as a proper partner of your life?'

'Yes, well, I suppose whether I am camp or just heterosexual or bisexual – just accepting it, without any sort of problems.'

'What they are trying to teach you there in the therapy course is to regard sex with a male as a normal thing?' the judge asked.

'Yes.'

'Now, looking back at this incident in the back road at Goulburn, sex with a male was the normal thing?'

'Well, Greta and I . . . speaking for myself, I set the situation up. That is not the normal way to have it, but . . .'

'How did you set it up?'

'I suppose I should have known, accepting a ride with Greta, you know.'

Margaret was allowed to go. She would, years later, remember the rope and the knives and the threat that she would be killed unless she had sex with Milat, but somewhere between the service station, the trial, and Milat's later infamy – under the influence of a psychiatrist trying to get her to accept her sexuality – her opinions changed, and changed back.

Greta was next into the stand. She too was still under psychiatric treatment, she told the court, barely audible. She described how a man picked them up.

'Can you see him here?' Tanner asked.

'Yes, the man smiling here,' she said, pointing to Milat.

She told of his demand for sex; of the knives coming out and the threat to kill them if they didn't give him sex. She wasn't very clear because of the Valium, but she described the sheathed knife with the curved blade.

'He said he made a habit of picking up hitchhikers and was also prepared with the knives,' said Greta. 'When he said he wanted to have sex with us and he had these knives, we said: "Oh, you are going to rape us?" and he said: "You could call it that".' Greta talked about him saying: 'You know what I am going to do? I am going to kill you. You won't scream when I cut your throats, will you?'

Her account was vastly different to Margaret's. It was full of the attack's menace. As Marsden tried to discredit her, Greta denied she'd taken the overdose of sleeping pills or any tablets.

He tried the lesbian line on her, too. She denied it.

'You go to a bar called Chez Ivy's which is a homosexual bar in Bondi Junction?' asked Marsden.

'Yes, but a lot of straight people go there too.'

'In fact, they have male homosexuals and lesbian homosexuals.' Greta stressed that she was not homosexual.

Marsden then pursued Greta's Valium taking. He established that she had smoked a little marijuana, and was into the zodiac. All points designed to reduce her standing before the jury. The court broke for lunch.

Joan Eldridge from the service station confirmed the story that Margaret had mentioned a knife and the Wanda Beach murders when she first came into the cafe, even though Margaret didn't tell that to the court.

A succession of police witnesses became largely irrelevant since consent had become the main issue. Marsden presented his client as a man with a low IQ, who stood firm against the allegations on the night of his arrest despite having no sleep all evening. The prosecution case closed and Marsden asked for an adjournment until the next day, Friday the 13th. It was granted.

When they came back the next day, Marsden submitted that, in light of Margaret's evidence, His Honour should direct a not-guilty verdict. Tanner submitted that there was still evidence upon which the jury could find lack of consent.

'Your Honour, the accused will make a statement,' said Marsden. With that, Ivan Milat, twenty-nine, rose to plead his case in an unsworn statement from the dock which the jury was instructed did not carry the weight of sworn testimony because it could not be tested by cross-examination.

Ladies and gentlemen: I am not guilty of rape. Margaret gave me permission then to have intercourse with her. At no stage did I threaten her with knives or force her into anything that she weren't agreeable to. It was a friendly trek down there and afterwards, when I run them back to the shops, she was real friendly, she was okay, and everything seemed to be all right. In the interview with the police, what I said was true and it is true now. There was no force. I didn't use threats or frighten her in any way. I am innocent. I don't know why she said this, but she has, but, please, I am innocent. I never did threaten her or frighten her in any way at all. Thank you.

Ivan resumed his seat. The jury went out and didn't take long. They found him not guilty and he was released immediately. His mother gave him a big hug. Mother and son caught the train home together.

Changing trains at Granville, the last thing they expected to see was Margaret – and vice versa – standing on the same platform. And Margaret didn't expect Milat to walk up and talk to her as if nothing had happened, beaming a broad smile. She was nervous. Didn't know what to say except to apologise. She felt she was to blame. Mrs Milat thought she had a hide.

EIGHTEEN

1975–1976

KAREN

The past year had been full of anguish for Marilyn. Nine-year-old Lynise was a constant reminder of the affair with Mac. She thought that by choosing to stay with Boris and the girls she had caused Ivan to run off the rails in 1971. Then she blamed herself for Ivan's arrest at the hospital. Now, he was finally free but, for the sake of the family, she could never see him again.

Boris said he was happy for his brother, yet he was still haunted by the thought that Ivan's reappearance could ruin his new life. He had re-established his construction-site cleaning business, and was building a new home – a three-storey Cape Cod – on the central coast.

They moved in as soon as the first storey was built and they saved money by doing most of the work themselves. Marilyn worked by Boris' side, passing bricks to him and even laying a few runs herself. But still Boris couldn't shrug off the thoughts of Ivan's betrayal. His drinking became chronic. His temper worsened.

Boris again came to imagine Ivan in every recess of his life. His paranoia reached new heights. Opening a kitchen drawer to fetch a knife one day, he found himself looking for Ivan inside. Then one afternoon, while returning home from working over the Easter long weekend, he spotted a lime green Valiant Charger parked off a road close to his home.

Boris' brain snapped. He raced home and grabbed a pistol he was minding for a friend. He got back in the car and headed for Guildford with one thought playing over and over in his head.

The Milat tribe had sat down to eat Easter Sunday dinner when Boris pulled up outside. He walked up the driveway and peered through the window to the dining room. Mum was on her feet, putting plates down in front of the family. Ivan was sitting facing the window as Boris raised the gun to the glass, clutching the grip with both hands. 'This is gunna fix him. Damn, get out of the way, Mum. Move!'

No one in the room heard his mutterings. Only one person felt his presence. Ivan looked up to see his brother with the pistol pointed at him. Boris would never forget that look. Ivan didn't flinch or even alert the others. Just sat there staring him down with a grin. The sight of Mum busying herself around the table brought Boris back to his senses. He lowered the pistol and walked away, despondent. For the second time in his life, he had pulled back from the brink of killing his brother.[74] Later, at Marilyn's urging, he sought psychiatric help.

Ivan was determined to go straight and, for the first time in a decade, it looked like peace had descended on 55 Campbell Hill Road, where Dad's grapevines were slowly taking a stranglehold on the back of the house.

It was a year of political turbulence. Gough Whitlam's Labor Government was sacked by the Governor-General, Sir John Kerr, but politics didn't count in the Milat household. Dad was a one-eyed Liberal and monarchist, and nobody else gave a hoot.

Ivan didn't have to wait long for a job driving trucks with a local driver, David Ward, who ran his own business out of Liverpool. His daughter Sharon was a friend of the family. 'Wardie' was a hardworking truckie who knew all the tricks in the dog-eat-dog business. Most of his trips were carting tyres to Goulburn, Yass and Canberra, but, one day, Wardie took him on a marathon drive lugging furniture to Perth, via Adelaide. Couldn't shut Ivan up about it when he came back. They did a couple of hauls to Melbourne, and a few up the east coast to Queensland's Gold Coast and Brisbane. He still didn't have a driver's licence in his own name.

One of Ivan's few mates was Wayne Duck, a grease monkey who worked on the trucks. Wayne lived at home with his folks, Elaine and Ronald, a local bus driver in Reilly Street, Lurnea, a brick and fibro Housing Commission suburb back of Liverpool. Wayne had a brother, Max, a chicken catcher at one of the local poultry farms, and a sixteen-year-old sister, Karen. She was an attractive brunette who caught Ivan's eye the moment he saw her at a party at the end of 1975. He flexed his muscles this night and homed right in on Karen, her dark hair falling over her shoulders. Ivan was almost thirteen-and-a-half years her senior, tanned, handsome, and with money to spend on a girl. He also had a Charger.

Karen had arrived with her boyfriend, Mark Needham, the Milats' cousin. That didn't count. Ivan, overcoming his usual reticence, swooped, and before the night was over, Mark Needham was no longer in the picture. For the third time in his life, he stole a family member's girl. It didn't matter that Karen thought she was pregnant to Mark. Six weeks gone, in fact.

'What can I do?' Needham complained to a sympathetic George Milat. 'Look at those arms. He's too strong for me.'

The warning signs were there early. In the first week of the relationship, she would later say, they were out driving when Ivan stopped, saying he was going to get some water from the back. He came to her side of the car, got in and grabbed her by the throat, demanding sex. She resisted at first, but: 'I got that way I just sort of lay there and said he could help himself, because I'd had it.' She was compliant, yet she resisted his efforts to have anal sex. He told her that was how they did it in jail.

Amazingly, Karen forgave him. He had staked his claim. She was his. Whatever the factors that brought them together – her naivety, his desire for permanence – they seemed inseparable. She was ignorant of his past, and it would be years before he confided bits of it to her.

He became a regular at the Duck home, dropping by after work, often staying for dinner. Karen's parents didn't mind at first. He seemed to be looking after her, but when the occasional row between them turned violent, Ron Duck stepped in and had to threaten him. Mrs Duck's attempts to talk sense into her daughter were fruitless. For all his faults, at least Ivan was prepared to do the right thing and stand by their daughter as her stomach grew large.

Ivan became a settling influence back at Guildford, but as ever there was a new generation coming through. Mac never said much, but he only had to look at the others and they knew who was boss. Dick's mate Scott Urquhart could see that the few words Ivan came out with, combined with a look, carried meaning. Richard was more like the type that thought they were best at everything. Ivan wasn't like that.

Mac dispensed little pearls to his younger brothers: 'Look after your money.' 'Be polite to your mother.'

The old man was still doing occasional work as a stonemason, well past retirement age. Urquhart would always be polite and say hello to him, huddled over his telly, but nine times out of ten wouldn't get a response. The only thing he'd say to his sons' friends was: 'Move your fucking bike.'

If he really had to communicate, he usually growled something at his wife as he sat playing his cards and she'd growl his instructions at the kids. He was an alien to his youngest boys who had never known the hard work of the tomatoes and the austerity of the dirt floors. He was from another time, another planet.

With Mrs Milat it was different. She was fit again and more than capable of laying down the law. She knew everybody who set foot in her house. Some people could come in 100 times and never see her. Those she considered undesirable, though, wouldn't get past the gate. She'd be keeping an eye out from the front room. If somebody she didn't like turned up – 'had the wrong tone of bike, or car, or walk' – it'd be: 'Get out! Get out of my house and don't come back again.'

Dick, Bodge, Urquhart and a few other mates used to all get about on their motorbikes, sometimes going up the coast or out bush. One time, Dick and another mate, Joe, headed off to Western Australia via Adelaide. They were gone for months, scrounging work where they could. They shacked up on the dole with girlfriends in a beach house near Perth, before heading to Port Hedland on the north-west coast and home.

The Milat yard at Guildford often resembled a panel beater's workshop. There were always blokes hanging around – their hair cut short on top, long at the back, 'animal' style – tinkering with their bikes. Engines roared and wheelies were dropped out the front. It gave the neighbours the shits. Police would cruise past, checking out who was around. If they collared one of the brothers, he'd say he weren't the one they were looking for, he was his brother, and have a great laugh about it after.

A few of them were out the front of the Milats' one afternoon when they heard the roar of Dick's bike coming down the road. He pulled up and started acting natural, tinkering with his bike. Moments later a cop car came along. Nothing unusual about that. All the guys looked up.

'Whose turn is it today?' they wondered. This day, as Mrs Milat pottered about the front garden with a shovel, the jacks in plain clothes and an unmarked vehicle stood on the grass verge and signalled for Dick to come over. They wanted to talk to him about a noise disturbance. Dick wasn't budging and said so, giving a bit of cheek. His mates stood up, watching. The officer stepped into the yard and went for him. There was a scuffle. Mrs Milat, apparently oblivious to their identity, went at a copper with the shovel. Thwack. Square cut to the boundary. 'Doug Walters would have been proud.' His nose and mouth were bleeding. The boys hit the deck laughing.[75]

The charges against Mrs Milat never had a chance, apparently. The bemused magistrate sized up the little woman before him against the six foot officer and dismissed the matter. They shouldn't have been on the premises to start with. There was no warrant, or so the story went.

On a hot summer's day, probably in early 1976, Wally's wife Maureen rang her mother to ask if she could bring the kids over for a swim in the above-ground pool. It was better than putting them under the sprinkler.

'Okay,' said her mother. 'You know Ivan's here.'

'No.'

'We're just having coffee. I'll get him to come and get you.'

'Fab.'

Ivan, who had time off work after coming back from a long haul in the truck, went and picked up Maureen and the kids. Robert was now four and in January 1975 she'd had a daughter, Susan.

They all had a swim and some lunch, then Ivan drove them home to Milperra. He helped Maureen get the kids and all her stuff in the house, and left. Wally came home from work a few hours later and Maureen had his tea in front of him straightaway like she was meant to, so there was no drama there, but the hint of fear was never far away. Like the time she started smoking again and he tore the packet from her hand and just threw it away.

She couldn't help thinking that Rob was being made to suffer for Wally's paranoia that Ivan was the real father. Wally was becoming so hard on the boy. So much of it was just because she was a friendly person, she thought, and it was just that she could relate to Ivan. Laugh and carry on with him. If Wally had a sense of humour, she'd never seen it.

As Wally sat down to dinner, Robert suddenly piped up: 'We went swimming with Uncle Ivan in Nanna's pool.' Wally stood and glared at Maureen as all the old jealousies rushed to the surface like the blood to his face. He picked up a jug and threw it hard across the poky little kitchen, smashing a hole through the fibro wall. He was sure Maureen was sleeping with Ivan, and he told her so.

'Yeah sure, in front of my mother and my kids,' she retorted, sarcastically. She knew the score. If Wally was in one of his moods, she couldn't even talk to the bloke next door because Wally'd think she was on with him, too. The argument ran – Yes, you did. No, I didn't – while Maureen tried to get the kids in the bath. Wally came into the bathroom, grabbed her head and pushed it into the bath, holding her under water. 'I'm going to kill ya.'[76] Maureen believed him.

He let her up, but he was still furious. Maureen saw him grab a gun and take off. She dressed the kids quickly, thinking Wally would head over to Guildford to confront Ivan. She was clearing out to her mum's, but thought she'd better ring Mrs Milat first, to warn Ivan. She put Susan into a pram and they went out the front to the red phone box, but Wally was in there, so she high-tailed it back inside and tried to act like she wasn't worried about anything, in case he came back. She waited. It seemed like forever. When Wally didn't return, she went back out. The coast was clear. She made the call to Mrs Milat but wasn't expecting the what-have-you-been-doing-to-my-boys tirade from the furious old girl.

'Nothing, nothing,' she tried to explain, over her mother-in-law's earful. She got her side out as best she could, then hung up.

Ivan had cleared out by the time Wally got to Guildford, so he went looking for him at Alex's place, 40 kilometres away at Yanderra, then up the road to Bill's at Bargo, where Wally ran around the yard with the gun looking for Ivan before taking off. Bill chased him along the highway trying to pull him over to calm him down. It was all madness. Maureen packed a few things in a laundry basket, and her mother took her away. Over the next week, Wally kept coming by, like a beaten dog with its tail between its legs, saying sorry and everything: 'I bought you a new jug and fixed the wall and I won't do it again.' They talked about it, and she pointed out how dumb it was to think she'd be having an affair in front of the kids. The tension eased and a couple of weeks later they went as a family to Alex and Joan's for the day. Ivan was sitting at the table reading the paper. Maureen felt like the filling in a sandwich.

She didn't look at Ivan for fear of inciting something, and Ivan didn't speak much to anybody, keeping his head in the paper. But basically the brothers just acted like nothing had ever happened and life went back to normal.

Karen Duck gave birth to Ivan Milat's cousin, Jason, on 24 July 1976. Ivan and Karen were still seeing each other, but they hadn't moved in together. It seemed to his family that Karen's influence had tamed him. Work became the dominant force in his life. He seemed to genuinely want to stay out of trouble, to work hard and earn an honest quid. A few months later, in October, he gave up the trucking life to go back to working the roads, but he continued to play the truck-drivin' man, the freewheeling cowboy. A rig would drive past while he was working on the road and he'd tell his workmates everything about the truck they never wanted to know. And he still listened to all that truckin' music like Slim Dusty's 'Black Smoke Over Eighteen Wheels'.

Big Don Borthwick was the ganger in charge of Ivan's paving crew. Borthwick had him pinned as someone who could do well and so started grooming him to be a boss. Within a fortnight, Borthwick had elevated him from common labourer to paver operator, running the machine which laid asphalt. Three months later, he was a ganger in charge of eleven men, second-in-charge to the foreman/supervisor. This was a meteoric rise in the Department of Main Roads scheme of things.

With Ivan, everything had to be spot on. He'd say it took the same time to do a good job as a bad one. This was not your typical road worker talking, and Borthwick appreciated him for that. Ivan's attitude was matched by his physical strength. He was a powerful little bastard. Borthwick had seen him throw things on to the back of a truck that normally took two men just to lift. He was the sort of bloke who'd do anything for you, too. 'Give his bum away and shit through his ribs if he thought it could help you,' as Borthwick's old dad used to say. Ivan had an inner strength when it came to pain. When his thumb was pulverised by a sledgehammer, he resisted advice from doctors to amputate and just wore the pain.

He was cheerful, a good bloke, but always apart from the others. During down times, he wouldn't join in their impromptu games of cricket by the road. He'd sit in the truck drinking his one-litre 'Crowd

Pleaser' bottles of Coke, and reading his trucking magazines. Most of the blokes got on the piss after work. Not Ivan. His crew niggled him about his tee-totalling, but soon gave up. He was just different.

A few months after he started at the DMR, Ivan moved in with Karen and Jason at her mother's house in Reilly Street, Lurnea, just up the road from his grandparents, the Piddlesdens. When Jason was about twelve months old, they started a routine of driving down to visit Alex at Yanderra every three or four weeks. The weekend excursions began with a stop at the small Hume Highway shopping complex at Casula which the Lombardo family had developed after giving up market gardening at Moorebank, ten years earlier. The stop became a ritual. 'We'll call into Lombardo's,' Ivan would say as they came to Casula, the last stop before the Campbelltown freeway. Karen never went in, but if she wound the window down, she heard the people with accents greeting him. She thought they must have been Yugoslavs and presumed they were friends of the family, because Ivan once pointed out their house across the road. He always came out with a can of Coke, a packet of Hubba Bubba bubble gum and a newspaper to read at Alex's.

Alex was an avid firearms collector. Ivan enjoyed the odd shot but, to Karen, he didn't seem overly enthused by guns. He just enjoyed driving in the country, getting away from the city. Once, when they were driving along, his memory was jogged by the sight of a young woman hitching. He told Karen he picked up a blonde hitchhiker on a trip up around the Gold Coast. She 'just got rooted' and dropped off, he said. That's all he said.

The DMR job took Ivan all over the state at all times of the year except winter, when it was too cold to lay the bitumen. They'd be on the road from August–September through April–May, starting at Singleton in the Hunter Valley, then Bowen Field out of Lithgow, over the Blue Mountains, then Bomaderry down the South Coast. They'd stay a week or a month at each – whatever had to be done. They lived in motels all week and came home Fridays.

When Ivan started, the Campbelltown freeway was being built and, because the spray gang wasn't needed all the time, they'd get home from Lithgow or Bathurst on Thursday, then work Friday, Saturday, Sunday sealing the freeway. Once other crews had prepared the road base, Ivan's spray gang put down bitumen with a light stone in it to form a membrane to weatherproof the road. The porous asphalt then went on top, so water would flow through to the membrane then run across to the drains. If water got through the membrane into the base, the road was stuffed.

They worked their bums off all weekend preparing kilometre after kilometre so the asphalt crews could follow them through the week. If there was no rain during the week, they came back and did the next stretch the following weekend. They doubled their pay with the overtime. There wasn't much home life, but plenty of beer, so Ivan's strange Coca-Cola habit was noticed from the start. As the size of Coke bottles grew, so did his appetite for the stuff. He'd buy two litres at smoko, another two at lunchtime and two more on the truck going home. Six litres a day, and then he'd hassle everyone else about all the grog they drank.

Borthwick asked him once: 'What's your problem with grog?'

'I went aggro, really aggro,' Ivan said, being unusually open. 'I could've done some damage to me girl.' He said he might have the odd scotch, but was frightened of the consequences.

While the gang was drinking in the bar at the motel, Ivan would be back in his room doing paperwork, sipping coffee. Even though the motels supplied it, the four to six satchels were never enough, so Milat always had his own jar. When he finished his paperwork he'd shine his boots so clean you could see your face in them, just so he could go back out the next day laying bitumen in them. Crazy. His leading hand, Terry Palmer, would come back to the room and Ivan might be doing weights or be settled in with a trucking magazine. *Truck and Bus*, *Trucking Life*, Trucking This, Trucking That. He could tell you cubic capacities and diff' ratios of every rig that went by and Palmer had to tell him he didn't give a shit, really, as they listened to truckin' music.

Sometimes, Milat drove Palmer back to base in the truck. He loved being behind the wheel and didn't seem to care that he didn't have a licence. Ivan felt comfortable enough with Palmer to later introduce him to Karen. She seemed attractive and sweet. Too nice for Ivan, he thought.

NINETEEN
1977–1978

NOVAK

There was a slump in road building in the mid-seventies, but after the Wran Labor Government came to office in 1976, business picked up and the road crews found themselves working harder than the one-armed paperboy. Ivan, long since reconciled with Wally, got his younger brother a job there. He was a good worker, too. Donny Borthwick would say you could cut the gang in half if what you had left were all Milats.

On the night of 3 January 1978, as violent storms raged across Sydney, Richard and Wally went out in Wally's yellow Land Rover and didn't come back. Maureen had no idea where they had gone – only a suspicion that they were up to no good. A knock at the door about 6.30 a.m. next day confirmed her fears. It was the police. Wally had been arrested. They barged their way in and started snooping around.

The first thing one of the policemen saw was a water heater with a doily and vase on top, then a CB radio base unit set up on the nearby buffet.

'Where'd you get this?' he asked harshly.

'I don't know,' said Maureen.

'Where'd you get that?' he said, pointing to Maureen's two-door fridge/freezer.

'I don't know. Wally told me he bought it from a guy at the pub.'

'What about that?' he said, looking at a Westinghouse dishwasher.

'Same.' She got in first and told him to have a look at the clothes drier in the laundry. Soon the cops were cleaning out the entire house on suspicion, including the kids' splasher pool.

Maureen had an inkling it was stolen, but her relationship with Wally was not built on communication. It was crumbling and she frankly didn't care what he did. She had kids to look after.

The policeman asked if he could go up to the bedroom.

'Have you got a search warrant?' she asked.

'You watch too much TV, lady.'[77]

Police were arriving in paddy wagons and rented vans, emptying the house. The Housing Commission neighbours had a great stickybeak. Maureen was so embarrassed. The police took everything except the toaster and they only left that because it blew up when one of them was helping himself to tea and toast. One sneered at Maureen: 'You're gunna go to jail, and your kids are going to end up in a home.' She was in tears. She believed him. They let her shower, then took her and the kids to Liverpool Police Station where all the property was being dumped into a cage in the basement. Maureen was so relieved to find Mrs Milat and Shirley were already there. The in-laws walked the kids around Liverpool trying to keep them occupied while Maureen was locked in an interview room all day. The police wouldn't even let her go to the bathroom unless she had a detective with her.

They took Wally down the basement and showed him a veritable Joyce Mayne warehouse of hot gear. Walter meekly gave himself up and was told he would be given the opportunity to read the record of interview and sign it if he wished.

'I can't read, though. Can you get someone to read it for me,' asked Wally.

Wally went on to admit it all, but he never mentioned Richard in any of the confessions. He lumped all the blame on a mystery man, Stephen Novak. Towards the end of the interview, he was asked: 'Could you describe the man Steve to me?'

'Well, his name is Stephen Novak. He's about twenty. A couple of inches taller than me. He's got light brown hair, long all over and messy about to his collar. He's got a medium build and last night he was wearing blue jeans and a dark blue shirt.'

'What vehicle does the man Steve drive?'

'He was driving my yellow Land Rover last night, but he drives a light blue Holden ute that belongs to a mate of his called Jim. Steve comes from Newcastle originally.'

Stephen Novak was a fabricated name, bandied about by the Milat boys and a lot of their mates as the fall guy whenever there was trouble. If Novak existed, he was a one-man crime wave.

Wally was initially charged with break, enter and steal, but his solicitor, John Marsden, managed to have that dropped and eventually Wally faced six lesser charges – accessory after the fact, stealing, and four of receiving. Marsden got him off on a $300, three-year good-behaviour bond. 'Novak' was never found.

As far as Maureen could tell, Wally went straight after that. He certainly didn't have any more dealings with police. Mostly he just stayed home making bullets in the garage. Not long before, he'd bought himself a bullet-making device that looked like a big vice. He set it up in his garage and spent hours on it. It was a quarter the cost of buying Winchesters, and you could increase the load to blow something to smithereens or decrease it to bring it down cleanly.

Whenever Ivan came around to visit, he'd always put his head in and say hello to Wally down in the garage, but he preferred being up talking to Maureen, the kids, and her mum over a cup of coffee. He never seemed gun crazy to Maureen. Not compared to Wally.

In early 1978, Ivan and Karen moved out of her mother's home and into the frying pan that was the Milat place at Guildford. They stayed in the house for a while, until Jason's asthma, which was turning out to be really chronic, saw them move out to the caravan. The backyard still had the feel of a farmyard, as the family's soul stayed firmly bogged in the backblocks of Moorebank. The goats and chickens and quails and pigeons were only reluctantly and slowly ceded to the motorbikes and the dinner table. The joint stank. The back part, anyway, where all the birdcages and animals were, and nobody went in the front. The old man's grapevines covered the back of the house which was falling down, but he wouldn't let them fix it because he didn't want his grapes disturbed.

When anybody came in the yard they usually passed Mac, out cleaning every inch of his precious car – polishing the dipstick – and if he wasn't there he'd be quietly sitting in the lounge room or at work. If he'd been away shooting until Sunday night, the car was pulled apart

Monday. He'd have the mats out, Armor-All the dash, put stuff into the seats, wash the roof liner and take the inside light out and dust it. Everything he owned, he looked after like that. He was a neat dresser, too. His pants always had a crease in them, like his shirts and jeans. He never walked out of the house untidy. His nails were always clean. His hair was clean, but he wasn't a wuss.

Mac projected a fatherly image to a lot of people around the house: the way he spoke to younger blokes. He had a demeanour like he was trying to impart some wisdom, without really talking down to them, or being smartarse or dictatorial. Helpful. He'd open the door for somebody else's missus. If they were still getting out of the car, he'd stop and wait.

Bodge's girlfriend, 'Toppy' Ambrose, thought Karen was a bit spacey but nice. Karen and Ivan argued like any couple, but it was always in the caravan. They seemed pretty happy staying at home, living the quiet life, saving money. Karen liked being driven around in the Charger which had a bulldog hood ornament from a Mack truck on the front. She struck people as unworldly. Done nothin', seen nothin'. That, of course, was a symptom of being pregnant at sixteen and hooked up with an overprotective man thirteen-and-a-half years her senior.

The house was chaos at the best of times. Partly because the boys were all so moody – best mates some days, enemies the next – and partly because the place was chockers. Especially after the boys brought girls back and they started spitting out the kids. George and his wife Patsy had their two girls in one room. There were usually three boys in another, sometimes sharing a double bed, and Steven and Margaret in another. Ivan and Karen were out in the caravan with Jason, and there were always people staying over – girlfriends, mates, and friends Richard was meeting in his travels and bringing back. Scott Urquhart reckoned they slept in shifts. No bullshit.

You couldn't get up and make one cup of coffee, you had to find twenty cups and make sure Mac's white mug was among 'em. They thought it was a hang-up from prison, where everybody has one plate, one cup.

The boys always seemed to be competing to get the attentions of their brothers' girls. They were trophies. Most of the boys thought of themselves as charmers. Especially Richard. He was 'Mr Grooming' and spent a lot of time in front of the mirror. He was reputed to have a 'dick like a donkey', but he had a bit of the gab as well. If he had a girlfriend, he'd be out pulling another on the side. Or trying. He tried with Bodge's girl, Toppy, with no luck.

But while they might have reckoned they were charmers, it didn't stop 'em freaking girls out with talk of guns and knives. One night, Toppy came in saying she thought she'd just been followed over to their place and Ivan told her: 'If anybody ever grabs you, make them a head on a stick.'

'Huh?'

'What you do, you just stick a knife down their back here,' he said, pointing to the piece of spine that juts out at the base of the neck. 'You put that in and they're paralysed from the neck down. They're alive, they know what's going on, but they can't do a thing. You do it with a pig stabber. You know what a pig stabber is? A hole puncher on a pocket knife. You only have to go in that far,' motioning a couple of centimetres. 'You go down and in an inch.' It was a trick he said he was told about by a Vietnam vet . . . take the gooks out and still get your information off 'em, or whatever. Have your way with 'em.[78] It became his standard sneer: 'Shut up or I'll make you a head on a stick.'

Urquhart and his mates were in awe at some of the knives the brothers had collected. Some were the sort that mercenaries carried – one, Urquhart reckoned could take half your head off. The blade was big and heavy enough. Inside the blade there were vents – the blood letter – designed to let the blood come out through the knife to let you pull it out cleanly without suction.

The legal age for drinking had been lowered to eighteen and all the young Milats hit the local, the Grand Villa, hard. If you didn't get up the Villa by 7 p.m. on a Thursday you had to park way out in the mulga, at the back of the tannery. It was Ugh boot and flanny city. Pretty tough too at times, and any Milat on the piss stood a good chance of getting himself in strife. A good chance of getting out of it too. It was known you had to hit 'em with a spade . . . and after that you still didn't turn your back . . . and didn't go to sleep because they'd come back. They all stood up for each other. Didn't matter what the problem was. They didn't ask.

Around this time, Toppy and Bodge were meant to be going away on his bike, a canary yellow 900 Kawasaki. He could ride that thing like nothing else, but he turned up blind drunk and Toppy refused to go with him. They had a big fight over it and she told him to come back sober. Bodge climbed on, opened the throttle right up and flipped it, head-on, into the first telegraph pole up from Toppy's place in Orchard Street, Chester Hill. He was hurt badly. Brain-damaged. Paralysed down one side.

Toppy went up to the Milats' a lot to help with his physiotherapy. She loved it. Loved the family. They were close, and there was a good atmosphere. Dad was quiet, of course. Old Steven would sit in his corner playing his Yugo solitaire, watching his TV. He only ever spoke to her once. He told her: 'They didn't have a TV when we were first married and that's why we have so many kids.' She was there trying to get Bodge's great big arms and legs back into working order and the old man was asking her: 'Why did you go out with this man, the bear?'

Bodge was a big, fat 114 kilograms. She was tiny: 41 kilos. She supposed it was because he was a funny guy. The old man was so different. He still didn't have an ounce of fat on him. Straight back, strong hands, and he definitely didn't have a sense of humour.

TWENTY

1979–1982

BLACKETT

Mick Milat walked out of prison having missed most of his twenties. He was thirty years old and hard. The cops reckoned he'd go straight back inside, so why not get it over with. They wouldn't leave him alone. If anything went wrong within ten k, they'd be around to see him. It was the sort of treatment Milats copped all the time. Mick got it worse, but he was determined to keep his nose clean.

Ivan got him a start on the roads. No interview or resumé required. Just a quick look at his biceps and he was in. Sometimes, on weekends, Wally, Mick and Ivan were all in the same gang together and Terry Palmer, Ivan's leading hand, remembered another brother working there under the name 'Paul Miller', but didn't know which one. Work was just wrapping up on the Bargo section of the Hume Highway, turning it to freeway almost into the Southern Highlands. They were also doing a lot of work on the freeway from Sydney west to Penrith at the foot of the Blue Mountains.

Mick was a typical Milat. A good solid worker. He was quiet, until he got a couple of drinks in him. Then he'd be off. Crazy. He'd get in his car, full of piss, and drive back to the motel two hundred ks an hour.

Early one Sunday morning they were out at Fairfield jackhammering. The Lady Mayoress, Janice Crosio, lived just across the road and she got on to the coppers and made them stop the work. The foreman said no worries. They were all on double time. But no copper was going to tell the Milats they couldn't work. Mick and Ivan got out the picks and started digging up the road by hand. As they warmed up they started competing to see who could take out the most bitumen. Everyone else was standing around watching the mad bastards, waiting for 9 a.m. when they could turn the compressor on again.

There would be jobs where they'd go away on a Saturday afternoon and they didn't know when they'd be getting home. Borthwick would throw the overtime and safety rules out the window and Ivan Milat and a few others, maybe his brothers, would be the first guys picked to go out and do the thirty, forty hours straight. It could be worth $600 for a weekend. Really good money. It wasn't unheard of to make $2300 in a fortnight, clear. Ivan had the inside running on the foreman's job, but he told Terry Palmer he could make more money as a ganger because it was easier to get overtime. He didn't have to get approval and fill in all the forms.

It was common knowledge Ivan was the highest paid worker out of 150 blokes at the Central Asphalt Depot. Palmer was pulling in $45,000 and he thought he was doing a lot of overtime, but the story was that Ivan made $75,000 one year when that was a fortune. First week of every July, they'd sit around comparing group certificates showing their annual earnings. Ivan never showed his, but Palmer remembered him always saying he topped the place. To make as much as he claimed, he had to practically live there – and he pretty much did, when he could.

Even though Ivan was happy as a ganger, he wasn't happy being told what to do and it led to the odd run-in over the years. And he'd never ask for advice. If he'd never used a machine before, he wouldn't even ask where the ignition switch was. He'd rather stand there for ten minutes trying to figure it out. It was like there was something in him – the Man – that just wouldn't allow anybody to be better at the job than him.

The jealousies between Wally and Ivan had faded. When Wally's yellow Land Rover broke down while the family was holidaying at South West Rocks, in October 1979, he was straight on the phone to Ivan asking him to come and get them. Ivan didn't hesitate. They knew he wouldn't. That was the sort of bloke he was. He hired a big trailer, hooked it up to the Charger, and pulled it 480 kilometres up there, then all the way back.

Wally and Maureen, though, were on the skids. Maureen wanted out, but was having trouble psyching herself up to ask for a divorce. She never really knew what sort of a mood Wally was going to be in. There were no obvious signs. Like when she said hello to these two old guys walking past the house, Wally came out and virtually dragged her inside by the hair. 'You're on with them, aren't ya?'

'What are you talking about?'

'Don't you talk to them. I don't want you talking to nobody.'

'I'm not doing anything,' she pleaded. God, they were nothing to look at – missing teeth and no hair.

She eventually built up the guts to ask for the divorce. She expected him to go off the deep end, but he was pretty calm: 'Why? Let's talk it over . . . I'll buy you a car if you stay till your birthday . . . we'll sort this divorce thing out.' He only seemed to go off over the little things. Like he didn't want the milk bottle on the table so he'd hit it for a sixer.

Maureen took Robert and Susan back to her mum's place at Moorebank anyway. The kids, however, were still going to their old school at Campbelltown, 20 kilometres away, and her car, a little Morris, wasn't well . . . and Wally did promise to buy her a new one. He kept phoning and kept being very nice. He would change, he said. For her birthday, he bought her the car – paid the deposit, anyway – and took her out for a meal at a Chinese restaurant.

Despite everything, they talked some more over the next few weeks and she let herself be persuaded to come back. He did change. He started doing things around the house. Maureen didn't feel like such a slave. They talked. It was different. For a time.

Then it went bad again and Maureen was back sleeping on the couch. One rainy Sunday morning, she was in her dressing gown having just made the kids breakfast. All of a sudden Wally appeared in the kitchen with a gun. He put it up under his chin. 'Go on, pull the trigger. Pull it!' He put her hands on the gun.

'No, no, Wally!' She was freaking out. She backed away and he kept coming towards her, as she backed up onto a chair.

'Go on, pull it. Pull it!'

And God she was tempted. It'd put an end to all the drama. But the kids were still in the house, and she'd have to clean up. Maybe another time, another place, she'd have done it. But, suddenly, he swung the gun around towards her: 'If I can't have ya, nobody else is gunna have ya. I can't live without you.'

'I'll stay, I'll stay,' she said, as calmly as she could. 'I'll do anything you want. I'll stay. We'll get this all together.' He let her go, and took the gun to the bedroom where the kids were playing.

'Oh my God, what's he gunna do? He's gunna kill the kids,' she thought. She didn't know what to think. She followed quietly, trying not to be dramatic. Settle him down. He had the gun beside him.

'See ya later, kids. Daddy's going. Goodbye.' He had this real sad sack face, but the kids were oblivious to what was going on.

'Yeah, bye,' they said casually, like they were just going to school, and went on playing. Wally gave Maureen a dirty look, and drove off in the Land Rover. Maureen was pacing up and down not knowing what to do. She just hoped he wouldn't come back.

But he wasn't gone long. He went up to the bedroom and was calling her. She imagined him sitting on the edge of the bed, in the middle of the doorway with the gun pointed right at her. She said to Rob, 'If anything happens to me, you go and phone Nanna straightaway.' She had hardly walked out the door when he got straight on the phone to his grandmother.

Wally was sitting on the bed, pulling the gun apart. He saw the look on her face. He was laughing. 'What's the matter with you? D'ya think I was gunna kill ya?'

'Well, I didn't know what you were going to do.'

'I just did that to see if you'd actually pull it. I had it on safety the whole time.' Maureen wondered what would have happened if she had pulled it, but now it was all a big joke.

She kept sleeping in the lounge room. There were episodes of sex at knife point. She felt like he got a kick out of seeing how scared she was. She wouldn't fight it. 'Okay, here you go,' she'd say, bored, impatient. 'Do it.' He'd finish and complain, 'You're like a dead fish.' She really hated him in the end and eventually got the courage to leave in 1980, taking the kids back to her mum's. She was the first of the Milat wives to walk, and she felt the pressure. Wally's sister Shirley came around a few times, begging her to go back.

'Think of the kids,' Shirley'd say. 'You don't know what you're doing to your kids.'

'Yes, I do. I'm giving them a good life, because they didn't have much with Wally.' Maureen eventually won a bitter custody battle and took the kids out of Sydney. Wally was working with a different crew to Ivan and his family situation didn't help his work at the DMR. During a lunch break while working in the Blue Mountains he and another bloke went to a pub and overstayed. The foreman came to get him and copped a tirade of abuse, so he sacked him.[79] Wally went into business for himself after that as a gyprocker.

Old Steven Milat still hadn't given up work completely but, at seventy-seven, was taking it a bit easier. He wanted to go back to see his homeland, Yugoslavia, and visit relatives. The family sent him off gladly because at last they could rip down the grapevines and do some work on the rotting old back part of the weatherboard house. When he returned, he was pretty cranky about losing the source of his white lightning.

Dick Milat was also on the move, his spur-of-the-moment wanderings on his motorbike took him to Queensland and more strife, this time in the Gold Coast hinterland. He was charged with malicious damage and the theft of cigarettes from the BP Service Station at Tallebudgera on 23 January 1980. The court record did not give a detailed account of what transpired, but it appeared to be a smash-and-grab robbery.

In sentencing Richard on 20 August, Judge Loewenthal took into account the fact that 'you have been out of trouble for something like four years, according to the information put before us... Ignoring petty matters, you have twice been convicted of offences of a like nature, but nevertheless I have decided to give you the option of paying a fine.'

Dick copped a $750 fine, a $500 good-behaviour bond and $173.10 compensation to the owners of the service station.

Ivan had long held it over Karen that she had the choice of a house or a car. She chose the house, and her one chance at a slice of suburban freedom was out the window. They wanted to get away from Guildford and go live on their own. All the quiet nights doing nothing in the caravan paid off when, in 1981, Ivan got a loan from the Commonwealth Bank to buy a house at 9 Sorensen Crescent, in the western suburb of Blackett. Their $48,000 bought them a two-bedroom, dark-brick box of a place in which you couldn't swing a cat unless you chopped off its tail. The bitumen outside bore the black rubber from some hoon's burnouts, while on the other side of the street there was a two-storey Housing Commission complex guarded by a high metal fence. Trees hadn't had time to grow from the cow paddocks which had recently preceded the property developers.

George Milat, who was living nearby, warned his brother not to buy in Blackett. 'It'll cost you your marriage. Women have got a lot of time on their hands out here, and there are women who'll lead her astray while you're away.' Ivan heard what George said but he didn't need to say it. Now that he had Karen on her own, he tightened the reins like never before. He would keep her in check as ruthlessly as he kept his front lawn. Nothing moved without his permission.

Ivan was earning good money, but Karen had to pay all the household bills from the single mother's pension she was drawing – despite having been in a de facto relationship for four years. Ivan kept all his money and just paid the mortgage so she was still dependent on him. Just the way he liked it. Wally sold Ivan the fridge and freezer and half the furniture out of the wreckage of his crumbled marriage. His divorce was still going through. Maureen never saw any of the money she was promised.

Ivan sold the Charger. It was in such good nick, he pretty much got back what he payed for it in 1974 – about $4000. They bought a little four-door Mitsubishi Colt and it looked like Karen, twenty-three, was going to learn to drive after all.

Ivan made himself up a set of weights in the garage: two buckets filled with cement, joined by a two-inch pipe. He also used the Bullworker – one of those Charles Atlas-type devices that stopped you getting sand kicked in your face. Later, he bought Jason a set of red dumbbells, but used them himself. Sometimes, he used Karen's exercise bike, too. At thirty-six, he was still a strong, fit man.

They were now a 20 kilometre cross-town drive from the southwestern suburbs where they both grew up. Karen was instantly isolated. Ivan hated her talking to anyone. The only neighbours who didn't pose a threat were an old deaf couple, the Normans, over the road. About four months after moving in, Karen asked Mrs Hilda Norman to teach her sign language. Mrs Norman was amazed Karen picked it up in two weeks. She used single-handed signing to talk to Hilda, and double-handed for Jim, Hilda's husband.

Hilda Norman became Karen's confidante – one who couldn't betray a secret even if she'd wanted to. Karen would come over for breakfast most mornings. They talked about everything, and it was plain from the start that Karen was unhappy. The Normans could see it in the way Ivan made her pick up all the leaves in the yard. It had to be spotless or she was in trouble. He'd give the house the white-glove treatment, yet leave garbage everywhere for her to clean up. She told Hilda how he'd eat an iceblock and throw the wrapper away, testing her, because he'd never be so slovenly otherwise. He demanded the house be completely dust-free because of Jason's increasingly acute asthma and he made Karen give up smoking, like him, for the same reason.

Ivan treated Jason like his own son. If the family ever went anywhere, they'd have to take his asthma machine and hook him up to it. Ivan told people how he was up through the night because of it. The five-year-old's attendance at Blackett Primary School was often made difficult by the attacks.

The move to Blackett seemed to change things for the worse. Ivan became more verbally abusive to Karen and swore more. She couldn't handle the isolation and the little tests. Perhaps inspired by Maureen's clean break, she made the big decision and left him, taking Jason to her parents' new place on the Central Coast, about 60 kilometres away. But Ivan promised to change. He called her often and wrote to her, begging her to come back. She relented because she loved him.

He was getting more interested in guns. His workmates noticed a dramatic change in his tastes. Suddenly, the trucking magazines were gone and it was all gun mags. There were days when it was too wet to work. They'd all be in the canteen at the Granville depot, 200 blokes bored and reading their under-the-counter 'smoot' mags. They passed theirs around, but he never even looked at them.

Around this time, Wally brought over a big, lethal-looking gun that took large bullets. Karen never knew if he gave it to Ivan or sold it to him. One day a little pistol appeared. Ivan said it was from the security firm Armaguard, but offered no explanation as to how he got it. He carried it on him every time he went further than the local shops. It went into his sock in his right boot. If he wasn't wearing boots, he wrapped it in a football sock and put it under the driver's seat of his car. Karen never saw him loading it, but he told her it was always ready to go. At home, he kept it in the linen closet.

Ivan pinched a grey leather apron from the DMR workshop, and he and Karen sat down at the sewing machine and turned it into a pouch and holster with some red velcro from a DMR jacket, though he never seemed to use the holster. His little armoury was growing. He had a ten-inch knife which folded up and which Karen knew was expensive.

Wally gave him a working replica of the earliest type of revolver where you had to pack the black powder in before the moulded lead bullets. Karen saw the rifle and the revolver a lot more than the pistol because Ivan continually had them out, taking them apart and cleaning each part separately. He kept the revolver under the bed or under the car seat in its own little wooden box with a Neighbourhood Watch sticker on it.

There had been a few robberies in the street, and Ivan became the driving force behind the creation of the local Neighbourhood Watch scheme. He became obsessed with security. He got an engraving kit and, after engraving everything in his own place right down to the toaster, he took it around from house to house, encouraging everyone to write their driver's licence number on all their electrical goods.

Sometimes, when he'd finished all his DMR paperwork, he'd sit at home and make model trucks which he painted camouflage colours. They never went out for a meal, never saw a movie, never went to a sporting event. They ate dinner and watched the TV at the table. They only ever visited his mum, or Alex.

In 1982, Steven Milat, aged seventy-nine, finally gave up work. Also that year, Ivan sold the Mitsubishi Colt and Karen's dreams of getting a driver's licence went with it. Her sense of isolation just got worse. He bought a Mitsubishi four-wheel-drive van, much the same as a normal delivery van with a sliding door at the side, but raised up for greater clearance in rough country. It was dark green with black and gold stripes and Ivan wanted to paint it camouflage colours until he found out how much that cost. If the Colt had seemed out of character to his workmates, the van just seemed strange.

His idea of going four-wheel driving was to find a couple of hills with dirt on them, drive up them a couple of times and go home. He didn't want to get the van too dirty, unlike his work vehicles which he thrashed about. Once he took Karen to a forest near the Jenolan Caves in the Blue Mountains, but they never did a tour of the limestone caves, just drove about the tracks of a pine plantation.

TWENTY-ONE

1983–1987

BREAKDOWN

Karen and Ivan were on shaky ground, getting wobblier. When Social Security found out she was living with Ivan, Karen lost her single mother's pension and Ivan had to start looking after her financially and he had no excuse not to marry her, either. She wanted the security that the institution seemed to offer, but she had plenty of doubts. He also had no excuse not to have kids. She wanted a girl, and while Ivan at first agreed, he suddenly changed, and threatened to blow her head off if she ever got pregnant. She didn't know how to take the threat.

Ivan had renewed his acquaintance with his old mates, John and Jenny Parsons, who were living in Smithfield. They had bumped into him one day outside a supermarket in Fairfield, where Ivan had been buying raw sugar in bulk for one of his father's brain-numbing concoctions. He had introduced Karen to the couple. They started to occasionally visit. On one visit, Karen and Jenny Parsons were sitting out by the pool in the Parsons' backyard. Jenny could tell there was something wrong. 'What's the matter with you?' she asked.

'I don't know. We're in bed at night and Rita's always ringing up crying, "Help me, Ivan, I've got to have help. Come over".' Jenny didn't know who Rita was, but presumed she was some sort of relation. Ivan would say he couldn't go because of Karen, then Rita'd keep on crying and Karen'd tell him to go, '. . . but if you keep doing this, I'm going to leave you'.

Even though she craved marriage, Karen really wasn't sure whether marrying Ivan was the thing to do. She showed bruises to some people, George Milat among them: 'Look what Ivan did.' But certainly the impression Karen and Ivan gave most people was that she was the driving force behind the marriage plans. Ivan agreed to it, but strictly on his terms. He'd marry her and pay her $200 a fortnight housekeeping. For that she had to keep the house spotless. She had to show him all the receipts for groceries. She couldn't spend it on herself or save it. She was his.

They ended up getting married on 20 February 1983. It was a no frills job at the registry. No guests, no party, no honeymoon. Karen told Jenny Parsons they would have had to get a babysitter for Jason and Ivan never let anybody mind him. He didn't even tell his own mother about the wedding. She was furious and wanted to know why. 'Mac didn't want you to come,' Karen told her.

Ivan treated it as a bit of a joke. 'Why didn't you come?' he asked his mother.

'You didn't want me there.'

'I said no such thing. Karen's mother was there and you didn't turn up.'

A month later, Steven Milat, eighty-two, having booked another trip back to Yugoslavia, became ill. They took him to St Joseph's Hospital, Auburn, where he was diagnosed with bowel cancer – the first time he'd ever been in hospital. They had him in for a few weeks before he made a slight recovery. But then on Easter Saturday when Margaret rang the hospital, the nurse told her to come quickly.

He went into a coma and died at 9 a.m., that Saturday, 23 April, from pneumonia which had arisen during his treatment. They buried him in Rookwood Cemetery after a Catholic service at East Granville. Ivan and Boris called another truce for the day to please their mum who got the impression they'd made up, but there was too much history for that. The wake was at Campbell Hill Road where a big silver bong floated between some of the brothers.

Just over a month later, their grandmother, Lillian Piddlesden, died in hospital and they buried her at Rookwood, too. It was a hard time for Margaret, compounded by Richard having yet another run-in with the law. This time a minor marijuana matter.

Around this time, Karen got the impression Ivan had done something wrong and would not tell her. He was real aggro, real fiery. She was too scared to ask what it was. Sometimes, when Karen and Ivan went down to Alex's place, Ivan took them into a quiet little state forest,

Belanglo. Karen thought Ivan knew the place well. He had no difficulty finding his way around. They went there four times in 1983. The first time, he wanted to shoot kangaroos but there were too many people about collecting firewood so they went home. The second time, they were in there almost an hour before they saw a mob. Ivan eased the green van off the dirt track, grabbed a rifle, aimed, shot one 'roo, then 'crack', another. He pulled a knife and walked to the second 'roo, its nerves still twitching. He bent over and slit its throat without hesitation, then kicked it to make sure it was dead. Light was fading, so they left the carcasses to rot and went home. It was the only time she saw him be cruel to an animal.

Ivan's workmates noted that the deaths in his family seemed to knock him around. Terry Palmer thought Ivan never had a great deal of regard for life or limb – here today, gone tomorrow – but he could see the death of his father shook him.

He noted a change in his behaviour, too. When a brown snake slithered out of the grass one day, Ivan sprang to kill it. Not content to just flatten its head, he chopped it up, all the while with a great smile on his face.

He got worse at home, too. He was a caveman, in Mrs Norman's eyes. Karen confided to her that he'd often pull her about by the hair, set off by stupid little things. And he began to display it in his choice of sex, too, pushing her without warning onto the kitchen table. She didn't mind so much at first but then his preference turned to the 'trick' he learnt in prison. She was brutalised by the first experience. She just had to cop it sweet.

His change became that much more worrying to Karen as his obsession with guns grew. If he was going to carry one all the time like he did, he was bound to use it. She went over the road to Mrs Norman's place one Sunday with her hands, feet and underarms all sweaty. They'd almost had an accident at an intersection in Granville after visiting the family. Ivan and the other driver started arguing and the other guy got out of his car and pulled out a rifle. Ivan made Karen hand him his pistol and a rifle. The two men stood there, pointing the guns at each other, shouting, threatening to pull the trigger as Karen and Jason huddled, terrified in the car. Eventually they both backed down.

Karen said that Ivan told her not to tell anyone, but Mrs Norman went and reported it to the police, but they never came to check out the report.

Always the mystery man, Ivan sometimes used to take off after work when they were out in the bush. One time, between 1985 and 1987, out on the Hay Plain in south-western New South Wales, it was above 40 degrees with no breeze and not even a tree for a dog to piss on. The crew drove back to the motel, and the boys headed straight for the pool. Ivan had a shower and got changed. 'I gotta go,' he told Terry Palmer. 'Keep an eye on the boys. Any problems, I'll see ya in the mornin'. Watch it, though, they're gunna get on the piss.'

'Yeah, so am I. What's the problem?'

Milat would get right up them if they were rude to motel staff. They'd be out there at Hay or some place wanting prawn cocktails and lobster. He'd go off his brain. But this arvo, he had his own agenda, piss or no piss, he took off with the little DMR Nissan Navara and was away all night. He later told Palmer he went over into Victoria to buy a crossbow, but that didn't make much sense to Palmer because the hours he was over there, all the shops would have been shut.

During the working day he could be anywhere, too. He'd tell the gang he was going ahead to check the job, and he probably was. He'd have to go and verify the road width for the sprayers, that sort of thing. He could be two kilometres up the road, or 50 kilometres, no one would know. But he always came back with the info.

Everything about Ivan was a mystery. Why he voted Liberal like he reckoned he did. Why he took rolls of sash cord home from work when he didn't have a dog or a boat or anything. And what he kept in his bag was anyone's guess. Anyone who picked it up knew he had more than his lunch in there. They saw him peel an orange with a foot-long Bowie knife he dragged out of there once.

Anne-Marie Breitkopf, the wife of one of Ivan's good workmates, Rolf, signed Karen and Ivan up to Amway. Karen did all the selling. The two women started to get to know each other. Karen would pick up all her stock from Anne-Marie. She was good at moving product, selling to her neighbours. Sometimes they had make-up parties to sell cosmetics.

Karen came to her place and they did make-overs for groups of women. Karen was good at it. All the women thought she was lovely. The parties were among the few occasions when Ivan let her go anywhere on her own. He'd drop her off: 'Well, what time are you gunna finish?'

'Maybe four o'clock.'

He'd be on the door, right on the dot. They'd hear him pull up, and she'd get agitated. 'Okay, I've got to go,' she'd say, timidly.

And he'd be at the door: 'Are you ready?'

She just didn't seem to be allowed to associate with anyone. She had to be inside, looking after him. Anne-Marie wouldn't encourage her to do anything either. It wasn't her that was going to cop it when they left.

Rolf used to say to his wife: 'Be wary of Ivan, okay. Just be careful of him.'

'You know I don't like him.'

'Well, that helps.' Rolf never explained the basis of his concern. Anne-Marie saw Ivan as very masculine, very macho. She could see something in his blue eyes that made her back away. They looked at you, like, straight through. Always in control. There was something she didn't trust, and she thought she was a good judge of character.

Ivan also used to let Karen associate with Barbara Brown, the daughter of one of his workmates. He used to say to Terry Palmer: 'All Karen wants to do is go shopping and spend money with Barbara.' But Ivan apparently made a pass at her once and Palmer thought that he might have been trying to drive a wedge between the two friends. For a start, he didn't want Karen spending money shopping and, secondly, he didn't want this woman around when Karen's job was to look after him and the boy. She couldn't even cook, he'd tell his workmates.

He told them she served him up this meal one time, and he just went: 'I'm not eating that shit.' And smashed the plate down on the glass coffee table, shattering both the plate and the table. Frightened the life out of Karen. He wanted it left there as a reminder and told her she wasn't to touch a thing and drew a picture of where the glass shattered, so he could tell if she'd touched any. 'Move a piece of that before I get home, you're dead.' The shards became a symbol of the marriage, left to linger long after they should have been cleaned away.

He upped and went to his mother's for a real feed – by the woman who had copped the same treatment from Milat's father so many years earlier. He told his mother Karen smashed the table for no reason. He took photographs of the mess to show his mum how untidy she was. 'Look what I have to put up with.'

Sometimes he'd stay at his mum's for a few days. Certainly the impression coming from Barbara Brown was that there were a lot of two- or three-day splits.

Ivan came back from seeing the movie *Rambo* and told his workmate Noel Wild what a good show it was. 'Gee, mate, you oughta go see it.' That sort of thing impressed him. Soldier-of-fortune stuff. It fitted his own self-image. Ivan was in raptures with the Stallone biceps. His own makeshift weight training intensified.

He loved the sight of Rambo blazing away with a machine-gun. Alex had a far heavier, unworkable antique in his collection – a German water-cooled machine-gun. Ivan struck a Rambo pose with it late one night in Alex's backyard for a series of photographs. Ivan, the soldier of fortune.

Anne-Marie Breitkopf was working at a local garage and was having problems with another macho man. He apparently expressed an interest in her and she told a co-worker she wouldn't touch him with a barge pole. His ego was bruised, so he started giving her a hard time, blaming her for everything that went wrong. She came home from work one day really distressed. Ivan and Rolf were in the front yard talking, and she told them what the guy was doing to her.

'Look,' said Ivan. 'Don't worry about it. Fifty bucks and I'll blow him away.'

'Ha, ha, it's not that bad,' she said, trying to play it down. 'Don't worry about it.'

'If you haven't got the fifty bucks. I'll lend it to you.' She never doubted that he meant it. 'I'll blow him away.'

After Ivan left, Rolf turned to her and said: 'You realise he's serious.'

'Yeah, but it's all right, I'll handle it. I'm a big girl.' She quit the job.

Ivan was forty-two now, and settled in as the ordinary family man. His short, dark hair was greying, especially the sidelevers which went down to the bottom of his ear. The full moustache went down past his lips to either side of his chin.

Jason turned ten on 24 July and Ivan gave him a rifle. It was going to come in handy because Richard and Wally were looking at a property to buy, something big enough to really go shooting on. A month later, the two brothers paid $25,000 for 149 hectares of bleak goat country west of Mittagong on the Wombeyan Caves road.

The family solicitors, Marsden's, did the conveyancing for the brothers. The land was good for nothing. Yet Wally and Richard liked it for its isolation, and the fact there were plenty of feral goats, kangaroos and wallabies straying in from the vast tract of bush bordering it, just waiting to be shot. In the middle of the property was a black peak known as Perpendicular Rock, which jutted straight up into the sky like it should have had a medieval castle on it with bats flying around the parapets. They called it 'Milat's Mountain' or the 'Big Block'.

Wally had a new, much younger woman in his life too, Lisa. They had moved on to a vacant block of land at Hilltop which Wally originally bought while married to Maureen. There, they set about building a new home while living in a caravan on site. Wally was still making his own bullets. It saved a lot of money, especially with all the ammunition they were firing down at the Big Block. It was nothing for them to go through a couple of thousand rounds in one session.

Wally was in his workshop making ammo when a hammer fell onto a live round which exploded. The bullet flew one way and the cartridge rocketed into his eye, obliterating it. He was lucky it didn't kill him. Doctors gave him a glass eye.

Soon after they bought the Big Block, Wally and Richard invited everybody down for a weekend. There was no house on the property, so Ivan bought a cheap, green and orange two-man tent for his family and a one-ring gas cooker. Jason's nebuliser for his asthma needed electricity, so Ivan bought a little generator too. They were the only bits of camping equipment he owned. It was the one and only time they'd ever go camping as a family. They didn't have backpacks or sleeping bags. They used pillows and blankets.

The weekend was spent exploring the property and shooting at beer cans, at rocks, pretty much anything that moved – and anything that didn't. Even the women joined in. Ivan was shooting the old black powder revolver, when he began to act silly, carrying on like a cowboy, much to Karen's embarrassment, wearing the weapon in the homemade holster on his hip and insisting he be called 'Texas' or 'Tex'.

Karen had a go at firing the semi-automatic assault rifle.

Karen had thought that getting married would change the world. It was a dumb idea. He owned her now. He paid for her, didn't he? Ivan the cowboy; Ivan the caveman. When Lyndon and Cathy Beattie moved in next door in 1986, they had a house-warming party. Ivan let Karen go alone, but she had to be home by 10 p.m. And she was. Cathy Beattie would see Karen constantly raking leaves no matter how many were on the ground. She kept the house spotless and Cathy could see she was too scared to say boo to Ivan as he sat there, forever doing his paperwork.

Cathy became a confidante of Karen, at least she thought so. She would hear tidbits prefaced with: 'Don't tell anybody, but . . .' She knew Ivan hurt her because Karen showed her bruises on her arm. One time, she also told Cathy she had an affair with a bloke down the road, but Cathy never saw the bloke and didn't think she was telling the truth. Certainly Karen never told Mrs Norman such a thing.

The Milats had one neighbour, 'Chris Thompson', who worked shifts. He was home most mornings and usually did a bit of shopping. Karen often rang. 'Can you get me some milk and bread when you're down there?'

'Sure.'

'Don't forget to ask for a receipt separate from yours.'

Once, when Thompson brought it to her, it was obvious she was in a bad way. Her palms and feet were clammy. He could see her nerves were going, that she was on the verge of a breakdown. She couldn't leave the house some days. Couldn't get out of bed on others. There were mental barriers all around. She was shaky, tense, full of fear. He knew about Ivan so it wasn't a mystery why she was cracking up, just the way she changed when he was about. Thompson knew how he made her account for every minute of the day, and had to explain why she wasn't home if he called and there was no answer.

She got on well with all the neighbours, but when Ivan was about, they didn't see her much. It was often hard for them to see why she was so afraid of him. To everyone but the Normans, he seemed like a quiet, decent sort of bloke. They just guessed that he was different in the house.

Even the Normans never saw any bruises on her, but they knew she was sleeping on the lounge – the same one Maureen had slept on six years earlier. Ivan pulled her off it by the hair and dragged her into the bed for sex. They called him the Caveman.

The marriage breakdown was almost complete by the end of '86. He would come home and find dust on something and throw it at her. He became increasingly agitated if she ever spoke to neighbours. Karen put a lot of it down to Ivan being under pressure at work to become a foreman. She was searching for a reason why things got so much worse as they went into 1987. She was now on large amounts of medication for her nerves.

She threatened to leave again and he told her she was staying whether she liked it or not. One day he threw a glass at her and just missed Jason. She ran into the bedroom with her son and wouldn't come out, vowing that it was all over.

Karen had earlier mentioned to Mrs Norman that she was thinking of leaving Ivan. Mrs Norman told her that she should ask her doctor for advice – the one she was seeing about her breakdown – 'but if I were you, I'd pack up'.

Karen said that Ivan had offered her a $4000 settlement if she left him.

'No way,' Mrs Norman signed. 'He is bluffing. He would give you no money.' Mrs Norman thought Karen should take the furniture, everything, and run. 'Best way to move out quickly while Ivan is working far away.'

But Karen seemed scared of that option. She knew it would send her husband crazy.

The Golden Eagle hotel/motel at Gateshead was about the cheapest place around Newcastle where you could still park all the DMR vehicles off road. Sometimes there were twenty or thirty blokes there.

On Valentine's Day 1987, Ivan rang Karen like he did every night he was away. He couldn't go a night without checking on her. 'Are you coming out to ring up, Tez?' he asked his roommate, Terry Palmer.

'Nah, I don't ring every night, mate. I'm home Friday.' Palmer always wondered what a nice young girl like Karen saw in Ivan, but he sure paid her a lot of attention. Palmer watched Ivan go off with his football sock heavy with two bob coins. One time he'd asked: 'Why don't you just reverse charges? You're feeding two bobs into that bloody thing. It's hungrier than a poker machine.' He'd picked up the sock and realised that there was something a lot more solid than 20 cent coins in there – and it was probably loaded.

This night, the phone back in Sorensen Crescent didn't answer. Ivan came back to the room, grunted something and just took off in the ute.

He rang some neighbours, the Cinconzes, that night. At 2 a.m. Jeff Cinconze answered the phone, startled at the hour.

'Have you seen Karen?' Ivan wanted to know.

'No, she went with the lady in the red car. I don't know if she's back yet, but I saw her taking off with her.'

'The trendy woman with the red Torana?'

'Yeah.'

'Right, I know where she is,' he said, apparently still calm.

The Cinconzes hadn't seen the removal van parked around the corner. Nina Cinconze used to have coffee with Karen sometimes and she looked happily married. She'd tell Nina how she didn't like Ivan going away too much because she missed him. She wanted him home all the time, so Nina thought she really loved him.

But the glass-throwing incident had been the last straw. She called in the removalists next day – Valentine's Day. She didn't even tell the Normans. She told no one except the Beatties who let her store some furniture she couldn't fit into the van.

Ivan was back at work the next morning. He never missed a day, but his workmates noticed a change in him after his mystery disappearance. He went strange. He was edgy, they could see it in the way he wasn't just sitting back reading his gun books. He was walking around, restless, always moving. Something was on his mind. 'Come on, Tez, fuck, get the boys going. Come on.' It was a few days before he started telling people Karen had done the flit on him. He was dirty on the world. Blamed the in-laws. 'They'll be sorry for meddling in my affairs.'

A few days later, Ivan went over to ask Lyndon Beattie if he or Cathy had seen her.

'What are you talking about?' Beattie asked.

'Come with me.' Milat, agitated and cranky, led Beattie into his home. It was completely empty but for the fridge. Beattie didn't let on that much of the gear was in his garage.

The Cinconzes saw him and he looked like he hadn't slept much. His eyes were red and half closed.

'She's emptied the house and took off,' he told Jeff Cinconze. He looked heartbroken. They felt bad for him. They didn't know about any of the shit that had gone down.

Ivan went home to his mum and the neighbours hardly saw him again. He had given it a few days before he phoned and broke the news. Told his mum she took everything, even a few thousand he had in the bank. He was worried about the little bloke, Jason. She couldn't understand why Karen left, but thought she had a 'rotten hide'. Ivan was crying on the phone, something he hadn't done since he was a toddler.

'Mum, I've got nowhere to go.'

'Come home. Come home.'[80]

Neighbourhood Watch collapsed without him. Jeff Cinconze saw him once a few months later when he was giving the house a final clean before selling it. It was a steal. Less than $50,000.

'Why so cheap?' asked Cinconze.

'Solicitor's advice to get a quick sale to make up the money she took and the furniture she took. He said: "Sell the house way under market value and she won't get anything. If you sell it at the right price . . . It'll go through court. She'll get half".'[81]

Cinconze wanted to grab it for that price, but he wasn't quick enough. It sold in a week. Didn't even get to an agent. The buyer was the father of his neighbour, Lyndon Beattie. Ivan, however, had a problem. Karen's signature was on the title. In order to sell it, he needed the signature. He offered Cathy Beattie $2000 to forge it for him. 'But I refused. I don't know who he got to forge the signature,' she'd say later.[82] He needed a woman because it had to be witnessed.

Ivan found someone – he told Palmer he got one of his brothers' girlfriends to do it – and so, on 21 July 1987 a person claiming to be Karen Merle Milat signed a childish signature 'K Milat' on the transfer document, then the witness, a solicitor, put his autograph below the words: 'Signed in my presence by the transferor who is known to me'.

The property went for $44,000 to Marilu Pty Ltd, a company

owned by Lyndon John Beattie and Marie Elsie Beattie of 10 William Street, South Strathfield. It was $4000 less than Milat had paid for it five years earlier. The property market was just starting to boom and it would have been worth almost twice that. They could have both had their $35,000 or $40,000, but that wasn't what this was about. This was revenge. A month later he blew most of it by buying himself a silver Nissan four-wheel drive for $24,500.

Then the sheriff turned up at the depot looking to serve some papers on him. 'Are you Ivan Milat?' he asked Ivan.

'No,' he answered. This happened a couple of times. He wanted the sheriff off his back and he thought the best way to do it was attack.

TWENTY-TWO

1988–1989

OLD FLAMES

Karen walking out on him gave Ivan more freedom to live up to his image as the freewheeling man on the edge. He told Terry Palmer how he'd go up to meet a contact in Queensland and bring back a load of marijuana to sell.

'Get a load of grass and a load of ammo,' he told Palmer, 'and the grass pays for the ammo. No questions asked on the ammo up there.' It was cheaper in Queensland and the firearms rules more lax.

He told Donny Borthwick he was in Queensland with his contact when they saw smoke in the distance. The contact started getting jumpy. As they neared the guy's plantation, he nearly broke down as he saw $20,000 to $30,000 of next year's crop gone up in smoke.

Ivan didn't smoke marijuana as far as his workmates could tell, but he did talk about knocking off laughing gas – nitrous oxide – from the dentist. 'You're a fruit loop,' Palmer told him.

Almost exactly a year after Karen walked out on Ivan, the DMR spray gang was back at the same motel in Gateshead on the old Pacific Highway in southern Newcastle. It was Saturday night, 13 February, and all the gang were in the pub out the front, except Ivan.

Palmer came back to the motel room expecting to see him there filling in his paperwork and drinking his Coke, but he was gone. Palmer heard him come in some time after 4 a.m. and thought that being single again, he must have gone out and got himself a bit of stray. Nothing was said.

Later that Sunday morning, Valentine's Day, they were out on the job and Ivan drove up in the Navara and parked it right in the middle of the gang. The radio news came on and he turned it up loud. There was a story about a suspicious fire early that morning in the Newcastle suburb of Hamilton.

'That was my in-laws,' Ivan declared. 'Serves 'em right.' He was happy as Larry.

'Hold on,' Palmer was thinking. 'They didn't say any names there. How'd he know whose place it was?' The other blokes twigged to it as well, but none of them said anything. Ivan seemed proud of it. He had been saying for a year that he'd sort out the in-laws for breaking up his marriage and here he was, showing them he was a man of his word. The soldier of fortune.

The official New South Wales Fire Brigade investigation of the blaze had the fire erupting in a car parked outside a block of units at 84 Glebe Road, Hamilton. There was no doubt it was the work of an arsonist. The fire had been lit in the passenger seat of the Ducks' Holden Torana and a chemical accelerant was used. The car was destroyed and a Ford Econovan parked nearby was also written off by heat damage.

The fire was enough to make Karen go running to the police. She told them Ivan had confronted her mother and threatened to burn the house down with the family inside if she didn't say where Karen was. She gave them a photograph of Ivan armed with a pistol, to press home her concern.

The police pulled him off the job and interviewed him. He denied it emphatically. They had no evidence, but then, they never interviewed Terry Palmer or the other blokes.

Word got around the yard that the police had been looking for Ivan. He was never the sort of bloke to go on about it, but he liked his workmates to know it; liked them to know what a tough bastard he was; an outlaw and all that.

Boris' drinking had not abated and his relationship with Marilyn continued to be turbulent and, at times, violent. He never let up on Marilyn about Ivan. His cure, finally, was to go out womanising. Never told the other women that he was still married. They usually found out when they rang him at home and Marilyn answered the phone. When she questioned him about these calls, he delighted in it. The tables had turned.

They eventually split up, and Marilyn stayed on the Central Coast. She started to get on with her life. She was living with Lynise, twenty-two, who had split up from her steady boyfriend, Paul Gould, a motorbike freak. Their other daughter, Charlene, had married a local car dealer.

It was early 1988 and Marilyn was driving to work through the northern suburbs of Gosford, when she got caught up in traffic. As the traffic moved slowly on, she saw the cause of the problem. A road gang. Then she saw something she hadn't seen in fourteen years – Ivan – standing up on a hot mix machine, tanned and handsome as ever. 'Ooh yeah,' she thought, her heart fluttering as the long-repressed love came pouring back. The years hadn't softened his physique, either. He didn't see her. She drove on wondering if there was still anything in his heart for her. It had broken hers when she was forced to make the decision between him and her daughters, so many years ago.

For the best part of seventeen years, Marilyn had been isolated from the Milats, and she was hesitant to ring them now to inquire about Ivan. Mrs Milat always blamed her for the split between the brothers. One day she was talking to Boris, so he would later claim, and she mentioned that she saw Mac working nearby. Boris twigged straightaway that she hadn't lost the old flame. He reckoned that for the first time in his life he didn't feel ill at ease about it. Thought he would do Marilyn a favour and ring Ivan at Mum's place and give him Marilyn's new address and phone number. That's the story he liked to tell: that, of all people, he brought them back together.

It was a Saturday in July 1988 when Ivan finally knocked on Marilyn's door. She threw her arms around him. He was as polite and quiet as ever. Ivan told her about Karen and how she up and walked out on him. He convinced her that he had never been violent towards Karen, that he was the injured party. Karen didn't deserve him, Marilyn thought. She felt as if she was the only person to ever truly know him. They resumed their relationship as if nothing had happened, though this time it was out in the open and in front of Lynise, who was still in the dark about her parentage.

Lynise didn't mind her mother dating one of her uncles. In the back of her mind, she thought her mother had once gone out with one of them anyway, but never picked it as Ivan. When he first came calling and Marilyn introduced Lynise, he had called her by the pet name, 'Kookie', that Ivan's mum had named her as a baby. She never knew it had also been Gran Milat's name for Ivan.

She was glad to see her mum happy for once and she let the two lovers do their own thing. Her mum seemed to come alive when Ivan dropped by. He was exciting and challenging. Ivan was always very nice to Lynise. Used to look at her funny, though. When Marilyn was in the same room, conversation was brief and limited to courtesies, but when she left the room, his whole manner changed. He'd become focused on Lynise, leaning forward and staring intently at her, as if studying her. She felt a strange bond, but dismissed the feeling.

The relationship was, however, still a part-time affair. Ivan and Marilyn were separated by distance and by his work. They were confined to Friday and Saturday nights at Marilyn's. Over time, she began to notice little changes in him, particularly when he stayed. She could tell that he had developed a temper in the years they had been apart. She saw it erupt for no reason. Some people would have been frightened by it, but to Marilyn it was nothing compared to Boris.

Marilyn noted he was still fastidious with his car. By God, it shone. Yet his obsession with guns, and the way he always carried a large hunting knife, disturbed her. He talked a lot about shooting down at the Big Block. He'd tell her stories about them going down and killing wild goats and sheep.

'How could you wound something and track it down like that?' she wondered.

Ivan often went down the property alone because he didn't like shooting around Wally. He thought Wally's gun safety was a bit lax and he especially didn't like Wally walking behind him with a loaded gun.[83] Both Wally and Dick had a real shoot-'em-up attitude, but then his brother George complained to both Wally and Richard that after Ivan had been there it took weeks for the game to come back, because he'd be shootin' everything.

Ivan began to take Marilyn out in his four-wheel drive, sometimes to remote areas where they did nothing but shoot. Occasionally, they stayed away overnight. During those trips, Marilyn noticed that he was still kind, but seemed to have lost some of the tenderness she knew in the sixties. He was harder, and she thought the marriage break-up might have been to blame. It was nothing for Ivan to kill a bird, but he seemed to get more satisfaction out of wounding it. Seemed to enjoy seeing the creature suffer. He'd get so incredibly pumped up from the adrenalin charge, it frightened her.

Marilyn told Boris about her concerns for Ivan. She told him that Ivan had shown her a large hunting knife, like Crocodile Dundee's and, on one occasion, had grabbed her from behind in a demonstration of how to penetrate flesh and avoid breaking the blade on bone.[84]

Out of the blue one day, Ivan told his workmate Terry Palmer: 'I've got to go.'

'What do you mean?'

'I'm gunna leave the DMR.'

'What about all these years you've been here? You've got more service than me.'

Ivan said he'd been tipped off by one of the bosses that they were going to start garnisheeing his wages to pay Karen's maintenance. He had stalled for as long as he could, but the march of bureaucracy was inevitable.

Some of the blokes were talking about buying him a present and giving him a little farewell, but he never wanted one. He didn't want to be confronted with the idea of someone doing that sort of thing for him so, after twelve years on the job, he just quietly stopped turning up on 9 September 1988.

Ivan found work at a place called Sweeping Services, where he drove a suction broom which was used for cleaning up industrial sites and road works. Don Borthwick bumped into him one day when he was driving the broom at a job on James Ruse Drive, sweeping up some loose asphalt. 'G'day, Ivan.'

'Sshh, me name's Bill.'

'What?'

'I'm working under a bodgie name, mate.'

Ivan didn't last long in the sweeping business. He quit after two months to go to a job at the Boral plasterboard factory at Camellia, near the DMR depot in Granville. He started there in November 1988 as Bill Milat, born 9 July 1947 – the real Bill Milat's birthday.

He worked there peacefully while the divorce went through. They called him the Phantom because he used to graffiti the comic book character in the toilets. It was his call sign. Lots of blokes did it, but they thought of him as an oddity because he was a bit of a loner. Strange.

It was only natural they'd have a bit of fun with a guy that didn't fit in. He was working down on the cutter where they cut lengths of plaster cornice that were coming out the end of a huge drying oven. One of the young forklift drivers, 'Northie', trying to be a hero, turned a hose on him. He did it a few times over several days. Next time, 'Bill' was waiting. Stuck a gun at Northie's head and said something like: 'If I could, I would.' The forkie never did it again.

Ivan's relationship with Marilyn began to sour. He was content to keep on seeing her, but she wanted more than weekends. She craved commitment. She wanted the one man she had always loved waiting for her down the end of the aisle. When she put marriage to him, in August 1989, he wouldn't buy it, so she told him they were through. There were other men interested in her. She couldn't confine herself to him if it was going nowhere. So, for the second time in her life, she made the decision to break it off. Ivan, she felt, was heartbroken. He turned his back on her and the phone calls stopped.

She would later come to think that leaving him sent him off the rails like it did back in 1971 when he had that trouble with the two girls and the rape charge. In her mind she was the love of his life – as he was of hers – and he just couldn't handle her leaving. Her thoughts broadly concur with serial killer profiles which often note some form of loss or rejection – in this case a 'narcissistic wound' – as the trigger for some force that was already building.

Within a week, he began making plans to take off, maybe to New Zealand again. He applied for his first passport. The photograph he submitted showed him wearing a thick, Zapata moustache. But he never used the passport.

Meanwhile, the matter of the signature on the title transfer for the property at Blackett was not going away. Karen took Lyndon Beattie senior to court over it, claiming that the two Lyndon Beatties and Ivan conspired to rip her off. Ivan was subpoenaed, but didn't turn up.

According to Lyndon Beattie junior: 'She turned up at court barefoot and pregnant looking for a new house or anything. We got dragged up to East Lambton Court House . . . She had a public solicitor [Legal Aid]. We had a barrister.' The magistrate threw out Karen's claim.

Cathy Beattie got a few threatening letters from her former friend as a result of the feud over the house. Mrs Norman received three letters from Karen. They were postmarked Queensland with no return address. Karen wrote in one that she had moved to Queensland after Ivan had set fire to the garage. In the third letter, she said she'd married, then separated again. She had a ten-month-old daughter.

In October 1989, with his divorce complete and the sheriff off his back, Ivan went back to working on the roads under his real name. Coincidentally, Lyndon Beattie junior worked there as well. Ivan laughed about the court case to him. Thought it was a great joke. Beattie always thought he was the sort of bloke you'd never cross. That look in his eye. Quiet, and a great worker, but always mysterious.

The DMR had been renamed the Roads and Traffic Authority with the election of the Liberal Government the previous year. The department was re-organised as there weren't as many away jobs any more. The furthest they'd go was Goulburn, but there was a lot of work going on at both ends of the Mittagong bypass. Ivan didn't want to go back to the spray gang, so they put him on the profiler, a giant machine that ripped up the bitumen so you could lay a fresh surface without the road rising forever upwards. One of his first jobs back was up at Gosford. They got called away from there to do the roundabout at Dural. They went there via the Galston Gorge – a route which would later become significant.

On 23 December, all work ceased for the Christmas/New Year break so Ivan Milat had a week's holiday. He had time to kill.

PART TWO

TWENTY-THREE

THE HIGHWAY

Charles Throsby, the youngest son of a noted historian, came to the colony of New South Wales as the surgeon aboard a convict ship in 1802. An apparently humane man, his prisoners were in such unusually good condition upon arrival they were sent straight out to work on the road gangs. It was a great bonus to the man's reputation for, after food and rum, roads were what the colony most sorely wanted. No track extended further than a day's walk from the fourteen-year-old settlement at Sydney Cove.

Granted 1500 acres near Liverpool after he resigned from the colony's medical staff in 1810, Throsby built a house, Glenfield, at a point which was then a frontier, but would become a gateway for travellers heading south out of Sydney.

A seventeen-year-old, locally born lad named Hamilton Hume had, by 1815, become the first white to edge into the country south-west of Sydney into what later became known as the Southern Highlands. In 1817, Throsby convinced Hume to show him around. Throsby had the means, Hume the knowledge.

Governor Macquarie offered Throsby his pick of 1000 acres of any new lands which he discovered. He chose a selection near present-day Moss Vale and became one of the earliest settlers of the district. He made several more journeys with Hume who, along with William Hovell, later became the first white to make the journey overland to Port Phillip, the site of present-day Melbourne.

To Throsby, the Southern Highlands, with its greenery and bracing climate, was more akin to home than the coast, 670 metres below. Macquarie put Throsby in charge of building a road into the district – the forerunner of the present highway. Throsby gave convict gangs extra bread because he expected them to work longer hours.

In 1821, Macquarie granted Throsby another 700 acres for his road-building efforts. He occupied an area which he referred to as being in Belanglo, which was one of the first, if not the first, written references to Belanglo – whose meaning is unclear. It is most likely an Aboriginal word but it could refer to an anglicised version of 'beautiful angel'. In 1828, overcome by depression caused by a drought, falling wool prices and a debt he acquired by going guarantor to a scallywag, Throsby committed suicide at Glenfield. A stain on the floor there – in what is now Australia's fifth oldest house – is said to be the ghostly blood of Throsby.

In the years that followed, the road which ran past Glenfield saw a flood south as bullock trains, large mobs of cattle and fortune-seekers on their way to the goldfields moved to what would become Victoria. The track they used roughly followed the route taken by Hume and Hovell. It became the Great Southern Road but, by the end of the century, had fallen into disrepair as the steam train replaced bullocks as the colony's main mode of heavy transportation. The road remained little better than a track until the rise of the car. In 1928, the Great Southern Road was renamed the Hume Highway as more money was thrown at roads under the weight of the emerging car lobby.

For decades, Australia's most important highway wound around hills and through the middle of towns – one potholed lane each way most of the way. Sections of freeway and overtaking lanes were added in a hodge-podge of planning, but it wasn't until the 1980s that the towns of the Southern Highlands, like Berrima, were to have the constant rumble of trucks and semi-trailers taken from their main streets.

The Mittagong/Berrima bypass rejoined the highway four kilometres north of the Belanglo State Forest. The new 35-kilometre section required 4.8 million cubic metres of excavation, thirty bridges, three interchanges and hard-working men like Ivan Milat to build it. There was little objection from any part of the community. About the only group which might have had a gripe was the gun club that Alex Milat belonged to. It lost its pistol range beneath the landfill, but still supported the road. That was progress. And, anyway, the RTA offered assistance in finding it a new location near the Belanglo State Forest.

Paul 'Bunny' Onions had been in the Royal Navy doing the air-conditioning on ships since he was a kid. He was twenty-three years old and sick of the regimented life. He was discharged just as the recession started to set in, so his prospects weren't great when he returned to live in his parental home in the brown brick terraces of a housing estate in Willenhall, in the industrial West Midlands of England. They call it the Black Country because of the soot that used to cover the area in the days before the Clean Air Act. All the men were said to have had hunches in their backs from leaning into the lathes of the locksmiths' workshops for which the area was famous.

After the navy, Onions couldn't settle down. 'There's nothing doin' here, Mum,' he said one day. 'I might as well be doin' it in the sun.' His mates in the navy had been down to Australia on the *Sirius* during the 1988 Bicentennial. He'd seen the pictures and thought it looked great. Land of milk and honey and all that.

His parents put on a big party at the Brown Jug up the road. They had a cake with the word Bunny written on it, and a toy boomerang on top. His mother hung the boomerang on the lounge room wall as Bunny set off on 8 December 1989. First stop: New Delhi. That was an eye opener. His doubts started immediately. He thought he'd done a lot of travelling with the navy, but in the services everything got done for you. In among the beggars and the smells, the food that didn't taste like a takeaway curry, and so many people, Paul Onions from good-old Willenhall knew he was out of his league. He realised he didn't have a clue about travelling. He booked into a hotel and hardly left it for almost two weeks.

Next stop was Singapore which proved a bit easier – a bit more western – before he headed to Australia three days later, arriving 22 December. This was more like it. He booked into a hostel, Hereford Lodge, in Glebe in Sydney's inner-west. There, he met all these other backpackers who'd been away for over a year and who knew the ropes. A good crowd. There were a couple of retrenched miners from up north of England. They'd been out for a while, and they set him on the right track. It was a world where you judged a person by how long they'd been on the road, living off the land, so to speak. He only brought £500 because he had an ethos of getting in amongst it and working his way round. He had to find work pretty quick, though.

He had been so on-guard before, but now he was dead relaxed. He wandered the streets of Sydney, just soaking up the place. His new mates took him down to Bondi Beach for a backpacker Christmas party where all the young travellers went for a rip-roaring, lager swilling debauch with sand between their toes. It was a party whose legend would grow in backpacker lore. They told him that for New Year's Eve they'd take him to the old part of town, The Rocks, where the original *Sirius* weighed anchor 201 years earlier.

Also planning their entry into the 1990s were Deborah Everist and James Gibson. The pair hadn't known each other long. They'd been introduced when Deborah and her closest friend, Marita, were seeing a band in September. Deborah and James were not really a boyfriend–girlfriend sort of couple, as far as anyone could tell.

Deborah grew up in Frankston on the southern fringes of Melbourne, where the city hugs the beaches of Port Phillip Bay. James – six foot and slim, with long brown hair usually pulled back in a ponytail – still lived with his parents a little further out, at Moorooduc, in a little tin-roofed country house surrounded by a stand of tall trees and old Morris Minors and Minis. His mother, Peggy, had been a nurse in London but came to Australia in the 1960s. His father, Ray, worked for Hastings Council as a road grader, but Ray's long grey hair marked him as an atypical council worker. Despite their modest means, the Gibsons sent their four children to a private school, Woodleigh, an open institution where the rules were few and students were encouraged to do their own thing. When James left there, the freewheeling spirit had hold of him. He deferred an art course for a year to go travelling. He went north, up through Nimbin – an 'alternative' town leftover from the Aquarius Festival of the early seventies and the old hippie trail which had turned into the backpacker trail. He hitched his way to various anti-logging protests up the east coast, sometimes using aliases like James Gordon or Stephen Gordon, a common practice among protesters who constantly faced arrest. Made him hard to trace, too.

He met a lot of people in a short time with his semi-transient ways, and had a wide circle of friends among alternative lifestylers. He moved around quickly and on impulse. Some friends thought of him as being a bit scatty. He apparently once hitched 870 kilometres from Melbourne to Sydney to meet someone, stayed 15–20 minutes, then went home again.

Just after he met Deborah, he went to Hamilton Island resort in Queensland where he tried to get work, but was foiled by the pilots' strike, which dried the island of its tourists. He knew his future was in art, anyway. His bedroom was covered by his own paintings and drawings and he was going to begin studying sculpture at the Chisholm Institute of Technology in March. After his return from Queensland, James started seeing more of Deborah.

Debbie was different. She was five foot four with blue eyes and shoulder-length hair, dyed black. She was in no way an alternative lifestyler. No hippie chick. She liked a warm bed and all the creature comforts. She had started first year of arts and psychology at Monash University, but she wanted to end up in journalism eventually. She had a wry sense of humour and loved to write. She could be wicked and funny. Everyone loved her. She had done some mischievous things, like at the end of Year 12 she was almost expelled because instead of running the school cross-country along the beach, she and a friend caught a bus. It was the sort of thing she did. Nothing serious. She was also one of a group behind an underground school magazine with slanderous caricatures of all the teachers they didn't like. She could have been expelled for that, too, except they never got caught. It was a hoot.

She loved writing. People told her she could be very funny and very sad at the same time. She'd get depressed, like any nineteen-year-old, but nothing chronic, and boys weren't the be all and end all of her existence.

Her hobbies were reading and clothes. Op-shop stuff. She had a thing for hats. It horrified her mother, Patricia. Stuck out in Frankston, oldies didn't see the inner-city fashions, so it made Pat wonder just what on earth her daughter was doing. Deborah shared a flat with Marita in Melbourne where they had some fun, stayed up late and slept all day, lectures permitting. She was free to do what she wanted.

But 1989 wasn't the year it should have been. Deborah's father was diagnosed with cancer. She wasn't committed to her studies and withdrew from university towards the end of the year to go home and manage the house while her mother tended to Dad. She thought maybe she'd start again at Melbourne University next year, when Dad was better; maybe do something with her writing. Life was too short, after all.

Her dad had a touch-and-go operation to clean the cancer out of him. It was declared a success, so Christmas 1989 became a joyous time to look to the future. Debbie's grandfather had died the year before but now the family was together. Stronger. They did the whole presents-under-the-tree thing and life was good. It was a family which knew pain, but which fought back. It was easy to believe that life was back to normal at last.

During James' travels, coming back from Queensland in spring, he had gone to a party at a terrace house in Bourke Street, Surry Hills, in the inner-suburbs of Sydney, eight doors down from the grungy rock'n'roll Hopetoun Hotel. He met a girl at the party, Katherine Sissons, and the two chatted about what interested them most – the environment. They got on well. About a month later, Katherine received a letter from James and in December he phoned her a couple of times. They arranged to meet at Confest – Convergence Festival – near Albury on the New South Wales/Victoria border. It was a celebration of alternative lifestyles with workshops and information tents and stalls selling vegetarian hamburgers, dope cookies and Indian-style spiced tea brewed in milk. James asked Deborah to come along with him, but she wasn't so keen on all the hippie stuff; camping and bucket showers. She told her mother that she probably wouldn't go, but Patricia had seen her work so hard through her father's illness. Now that he was getting better, she urged Debbie to have a holiday.

'Oh, I'm not that keen. I hate these things,' she said.

'It'll do you good. You need a break.' How those words would resonate in Patricia Everist's mind as the worst thing she ever said.

Deborah agreed to go, joking that they'd never get her up a tree singing protest songs. Pat had met James once or twice and quite liked him. There were always so many young people coming around, she forgot who a lot of them were, but she knew she liked James. He didn't seem so alternative to her. After all, he was still living at home.

The mothers, Peggy and Patricia, had never met. Yet, somehow, they both feel worried as they drop their nineteen-year-olds off separately at Frankston Railway Station around 9 a.m. on Thursday, 28 December 1989. Peggy knows James is hitching and doesn't like it one bit. 'There's no worries if you're travelling as a couple,' he tells her. 'You've been watching too much television.'

What can she say? You can't tell them. He doesn't tell her he plans to go to Confest, only to see friends in Sydney. He is wearing his trademark black felt floppy hat, green and black checked shirt and jeans; lugging a much-travelled red and greeny-beige backpack with, among other things, oatmeal, a notebook and camera inside. Peggy Gibson doesn't know how cashed up he is. Just that he has his credit card.

Deborah tells her mother she is getting a lift with friends, but still Patricia feels concern. As far as she knows, Deborah has never hitched and wouldn't be so stupid. Deborah doesn't take much money, $50 or $60, because she only intends to be away for a few days.

It doesn't help Patricia's worrying that within hours of farewelling her daughter, Newcastle, 150 kilometres north of Sydney, is hit by the most destructive earthquake ever to strike Australia. It eases her mind, then, that Deborah rings home from Sydney on the evening of the 29th, with James audible in the background.

'Hi, Ma, we've arrived safely. I knew you'd be in a panic until you heard from us,' she says. 'Don't worry, we're nowhere near Newcastle. We had a trip on the harbour today and we'll be heading off and I'll send a postcard and ring.'

'Don't worry about a postcard, you'll be home before it gets here,' her mother says.

'You know how I love writing.'

Deborah doesn't mention that the friends from Surry Hills who James had arranged to meet have gone without them. James' plan was for them all to go down together – turning a simple 400 kilometre journey from Frankston to Walwa, 60 kilometres east of Albury, into a 1400 kilometre odyssey. His friends had waited until Friday morning, 29 December, before heading off. They just missed each other.

Katherine Sissons and her friend Mark Wilson hitch the 560 kilometres to Walwa in a day. The festival hasn't really started when they get there. People are still putting up tents and only a few stalls are open.

Deborah rings her friend Marita, in good spirits. Marita is off to India and she wants to say goodbye. Deborah says she is thinking of not going to university next year, after all, but maybe moving to Sydney to work for a year.

She and James crash in the lounge room. Next morning, the flatmate, Stephanie Wilson, encounters James preparing to leave some time between 9 a.m. and 9.30 a.m. 'How are you getting there?' she asks.

'Hitching.'

'Best of luck, we'll see you some time in the future.' She doesn't see them to the door and doesn't see them go, James in his distinctive hat, Deborah in a sleeveless Nick Cave and the Bad Seeds T-shirt.

Saturday, 30 December 1989 is a pleasant day, fresh in the city when they leave, but getting warm at Liverpool and hot as they go further inland. Emergency workers are still trying to reach the bodies of six people trapped in the rubble of the Newcastle Workers Club. All hope of finding anyone alive has faded.

Down at Confest, Katherine and Mark wonder where James and his friend could be.

TWENTY-FOUR

1990

THE VOID

Patricia Everist is beside herself with worry because Debbie promised to call her on 30 December. She is good at calling so as each moment of the new year passes, Patricia's fear grows deeper. Pat decides to ring James' mother, Peggy Gibson, on New Year's Day or the day after to ask if she's heard anything.

Peggy isn't so worried. 'Look, they're probably somewhere where she can't ring,' she tells Pat, who she's never met. James has been away before, up in the hills and through the obscure, alternative-lifestyle country of northern New South Wales, and he always calls eventually. The longest he's gone without making contact is about two weeks, so Peggy is sure she'll hear from him soon.

Pat tries to contact all Deborah's friends to see if they've heard anything. Half are away on holidays and the others haven't heard a thing. The days pass without word and Peggy Gibson begins to take on all Pat's fears. Peggy is now ringing Sydney, too, trying to pin down James' friends, but so many of them are away, enjoying summer. One of the calls is to Kathy Sissons' home at Warrawee. Pat speaks to Kathy's mother who tells her that James rang looking for her daughter and said he was hitching to Confest.

By 15 January, the women can wait no longer. Together they go to the Frankston Police Station. It is not a serious case in the eyes of the police – two nineteen-year-olds off on a bit of a skylark. If they investigated every such case, they'd be doing nothing else, especially in mid-summer. The police quote the mothers statistics about all the thousands of people reported missing each year. Eighty-six per cent turn up within a fortnight, they say.

But when James doesn't show up for his sister Mary Ann's wedding on 21 January – three weeks – Peggy and her husband Ray know it is serious. James and his sister get on so well and he promised to be there. Something is terribly wrong.

Paul Onions' visa is good for six months working in Australia, but he learns from the folklore of the hostel that if he gets to like the place he can always overstay a little. What he hasn't counted on is the recession closing in on Australia just as bad as, if not worse than, home. He potters around a bit looking for jobs, but it is pretty tight. Towards the end of January, the 500 quid he brought with him is draining away, out of the beer tap and down the urinal.

He thinks fruit picking looks an easy way into work, and so announces to his mates that he's going down the Riverina. They have a good laugh at that. 'It's too bloody hard,' one of them says.

'I'm running out of money, mate,' Paul explains. They offer to tide him over until he finds something in Sydney, but Paul tells them it's time to see the country, meet the locals.

'You'll be back by the end of the week,' predicts one of the lads.

Paul plans to go to Melbourne by bus then head back up to the fruit-growing areas, but on the way to buy his ticket, he runs into a guy he knows who tells him he's mad. 'You don't want to go by bus. You want to hitchhike. You meet loads of Australians. Great people. I've just done it. Got taken home for dinner, met their daughters, everything. It's brilliant.'

He doesn't need much convincing. He goes straight back to the hostel and starts packing. His mates come out for a farewell drink and help him piss away a few more quid before he sets off bright and early next day, 25 January 1990.

Paul looks at the map and sees the Hume Highway is the straightest way to Melbourne, and that Liverpool looks like the first town out of Sydney to get onto it. He catches a bus to Central Railway, then a train which takes him from the old inner-city, the harbour, skyscrapers and Victorian terrace houses, all stations to post-war suburbia. The backyards he looks down into get bigger and the houses – all weatherboard, fibro and aluminium cladding – get flimsier. The double-decker train cuts through large open playing fields, blocks of blond and red-brick flats, warehouses, stormwater drains and dobs of industrial ugly.

Out of the postcard, into where the people live. He goes by the bottom of Campbell Hill Road; past the Vietnamese signs of Cabramatta; the Ukrainian club; the Austro-German Club to Liverpool – 30 kilometres from the city and three degrees hotter.

Paul gets there in the stinking heat. He's expecting some little hick town from *Crocodile Dundee*, so the bus interchange and mirrored office buildings are disappointing. He thought there'd be a trickle of cars and a lift would come dead easy. He is about forty-five years too late and it makes him sad for the world. The cars have taken over everywhere. Australia is the last place that should be like this.

'Where's the Hume Highway?' he asks two old ladies.

'That's it just there,' they say, pointing up the road to an intersection 400 metres away. Just a normal big road thick with cars. What a disappointment. He walks there and drops his army rucksack containing the basics – jeans, shirts, jumper, a camera and a Sony Walkman – by the side of the road. He sticks out his finger. Nothing happens. No great people. No dinners. No daughters. An hour of nothing. Stinking hot nothing.

He decides to start walking in the hope the traffic will thin, but after maybe another half hour of slowly dehydrating in the fumes and humidity, he sees a red sign in the distance. That's it. He'll go as far as the sign, see if he can get a drink, then he'll pack it in.

As the one-time bullock track to his right rumbles with six lanes of traffic, and the ghostly stains on the floor of Charles Throsby's old home lie just 200 metres to his left, Paul is stuck in the here and now. And it's lousy. He reaches the red sign, part of a little shopping centre. He goes straight for the newsagency to get a drink, his pack still on, and has finished it before he gets back out the door. He is wondering what he'll do now that hitching has proved such a disaster. A strong-looking guy approaches. 'Where you headed? Do you need a lift?' he asks.

'Yeah, mate, yeah. I'm going to Melbourne,' Paul tells him.

'Fine. I'm going to Canberra.'

Yes, yes, yes, Paul is thinking, likening his success to chatting up a bird after a night of failure, just as they're calling last drinks. 'I was just about to get a train,' he tells the guy, beaming.

'That's my four-wheel drive over there.'

This is even better. Four-wheel drives are still rare in England. And the bloke looks just like Dennis Lillee with this bloody moustache. Or the other Aussie cricketer, Merv Hughes. Paul's first encounter with an Australian was during a cricket test at Edgbaston when he was a kid. Dennis Lillee, the legendary fast bowler, was fielding in front of him and his mates, and they gave the big man a bit of lip. Lillee turned around, dead-cool like, and winked at them.

This dark-haired guy has the look of a fast bowler, too. He looks big to Paul – who is only five foot six – maybe five foot ten to six feet, wearing a T-shirt, shorts and sunglasses. The guy goes into the shop and says he'll be out in a minute. Paul walks over to the vehicle and waits for him, laughing: I've got Dennis Lillee and a four-wheel drive. Magic. And it's a 'real Australian', with the accent and everything. Paul hadn't met any after five weeks in Sydney.

Paul opens the passenger door, climbs up on the running board and throws his pack over the seat into the back. It is the first time he's ever seen a bullbar and the sheepskin seat covers seem a bit scruffy inside such a nice car. Paul introduces himself and the big guy says his name is Bill. As the pair drive down the highway, past The Crossroads and onto the freeway, Bill is full of questions: how long you been in Australia? Who you just left? Meeting up with anyone tonight? Anybody know where you're heading? Where's your family? How long till you're due home? What did you do for a living? Paul answers away innocently enough at first, but after a while the questions start to seem a bit too inquisitive. Still, he is happy to chat.

Bill tells him he lives locally, around Liverpool, works on the roads and is on a bit of a holiday. He is heading for Canberra to stay with a few friends. His family is originally from Yugoslavia, and he is divorced.

Paul had been feeling tired but sparks up when the country starts to open up. It is his first look at the Australian bush. It's great really, that first hour, as they rise up into the highlands. But, at around the hour mark, something about Bill changes. He asks Paul if he had any special forces training in the navy. No. Then Bill becomes anti-British, ranting about the occupation in Northern Ireland. His voice and manner seem strange.

Just trying to make conversation, Paul says something about seeing so many Asians in Australia and Bill starts going off about all these fucking gooks. Paul is getting edgy, but there's a part of his brain saying, 'calm down, this guy has given you a lift, you should be happy about it'.

Some time between 2 p.m. and 3 p.m., they come to Mittagong.

Sitting at traffic lights on a fork in the road, Bill really changes. He stops talking. Paul can't get a word out of him, so stops trying, but senses that he's angry, weird. All the gaps in conversation are filled by paranoia creeping into Paul's head. He wants to put it back where it came from.

They are soon back on the dual carriageway and the steady rhythm of the road is making Paul sleepy. He is absolutely knackered, really tired, but isn't going to allow himself to nod. He wonders if he is being so wary because it's his first time hitching. He looks at the driver differently. The grey flecks in the hair. The strong mouth with lips which protrude a little in profile. His build. Huge biceps. God he looks strong. Seems a little bit older than Paul's first impression, maybe mid-thirties to early forties.

Paul had slept on so many train stations coming home from the naval bases at Plymouth or Portsmouth every weekend, he was used to being guarded and keeping one eye open. The navy also taught him to read people and to expect a bad side in everyone – something that comes out readily in the close quarters of a ship. Now he is watching Bill drive strangely, slowing down, looking up to the rear-view mirror, accelerating.

'When you get this far out of Sydney,' Bill says, 'you start to lose the radio.' It's the first thing he's said in ages, but it sounds fair enough. 'I'll pull over and get some tapes out of the boot.'

That doesn't sound right. There are a load of tapes between the two of them in the console. Bill keeps looking in the mirror as he waits for a place to pull over. Paul is getting edgier, but keeps telling himself to calm down and not be stupid. They pull up just over a rise and Bill gets out. He is messing around in the back, so Paul decides to get out, stretch his legs and check out what the geezer is up to. That makes Bill real stormy: 'What are you getting out of the car for? Get back in there.'

'I'm just stretching me legs, Bill, you know, just want to stretch my legs a bit.' His adrenalin is pumping as he tells himself to get a grip. Calm down and deal with this. But stronger instincts are at work, and all those questions Bill was asking earlier are now thick in his head. Who does know I'm out here? Special forces? Timetables? And what's with the tapes, his mood, and all this messin' about? Paul starts looking to see how much traffic is on the road. A couple of cars. It's pretty quiet. His mind is racing: 'How do I get out of this? Am I being stupid?'

Not wanting to inflame the situation, Paul climbs back into his sheepskin seat, like Bill told him. 'You're just being paranoid. See if it's just you,' he tells himself as he reaches for his seat belt. 'It'll be okay.'

Bill gets back in the car and buckles up. Paul instantly calms. 'I'm all right. I'm all right.' Then, in a second, Bill is back out: 'I'll just have a look under the seat one more time.'

He fiddles about under the driver's seat and quickly comes back up with a black revolver. 'This is a robbery. Do you know what this is?'

Paul sees the gun for only an instant – a distinctive thing with copper-tipped bullets in the chamber and a brown handle. He knows a little about guns from the forces. He knows to respect them, but he isn't as scared as he would have thought. 'Calm down, Bill. What's going on, mate? What are you doing? Calm down.'

'Shut the fuck up and keep your seat belt on.' Bill is aggressive, but in control. He has the edge. He looks under the seat again and pulls out a bag full of dirty rope. That scares Paul more than the gun. All the earlier conversations, the oddities, and the fact he only has a smelly rucksack. It adds to a simple, instantaneous conclusion... This is no robbery. This is serious. He hears himself thinking: 'Fuck you. You make the decision. Shoot me, or I'm outta here.'

He goes for his seat belt.

'Put it back on,' Bill snarls, but Paul's feet are already on the ground, and he's legging it up the road. It feels like suicide, but he isn't prepared to face the alternative. The next few seconds will become a dream scene. Something black and white, grainy, out of focus and out of sequence. There are words: 'Stop or I'll shoot.' But no dialogue in the *verité* of his mind. He's heading towards the back of the vehicle, towards oncoming traffic. A shot cracks the air. He doesn't look back.

His mind just has him running. Zigzagging. Waving. A car slams on its brakes, and he sees a face looking blankly at him from behind the windscreen, before it speeds off. The next goes past too, then the next and maybe another in quick succession. He doesn't feel badly towards them. Maybe it's now he turns and Bill is right there. They struggle. The bastard doesn't seem so strong; doesn't seem so in control. Now Paul is away, his shirt sleeve is torn. Looking back, the bastard is standing by the car grinning like he knows his quarry has nowhere to go. He's got that dead cocky look of control back again. 'Get back in here you,' he says, dismissively, or maybe Paul is just thinking he says that.

To Paul, Australia seems so massive, like he'll have to run for ever and ever to get away. He's in the middle of nowhere, there are no houses in sight, and there is no way out. He stops running. He looks at the bastard – maybe 20 metres away – at the grin, so casual, telling him: 'No one'll stop. Get back in here!' He's about to do what the grin says. Go meekly to his death. The grin has won, he knows . . . unless he can stop the very next car. Doesn't matter if it runs him over.

Joanne Berry is driving from Mittagong to Canberra with her four kids – aged ten, nine, and twins aged three. Her sister, Gay Barnes, is in the passenger seat of the cream Tarago van. They have been at their mother's place for lunch, leaving just before 3 p.m. Berry notices a car stopped up the road with two men standing at the back of it. She starts braking as one of them runs onto the road waving his hands at a car up ahead, like he's trying to get help. The other man chases him across the southbound lanes and tackles him onto the grassy median strip. They struggle there. They roll over maybe three or four times. The first man struggles free and comes at her waving again. She isn't going to stop, but he jumps right in front of her. She brakes quickly, one-and-a-half football fields from the parked car, she'd estimate.

The guy is distressed, and close to tears as he comes to her window, pleading. 'Please help. Please help. He's got a gun. Help me!'

'No. Get away. Get away. Look, I've got all these kids. I can't.' She doesn't want any trouble. Suddenly, the guy rips open the door. He dives in and puts the button down.

'Get out,' she yells, with the children crying in the back.

'No way. I'm going nowhere. He's got a gun. Believe me.'

Paul looks up at the driver, sees her attitude change. He sees her speak to the person next to her – something about a police station – then she jams the van into reverse. Berry looks up as she reverses and sees the other man running back up the road to his car. His arms aren't swinging like a normal person running. They're held in tight, perhaps carrying something.

At a safe distance, she turns the van right and bashes her way across the sapling-covered median strip. As they bounce away, the bodies of Deborah Everist and James Gibson lie about five kilometres ahead to the west, three-and-a-half weeks decomposed in a grave of leaf and twig.

Paul is hiding behind the seat. He briefly dares pull his head up for a look and sees the bastard standing on the side of the road maybe fifty metres away, watching, weighing the situation with that stupid grin, his sunglasses off for the first time. They turn right into the north-bound lane and Berry drives hard towards Berrima Police Station. Not hard enough for Paul, who thinks the guy will come after them. It is a tense ride. There is no conversation beyond: 'Are you okay?'

'Yeah. Let's get there fast.'

They're annoyed when they arrive at the police station to find it closed. Berry takes him to Bowral instead. There, he speaks to Constable Janet Nicholson at the desk. He is so distressed she can hardly understand what he's saying. He calms down and gets his story out, but becomes upset again when he shows her his ripped T-shirt. She asks him about the gun, and as he tries to explain, she pulls out her service revolver, a .38 Smith & Wesson. It looks similar, he says, but can't say for sure. He tells her that Bill stole his backpack, camera, airline ticket and passport. All he has left is his MasterCard and a little cash in his pocket. He makes a statement, then a more senior copper pulls him into a side room. There are pictures all over the wall.

'These are all missing people,' the policeman tells him in a fatherly lecture kind of way. 'You don't realise, Australia's a big place and there are hundreds of people who are missing out there. I just want you to realise how lucky you are. You might just have become one of them.'

The realisation hits Paul hard. 'Sorry. It is me first time, like. Won't be doing it again.'

'Good . . . Look, hitchhiking, you might think it's okay, mate, but them days are gone. We could be looking for you for years. No one would ever find ya. It'd be a needle in a haystack.'

'You're right, mate. Sorry.'

Paul hears the report go over the police radio and one of the coppers explains the police codes: be on the lookout for a silver four-wheel drive with a driver that looks like Merv Hughes. Wanted in connection with a robbery. A firearm was discharged. It appears to Paul that they're taking it seriously. The older copper tells him then, though, that there is little chance of finding 'Bill'. 'You don't get the numberplate, there's not much we can do. He could be halfway to the Victorian border by now.' They give him $20 to get back to Sydney and he is thrilled with the kindness. He hasn't asked for it, but he needs it.

Nothing more is done in pursuit of his attacker, but Paul would never carry any grudge against the Bowral police. He thinks they had little to go on, and even if they got him, there'd be little evidence. He got himself in a bad situation and he got himself out. That was all.

He is still edgy though when he arrives at the Bowral Railway Station. He is shitting himself, really, standing there on the platform with a clear view in both directions, feeling way too exposed. The train eventually comes and there are these two friendly blokes sitting near him in the carriage and he won't speak to them. They sledge the little Pom all the way to Sydney.

He gets back to the hostel where he knows a ribbing is waiting for him. The boys see him and their eyes light up. 'One day?' they jeer. 'Too tough for ya, Paul?' They're hysterical with laughter. He tells them what happened. Don't matter. It is too good an opportunity to pass up. The ribbing goes on for weeks, although he does notice that whenever anybody says they're going hitchhiking, people in the hostel tell them: 'Hey, go and see Paul first.'

A lot of people come and ask him about it. Even then, he doesn't tell them outright not to hitch. 'I was a bit stupid, really, mouthing me head off,' he says. 'Just lie your head off. Every man and his dog said goodbye to ya. And every man and his dog's going to meet you tonight, on the beer for a piss-up . . . You know everybody in Australia, the Prime Minister, everybody.'

He goes to the British High Commission in Sydney to get another passport and maybe some financial assistance. His own government is less helpful than the New South Wales Police Service. They won't give him a penny, but an old lady in the queue behind him says, 'Oh love, you poor darling, here's $20.' That's two days' food or lodging. After all he's been through, it feels like $200. 'You've just made up me mind,' he tells her. 'I'm staying.'

'Hope you have a great time now.'

'I will. I'm going crazy now.'

And he does . . . but not quite the way he meant.

His mates loan him some cash and a few bits of clothing. He has a couple of days on the beer still weighing up whether to go home. It's January. It's sunny. 'They'll all laugh at me for coming back to the shite weather.' That's it. He'll get a job and he'll bloody well have a good time.

His girlfriend, Michelle, back in England, is onto him wanting to come out, but he keeps telling her to wait. He can't get it out of his head that if she'd been with him that day they'd both be dead. She is getting annoyed with him, thinking he doesn't want her to come. He tells no one at home what happened except his brother Simon. He doesn't want his mother worrying. Mrs Onions won't find out for years.

He finds a job at a flour mill in Pyrmont. Best job he ever had. He meets his second real Australian, Bruce Hawker, a lad just off a sheep farm and on his first visit to the big city, suffering more culture shock than Paul. Hawker is a kid in a lolly shop. He gets jobs and loses them straightaway because he's out having too much fun. Paul has as much fun just watching him.

The families of James Gibson and Deborah Everist have entered a vacuum known only to those whose loved ones have fallen off the face of the globe. Every time the phone rings, they jump. Every car that pulls up outside represents hope or, if it looks like a police car, fear. Days blur into each other as one by one the options, the plans, the possibilities are tried and proven failures. They survive because they have to, because there is always hope, no matter how slim, no matter how unreasonable. Patricia Everist already knows in her head that Deborah is dead, but she won't give up.

The two families hire a private detective but that comes to nothing. Deborah's dad takes a turn for the worse. His operation wasn't a success after all. The doctors say he only has months to live. Thank God Pat is able to keep the news about Debbie from him. The cancer has spread to his brain. As he slips in and out of lucidity, he'll ask, 'Where's Deb?'

'She's on holidays. She'll be here soon.' It is awful.

He wants to die at home, and needs constant attention, and Patricia feels like she should be doing more to help Peggy Gibson with the search, but Patricia's life has descended into hell. The only consolation is that as the cancer eats out more of her husband's capacity for thought, it becomes less likely he'll ever know about Deb.

Peggy runs the search. She and her two older sons go up the Hume dropping into truck stops wearing MISSING T-shirts emblazoned with a picture of James. They have three posters made up and photocopied: one with four pictures of James, another with two pictures of Deborah and a third with a picture of each. They plaster them on walls and windows up and down the highway; signposts to another tragedy. Police have started taking the case more seriously now, and the families are in contact with the missing persons detectives in Sydney.

Missing Persons week in March enables Peggy to generate the first vital publicity for the cause. PARENTS CAN ONLY WAIT AND WONDER says the headline in the Melbourne *Herald Sun*.

> **WHEN Mrs Peggy Gibson cleans her Moorooduc home she stops at the door of her youngest son's bedroom and wonders... Wonders whether she should tidy up the mess any teenager makes; wonders what to do with his mounting pile of letters; wonders whether her son, James, is still alive.**

Then, on 13 March, the whole nature of the case changes. Switchboard operator Wendy Dellsperger sees a red pack by the side of Galston Road – a narrow hairpin route which winds down and up Galston Gorge, 30 kilometres north-west of Sydney, running from Dural to Hornsby. The pack is on the north-western side, leaning against a sandstone wall. She thinks maybe a school kid has lost it. She stops on the narrow road and throws the weathered and mouldy pack into her boot. Lying on the ground near the pack are some bread wrappings. Later that day she looks inside the pack, but the top has been cut off where she expects to find a name tag. Its only contents are a black plastic pen and an unopened can of sardines. She also sees some dirt and pine needles. That is odd, she thinks, there are no pine trees for miles from where she found it. At home that night, she takes a better look inside the bag. It looks like the owner has planned to outwit any thieves because down the bottom in a boot compartment she sees his name in marker pen – 'Gibson 80 Loader Rd, Moorooduc, Vic, 3933, Australia' – and a telephone number. Dellsperger rings the number the next afternoon. Peggy answers.

This is important – and terrible, says Peggy. 'My son's missing. Give the pack to police urgently.'

She gives it to Hornsby police. Later that day, Constable Guy Nicholson goes to the approximate spot where Dellsperger found it, but finds no more clues.

After talking to Mrs Dellsperger, Peggy rings Patricia Everist, who bursts into tears because it seems to confirm all their worst fears. The runaway theory is now even less plausible. The next day, 15 March, Ray Gibson and his son Peter head to Sydney to formally ID the backpack.

Steve Barrett is working police rounds for Channel Nine News, Australia's most watched news program, on a quiet Sunday looking for a story. He rings his mate Detective Barry Keeling at Northern Region Major Crime at Chatswood. There was a serial killer loose on the North Shore who had killed five elderly women in the previous twelve months and Barrett was fishing around for stories. (John Wayne Glover was caught next day having claimed a sixth victim. Barrett and the authors both wrote books about the case.)

'What have you got, mate?'

'Mate, we've found a backpack at Galston Gorge that comes from Melbourne.'

'Why have you got it at homicide?'

'It belongs to a couple from down there and we can't find 'em.'

Keeling had smelt trouble. Two other couples had disappeared from the Hornsby area without trace – Michelle Pope, eighteen, and boyfriend Stephen Lapthorne, twenty-one, on 25 August 1978 in their green panel van, and on 12 January 1979 Anneke Adriaansen, nineteen, and boyfriend Alan Fox, twenty-one, from nearby, vanished after hitch-hiking up the north coast. There was no link between the three couples, only the locality, and police didn't want to draw any long bows.

It is a slow day. Barrett does a grave-fears-are-held story. It goes out around the country and the publicity kicks on from there. Within a day or two, Steve Mangan, a video company director, remembers the camera he found while riding his bike through the gorge training for a triathlon. He saw it sitting on a rocky slope near a small bridge. He kept it and didn't think much more about it until this. He checks his training diary to help the police with the date – 31 December. The day after Gibson and Everist disappeared.

They were going south down the Hume. How could the pack and the camera have come to be in this obscure little pocket of bushland on the north-western outskirts of Sydney so soon after?

Police know it looks bad and mount a search of the gorge on 29 April 1990. One hundred and fifty police and State Emergency Services volunteers go through looking for more gear – and two bodies. They find nothing. But local resident Peter Butcher, the live-in manager of the Crosslands youth camp, tells them he saw a red backpack on the side of the road. He was certain he'd seen it on the Hornsby side of the gorge about January. He didn't know it had been found on the opposite slope, the Galston side. Consulting his diary, he put the date at between New Year's Day and 5 January. He remembered because he had a group staying at the youth camp around that time when another rowdy group of hikers came through. A bit later, he was driving down Galston Road when he first saw the pack. It stuck out like a sore thumb, leaning against a culvert rail. There was clothing and a towel draped over the rail like they were on display. He didn't stop because it was too dangerous on the single-lane road. So dangerous that signs warned hikers not to use the road. The pack stayed there for two months. The clothing and towel fell to the ground, then disappeared.

Three weeks after his attack, Paul Onions is thinking this geezer done him a favour, getting rid of all the gear he overpacked. Don't need half of it. The lads give him a little Adidas sports bag and a few T-shirts. Anything else he needs, he buys. Anyway, after a month or two, Onions feels he has some stability back, and tells his girlfriend Michelle that she should come out. When she arrives, he has a go at her for packing too much. They travel up the east coast by bus and each time he gets off he has a little giggle at all the backpackers struggling under their huge packs.

He hires a four-wheel drive and they do Fraser Island and drive along the 100 kilometre beach. They see dingoes, and brumbies whose hooves have evolved soft and splayed to cope with the sand. They go inland to the rainforests and the sandy lakes full of little turtles. This is Australia. Brilliant. They go by bus up to Port Douglas, and across to Katherine Gorge, down the middle and back to Sydney. He wants to stay, but Michelle has to get back to her job so they leave for home via the United States on 21 June, the day before his visa runs out.

As much as Paul thinks he has put it all behind him, they are in a cab in New York which breaks down in a tunnel under the Hudson River. Subconsciously, Bill is with him again. Paul loses the plot, freaks out, sure they are about to be mugged. Still, he thinks the attack hasn't affected him. Over the next year, however, he starts getting sick for no apparent reason. He doesn't attribute it to the highway robbery. If he thought about it more, he might call it post-traumatic stress disorder, but he doesn't think of that until much later.

Deborah's father dies without seeing his daughter again, unaware she is gone. Deborah's friend Marita – who left for India two days after they talked on 29 December – phones the Everists' house to tell Debbie of her travels. Patricia gives her the news. Marita confirms all of what Pat has already told investigators. Deborah doesn't hitchhike, wouldn't camp out, certainly wouldn't have gone feral. But, she adds, if Deborah did hitch, she wouldn't tell Pat. Marita goes through Deborah's wardrobe. Just about everything is there. She knows Deborah wouldn't go far without a good wardrobe.

Patricia Everist's stress is constant. She has been unable to go into Deborah's room for months. Deborah's cat sits outside Deb's door each night, waiting to be let in to curl up around her feet. Patricia's moods swing from hope to despair. Her imagination, from positive to the most awful scenarios. Every time the phone rings: 'Please God, let it be her. I don't care what she's done.'

The families check to see if Deborah and James vote in the federal election. They haven't. 'Deb is a mad voter,' Patricia tells a local reporter. 'Politics is her best subject at school.' Her grandmother's eighty-third birthday passes on 24 July 1990 without Deborah. Every milestone she misses just adds to the despair.

There are more newspaper stories. In one, the reporter, Paul Amy, notes that Peggy Gibson talks about James in the present tense. She poses for the camera absently fondling a trophy James won playing Dungeons and Dragons.

'He's very good at it,' she says quietly.

'Yes, I like a game of Dungeons and Dragons myself,' the photographer, Ric Clarke, replies.

'Well, when James comes home, I'll have to give you a ring, Ric, and you can pit your skills against him.'

A year after Deborah and James disappear, James' twenty-four-year-old brother Chris, and his sister, Mary Ann, twenty-six, go to Confest wearing the MISSING T-shirts. They come back with nothing. Patricia has bought Deborah a Christmas present. Just in case.

TWENTY-FIVE

Early 1991

HORNETS AND WASPS

Wally's ex-wife, Maureen, hadn't had anything to do with the Milats since 1980, and nothing to do with Wally since the divorce in 1982. She had been very good friends with Bill's wife, Carol, but Wally and Bill were brothers and after all the garbage that went down with Wally, she had to become a single person again, something she hadn't been since she was sixteen.

Maureen stayed in Sydney for a few years, got involved with a policeman, but that didn't work out. Then, in 1985, she headed up to South West Rocks, 480 kilometres north of Sydney, where she and Wally had gone for holidays back in the seventies and where her parents were now retired. She had in the last few years met a good man, Russell, a chef, and was engaged to be married. The last thing she expected to see was Ivan Milat on her doorstep in Gothic Street.

He hadn't changed at all. Maureen looked over his shoulder. 'Where's Karen?' she asked, expecting to see her coming from the car. 'How is she?'

'I don't know,' he said. 'We're divorced.'

Maureen was shocked. She had been happy for him and Karen. It seemed like Ivan had at last found someone who he could spend his life with. He was such a good fellow, she was sure they'd have a good life together.

He came in, and she made him coffee. She hadn't forgotten that he had it in a white mug, black, no sugar, but she made the mistake of using a plunger. 'Can I have a real cup of coffee,' he complained. He wanted instant because it came out hotter. They chatted about old times and about the family. He told her that Shirley was divorced from Gerry

Soire. That Wally and his new wife Lisa were expecting a baby. He told her he had gone the heavy on this bloke who got one of his nieces pregnant. 'I think he's going to behave himself now,' he said. 'He'll do the right thing by her.'

She asked about his divorce. 'I was at work and came home and she was gone with everything . . .' He thought about Jason a lot, he said. 'I hope he can find me . . . I'd like to see him. I'm the only father he'll know . . . You think he'll ever contact me?'

'Yeah, well they get curious, just like what my kids have been through. If you haven't really offended or hurt the mother, of course he'll want to find you one day. I always told my kids, "You're not going to find your father until you're eighteen. I went through too much to get your custody. I've brought you up. He hasn't helped me at all. When you're eighteen, you're an adult, you go off on your own terms."'

Then Ivan told her about Karen. 'I tracked her down to her parents' house and set fire to the garage. I went to another street and saw the fire engines and all of the commotion.' He sounded amused, and it was hard to tell if he was being serious, but she thought he was. It was night, he said, and he poured petrol all over her parents' car.

'You're an idiot,' she told him. 'Jason won't want to see you now. He won't respect you, because you've done this to his grandparents, more than his mother. He'll hate you for that.' Ivan sat there without comment, but she could tell he didn't like being told basic truths. She told him how her own daughter Susan had become more curious about Wally because she was too young to be affected by all the troubles like Robert had been. Robert didn't want to know about Wally.

They talked for about three hours. He and Maureen always had an affinity. He told her he was in the fourth week of a six-week holiday, on his way to visit Mick and his wife Sherie, up at Nanango, 200 kilometres north-west of Brisbane. 'And I'm going to see a lady friend on the way.'

Maureen had some fun with this. 'Who is it?' she hassled him. 'Come on. You can tell me. Who?'

He reluctantly confessed: 'It's Marilyn. She's at Austral Eden.' Maureen knew all about Ivan and Marilyn, but was surprised to find Marilyn was living in the tiny village only a half hour's drive away.

Maureen walked him out to his car about five o'clock and her strong sense of family history demanded she should get a picture of the occasion. Not that the kids seemed to care that they didn't have any pictures of that side of the family. Susan had already come in, paid Uncle Ivan no attention and left. Robert didn't want to be in the picture, so he took the shot of Ivan and Maureen in a light embrace in front of Ivan's Nissan Patrol.

'That's a nice car,' she commented.

'Yeah, it's okay'. She wrote the date, 9 January 1991, in her diary and sent a copy of the picture to Ivan.

After Marilyn split from Ivan in 1989, she found a bloke and married him on the rebound. They moved to Austral Eden, but the marriage was on the rocks by the time Ivan caught up with her that Wednesday night. She had been living alone for two months. Ivan didn't tell her he'd been to see Maureen first.

They hadn't seen each other for eighteen months. She still wanted commitment. He still wanted passion. As much as she wanted him, she couldn't give him one without the other. Ivan moved on the next day, heading north, and as soon as he left, Marilyn decided to move back to the Central Coast to her caravan by the sea. Work had dried up in the Kempsey area and Lynise was pregnant and having problems.

Born on 8 June 1969, Simone Schmidl had been such a friendly little girl. She had this bright, open personality. When she was young, her favourite television characters were Pumuckl, a cheeky character who lived with a carpenter in Bavaria; and Biena Maja, a trusting little bee which went off having adventures in the forest, naively encountering all the baddies – the wasps and the hornets – and ultimately triumphing.

She lived in an apartment in Regensburg, a beautiful old town on the edge of the Bavarian Forest with its spectacular autumnal reds and browns. She first went overseas, to Canada, with her family when she was eleven. It seemed natural that Simone would come to love travelling and the outdoors.

Her father, Herbert Schmidl, a bus driver, saw this self-confident woman – a traveller, studying her destinations intently in books and videos – and he could not help but wonder how his blue-eyed daughter had bridged the gap from childhood into adulthood so quickly. She still trusted people. She was still outgoing.

She had all her *klamotten* – her skis and pushbikes and ice skates – in the cellar of the apartment building. She skied in Austria. She swam, rode, jogged and played handball for the Regensburg athletic club, Regensburger Turverein, which took her all over Bavaria. She made time to watch TV and eat out – Italian and Greek – with her friends. She was, in short, making the most of modern life.

She went back to Canada with a friend in 1986, the year her parents separated. She moved in with her mother, but she visited Herbert regularly. Later, he got her a job in a business consultancy as secretary to the woman who became his second wife, Helena. But Simone was well and truly bitten by the travel bug and went back to Canada in 1989 and then on to Alaska where she met some Australians on a four-wheel-drive holiday. Simi was always the most adventurous of the group, always wanting to push on and explore more. At the end of a month or so, the group broke up, exchanging addresses, full of vague intentions to catch up again.

In the middle of 1990, Simone declared to her parents that she was tossing her job in to go travelling in Australia and catch up with her new Australian friends. She wrote to Kristine Murphy who wrote back that she had a place to crash.

As the date approached, Herbert took his daughter to his preferred camping store, Sports Tahedl in Regensburg. The salesman, Georg Wolff, recognised Herbert, but did not know the young lady with him. Wolff would remember their visit because the tent Herbert wanted had to be ordered from the manufacturer. As Simone wandered around the shop, Wolff asked Simone where she was heading. 'Australia,' she said, picking a backpack for its snappy colours – lilac and pink. She also bought a sleeping bag, and a band to tie up her sleeping mat.

She was really relaxed about the trip because all the books were telling her how safe it was and she also knew people there, so it was hard to imagine any problems, but still Herbert warned her against taking lifts with strangers. She promised she wouldn't. He was happy to see her go to a safe place.

He farewelled Simone at Regensburg Railway Station at the end of September 1990. He helped load her pack on the train. 'Simone, take care of yourself. If something happens to you, I am so far away, I can't do anything for you.'

'Papa, you take care of yourself. Besides, even if anything happens to me, you will find out about it because they will send me back in a black coffin.' She meant it as a joke. She caught the train to Frankfurt Airport and flew to Australia. In transit, at Athens Airport, she met a fellow German, Jeanette Muller, twenty. The two hooked up to travel together. Within a week of arriving in Sydney on 1 October 1990, they decided to hitch the 870 kilometres to Melbourne. They were told that the way to go was a train to Liverpool, then a walk to the Hume Highway. They had a great time getting there, meeting some good people on the way.

They stayed in Melbourne for a week, bought a Datsun and drove it back to Sydney, staying overnight at the Murphys' home in Guildford, before setting off for the long drive up to north Queensland, camping out to save money. The distance was the equivalent of driving from their homes to Moscow on secondary roads – with sun. They returned to Melbourne in mid-November staying one day then leaving the car with some friends to sell, before hitching back to Sydney, well-tanned and ready for more adventure. They stayed overnight at the Murphys' and left for New Zealand the next day, 20 November.

The girls headed from Auckland to Rotorua where they bought identical plastic green army water bottles. Simone wrote her nickname, Simi, on hers with a marker pen. She called her father just before Christmas. She was having a great time, she said. The people were very nice, very friendly, and again Herbert told her not to take rides from strangers, and again she promised. He couldn't tell her any more.

Simi and Jeanette returned to Sydney on Saturday, 19 January 1991. Simi's mother was flying into Melbourne on the 24th and she was to meet her at the airport. Simi planned to buy a campervan for them to travel around the country in together, so she wanted to get down there as soon as possible to have everything ready. That day, she went to Manly to collect some travellers' cheques she had left with a friend. She had a bad habit of losing things so she left money and tickets with others to look after. The people at Manly weren't there, so she returned to the Murphys with only ten dollars on her. She was going to have to wait until Melbourne to get to a bank.

It was evening by the time she got back to the Murphys', but she was intent on leaving immediately. Kristine's mother, Doris, tried to talk her out of hitching, but the young backpacker pulled out a travel book and pointed at a passage which said hitchhiking was safe in Australia. No argument would be entered into. 'It says here, Australians are warm and friendly,' she insisted in her thickly accented, but clear English. The Murphys told her about all the drunks and idiots who'd be on the roads on a Saturday night and managed to convince her it was not a good idea. She agreed to wait until the morning.

So, twenty-one-year-old Simi set off from Guildford – the Murphys lived about 1500 metres from the Milats – at 8.15 a.m. on 20 January, wearing a yellow singlet, khaki shorts and hiking boots. An ankle support from a sprain in New Zealand peeked over the top of her right sock. Her money belt was hanging around her neck, under the singlet.

Jeanette offered to lend her the bus fare, but she refused. 'No, I'm just taking the train to Liverpool to hitchhike again. We had such a good experience last time.' They walked halfway to the station before Simi headed off alone. Her wild dark-brown dreadlocks were tied in a purple scarf, cutting quite a figure in the drab, fibro streets of Guildford. Their parting was no big deal. Simi was due back in Sydney with her mother before long. Her plan was to catch a train to Liverpool, then hitch, but the trains weren't running that day, due to track work, so she caught a bus. She planned to walk to the tourist information centre near Lombardo's at Casula where she thought she might be able to find a truck driver with her 'Melbourne' sign.

It was a funny day, 20 January, hot and sticky. The US military had just begun carpet bombing Saddam Hussein's Republican Guard, making way for its planned invasion of Kuwait. Thunderstorms moved across Sydney, hitting some suburbs like a B52, missing others.

Local resident Jeanette Wallace left her Moorebank home to drive to McDonald's on the Hume Highway about 9 a.m. She noticed a person walking with a huge backpack towards the highway from the station. When she stopped at the Hoxton Park Road lights – the intersection where Ivan Milat's car had been found full of stolen car parts in 1967 – she looked back and was surprised that it was a girl, because the pack looked so heavy. The McDonald's was a block ahead. Wallace was in there three to five minutes and when she came out, there was no sign of the girl.

Ivan Milat returned to work on Tuesday, 22 January. When workmate Tony Sara asked him what he'd been up to, Ivan told him he'd seen a relative at South West Rocks, before driving on to Caloundra in Queensland.

'How was it? What'd you do up there, eh?' asked Sara.

'Went snorkelling and cruised around. Wouldn't mind movin' up there one day.'

He hadn't stayed up north very long though because, on Wednesday, 16 January, a week after he had visited Maureen and Marilyn, his Nissan Patrol was snapped going through a red light camera at 12.12 a.m. on Pennant Hills Road, Carlingford, in Sydney's north-west.

Simone Schmidl had agreed to ring Kristine Murphy as soon as she got to Melbourne, but the call never came. Simi's mother, Erwinea, flew in on Thursday, 24 January, and was met by a friend, Cindy Schuster, who told her that Simone hadn't turned up. There was no doubt that something was terribly wrong. They knew Simi had left the Murphys' house four days earlier and they knew she had no intention of going anywhere else. Mrs Schmidl reported her daughter missing to both Victorian and New South Wales police the following day, 25 January, one year to the day after Paul Onions had his narrow escape on the highway.

Erwinea rang her ex-husband. 'Herbert, Simone was not at the airport. I'm very worried I've just told the police here in Melbourne.' The police didn't seem too concerned, but nor was Herbert at that time. 'Maybe she got delayed or had a small accident.' She was a very punctual sort of person, so he knew something had gone wrong, but presumed it was something inconsequential. Then, as each day went by, the possible explanations became less realistic and the fears grew. Erwinea, still desperately waiting in Melbourne, made contact with the ethnic broadcaster SBS, and they helped start getting the message out that she was missing.

Jeanette Wallace rang the Liverpool police with the last probable sighting a week later, after reading a small article in the *Liverpool Champion*. But no investigating officer called her for another three years. Throughout February, sightings of a woman fitting Simone's description came in from all over. Two in Albury on the New South Wales/Victorian border stood out because they sounded a lot like Simone.

Erwinea Schmidl waited for six weeks in Australia, but knew long before she returned to Regensburg that something terrible had happened to Simi. Back in Germany, Herbert Schmidl wanted to fly to Australia but couldn't think what use he could be with neither English nor any idea where to start looking. The size of the place was daunting. Even if he confined the search to the length of the Hume Highway, he could see the distance was something like Munich to the English Channel. He was forced to do what he could from Regensburg.

He had 1500 posters made up with two pictures of Simone. Some friendly people from SBS Television and some Australian friends of friends helped make sure they were put up in schools, universities, bus stations, churches, every place they could think to send them along the length of the Hume Highway. They sent them to the German cultural group, the Goethe Institute, and backpacker hostels. The Salvation Army helped too.

Because of the language problem, he tried to get the local German police to help him find out what was happening back in Australia, but they were useless. Didn't want to know about his problems. He asked if they could ring their Australian counterparts, but they told him to do it himself. 'We can't do anything about it,' they said. He was furious. Of course he'd do it himself – if he could. He only wanted to find if there was any news. He wrote to the Bavarian police headquarters and the Federal Police, but they each said the same thing. Besides, they said, it couldn't be that bad. These missing kids always turned up. They gave excuse after excuse.

Bizarre stories appeared in the German press about white women being kidnapped and taken as slaves to Asia. Such snippets, as unlikely as they seemed, fuelled terrible fears in Herbert's mind. He received a letter from the Bavarian police department saying it was scarcely possible to kidnap a grown adult and take them over a border or hold them prisoner for any length of time. That just made him angry. He wasn't talking kidnaps and borders. He kept pestering police and eventually was told to lay off. So he wrote to the German President, Richard von Weizsaecker, complaining about the lack of support. He got a polite response. *'Dear Herr Schmidl, the president has asked me to thank you for your letter of 12 April and advise you that the foreign ministry has been advised to assess the situation and in the case of no action to ask the relevant authorities to pursue the matter with the appropriate foreign agency . . .'*

Herbert just felt so helpless. He was shocked by the lack of compassion. He came to think that so many of his countrymen who were otherwise friendly and helpful just turned their backs when things got difficult and outside their direct area of responsibility. He made contact with the German consuls in Melbourne and Sydney and found them far more helpful. Maybe the letter to the president had helped after all. They passed on information as soon as they heard it and were more supportive.

Herbert gave others the impression of pessimism, but he never fully gave up. So long as there was a chance, he would hope. The passengers on his bus would always be enquiring if there was any news, meaning that he could never escape his worst thoughts. He tried booze and pills to sleep, but the thoughts remained and he eventually had to take a long spell from work. That just left him with nothing else to think of, so he went back to the buses.

TWENTY-SIX

Mid 1991

THE UNLOADER

When Nick Collins started work at Boral in 1989, it seemed like a great place except for this bloke Paul Miller who wouldn't have a bar of him. Collins had short hair and a friendly way about him, so Miller thought he was an undercover cop planted by the company. Miller just wasn't going to like him, no matter what.

Collins brought in some mull one night as a peace offering. 'You want a blow?'

'Fuck off, man,' Miller told him.

Collins shrugged. He'd have the joint himself.

Miller had only been there about three months so it wasn't like he was some old hand. Even so, he seemed to have everybody scared. It was a cushy job, but Miller was the laziest worker Collins had ever seen and the foremen just wouldn't take him on. 'I'm not doing it,' he'd say, walking back to the tearoom, or out to his car, and they'd just watch him go. Then there'd be some fight about who was going to get overtime. Miller would want to work then because the pay rate was time-and-a-half or double, and he'd be arguing with some bloke about whose turn it was, and he'd say: 'I hope your wife's good looking', implying all sorts of things. They backed down every time. It wasn't as though he was that big or tough. There were a few blokes there who would have done him for sure, but none of them ever stood up to him. They knew what he could do. Sometimes, he'd just go missing for hours. On the rare occasions a foreman said anything, they'd find two flat tyres or some similar problem at the end of the shift.

It took a few months, but Miller eventually started trusting Collins.

The ice melted and the air filled with bong smoke. Collins sold Miller his overtime for the price of the meal allowance – tea money – that the extra shift entitled you to. Collins was making enough money on the side selling pot. He didn't need the shifts.

Collins and Miller worked the unloader, where lengths of hot-cooked plaster cornice slide out of the drying oven, ready to line the ceilings of suburbia. They packed them up five at a time into lots of 300-odd. It was hot and boring. Bastard of a job, except for one thing: there were two unloaders, each manned by two workers, but the cornices came out at such intervals that it was possible for two men to handle both unloaders, so the other pair would have an hour off. The teams swapped on the hour. Hour on, hour off, hour on, hour off, lunch hour. It was the biggest bludge. The money was nothing special, but if you did overtime it was okay, and there was plenty of overtime to be had back then.

Even though they were only working four hours of an eight-hour shift, that was still too much for Miller. People would talk about it for years after, the way he had this great knack for fixing some things and blowing others up. He'd stop the oven by pulling a chain off and the whole line would come to a halt. He'd open up electrical cabinets and put one wire on another until it blew. When he went to the fuse box, it was something to see. These weren't your standard home fuses, they were great big blocks with an industrial current pulsing through them. He'd pull one out a bit and the current would make a blue arc the width of your finger. Phooom. Everything would go dead. He'd whack it back in real quick, and everyone would retire to the tearoom for a few hours break.

No one ever dobbed him in because Miller was Miller – a scary bloke – and, besides, they all got to have a rest. When the machines were going to be down for a long time, they might buy a case of beer and drink it for the first half of the shift then sleep the rest. Miller would drink so fast you had to go flat out to stop him drinking the whole case himself. Same thing if you went halves in a pizza, he'd go two pieces at once, and you'd be lucky to get two, total. They called him a coffeeholic, he'd drink it all day, but he never bought any milk, so one day Collins thought he'd teach him a lesson.

'Don't drink the milk,' he told everyone. 'I pissed in it. I'm gunna get Miller.'

They were sitting around and Miller came in and passed his cup, but someone told him before he drank it. He went crazy.

'Did you piss in it?' His eyes were wide and manic. 'Did you?'

'No, mate. I wouldn't do that.' Collins had to leave the room to keep from laughing, knowing that he could be in big trouble from Miller.

More often than not they had a bong there: a little Orchy Orange Juice bottle, with a piece of garden hose for a stem. Collins and Miller always had gear on them. Sometimes, Miller would bring in large bags of his own home-grown, and Collins would move it for him. Miller had the gear, but Collins had the contacts. It was average sort of gear. Typical home-grown, but it was a fair price. Hell, it wasn't costing Miller nothing. Sometimes he brought in as much as a pound. Collins could move it in a week.

'When will you have the money?' Miller'd ask.

Collins knew that if he told him a particular day, it had to be there that day, otherwise Miller'd get really funny. Then, if he got it to him on the right day, Miller'd be handing him hundreds back saying, 'Here take this.'

Collins would pack him a cone then try to get away from him before being cornered by one of his legendary rants. He'd get right in their personal space, raving, with his little gut sticking out his dirty shirt, belly button exposed. He lived in a caravan in the backyard of his mum's place and it seemed like he didn't get inside for a shower too often. The poor cornered bastard felt Miller pressing against him. He'd be leaning back while his workmates laughed, pulling faces:

'Hah, on with Miller Havachat. Sucked in.'

It happened to them all. He wouldn't stop. Talk, talk, talk. They wouldn't listen. They'd nod: 'Yeah Paul . . . Yeah Paul . . . Yeah Paul.'

And even when they didn't nod, he just went on and on talking garbage as their white-lit plasterboard factory hummed quietly through the night.

They called him 'Killer', 'Miller the Killer'. No one thought he murdered people. It was more because he was into guns, and it rhymed, and he was so way out there. He could go on about anything: lollies he stole when he was a kid, then in the same sentence he was talking about robbing banks. He talked a lot about his travels: riding his bike, picking up hitchers, stealing things, meeting people on the road, making friends with them, having beers with them; driving a Land Rover through a showroom window in Parramatta, and travelling around Australia in it.

When he was stoned, you could pick him a mile away with his head cocked sharply to the right and this pimp-roll, Leo-Wanker stagger. You'd know to clear out. Collins would climb three decks of pallets in the forklift forest to get away.

Miller wasn't only good at blowing things up, he was also a wizz at fixing cars. Just about everyone brought theirs in for him to fix. He'd do the simple things in the Boral car park during the down times. The more difficult ones he took home. Everybody used to think he was a dope, but Paul Douglas, who used to have a few beers with him while he worked on his Commodore, knew better. And he wasn't such a bad person, either, Douglas thought. Nothing was ever a problem for him. Somebody at work would whinge about an oil filter problem, next day he'd turn up with an oil filter, unrequested. One night he came in with a chainsaw and spent the entire shift chopping up Boral's specially built pallets for some old lady down the road who needed it for her winter fire. He filled his car – the boot, back seat and front seat – to the roof.

Paul Douglas was a New Zealander who worked on the mixer at the far end of the line from the unloader, pouring bags of gypsum into tanks, and watching machines swirling the plaster before it went into the moulds and the ovens. He looked a bit like Miller but for the gaps between his teeth, and the bald spot.

Miller used to drop around to Douglas' place at Railway Street, unannounced at 11 a.m. before afternoon shift and they went to the pub together once or twice. They were working eight- to sixteen-hour days then. Douglas was tired and knew to ignore his workmate when he was high, just answering 'Yeah . . . Yeah . . . Yeah'.

He thought they got on pretty well but, because Douglas worked at the far end of the line, he was about the only worker in the place who didn't know that his friend was sabotaging the line and causing the plaster to overflow everywhere. It was Douglas' job to clean it all up. On hot days, the plaster would set in great rocks on the floor before he could get to it, and he'd have to chisel it away while the others were enjoying their beer and bongs in the tearoom. He thought all the breaks were caused by faulty machinery and couldn't believe anyone would do it on purpose.

Management had their suspicions about Miller, though, and they started noting when these incidents were occurring, compared to his shifts. They found it was happening across all shifts, and so felt it must have been the equipment. Another colleague, Des Butler, eventually told Douglas what was going on because he could see that they were creating work for him.

For all this, Miller did seem to get on with people. He was always inviting them to go shooting at what he called Miller's Mountain, a property he and his brother Wally owned on the Wombeyan Caves road. The only one to ever take him up on it was Des Butler, the Irishman. It was a holiday Monday and Butler was feeling a bit rugged after a weekend of excess, but Miller insisted, so he did. They drove to Wally's place and Butler wondered why Wally kept calling Miller 'Dick' instead of Paul.

They got out to the property and he was less than impressed. There was no road in the last bit and the walk damn near killed him. The two brothers had fifteen years on him and both seemed pretty fit. Butler was buggered. He'd go up five minutes, then have to rest. It took him four spells to make it. He got there and lit up a cigarette. The two brothers lit up a joint. Butler was a heavy smoker and noticed that for the rest of the day, every cigarette he smoked, they matched him puff for puff with the funny stuff.

Wally had converted an SKS Chinese assault rifle to fully automatic. It was only a matter of filing down some part of the gun, Miller explained. Des timed the thing. Thirty rounds in three-and-a-half seconds. They stuck paper targets on trees and blew them away. They shot at rocks. Blew them away. They shot at anything. There was only one rule, Wally made very clear: 'No shooting at birds.' They fired about 1200 rounds in the day. Most of that was from the SKS which took steel bullets – none of this lead or full metal jacket stuff – so it worked out reasonably cheap at about $30 each.

Des got back to work and told his workmates: 'Never again. They just smoked the funny stuff the whole time and fired off everywhere. It was madness.' Des also had an unnerving experience. Wally had the gun leaning on a tree. It slipped and went off not far from Des as Wally tried to grab it.[85] He told them how Wally's wife yelled out as they left his place at Hilltop: 'Get some roos for the dogs, Wally.' It was another world.

Miller invited Collins up to the mountain a few times, but he never went. Didn't like the idea of blowing things away. He knew Wally, too. When they'd met, Wally came over to Collins' place and pulled his eye out before they shook hands. Charming.

'Do you want a bong, mate?' Collins had asked.

Wally said yeah, and punched the cone back in one. Then packed himself five more. Collins was annoyed by the bad etiquette. He didn't have much in the bowl.

'You pull bongs like your brother eats pizza,' he said.

Collins also met his other brother, Ivan, when Miller was servicing his car. They were round at Guildford. The house smelt of dog, and there was a picture of the dead sister, Margaret, on the mantelpiece, but Collins already knew that was a no-talk subject. Ivan was there in his tight blue T-shirt and Stubbies, built like a brick shithouse, his reputation preceding him. Collins knew the story from Boral about the time Ivan worked there and got jacked off with the forkie who kept spraying him with water. The way Collins heard it, Northie found a live bullet sitting on his bundy card one day, but didn't get the hint. Next time he sprayed him was when he had the gun put to his head.

Ivan freaked Collins out in a way he couldn't really explain. He told his wife, 'Some blokes can walk in and there's an aura about them. There's something about that bloke. I don't feel comfortable around him. He's strange as shit, man.'

There were a few boxes covered with Chinese writing lying around. 'What's that for?' Collins asked.

'Oh that, that's for Christmas,' Miller explained. Five hundred bucks worth of ammo to blast in the New Year. Miller came back from these yuletide celebrations showing off pictures of dead goats, and other carcasses. His colleagues humoured him. 'Yeah, that's great, mate.'

Miller started going round Collins' place fairly regularly. Collins' wife Diana liked Miller – she liked the way he'd tell a story when he was a bit stoned, talking in 3D. He'd make you feel like you were there, with every gear change, the wind going through his hair, and every tree by the road. When Miller brought his de facto, Liz, along, she'd go on a bit like him, but couldn't actually hold a conversation, especially after a drink. That was another thing about Miller, all the time Collins knew him, he never heard him say 'she's a good sort', or any sort of sexual comment. He never talked about sex: getting any, not getting any. He'd rather talk about valve clearances and shit.

Only time he talked about Liz was to badmouth her. One day he even came in and said: 'I just beat up my girlfriend.'

Paul Douglas asked him why.

'She's too hard on the boy.' He told everyone how much he loved his son, and he wasn't going to have this drunk woman beating on him. Gave her a black eye and all that, you know, he said.

Miller just seemed to be getting weirder. They never knew what to make of anything he said. They thought he was full of it. Like the time they were sitting around during down time, in winter 1991, talking about nothing in particular. Miller was high. Out of nowhere he just said: 'I know somebody who goes around killing people. He's pretty well off. Drives a white Mercedes.'[86]

'Oh yeah. Why does he do that?' asked a sceptical Paul Douglas.

'Just to see the shock on their faces . . .'

'Yeah right.' He was obviously off with the fairies, trying to get a reaction out of Douglas.

One time in the meal room, they were talking about a court case where some rapists had been let off lightly.

'I can't understand the Australian justice system,' said Douglas, a New Zealander. 'They keep letting these guys off lightly . . . The justice system's no good.'

Miller replied, way out of context: 'Stabbing a woman is like cutting a loaf of bread.'[87]

Douglas didn't reply. Miller was sober this time and he wasn't smiling.

The blokes weren't surprised by Miller's reaction to the Strathfield massacre on Saturday, 17 August, when taxi driver Wade Frankum went berserk in a coffee shop in the Strathfield Plaza shopping mall. Frankum stabbed his first victim with a large hunting knife, then shot six others dead with a Chinese SKK military assault rifle, the same as the one Des Butler had fired down at Miller's place. The only difference was Frankum hadn't converted his to fully automatic.

The talk in the tearoom at Boral was along the lines of what a maggot this guy must have been. Miller came out with the line that 'the guy obviously doesn't know what he's doing'. He didn't seem to have any moral problem with Frankum at all. His words didn't surprise anyone, though. This was a guy whose solution to world hunger, after all, was to blow up the starving.

Over at the RTA, his brother Ivan was talking about the massacre with Noel Wild. Wild had given Ivan a lift back to the depot and had wondered how tough Frankum would have been if someone fronted him and started shooting back.

As Ivan got out of the vehicle he turned to Wild: 'I woulda shot more of 'em.'

To Ivan, the bloke hadn't appreciated the capabilities of his weapon.

TWENTY-SEVEN

Late 1991

BONDI BEACH PARTY

There is no tourist information bureau in Maesteg, South Wales. Pronounced my-steg, it is a hard town in a rough green valley. Beer and petrol are cheap. It grew up last century with the prospect of jobs in iron and coal; its terraced houses are the colour of the brown rock of the hills. Popstars Kylie and Dannii Minogue's ancestors came from Maesteg and their great aunts and uncles still live there. That's about it for claims to fame.

The Walters family lived in a plain row of pebbledash terraces, with rough tin sheds in back gardens which dropped away to a weedy stream. Joanne Walters was born on Australia Day, 26 January 1970, at Bridgend Hospital, near Maesteg. She was a bright student at Llangynwyd Senior School, gaining eight O levels before doing a nannying course at Bridgend Technical College. She loved kids and she loved the idea of travel, so she figured it was the sort of training that would get her work anywhere. After graduating, she got a job at the local Sony plant to save for the big trip.

Her first venture out into the world was in 1990, when she found nannying jobs in Italy, Greece and Sardinia. In Greece, on the island of Rhodes, she met Pauline Reid from the Shetland Islands. The two got along well and decided that the following year, they'd travel to Australia together.

They spent a week in Singapore before flying to Sydney, arriving 4 June 1991 – just another two of the 45,000 young Britons arriving each year on working holidays. On the immigration form that she filled in on the plane, Joanne wrote her local address as 70 Thunderbolt Drive, Raby, the address of friends of friends of her grandmother's, just a few doors down from where Ivan's sister Shirley and Gerry Soire had lived until two years earlier.

It was winter, so Pauline and Joanne went north, chasing the sun. Arriving in Brisbane, Joanne worked briefly in a rubber factory and in a Chinese restaurant. They hitched on to the Sunshine Coast, then to the tropical north, Cairns and Airlie Beach, whose winters would make a Welsh summer blush. They worked for a few weeks on a yacht, and they picked fruit near Bowen. They were doing the backpacker business, well and truly. Then Pauline went to Magnetic Island, off Townsville, while Joanne headed south to Sydney to find work and save money. Pauline followed a week later.

Joanne was the sort of girl who was very close to her parents. She phoned home just about more often than anyone else in all the hostels they stayed. She was the type of girl to send her father a boomerang for Father's Day, and he was the sort of father to proudly hang it above the fireplace: Greetings from Australia.

The place Joanne came to stay at was one of Australia's most significant tourist developments of recent times – the Original Backpackers Hostel in Kings Cross. It was a big old home, converted in 1980 into Victoria Street's first hostel by John Cook, the man who, two years earlier, had opened the first backpackers hostel in the Cross. By the time Joanne Walters arrived, his grand Victorian building had hosted about 100,000 young travellers. When Cook started out they'd all been hippies and counter-culture types wandering the streets looking for somewhere to crash without the restrictive rules and curfews of the youth hostels. If they couldn't find somewhere cheap, they'd crash in a park or wind up in one of the nearby doss houses.

But the Aussie dollar crashed in the mid-1980s, and Australia suddenly became a cheap destination. Backpacking boomed. As Victoria Street became crowded with fluorescent packs and plenty of competing hostels, Cook saw the kids become nicer, more middle-class and less intrepid. They had brochures and package trips. Buses ferried them from the airport. It disappointed him to see the adventure taken away. Where once everybody had either hitched or bought old bombs together, now the majority took the bus. Backpacking had become pedestrian.

While staying at the Original Backpackers, Joanne Walters met a girl from the other end of the British social structure. Someone whose path, in other times, would simply not have crossed her own, except perhaps as employer/employee.

Caroline Clarke grew up the youngest of three children in a large house in Hindhead, Surrey, a hopelessly green village which daily feeds a good portion of its inhabitants, like her father Ian, into London's City district. From an early age, she struck her parents as a strong-willed girl. Being the youngest child, she learned to hold her own with a sharp tongue. She was a character, a great mimic who had an answer for everything, always having the last word. She possessed a wonderful laugh. Just to hear it made everybody else laugh with her. She had sparkle and a why-worry attitude.

The family always kept labradors and her godmother gave her a puppy for her birthday when she was about nine. He only lived for eighteen months. Died quite suddenly of stomach cancer. One of the worst moments of her happy life.

She was a bit of a butterfly, and would dip her toe into all sorts of sports. She rode, of course, and later got into skiing in France. She always wanted to go parachuting and intended to do bungy jumping when she made the trip to Australia she'd always planned.

Never academic, she left school, St Margaret's Convent, Midhurst, Sussex, at sixteen, and did a two-year catering course at Guildford Tech where she met Gill Baker, who was to become her best friend. Gill was Scottish and, when she moved to England, Caroline was the one person who accepted her straight off, took her under her wing. At catering college, Gill liked doing sweets and Caroline liked doing main meals, so they'd each do their own thing, then swap without telling the lecturer.

What she really wanted to do was join the police force. She went along for a preliminary chat with them when she was eighteen, and was told to go away and get some experience. What better experience, she thought, than to follow her brother around the world. Right from her early teens, she had a fixation with Australia.

Caroline lived at Hindhead until her parents moved up north to Slaley in 1988. Her father had become the Agent for the Bank of England in Newcastle, which meant he ran the northern section of England's central bank. Her parents sold the family home and bought a small townhouse in Farnham, Surrey, for the children, who all wanted to stay down south. No sooner had they bought the house than their son, Simon, announced he'd given up his job and was going around the world, and their eldest daughter, Emma, declared she was getting married, leaving nineteen-year-old Caroline with a flat to herself. She wasn't too displeased with that. She had various pals lodge with her from time to time and they had a few parties there, too.

She started to save money for her trip, working her way up to assistant manager at the Guildford Pizza Hut. Simon left in 1989, aged twenty-three, and was still away in 1991 as Caroline planned to go. He was sending back long descriptive letters as he made his way through Europe on a Eurail pass, then Athens to Turkey, then Delhi, around India, and on to Sydney. He did a spell 'cotton chipping' on a cotton farm at Narrabri in north-west New South Wales and talked about fossicking for opals in Lightning Ridge and all the weirdos he'd met. It wasn't glamorous, but for a nineteen-year-old dreaming of adventure, it was as good as Marco Polo.

Caroline was determined to do just as much – and even more. Simon had only hitchhiked once the whole time he'd been away, but Caroline was determined it was to be part of her agenda. Her parents had a long chat with her about it, but she had made up her mind. It was the way to meet people, and it was cheap, she said. The best her parents could get from her was an assurance she'd never do it alone.

The big journey was to start in Europe, the day after her twenty-first birthday party on 10 August 1991. Simon was quite literally somewhere up the Khyber Pass at the time. Her parents threw a party at their beautiful home converted from a farm building. A load of friends came up from the south. Her cake was in the shape of a Volkswagen Beetle, her dream car. They partied on at a nightclub on a boat moored on the Tyne at Newcastle.

At one point, Gill Baker pulled her aside: 'Caroline, I don't want you to go.'

'Shut up and don't be stupid. I'm going and that's it . . . If I don't go, people will think I'm chicken.'

She left the next day, leaving her Peugot 205 for her parents to sell. The big adventure had begun. She travelled to Europe with twenty-three-year-old Noel Goldthorpe, a friend who got fired up about travelling from listening to Caroline's plans. They travelled all over Europe on their Eurail passes. She dragged him from church to cathedral to museum with her *Let's Go, Europe* firmly in hand. She had loads of get-up-and-go. Too much for him.

Noel was skint and got a job in Athens spruiking backpackers into Zorba's hostel. A fast talker, he was in his element working for food, accommodation and five pounds a day. She was free now to do what she wanted. She was living her dream. She met an Australian girl, Janice Tsimiklis, and started travelling with her; off to Germany where she wanted to see the Belsen concentration camp, and then the Netherlands. She returned to England for one night, before catching a 5 a.m. flight to Australia.

Noel hitched back to England from Greece in six days, well aware that the traveller's ultimate destination, Australia, was out of his reach. He never could get over what hard work travelling was. So much time spent sitting in stations.

Caroline arrived in Sydney on 19 September, with just enough money to prove to the authorities she wouldn't be destitute, and found work straightaway packing T-shirts that responded to one's body heat. Horrendous things. They paid her well, though, she said.

Her parents always received short calls, with just the basic information, before her money ran out. Much of their information was from letters and friends. She told her parents she caught a really bad throat infection and had a few days in hospital. She told her friend Gill there was something in the chemicals in the T-shirts that had done something to her brain. Her letters weren't always entirely factual. She was, however, definitely in hospital for thirteen days being treated by a neurologist. When she came out, her new friend from the Original Backpackers, Joanne Walters, and a group of others had rented a flat on Kings Cross Road.

Joanne had been the driving force behind the flat. She and a group of Britons planned to stay and work for a while, so it was cheaper for them to cram into a flat than stay in a hostel. There was Joanne, Simon Wharton, a lad from Yorkshire who just had come in from Fiji, Nina Tunnicliffe from Derby, Ben Hitchcock from Hertfordshire, and another chap from Merseyside.

At $60 a week each, they were saving about $20. The flat only had two bedrooms. Three guys in one, two girls in the other. The furniture was crap. The landlord told them: 'If you want a telly you'll have to pay a bigger bond.' They paid the bigger bond. One of their neighbours dressed in drag with stubble sticking through loads of makeup. First time Simon saw him/her he thought he/she was going to a fancy dress party. Welcome to Kings Cross.

They all got on pretty well. Joanne and Simon tended to do most of the cleaning. During the week, they'd all be off to work. Most of them were into saving, so they usually stayed home at night, although they did go out for the odd lager. Most of the crowd in the flat only met Caroline after she came out of hospital in late November. She moved into a hostel in Tusculum Street and met a Dutch girl called Resy. They became good friends. They both smoked a bit and shared each other's cigarettes – Horizon 50s or Longbeach 30s, the medium-strength ones.

In early December, Joanne answered an ad in the *Sydney Morning Herald* for a job nannying at Kirribilli. Dr Deborah Jensen had just returned from doing postgraduate work at Stanford and needed someone to look after her thirteen-month-old son, Nicholas. Joanne was the first applicant to be interviewed. Deborah and her mother, Jean Jensen, both thought she presented well, was well groomed and had very good qualifications, but they particularly noted the way she didn't pay too much attention to them. She was too busy talking to Nicholas. The Jensens must have interviewed another thirty applicants that day and just kept looking at each other: 'That one we interviewed first.'

Joanne started immediately on Monday, 2 December – 9 a.m. to 5 p.m., five days a week for $240 a week. She'd bath and clothe Nicholas and feed him with the most daintily presented little plates of food Jean Jensen had ever seen. And when he was napping, she'd set herself up on the balcony by the pool and write to friends and family back home. She could sit out there overlooking Careening Cove and write for hours, or Jean would come out and they'd chat. The two women got on well despite the forty-two-year age difference. For Jean it was like having one of her own daughters back again. Joanne spoke of her family often. She was obviously very attached to them.

Caroline Clarke went over to Adelaide to spend Christmas with the girl she met in Greece, Janice Tsimiklis. She arrived to find herself the guest of honour at a large family gathering, much to her surprise and embarrassment. Surrounded by such a wonderful family, it was the first time she'd become homesick, she told her mother.

For the crowd in the flat at Kings Cross, Christmas meant the Bondi Beach backpackers party which was becoming a travellers' institution. The party took Sydney by surprise that day. Tens of thousands of backpackers carted lounge suites, fridges, Christmas trees and truckloads of beer down to the beach. Face-painted Poms with white legs and Union Jacks thought they were in the terraces. Ethnic chants competed with huge sound systems in vans backed over the promenade with the doors wide open. It was a hot day. Really hot if you were in it all day with a bellyful. Dozens of young travellers were pulled out of the surf by lifeguards.

Also on the beach that day were two Germans who had stayed the night at the Original Backpackers having come in from up north two days earlier. Their paths probably never crossed the Brits' from the flat and, even if they had, they probably wouldn't have had much to say.

Gabor Neugebauer was born on 6 April 1970, the day that, in another world, Ivan Milat got out of jail after two-and-a-half years away to find his brother Mick and John Preston were being convicted of assault on two soldiers. Gabor's father, Manfred, had to rush his pregnant wife Anke to a hospital in Sulz, in the Neckar Valley, near Stuttgart. The baby was several weeks premature and came out feet first, but the doctor performed brilliantly to bring him out smoothly.

Manfred rose to become a lieutenant colonel in the West German air force and was on the regional command staff. Germany was settling in to the thawing cold war peacefully and prosperously. Threats of a Russian attack had subsided since 1961 when their eldest daughter, Ilka, was born and the Cuban crisis was beginning. Those were scary times. Manfred was at a fighter bomber squadron and night after night he was called in on alert. The whole military structure went underground, waiting for the big one. Manfred was in charge of fire brigades and ambulances and logistics.

The seventies were blissful, by comparison. By 1979 the family made the last of its eleven moves to settle in Heimerzheim on the Swisstal River, a quiet little village half an hour's cycle from Manfred's headquarters in Bonn.

They hadn't been in Heimerzheim very long when their oldest son Tibor, thirteen, and Gabor, nine, hopped on their bikes to visit friends in a village about ten kilometres away. They took off along a bicycle track, out across the flat fields of sugar beet surrounding the village and into a small dark forest of spruce trees about two kilometres away.

A man in his twenties stopped them. 'My rabbit is lost. Come and help me search for my rabbit,' he implored them. 'This way.'

Tibor was older and more suspicious, but they got off their bikes and followed him in about 20 metres. In the summer darkness of the deciduous woods, they were out of sight of any passersby when the man suddenly pulled a Swiss army knife from his pocket. 'We should undress now,' he ordered. Tibor had been watching too much murder on television and knew enough about this sort of thing to know it was very serious. If they undressed, they'd be a lot worse off. They stood there in silence for a moment looking at the man, then Tibor flew at his hand. 'Run, Gabor! Run!' His little brother ran – but slowly, thoughtfully, like he was scared to leave – as Tibor held the knife arm for dear life. He didn't see where Gabor went as the two struggled. Could have been ten seconds, could have been thirty. He didn't know. When his little brother was out of sight, he broke free. The guy grabbed him again and his T-shirt ripped. Then he was free again and on his bike, peddling furiously in the direction away from home because he knew there'd be more people in that direction. He found a family coming along the trail and told them what happened. They took him to the Neugebauer home and Tibor ran in.

'Gabor? Gabor? Is Gabor not here?'

Manfred looked a bit perplexed. 'Gabor came in a few minutes ago and went straight to his room without saying a word.' Tibor couldn't believe it. He thought he'd risked his life so his little brother would run and get help. He expected the search parties to be out already. Gabor had been so shocked he couldn't talk. Maybe he felt guilty for leaving his brother. Tibor would never know. Gabor never did talk about the incident, nor so many other things in his life. His parents had to hear it from others. It was his nature. He opened up sometimes to his sister, Ilka. Years later she explained to Tibor just what a profound impact the incident had on Gabor. She said that after Tibor escaped, the man found Gabor again and then let him go, saying 'see you later'. Gabor told Ilka about a feeling of violation which stayed with him always. He had nightmares and would wake up sweating. His trusting nature was never the same. He might still have faith in people, but he knew they weren't all good.

He was the type of boy who didn't make friends easily. He had a few very close friends and that was it. With them he could talk and talk, but generally he was quiet. He never gave trouble. Tibor considered his brother the best friend you could imagine. He never heard him say a bad word about anyone. He was calm and relaxed and laughed a lot. He started weight training in his teens. Tibor thought maybe the attack in the forest was the deep-seated motivation. He wanted to be able to defend himself and the people he loved.

Gabor finished his thirteen years of schooling in May 1989, never having exerted himself scholastically, but always bright enough to get by. He went straight into his compulsory military service, wanting to be in an alpine unit, but couldn't get in. His next choice was anything in Munich, with its nightlife and its proximity to the skiing and hiking. Manfred pulled a few strings to get him posted there as a pioneer – an engineer infantry soldier. When he enlisted, they went down together on a military cargo plane.

It was in the last month of his fifteen-month military service, around August 1990, that Gabor went to a disco with a friend. He wasn't a dancer, and neither was the girl with the long, reddish-blonde hair he was looking at. She looked at him. They talked. Her name was Anja. She was studying technical drawing at Munich. They talked some more. She became Gabor's first girlfriend.

Anja's alternative style of dress did not reflect her lifestyle choices. She was non-drinking, non-smoking and ate healthy food. She and Gabor had a lot in common that way – and they both had the travel bug. They started roaming almost as soon as they met. It was their bond. Gabor wasn't worried about letting it interfere with his studies, much to his parents' dismay. 'If I'm old or if I'm married, I'm never going to have the chance to do this again,' he told his father who was born in times when such attitudes were impossible.

The Neugebauers only met Anja once, when the couple missed their bus in London and were forced to catch a ferry to Dieppe in France. Manfred had to drive 500 kilometres in the snow to pick them up because they had no money. Like Gabor, Anja struck Manfred as shy but nice. Manfred thought they had great *sympathie* for each other, they complemented one another.

After his national service, Gabor wanted to study in Munich to be with Anja. He had always wanted to do interior design so in order to do that he had to first learn a handcraft trade. He chose carpentry, but soon realised he couldn't cut it with the practical skills. He was not quick or accurate enough.

In 1991, he enrolled in philosophy at Munich University, giving him all the advantages of being a student without the heavy loads. He assured his parents he would do a more serious degree when he had seen the world. For now, he was working in a home for immigrants and as a hotel porter – always saving to travel.

The couple travelled to Spain, France, Austria, Italy, Greece and the Netherlands. Gabor also went to Hungary by himself. Anja was just finishing her degree, qualifying as a draftsperson in mid-1991, when Gabor told his mother over the phone that he and Anja were going to Indonesia. She wanted him to wait until he'd started his 'serious' degree – he'd decided on geology – but Gabor was determined.

'It's more important for me now to go and travel,' he told her.

Anja's mother was concerned at her daughter going such a long way and her father insisted that she must call regularly. The focus of the trip was to be the temples of Bali and the volcanoes of Java, Bali and Lombok. Gabor thought it complemented his interest in philosophy and geology quite neatly. They left Munich on 21 October 1991, into what was for their parents a world pieced together from postcards and conversations rushed to the rhythm of coins clunking through payphones and warning beeps as they said their goodbyes.

Java, Bali, Lombok. The weather turned bad up on a volcano so they made a spur-of-the-moment decision to head for Australia. They came down through Flores and West Timor to Darwin, arriving by air on 20 November 1991, 'back to civilisation' wrote Gabor. The Neugebauers were glad he was there. It would be safer. He had learned a bit of English, but Anja had almost none.

She was more diligent at keeping in touch with her parents than he was, but he was still pretty regular. Anja rang home from Darwin on 22 November, her twentieth birthday. Gabor with his interest in geology wanted to see Ayers Rock. Of the six people they travelled there with, Anja noticed that they all considered seeing 'Uluru' to be a lifelong dream. When they saw it, Gabor was awestruck, but she thought it was just a big stone in the middle of the desert.

They saw the bones and carcasses of hundreds of dead kangaroos by the side of the road, but also live wild horses and a camel. They went on a two-day canoe safari with a group of Germans in the Katherine Gorge, but had to carry the canoe for much of the time because the rainy season hadn't yet come. They appreciated the rugged beauty of the place, nevertheless.

Gabor didn't call home again until 7 December, from Cairns. They were going to Brisbane, then Sydney, he said.

Manfred asked about money: 'You will get some for Christmas.'

'We have enough money,' said Gabor. 'We don't need it.' Manfred wondered how they could travel such distances without burning up large amounts of cash. He didn't understand the frugal culture of backpacking. He presumed they must be catching buses or sometimes getting lifts with travellers they had met. This turned out to be correct. Anja sent her parents a letter from Cairns telling of how, after they'd travelled 400 kilometres from one of their campsites in western Queensland, Gabor remembered he'd left his money belt – containing travellers' cheques and the tickets home – on the roof of the car when they left their campsite. They got to the next town and called the police at Richmond, the closest town to their overnight campsite. 'They drove those 120 kilometres for us and searched there on our behalf for an eternity in such a heat too,' Anja wrote. They found the money belt, intact, and sent it on by express post. 'Really unbelievable,' she wrote, continuing, '. . . We decided to celebrate Christmas in Sydney. There will be a big party of all travellers and Sydney itself is also said to be very beautiful. It will be a little difficult after Christmas, because we will need to travel the 4100 kilometres to Darwin uninterrupted.'

Anja said she might change her plans. She wanted to find a single female who she might travel through Malaysia or Thailand with. Then right at the end, she said they both might change their plans. 'We have just heard that there will be a four-day festival on New Year's Eve.'

Gabor next rang on Tuesday, 24 December (German time), from Sydney. Anke and Tibor were working in the kitchen on the Christmas Eve meal. She was busy making Bratwurst which Manfred always insisted on having at Christmas because, in the poor times after the war when he knew real hunger, it was such a great delicacy. Nobody else in the family liked it, but every Christmas Eve he would make them eat this damn cheap Prussian version of the sausage. Anke was a little annoyed at being disturbed from her task – until she heard it was Gabor. Then she raced to the phone.

'What time is it there?' she asked.

'Between three and four in the morning. On the 25th.'

'Where is Anja?'

'She's still sleeping.'

Gabor was finding the hot weather difficult. He and Anja were going to a beach festival, he said. The last thing he said, before the beeps of a broken line cut in, was, 'we have to get out of this land as soon as possible . . .' He had sounded a little agitated. That was easily explained at the time by his need to hurry to get back to Darwin to catch their flight back to Indonesia, but the words would grow to take on more ominous tones over the following months.

Anja rang home, too. She told her family that she had enjoyed Bali more than Australia. Now they had to hurry back to Darwin to meet their flight. She was running out of coins and the line went dead. She didn't sound distressed.

Gabor and Anja checked out of their hostel next day as an old fridge and a Christmas tree still smouldered on Bondi Beach from the party the day before. They needed to cover almost 700 kilometres a day for six days across the desert to make their 1 January flight out of Darwin.

It was a typical Milat Boxing Day. Margaret visited Steven's grave for his birthday. She visited her daughter Margaret's grave, too, before returning to Campbell Hill Road to prepare the lunch like she'd done the day before Ivan was born forty-seven years earlier and every Boxing Day since. The other Milat women arrived to help, and the men grouped outside, drinking and smoking a bit of pot while the kids ran around shooting at each other with their Christmas presents. Uncle Ivan had given one nephew a pump-action water pistol and another, just nine-months old, received a black toy AK47 machine-gun. Bill's wife Carol was wearing a new blouse and was blasted when she came through the door. 'You dirty little kids,' she yelled at them. She was certain it was Mac who'd put them up to it and primed the Super-Soaker water pistol. She was soaking, and she would remain adamant that he was there laughing but, if he was present that day, he managed to stay out of all the photos.

Three days after Boxing Day, Ivan put in his Lotto form at a newsagent in Mittagong, in the Southern Highlands. He had started his annual leave on 20 December and wasn't due back at work until 22 January 1992. Normally, he would have lodged his Lotto form at Lombardo's newsagency at Casula.

TWENTY-EIGHT

Early 1992

WORLDS APART

Samir El Hallak and his wife moved into 53 Campbell Hill Road just before Ivan moved back next door in 1987. Samir came to Australia from the Middle East in 1981. His English was broken, so he didn't talk to his neighbours much, but his children, particularly the youngest son, Khali, would scramble over the fence to play with Mrs Milat's two dogs or to talk to Ivan whenever he saw him out ritually cleaning the Nissan Patrol.

When Samir first arrived in Australia he worked in a factory spray painting cars but, by January 1992, the recession had left him unemployed for some time. To help pay the bills, he became a backyard car dealer. Every four months he'd buy a second-hand car, fix it and sell it. On Monday, 6 January 1992, Ivan saw him spraying a car and asked if he could do panel beating, too.

'Sure,' said Samir. Though no expert, he knew what to do. Ivan showed him a small hole which he wanted patched and re-sprayed. Samir could tell it was a bullet hole and that it had been fired inside the vehicle from the driver's side into the front passenger-side door in line with where the passenger's hip would be.

Ivan didn't hide the fact it was a bullet hole. Told Samir it was a stupid accident. A gun went off as he put it down inside the car. It was no surprise because the handful of times that Samir did talk to Ivan, the conversation was dominated by camping, hunting and shooting. Ivan once told him it was nothing for him to fire between 4000 and 5000 rounds 'just for fun'.

A few days later, Samir filled the hole and sprayed it, but the colour was not a good match.

On Friday, 10 January 1992, Ivan recorded the repair job in his owner's manual. He was methodical like that, recording every grease and oil change, every service, and all the kilometres racked up.

He was back at the RTA from holiday on Wednesday, 22 January. Although not sure of the exact date, Noel Wild remembers pulling up in the car park beside him around this time. 'Look what I've done,' Milat said, excited. He showed him a bullet hole in the car door. He told all his workmates about it. 'Nothing to worry about,' said cowboy Ivan. 'No one was shooting at me. Me gun went off accidentally . . . I threw it down on the seat and it went off.' Noel Wild couldn't help thinking it was strange. Ivan was so good with guns. It wasn't the sort of thing an experienced bloke would do. And the way Ivan only ever half told a story you never knew what to make of him. Why should anyone shoot at him?

The calls home from Anja and Gabor dried up after Christmas. There were no more postcards, but it caused little concern because they were due back soon, anyway. When Gabor got home, he was going to stay with his parents for the last week of his holidays before he returned to work. Anja was going skiing with a friend in the Alps.

On Friday, 24 January, Anja's father, Guenther, went to Munich Airport to meet their flight from Singapore. Waves of people poured through customs. He waited and waited, but his daughter and her boyfriend never came through the gate.

He rang Anke Neugebauer. 'They are not on the flight. Have you heard anything?'

'No. Are you sure?'

'Positive.'

It was now exactly a month since the parents had heard from their children and Anke panicked a little, but Mr Habschied soothed her, saying that they would have had trouble making a call from Indonesia. There wasn't a lot to worry about. After all, the couple had missed their bus in London that time. A call explaining everything would surely be coming in the next few hours.

The hours turned to days. Nothing. The families knew it was bad. Anke Neugebauer went to the foreign office after three days to ask what could be done. Not much. She reported Gabor and Anja missing to the German police three days later, on 30 January, but, as is usually the case, a couple of travellers missing for only a week did not rate highly on police priorities.

Anke rang the Australian Embassy and was told she shouldn't be worried. It's a big and interesting country, young people are always overstaying. Thank you. Bye. Manfred rang the German honorary consul in Darwin and asked him to find whether there was a flight out of Darwin to Timor on 1 January, and if a parcel with Christmas cookies, vitamins and sweets for Gabor had been collected from Post Restante in Darwin. The consul rang back a day later and said there was no flight (this proved incorrect) and the parcel had not been collected, indicating they hadn't made it to Darwin.

About a fortnight after the pair had failed to arrive, Manfred talked to his brother-in-law who immediately offered to go to Australia with him to search. But Manfred wasn't so sure. 'Where would we go? I don't know where they have been.'

'We should first look where they were at the end, when he rang you . . . I know someone in Australia who might help us.' Through a network of bank contacts, the brother-in-law came up with private investigator Neville Clarke, a former provo marshall in the Royal Australian Air Force who had only recently taken out a private investigator's licence and was working for private investigators, Hudsons.

At first the Habschieds did not agree to retain him. Guenther Habschied seemed, to the Neugebauers, resigned to the worst. He thought an investigator would achieve nothing, and the cost might blow out to anything. Manfred, however, convinced him it was the only course left open. 'If you don't pay, we will take it ourselves. We will not wait for your approval.'

They agreed, but Manfred felt that he was always having to convince the Habschieds of the necessity of all his actions. At first it was like they were putting their heads in the sand. To see and hear nothing. Then, knowing that their daughter would not run away, they seemed to lose all hope.

Not that Guenther Habschied was inactive. He had faxed youth hostels all over the couple's possible routes. Anke Neugebauer had found the addresses from a Youth Hostels publication, but she didn't know about the informal network of backpacker hostels where the majority of young travellers stayed.

The investigator, Neville Clarke, received his first briefing from

Manfred on 12 February. Manfred told him that owing to difficulties with the German Consul, Clarke should go about his inquiries discreetly, with no media support. They didn't want to disrupt any official investigations being got up through diplomatic channels.

Clarke would have bet the couple were going to show up; that they'd decided to change their itinerary or were working in a pub somewhere and they just couldn't bear to tell Mum and Dad about missing university. All Clarke had to go on was that they'd been at a hostel-type place in Sydney. He looked into it and found that the Cross was the most popular destination for backpackers.

He was also told that Anja had commented on the lovely Christmas tree in the hostel where they had stayed, so this gave him something to go on when he began canvassing around Kings Cross on 11 March. Everywhere he went he showed pictures of Gabor and Anja and asked the hostel staff if they had had a Christmas tree. The silver-haired investigator had only been out of the RAAF for a few months and still carried the bearing of a military man or, perhaps, a policeman. He made it clear that he wasn't from the constabulary, but he got the impression they thought he was maybe a father looking for a runaway teenager, or a process server or debt collector – and he wasn't always given the best answers. Over the next few days, he started to dress down and didn't shave, trying to look grubbier. He found he fared better.

Clarke had been a Queensland policeman up until 1969 before he joined the air force police where – apart from drug suppression, counter espionage and counter subversion – the main task was tracking AWOL servicemen. It was the era of the Vietnam War, so there was no shortage of men who didn't want to be found, just as he thought these missing Germans might not want to be found. The main thing he learnt from all those years in the service was persistence – keep going back.

He spent a few days in the Cross. He checked nineteen hostels, flop houses and rooms to rent around Victoria Street and came up with nothing. While his appearance was getting shabbier each day, his bearing was such that he was never going to look completely at home.

When he tried the Original Backpackers, he showed a young woman the photos and she didn't recognise them. She wasn't there at Christmas. There were so many young people, so many languages, coming and going with all their gear. He could see he was up against it. He knew that many of the staff of these places only worked for a few weeks or months and wouldn't have a long corporate memory.

He left and had a cup of coffee on Victoria Street, about to give the hunt away, saying, 'they haven't jolly-well been to Sydney, certainly not Kings Cross', but he couldn't help thinking he should have another go. He went back over the road and this time an older woman was at the desk.

'Did you have a Christmas tree here?' he asked.

She said yes, and Clarke flashed her the pictures. The woman instantly recognised the couple – Anja had changed $20 to phone Germany on Christmas Day. She took out the books. They booked in on 23 December 1991. They'd occupied room five – a double. Not a dorm. Most importantly for Clarke, she thought she recalled them saying they were heading north, to the Gold Coast and Cairns.

He telephoned the Neugebauers that night. Manfred said he didn't think they would go north, back up the east coast, because they'd already been that way. Clarke also had news from the German Embassy: 'Mr Kalinowski told me that he didn't think you coming to Australia would serve any useful purpose.'

Clarke's next step was to find where they went after leaving Sydney. Since it appeared they had gone north, he thought about checking out Nimbin, in northern New South Wales, to see if maybe they'd taken up with the alternative lifestylers – gone feral, to put it unkindly. But a police friend told him he'd get nowhere with the locals there. Clarke phoned the Cairns Backpackers Inn and dozens of hostels all the way down the Queensland coast. He drove to Coffs Harbour to check out a transient hippie-type community he was told about, but drew a blank. He tried some sources up in Darwin but they came up with no traces either.

Everything was pointing back to the Original Backpackers. Clarke's earlier prediction that the couple would turn up had soured. He started to think of different scenarios: did they go swimming and get washed out to sea? Were they caught in a gorge or climbing in the mountains? But the more he thought about it, the more it looked like the pair had been done away with.

Clarke gave the Neugebauers his report on 22 March. It wasn't much, but it was the first time the parents had something definite, a starting point – the Original Backpackers. Manfred – supporting two students and a mortgage – could no longer afford to retain Clarke.

'Now we will go to Australia and take a look for ourselves,' he announced to Anke. She had at first been reluctant to go because she feared that Gabor would phone and nobody would be there but, as time went by, this became less compelling. They booked a flight immediately. Shortly before they left, Anke rang the Habschieds. 'Come with me to Australia,' she urged Olga. Mrs Habschied didn't want to go, but said her son Norbert would.

Neville Clarke did another report for them on 7 April. 'A very reliable and experienced source here in Sydney suggests that the pair may have been disposed of and their passports altered and used by others to exit Australia. No passports under the names have been recorded as having departed Australia to date.' A former detective had told him there were so many missing people on the books – many of them couples – a task force should have been set up.

Joanne Walters was still working as a nanny in Kirribilli in February 1992. Next door, a young Australian, Liz, was doing the same for an English couple. The two girls often got together with their young charges by the Jensen pool and just nattered away. Liz was going to England with her employers and the two girls made plans to meet there the following year to go travelling through Europe. It was easy living. The dreams were free. Kirribilli is one of Sydney's more sought-after addresses – the prime minister and governor-general keep their official Sydney residences there. Anything was possible as they looked out across the harbour to the Opera House.

Then, one day, Joanne announced that some friends were going fruit picking and she was joining them. Jean Jensen thought Joanne quite intrepid, perhaps even fearless, in her ability to get around town at all hours on public transport. Jean wouldn't walk down the street to the Royal Yacht Squadron by herself at night. She thought Joanne had met so many good people that she assumed all Australians were equally as friendly and trustworthy. Jean knew better, and she recalled to Joanne a saying from her childhood in the bush. 'There are nuts and bolts in every community, so just be careful.' She knew that in these small towns the itinerant workers weren't always welcomed by the locals.

Just about all backpackers had been hitchhikers a few years earlier. Trains held a legislated monopoly for travel within New South Wales.

They were slow and infrequent and not always cheap. More importantly for backpackers, they didn't go to a lot of coastal towns. So the only way to get around on short hops up the coast had been to hitch or buy a car. Victoria Street had turned into a de facto car market as the FOR SALE signs went up in the windows while travellers waited in the gutter for someone to buy the car and take it on another lap of the country.

But, in the late eighties, buses had taken over the coastal transport business. They offered dirt-cheap fares and quickly became the most common mode of transport for young travellers. Hordes of spruikers would greet them at the major stops like Byron Bay and ferry them to hostels with swimming pools and float tanks for just $10 a night. Backpacking just got easier and easier. By 1991, only one in five backpackers did any hitchhiking and considerably fewer used it as their main mode of transport. The opportunities to get out and meet the people – to have a 'real' experience – were dwindling.

Joanne and her new friend Caroline knew this.

Grape grower and winemaker Vince Capogreco had rung a hostel looking for workers for his family's vineyard. The picking season ran from early February to late March. Backpackers had become a vital source of labour as locals became increasingly reluctant to adopt the itinerant lifestyle.

Joanne answered the ad telling Capogreco that a group would be down in early February. He told her in his broad Australian accent with its strange twist of Italian, that he'd pick them up in Mildura.

Joanne, her flatmate Nina, Caroline, and a Dutch girl, Jantina, set off to go fruit picking. They took a train to Liverpool and split up. Two girls never had problems getting a lift. Nina and Joanne didn't even have to walk to the highway. They got a lift from the station to a 'nite spot' called the Copacabana on the Hume Highway, right next to Lombardo's little shopping centre.

Then they were away: a lift from a truckie 460 kilometres to Wagga Wagga, then a 560 kilometre ride to Mildura, a town built on the irrigation systems on the Victorian side of the Murray River. Tina and Caroline got a lift straightaway, then picked up a truck going to Mildura. They stayed the night in the truck and arrived in Mildura around 11 a.m. Joanne and Nina arrived one or two hours later. Caroline's friend, Resy, followed them down by bus.

Caroline wrote to her friend Gill Baker.

19/2/92

G'day, how the devil are you . . . I'm no longer in Sydney but actually in Victoria in a place called Mildura for 6 to 8 weeks. I'm doing some grape picking. Been here about two weeks and to be honest, two weeks too long. But the money's not bad, about 40 pound a day. I'm not paying any rent so it's even better. Came up here with four other girls so it's not so bad and we all get on really well and have a good laugh in the evening. Great farm situated about 10kms away from the extremely exciting town of Mildura. So it's very difficult to get in, so all the more money is going into the bank. Makes a change doesn't it. Well my plans have changed from the last time I wrote because I've met up with this girl called Joanne from Wales and the two of us have decided to go back to Sydney for another couple of months and work to get about $5000 (that's 2500 pound) and travel around Australia for a couple of months, which is a bit disappointing really because I wanted to spend longer, but the best bit is yet to come and we've both decided to come home through Asia, starting from Darwin, over to Indonesia, Malaysia, Thailand, Singapore, Nepal, India, Pakistan Afghanistan, China, Hong Kong and catching the trans-Siberian railway home, so I may well be back around Christmas time but don't count on it . . .

By 23 March, the grapes had been picked and the Capogrecos put on a nice spread for their pickers. They didn't usually do it but this was such a good bunch, they thought they'd do something special for them. Pictures and home videos were taken. Next day, Vince Capogreco dropped them at a roadhouse near Mildura and they split into groups: Joanne and Caroline picked up a truck heading towards Sydney, where they all met up again at a hostel in Tusculum Street, Kings Cross.

When the girls got back to Sydney, it was obvious to Simon Wharton that they were having the best time of their lives. They couldn't stop talking about it all. How Joanne was the lucky one. She could lose her purse in Kings Cross Station and still have it handed in. Nina was going on about how, no matter what she did, she couldn't pick as many grapes as Joanne. Joanne would be nattering away, while Nina would be hard at it but still pick less. Joanne just seemed to get the healthiest most easily accessible vines. Fortune smiled on her.

Caroline, who'd been cooped up in the T-shirt factory, working her bum off all summer, as well as getting sick and going to hospital, had been pale and English-looking when she left, but now she was tanned and healthy. But they immediately started wondering what the hell they were doing back in the city. They decided Tasmania was the go – apple picking or whatever. So they up and left on 28 March, just days after getting back. This time, they took the train to Casula, one stop past Liverpool, because they heard it was closer to the highway and generally unmanned so you didn't have to buy a ticket. They then walked out to the highway, turning left at Lombardo's. They split into pairs: Steve Wright, a south Londoner they'd met at Capogreco's, with Joanne; Nina with Caroline.

They boarded the Abel Tasman ferry bound for Devonport, arriving 30 March. They soon moved on to Launceston. Steve, Joanne and Caroline went shopping and bought a little cooker and Joanne bought a blue and mauve Caribee 'Blaze' sleeping bag. There was no picking work to be had, however, in the Apple Isle, so they split into pairs again and hitched to Hobart to look for work. Again a blank. The weather was awful, reminded them of home, so on 12 April, the group split. Joanne and Caroline decided to head back to New South Wales.

Steve had no real use for the tent he bought six weeks earlier in Mildura. It was too big for him, so he did a swap: Caroline's small tent, which was falling apart, for his brand new three-man one, which the girls planned to share. He handed it over, complete with a hole he'd made by accident with his grape-cutting knife. He had meant to stitch it, but hadn't got around to it. Instead, it was held together by the little sticky labels he'd had made up with the addresses of friends on them for sticking on postcards. Also in the tent bag was a clothesline he'd meant to keep. It had snapped and he'd repaired it.

On their way back to Sydney the girls scored a job in Batlow, in southern New South Wales, picking apples, but were found to be bruising too many and were told on their first day that they were no longer required. They all met up again around 15 April in Kings Cross where Joanne and Caroline were staying at a hostel on Darlinghurst Road, the main sleaze strip of Sydney, directly opposite the 'World Famous Love Machine'. Similar joints were dotted all the way along the street, punctuated by takeaway food shops, dutyfree stores and mysterious doorways.

Joanne and Caroline didn't have a television in their room but it probably wouldn't have done them any good if they'd seen the story that night about the missing Germans; or even if they'd been stopped in the street by the well-dressed couple working the hostels of Kings Cross that day and the next showing two pictures to anyone who would stop.

'We are the parents looking for our children who visited Australia and Kings Cross,' said the mother on that night's episode of 'Real Life'.

'They are Germans?' asked a young traveller.

'Yes and she is here with red hair,' the mother's words cracking with stress. 'Their names are Gabor and Anja.'

Heads shook. 'No, sorry.'

Over and over.

TWENTY-NINE

April 1992

DOPE TALK

The Neugebauers and Norbert Habschied flew into Sydney on 10 April. The German foreign office was still telling them not to go; that everything that could be done was being done. Mr Kalinowski was really annoying Manfred telling him that making a fuss about it wouldn't help. Manfred felt there had not been any trouble and even if there was, they no longer had anything to lose.

For Manfred, the fact that Anja and Gabor had not drawn any money since Anja cashed $500 on 16 December (Gabor hadn't drawn anything since 5000DM [$4000] before leaving Germany) should be unavoidably compelling, even to the most cynical authorities.

From the time they hit the ground, the media were interested. The Australian Federal Police media officer, Phil Castles, had issued a press release flagging their arrival and the media had responded. Manfred would continue to be amazed at the way people rallied around.

When they flew in they were shocked by the reception. They were only expecting Neville Clarke, the investigator. But relatives of their daughter's partner, the Klaasons, had turned up with their friends Rita and Peter O'Malley, who spoke German, plus the Federal Police and several newspapers.

The Federal Police whisked them through customs and into a brief interview. They declined press interviews at the airport. They were too tired. The Klaasons took them to their home in Coogee.

The Sunday papers came back to talk to them next day. Then followed television. 'Good Morning Australia' flashed up a phone number for people with information. They hadn't left the studio building before it started ringing. Some of the calls were interesting, but mostly they were misleading. People had recommendations and observations. 'I have seen your children on Bali,' said one caller who insisted they were on a Russian ship. Manfred would always remember that caller and wonder if he was a guilty party trying to take them off the scent. But at the time he was just grateful for the information. He noted it and asked for specifics. He was still struggling with the Australian accent so it was difficult. Police logged some 200 calls during the next week.

The Neugebauers were told to get on 'A Current Affair' because it was the highest-rating current affairs show, but its people weren't interested. The Klaasons were ringing all the media up, proving to be an effective PR machine. On Monday, 13 April, they were run on Channel Nine News with the top-rating Brian Henderson telling viewers: 'Australian police hold grave fears for two German tourists who haven't been heard of since Christmas.' Reporter Russell Bishop showed Mrs Neugebauer obviously upset: 'I hope he will turn up and I hope we will bring him back to Germany with Anja together.'

Norbert Habschied said of his sister: 'She is very realistic. She don't get into a car where a crazy man in it. She says, "No thank you, go away". She absolutely has something against drugs. She don't want that. Also she didn't like alcohol or smoking.'

Bishop: 'The families are confident someone will remember the couple. Both have nose studs. Gabor has an ear ring and Anja a shock of red hair.'

Manfred: 'Tell us where you have seen them or if you cannot inform us, please inform ze local police.'

Then, on the night Joanne and Caroline were planning to head off on their big adventure, Channel Seven's 'Real Life' became the first to start linking the disappearing tourists, connecting Neugebauer, Habschied, Schmidl, a missing Zimbabwean student and a Japanese tourist, Naoka Onda, who disappeared after checking out of a Queensland hotel in the company of a man.

The cameras followed the Neugebauers as they launched into search mode, canvassing young travellers around the Cross. The reporter said that Anja was at first thought to be 'Jane Doe', the body of a young woman found at the time Anja went missing and whose identity was still baffling police. (The body was later found to be Vivienne Lynda Ruiz, murdered by her boyfriend Richard White, when she told him she was working as a prostitute.) 'Police are tight-lipped about the possibility of a pattern emerging from the string of missing tourists but it is a trend they are closely monitoring.'

Nick Collins and Paul Miller had become good mates with their mutual love of mull and motorbikes. When they were driving about, if Miller ever seen any hitchhikers, he'd go off. 'If the cunts can't afford their own car, fuck 'em. Fucking bums.' He told Collins his trick was to drive up to 'em fast, then brake in the gravel, spraying it into them.

One night at Boral, Collins had a few bongs and was crashed out in the tearoom when someone stole his wallet with $500 in it. He was sure it was a distant relative of Miller's. It wasn't just the money; that wallet was the only thing his father ever left him and the little maggot threw it in the furnace after he got the cash out. Collins, a tall lean muscular guy, was looking for him. He told Miller, knowing he was his relative, 'I'll kill the bastard.'

Miller could see his point. 'I won't touch you, but the brothers will get ya.' Nick knew what he meant.

This same relative had shot a guy through the door of his house in early 1991, late '90, around Lurnea. He had given the guy $400 for an ounce of pot which never came through. So he shot him in the elbow. Ivan took an exceptionally rare day off work to give character evidence in court and the cousin got away with weekend detention until he screwed up some credit card fraud and was put away full-time. There was talk that, another time, Ivan was involved in bashing a guy as payback for this cousin getting beaten up.

Nick Collins came in for the afternoon shift at Boral one day in early 1992. He hung up his jacket with his stash in the pocket. In walked a much-hated company executive with two detectives. Someone had tipped them off about the drug dealing going on.

They took him to the office, frisked him, searched his locker, took him out to his car and searched that. There, they found four grams of leaf lying around loose. The stuff he'd throw out when he was putting bags of bud together. It was enough for the cops to bust him anyway. They hammered him about being the site's resident dealer and he kept denying it. 'What about Paul Miller?'

'No. Not him either.' Collins was thinking how lucky Miller was, being rostered off that day. Half the pot in the jacket was his.

'Tell us about Miller and you can go.'

'No. I don't know nothing about him.'

They took Collins to the police station where he was told he had $1700 worth of traffic warrants outstanding. 'You pay these if you want to go home.' He was sure his wife had paid them already, but he wasn't asking any questions. He paid cash, and they threw him out the door with no charges and no receipt. One of Collins' colleagues had already picked up his jacket and found the big wad of pot in the pocket and put it away for safe keeping. He had a hell of a lot in there.

In early 1992, a new bloke came on, Steve Scott, thirty-six, same age as Miller. He started on the nightshift – 10.30 p.m. to 6.30 a.m. – on the unloader with Miller. No one had told him what to do so he was pretty hopeless. There was a knack to picking up the cornice and stacking it. The pain in his arms was intense. He had to hold it a certain way and if he went the wrong way he could hurt his partner. Miller straight up refused to work with him. Scott was amazed that no one stood up to this guy. Scott had been a supervisor at his previous job and this sort of thing wouldn't have happened. He had the build of a rugby league footballer, only taller, and he had short spiky hair. The rumour went around that he was a copper trying to find the drug dealer. The way he looked, it wouldn't have taken any stretch of the imagination to believe.

Miller'd come in half pissed from the pub. He'd have his first hour off, while the other crew worked, then say, angrily, 'I'm not working with you. No one's trained ya.' Then to the foreman: 'I'm going home.' And he'd storm off. No one said a thing. Scott wanted to belt him that first week. He complained to the foreman, who just said: 'Come on, fellers, work together.' They were all gutless.

Scott eventually got to know him. He learned the unloader and, like Miller, considered himself a pretty good gambler. Especially at backgammon. They used to bet a dollar a point, and have some epic struggles as the factory hummed away through the night. Other times, they'd just sleep. He'd get home after dawn and couldn't sleep because work had left him too well rested.

As Scott came to know Miller, he found himself thinking he was a nice bloke. Then in the same breath he'd say he was an arsehole. It was hard to know what to make of him. He certainly didn't fit the 'Aussie larrikin' mould. Scott couldn't work with him when he was falling-over drunk or full of drugs. The nights when he came in pissed, you'd write it off. Bong after bong after bong. The little orange juice bottle was never without wisps of white smoke, licking out of it. Then he'd be off on one of his rants and Scott – who wouldn't have known what a dope plant looked like – was stuck. Miller talked about his girlfriend 'drinking that bloody scotch before breakfast... bought me son a $2000 little toy car you drive... You shoot a goat you don't just shoot it you blow it to smithereens.'

Steve Scott also helped Miller make bullets for his black powder musket. For some reason, Miller didn't like doing them, and so would go out and actually work Scott's share while he sat in the tearoom with these flat sheets of lead and a little Bunsen burner. He'd spoon it out of the bubbling crucible, happy as Larry. Scott wouldn't know a bullet if it hit him. He just followed Miller's instructions and either put the lead in the ball moulds or the ones he equated to those he saw in cartoons – standard bullet shape. It was fun. Better than working. Scott was just amazed at what you could get away with.

Miller brought in a crossbow one night. Shot it down the production line. He brought guns in to work too. Collins saw him shooting one with a silencer into the gypsum pit. 'Ph... ph... ph.' He was such a kid. Another night, Paul Douglas was in the computer room, his head down, writing up something. He heard the door open, but didn't look up. Suddenly there was an almighty bang next to his ear. He looked up in fright and Miller had a hand gun at his forehead. There were two people outside laughing. Douglas went off his brain with his ears ringing around his head.

Collins got to know Miller better than most. He rang him at home a lot, asked for Paul and then heard whoever answered the phone yell out: 'Richard, it's for you.'

'Eh mate, what's this Paul/Richard business?' Collins asked.

'Richard's me real name.'

Some time after photo driver's licences were introduced in 1991, everybody in the tearoom was showing theirs around. Miller took his out, showed a few guys it was in the name of Richard James Milat.

'What have you got that for?'

'Never know when you might need it.' He also had one in the name of Paul Miller, and Paul Douglas wondered what he'd need two licences for. Another piece in the strange jigsaw of Paul Miller.

It reminded Des Butler of the time Miller had come in with his hair dyed light brown. Then a while later his hair was dark again. 'I've got to get a new licence,' he said, as if that explained it. His appearance changed regularly. He'd have a beard, let it grow, then cut it back to a goatee, then a mo, and back to square one again.

They never asked for an explanation because with Miller – they continued calling him that even after they learned his real name – you didn't want to get him started. You didn't delve. They were stuck on this machine with him and questions risked hours and hours more bull.

It was a night like that, just before Easter 1992, Miller was working the unloader with Des Butler. They were talking about something or other which triggered something in Miller's scattergun brain. 'Oh yeah. I know who killed those Germans,' he said.[88] And just as quickly his mind was off in other directions. Butler didn't say anything because he didn't believe him. It had to be the marijuana talking, and if he asked any more questions, he just risked more babble. He remembered it though, because he'd been reading about some missing Germans – their parents had been out looking for them – vanished off the face of the earth. Maybe Miller read the same articles.

THIRTY

Mid 1992

LIMBO

Joanne and Caroline had a farewell on Good Friday, 17 April, with most of the gang from the old flat. They were breaking up. Resy had already gone home to the Netherlands to begin an agriculture course and Tina was leaving next day to go home via Bali. Nina Tunnicliffe was doing her own thing.

The girls were still bubbling from their travels, and they were showing their pictures off to Ben and Simon who'd been stuck in the city. They were keen to get back on the road, but their plans were hazy. Plan A was to organise a lift with a truckie, plan B was to just hitch, Simon thought. He and Ben left to go to a birthday bash at a pub in Paddington.

About 10.30 p.m., a fellow backpacker, Dennis Sisterson, manning the desk of the hostel on Darlinghurst Road, saw Joanne and Caroline leave. They told him they were catching a late-night coach for Alice Springs, but he couldn't understand why they didn't have any packs.

Caroline snuck back upstairs into Steve Wright's room where she and Joanne were to crash the night for free. Joanne went over the road to Studebakers for a few hours with Pauline Reid, the girl with whom she had come to Australia. Pauline thought the girls were waiting on a telephone call from a woman in Western Australia, or 'that sort of direction', to go fruit picking. It would be hard to remember. Nina thought they had a contact in Kununurra at the very top of Western Australia. Their visas were running out and everybody knew you couldn't extend your visa – so they were thinking they might overstay. That was easy.

The girls left early next morning to get past the desk unseen. Their plan was to go the same way as before: train to Casula; walk to the highway, near Lombardo's. Steve Wright saw them go at about 7.30 a.m. He thought they planned to hitch to Melbourne and then west along the Great Ocean Road with its spectacular rock pinnacles, then on to the far north-west. He left the same day and hitched north to Byron Bay, then Cairns, before flying home to a job in the city.

No road crews were working that Easter Saturday. There were plenty of coppers about. New South Wales police had already booked 2248 drivers in the first twenty-four hours of the long weekend road blitz. Still, by Saturday, ten people were already laid out in morgues across the country – victims of road accidents.

Across town at the Royal Easter Show, Kevin Burgess was fuming. Phil Polglase had done it to him again. Burgess had got Polglase this plum job at the Show. It was big money, but it took a bit of responsibility; something he should have known Phil didn't have. First, Phil had missed the bus down from Taree on the New South Wales mid-north coast. They had to set up the rides and, since Phil was a carpenter, it was one of the reasons they employed him in the first place. Then he turned up out of the blue, days late, expecting to get a start. Most of the work had already been done . . . but it must have been something about Phil that persuaded them to give him a chance. Nice bloke 'Polly', you couldn't help liking him but, Geez, you could choke him.

He was working on the rollercoaster and the Ferris wheel. He'd do fourteen hours on that, then they'd have to go in and sleep with the stock from the stalls. The showground at night was full of thieves. You had to watch everything. Burgess never saw Phil during the day, but he expected to see him back at their little makeshift camp in the shipping container each night. They had beds, power, and a little TV in there, so it wasn't too rough.

Now, here he was, missing two nights in a row.

Phil had built most of Burgess' home up near Taree. 'Most of it', because he'd gone walkabout when it was 90 per cent done. When he actually did work, it was good quality, but you'd have to chase him for everything. He was always going to finish it tomorrow, no worries.

Burgess forgave him that, but he could have decked him now. Burgess had been a 'showie' since he fought as Kevin Rose taking on all comers in the old tent boxing troupes like Jimmy Sharman's. The show had to go on. Phil should know that. The bosses were having a shot at Burgess so, when Phil did get back on Easter Sunday, Burgess had a shot at him. 'You're supposed to be here. You're making me look bad now, you know . . . Where was you last night, anyway?'

'I come in, you were asleep. And then I left early.'

'Nah, nah, you never come home.' Burgess had got up at 6 a.m. like he did every morning, and he was a light sleeper, so he wasn't buying Phil's crap. But wherever Phil had been, he wasn't saying.

Phillip Polglase had in fact been around to his mate Paul Foster's place at Guildford on the Friday night but then he'd run into his old mate 'Bodge', David John Milat, up at the Golf View Hotel (formerly the Grand Villa). Bodge told Phil he could crash at their place.

Phil was sleeping on the lounge when Ivan came back, about 5.30 a.m. He got up, and they had a cup of coffee. These Milats could really drink the stuff. Phil saw that Ivan had a gun painted in camouflage colours and this dirty-great hunting knife with a 20 centimetre blade about four centimetres wide. It was in a brown leather sheath with what looked like a brown and white ivory handle. He also had a revolver and a machete. Polglase pulled the razor-sharp knife from its sheath. There was a dark stain up near the top of the blade. It looked like it had been wiped, but it was tacky. Not dry yet.

'There's still blood on the knife,' said Ivan.

'Did you go out shooting?'

'Yeah, out hunting.'

'Did you shoot a goat or something?' Polglase asked, knowing they had goats out at the Wombeyan Caves property, although he hadn't been there.

'That's human blood,' Ivan said, as if he was joking, 'I stabbed a bloke with it . . . stabbed him through the spine.'

Somehow the conversation got on to hitchhiking. Polglase told how he'd hitched up to North Queensland in January 1983 and that there were all these murders going on up there then.

'Yeah,' said Ivan, 'there's a heap of unsolved killings around the Canberra–Queanbeyan area.' Phil didn't know anything about that.

Ivan asked Polglase if he could stab someone.

'Not me, mate.'

It was all a bit surreal for Phil, getting up in the middle of the night, having this dream scene going down. Ivan offered him a German male's passport and he saw at least one other passport of a female German: blondish hair, with glasses, he'd recall.

Phil didn't take things any further. It all seemed like bullshit talk to him.

Bodge drove Phil to Granville Railway Station and, as they were going, Bodge told him: 'You shouldn't come around and stay while Ivan is here 'cause he's easily upset. He's a bit of an aggro type . . . Ivan's been doing something bad, years ago . . . We stopped him, but now we think he's doing it again.'[89]

Phil asked Bodge if he meant armed robberies.

'No, it's worse than that.'

At the end of the Royal Easter Show, Polglase told Kevin Burgess he wasn't going back to Taree with him. He was going to hang around down in Sydney. Burgess felt sorry for Phil's wife Gail and the tribe of kids he always seemed to be running away from – then running back to. He was his own worst enemy, Phil.

The Neugebauers and Norbert Habschied hired a campervan, leaving on Easter Sunday, just hours after Phil Polglase had been woken by the hunter's return. They headed north because that was the way the people at the hostel thought Anja and Gabor were going. First night, they camped by a beach, then they did Nimbin, where they had been warned to expect the psychedelic decor and the hardcore feral culture. The dreadlocked young people there seemed to genuinely want to help. In a cafe with bad coffee and sweet-smelling smoke all around, a girl thought she recognised the photographs. Thought she'd seen them in January, but they dismissed the sighting because of the date. The Neugebauers didn't know it, but Gabor and Anja had been there in December. They later found the driver of the car in which Anja and Gabor had come down the east coast. The driver had the first joint of his life there, but Gabor and Anja had declined.

Manfred's English was a lot better than Anke's and improving as they canvassed up the long Queensland coast. His English lessons had been terminated when the Russians arrived in 1945. He went to Berlin in 1952, aged eighteen, and caught a train into the west. Everyone was poor on both sides of what would later become the Berlin Wall. There were still great plains of rubble stretching across the city. He knew days of hunger. He joined the air force and wanted to be a pilot, but he was cut from the initial intake because his English wasn't good enough. So, he went into infrastructure, building airfields and underground defences, and continued working on his English. He met Anke, a dark-haired woman with the most regal bearing, while doing security at an air force open day.

In Brisbane, they had a radio interview and an ABC television interview which was seen in Darwin. A woman called from there, saying she'd seen Anja and Gabor in a tent at her caravan park. The woman was convincing, despite the evidence of the parcel not having been collected at Darwin's post office. Perhaps they hadn't had time to collect it. Manfred and Anke decided they must go to Darwin, despite the great distance.

Before they left, they attended a meeting of a missing-persons group in a park – a sad assembly whose faces told the stories, all caught in the limbo of not knowing what had befallen their loved ones. The Neugebauers knew they were not alone in this unhappy fate, but they couldn't resign themselves to it yet.

Norbert left them in Brisbane. He had to return home. The Neugebauers headed up the Queensland coast, 1356 kilometres to Townsville, then 886 kilometres to Mount Isa via Richmond where the police had been so kind to Gabor after he lost his money belt. They were going to buy the policemen some beer, but the station was empty. Then from Mount Isa to Tennant Creek, 636 kilometres. These weren't European kilometres. These were dusty-hot-and-bumpy kilometres. It was their first experience of the outback, and the huge distances between nothing and not much. The road trains took them completely by surprise – having to get off the road when the huge two- and three-trailer trucks came at them. Such dust. Red clouds all around and cobalt blue above. It was worse than any fog in Germany. And having to overtake the road trains was worse still.

They talked a lot on those straight, lonely stretches of road; always about what could have happened. How could they trace them? Where are the clues? Still they had to think of where to stay each night, where the next petrol was. There was no time to become despondent; no time for the indulgence of feelings. There was, however, time to think. Manfred had known as a child all about missing loved ones. He had a brother missing on the eastern front for months after the war. When the Russians came in '45, the war was already over. All girls and young women had to be hidden away, and all possessions too. Some girls tried to get around in old women's clothes, but mostly they hid. His family joined the columns of refugees fleeing to Czechoslovakia, only 50 kilometres away. In the chaos of the road, on a black night, his sister was suddenly gone.

The family drifted back to its village and the little bakery they ran, but still no sign of the sister. The rapes had stopped as order was restored, but he watched his mother fret for his sister and, of course, that infused itself in young Manfred, eleven. And then one day somebody knocked on the door with word that his brother was alive in Czechoslovakia. He turned up much later looking like a stranger. Then word came, again by messenger, that his sister was safe over near the French border, working for her keep on a vineyard.

There was no solace in these happy endings as the Neugebauers battled the tedium of the Barkly Highway. Germany then was in chaos. Australia now was peaceful, the people so friendly, and the communications so accessible, there was only room for the worst of conclusions in this best of all possible worlds.

On the 984 kilometre run from Tennant Creek to Darwin, they picked up a young girl, hitching out of Katherine alone. They told her why they were there. 'Do you know how dangerous it is to hitchhike?' Manfred asked.

'I don't believe it,' she said, saying that she'd been hitching around the United States and New Zealand since leaving high school and never had any trouble. They had been conversing in English and it was only later they realised she, too, was German. They told her about Gabor and Anja, but it didn't seem to faze her.

The Darwin caravan park was fruitless so, returning south, they stopped at the Kookaburra Lodge in Katherine. The pictures of Gabor and Anja which had been mailed all over Australia were on the wall. The staff didn't remember them, but they had a look at the registry and sure enough the couple had stayed there. Then someone remembered them being in a group which went canoeing in Katherine Gorge. There were some addresses for others who went with them. Anke later wrote to them but didn't get much response. A Swiss remembered them, but said they kept to themselves.

Time was running out and the Neugebauers had to start driving hard. They did another TV interview in Alice Springs, but never heard if it created any response. There was no longer time for canvassing.

They had to make 1000 kilometres a day to get back to Sydney for the flight home. They didn't want to drive at night because of the kangaroos' habit of jumping in front of headlights. The country was in drought and kangaroos are drawn to the side of black-top roads at such times. Water vapour is drawn up from deep below the hot bitumen, then condenses and flows with the camber to the sides of highways, bringing grass and 'roos. The Neugebauers had seen thousands of 'roo and emu carcasses and skeletons. It was carnage. Even after thousands of kilometres they hadn't seen a live kangaroo until one bounced off their bullbar and hopped back into the night, north of Katherine.

They had found nothing useful. The room for hope was being squeezed. In those last few days as Anke refused to give up, wanting to believe Gabor had run away or something – anything to give her hope – Manfred would snap back, a little angry, 'Why do you say such bad things about our son? He wouldn't behave as you think. He would always tell us where he is. He would never disappear.' Manfred could only entertain the possibility that he was alive if perhaps he was being held against his will somewhere. Somebody told him farmers kept slave labour on farms, but that didn't sound right. Now, having seen the outback, he could see the possibility of them dying of thirst somewhere out there.

They returned to Sydney on Saturday, 9 May, having travelled more than 9000 kilometres in twenty days. On their travels, they had met a woman who told them of a fortune teller in Sydney, Margaret Dent. They were walking around blind, why not clutch at straws? So they visited her a few hours before their flight home.

'You should have come to me earlier,' said the seer. 'It would not have been necessary for you to go searching such a long way.' She told them both children were dead. Anke burst into tears. Anke's recollection would differ from Manfred's. Anke was sure Dent said their bodies were lying in a forest with other bodies. Manfred would recall only that she said, 'The girl suffered very badly. She died an awful death, but your son died very quickly.' Anke was distraught. For Manfred, the prophecy concurred with what he already guessed. 'Can you tell us where it happened?' he asked.

'I see wood and timber.'

'Is it possible to say north or south?'

'Only wood and timber.'

'Will they ever be found?'

'It will not be long. Maybe two to four years.'

Back in Germany, an Arabic neighbour who claimed some psychic ability told Anke Gabor was alive. She found solace in that.

The following months saw Manfred and Anke descend into that nether world inhabited by the people they saw in the Brisbane park; the people for whom the phone can never ring without a twang of hope nor the doorbell without a little dread.

Father's Day passed and Joanne Walters hadn't called her dad, Ray, for over a month. She was the sort of girl to go out of her way for that sort of thing. Ray Walters had already rung the bank to find out when her account had last moved. They told him 18 May, just a few days earlier. That had been a huge relief. She was alive. Then the teller rang back an hour later. He'd made a mistake. It was just a bank transaction. She hadn't withdrawn anything since 16 April, the day after her last call. In that call, she said something about hitching to Melbourne. Joanne had never mentioned hitchhiking before. Her mother warned her against it and as she was about to hang up, Jill said, 'Ring me in a fortnight's time.'

'I'll ring you before that, just to let you know where I am.'

And that was it.

Now as their fears began to set in, Ray rang the Capogreco vineyard and the few other contacts he had. Joanne's return ticket was due to bring her home on 27 May. Her visa ran out on 28 May. If she wasn't back by then, it must be serious.

Jean Jensen, the grandmother of the baby Joanne Walters had looked after, had also been thinking a little about Joanne who seemed like the sort of girl who would let her know how she was going, and would certainly have said goodbye before leaving the country. But one postcard from Mildura and one from Huonville, Tasmania, on 10 April and that was it.

Then the phone rang on Thursday, 28 May, with a male Welsh voice on the other end.

Ray Walters explained that he and his wife were worried about Joanne.

'That's funny, I've been wondering too,' said Jensen. 'Joanne promised to stay in touch and I'm sure she would have come by to see Nicholas before leaving.' They agreed that the police had to be called.

Walters reported her missing in Wales and Jensen went to North Sydney Police Station the next day, Friday, 29 May. Constable Gary Booth asked her: 'Do you just wish to make contact, or are you concerned for her safety?'

'I'm concerned for her welfare,' Mrs Jensen replied, somewhat peeved.

Caroline Clarke had rung home from somewhere out in the bush on 12 April. She was all bubbly, saying that she and her new companion Joanne, a Welsh girl, had a promise of a job picking melons near Perth. It was a quick call, as usual, the coins clunking through the phone. Her parents, Ian and Jacquie, expected a letter every three or four weeks to fill in the detail. Caroline had no definite routine, so the Clarkes hardly thought to start worrying until she didn't call for her sister Emma's birthday on 8 May, and then her father's on 24 May. She was always very good with birthdays. The family was beginning to twitch fairly seriously, but not too seriously. For Ian Clarke, it was a case of: 'Hmmm, odd that Caroline hasn't called, but perhaps she's out on the road. Perhaps she's in the bush and can't reach a phone.'

Joanne had given her parents more details about her travelling companion than had Caroline – enough for Ray Walters to track the Clarkes down by phone. Walters got hold of Simon, five months back from his two-and-a-half-year odyssey, minding the labradors in Slaley. Simon told Walters his parents were with friends in Cornwall. Walters tried the number, but the Clarkes had just left. With the doggedness that was to become his defining quality, he tracked them to a hotel on the way back. He introduced himself and explained his fears. 'Have you heard anything?' he asked.

Walters' question set the alarms ringing in Ian Clarke's head. Now it was clear his butterfly daughter was with a more disciplined person. Clarke went into a spin, as all the subtle fears he had resisted expressing were suddenly illuminated. They started running through all the possible excuses. They were on a remote farm? An Aboriginal reserve? A fishing boat?

Walters had had little success with his own police force in South Wales, but Clarke was lucky to have good connections with the police through his job at the Bank of England.

He needed to have a close liaison with police. The Bank of England is, after all, a very secure place. One helped maintain that by being on good terms with the constabulary. Clarke put Ray Walters in touch with the head of security at the bank, Philip Corbett. Clarke's link to Corbett was fortuitous. The security chief was the former head of the International and Serious Crime Branch of the Metropolitan Police, which liaises with other countries on the practical crime-fighting front.

A slim, precise man who ran marathons, Corbett now had responsibility for all security matters relating to the bank: the guards, the gold, and Clarke's personal security. So, Ray Walters' hard slog had taken him from the simple offices of Maesteg's paper mill and union rooms, to the seat of real power: the Old Lady of Threadneedle Street, as Londoners call the edifice with its 1730s granite facade. It's never been robbed. Indeed, it was as safe as the Bank of England. And the man whose job for the last four years had been to keep it that way was Corbett. England's gold reserves sat somewhere deep below his desk in the basement. The man had weight. He was glad to be able to use some of it to help. Walters told him about the two girls and their last movements. He had already contacted police and the Flying Doctor at Alice Springs.

Corbett was impressed by the amount of work Walters had already put in. He'd done all the basics – amassing a huge phone bill. He struck Corbett as being a very determined, constructive and logical researcher. He was a union convenor and he was bringing all his negotiating skills to bear with people he was speaking to in Australia and doing his damnedest to follow any clues.

Corbett's gut feeling tended towards the sinister even at that stage. He was perhaps over sensitised because one of the last cases he'd done with the Metropolitan Police was the paedophile murders of Jason Swift and Barry Lewis. A case which rocked Britain and which showed him the awful things people could do.

On 1 June, Corbett rang Detective Sergeant Cliff John at Bridgend in Glamorgan to see what they'd done regarding Joanne; let them know people were watching. Of course, there wasn't a lot that could be done from that end, but they had to get the ball rolling officially to put pressure on the Australians.

In Australia, Jean Jensen went back to the North Sydney Police Station on 4 June feeling like she hadn't forced any progress. Then Caroline was officially reported missing on 5 June. Corbett made some confidential recommendations to Clarke on the practicable way ahead. Among them: go directly to the Australian police rather than Interpol whose bureaucracy was a nightmare. Corbett made contact with the Australian High Commission, but it was hard convincing the two seconded Australian Federal Police officers, Alan Sing and Alan Bilby, of the case's importance. He knew that if he'd been in his former position, he would have found it very difficult to make a high-level commitment, costing thousands of pounds, when nobody knew where to start looking.

Ian Clarke rang the editor of the *Newcastle Chronicle*, Graham Stanton, whom he knew quite well. They had a long talk about the way to plug in to the media. Stanton rang the press office of the Australian High Commission, from which came the suggestion to enlist News Ltd Australia because the Murdoch papers had the greatest reach around Australia. Sarah Harris, who represented all Murdoch's dailies in Australia except *The Australian*, came in to the Bank of England on 8 June. She didn't need any convincing that it was a good story. Her article, the first on the case, appeared on 10 June, and it seemed to have some effect. Glenn Drake from Missing Persons came to interview Jean Jensen that day.

'It took you a while,' the spritely woman told him. 'I reported this on 29 May.'

'We have got to come in big on this one,' Drake told her.

Television picked it up that night. Ian Clarke told the camera in his very English way: 'We hope that she's having a good time somewhere and will surface in due time, but it is a long time and she is a responsible girl and I would have expected her to have spoken to us before now.' The report linked the disappearance to Neugebauer and Habschied, saying they all stayed at a Kings Cross hostel and were heading for South Australia's Riverland.

Because the girls had gone missing from Kings Cross, the investigation fell to Kings Cross detectives. It was, to say the least, a step down from Threadneedle Street. Some of the police were owned by drug dealers and pimps and so much of their time was spent on bag snatchers and collecting bribes that serious investigations suffered.[90]

A day might start down at the casualty ward of St Vincent's Hospital interviewing some assault victim. There were rarely any witnesses so the matter invariably went nowhere, but the job had to be done. A murder might happen; a reprisal for some druggie who'd burnt his ex-friends. There'd be no witnesses and no time to look for any because there'd be another assault victim down at Vinnie's.

Missing persons jobs usually went the other way. Kings Cross was at the receiving end, as the suburbs sent in their crazy mixed-up kids, the victims of abuse and boredom, to join some or all parts of the drugs/prostitution/victim spectrum of Sydney's underbelly.

Burnout among Kings Cross detectives was high, morale low. The twenty-five Ds shared just two cars and there was no system of working with a partner. Whoever was rostered on got the job. Whoever was free, went with him. And so it was that Detective Sergeant Neville Scullion was given the Clarke/Walters investigation.

When Scullion first started working the Cross as a constable out of the old Darlinghurst police station, he could sense a whiff of corruption among the senior officers, but it was only upon his return to the area as a detective sergeant that he was high enough to sniff out the source. An older officer pulled him aside and said the only thing that'd keep a cop at the arse end of the world – Kings Cross – was 'a drink or a quid'.

There was a feeling that this kind of thing had been happening since the First Fleet, and maybe it had, so why fight it. Scullion's first 'drink' came one night when his superior, Kim Thompson, handed him a $50 or a $100 note and said: 'You're on the late shift. That's yours to have a drink.' From then on, the envelopes came regularly.[91]

Money started rolling in for the boofy cop with the sagging jowls and the jug ears. He didn't have to do much for it, just leave the sleaze merchants alone. Favours, however, cost extra. It's just as well Ray Walters knew none of this. Scullion and he got off on the wrong foot from the start. Perhaps Walters was being unreasonable, complaining that there was only a sergeant dealing with his case; he thought it should have been the chief of police. But the focused, passionate Welshman and the cynical, corrupt copper weren't a good match.

Jean Jensen, however, noted how well dressed Scullion was. Very professional too, she thought.

Pauline Reid from the Shetlands was the first travelling companion to be made aware of the disappearance, and she helped Corbett round up others. Simon Wharton came back on 31 May. He was at home at Well in Yorkshire when his old man came upstairs after watching the local news. Because Caroline's parents lived up north, it was on the regional news. 'Do you know a Caroline Clarke?'

'Yeah, I went to school with her.'

'No, in Australia.'

'Yeah, I did.'

'Well, people think she's missing.' It was only nine weeks since he'd seen her, so he rang her parents. They'd swapped addresses, like you do. He might have come back with forty addresses, never really expecting to catch up with any of them, but maybe he and Caroline would have because they only lived an hour apart and they did have a bit of a thing – going for coffee and a trip to Taronga Zoo together. He rang her mother, but couldn't tell her anything they didn't already know. The last he heard, the girls might have been going to Queensland.

Corbett's influence did not go astray when his old colleague, the Chief Constable of Northumbria, John Stephens, very kindly introduced Detective Sergeant Tony Noble to the case on a permanent seconded basis. Noble worked night duty so he was able to communicate with people in Australia. He became the link between the two countries' police forces. He took the statements that Corbett hadn't already done.

While the Walters had great cause for concern, owing to Joanne's organised nature, the Clarkes could still have hope. What Caroline intended to do before breakfast might be totally different to what she was going to do after lunch. Ian and Jacquie were only too aware that the great attraction of backpacking was its freedom to change plans. They held onto this. It was all they had.

As the case generated publicity through July, and more than 100 sightings came in from all states, Glenn Drake from Missing Persons was able to say police were confident of finding Clarke and Walters alive. A large number of calls had come from the Northern Territory and Darwin. One of the best sightings – that the girls were working as cooks on a road construction site near Mount Isa in western Queensland – held currency for a few days before it fizzled. But a truck driver said he saw the women hitching near Mount Isa on Saturday, 2 May, carrying a sign saying 'Darwin'. That fizzled. Ayers Rock in a hire car: fizzled.

Then, out of the blue, two women rang the task force saying they'd picked up the girls and dropped them at Bulli Tops on the Princes Highway, overlooking Wollongong, south of Sydney.

Next thing, Ray Walters rang the women – Susan Burns and Myrna Honeyman – and wanted to have a chat. The police had faxed their statements to him and he believed it was a genuine sighting. When news of Burns and Honeyman's sighting broke, Ray Walters told the *Express*: 'At least now we know the girls left Sydney safe. Any news now is good news, but we are still anxious because it has been such a long time.'

Scullion announced the next day that they were working a new theory that the girls could be in the ski fields, because they'd had several consistent sightings down that way. So they thought the girls could have got back to the Hume Highway from Bulli Tops and down to the Snowy Mountains.

'We've developed a theory that the girls were given a lift in [a Pantec] truck from that location to a point near Canberra,' said Scullion. 'A woman has given us information which co-ordinates with this, because she says she picked up two British girls near Canberra around this time. She said the girls told her they were headed to Cooma where one of the girls said she wanted to visit distant relatives.'

On 10 July, Kings Cross police arrested a doorman suspected of cutting open a safe in Alice Springs and stealing $13,800, of which about seven grand had been burnt by his oxyacetylene torch. Scullion and some of his police mates went around to the doorman's hotel room and allegedly pocketed about $7000 in the unburnt notes and recorded that they found $5,120 there.[92] The deal was, the cops kept the money, the doorman shut up and the girlfriend walked with $200 to get her back to her home town. Rather than telling the guy to come clean, however, Scullion allegedly told him to plead not guilty so Scullion could get a free trip to the Alice to give evidence. His love of travel might also help explain his interest in the ski-field theory.

By late July, New South Wales Police Missing Persons had identified six young overseas travellers, each with plenty of cash and unexpired visas, who had disappeared inexplicably – Walters and Clarke, Neugebauer and Habschied, Simone Schmidl and Japanese tourist Naoka Onda, twenty-two, who disappeared four years earlier from Queensland's Gold Coast. All were regarded as reliable with strong family ties and friendships in their homelands.

The head of Missing Persons, Sergeant Marcon, told *Sydney Morning Herald* crime reporter Sandra Harvey that detectives in three states had been investigating the cases. 'I have to suggest that we've got nothing at this point to suggest they've been killed, but we've had a massive media campaign and we haven't been able to come up with anything positive. We have to call on the resources of other people – like the homicide squad.'

For the parents, the entry of homicide was a double-edged sword. The police were at least taking it seriously, but there was little comfort in that.

In June, Shirley Milat took Ivan along to the movies with a friend of hers, Chalinder Hughes, from the accountancy firm where they worked. They saw *Basic Instinct*. To Chalinder, Ivan seemed embarrassed by the content of the sex thriller and said he wouldn't have taken her if he'd known what it was about. She saw him as very conservative.

As far as she was concerned, though, any brother of Shirley's had to be all right. They got on well enough. There was no flaming passion, but they slowly fell into a relationship – dinner and the movies, nothing flash. Chalinder had come through a divorce in 1990 and was looking for companionship. They didn't see much of each other during the week. He was always so tired from work.

They'd be together most weekends and they'd go visiting people. She felt a bit awkward with Shirley around, now that she was going out with her brother, even though Shirley approved of the relationship. He introduced her to the family and they all seemed to like her, even though she was a foreigner.

As time went on, they went out less on the weekends too. They'd watch the telly. He liked westerns. She liked 'Star Trek'. He liked watching motor racing, so she read books. Ivan had dropped in on John and Jenny Parsons at Smithfield, on one of his occasional visits coinciding with a trip to the Horsley Park Gun Shop. Jenny offered him a chocolate Golly-Wog biscuit to go with his coffee, and Ivan got the giggles.

'You know, John, about my views about Asians and blacks?' he said. John nodded, knowing Ivan to be a bit racist. Ivan grinned: 'Well, this is gunna come as a shock. Me girlfriend's Indian.' It was a shock, but people do change.

One day he pulled up outside the home on his new red Harley-Davidson with Chalinder on the back.

'John and Jenny, this is Cylinder.' Jenny had cooked a roast lamb, but discovered Chalinder was a vegetarian. She also gave the impression that Ivan was pressuring her to lose weight. Jenny gave her a carrot to gnaw on. Jenny thought them a strange pair, but Ivan was as happy as she'd ever seen him. Finally, there seemed to be some stability in his life.

He wasn't very romantic towards Chalinder. He thought he was. Thought that looking after her was romance enough. She wanted to be sent flowers and be taken to dinner. But they were comfortable together. He was trustworthy, and over time they would come to an implicit understanding that marriage would sort of happen somewhere down the track, but nothing like that came out for a long while.[93]

Ivan was flush with money mid-1992. All the blokes at the RTA Central Asphalt Depot were, thanks to the New South Wales Liberal Government which determined that the business of building roads would be better run by private enterprise. On 30 June 1992 the RTA retrenched them all and sold off the depot to Readymix (CSR). The new bosses rehired eighty of the 130 retrenched workers, including Ivan. Don Borthwick put on a big $3000 piss-up, courtesy of the new company. He stood on a truck and took a photo of them all gathered around. He couldn't recall Ivan being there, but the photo shows him standing at the very back, distinguishable only by the moustache and his black Batman cap.

Ivan went saying he got $11,000 in redundancy.

'But you've already been paid out last time you left,' Terry Palmer queried.

'Oh, well. They're stupid. They've given me eleven grand for shit.'

Palmer used to think the RTA was inefficient, but as soon as private enterprise came in, having cut a third of the actual workers, they tore down half the stores and put up offices. They used to get by with six engineers, but now you couldn't move in the yard for all the shiny new company Commodores. And as soon as business went down, the crews were first to be cut.

With plenty of money at his disposal, Ivan started building a house at Eagle Vale, near Campbelltown in the far south-western outskirts of

Sydney, eleven kilometres past Lombardo's. He told his workmates 'I'm going to build it with this sheila.' Both Noel Wild and Terry Palmer were under the impression he was shacking up with some woman as well as having 'Cylinder'.

'What's your girlfriend think of that?' Wild asked.

'It's all right. She's very much like me.'

'What, have you got 'em on a roster?' Palmer asked. 'You can't service both of 'em together.'

'Nah, it works out all right,' said Ivan the stud. 'One doesn't mind. The other's a bit pissed off about it, but it's working all right.'

Ivan didn't talk about his family at all. Wild didn't even know he had a sister, let alone that it was his sister Shirley he was actually building the house with. He was a real mystery man. If you rang him up at home, you'd get this strange voice answering.

'Can I speak to Ivan?' Wild would ask.

'Oh, it's you, Noel,' Ivan would say, changing his voice back to normal.

The Clarkes and the Walters became comfortable with the media. They had managed to keep the press interested for over a month. When Ian and Jacquie were away, their children Simon and Emma handled it. They were busy mailing everywhere: unions, universities, and Simon's employer Peat Marwick helped too. They had a list of hostels which all received the MISSING posters, and all the while they hoped.

Doubt, however, is an insidious thing. It gnaws. Over time, their worst fears became rational; the only logical explanations were the sinister ones. They kept the dark thoughts to themselves, as if voicing them might give them substance, animate them.

Ian kept telling journalists: 'Whatever you do, you must never give up hope.' The two families never did give up: fighting always to think up new ways of tracking their daughters; more people they ought to be talking to; shaking people who needed a good shake. But by the end of July, maybe the beginning of August, in their hearts, the Clarkes knew. It was never so much expressed, but it slowly, imperceptibly, became reality. One night in August, Jacquie turned to Ian out of the blue, crying, 'She's not coming home, is she?'

'No,' Ian said quietly, 'I don't think she is.' That was the first time they'd voiced it. Let the genie out. Still, they hoped. Ian might have allowed himself to think about the possibility of murder, but neither of them could cope with expressing that fear. It would have been too frightening to fall into a low together. They had to be strong for each other.

In August, the Walters decided that they had to be a part of the search. They had to keep the case in the media. They gained sponsorship from a television station to travel to Australia. Depending on how they went, the Clarkes would follow them out at some point. Ian Clarke sent Ray Walters a resumé of his and Corbett's thoughts. They wanted more attention paid to the Adelaide/Perth line because Caroline had mentioned that, and there were fishing boats out there. That was an explanation they had clung to . . . 'Are the police still checking post restante? . . . Have the police considered the possibility that the girls could have been propositioned by the Scientologists or similar "religious sects"? If not, perhaps they should . . . Do the police ever work with clairvoyants – if so is there any way we can help . . . Jacquie and I wish you and your wife a safe journey and pray it may bring success . . . With all our thoughts and prayers . . .'

Ray and Jill arrived in Sydney on Tuesday, 25 August. They had a hectic schedule ahead and thousands of kilometres to cover by road. Despite the jet lag, they began giving interviews next morning to anyone in the media who would listen. The first was at a press conference at police headquarters during which Jill, full of emotion, pleaded: 'There is bound to be someone out there who knows something. There's got to be.' The tears welled in her eyes: 'Joanne is in our thoughts every minute of the day. It's the not knowing of what has happened which upsets us.' Ray appealed for a Melbourne man by the name of Bob who sent letters to Joanne in Wales saying he loved her, to come forward. He said he had received information which suggested they had been looking for work on an Aboriginal mission.

By the time they appeared on the 'Midday Show', Ray Walters' frustration could not be contained and he accused the relevant authorities of dragging their feet in the search. The couple left the studio for Kings Cross, visiting the hostel where the girls last stayed, before canvassing Victoria Street and pinning up pictures, unaware of the indignation they had caused among investigators. The Media Unit, at the behest of Kings Cross detectives, was anxious to put the record straight. The next day, they issued a joint statement by Walters and Scullion: FATHER OF MISSING UK GIRL TAKEN OUT OF CONTEXT.

The Walters went down to Thirroul to have a drink with the women who may have dropped the girls at Bulli Tops, Susan Burns and Myrna Honeyman. They talked about a signet ring and some others that Susan remembered seeing while the girl showed her a map. Myrna asked Ray if Joanne worked for a doctor. 'Yes, she was a nanny for one.' To Myrna, that gelled with what the girl had told him.

They hadn't received any information about the girls at this point. Near the end of the evening they were talking and Susan remembered something which she hadn't mentioned to the police: 'We were talking about China and I said, "You should go there if you possibly can wangle it on your way back." We were in China not terribly long ago. And the English girl said, "My brother's been on the Trans-Siberian Railway. We'd love to, but whether or not we can afford it or fit it in we don't know."' This and other details helped convince the Walters that the women had given Joanne and Caroline a lift, even if it had been three days after they were supposed to have left their friends at Kings Cross.

Ray Walters went back to the police and insisted they come back and talk to them.

THIRTY-ONE

September 1992

THE FOREST

It is Saturday, 19 September. Friends Keith Siely and Keith Caldwell are running through eucalypt scrub in an orienteering training exercise for their Liverpool-based Scrub Runners club. The object is for one of the pair to take the map and compass and navigate the other into a predesignated area, then hand the map and compass over to the other to then guide them on to the next marker. It is all pretty routine and relaxed. They are making good time, running for the fourth mark, about 3.45 p.m. They cross a fire trail and turn south over a rise towards a boulder marked as a dot on their map.

As they approach the sandstone outcrop, there is the unmistakable whiff of death in the air. They go towards it, and Caldwell lingers to find the source. He sees something under a ledge in the rock. A wombat under branches and leaf litter? A kangaroo limb? There is a boot, a patch of shirt. His friend has joined him. They stay maybe half a minute, peering but not touching, as the truth becomes clear. 'It's a body,' says Caldwell. The kangaroo leg is a human elbow; the wombat fur, the hair of a human head. They stand there, unsure what to do, until they hear others approaching on the same course. They tell them what they have found and, charged with a profound sense of uneasiness, the four run back for Caldwell's mobile phone to call Bowral police.

Darkness had descended by the time Senior Constable Andrew Grosse from the Goulburn Police Crime Scene Unit – 'Scientific' – was guided into the Belanglo State Forest. As the group of police made its way slowly through a small glade, he noticed a rock outcrop in the torch light with some broken house bricks made into a fireplace. It seemed out of place.

They stopped near a rock overhang in a boulder, about 90 metres from the bumpy dirt track called the Longacre Creek Fire Trail. Landmarks they would come to know well.

Grosse set about his grim task in the hard light of portable floods. He observed a right elbow, the skin hardened and yellow, protruding from the side of a pile of dry sticks and leaves. The top of a head and boots were sticking out each end. The sticks, up to one-and-a-half metres long, were placed lengthwise, horizontal to the body. He photographed them, then slowly began lifting the covering away, revealing a layer of smaller twigs which were photographed and removed. The decomposing body was on its stomach. Female. Her right arm was extended above the head. The left arm was to her side. Both legs were straight and slightly apart, the feet pointing inwards. She was wearing a dark blue T-shirt, blue jeans and black shoes all turned a ghastly black and purple by the fluids of decomposition.

She wore two rings – one buckle shaped, the other with a stone in it and a bracelet on the left hand.

Once they had examined the area, their gloved hands rolled her gently onto a body bag. It was then that they noted that her T-shirt and bra, stiffly frozen in position, were pulled up over her breasts, but her shirt was still down around the waist at the back. The fly of her 501s was unbuttoned, but the top anchor button was still fastened.

A late-night call to Neville Scullion from Kings Cross police with details of the jewellery confirmed that it was Joanne Walters long before the dental charts made it official.

The police Media Unit had earlier been told of the find, but the significance was not conveyed. Not even local cops knew. In the late editions of the next morning's papers, a news brief gave the impression that perhaps it was a hapless bushwalker who perished on a lone trek.

Detectives at the scene had no doubt as to who they had found, but where was her travelling companion, Caroline Clarke? Where were their belongings? Equally intriguing was the state of decomposition of the remains. If this was indeed Joanne Walters, she looked too well preserved to have been there since April. Where could she have been those missing months? Maybe it could be attributed to the cool Southern Highlands climate. The post-mortem would soon sort it out.

Dawn was fast approaching when the body was removed. Shortly after, on that cold Sunday, police and the Berrima District Volunteer Rescue Squad gathered on the Longacre Creek Fire Trail, dressed in an assortment of blue, orange and white overalls. At 7.30 a.m., under the guidance of police, they commenced a spiral line search. Starting where the body was found, the line moved in a circle around the taped-off rock overhang, swinging slowly out. They'd been at it some time and were only 30 metres from the boulder, when the search was brought to an abrupt halt. Senior Constables Suzanne Roberts and Roger Gough spotted something in a pile of sticks under the arched, black-barked trunk of a fallen gum tree. It looked like clothing and the form of a human limb. At first glance you wouldn't even notice the brown hiking boots and blue jeans sticking out the end. Roberts called to Andy Grosse from the Crime Scene Unit a short distance away. The search party was withdrawn.

Detective Sergeant Steve McLennan had come in to the office of the South West Region Major Crime Squad Homicide Unit at Flemington that Sunday to pore over an old unsolved murder brief. No sooner had the snowy-haired and bearded detective arrived than he was told to get on the road. Another body had been found in this forest he'd never heard of. As he and detectives Keith Smith and Mick O'Keefe drove south along the Hume, they had only the basic overnight info. Joanne Walters' disappearance had fallen under the ambit of the Southern Region Homicide Squad, so McLennan's knowledge of it had been confined to newspaper reports. But the bodies had turned up in his region, so the case now belonged to South West Major Crime. To him and his team.

They arrived about 11 a.m. A uniformed officer waiting beside the highway guided them along almost five kilometres of dusty logging tracks cutting through dense uniform stands of European pine, then on into native bush.

McLennan stepped from his vehicle and took in the surrounds. He was struck by the isolation of the area, the loneliness. The low scrub was not picturesque, not the place for a picnic. After receiving a briefing from the local detectives, all the officers could do was wait behind the blue and white police tape for forensic pathologist Dr Peter Bradhurst to arrive. Only then could McLennan and his team get their first close look at the scene.

Dr Bradhurst had been at the morgue in Sydney X-raying Joanne's body – still fully clothed and zipped into the blue plastic body bag – looking for bullets. He was just about to ring the investigators to tell them there was no metal in the corpse, when they rang him to say there was another body and he'd better get down there. He arrived to find an atmosphere of tense expectation; a quiet professionalism which said there was a big job at hand. The doctor was taken over to the pile of sticks and, as they all studied the scene, the silence was broken by a disconcerting volley of gunfire in the distance. Local police knew the source as the Bowral Pistol Club, set in a disused quarry a few kilometres north-west, off Bunnygalore Road, a track leading to nowhere in the rugged gullies beyond.

Grosse photographed each phase of the removal of the dry branches from the second corpse, noting that again there was a layer of smaller twigs and leaf litter under longer branches. The body appeared to be female. She was lying on her stomach, wedged into the side of a tree. Her head was wrapped in red cloth which looked like it had bullet holes through it. Both arms were extended above her head. Her legs were straight out and the feet were pointing slightly inwards, same as the first body. She was far more decayed than the first body, probably due to her more exposed position, Bradhurst thought.

Under the doctor's instructions, they lifted the body and all the matter around it gently onto the body bag. Dressed only in gloves and civilian clothes, Bradhurst always found this unpleasant, but like all around him, he had learned to switch off, concentrating on the important details. He knew nothing of the missing backpackers, but he picked up from the police that there wasn't much doubt this was Caroline Clarke.

The 'government contractors' arrived to take her back to the inner-city Glebe morgue in a non-refrigerated van. She arrived there via the loading-dock entrance, where she was wheeled onto a hydraulic platform and lifted to the level of the bottom floor, moved to a bigger trolley where the mortuary clerk weighed her on an industrial-sized roll-on scale, then measured her. The police were filling in a P79(a) report on the circumstances of the death and the deceased, before she was taken into the X-ray room. The morgue's radiographer and photographer, Ian White, unzipped the bag so that he got his angles right, then took a series of X-rays down the length of her body. They showed that her head contained four 'radio-opaque' objects, undoubtedly spent bullets. Then she was wheeled into the refrigerator with Joanne and fifteen or so other anonymous blue bags.

Back at the scene, Grosse had measured and photographed a three-metre-by-one-metre patch of broken and trampled shrubs, some snapped off at ground level, which had started to regenerate. Situated between the two bodies, it looked like a 'struggle area'. On the edge of it, five metres from the second body, Grosse found six cigarette butts – later identified as Longbeach, a brand which Caroline sometimes smoked – and a fired .22 Winchester cartridge case. Another interesting feature of the murder scene was the absence of so much. Packs, camping gear, tents, clothes, toiletries, cameras – all missing. Already, a certain difference between the two murders was becoming apparent and McLennan was pondering whether one or more killers had been at work.

After withdrawing to Bowral Police Station, McLennan, who had now been put in charge of the investigation, ordered all files on the two women moved from Southern Region Homicide to his team. The phones were running hot with calls from the media. By midday, word had got out about the second find. News crews were all over the scene by early evening.

Ian and Jacquie Clarke were due to fly to Australia to take over from the Walters at the end of September. They had been to a wedding and were approaching London when Tony Noble rang on the car phone: 'Where are you?'

'Approaching the M25.'

'Look, pull over. We've got some bad news.' They stopped. 'Two bodies have been found in a forest and it looks as though it's the girls.' It was a king hit, but just open-ended enough to leave them hope. Ian turned back to their daughter Emma's house. It was fortunate Noble reached them when he did because ten minutes later they heard it on the radio when they would have been in the fast lane of the M25 and anything could have happened.

Then Jacquie decided there was no point moping around down there. She'd rather be home. So they began the six-hour drive north. The media had descended on Simon who was dog sitting again: 'My parents are down south. They won't be back,' he told them. So when they did get back, everything was quiet. Next morning, though, cameras were everywhere. They had used the media unashamedly when they needed it. Now the same reporters still had jobs to do, so the Clarkes saw it as an obligation to give them something, but they could not have done interminable one-on-one interviews that day as they awaited the official identification. They did a 'piece to camera' – familiar now with TV jargon – which was pooled and fed to all the networks.

The Walters had it tougher, still in the eye of the storm, in Australia. The police had been unable to find them, but fortunately Ray Walters rang Neville Scullion to ask if there were any developments. The couple were at the Opera House, sightseeing, and the copper went out to tell them in person that Joanne may have been found. So, in the shadow of the white sails, he had the horrible job of breaking the news. Maybe it was a mistake to do it in such a public spot, but there is no good place for such a task. Mrs Walters broke down in the very truest sense of the expression.

Dr Bradhurst began the post-mortem examination of Joanne on Monday morning. It wasn't the sort of thing that he could have done the previous afternoon, you've got to be fresh and alert for a draining day of this minutest of investigations. He'd done about 1500 of them in the ten years he'd been at the New South Wales Institute of Forensic Medicine. Some could still shock him. He can turn off emotionally, but sometimes he can't help thinking what it was like for the victim. This would be one of those cases.

He came in the 'infectious' or 'd' room, dressed as if for surgery in pale blue gown with a plastic apron over the top and with black galoshes on his feet. It was a room just off from the main autopsy room, reserved for either infectious cases or decomposing bodies – hence the 'd' – and was equipped with large extractor fans to take the odours away.

The external examination was the slowest part of the process. It was a matter of removing layer after layer, slowly placing all the sticks and dirt that were stuck to her clothes and skin over onto a second table behind him, carefully looking for evidence. He found dark hairs on the front of her shirt and jeans, and eleven in her hands which seemed locked in position. He noted extensive maggot infestation, especially about the face, neck and chest. The gag was discoloured to the same uniform black and purple as the rest of the clothing. There was also what appeared to be an untied ligature lying around the front and sides of the neck which suggested strangulation. He cut the gag so as to preserve the knot for evidence.

The body was undressed layer by layer. Bradhurst noted that she had no underwear on. Combined with the undone fly and the still stiffly pushed-up shirt, it indicated a sexual aspect to the murder. There was no evidence of any penetrating injury to the vulva, vagina, anus or perineum – between the vulva and the anus. However, because of decomposition, it was not possible to tell if there'd been bruising or abrasions there. A vaginal swab and smear were taken. Sperm can remain identifiable in a dead body for months. Nail clippings were taken for examination in case she had been able to scratch her attacker. Scalp and pubic hairs were pulled for matching with the other hairs found.

As she lay on her back, it was clear she'd been stabbed. With each observation, he'd have to move to the head of the stainless steel table and wash his hands so that he could make a note on a diagram with little red crosses, and scribble a few words, without dirtying the pages. He drew red elliptical shapes to show the shape of the three stab wounds to the right side of the chest; plus one to the front left of the chest; and one to the front right of the neck. Each wound was noted and measured by his assistant, Tania Edwards.

Joanne was gently rolled over onto her stomach and the red ellipses in the reverse diagram slowly cluttered around the upper spine. There were two stab wounds to the back left side of the chest; five to the back right of the chest and two to the spinal cord at the base of the neck. There were fourteen stab wounds in all. This was a frenzy.

As Dr Bradhurst cut open the body and began examining the extent of the internal injuries, he saw that the knife had cut deep. One of the two wounds to the back of the neck cut hard into the spine and would have paralysed her. Other blows had cut off the tips of the transverse processes, the little projections of bone that stick out on either side of the vertebrae. At least five of the stab wounds had cut the spine. There could have been more because the transverse processes on the right side of the fifth, sixth and seventh vertebrae could have been cut by one or more stabs. It was certainly feasible that the paralysing blows would not have killed her. They could have been delivered well before the fatal blows to the vital organs. He thought that maybe, if there was one killer, he could have done this to quickly overpower her before moving to the other victim.

The seventh and ninth right ribs had been cut clean through. It looked like none of these wounds would have penetrated the heart, but both lungs were so severely decomposed it was not possible to assess how many stab wounds had punctured them. Because of the decomposition and maggot infestation of the chest cavity, it appeared that the weapon had penetrated each lung as well as the oesophagus, the aorta – the main artery leading from the heart to the rest of the body – the trachea and the larynx. The organs were taken out and weighed on the greengrocers' scales at the head of the table.

All soft tissues from the face and neck had decomposed so it wasn't possible to assess the presence or absence of soft tissue injuries there, or of strangulation. It was likely that there were more stab wounds there which did not cut bone. So, while he counted fourteen, it was likely that there were many more.

Two fingers had been eaten by animals, but there were no defensive wounds on her hands. That, combined with the gag, indicated it was a very controlled murder. It looked like only one knife had been used. Five of the stab entry wounds were still present in the skin, measuring 30 by 10 millimetres. It was a single-bladed knife. Bradhurst thought of a Bowie knife or cavalry sword or similar.

The cause of death was given as stab wounds to the chest and neck. The time of death, given the cold climate, was consistent with any time between April and June 1992.

McLennan's team had ensconced itself in the Bowral detectives' office, a red brick cottage adjoining the police station. It looked more like a family home than a cop shop. Detective Inspector Bob Godden was brought in to take command of the overall investigation while McLennan was made chief investigator. Godden towered over most blokes in stature – 195 centimetres or six foot five – and reputation. He was one of the state's most experienced homicide investigators. He joined the force in 1965, following in his father's footsteps, after serving a two-year cadetship as a patrol officer on the island of Bougainville, Papua New Guinea. Like most detectives of his era, he served an apprenticeship with 21 Division, a flying squad set up to target street violence, gangs, hoodlums and drugs. He once disarmed and arrested a notorious bandit by sticking his thumb in the cocked hammer of a pistol levelled at his gut. By 1972, with seven years service, he had been promoted to the Special Crime Unit, the then homicide squad of the Criminal Investigation Branch. The following year he was part of the team that arrested Scottish-born Archibald McCafferty for the serial murders of three people, but back then the term serial killer had not been coined. McCafferty's were dubbed 'thrill killings'. Godden went on to survive an encounter with fugitive bank robber and notorious escapee 'Jockey' Smith who tried to kill him during his arrest. In 1990 he found himself overseeing investigations into the Strathfield massacre.

The South West Region Major Crime Squad briefed the Godden–McLennan team later that day on all the sightings, travel intentions, acquaintances and a list of missing belongings – backpacks, clothing, credit cards, cameras. McLennan and Godden concurred that everything would have to be re-examined in the event that something had been overlooked. A widened search of the crime scene would also have to be conducted. Telephone calls to Bowral detectives from media in Britain and Australia were clogging the lines.

In an extraordinary move, the head of the Institute of Forensic Medicine at Glebe, Professor John Hilton, revealed the first details of the girls' fate to more than forty reporters and photographers – half from the British press. They gathered in the morgue's auditorium to hear the crew-cut Scot speak in a halting voice.

'The, um, apparent cause of death of Joanne Walters, was, ah, penetrating wounds to the chest, consistent with them being stab wounds.' He paused, looking up through his silver glasses, and continued as cameras flashed away. 'And the preliminary investigation of the other female body suggests the cause of death there may well have been gunshot wounds to the head.'

The London tabloid, the *Sun*, didn't need such detail. It made its own:

BEAST OF THE BUSH
BRIT GIRLS VICTIMS OF OZ SERIAL KILLER
Two British girl backpackers were murdered by a serial killer who held them prisoner for three months in the

Australian bush, police feared yesterday . . . Their killer could be a fiend responsible for the disappearance of 20 people in the area over 20 years.

Ray Walters told the *Express*: 'The miracle we'd always hoped for just didn't occur. We have cried so much since she went missing. Now we're too numb to take it in. It's unbelievable.' He said Jill was under sedation: 'If she had a gun she would shoot whoever was involved in the killings.'

Ian Clarke was crying, too, but his perspective was different: 'Now we know rather than wonder, obviously it is a relief. We now have to look back on the happy times she did have, although it is so sad.'

The police had immediately downplayed to the media the possibility that the murders were connected to any others and that there were more graves out there. But even as the media flacks were spreading one line, the investigators *were* looking at such links. The police don't like the public thinking too much about serial killers, despite the multitudes of highway disappearances over the decades.

On Tuesday, 22 September, ballistics expert Sergeant Gerard Dutton found himself dressed in a gown in the 'dirty room' at the morgue for Caroline Clarke's autopsy. Veteran officers often went to such examinations with Vapour Rub to apply to their nostrils.

Dutton and his colleague from the Forensic Ballistics Unit, Constable Jason Donnolley, had been heading for Katoomba on Sunday morning in response to a suspicious parcel at the front door of the council chambers. Weeks earlier, a powerful homemade bomb had gone off in the same place, so it looked like an interesting job. As they drove up the mountains, a report had come on the radio news about a decaying body found in bushland south of Sydney. Dutton quipped that he hoped the victim hadn't been shot, because if it had, there'd be a foul-smelling autopsy waiting for them.[94] Whoever was on-call for the Ballistics Unit had to attend autopsies on all gunshot victims. The suspicious parcel had turned out to be a furphy, and the victim in the forest had not been shot, but as they were ruling out the bomb, searchers were uncovering the bullet-riddled skull of Caroline Clarke.

At the morgue, Dutton and Donnolley looked on as Dr Bradhurst and Andy Grosse from Goulburn Police Crime Scene Unit peeled back the maroon material from her skull, counting ten bullet entry holes in her skull from a small-calibre weapon. The maroon sweatshirt had ten corresponding entry holes. She never saw a thing. There were four exit holes. Entry wounds are distinguished from exit wounds by the sharp edge of the hole on the outside, whereas exit wounds flake the outside of the skull and leave a sharp edge on the inside.

There were two bullets in her hair. They had exited the skull but had lost velocity and caught just under the skin. With decomposition they had matted themselves in with the hair. Another was found in the dirt covering her left shoulder.

Caroline was more decomposed than Joanne. Most of the skin was missing from her neck and head. There was massive maggot infestation. The head came away from the body because all the soft material had gone. The skin of the limbs had mummified rock hard.

Bradhurst used a circular saw to cut off the 'skull cap' in a line just above the eyebrow. The brain, after five months of decomposition, had settled into a small pool of green/grey paste against the right side of the skull. Dutton wouldn't be able to eat avocado for a long time.

Bradhurst pulled four bullets out of the paste with his hands. Tweezers might mark them. He ran them under a tap, with the drains covered, and handed each to Dutton who stood there contemplating the meaning of the ten bullet entry holes.

The size of the holes appeared to be from a .22, and Dutton could see marks on some of the bullets that suggested a silencer had been fitted. The pattern of the holes in the skull, however, was just as interesting. They appeared to have been fired from three directions. Four bullets had entered the left side of the head; three entered closely grouped on the right; and three entered closely grouped in the rear. Six bullets had exited, causing only four exit holes. Some of the front bones of the skull were missing, so it was possible that the two other bullets had exited through the skull there.

Dutton knew it was relatively uncommon for murderers to shoot an excessive amount of bullets into victims, except perhaps the occasional underworld hit where they might be making some point. Combined with the savagery of the Walters attack, this one had all in the room wondering who could do such a thing.

There were fractures of the skull and upper jaw, consistent with shattering caused by the force of the bullets hitting the bone. Dr Bradhurst also noted she had suffered one stab wound to the back, just below the right shoulder blade. It had been inflicted with a long-bladed weapon similar to the one used on Joanne, but had not damaged bone. He could not determine what damage the knife had done because all the chest organs had decomposed and the ribs were all disorganised. Her khaki shirt showed a 30 millimetre cut in the back, corresponding to the stab wound and consistent with it being the same knife that stabbed Joanne. There was no evidence of any defensive wounds.

The decomposition around the head and shoulders and part of each side of the chest made it impossible to exclude stab wounds to those areas. Her hyoid bone, at the top of her throat, was missing, so strangulation was a possibility.

Strands of hair were collected from her right hand and bagged for further examination. Likewise, elimination samples of hair from various parts of her body were also collected and swabs taken. There was no penetrating injury to the vulva, perineum or anus but, as with Joanne Walters, decomposition meant Bradhurst could not determine if there had been any bruising or abrasions there. The only evidence of a sexual nature was that her bra was unclipped at the front. Maggots and beetles were taken for entomological examination. This can often help determine the timing of a murder.

Bradhurst gave the cause of death as gunshot wounds to the head associated with stab wounds to the chest, but he was unable to determine which was the fatal blow. He could be more sure about the time of death being around the time of her disappearance in April.

Bradhurst left the post-mortem, walking through the phenolic solution at the door to disinfect his boots, thinking that the different manner of the two deaths pointed to there being two killers, but he was still open to the possibility that there was only one, if the women had been subdued in some way.

Ray and Jill Walters were shattered wrecks, but the police needed publicity to generate leads from the public, so it fell on Bob Godden to persuade them to talk. On Wednesday, 23 September, the Walters spoke at a press conference at Sydney Police Headquarters. Ray's eyes were reddened by tears and little sleep. It was meant to be a brief appeal for public help, but he continued on, his voice wavering: 'Whoever has done this thing I wouldn't call them sick, because sick people can be cured to some extent. These are evil-minded people and like dogs with rabies, there is only one way – they've got to be put down, because the world has not got the resources to keep these people in jail. There's got to be some system whereby we destroy these people so they don't put their evil genes anywhere else.' Jill Walters sat beside her husband, head bowed, hands clasped together. Her voice was weak from a broken, angry heart: 'These people who have done this to these girls, they are just proper animals and they deserve to be shot. They are proper animals, that's all I can say.'

As they spoke, Andy Grosse and his colleague from Goulburn Crime Scene Unit, Detective Sergeant John Goldie, were showing the ballistics experts Gerard Dutton and Jason Donnolley the site in the Belanglo. Two fired .22 calibre Winchester cartridge cases had already been found a few metres from Clarke's body. Dutton and Donnolley set about scouring the area with metal detectors. They searched around where Joanne's body was found but came up with nothing. Then, in long grass, close to the first two cartridge cases, they found eight more fired .22 Winchester cases in front of a small tree about ten metres from where Caroline was found. The cases were so close it looked like the killer had stood in one spot and fired all ten shots. Yet the entry wounds were from three directions. Grosse told them that was where he'd found the six cigarette butts, too. It looked like the shooter had lingered and savoured the moment, moving the dead girl's head on some whim, dragging on a cigarette. But it could have been Clarke awaiting her fate as Walters was attacked.

Nearby, in the 'struggle area', they also found a bracelet, later identified as Joanne's, despite its proximity to Caroline's body, and a coin, quite close to where the cigarettes and the cartridge cases were found.

Andy Grosse dug the dirt from where Clarke's head had been. Using a mechanical sieve and a metal detector on site, he found three more spent bullets. That made a total of ten to match the cartridge cases and the entry wounds in the skull. This was important because, knife wound notwithstanding, it meant she had probably been killed where she lay. All the while, the idle speculation of those at the scene ran to the question of who they were dealing with: one killer or two? It was all academic at this point because they knew that only by doing their jobs perfectly now might the question be answered.

The exact position of the cartridges was important, because it might point to the ejection characteristics of the murder weapon, and the killer's exact position. So they put little numbered flags next to each case before they were collected. To plot the positions, they used 'terrestrial photogrammetry' – photography in stereo where two images are used to plot a 3D image and give an exact location by triangulation. The flags were left overnight for the Photogrammetry Unit to plot them the next day, but when they turned up in the morning all the flags were gone. It turned out a uniformed constable guarding the scene thought they'd been left behind. The Walters were coming to visit the next day, so he collected the flags to avoid upsetting them. Measurements had already been taken, though, so it wasn't as disastrous as it could have been, but Dutton was annoyed.[95]

Jill and Ray Walters had asked to see the murder scene, to lay some flowers and say a prayer. They came into the Bowral Police Station to meet Steve McLennan. It was clear to the detective that the couple were emotional wrecks, more so Mrs Walters. Ray Walters, in his action-orientated way, had a million questions and he wanted answers which McLennan couldn't give.

McLennan drove the couple to the forest from Bowral. Few words were spoken during the twenty-minute journey. The area was still sealed off and under guard. There was much work yet to be done by the crime scene boys but McLennan cleared them away and led the parents to the rock overhang, leaving them to grieve in peace. It was a horrible time. Mrs Walters' sobbing punctuated the silence as they lingered for almost an hour. Both Bob Godden and McLennan promised then to catch the killer.

The bullets were the only solid clues which the detectives had to work with and the two questions they most needed Gerard Dutton to answer were: what sort of gun was it? Did the same weapon fire all ten shots? The second question was easier. Back at the Ballistics Unit in the concrete bunker that is the Sydney Police Centre, he pulled up the image of each cartridge case and each bullet on the 'comparison macroscope'. It magnifies two images at a time to allow for each to be quickly compared. Two bullets were too badly damaged for any worthwhile characteristics, but the remaining eight and the ten cartridges were all in good order.

As he started to work through the cases, he knew he had one stroke of luck, the firing pin was leaving a peculiar upward curve on the heel of the case, a very distinctive signature. When a firing pin strikes the rim of a cartridge, it crushes a sensitive chemical compound which ignites the gunpowder. Peculiarities of the firing pin are imprinted onto the soft metal of the cartridge case. All ten cases had this upward curve, and some other distinctive marks, so it looked like the same gun.

Identifying the weapon became a process of elimination. Dutton had a few signposts to look out for: the firing pin marks; scratch marks left on cases as gases expand and push the soft brass case up against the hard steel of the chamber as the bullet is fired; then more scratches can be left as the case is ejected. Putting the size, shape and location of these marks under the macroscope can indicate certain weapons and, more often, exclude others.

All rifles have 'rifling grooves' – spirals cut into the barrel to spin the bullet as it is fired to give it stability through the air like a quarterback's pass in American football. Rifles can have between two and twenty-four twists of the groove along the length of the barrel, although four to eight is more common – either clockwise or counter-clockwise. A good ballistics man can pick up both the number of twists and their direction just by looking at the scratches they leave on a fresh bullet.

Often these characteristics leave a list of possible weapons pages long. An exact fit is rare, but again Dutton was lucky with the upward curve at the bottom of the firing pin impression. All Ruger 10/22s made before 1982 left a peculiar crescent-shaped firing-pin impression owing to a fault in the manufacturing process, but this upward curve at the bottom was an exaggeration of that and quite rare. Combined with all the other markings, Dutton was able to say with reasonable certainty that it was the weapon. The Ruger 10/22 was self-loading, with a standard ten-round rotary box magazine, so the killer had emptied a full magazine on Caroline Clarke.

The identification of the Ruger didn't help investigators much. The 10/22 was one of the most popular .22s ever made. More than 4.5 million had been made in the previous twenty-five years. Tens of thousands had come to Australia. And there was always the vague possibility that it wasn't a Ruger at all, but some obscure, unknown firearm.

There were other good marks left by what he concluded must have been a tiny metal burr on the breech face, impressed on the cases by the expansion of the gases when the bullet is fired. There were also good 'chamber marks' caused by slight irregularities in the chamber. When the cases are ejected automatically, they are still expanding and so more prone to be marked and scratched by the irregularities. These were going to be good identifiers.

Turning to the ten bullets, he could see they all had a strange gouge along their length. It appeared they had to have been made by some attachment to the muzzle – most likely a faulty silencer. Silencers work because the bang from a fired gun is mainly caused by the rapidly expanding gases which generate a shock wave much the same as uncorking a champagne bottle. Most bullets travel faster than the speed of sound – approximately 335 metres per second – so a second crack comes from the sonic boom. That is why, when you stand a long way from a gun, two distinct cracks can be heard from the one shot. Therefore the first thing when using a silencer is that the ammunition has to be subsonic – slower than sound – to avoid the secondary crack. The silencer then slows the expanding propellant gases, releasing them over a fractionally longer time, muffling the loud bang. The baffles used in the silencer are merely a line of washers within a tube. The hole in each washer has to be just slightly larger than the bullet. The gases then get diverted into the little chambers between the washers, slowing them sufficiently to stop the bang. So, if a washer is only slightly out of alignment, it will scrape the bullet on the way through.

But Dutton noted that the gouge in some bullets wasn't in exact alignment with the scratches from the rifling grooves. The fact the gouge moved was good in that it ruled out a defect in the barrel or a burr left from sawing it off. Such a defect would be constant. It meant the defect had to be caused by something moveable attached to the gun. A screw-on silencer fitted the bill and it must have been moved between shots. Dutton wondered why the shooter would do that. His mind went back to the crime scene. Since three bullets were found in the soil beneath Clarke's head, it was clear she had been shot at least three times where she lay. Probably ten times. The cartridge cases showed that the shooter fired a full magazine from one spot. Since the bullets hit the head from different directions – the right, left and rear – the head must have been moved. The shooter must have either put the gun down to move the head, or put it down and adjusted it while an accomplice moved the head. Maybe the shooter bumped the silencer as he put it down or fiddled with it as he passed it to an accomplice.

Bob Godden had ordered the forest searched for any foreign objects within 300 metres of the crime scene – essentially, the belongings of Clarke and Walters. The sweep began with 100 officers, but by day four had been scaled down to a core of forty who were then tasked with scouring an area 150 metres to 200 metres either side of the Longacre Creek Fire Trail heading back to the highway.

In charge, Steve McLennan reasoned that the killer might have stopped on his way out of the forest to discard the gear. Going over such a vast tract of bushland for clues which may or may not be there was a lottery, one that was very expensive to play, tying up so many police.

The activities of a large force of police in overalls searching a wider perimeter of the forest heightened speculation about the nature of the killings. The media were hungry for any skerrick of information. The *Daily Telegraph Mirror*'s front page on Thursday, 24 September, carried a photograph of a line of police in a fire break, saying they were searching for more bodies.

The same day, the *Sydney Morning Herald* published a story which stated investigators were examining links to the murder a year earlier of Dianne Pennacchio, a thirty-year-old mother whose body was found ten months earlier in the Tallaganda State Forest, near the town of Bungendore 120 kilometres south of Belanglo. Two forestry workers made the discovery about 30 metres in from McCurley's Road. She was lying face down, concealed behind a log inside the pine plantation, about ten metres from a fire trail. The body, its jeans wrenched down around her ankles, had been covered with pine needles. A post-mortem found she had been stabbed a number of times in the back. She had possibly disappeared while hitching, but her lift came at 11.30 p.m., after leaving the Lake George Hotel at Bungendore. (At the time of publication the Pennacchio murder remains unsolved.)

The investigation team hit the roof over both reports and were quick to issue denials. The normally reserved Steve McLennan was the angriest. He wouldn't have anything more to do with the *Herald* reporter. The last thing police needed was public hysteria and for investigators to be led down unrelated paths.

He was quietly convinced the Pennacchio murder had been committed by a different perpetrator, but for 'operational reasons' didn't want to state the differences. For one thing, Pennacchio had been murdered elsewhere and her body dumped. There were also indications that she had not hitchhiked and may have got into a truck, possibly with someone she knew. But even though they didn't think there was a link, they kept the file on her murder, just in case.

The *Telegraph Mirror* report added to their consternation because as far as they were concerned the search had effectively ended speculation that the forest was a killing field. The police issued a denial, saying: 'There is no evidence to suggest a serial killer is on the loose.' It said there were 'more differences in the two cases than similarities'. However, it added: 'Whilst we are keeping an open mind on the subject, and we have obviously spoken to detectives at Queanbeyan, there is nothing to suggest the murders are linked in any way. To suggest a serial killer is responsible for the deaths could impede the investigation.' The search finished a little over a week after Joanne's body was found.

THIRTY-TWO

Late 1992

WHICH WAY SOUTH?

At the unloader, about 10 a.m. on Monday, 21 September 1992, Paul Douglas and Nick Collins have the papers with them and are talking about the day's front page: the bodies of two British backpackers, Caroline Clarke and Joanne Walters, have been found in forest graves. It is big news in a way that only a country as self-conscious as Australia can manage. It becomes dinner conversation. Workplace conversation. 'Isn't it terrible . . . What kind of bastard would do this?'

Miller drops in, mid-conversation: 'There's more bodies out there. They haven't found the two Germans yet.'[96]

It is hard for Douglas to tell if Miller is sober. Even though it is still morning, Douglas decides he must be ripped, for the simple reason that he almost always is. It makes it easier to disregard his bombshell.

On the same day at the change of shift, about ten past two, the death of the British girls is still the subject of the moment in the tea-room and again Miller has his two-bobs worth: 'You could pick up anybody on that road and you'd never find them again. You'd never find out who did it either.'

Most don't know where the Belanglo State Forest is and don't give it any more thought. Des Butler does, though. He remembers Miller's comment months earlier about the Germans. The case of the British girls and the German couple have now been linked in the media and Des knows that 'Miller's Mountain' – where 'Killer' goes with his brothers to fire off their huge arsenal of guns – isn't far from where the girls were found. He doesn't say anything, though. There is a sense of fear around Miller. Butler has been to their mountain and seen their firepower. He knows what Miller and his brothers are capable of. Like when one of his workmates was in the car park with him. 'That's Pfanner's car,' Miller said, going over to the company car of their most hated boss. Boot! He kicked the headlights in.

'Oh shit,' said his co-worker wanting to bolt. It was broad daylight.

Everybody hated this Pfanner. He'd been brought in to shake things up and he'd shaken too hard for some's liking. Miller began a vendetta against him. He'd ring Pfanner every night when he was on nightshift. He'd wake him up. Hang up. Wake him. Hang up. Trying to drive the boss crazy. A rumour went around that the company put on a phone tap to catch the culprit.

Towards the end of 1992, Miller brought in a photograph of Pfanner and told a mate that he was going to print up some copies and distribute them around his neighbourhood with the words: 'This man is a known paedophile.' His colleagues, who hated this boss too, thought maybe that was going too far. He never carried it out as far as anyone knew.

Another time, he snickered to a workmate, 'Just wait, the phone'll ring and it'll be for Pfanner.' The phone soon rang and a message came over the PA system. 'Bill Pfanner, you're wanted on the phone.'

'What's going on?' asked the curious colleague.

Miller was smiling. 'I rang his wife and said, "Are you sure your kids are at school?" I don't like doing that, involving kids and all, but Pfanner's such an arsehole. Arrogant prick.' Miller could be so cunning it was scary. Told him he poured a can of oil under the front door of some guy he held a grudge against. You didn't want to get in Miller's bad books.

But Miller was forced to leave Boral when the paymaster started to hassle him about the bodgie tax file number he gave. The recession had well and truly settled in and Boral were offering redundancies so Miller took it at the end of 1992 – four weeks pay for every year he was there. His colleagues thought he got about $10,000. The company was glad to see the back of him, and he had the tax man off his case.

Bodge's mate Phil Polglase had been in a car accident and had to come down to Sydney on 24 September to visit a specialist. He booked himself a room at the Golf View Hotel/Motel, Guildford – $50 a night for a single.

In its Ugh boot glory days, when the tannery and the dunny depot were out the back, the old Grand Villa was the local for all the younger Milats who lived only 800 metres away. The 1969 mock-hacienda, with the horse races drowning out the jukebox, had seen better days.

Polglase saw Dick Milat there as he might have expected. Milat approached and asked him about some money Polglase had owed him for a while. That was typical of Phil. Always owed money or something to someone. Then Milat brought up that night a few months earlier when Phil had stayed over at his place and spoken with Ivan. Did he remember it? Milat asked.

Nah, mate, Polglase told him nervously. He couldn't remember shit these days, since the car accident. Milat left. Later, one of Milat's friends, Craig Dyer, came up and asked Polglase why Dick Milat was going round saying he was going to kill him.

'Fuck, I don't know, mate.'[97]

But he knew all too well.

The fact that the double murder took place in such an isolated spot made everybody think the killer was a local. It placed the town of Bowral under intense national and international scrutiny. Bowral prided itself on its gentrified charm – its private boarding schools, the Tulip Festival and, more importantly, giving rise to the career of cricketing legend Sir Donald Bradman. Many locals took offence at the town being linked to the murders when it was only the base for the police investigation. The nearest town to Belanglo was historic Berrima, 15 kilometres away, they pointed out.

'We're all hoping it wasn't a local but it looks as if it was someone who knew the area,' Trevor Johnson, publican of the Surveyor General Inn at Berrima told a wayward reporter. 'That's our biggest fear. No one else would have known about the place. Nothing like this has ever happened down here. It's a nice quiet peaceful place.'

The investigation team had grown to ten detectives by the fifth day. The appeal by Mr and Mrs Walters had produced a rising tide of information, so they had plenty to get on with. There were hundreds of bits of information, much of it trivial and of no use, yet all of it had to be sifted through and checked. One such report came from a man who claimed to have met Caroline Clarke at a ski resort in the Snowy Mountains. He said the two women had stayed in a caravan park on Sydney's northern beaches on the weekend they disappeared, which concurred with Susan Burns and Myrna Honeyman's story of picking up the two hitchhikers. Suddenly, the time lag between leaving Kings Cross and being dropped off at Bulli Tops could be explained.

Another report came from a Canberra couple who had stopped at a roadside rest area at the top of the Boxvale Walking Trail, ten minutes drive from Belanglo, on Sunday, 26 April – eight days after the girls left Kings Cross. Although the couple could not recall seeing two women, their ten-year-old daughter insisted they call police when she saw photographs of them on television. The girl was called in and a statement taken in the presence of her parents. She said they were making dinner over a camp fire with a man. Parked next to them was a white Volkswagen kombi van.

Her account coincided with a report of two women matching the descriptions who had been drinking and singing two nights earlier – 24 April – at Bowral's Blue Boar Inn. The women had been asked to show proof of age and had produced their UK passports. One spoke with a distinct sing-song Welsh accent and her friend was clearly English. They had left the hotel late that night with a group of men and were thought to have got into a kombi van.

It now looked like the girls might have travelled from Bulli Tops to Bowral, probably along the Appin Way. Bob Godden hoped that more motorists saw them travelling the route.

On Monday, 28 September, Godden went public with the possible sightings at the rest area. He said the kombi had a spare tyre cover with a 'smiley face'. Virtually overnight every light-coloured kombi owner in New South Wales became a suspect or at least the butt of jokes. Smiley covers became more rare. The motor registry provided investigators with a list of more than 1000 white kombi vans. Coupled with trying to locate the murder weapon, locating the owner of the van was a nightmare.

Police began canvassing property owners surrounding the forest, trying to ascertain the types of people likely to frequent the area. It was soon apparent that the seemingly quiet spot was heavily visited by possible suspects. The most obvious were forestry workers and members of the Bowral Pistol Club. Then there were the Water Board workers who maintained pipelines, and truckers who came to empty treated effluent in the pine plantation. Many people in the district also had permits to chop firewood. The Police Rescue Squad used the nearby gorge country for exercises, as did the army, reservists, school cadets, scouts and orienteers. Then there were the four-wheel drivers.

Paul Onions' illnesses had continued for almost three years, and got worse whenever he was away from home, which was often, because his work as an air-conditioning engineer took him all over Britain doing installations. He was tired all the time and losing weight. He never connected the sickness to the attack on the Hume Highway, but he knew the panic attacks must be related. He and his brother Simon went over to Paris in 1992 to catch a Simple Minds concert. Onions was already getting vertigo often, and he got it badly up the Eiffel Tower. He'd go in a bar and be paranoid about who he could talk to. Once, he was in a car with a friend when, suddenly, it was as if the mad bastard with the moustache was sitting there beside him driving through the green fields of home. The grin would not allow Onions to escape. 'Get back in here, you.'

Onions always felt that what happened to him wasn't a robbery and this guy 'Bill' would be doing whatever he was doing to others. Onions feared for those who followed in his steps. He knew that 'Bill' wouldn't muck about again, but he felt powerless to do anything about it.

He had been down in London for work and, reading a tabloid one day, there was a story about this Welsh couple going out to Australia to look for their daughter and her English friend. The story mentioned how their bank accounts hadn't been touched. He turned to his workmate, Phil: 'I think there's something bad here, because the girls ain't answered their parents' birthdays. What do you think? Maybe they don't want to be found because they're having such a balling time . . . but I think there's something bad here, mate.'

A couple of months later, he was working up in Scotland and Phil came in with the paper. 'It's true what you said, like, about those girls missing in Australia. They're dead.'

Soon afterwards, he was back home and his brother Simon came into his room carrying the *News of the World*. 'This is exactly the same story you told me, Bunny,' he said pointing at the article about Clarke and Walters. 'It's all in there.'

Even Simon could tell that the bodies were near the same road Bunny had been on. Paul saw Bowral on the tabloid's map and felt ill.

He wanted to dismiss it – did dismiss it – yet all the while it gnawed away at him: how massive Australia was, and yet these bodies turn up so close to where he was attacked. It seemed like more than coincidence. But what could he do?

The weather was coming in grey and blustery on the day of Joanne and Caroline's memorial service. Susan Burns and Myrna Honeyman sheltered from the rain in their car, waiting for everybody to turn up. The track had turned into a quagmire. A car stopped nearby and a woman got out. Susan grabbed Myrna like she'd seen a ghost. 'Look at that girl!'

It turned out to be Nicola Burge, a cousin of Caroline Clarke from Adelaide. She was terribly similar to her cousin, thought Susan. Bigger, but so alike.

The rain continued bucketing down, but the moment the Welsh choir started, it stopped. The sun burst through the clouds and filtered down through the mist-covered trees in great cathedral shafts, enveloping the 150 mourners. It was cliché perfect.

'Spooky,' thought Susan and others, going by the looks on their faces. The piercing sweetness of thirty lilting Welsh voices rose through the bush, some cracking with emotion as they sang: 'Ye, though I walk in death's dark vale. Yet I will fear no ill.' Jill and Ray Walters walked slowly past the members of the Sydney Welsh Choir and the Australian Welsh Friendship Club, towards the moss-covered boulder which had sheltered the body of their daughter. A Welsh flag, the red dragon, now draped it. Jill leaned more heavily on her husband as they drew closer, cradling a posy of pink roses. Supported by her son Jonathan and her sister Maureen Williams-Jones, they covered the ground in a bed of flowers, before lighting a candle. They then placed flowers and lit a candle where a Union Jack was draped over the fallen tree which had concealed Caroline's body.

'We have come here to this place, a place that something wicked happened at,' Anglican Reverend Stephen Gray began, his voice disappearing into the bush. 'We are going to say today that evil doesn't have the last word.'

Afterwards the Welsh community had put on a lovely spread in a small church at Berrima, down in a little valley. It was bitterly cold and the fire was crackling. Reporter Marie Mohr grabbed Susan: 'Come and have a look at this.' There were two rainbows, back towards Belanglo. Unbelievable. Susan went back and got Jill Walters. 'Come and have a look.' Just beautiful, they all agreed.

The Clarkes had been due to fly to Australia, but stayed in England to wait for Caroline's remains to come home. In early October, Jacquie got a call: 'This is the international undertakers. The body has left Sydney airport.' It rankled. It wasn't a body. It was Caroline. The local undertaker in Newcastle was also Ian's driver on official occasions. He warned them not to come to see her at the airport because she would just be in a crate. 'I'll meet her and take her back and then you can come and be with her.'

They came and sat with her in the 'Chapel of Rest'. They talked to her, told her they loved her and how proud they were of her.

The tiny village church at Slaley had about 200 people crammed in for the funeral, with people spilling into the yard. Lots of her friends had come all the way from Surrey, just over a year after coming up for her twenty-first birthday. Neighbours gave beds to mourners so they could stay the night. There was a wreath in the shape of the little dream car she never had, the blue Volkswagen Beetle. Same as her birthday cake.

There were a lot of letters from outraged Australians. 'You don't know me, but . . .' horrified and ashamed that such a thing could happen. The Clarkes appreciated every one of them. And appreciated how much good there was out there. That these people took the trouble to write.

They left England four days later to come to Australia. The Walters had waited to meet them. The police asked them to do a press conference. They pulled a crowd of thirty or forty media. Even after a month, the story was still strong. At one point, the police media people said 'that's enough', but the Clarkes were quite happy to go on for as long as the media wanted, on the understanding 'that for the rest of the time we're here, we're on our own'. It worked out with no problems at all.

The Walters took Joanne home and buried her in Maesteg on 25 October. There was another little service in the forest in late October, but unlike the Walters, the Clarkes found no solace there. It was beautiful yet horrible. Impossible to imagine its secrets.

A month had passed since the discovery of the bodies. The search of the crime scene had been called off. On Thursday, 23 October, Steve McLennan admitted the Blue Boar report had been a case of mistaken identity. Two female backpackers, one English, the other Welsh, had come forward to say it was them in the pub. They had been staying with friends and working in Berrima. They only realised police were barking up the wrong tree upon reading about the sighting in the British press when they returned home. Further investigation proved the guy who claimed to be with the girls on the northern beaches was a hoaxer. The thirty-four-year-old was known for similar pranks. He was charged with public mischief.

Yet the Boxvale sighting of the kombi still had legs, especially after an old fellow reported seeing two backpacks at the Welby rubbish tip that weekend. The dump was less than two kilometres from the Boxvale picnic area. The man's description of the packs matched 'fairly closely' those owned by the women and so twenty-five recruits from the police academy, detectives and council workers were sent to dig up the tip. The cadets, in surgical masks, gloves and white overalls did all the digging, of course, spending all day in the garbage, dating it as they went by the use-by dates on milk cartons. They found nothing resembling a backpack.

Godden and McLennan were beginning to have misgivings about the Bulli Tops sighting, too. The time frame wasn't adding up. There would surely have been more witnesses to them in the missing weekend. More and more, their inquiries took them back to Kings Cross as the last known whereabouts. Investigators had re-examined dozens of other 'sightings' of the girls, either together or apart, all over Sydney. Most didn't make sense. The investigation was losing momentum.

What investigators had up their sleeve, were the strands of hair both girls had held in their hands and the vaginal swabs which were all still away being tested at a series of laboratories. It looked like sperm had been taken from Walters but the scientists were struggling to extract the DNA from it which could convict a killer.

THIRTY-THREE

Late 1992

OFFENDER 2

Dr Rod Milton had dealt with some of Sydney's biggest crimes and criminals in his twenty years of forensic psychiatry. He never knew if the police would call him in on any given case. Sometimes they'd phone months after the event, when he thought it was all over, depending on the individual detective. He'd helped police with a profile of the serial killer who was attacking elderly women on Sydney's upmarket North Shore. His predictions there were quite accurate except for perhaps the single most important point, the offender's age. He had predicted a young man, a teenager, whereas in fact the killer had been almost sixty. He certainly understood that this was an inexact science. He had given important evidence at the trial of Gregory Alan Brown, a habitual arsonist who set fire to the Down Under backpackers hostel in Kings Cross in September 1989. Six young travellers died in the blaze, 100 metres from where Caroline Clarke and Joanne Walters were last seen alive. Milton had also worked with Bob Godden on the Strathfield massacre.

Now Godden and McLennan were driving him to Belanglo. The leads had started to dry up. There was still plenty to be followed, but it was hoped the psych could provide some sort of fresh perspective. Milton felt it was vital to see the spot where the murders were committed. Whoever it was *chose* that spot as their stage, and so they were leaving behind just a little bit of themselves. He or they also chose to leave the girls the way they were left – the final act of some fantasy that had played out in their minds many times. So he had all the crime scene photos and diagrams with him in the back seat. To Milton, they were not pictures of two dead girls, they were images from the mind of the killer.

Milton grilled the detectives on the details as he flicked through the photos. As they entered the forest, it took no professional training for Milton to conclude the killer or killers were familiar with the area. His experience was that killers rarely did it in unfamiliar surroundings. That was just common sense. The further they went over the bumpy roads in the police car, the more the crime revealed itself as less opportunistic, more planned. They went through the pine plantation closing in darkly above them, then the light, scrubby eucalypts – unappealing country, Milton thought. Certainly not the kind to attract daytrippers.

The cars came to the murder scene in the mid-morning. It was a relatively open, accessible spot. Some black plastic military-calibre shells lay on the ground, relics from some imaginary battle. Andy Grosse from the Crime Scene Unit had come to meet them, to help explain the physical evidence. The policemen walked Milton through the scene. They could still see bits of broken sapling in the struggle area. Tiny plants were growing up there. Grosse explained that they'd found a necklace there. He described how the bodies were found: the wounds, the clothing, the little group of ten cartridge cases; the six cigarette butts. Milton took photos as they went, but he knew his were never any good. Too flat. Too one-dimensional. Then, as was his practice, he sat down in the middle of the killer's stage and examined the set design, running it through his mind. Over and over. There was no substitute for sitting in the spot itself to gain an insight into what it might have been like that terrible day.

He pondered the way they were killed separately, in totally different ways. Miss Clarke, as he would call her, was murdered in a deliberate, cold and callous fashion. Little more than target practice. The killer fired a shot which must surely have caused death very quickly. Then he kept firing – nine more shots, turning the head around a bit and firing at different places and, as far as Andy Grosse could tell him, firing through a sloppy joe wrapped around her head. Grosse, who struck Milton as very thoughtful, explained to him the way the holes through the windcheater had aligned with the bullets in her head. It was such a typical way to depersonalise a victim, to stop any thoughts of the victim as a real person intruding on the fantasy. Her front-fastening bra had been unclipped, but the rest of her clothes were in place. This could have meant she was sexually assaulted elsewhere, and had time to get dressed, but more likely not. Her lower clothing was intact. The murder might be sexually driven, but an act of sex wasn't part of the plan, he thought. The way Grosse described the groupings of bullets in her skull, it was likely she was kneeling when the first bullet struck her. This killer wasn't here for sex. It was so deliberate and calculated, it was almost ritual; an execution for its own sake. She was left on her stomach with both arms over her head, suggesting that they had been placed that way after death. Maybe it was accidental, but more likely that he wanted the arms up in supplication, begging . . . or something like that. This was part of the picture in the killer's head, his own private emotional creation. Its meaning would be intensely personal.

Grosse explained that the knife wound in the back would not have caused death. Milton reckoned it was done after death and was an act of participation by someone else.

The bullets in the soil showing she had been killed where she lay indicated organisation and planning by the killer – walking her to somewhere that would be easy to cover in death, avoiding having to move the body. The cigarette butts suggested a leisurely approach to the killing, and also considerable enjoyment.

This scene was quite different to the incredible outpouring of violence perpetrated on Miss Walters. The rage. It was not clear if she had been killed in the little hollow under the boulder, or if she had been dragged there. The arrangement of her clothes was not consistent with dragging. The disarray looked more sexual – more like the dozens of sexual homicides Milton had seen in two decades trying to unlock homicidal minds for police. She was not wearing underpants, something he would expect a female traveller to do. He pondered the unbuttoned fly and the bra pushed up above the breasts, but still fastened at the back. She too had been depersonalised with a gag. The wounds were so violent, pieces of the spinal cord had been cut off, ribs sliced, and the aorta probably severed. This was very violent, very messy. There were no cigarette butts lying around here.

Sitting out on the sandstone, Milton reasoned that, generally, two people who were killed separately, in different ways, when the motive has been pleasure, have been killed by different people. His internal dialogue went that those who kill for enjoyment tend to stick to one pattern – not always, but there's a tendency – because they enjoy doing it in a particular way so they are going to do it that way over and over again. It's like a preference for a particular piece of music which the killer wants played in rotation.

The psychiatrist tossed the idea around with the policemen, and there was some robust debate about the theory's merit. He certainly wasn't the first to come up with this two-killer hypothesis. Some others thought the different MOs could be explained easily on the basis of one person trying to enjoy two different ways of killing. Two favourite songs was something the psychiatrist knew was perfectly feasible, but from his experience and his reading, he thought two killers.

He was pondering all this with his nervous habit of holding his collar between his fingers, closing his shirt up around his neck. His body language belying his calmness in the presence of evil.

There were certainly two personalities at work. That was certain. But how did those personalities interact? The bodies were old, the circumstances vague. The rotation of Miss Clarke's head, he thought, was for fun, to say: I'll put a shot in here and I'll put a shot in there; I am in control. But she had also been stabbed in the back. Had she been stabbed first, then shot? That was a possibility, but Milton tried to make sense of it in relation to the multiple stab wounds of Miss Walters. Her death was so violent, so vicious. What sort of a person is going to kill like that? Someone who is young and very violent? Yes, there was a kind of youthful violence about the scene. It might have been what they called a frenzy, but certainly it was a very deliberate killing. With her shoes laced up, he couldn't have taken the jeans right off. Her panties were probably cut off and kept as a souvenir. That would indicate the killer had pulled her pants down and perhaps raped her anally, face down – a final act of humiliation. She was then able to pull her jeans back on, but didn't have time to do them up properly. Her bra being pushed up over her breasts, in a kind of a display, lent itself to the sexual possibilities, but none of this was why they were all here. It wasn't sex. The pleasure here was from the stabbing and the power over this poor thing. The force was far in excess of that required to cover up a rape. Yet this was so different from Miss Clarke who was stabbed only once. How could you make sense of this? Was it that someone in a frenzy stabbed Miss Walters down behind the rock and came over and stabbed Miss Clarke once and then shot her? Or, had he stabbed Miss Clarke once, then used her head for target practice, before raping Miss Walters. Milton was trying to make up a template to fit the page. There were any number of permutations of the fantasy come to life, but the one Milton couldn't help coming back to was that there were two killers and they were brothers. One was older and dominant;

the other, rebellious, but still submissive to the elder. The scene made sense in those terms. Then he said to himself: you get the younger brother – who is more sexually inclined – goes up and rapes the girl and he likes to be a bit private, away from his brother. Guys who weren't related might not worry about privacy and might do the rape in front of each other – and the shooting and killing. Well, this older one did the shooting and the younger one left his mark by putting a stab wound in the body. It was fanciful, he knew. There were a lot of guesses, but this wasn't science. It was informed guesswork. He didn't think it possible, nor helpful, to go on surmising much further.

Milton deduced the killers more than likely lived locally and might even belong to a local gun club, something like that, but they weren't very sociable, he thought. They wouldn't participate in a lot of social activities, probably some hunting and surely an interest in weapons, and if they were in a gun club it was only for the chance to shoot their weapons off. The shooter had an obsessional nature. The shots had the mark of a person who really needed to be in control. He thought the killers might be the types to work for a while, then go on the dole, live in the bush, isolate themselves in their world.

It wasn't in the psychiatrist's brief to raise the issue of whether they were looking at a serial killer or more bodies.

And so Milton stood up from the rock. The four men got back in their cars and drove to a nearby dam, then to a lookout where they gazed back at the forest which had seen so much and had given up so little. They talked about their theories, and about the Volkswagen kombi which was still current, but fading, as a viable lead. Milton didn't think it sounded right. They sounded like travellers at a rest stop. Locals don't tend to go to them. However, while there were only two bodies, a random killing by a psychopathic tourist could not be ruled out. Yet there were so many equally secluded spots more accessible to the Hume Highway. Someone with knowledge of the forest, on the other hand, might have had the place by the big boulder in mind for some time as a suitable place to enjoy such a crime – a local or someone from the greater Sydney area. Milton took all the photos and diagrams back to his suburban office, the walls covered in certificates, diplomas and books on crime and criminals, some acutely academic, some downmarket commercial, as well as the requisite clinical psychiatry texts. He still had the classic Freudian couch in the corner: leather with pillows right out of Vienna, circa 1900.

He thought of the similarities between the deaths. Both girls were face down with a head covering. The wounds were inflicted through cloth, and each had her arms arranged in a deliberate way. This all pointed to there being one killer.

Two weapons suggested two offenders. The lack of restraints also indicated two rather than one person, he thought. One killer would need to tie one victim down while he did what he wanted with the other. Maybe the similarities were the result of the dominance of one killer over the other.

Milton thought the shooting of Miss Clarke had such a deliberate, ritualised quality that the offender would show some of this quality in other aspects of his life. There was something experimental about the bullet holes. Perhaps it was someone with fantasies of being a marksman – or hit man, or executioner. There was no indication of mental illness – too much organisation. Miss Walters' killer was someone far more immediately violent and without the need to distance himself from his victim.

Milton began his offender profile with a disclaimer that a psychiatrist cannot hope to give better than informed guesses. 'Please be sure not to take these guesses too literally. It is possible for a profile to be partly right – a suspect could have some of the qualities described, but not all. Therefore do not depend on a particular prediction, e.g. age or occupations; rather form a general idea.'

If there were two offenders, they would live together in fairly humble circumstances. They wouldn't worry about personal comfort and the place probably wouldn't be well looked after. The fact money, backpacks and the contents had been removed meant they perceived them as valuable. Someone well off wouldn't have bothered with much of it, just a few small souvenirs.

Miss Clarke was shot by the dominant partner, he thought – Offender 1. Offender 1 would be late twenties to mid-thirties, though he could be older; average intelligence; a relatively quiet person with a semi-skilled manual job like a garage attendant, panel beater or general rural worker. His car might be powerful, but he wouldn't worry about its appearance.

He would live in an isolated place, like a run-down farmhouse with plenty of land around it or, if he lived in a built-up area, he'd distance himself from neighbours. Milton doubted he'd have stable relationships with women, certainly not a satisfactory relationship. There would be some chance of homosexuality or bi-sexuality – possibly with Offender 2.

'Though essentially a hostile and aggressive person, he probably would not show his aggression by getting into fights when drunk. He might be aggressive when pushed e.g. in conflict with neighbours or to an earlier spouse.' He would dislike authority and probably wouldn't pay fines. There'd be no mental illness and probably not illicit drug use.

Milton advised the police that he could be in a rifle club but would prefer hunting and probably prided himself on his bush skills.

Offender 2, the stabber, would be younger, not very bright and subservient to Offender 1, although he'd rebel in minor ways. He'd be less likely to be in employment. He'd probably have a history of offences of an indiscriminate nature – drugs, stealing, break and enter, and assault. He'd like drugs and alcohol more than Offender 1. 'He does not form stable relationships and is unlikely to have a girlfriend for any length of time. If in a homosexual relationship with Offender 1, he would accept this as an obligation rather than by preference. He takes sex where he finds it, in a fairly indiscriminate manner.'

Neither would have talked much to their victims. 'The fact they depersonalise their victims is an indication of their difficulty dealing emotionally with other people.' The depersonalisation: covering their heads and inflicting wounds from behind were 'avoidant qualities' which tended to be associated with limited personalities, 'and in my experience with offenders living fairly close to the scene of the crime'. They may have discussed killing and planned them broadly, but Milton thought the lack of restraints and the fact they hadn't buried the girls – didn't have a shovel, perhaps – indicated a certain opportunism rather than minute planning. They may have been driving along with no immediate intent, but when they saw the girls, the rough plan clicked into action.

Dr Milton's profile pretty much confirmed what McLennan and Godden were both privately thinking anyway, though they did feel there was just as compelling an argument for only one killer being at work.

On Armistice Day, Wednesday, 11 November, came the first sign that the murders would not be solved so easily: the posting of a $100,000 reward for information. In the past, the offer of a reward on any crime in New South Wales was made only when all leads had been exhausted.

Godden's team certainly hadn't given up on this one. Gun ownership records and the kombi van registrations were still being laboriously examined, but they needed a breakthrough. They thought a big reward was a good way to keep the case in the public eye and elicit fresh leads.

In announcing it, Police Minister Terry Griffiths echoed the police view, then alluded to the possibility of a second killer. 'The Governor will be advised to extend a free pardon to any accomplice who did not commit the crime, but supplies information.'

Investigators had no doubt their task would be a frustrating slog. Every week that passed made it look less and less like they'd get him. The pressure from not producing a result was compounded by the very real fear that the killer would strike again.

As the year wound down, so did the momentum of the case. There were no good suspects, no decent leads. Only a few detectives were left on it and it was starting to look like so many other highway mysteries of the past two decades: insoluble.

Someone out there had to know something.

THIRTY-FOUR

January–October 1993

THE POTTER

Alex Milat was laid off from his job as a coalminer in January 1993 for medical reasons. He had the skin disease psoriasis. The doctor told him to go to a warmer climate. Far as he was concerned, there was nothing wrong with living where they were. His wife kept going on about it, though.

'If you want to move to Queensland,' he told Joan, 'you go and find the place. So long as it's big enough to shoot on.'

She found a place at Woombye, near the Big Pineapple, back of the Sunshine Coast. By February, they were moving all their belongings up in a one-and-half-tonne truck. There was hardly an inch to spare in the back, right up to the roof. Every item that wasn't solid had something else squeezed inside. Virtually the last thing squashed in was a backpack Ivan had given Joan as a Christmas present when she was planning to go to Tasmania. 'IM' was marked in black Texta under the flap with arrows on the legs of the letters, the way Ivan used to do it.

They were booked for overloading on the long drive up the coast.

Ivan and Chalinder's relationship continued, slowly building into a more regular, more serious entity. Some people just didn't get it. Ivan brought her around to meet Bodge's old mate, Scott Urquhart, and his ex-girlfriend, Toppy. They both knew that all the younger Milats didn't like Poms and didn't like gooks. The way they saw it, Chalinder was black and Toppy couldn't help thinking of a line she always used to hear around the Milat place. 'You need two blacks. One to kick and one to whip.' They all thought that way, she was sure.

But they liked Chalinder. Quiet, but nice. They came round a couple of times. Ivan, of course, was never lovey-dovey with her but he was always the perfect gentleman. They'd go to leave, and he'd race up to get the door for her, then shut it behind with his hand gently on her back, then open the car door for her. Richard was the complete opposite. He was more like. 'Open the gates, yu fucking slut.'

Dick's girlfriend, Lizzie, the mother of his child, turned up at their place once with the imprint of a Dunlop work boot in her side. You could see it. And that was a couple of days after he put it there. They used to go off at each other. They called her 'Dizzie Lizzie'. She used to pull up at their place and say, 'Oh, I've left me bag in the car.' They'd see her, the baby in her arms, go out to the passenger door and be down on one knee under the dash, guzzling down half a bottle of Brandavino. Just looking at it would be burning Toppy's chest.

'You can't drink brandy like that and keep wantin' to live,' Toppy would say. And she'd been doing it for the dozen or so years Toppy knew her. Richard was always on at her about it, but then he had his own problems as well.

She'd push him with some jibe. Yak, yak, yak. Grind him down. But he wouldn't just tell her to shut up. Toppy and Scott'd be sitting out on the back veranda, he'd be kicking the shit out of her in the caravan, then walk outside and be nice as pie.

Patricia Everist and Peggy Gibson were still plugging away, getting publicity when they could. Missing Persons week would be good, they'd be sure to get publicity then. There wasn't much else they could do. They kept in touch with missing persons police in Victoria and, later, with New South Wales homicide.

A woman came forward saying she met James Gibson in Eden, in far-south New South Wales, at an anti-logging protest in late September 1991 – more than a year-and-a-half after his disappearance. She compiled a Penry picture of a man with dreadlocks. It wasn't impossible that his hair had changed. Peggy Gibson went up to check it out, then Patricia Everist went up in August.

She never believed it, but she had to do something. Neither Deborah nor James had used social security or touched their bank accounts, so it just didn't suggest a feral lifestyle. She could still hope that something would jog someone's memory and they'd at least get an idea what had happened to them. She'd go to bed and lie there and imagine everything possible. Somehow she just never imagined – couldn't let herself imagine – the truth.

When Manfred Neugebauer had heard about the two British girls found in the forest, he couldn't help feeling they were closer to finding Gabor and Anja. 'It can only be connected,' he said to Anke. 'They were there at the same time and they stayed in the same area . . . Should I take a year off my studies, to go to Australia and search every square metre of that forest to find them?' He was told it was a vast area of impenetrable scrub and so the idea lapsed. He later saw that the forest wasn't so huge, nor so impenetrable compared to many German forests, and he would regret not doing it but, fortunately, someone else was thinking along similar lines.

Bundanoon potter and househusband Bruce Pryor had been as shocked as anybody that the murders had happened in his district. He was surprised that no evidence had been found in the forest and thought there must be clues out there somewhere. Like many locals, he had a $40 permit to gather firewood in nearby state forests. You could take out up to four tonnes in the designated three or four months. Often, the millers would lop a tree and only take the first five or six metres, up to the first limbs, so there'd be plenty of logs lying around for the taking. He'd pull up next to a tallow wood tree and get into it with his chainsaw and in two hours have enough in the back of his little red Mitsubishi ute to last most of winter.

After coming down from Newcastle five years earlier, he was still familiarising himself with the district. He usually went to Wingello State Forest. Then, one year, there was what looked like a professional team through, probably illegally, with three trucks and quickly cleaned the Wingello of its best scraps. So Pryor checked out Belanglo. It was a bit further away, but there was a brilliant amount of timber out there. Heaps of snappy gum which was easy on the chainsaw.

So he came to know the forest and when the bodies were found out there, he thought: well, if there's anything out there, I'm going to find it. He had spent a lot of time in the bush as a kid. His dad was a stone polisher, and family holidays saw young Bruce up and down every second creek looking for stones. He was the best in the family at it and always came back with great finds. So now it seemed natural that while he was in the forest, he'd try to help out by finding something. He thought the police had ended their search way too soon. He was a parent and the thought of those poor people suffering on the other side of the world was always in mind.

No one told him where the girls had been found, but he had a vague idea from the television reports. He'd cut a lot of wood in the area of the Longacre Creek Fire Trail and he thought it looked like the place. It took him three trips, just following his nose, to come across the strips of blue and white checked crime scene tape scattered all over the place, and then he found the withered floral wreaths stuck out there in the silence. Having found it, his subsequent walks radiated out from the site in all directions. He was going out regularly, slowly becoming absorbed by the hunt. Firewood didn't come into it so much any more. He might throw a bit on the back of the ute to make it worthwhile, but that was more an excuse to be out there almost every weekday. If he went there with the killings in his head, the forest was an oppressive place. But he loved some of the beautiful spots, hidden away from the fire trails. He'd take his camera sometimes and shoot the amazing sandstone formations down over the cliffs where the water had worked the rock into great overhanging galleries of absolutely stunning stuff. He rarely saw any wildlife. There was a sense of deadness about the place. The only human noises were harbingers of death – chainsaws cranking up in the distance; an occasional truck belting through the scrub with a rattling trailer load; cracks from the pistol club.

He received a fright walking around one day. There was this incredible stink. 'Oh no. Something's died somewhere.' But it wasn't nearby. These fetid waves were coming across from somewhere and he spent an hour wandering around the rocks, scared of what he might find, but never able to pin it down. It was getting stronger and stronger. He heard machinery droning a long way off, so he got back to his car and drove until he found that it was trucks bringing sewage sludge to fertilise the pine plantation.

One time he found a double mattress. Not far from it were thirty wine bottles and not far from that another couple of wine bottles and then a few more. It made him wonder. Another time, he found a floppy hat – like an ex-army giggle hat much favoured by orienteers – about 500 metres from the murder scene. He took it to local detective Bill Dowton, but never heard anything more about it.

And, as the months rolled by, his commitment to the search slowly waned until, by the anniversary of the bodies being found, he hadn't been out there for weeks. The homicide detectives had long since moved back to Sydney. But the case was not filed away yet. Bob Godden had begun organising a public meeting to be held at the Bowral Town Hall.

He'd organised the Walters and Clarkes to prerecord video interviews for the gathering, in the hope that if the killer had a local tie, someone might give them up. He was also planning to reveal a clue he'd been holding, in the way that police do in order to keep publicity going. It was a gold locket sent to Joanne Walters by her parents for Christmas which had not been found. The killer might have given it to someone as a present.

The pre-meeting publicity brought the case back into Pryor's consciousness. He lay in bed that Monday night wondering what was irritating him. He thought about Belanglo; the Morrice Fire Trail. 'I've never been up there.' He had the following day off work and was planning to go down and have a fossick around the Fitzroy Falls gold fields near Nowra. About 11 a.m., he was halfway there with the metal detector in the tray of the ute when he pulled off the road and didn't know why. 'What the hell's going on?' He didn't have an answer, so kept driving. A couple of hundred metres further down the road, he pulled over again. Couldn't help himself. 'What am I doing going to Nowra? No. I'm not.' He turned around and rang his wife Fiona. 'I've changed my plans, I'm going out to Belanglo.'

As he drove in, forestry workers were bulldozing stumps and debris from felled pines into great pyres, in preparation for the planting of seedlings. He realised what had irritated him the night before was that he'd never been down the Morrice Fire Trail. When he was driving into the forest, the angle at which it met the road was sharp and he just tended to drive on by. When he was driving back, the angle was an easy fork in the track, but he was always going home then. He turned hard into it, stopping to examine an old bush shelter. Spooked, he continued along until the track descended towards a T-intersection, the right arm of which was the Cearly's Exit Fire Trail.

'Well, if I'm hiding stuff which way do I go? Left or right?' He put himself in search mode and went left. The track suddenly widened onto a flat rock platform near some small rock outcrops. On the rock shelf he noticed an old camp fire – a small circle of stones with a pile of ash in the centre.

He sat in the vehicle wondering whether to get out. He noticed some rock outcrops and thought they were worth a look. He took a torch to search all the little caves and cavities. Fifty metres from the car he was stopped in his tracks. A bone was lying out in the open. Immediately, he thought it was human. Fi, his wife, was a radiographer and she'd left books lying around that he'd skimmed through. This looked like a human thigh bone. He knew what a kangaroo femur looked like, sort of flaring at the end. This didn't look like that, but then, maybe it was.

The adrenalin was pumping, willing it to be a kangaroo bone. He picked it up and stared. Didn't look kangaroo. One end had been gnawed a little. He measured it against his own leg. 'Well, if it's a human, whoever it is, they're about my height.' He put the bone back down, and mentally gridded the area. 'Okay. Let's go and find the kangaroo skeleton and sort this out once and for all.' He reckoned it would have to be within, say, 50 metres. He was at the bottom of a slope and figured there was more chance the bone had been dragged down than up.

He zigzagged up the hill, back and forward to the ridge. Then, coming down towards the ute, he picked a line which took him through thick, waist-high prickly pea brush. He was battling through it when another flash of white caught his eye. He stared at it. It looked like a human skull. A little voice was in his head: 'Well, there you go. You've found something. Are you happy now?' The hair on the back of his neck went up. He tingled. He wasn't happy. 'Boy, Oh boy . . . Christ.' He went through stages of realisation until he came to an inevitable conclusion: 'You are standing on what is obviously another murder scene.' He had only ever come out into the forest searching for evidence. Media speculation about a serial killer's graveyard had passed him by. This was wild.

He picked up the skull and looked at it. He knew the teeth would give an idea of the age of the victim. The skull was small so he figured it was female. He stood there gazing, pondering the enormity of what had gone before. One minute, two minutes. The joint at the top of the jaw had been broken off on the right side. She had obviously been smashed pretty hard in the jaw. There was a stab mark in the forehead. Five minutes, six minutes. 'Shit, better get the police in on this. Now, do I leave everything? Do I put it back and do I bolt out of here now and bring them back? What if this is the day that someone comes back and decides they are going to clean up? That'll leave you in a very awkward situation.' He decided to take the skull with him. 'This will convince them that there's definitely something gone on.' He wrapped it up in a jersey, put it on the passenger seat, locked the doors, and drove out as carefully as he could until he came to the orienteers' hut at the entrance to the forest. He saw that someone was there.

John Springett, a builder by trade and a keen orienteer, was out the back doing some maintenance on the old hut which the Orienteering Association of New South Wales rents from the Forestry Commission as a headquarters. It was an old place. The gutters were falling off and it needed painting. Orienteering was getting bigger so they needed extra space. They bought two old containers and Springett was putting them together to form a new meeting room with kitchen.

It was about 1–1.30 p.m. when Springett saw this guy in his early forties – 5'6", fit and tanned with a neat moustache – coming towards him. He was calm. 'You got a phone there?'

'Yeah, I've got a mobile in the truck.'

'You wouldn't know the number of Bowral detectives would you?'

'No, I wouldn't. I've got a phone book here.' Springett kept it under the seat of his truck. Pryor tried calling the local detective Bill Dowton at home and at work, but didn't get through, so he tried Bowral detectives.

'What do you want the detectives for?' Springett felt compelled to ask.

'I think I've discovered another body out in the forest.'

'Oh no, not again.' It was a little over twelve months since Springett's friends, Keith Siely and Keith Caldwell, had found the first body. He should have been on the same orienteering exercise that day, but hadn't been able to make it. 'What do you mean you think you've found another body?'

'I've found some human bones. I think they're human. I've got them in the car with me.' Pryor wasn't going to tell him it was a skull. Didn't know who he was. Could have been the killer for all he knew.

'Are you sure they're human?'

'Yeah. Pretty sure.' Pryor dialled Bowral detectives but got no answer. It took a few calls but they got through to Bowral Police Station.

The police asked where he was. He described it. 'Whose phone are you ringing on . . . Stay there. We'll have someone out there in half an hour.'

Springett and Pryor started walking back towards the ute. 'Why'd you pick up the bones?'

'I thought no one would believe me.'

That sounded fair enough. Pryor would later be certain he didn't tell Springett he had a skull with him, but Springett remembered asking him: 'Are you sure it's a human skull?'

'Yeah, yeah.' Whatever, Springett didn't feel the need to have a look. There was no reason to disbelieve the guy's sincerity.

'Whereabouts you find it?'

Pryor pointed off into the forest.

'What were you doing up there? You weren't orienteering or anything.'

'Oh no, I get firewood occasionally. I just had an hour or two to spare this afternoon so I thought I'd come out and see what trees had fallen over and how close to the road they are.'

As they walked over to the truck, Springett's phone rang. It was the police. 'Did a guy just use your phone? Did he have a skull in the front seat?'

'I haven't seen anything, but the guy looks pretty serious to me.'

'G'day,' said the uniformed policeman getting out of the paddy wagon and shaking Pryor's hand. 'Have you got something for me?' he asked, casual, like he had nutters calling in with weird shit from Belanglo all the time.

'Yeah, on the seat of the truck,' said Pryor, letting the coppers open the door and unwrap the jersey for themselves.

'It's a skull!' exclaimed the cop, surprised. He got straight on the radio and called it in. Pryor led them in to the north-west corner of the forest where he found it. They parked close by, and the two coppers asked him to show them the scene. They crash-bang-thumped their way in, walking over everything as they went up the hill.[98] He showed them the spot where the skull had been. He showed them the femur and a felt hat. 'Listen,' said one. 'We haven't been up here, you know, so don't tell anybody.'

Detectives Peter Lovell and Stephen 'Murf' Murphy soon arrived to take charge. They had a look at the skull and put it in a plastic bag. Then Pryor walked them slowly up the hill. There was a little bit of chat, but not a lot. Murphy saw the camp fire in the clearing where Pryor's red ute was parked. It was a boy-scout type fire with rocks in a circle around the coals. The rest of the remains were 30 metres up the hill from the femur, at the base of a tall gum tree. They were partially covered in forest debris. At first it had looked like there were a lot of stones on the ground, but Pryor only now realised they were actually bits of bone scattered everywhere. As Pryor ran through what he'd done, Steve Murphy – who had been seconded to work on the Clarke/Walters investigation – wandered away 20, 30, 40 metres. Then came back.

'There's a pair of sandshoes, looks like a pair of sandshoes, sticking out of some leaf litter up there.' He had quickly started a plan for isolating the crime scene. 'What we'll do, we'll run a tape out and seal this area off from there to there down these trees. We'll do that now before anyone else arrives.' As they went down, 'We'll be a little bit more careful, now. We'll walk over here and down past that tree and back to the car.' He was designating a pathway to disturb as little as possible. As he said it, Pryor realised there was all this stuff on the ground like bits of clothing he hadn't seen before. Looking back above the slope where the sandshoes had been found he noticed that 30 metres away timber getters had been working away at some stage, oblivious to what lay nearby.

Lovell and Murphy were fairly reserved towards Pryor. Very straightforward. A little curious as to what the hell he was doing out there. Other people were arriving. The blue and white checked crime scene tape went up, and a female sergeant was noting everybody who went under or over it, so that footprints or cigarette butts or any other damn fool thing left behind could be accounted for.

The crime scene guys turned up and Pryor was introduced to Andy Grosse and John Goldie. He walked them under the tape and took them through what had happened again. To Pryor, the difference between them and the first two plods on the scene was absolutely amazing. The older guy, Goldie, barely said a word. He walked in three or four metres, then stopped, asked a couple of questions, and stood there looking. Silent. Then, 'Okay', and they moved another few metres. 'Step on rocks where you can so as not to disturb the undergrowth.' . . . 'Show us where you found the femur bone.' . . . 'Show me exactly what you did afterwards.' It took fifteen minutes, just pointing everything out to him. When they got up to where the skull was, they spent twenty minutes just standing in the one spot. It was difficult finding the exact location where he found the skull, but he was pretty sure he pointed to it within a few centimetres. Goldie put the skull back in the position and silently took in the minutiae of the scene.

Grosse, who'd been one of the first on the scene at the Clarke/Walters site, knew already that it was probably the same killer, just from the way the leaves and branches appeared to be stacked up on the bodies. And the fireplace, too.

Goldie said to Murphy: 'Okay, where were the sandshoes?' They went around the base of a tree, a big blackbutt, with the roots jutting out of the ground, amid piles of leaf litter. There was a rock at the edge of the leaf litter. Goldie stepped onto it, and stood there looking down for about three or four minutes. He pointed into the leaves, subtly, understated, and stepped back. The other forensic guy stepped up on the rock and then the two detectives had a look. Pryor had been standing there for ages before he realised. Oh shit. 'There's another hat there.' The police just nodded knowingly. 'Well, that's two,' Pryor said, stepping up onto the rock for a look. He had to look hard. He didn't see anything immediately. But after about twenty, thirty seconds it dawned on him. He was looking at the side of a skull just under the leaf litter, obscured by the mulch and the small branches and sticks the thickness of a finger. The covering was flush to the ground so Pryor presumed whoever left it there had dug out a little hollow and piled all the leaves and branches on top. He could easily have walked all over it and never known there was a body underneath. It was amazing.

Pryor was taken back to the cars via an indirect route up the hill. Steve Murphy took a brief statement, jotted in his notebook. The place was going crazy by this time. Police helicopters had flown in with the heavies from Sydney, and the media were onto it already, buzzing above the scene. He was introduced to half a dozen detectives and then he saw what looked like very senior guys in dark uniforms fly in. One of them gave him a cursory nod and was chatting to one of the forensic guys with dust and leaves being blown up by helicopters overhead. He turned to one of the other guys. 'We don't have to put up with this shit. Where's your phone?' He grabbed the phone and punched in a number. Two minutes later the helicopters were gone.

Pryor was told he could go, and they'd be back in touch over the next few days so he could come in and make a formal statement.

Springett had continued working on the hut, and noted the steady stream of traffic driving in. Then the helicopters. 'Yep, the guy was for real.'

THIRTY-FIVE

October 1993

EXECUTIONERS DROP

Steve McLennan was called by Harry Potter from Channel Ten News. 'I suppose you're going down to Bowral, Steve?' the silver-haired reporter asked the cop.

'What are you talking about?'

'Four more bodies have been found in the bush at Belanglo Forest,' Potter said in his dramatic voice.

McLennan thought he was joking. 'Oh yeah, bullshit.'

Potter, however, was adamant, so McLennan checked it out – only one body had been found – and a few minutes later, the homicide detectives were like firemen rushing to a blaze. If the four detectives – McLennan, Gary Miller, Mick Ashwood and Anne Marie Andrea – had poles, they would have used them. It took them ninety minutes to reach the scene, 114 kilometres away.

Word of a second body had come through and McLennan was desperate to be shown where. He had been happy with the search a year earlier, but now felt a great uneasiness about it. Had they walked over bodies? Were these new corpses dumped after his search?

His concerns abated, however, as he was being taken to the scene and they passed Longacre Creek Fire Trail, then turned left onto the Morrice Fire Trail. It was about one kilometre by road and about 600 to 700 metres in a straight line north-east of where Clarke and Walters were found. The search had stopped 400 metres away and he was at first pleased that it had not fouled up, but then he and those around him realised the implications of the second find. How much of the forest should they have searched? Could there be even more bodies? Everyone was thinking serial killers.

Word of the discovery spread like wildfire and teams of reporters were on their way. Light was fast fading, bringing 'roos onto the tracks, as McLennan emerged with the stony look of a man with many burdens. The last thing on his mind was talking to the media, but he reluctantly made a brief statement. 'You have to understand the investigation is still under way and I am limited in what I can say. Yes, we have what we believe to be the remains of two people. They were found by a bushwalker after lunchtime. Crime scene officers are examining the area and it has been sealed off.' That was all. He would not be drawn on the sex or possible identities of the victims, their manner of death, or links to the first two. He departed shaking his head at the persistence of some reporters asking the same questions over and over. He wanted the same answers himself.

Suddenly, the forest began to echo with rapid volleys of gunfire, as if a machine-gun was being fired only a couple of hundred metres away. Reporters stared at each other. 'It's just the Bowral Pistol Club,' said the officer on guard. 'The blokes go down the range after work and shoot a few off. It's over there.' He pointed north-west, through the scrub. They were several kilometres away on the other side of a gorge but, in the still mountain air, it reverberated in a menacing overture.

Senior Constable David Carroll from the Media Unit was equally spooked by the gunfire as he began telling reporters that the remains were skeletal. They had been found in what detectives described as a 'million-to-one' chance find by a bushman collecting firewood. The 'bushman' had been ushered past media by police and told not to talk as he drove off in his ute. 'At this stage, it appears that the remains have been there for at least a year,' said Carroll, as the reporters struggled to write their notes in the poor light. He added that the discovery was made in an area partially searched by police a year earlier for clues to the murder of the British girls. 'Further details will be released at Bowral police.'

There, the phones were driving officers to distraction. Most were from media unable to reach the area. The senior echelons wanted to know what was happening, too. Police were tiring of answering the same questions from everyone as they spent the first couple of hours trying to catch their tails.

Detectives at the scene had seen the felt floppy hat, but had not reached any conclusion on who it belonged to. But back in the office, while correlating old missing persons reports, the link was made to the hat worn by James Gibson. If that was the case, they had to explain what his backpack and camera had been doing by the side of a road in Galston Gorge, 130 kilometres north, the day after he went missing. Was it a red herring? Was the killer tied to that area? The file also showed that the pack had contained pine needles. That raised all sorts of scenarios because the remains were found several kilometres from the pine forest.

Police telephoned the Gibsons to prepare them for the worst.

Meanwhile, Andy Grosse and John Goldie from the Crime Scene Unit worked into the night, but then left the bodies there under guard. They came back the next day with Dr Peter Bradhurst and the forensic odontologist – or dentist – Dr Chris Griffiths.

Grosse and Goldie did the photogrammetry work and ran the metal detectors over the bodies and the immediate area surrounding them, but didn't come up with any bullets. Around the first body, Grosse found a silver fob chain, a silver crucifix, a bracelet with multi-coloured stones and some smaller jewellery.

At the second body, Bradhurst could see they had a full skeleton. The deceased was lying on his/her left-hand side in a foetal position. It was hard to see exactly what clothing there was because it was so badly rotted: denim jeans, perhaps a green shirt. But this one was male. His strangely white, size 11 Dunlop Volleys were still on his feet.

Griffiths had some dental charts and a toothbrush to clean away the dirt, and so was able to perform an informal ID on the spot to allow police to get on with the murder investigation. It was James Gibson.

Bradhurst and Griffiths went over to the first body in its shallow grave at the base of a tree. Now the debris had been cleared, a lot of bones could be seen scattered about. Looked like ribs and some vertebrae. Seemed like they'd been spread by animals. They also had small marks on them typical of animal teeth. There was a lot of decomposed material in the area; either vegetable or clothing, it was hard to tell. This body was going to be difficult to identify because there was only a small piece of lower jaw for Griffiths to work with. But the presence of James Gibson seemed to point in only one direction.

At this type of scene, all the bones collapse and get jumbled up, but they were carefully put into the body bag in some semblance of the order in which they were found, including all the dirt and leaf litter around them, which may also have contained bones and clues.

The sets of remains were taken to the morgue and Bradhurst began the post-mortem on James Gibson the next day, with Andy Grosse observing and taking photographs. Grosse had removed soil from beneath the second body. While sifting it at the morgue, he discovered smaller hand and foot bones plus some small decomposed clothing scraps: a silver-coloured ring, neck chain with pendant, and some buttons. It was hard to even tell what colour they were. But they found the fly among the scraps. The top button was done up, but the zip was fully down – the same as Joanne Walters' jeans. It looked like there was a sexual aspect with the boy as well.

The only bones missing were the hyoid bone (above the Adam's apple) and the left kneecap and possibly one or two of the small hand and feet bones. As the doctor laid the bones out in anatomical order, he noted they had no tendon tags (small gristly remnants of tendons attached to bone which, if they are still present, indicate as a general rule that the remains have been there for less than two years) but they also felt greasy which meant they weren't ancient either. That was as precise as it got. The time of death was estimated at more than two years and consistent with four years.

Gradually, as he built the skeleton on the stainless steel table, a partial picture of the murder came fuzzily into view. As with the unzipped fly, this murder seemed more like Joanne Walters'. One of his stab wounds went through the mid-thoracic spine (between the shoulder blades), cutting lengthwise up through three vertebrae, from the top of the sixth, through the entire fifth and the lower part of the fourth. It passed through the canal that holds the spinal cord and would have paralysed him. This would have required an extreme degree of force, Bradhurst thought, because it cut so much bone. Young healthy bone. If James was standing, the doctor visualised the killer striking with a hefty uppercut motion.

Two stab wounds went through the full thickness of the sternum, or breast bone. Both would have penetrated the chest cavity into either the heart, or the arteries coming from the heart. Two stab wounds to the right side of the chest would have penetrated into the right lung. He'd not only have his air capacity halved, but slowly the lungs would collapse under the weight of blood filling the chest cavity. There was another knife wound to the back right of the chest and the seventh was in the back left side of the chest, close to the spine. It would have penetrated the left lung and the aorta or the heart. It may have also penetrated into the liver. Again, it was overkill. The size of the cuts indicated that the blade would have been somewhere between 30 and 35 millimetres wide. Same as the Clarke/Walters weapon.

The cause of death was given as multiple stab wounds to the chest (which included the stab wound to the spine). But that was based only on the injuries that had left a mark on bone. The zip indicated a sexual aspect but it was impossible to know. They couldn't even tell if he was wearing underwear or whether it had just disintegrated.

Bradhurst might have been able to switch off from an emotive response to all the suffering but it was a full day of extremely draining and intense work, and he knew he had to go home to his wife and child, then face it all again tomorrow.

John Springett, still fixing the orienteers' hut, watched the passing parade tear along, kicking up stones and dust all day. The media were swarming over the forest and Bowral, trying to cover every possible angle. Everybody wanted Bruce Pryor, but the next best thing was the bloke whose phone he'd used to call in his find. Springett was showing cadet reporter Andrew Burke the orienteers' map of the forest, when Burke called out to Les Kennedy that he'd better come and have a look at this. Kennedy couldn't understand Burke's insistence until he saw the name of the map – Executioners Drop. There was no actual spot called Executioners Drop. It was an amalgamation of two features – Kelly's Drop and Executioners Point.

It freaked the reporters out – like Cannibal Creek in Victoria where the bodies of four murdered women had been found in the eighties. They drove straight to Bowral police and knocked on the door of the detectives' office. Whatever the detectives were doing came to a sudden halt and they huddled around the map. 'Shit, where did this come from?' No one had seen it before. Their maps didn't give names to bush roads or key features. Clearly they needed better maps and to find out just how many of these orienteers' maps were in circulation. Registers of orienteers were later examined by police. The headline about Executioners Drop went around the world, distorted to make it look like that was an actual place where the bodies were found. The British tabloids loved it.

That day, police in the forest were down on their hands and knees going minutely over the crime scene. Senior Constable Steve Inglese found a pair of faded black panties 50 metres from where the female bones had been found scattered. Later, four metres from the body, Senior Constable Roger Schiels came across a pair of greying tights, which had been tied in two knots.

John Goldie was measuring the scene. He recovered lead fragments from a tree 40 metres from the murder scene. One was clearly a .22 bullet. He noted that the two deceased were 22 metres apart. There was a black bra ten metres from the first body. It had a stab mark through one of the cups.

All the clothing, still covered in dirt and sticks and mulch, was ferried urgently to the morgue where the post-mortem on the still-unidentified body was beginning. It was a girl. Andy Grosse examined the tights and noticed that the knots were slip knots. It looked like they'd been used as a restraint, maybe a hog tie. It was hard to tell exactly how it had worked, but bondage was definitely a part of this murder.

Autopsies on skeletal remains are more time consuming than on complete bodies. After they were X-rayed for bullets in the body bag, all the bones had to be meticulously separated from the leaf litter and reassembled into their natural order. An inventory was then taken of what was missing. Following this, the bones were boiled in a special solution for a few hours in order to clean them and expose any wounds.

Even before they had been cleaned, Bradhurst could see she suffered a beating. There were two fractures to the skull above and behind the ear caused by a blunt object – a block of wood or a rock, perhaps. It looked like a blunt injury to the lower jaw too, because all that was found was the left part of the jaw and the first part of the right jaw and then the fracture line. The right chin was missing, probably dragged off by animals.

The injuries that caused the two fractures to the head and jaw may have led to unconsciousness, intracranial haemorrhage (bleeding inside the skull), brain damage and possibly death. But her skull was also marked by four blows with a sharp blade to the forehead; two on each side at about the hairline. Two of the cuts were straight lines and two had flaked up bone, making it look like they'd been made with a hard, slashing blow from the blade of a large knife or sword, rather than a stabbing action. They were probably not of sufficient severity to have caused death, but would have bled profusely.

There was a stab wound through the lower left rib which would have entered the chest cavity from behind – about nine centimetres left of the spine. It would have penetrated the left lung, and probably the heart or aorta.

Only a few hand bones were ever found and none of these had defensive wounds. The knotted tights explained that well enough. Bradhurst could not give a specific cause of death. He went with 'multiple injuries'. This was based only on the injuries to the bones found. There could have been many more.

Reporter John Mitchell from the *Australian Women's Weekly* was with James Gibson's family in their country cottage at Moorooduc as they awaited news of the official dental identification. The MISSING T-shirts with the colour photos of Debbie and James were sitting there in bundles. 'Surrounded by sweet-smelling wisteria and spring bluebells, Peggy Gibson is waiting for the telephone call that will confirm all her darkest fears. Inside, friends and relatives are answering the constantly ringing telephone. Outside the front gate, a TV crew is waiting for the inevitable arrival of police to break the official news that James Gibson would not be walking up to the gate of the family farm this fine early summer day, or ever again.' Mrs Gibson hugged her dog, Perot, in the garden and said: 'Whatever the outcome of today, I just hope they go over that terrible forest with a fine-tooth comb to discover any clues. Whoever is out there killing these young hitchhikers must be found.'

He was there later in the afternoon when the phone rang. 'Her face shocked and drawn, Peggy Gibson dissolves into tears. "Oh God, it's James . . ." she whispers. With all the anguish of a mother whose hope has been destroyed, she collapses into the arms of her family, gathered around her in mutual grief.'

Patricia Everist knew there was no hope, but she was still hoping. At the time Clarke and Walters were found, the police had assured her the two cases weren't connected. In all those nights she lay in bed imagining everything possible, she hadn't imagined anything like this. Now they had identified James it seemed just a formality that Deborah would be named as the other victim . . . But maybe . . . She used to say that the worst thing was not knowing. Now she wasn't so sure. The identification was being done by dental records, so Patricia was spared the ordeal of identifying her daughter.

The phone was running hot. One call from Sydney said it would be a couple of days before they could be identified. Then she received a call from Frankston police. They were having trouble identifying the female body. Didn't matter. Pat already knew. Who else could it be?

Bob Godden rang the Neugebauers shortly after saying they had found two bodies but it probably wasn't Gabor and Anja. There was no relief, just blankness. It didn't help them. Their uncertainty, their vacuum, continued.

Bruce Pryor, the potter, hadn't had a chance to sit down and ponder the nature of what he'd done; hadn't the time to grieve for the still unidentified bodies. He discussed his emotions with his wife Fiona and they decided that finding a skeleton was less horrific than finding a decomposing body. It was further removed. But that Friday, when he saw the ID of James Gibson in the papers, a large picture of the still unidentified Deborah Everist smiled out at him, and he knew it was her. He recognised the big teeth, and the pain really hit home. They were such nice-looking kids.

Detective Steve Murphy called him on Thursday morning for an interview that afternoon at three.

'Yeah, sure. How long will it take?' asked Pryor.

'About ten, twenty minutes, it won't be long.' The interview at Bowral cop shop was in a converted garage full of computers. Flow charts on the wall detailed the four murders. The interview started out pleasant enough, but Pryor slowly felt the tension rise.

After about two-and-a-half hours, they had coffee and when they returned the pressure rose some more. They started probing his background asking about whether he picked up hitchhikers and what his interest in bushwalking was. Why was he wandering around such a remote place?

'I just walked where I walked; what do you want?' he said.

'But there were no paths, you were just pushing your way through the scrub?'

'Well, I don't remember it being that dense.'

'You couldn't see the bone. You'd have to stand on it. The bush was so dense. Why were you out in the forest?'[99]

It didn't look good when he told them he had pulled over to the side of the road and 'had this urge to go to the Morrice Fire Trail. I was just drawn to it.'

'Drawn to it? Why were you drawn to it? . . . What do you mean drawn to it?'

He could tell they were reading it really differently to the way it was meant. He felt the whole body language thing and the tone of voice showed that Murphy thought he was about to crack the case. Pryor couldn't help thinking if he had just spoken their language, said something like, 'Listen, mate, I just had a gut feeling that I might bloody find something out there so I went for a fucking bushwalk', everything would be all right, but he didn't have the lingo. And these coppers had the scent of a psycho killer in their nostrils.

Then it got heavy. 'I have to ask you this: are you responsible in any way for the death of Deborah Everist?' . . . 'Are you responsible for the death of James Gibson?' . . . 'Do you have any knowledge as to how Deborah Everist and James Gibson came to be in the Belanglo Forest?'[100] No. No. No. Pryor felt himself being sucked into the floor. What was going on?

He was trying to explain: he'd been out there *helping*. He spent nine months looking and always thought he'd find something, not someone. Then they asked him the same questions again, looking for contradictions and let him go at 8 p.m., after five hours of interrogation. He was pretty shocked. Off the planet, really. He wouldn't sleep properly again for years. He left thinking that if they felt like it, they could pull the rug out from under his cosy little potter's world just like that.

As a mist settled over the Southern Highlands that night, local residents gathered in the Bowral Town Hall. It was a disappointing turn out. Police wondered if the fact no locals had been killed had lessened the impact of the murders. Since one of the purposes of the meeting was to allay fears, that wasn't so bad.

The 200 or so people who filed in were secretly filmed, while a dozen investigators stood at the rear scanning the crowd. The fifteen-minute video of the British girls' parents was played. 'I am sure somebody must have a suspicion amongst the community and it would be wonderful if they came forward,' Jacquie Clarke said with tears in her eyes. 'I'm terrified it could happen to someone else.' When the interviewer asked them if they believed the killer came from the Bowral area, the Clarkes both nodded. Ian Clarke suggested that maybe locals or tourists had inadvertently photographed the two women, possibly in the company of a person, and asked people to check their albums. Jill Walters spoke repeatedly of the many photographs her daughter had taken during her Australian adventure which were still missing. 'I do appeal to anybody, even to the person who has done this terrible thing, if they could just post them to any nearest police station. They are the only things I have got left of Joanne . . . of her stay in Australia.'

When the tape finished residents and police sat quietly. There was no movement and heads were bowed.

The Liverpool District Commander, Superintendent Clive Small, had been sent down to find out for the hierarchy what was going on. He'd been briefed and taken to the scene. The investigators told him from the start that there were potentially big issues going on here, very possibly more bodies. Small was quickly put in charge of the whole operation – the search and the investigation – and now a day later he was taking the podium and fielding questions from the worried people. The concern on all their faces was clear, the elderly, teenaged girls, a fireman in uniform, a man in a wheelchair, farmers, businessmen, forestry workers, a woman feeding her baby. The questions revealed the community's expectation of police omniscience. 'Are women at risk walking in the Bowral district?' a woman asked. 'Is there more than one person involved?' . . . 'Are there possibly more bodies in the forest?' But there were also people volunteering to help and giving practical suggestions. One man was critical of police for not getting back to him over his reported sighting in April 1992 of two girls similar to the British girls with a man near Ulladulla on the South Coast. He was told that police had discounted that theory, but he wasn't happy with the answer.

Small, feeling very much the new boy, tried to ease the fears, but he didn't want to expose his lack of detailed knowledge of the case, so he let Bob Godden and Steve McLennan take the specific questions. Godden said it was difficult to tell if there was one killer or more on the loose. McLennan outlined the last known movements of Clarke and Walters and the possible sighting of them at the Boxvale rest area. He said the public had given more than 30,000 separate pieces of information to police since their disappearance. Some of it had been given to police interstate and had led to the arrests of a number of people for murder and serious sexual offences.

Clive Small, the new man in charge, had a big reputation, but his career was stalled owing to the enmity between him and the Commissioner, Tony Lauer. Many believed this was a mission impossible – four old murders, no leads – and that, so the theory went, was precisely why Lauer gave Small the job. Regardless of its veracity, the story illustrates the daunting task ahead, and the intrigue behind, for the New South Wales police. Small's career had been eventful. He joined up in 1963, was a detective by 1968, and in the elite CIB two years later. He was an investigator with the Woodward Royal Commission, then led the enquiry into the mysterious Nugan Hand Bank.

When the staunchly Christian commissioner, John Avery, took on the CIB detectives who ran Sydney's organised crime, Small was on his policy unit. Then in 1987, he was called in to re-investigate the shooting of an undercover drug squad officer, Mick Drury. Small's investigation led to the charging of Detective Sergeant Roger Rogerson over the shooting, as depicted in the television miniseries 'Blue Murder'. Rogerson was acquitted, but Small's reputation soared. He had taken on the toughest bunch of cops in the force, and he hadn't lost.

When, on 24 July 1989, a former police superintendent, Harry Blackburn, was arrested and charged with twenty-five offences relating to a series of rapes over twenty years, it was seen as a sign that the 'Service' was at last prepared to deal with its own. It was a symbol of the victory of the good guys. They wanted to tell the world, and they did. The story, with a picture of Blackburn, even made it into *The Times* in England. And what a story: a kilted rapist who terrorised Sydney's southern suburbs turns out to be the former head of the Crime Squad, and had been a part of the rape investigation.

As in all such triumphs of justice, the investigating officers marked the occasion by getting thoroughly drunk. Driving home that night, two of the detectives were involved in a car crash which left the chief investigator, Sergeant Phil Minkley, seriously injured. Small, fresh from the Drury case, was brought in to replace him with nods of approval all the way up to the commissioner.

The belief in Blackburn's guilt had originated with Detective Chief Inspector Jim Thornthwaite who had harboured a twenty-year-old hunch – based on rumours and an early identikit picture – that his former superior, Blackburn, was the 'Georges Hall' rapist. Having become head of tactical intelligence, Thornthwaite enlisted Minkley to link Blackburn to the Georges Hall attacks and to the more recent 'kilted rapist'. It was a narrow-minded witch-hunt founded on a hunch, but its fervour came from a righteous need to clean up the force.

It took Small only a couple of weeks of re-investigation to realise that the police had no case. Alibi evidence had been overlooked, blood evidence had been ignored, innuendo and rumour had been built into fact. But then Deputy Commissioner Lauer had – aggressively – made him delete his recommendation that charges be dropped and continued to support Thornthwaite's contention that the matter should proceed to trial. Blackburn was being tied to the stake. When Small tried to point this out before they lit the pyre, the righteous turned on him. The reasoning was that since Lauer fought against corruption, anybody who stood to embarrass him must be corrupt.

Small became the victim of a slur campaign, but he stuck to his guns and when the dropping of the charges was imminent, rumours started circulating from Lauer[101] about how he was a 'Black Knight' – a member of the 'Barbecue Set', a bunch of corrupt officers who socialised with criminals – and had gutted the Blackburn brief in a conspiracy to discredit Lauer and the forces of good.

The rumours were easy to believe after all the public had been conditioned to believe about its police. A royal commission was created to investigate the scandal and root out these forces of evil once and for all – if they existed. Blackburn's guilt was taken as a given by those 'in the know'. The royal commission began in an atmosphere pregnant with the possibility that Small would be tied to the stake with him.

But the evidence went all the other way. It was extremely embarrassing to Lauer and the hierarchy. Royal Commissioner Justice Jack Lee found: 'Mr Small had done all that any man could have done to get the senior police to recognise the appalling predicament in which Mr Blackburn had been placed at the hands of the investigation police, but the senior police clung tenaciously and blindly to a hope that Mr Small might be wrong, and they did so, it seems, without either really acquainting themselves with the fine print of the evidence in the brief, or treating the evidence with objectivity, as every competent investigator into crime knows he must do.

'Mr Small deserves the highest commendation for the work he did, which so speedily established the innocence of a man who at the time was, no doubt, held in loathing by a good section of the community of New South Wales. His meticulous attention to objective appraisal of evidence and his willingness to press on and discover the truth are characteristics which ought to belong to every police officer.'

The then Deputy Commissioner Lauer was criticised in the report for, among other things, allowing Blackburn to be walked in front of the media on the night of his arrest.

Lauer hated Small.

Justice Lee expressed a fear that Small's career might be hurt by his Blackburn investigation. 'The public of New South Wales will watch with interest Mr Small's future.' Indeed it would. The four senior officers most heavily criticised by the Royal Commissioner were, within the year, all promoted – Lauer being made Commissioner. Small, on the other hand, was overlooked twice before finally getting a promotion after a few well-timed media stories on his career stagnation.

Appointed to this new murder investigation, the now Superintendent Small was plunged into days of chaos as everything was sorted out. His growing team was crammed into Bowral detectives' brick cottage, converting the garage out the back into an operations room.

The media had already dubbed them the 'Backpacker Task Force' even though it didn't have task force status. Nevertheless, Small's arrival marked a step up in the operation and sixty extra uniformed police were drafted in for the ground search.

Small was regarded by his officers as a good case manager, a person who could get results – and the resources to do so. The fact that the murders had occurred in the electorate of the Premier of New South Wales, John Fahey, was also in the minds of investigators, though no overt political pressure was put on them for a quick result. This time, no stone could be left unturned, particularly since – in the public mind – police had not searched hard or long enough the first time. It wasn't his fault but he did make excuses for the failings of the previous search. 'Just look at how much bush there is. Where do you begin to search? You could search here for months with a small army,' he said.

Small became the public face of both the search and investigation, continuing to wear a uniform rather than don plain clothes. It was felt the uniform would project the right reassuring message. At his first press conference outside the police station, he would not be drawn on talk of a serial killer, but reporters persisted with the obvious question: are the four murders connected?

'Due to the closeness of the two lots of two bodies we certainly are not ruling out a connection' was the best he would do.

While Small stayed at Bowral, his newly appointed second-in-command, Detective Inspector Rod Lynch, was delegated to set up an office for the growing team of investigators in Sydney and to set up an infrastructure for a long investigation. They planned to be based in Sydney once the initial flurry of enquiries were completed at Bowral. A lot of the calls flooding in to Bowral were matters that were going to have to be followed up from the city. They were given a floor of the old Hat Factory, now a run-down old building, long since deserted by the defunct and discredited CIB, who had interrogated Ivan and Mick Milat there in 1971. The big room they were allocated was a shambles. It was dusty, had no phones, no computers, no air-conditioning and limited plumbing. Lynch had to get furniture and computers and see that they were linked to the office at Bowral and the State Intelligence Group. He had to get everything ready to set up a hotline: enough phones, enough computers, enough officers to man the phones. Had to ensure the way they recorded the information on hard copy was compatible with their other records and their computers.

All the while he was reading broadly through the files, trying to get on top of the case while recruiting people to put behind the desks, and always answering the phones as the calls came flooding in. This was the time when all murder investigators knew the crucial lead would come.

Lynch drew on his experience to make sure there was a good cross-section of people; a mix of analysts, experienced investigators with background in these motiveless, serial-type investigations, and young enthusiastic workers. He needed the type of investigator who could hack a long haul. There was no room for flighty brilliance. He told each new prospect that 'unless we get a breakthrough, you can expect to be here for at least three years'. That's a long time to be knocking on doors, chasing spurious leads, getting nowhere. A lot of people can't cop it. It needed a particular type of mind.

He didn't have one knock-back, though, because he knew the people he approached. Small and Lynch had worked together in the 'Breakers' in the seventies, doing major break-ins, arsons. It was the elite squad of the day. Full of tough cookies and streetwise investigators, tarnished now by the presence of bad and brilliant cops like Roger Rogerson. Small had been Lynch's junior then.

A coroner, looking at Lynch's re-investigation of a series of fires in Kings Cross in the early eighties, described him as having no peer as far as investigators were concerned. His characteristic thoroughness was what was going to be needed in a long investigation like this. He required the same standards from those who worked for him, and they knew it. Experience had taught him to think broadly and laterally. He didn't know where the nickname 'Sheep Dog' came from. Might have been the hair cut.

He'd never been much of a drinker, maybe a couple of beers a year, and that set him apart from a lot of his colleagues.

The search of the forest was called off for a few days, so it could be re-organised and expanded. Chief Inspector Bob May from the Tactical Support Unit had been sent to check the lay of the land at Belanglo and marshal what officers he felt necessary for the coming search. He arrived in Bowral on the same day as Small. Given that the bodies were found 30 metres off fire trails, May devised a search strategy whereby a team of forty stood at arm's length and swept the sides of all tracks in slow-moving lines. There were finite boundaries to the search area. The tracks just petered out to the west. Rugged gorges blocked the north, and pine plantations blocked the south and east, towards the highway. The treated sewage sprayed onto the pines made large tracts unfit for humans to walk through. But that didn't matter, because they had examined the pines a year earlier with no result and they surmised that the killer preferred the quieter native bush area. Although the pine needles in James Gibson's pack were worrying.

The remaining area was gridded off into squares. Every centimetre of each square – representing 250 square metres – was to be covered, if the terrain allowed.

As the search swung into gear, officers coming across a foreign object such as an old bottle would raise their hand and shout 'find'. They would remain stationary until a scientific officer had photographed it, noted the location on a map, tagged it with a serial number and put it in a paper bag. If something of significance was found, then a second search of the area would be done by officers on their hands and knees, crawling shoulder to shoulder, sifting through leaves with their hands. It was a slow, painstaking slog through sometimes harsh, prickly scrub.

One of the most intriguing early finds was a key ring located between the two crime scenes. Engraved on it was a number and the name of the Backpackers Connection Hostel in Kings Cross. It caused a flurry of concern that it belonged to a backpacker who had not been posted as missing. The hostel was contacted and the name and nationality of the man issued with the number found. Australian Customs and Immigration confirmed that a person with that name had left Australia in 1991. Detectives weren't satisfied, but they found him overseas and he could offer no explanation as to how the key ring ended up at Belanglo.

THIRTY-SIX

October 1993

TASK FORCE EYRE?

Paul Miller, aka Richard Milat, had been gone from Boral almost a year. His comments about the Germans, though, would not leave the minds of Des Butler and Paul Douglas. Douglas was at a barbecue on a Saturday just after Everist and Gibson were found. He was telling his brother-in-law about his former workmate and what he had said. The brother-in-law told him to report it, but Douglas knew it wasn't that easy.

He remembered a day when they were all sitting around eating lunch and talking about nothing in particular, well before any bodies had turned up, and Miller said, 'Anybody rats on me for any reason, I'll get 'em. What have I got to lose, if I'm up for murder or anything, you're going away for life, so what's the difference?'

It was another one of his clangers that were easy to ignore at the time but which were now starting to resonate with meaning. Even though no Germans had been found, why would he say such things without reason? And Douglas feared he was capable of backing up his talk with actions. Guns and vindictiveness seemed to be his thing.

Miller told him one time: 'I'm no fighter, but if I know someone's going to get me, punch me out, I'll get 'em first. I'll surprise 'em from behind. Whatever.' Douglas had no reason to doubt him.[102]

After more bodies were found, however, Douglas couldn't ignore it any more. It was time to stick his neck out, no matter the consequences. Douglas and Butler lived close to each other and drank at the Albion Hotel, Parramatta. Miller had drunk there too.

Douglas popped in for a beer this night, 11 October, around 7 o'clock and saw Des sitting at a high table near the door of the wood-panelled front bar hung with pictures of the great Parramatta rugby league teams of the early 1980s. It was crowded for a weeknight, and all the windows were wide open, letting in the fresh spring air, and letting out the warm hubbub of voices on to the street.

They said their hellos. Douglas bought a middy of VB and a scotch for Butler.

'I've been thinking about what Paul Miller said to me,' said Butler. 'Some of the things that Paul Miller's been talking about.'

'Yeah, I've been thinking about the same thing,' Douglas replied, strangely excited that someone else was sharing his concerns. Each man knew that the other had heard Miller say strange things, but this was the first time they'd sat down and taken his ravings seriously.

'Yeah, it looks a bit suss to me, you know. There's got to be something in it,' said Butler, as they pulled in close so no one could hear. They began exchanging Miller stories. Butler's wife, Lynn, turned up and listened in as the grog loosened their talk and firmed their resolve. Butler and Lynn had been meant to have a meal together. It was Lynn's birthday, but the talk of Miller came to dominate the evening. She didn't mind because she already knew her husband's fears about him.

'You've got to do something about this,' she told them. 'You can't have four people murdered like this and not do something about it.'

But the men weren't so sure. They knew Miller better. They'd heard him there in the tearoom babbling away about how his family all looked after one another. 'You want to tangle with Boris, boom boom boom, you want to tangle with Alex, boom boom boom,' and he'd go through a list of six or seven of them. On and on. He told them how there were some Italians building a house over the road from his place at Guildford and one of them said something to his sister. She went back to the house and told the boys, so four of them went over and kicked the living shit out of them. The next day there was a FOR SALE sign out the front. That's what he said, anyway. He told them that the brother Mick, the one that did the armed robberies, used to go the knuckle. He said he was mad. And that his mother had hit a cop over the head with a shovel when they came to arrest him.

All this was swirling in the heads of Douglas and Butler as they contemplated what to do. The three of them went back to Des and Lynn's place at Rose Hill, about 9 p.m. They'd had quite a few by this. Lynn fixed a bite to eat and the talk continued.

'Leave it with me,' Butler said. 'I'll contact the police now and handle everything. We'll keep you two out of it.' He got on the phone and rang the anti-crime hotline, Crimestoppers. He told the officer about Miller and his family. The grog told on his voice.

The policeman asked: do they have guns?

'Guns, he's got enough for an army. I've seen the bloody things. I was out shooting with 'em.' When Douglas heard him say he didn't want to give his name, it took him by surprise. He thought that once they'd decided to do it, it would be all the way, but he could tell Butler was trying to protect him. They knew what Miller was like. Lynn was sitting there, imagining some policeman on the other end, just shaking his head. She imagined there'd be plenty of nutters calling in, and thought this was too important to let go that way. But Butler had felt the power of Wally's fully automatic SKS, and now here he was walking round Parramatta without a gun, without even a car. Of course he was frightened.[103]

Next day, Deborah Everist's mother Patricia and brother Tim came to Bowral from Victoria for a meeting with detectives. Under grey skies threatening rain, she emerged to face the media cradling two large bouquets. Tim hugged her while she spoke of the dangers of hitchhiking, tears running down her cheeks. 'You don't think it will ever happen. This was the first time my daughter had ever done it and look what's happened. I would like anyone who has any information to come forward. It could save this from happening to other young people and other families.'

Tim was more bitter as he urged that the killer or killers be given up by anyone who knew them. 'How would they feel if it were their sister, or mother, or daughter, or brother?'

They were then taken to the scene. Detectives left the clearing to allow the pair privacy. Patricia broke down in tears when she saw the place her daughter died. Tim comforted her. She left the first bouquet next to flowers which had been laid the day before by Peggy Gibson.

Lynn Butler had taken her husband's stories about Paul Miller seriously since he first came home from work talking about him, well before any bodies had turned up. Then, when the English girls were found, it really connected for both of them that Miller's brothers all seemed to live down that way – two or three of them, anyway. She didn't need convincing.

Now there were more bodies turning up, it seemed too serious to ignore. She didn't want to broach it with him, though. Didn't want to start a row.

She worked for a pawnbroker, Aceben Loan Brokers, and they often had dealings with police, so at work on Wednesday, 13 October, two days after the night at the Albion, she rang one of the detectives she knew, Ewhen Hreszczuk. 'There's something I want to talk to you about. It's about these murders in the forest.'

Hreszczuk was surprisingly receptive to it. He and his partner, Brett Coman, came straight out to meet her. She told them what her husband and Douglas had told her, but she wanted her name kept out of it. So the running sheet read simply: 'Informant name: Detectives Coman and Hreszczuk.'

She was afraid how her husband might react to her going behind his back to make the report, but the policeman assured her she'd done the right thing, and if there was any trouble to contact him. 'We'll put him right.'

Coman rang the human resources manager at Boral, Jim Aked, who gave him a few details and mentioned that Miller's 'uncle', 'Bill', had also worked there a few years earlier. They had both given two addresses – 22 and 55 Campbell Hill Road. Coman put the name Paul Thomas Miller into the COPS (computerised operational policing system) to do a criminal record check which contained the interesting titbit that this Paul Miller from Campbell Hill Road was aka Paul Milat aka Richard Milat.

Coman and Hreszczuk thought the information seemed fairly good. Worth faxing down to Bob Godden in Bowral. Hreszczuk asked Godden if he wanted them to follow up the enquiry, but Godden said his team would be happy to do it.

Owing to the size of the job ahead, the State Major Incident protocol was enacted, allowing the creation of a task force that would draw investigators from the three remaining police regions. The task force was officially formed the day after Lynn Butler made her statement, and Brett Coman found himself assigned to it in what was going to be an intelligence cell. Also starting that day were detectives Bob Benson, Steve Leach, Angelo Bilias, Andy Waterman and Stuart Wilkins who would all come to play vital roles in the investigation. But in these early days, with lots of manpower, and nowhere to sit, their main job was moving furniture into the office.

The task force was going to be called Eyre, as in Lake Eyre. The police at that time chose their task force code-names from the reference index of the State Library. They were slowly working their way through geographical place names. But when the announcement was put to paper and faxed to newsrooms, the official press release misspelt it as Task Force Air. Many believed it came from the victims or killer having vanished into thin air. Whatever, the name stuck.

Its terms of reference were to investigate the murders; to search the forest for more evidence or more victims; and to review possible connections between the four murders and the disappearance of any other people. It had a core strength of twenty investigators and intelligence officers.

The media had quickly lost interest in the forest and returned to Sydney, but they came back to have a look at the wizzbang dogs brought in to sniff out human remains. When we die, we emit phosphorus and nitrogen for a long period after death. It was claimed that dogs, similarly trained with synthetic mixtures of the chemicals, were being used in America to sniff out old Civil War graves. At $1000 a day, they were a gamble. The searchers had the black labradors, Asia and Narcs, out in front, sniffing the fresh ground, followed by lines of shoulder-to-shoulder police, then another line of officers with metal detectors. On their first day, the dogs caused some excitement when they sniffed out some bones, but they turned out to be from a feral pig.

The Ruger 10/22 from the Clarke murder remained the only solid clue. Detective Steve Leach and his team of four detectives were given the task of finding it – a seemingly impossible job. The first point of call was Ruger's representative in Australia who informed him that the weapon capable of producing the particular crescent-shaped firing pin had been imported into Australia between 1964 and 1982. There were more than 50,000 out there, but it was also possible that the killer had put an old bolt into a newer Ruger, and so the actual number of possible murder weapons was closer to 100,000. The company held records of all the 10/22s imported into Australia and the gun shops which bought each one. The shops, in turn, should hold records of who bought each weapon from them. Beyond that, they were on their own. Guns can be bought and sold a dozen times with no legal requirement to record the sales.

At this point in the investigation, there was nowhere else to go. As Leach saw it, there were four dead kids in the forest, no suspect, and no solid clues except this one. His team at first concentrated on those weapons which had been sold in the Southern Highlands. But they knew that unless something better came along they would eventually have to try to trace every single one in the country.

They were lucky in that the murdered Federal Police boss Colin Winchester was shot with a Ruger 10/22. The Federal Police had already built up a useful little database with lists of owners of the weapon, many of whom were in the Southern Highlands, thanks to the relative proximity to Canberra where Winchester was murdered.

The news that there were orders to test-fire all .22s in the district had travelled quickly on the bush telegraph between gun owners, but detectives had managed to convince a number of reporters who came across the story not to run it. When they explained that the killer would dump the weapon if the news got out, the reporters had all agreed. But that was blown away when the *Sun-Herald* ran the story. So Small was forced to go public about it, although he stopped short of naming the brand. It was a small disaster, but there was the consolation that maybe the added information would prompt acquaintances of the killer to link him to the murder.

The Bowral Pistol Club was a natural place to go looking for information. Some of the shooters took affront to this, but had the murder weapon been a hockey stick, you'd expect the local hockey club to be queried.

Detective Sergeant Kevin Hammond was the head of the local Bowral detectives office, seconded to the task force to do a lot of these local inquiries. Hammond and another detective went to the club on the edge of Belanglo on Saturday, 16 October, during a competition shoot, asking if anybody had seen anything strange or had any ideas about people acting funny. One of the club leaders, Bill Ayres from Buxton, told Hammond he should speak to one of his members who'd mentioned seeing something the previous year – and he wasn't short of theories either.

Hammond spoke to this fellow and arranged for him to come in and make a formal statement the next Monday. So on 18 October, the man walked into Bowral Police Station with, seemingly, the strongest lead of the investigation. They went through all the preamble then got down to business with a detective typing. The man said that between 4 p.m. and 4.30 p.m. on Sunday, 26 April 1992, he left the pistol club with Bill Ayres. He described how Ayres was driving his Holden Rodeo along Belanglo Road towards the Hume Highway at no more than 30 km/h when he saw two vehicles approaching.

'When we were approximately 30 to 40 metres from these vehicles I noticed that the front vehicle had its right-hand indicator flashing. This vehicle I would describe as being a 1980 model Ford Falcon sedan which was a chocolate brown colour and from my observation it appeared to be in good condition. The vehicle rode level with the ground and didn't appear to be sagging at the rear which a lot of these models seem to do with age. It appeared to be fitted with just the standard wheels. I cannot recall any other significant features such as striping, dents or other damage on the body.

'The vehicle was being followed by a two-tone colour 4WD dual cab utility which was coloured beige on the bottom half . . . and brown colour on the top half. In my opinion this vehicle may have been a Holden Rodeo but it could have been a Nissan Navara which is similar in appearance to the Rodeo. This vehicle was travelling a distance of about three metres behind the Falcon sedan at the time and appeared to be in almost brand new condition. I can't recall any other significant features about this vehicle.'

He said Ayres slowed down to 20 km/h and went over to the incorrect side of the track to let the two vehicles pass.

'The front rearside door of my vehicle would have been only a metre or even closer from the front nearside passenger door of the Falcon sedan. At this time I looked down into the cabin of the Falcon through its front windscreen and the first thing I saw was the driver's hands which were on the steering wheel at the 10 to 2 position. On the fingers of his left hand I noticed shadows on the upper knuckles area which suggested to me that he had some form of tattoo on his fingers. When I looked at the driver he appeared to be a tall person as I noticed that the front seat in which he was seated was reclined to the rear further than what a person of average height would require. It appeared to me that the front seat of the car was not a bucket seat but more likely a bench seat although it may have been a seat which has an arm rest separating the two front seats. The driver appeared to be a Caucasian of medium complexion. He was of thin build. I would estimate about 100 kg in weight, aged in his mid-20s and he appeared to have a prominent nose and Adam's apple. He supported a flat-top hair style and appeared to have mutton-chop style side levers. His hair was an orange, red colour which gave me the impression it may have been dyed. I can also recall that he had acne spots or marks on the cheeks of his face.'

He described the person in the front passenger seat in even greater detail, then said:

'His right hand was beside him on his right side holding what appeared to me to be a shotgun 410 model. He had hold of its barrel which was pointing upwards towards the roof of the vehicle and the stock appeared to be on the floor beside him.

'In the rear passenger seat of this vehicle I saw a female person who I describe as being aged in her twenties, with shoulder length or slightly longer, mousy-coloured hair, a Caucasian of fair complexion and she appeared not to be a heavy build. I saw what appeared to me to be a gag which consisted of a length of heavy, coloured material which was wrapped around her head across her mouth. Outside the mouth, the material appeared to be knotted a number of times. As my vehicle was passing I saw that this female was looking at me and she appeared to sit up in the back seat with her arms by her side as if she was trying to attract my attention. I am not able to comment to any great extent on her clothing other than she may have been wearing a top which was light yellow or primrose coloured.

'On each side of this female there was a male person seated. However, I am not able to comment on any of these persons.

'As I passed the rear of the Falcon I noticed the rear tail-lights and saw that they had ridges which were spaced about an inch and a half in width. I also noticed that the stop lamps were not illuminated at this time so I formed an opinion that the vehicle's brakes were not being applied at that time.

'After passing the Falcon and as my vehicle approached the front of the dual cab 4WD utility, I saw that there were two male persons seated in the front of the vehicle, a male person seated in the back seat on the near side and a female person seated in the centre of the back side. As my vehicle drew alongside the dual cab which was only about a metre away at the most and on a slight angle to my vehicle, I looked inside the cabin and immediately focused on the female person in the rear seat. I saw that this female person had a gag consisting of a piece of a honey-coloured material although from memory it was a different colour to the material I had seen wrapped around the female in the Falcon which was wrapped around her head across her mouth. Her arms were down her sides and as we were driving past she also sat up in the seat and looked at me with her eyes wide open as if she was frightened. I would estimate that this female was aged in her 20s, a Caucasian of fair complexion. She appeared to be a heavier build than the female I had seen in the Falcon sedan. She appeared to be dumpy or more solidly built than the female in the Falcon sedan

and she had what I considered to be dark brown coloured hair which was styled in a Prince Valiant style which was cut collar length.

'Of the two male persons who I had seen seated in the front of the utility and the single male who was seated in the rear seat on the nearside next to the female, the only one who I had an opportunity to observe was the male passenger seated next to the female.

'I saw that the male passenger in the rear seat, next to the female, appeared to be aged in his mid-20s, a Caucasian, fair complexion with brownish colour hair which was neatly groomed and cut to the ears and neatly trimmed around the sides to the rear. He was clean shaven and appeared to be well dressed. From memory he was wearing an off-white colour, collar-style, long sleeve shirt. As I became closer and almost level to this person, he raised his left hand and placed it beside his face so it blocked my view of him. At this time, I noticed his hands were not rough as if he was an office worker as opposed to a labourer and his hands were clean.'

The witness said he wrote the numberplate on a piece of cardboard and had lost it, but to the best of his recollection it was ALD 537 or ALO, or DAL, or ACL.

'. . . At the time I was of the opinion that it was just some young blokes taking some girls into the forest to have a good time and I didn't give much thought to it being anything more than that. I didn't wish to get involved, so I didn't contact the police and inform them what I had seen. From my knowledge and experiences in that area I am aware of countless times when young men and women are observed driving around the forest looking like they are lost or looking for somewhere they can have a good time and I didn't think that this instant was any different.'

He went on to say he'd seen the same Falcon in there twice before, both times about nine months prior to April '92, once with five men, all but one of whom had a rifle. One of the rifles was a Ruger, he said, because he noticed the thick barrel. One time there was a male with an SKS. The policeman showed him photos of Clarke and Walters. He said the photos, 'do not in my opinion do these girls justice'. One appeared thinner, one heavier than in the photos.

The man read the statement back, then signed it: 'Alex Milat'.[104]

Hammond took the statement into the garage occupied by the task force detectives at the back of the police station. 'Have a look at this,' he said to Clive Small and Bob Godden. 'I think this guy knows something.' He put the statement down in front of them. 'Either that or he's putting up a smoke screen.'

Small and Godden started to examine the statement. Neither said anything, just studied it. Hammond urged them to look at Alex Milat, but got no response. He left the room without any impression of what they thought.

There was an undercurrent of tension between the task force and local detectives. Even Alex Milat noticed it. He claimed a task force officer asked for a pen and a local told him, 'Go and get your own.'

A few days after Alex made his statement, the police came back to the Bowral Pistol Club to check out firing pins. 'Most of 'em don't know which end of a gun to look at,' Alex Milat sneered. The 'Silver Fox', Harry Potter from Channel Ten News, came up and did a story which got right up the nose of the club members. Alex thought his mate Billy Ayres was going to knock Sydney's smoothest reporter 'arse over tit' the way he was making out they were all crims. Ayres would handle media enquiries for the gun club and wouldn't even answer questions like how long it had been there.

When police went to Ayres to see if he could corroborate Alex's statement, he told them he remembered being with Milat on the day in question and remembered seeing the cars, but was too busy driving to notice any peculiarities. He added, though, that if Alex Milat says there's fifteen bullet holes in a signpost, there'll be fifteen holes in it because he knows those sort of things.

While Alex was making his rather detailed statement, Bruce Pryor was back in the forest. His peaceful life had been collapsing around him in the last two weeks since he became a suspect, perhaps the main suspect. His guts had been in a knot all weekend worrying about this police invitation to go back to Belanglo: 'Why would they want me out there if they didn't think I was involved?'

They went out in the morning and parked on the Longacre Creek Fire Trail; the forest was alive with police in overalls. Bill Dowton, the local detective whose kids went to the same school as Pryor's two girls, was handling him.

'Let's go for a walk, we might be able to come up with something.'[105] This was the most unpleasant part for Pryor. Like he was being paraded: bring the killer back to the scene and see if he cracks. He knew Dowton was only doing his job. He resented it anyway.

'What are we doing?' asked Pryor.

'Well, you lead and I'll follow.'

'Yeah, but what are we doing?'

'The boss seems to think that you've been out here and done a lot of work already, so we figured you may as well come and do more work. So, show me around?' They started walking. Pryor thought he might as well show him where he found the giggle hat months earlier. That took them towards where Clarke and Walters had been found. Pryor's guts were churning. He was walking along thinking: 'I can't look up there . . . Do I look up the track where the girls were or do I just keep walking? Do I make a joke about where they are? No, it's best to just keep walking.' He'd already told the police he knew where they were found, but still he thought any reaction now would only be misinterpreted.

He showed Dowton where he found the hat. 'Where else do you think would be a good spot to dispose of bodies out here?' the policeman asked.[106]

Pryor nearly lost it. 'Look, if I'm ever involved in having to dispose of someone's body and I ended up out here, I'd dig a fuckin' hole eight foot deep, I'd put four tons of rocks on it, lime the body and put fast growing natives on it. I'd come out here each day and water the fucking trees, nothing short of God would present that body back to humanity again.'

'All right, okay. Let's walk on.'

The officers back at the Hat Factory in Sydney were still preoccupied moving furniture and setting up the office. The only piece of paper that had come in from Bowral was Alex Milat's statement attached to an intelligence summary of it. It was passed around the office as the new investigators familiarised themselves with the case.

When Brett Coman read the summary at the front, he thought it looked like a great lead. Then he read the whole thing and wasn't so sure. It quickly dawned on him, however, that the name rang a bell. He had something on the Milats. 'Shit, this is interesting.'

He went in to Rod Lynch. 'This Milat statement, I've got a running sheet on a Milat.' Lynch sent him downstairs to his old office in the breaking squad to get Lynn Butler's brief statement about 'Paul Miller'.

Coman's senior officer, Royce Gorman, liked what he saw too. The trouble was, the phones were ringing all day from 6 a.m. to 11 p.m. They were inundated and for weeks could do little other than pick up the phones and record the information on the running sheets. Even Small and Lynch were doing it. They were like the boy with his finger in the dyke trying to contain the flood. And they were running out of fingers. There was some informal discussion about putting the dogs on the Milats, but nothing came of it. Lynch was keen to follow them up. Clive Small seemed keen, too. He wanted Alex Milat hypnotised to see if he could remember any more about the two cars he saw, particularly the numberplate, or perhaps if he was lying. It took a bit of persuasion to point out that Alex's level of detail was already unusually precise. Nevertheless, the hypnotist went to Alex's house at Buxton to put him under.

Of the experience, Alex would remember being told he'd forget all about it, and he'd remember that it took ages. He blurted out a few letters from a numberplate then fell asleep. His daughter, Rachel, could hear him snoring from another room.

Ivan Milat's workmate Rolf Breitkopf had been made redundant with the privatisation in 1992, so he and Anne-Marie had moved to their property near Mudgee. Rolf died suddenly up there in October 1993, and Ivan went up for the funeral. All the boys from the roads came up in the one car on 22 October.

Anne-Marie had never been too comfortable around Ivan and this day she just recoiled from him with his huge black sideburns and a black Al Capone suit. There must have been 250 people at the funeral all comforting her, but when he came up and put his arms around her and cuddled her, she shook. She had to walk away and back into the arms of her old friend Chris Thompson who had, coincidentally, been Ivan's neighbour back in Blackett.

THIRTY-SEVEN

November 1993

AREA A

Sergeant Jeffrey Trichter had his team of forty-odd searchers way out the eastern end of the search area, five kilometres from where the other bodies had been. They'd found a lot of garbage, but nothing of great interest in the twenty-six days since Bruce Pryor found Deborah Everist's bones. And not much action was expected out here. He had blisters on his feet, scratches on his face and hands, but it was all going to be over in a day or two. The single team had just about covered the entire 22 square kilometre search area. It was getting difficult keeping the searchers focused.

As they worked, a press release was being written stating that police were satisfied there were no more bodies in the forest. The search was to be called off in a few days. Trichter was reconnoitring out in front of the line when he came into a small clearing to the right of the track and saw an empty bullet packet, then a length of blue and yellow rope next to a pair of pink women's jeans. It was interesting, but nothing out of the ordinary. They'd found a lot of bizarre stuff in the forest and a lot of ammunition. But as the line inched forward into the clearing they began to uncover all manner of oddities: cans riddled with .22 bullet holes, a length of wire twisted into a loop, a fireplace, empty alcohol bottles and some fired .22 cartridge cases. It was starting to look very interesting.

It was getting on for lunch. The Crime Scene Unit was there, and so Trichter took his troops back to the command post to be fed. After the break, they only had a couple of hours so he took them out to the furthest end of the search area, a headland overlooking a valley about a kilometre from the pink jeans. It would be easier to cover in the time they had. About 3 p.m., he lined them up for the last bit of the grid. 'Okay, keep your heads down. We'll have one more good search, then knock off for the day.' They hadn't gone far when Senior Constable Martin Rullis crossed a flat rocky outcrop and saw a flash of white. He looked closer. It was a bone.

'Find,' he called out in the prescribed way. Trichter came over and marked the scene and called for the Crime Scene guys over the radio. Rullis continued searching over towards a tangle of heavy, gnarled wood, three metres further on. There was no doubt as he bent down and looked into it. A human skull. 'Find!' His eyes cast around in that instant, and he saw a large bone and an ankle-high brown boot at the other end of the pile of sticks.

One of the police in the line, Detective Mick Adam, came over for a look. Standing there in the scrub he imagined the victim alone at the hands of a killer pleading for her life. His head was filled with the sounds of her desperate screams. It seemed real, like that terrible moment had been left clinging to the air. A strange feeling rippled down the line, a mixture of horror and jubilation. They were looking at something deeply shocking, yet after almost a month of fruitless bush bashing, they had succeeded. They'd done their job.

The Crime Scene guy, John Goldie, had just turned up. He noticed the telltale sticks stacked roughly parallel. He skirted around the pile. This one appeared to have been put in a shallow cavity dug out of the poor white soil, then covered with the characteristic layers of light brush. The remains were closer to a track than the others, but there would have been no chance of spotting it without coming in close to investigate. Fearing more bodies, Goldie searched the undergrowth in the vicinity, but this victim seemed to be alone.

There was a piece of wire in the shape of a loop, and a piece of greyish material found, perhaps another bondage device. Some other bits of old wire and iron were turned up but no importance was attached to them.

Detectives who drove from Bowral to the site that afternoon recognised the purple headband on the skull from photographs of the missing German girl, Simone Schmidl. She was dressed in the clothes she was last seen in but, again, her backpack and camping gear were nowhere to be seen.

The area was sealed off and the body left 'in situ' overnight, one more night in the bush, this time protected by a plastic sheet and a police guard, awaiting more detailed examination next day.

Clive Small was in Sydney attending a conference. As soon as he heard the news he got in a car and raced down to Bowral. He might have been breaking the speed limit but news cars wizzed by him in the wake of the helicopters above tracking down the highway for the forest.

The television crew that was right on the spot when Simone's body was found was with Australia's most renowned investigative reporter, Chris Masters from the ABC's 'Four Corners'. For years a hound snapping at the heals of corrupt police, Masters was in the forest to record the other side of the equation. Cops doing some honest toil.

Masters had known Clive Small casually for years. The cop had a reputation for being one of the good guys. Masters saw him as an interesting study because he provided a good rebuttal to the argument put about by the old guard that all the best coppers in the force had been purged during the Avery years – they pushed the line that you needed to be a crook to fight crime. Masters also knew that Commissioner Lauer hated Small. Masters was puzzled over whether police practices in the past, however corrupt, really meant they were good or bad at what they did. 'Here's a real crime,' he thought. 'Here's real public pain. Here's a perfect occasion where you really need police to perform to their optimum.' He knew the old-school attitude: just put the A-grade team on it; round up the usual suspects; give someone a thumping; stick something in their pocket and, if they didn't do it, well, they were probably guilty of something. This didn't apply now. There were no usual suspects. It was put up or shut up.

It was a challenge for him, too. Masters had trouble convincing some at the ABC that a highbrow show like 'Four Corners' should do a murder story. He was of the view that murder could be very worthy; that it depended on how it was done and what sort of meaning you could draw from it. He hoped that by doing quality reconstructions and associating disappearances with events of the day, like the earthquake before Everist and Gibson disappeared, they might be able to jog someone's memory and make the story very justifiable.

He was acutely aware of the problems of reporting on tragedy and grief. Digging up all the gruesome details could exacerbate the grief of the families but, on the other hand, he knew as a parent who had lost a child himself, that parents frequently wanted you there. They wanted the world to see what had happened to their child. That the death was important.

So, with some resistance, Masters made up his mind to do the story.

He went down to the forest watching the search. It was always kind of tense being there. He felt the police didn't want him near. After getting what seemed like hours of footage, one of the search leaders said, 'You must have had enough now? Surely you've got enough.'

'Okay, it's your call.' As he and the crew walked away, he joked: 'They're going to find somebody.'

The searchers hadn't gone 100 metres before they found Simone. Masters was on the mobile, 300 metres away talking to the forensic odontologist, Dr Chris Griffiths, when the dentist got the call to come back to the forest. One of Masters' crew rang ABC Radio News which broke the story.

Back at the command post, the forward search commander, Chief Inspector May, made an ominous prediction in the late afternoon sunshine. 'Five bodies have been located and there are indicators there could be more out there.' What those indicators were, he wouldn't say.

The new find had disturbed Small. They could so easily have missed Simone, out where she was, on the far perimeter of the search area. Small and his senior officers discussed the problems the find threw up. There wasn't too much more of the forest left to be searched, but they wondered if they should start looking at other forests nearby.

They all agreed there was only one way to go about it now. They needed more officers on the ground to finish this off. Small would make sure the hierarchy gave him everything he needed. They would have seven teams of forty officers, go back over everything. He also decided to give the cadaver dogs another go.

At the Bowral Hotel that night police and media broke the tension of the fifth discovery with a few ales backed by a country and western band. Harry Potter, 'The Silver Fox', crooned a sensitive rendition of Elvis Presley's 'If I Don't Have a Wooden Heart'. But this night, as more than 100 people packed the front bar of the Bowral Hotel, locals, police and media, all the beer talk was about the missing Germans, Gabor Neugebauer and Anja Habschied. Were they out there?

The news of a body in the forest reached Germany before Simone's body was officially identified. Herbert Schmidl's wife, Helene, heard it on the radio and raced out in her car to find Herbert's bus, somewhere between Regensburg and Worth. She had to tell him before one of his passengers did. She flagged down the bus and gave him the news. He wept by the side of the road and a replacement driver was sent out to take over his run. They had trouble getting official comment from the German police and, indeed, would not receive official confirmation that the body was Simone's for some two weeks – after her remains had been flown to Germany and buried. His contempt for the German authorities grew deeper.[107]

Simone's mother Erwinea told German-born *Telegraph Mirror* reporter Frank Zeller: 'In Germany Simi never used to take lifts, maybe she knew the people who were driving.' She had been informally warned by New South Wales police to expect the worst.

The next day, a cold, sunny Tuesday, was Melbourne Cup day. A decision was taken to rest the search teams that afternoon and one of the television news teams tried to organise a link up for them to watch 'the race that stops a nation', but it never materialised and the searchers were sent back into the field.

The Crime Scene Unit's John Goldie was back in the forest with Andy Grosse. They began a close search of the immediate area around the Schmidl scene, all being videotaped. They ran the metal detectors over the body without result. Dr Bradhurst arrived so they could get down to business. The wood was slowly removed. The body was face down, head turned to the right. The upper-body clothing, stiff with time and decomposition, was bunched up to the shoulders – much the same as Joanne Walters' – again denoting a sexual aspect. Bradhurst noted what appeared to be a gag but, as they cleared all the sticks and debris away, the material disintegrated so they couldn't keep it as any sort of evidence. He noted that the right arm was stretched outwards with the forearm and hand above the head. The bones of the left arm were found one to two metres away from the main skeleton. Close to the body on the left side and in the place where the left hand may have been, there was a ring, a two dollar coin and a fifty cent piece. In the neck region was a bead necklace. Around the skeleton's pelvis was a pair of green 'Kiwi Lager' shorts in the normal position with the cord undone.

For the first and last time, the media were allowed briefly into the site, ordered to stand ten metres away on the track as the forensic scientists went about their work, speaking in hushed tones. Some photographers and cameramen climbed up the side of police vehicles for a better vantage. As the bones were removed a scientific officer swept the scene with a metal detector, its alarm bleating, constantly triggered by the mineral content of the soil. The terrain had played the same trick at the Gibson scene. About 250 metres away, they found a white necklace belonging to Simone.

When he emerged from the bush mid-morning, Clive Small confirmed that the remains were those of Simone Schmidl. Fielding a barrage of questions, many of which he could not answer, Small said it was possible the killer owned a four-wheel drive to overcome rugged aspects of the tracks. He had 'no doubt' the 'killer or killers' knew the area well. But he added: 'Whether that person is a local or not we don't know. The reality is, we don't have any prime targets in this matter at this stage ... A pattern does seem to be emerging. We are considering all possibilities. There are a number of other missing people – I'm not saying that as a scare tactic – but we are looking at the files of a whole range of people.'

When asked if he thought Anja Habschied and Gabor Neugebauer would be found in the forest, Small, previously so guarded, said: 'I would not be surprised given what we know ... I would not be surprised.'

What Small knew was that the pink jeans and the bullets found in what would become known simply as Area A were probably part of another crime scene. Gerard Dutton had found that the empty ammunition box had contained Winchester 'Winner' .22 bullets. They fitted the type used on Caroline Clarke several kilometres away. And the pink jeans looked like Anja Habschied's – and the zipper was broken.

Dr Bradhurst began the post-mortem of Simone Schmidl on 3 November. The skeleton was complete except for the hyoid bone, some of the small hand bones, and the left radius and ulna – the forearm. The remaining ends of these bones had been chewed by animals. Animals had also chewed the upper and lower ends of the left fibula – one of the two bones in the lower leg. There were no tendon tags or other soft tissue attached to the bones, which felt greasy. This was consistent with death having occurred two to three years previously, given the nature of the grave site and climatic conditions. There was no evidence of underpants.

The washed bones were laid out in their place on the stainless steel table. The skull looked okay. Bradhurst moved down to the spine and was confronted by a sight which was becoming all too familiar. There were two stab wounds there. One through the cervical spine – the neck – about halfway down. The other was in the thoracic spine, below the neck. Both were from behind. They would have caused paralysis and difficulty in breathing. The wound in the back indicated that if Simone had been standing, the blade would have been at a flat angle, horizontal, through the spine, and would have required a severe degree of force.

There were four stab wounds to the back of the left chest, and two to the back of the right chest – all of which left cuts in the ribs. They were all either from behind or from the side, but mainly from behind. Some of the ribs had cracked under the pressure of the knife. Bradhurst could guess from the angle of grooves that the blade would have penetrated both lungs and – two of them – probably the heart and possibly the aorta or pulmonary artery, the large blood vessels coming from the heart. Extremely bloody, but it wouldn't have come spurting out over the perpetrator. Most of it would first drain quickly into the chest cavity.

The cause of death, based only on those injuries which left marks on bone, was given as multiple stab wounds to the chest and spine. And, as with the others, there were no defensive wounds. It was difficult to determine the type of knife, but one of the spinal injuries was 27 millimetres wide so Bradhurst concluded that was, at least, the width of the weapon. Andy Grosse took away the clothing that had been rolled up to the chest and found stab marks through it. He also found stab marks to the seam of the shorts.

On the morning of 4 November, Bradhurst was just finishing up elements of the autopsy when the phone rang. It was a detective down in Bowral. 'Doc, we think we've found the other two now. The two German kids. We've got a helicopter waiting for you and Dr Griffiths.'

He took it with a shrug of the shoulders. This was his job. Didn't necessarily like it at times like this, but this was it.

The search team had been tied up doing a hands-and-knees search around the Schmidl scene for the two days after finding her body, but on the Thursday turned their attention once again to fresh ground near Area A. Around 11 a.m. they found a sandal and, shortly after, a set of skeletal remains covered by a metre-high pile of loose logs and large branches. They were all piled next to a burnt fallen tree. It took three to four officers to lift the larger logs to expose the remains. By 12.15 p.m. the remains of a second body had been found covered with branches, about 50 metres away.

At police headquarters plans were under way to announce a major reward. Those reporters who hadn't already left Bowral were under orders from their news rooms to clear out by the end of the day, so there were plans for a long lunch at the Surveyor General Hotel at Berrima. It was to be the only real lunch of the search.

The Australian newspaper's Janet Fife-Yeomans had spent the late morning interviewing Bob Godden and was wrapping up when his phone rang. 'Ah huh, okay . . . right, okay.' He put the phone down and bade her farewell. She headed off to Sydney unaware of the significance of the call.

Other reporters were making their way out of the forest in a small convoy when they saw a cloud of dust in the distance behind two fast-approaching vehicles. As the cars swept by, they saw they were full of detectives. Something was on. They swung around into the trail of dust, but the detectives disappeared into a restricted area south-east of the Schmidl scene.

The command post was abuzz with talk of another body when a four-wheel drive pulled up. Two young officers got out with huge grins. 'We found them, we found them,' one of them said, taking his cap off.

Reporters were quick to their phones. Within an hour police had unofficially confirmed the discovery of two more bodies. The *Daily Telegraph Mirror* kept its presses working all afternoon to bring out a special commuters' edition.

By 3 p.m., the sky over the forest resembled a scene from *Apocalypse Now*. A strong hot easterly was forcing helicopters to jockey for landing positions in the little-used east-west fire break. The last chopper to land was from the Police Air Wing carrying forensic odontologist Dr Chris Griffiths and Dr Bradhurst. Clouds of dust thrown up by the rotor blades stung the faces of reporters, police and SES workers taking shelter in the pine trees.

As Griffiths made his way to the command post clutching a small leather folder, he was suddenly surrounded by reporters. 'Have you brought the records of the German couple with you?' Australian Associated Press reporter Jennifer Ezzy called out over the din of the still-whirring rotors.

'Only the boy, Neugebauer. I'm still waiting on the charts for the girl,' the doctor replied as he continued walking. A muscular officer interceded, saying the press weren't to ask any questions. But the cat was out of the bag, everyone within earshot knew it was the German couple.

Those who had followed the searches and been present for all the finds, who had weathered the pressures of changing deadlines and demands from news editors, seemed to lose their sanity. More in anger at the perpetrator than anything. Seven people murdered. Out here in this miserable scrub. Seven! 'I don't believe it, Geezus.' 'What the fuck are we dealing with here?' 'Fuckin' hell.'

The media pack grew with the arrival of more television crews, feature writers, artists, current affairs and magazine journalists, technicians with equipment for live-to-air crosses. Reporters shouted and jostled each other in frustration. Everyone cramming for a piece of information that no one else had. Then, suddenly, Clive Small emerged. 'We now have seven bodies recovered and, notwithstanding that we don't know the cause of death in the present case, we do have a serial killer.'

Hooray. He'd just told everyone what the world had been presuming for a month, if not a year.

Were there more bodies in the forest?

'I can't answer that. Our search has been extended and we will keep going until we do everything we can. We are taking into account every possibility.'

Dr Bradhurst saw the first body lying well hidden next to a burnt fallen tree trunk, covered with branches and leaves like all the others. He could tell by the position of the pelvis – to which was attached a strip of parched, mummified skin – that it was lying front down like all the others. But this time, as the branches were carefully lifted away, there was no skull to be seen. It was also clear there was no lower clothing or shoes. They went over to the other body. It was again well hidden close to a thick, forked trunk of a fallen tree, covered by branches and leaf litter. There were fresh wood chips on the ground, as if someone had recently used the larger log to chop smaller pieces. Looking at this body, it was clear that the forensic expert Gerard Dutton had another job on his hands. The skull clearly had several small-calibre holes. They held a metal detector to the side of the head and the loud buzz confirmed it. Bullets for sure. Dr Griffiths went in with his purple toothbrush to get an ID from the teeth. It was Gabor.

The bones were again packed away as carefully as possible in the blue plastic body bags and reassembled the following day on the autopsy table. There wasn't much doubt the first body was Anja Habschied. The only clothing found on her was a faded purple halter top – stained brown and collapsed in around the ribs – a wrist band and an ankle band, a ring and a wristwatch. There was no head for dental identification so they had to get skin tissue for DNA analysis.

It was only upon cleaning all the bones and laying them out anatomically that it became clear she had been decapitated. Everything was present except the head and the first three vertebrae, most of the fourth vertebra, the hyoid bone and most of the small bones of the hands, wrists, ankles and feet. There was no evidence of animal bite marks.

The only injury that was evident was the oblique cut clean through the spine, from the lower part of the fourth vertebra, upwards as it went through, from back to front. The cut was such that it left only a wedge-shaped piece of the fourth vertebra, the rest of which had remained connected to the head. Only a single powerful blow with a heavy, sharp weapon such as a machete, a large knife, a sword or a sharp axe could make such a clean cut. Bradhurst was unable to say definitively if she was alive when she was beheaded, but the angle of the cut suggested strongly to him that she must have had her head bent forward with her chin down on her chest as far as it could go. He couldn't help thinking she had suffered some sort of ceremonial execution. Kneeling perhaps. There were no defensive wounds.

Taking account of the location of the body and the climatic conditions, and that tendon tags were present as well as remnants of skin, the estimated time of death was consistent with her disappearance almost two years previously.

And so Bradhurst went home to his wife and two-year-old son, feeling the full pressure of the case hanging over him. He was a softly spoken, behind-the-scenes kind of guy and it was strange now to feel the media's glare, even if it wasn't directly shining on him. It was impossible to relax at home, knowing that he was going to have to go back in and do it all again tomorrow.

The discovery couldn't have come at a worse time for Bowral businesses, right in the middle of the annual Tulip Festival. Some years earlier the festival had been ruined when vandals Wipper-Snipped entire beds of flowers. Now this. The media and police had solid bookings in the hotels and motels, but the message they were sending to the world was hardly from the brochures.

Media and police inevitably found themselves drinking at the same places. Both sides used it as an opportunity to square off over misreports and misinformation, but it was amicable. Small made a point of letting the media know where he'd be eating his meal so that they always knew where to find him and his detectives. It meant there was no down time, but it took a lot of pressure off both sides. The media weren't always fretting that a rival was out drinking with the police, and the police didn't feel like they had to hide away.

Sometimes the detectives took the piss.

'Surprised you fellers haven't picked it up yet?' said one.

'What?'

'On the map, the pattern that seems to be forming with the location of the bodies.'

The next night a theory that the bodies were being disposed of in some occult pattern hit the television news and next day the wires and newspapers carried it too.

The one hotel where nobody drank was the Blue Boar. The owner didn't like the way it was reported when the British girls were thought to have been seen drinking there. Many an innocent reporter was shown the door.

By first light on Friday, 5 November, satellite transmission dishes had been trucked in and set up at the command post so Channel Nine's 'Today Show' could broadcast its entire program from the forest. The Premier, John Fahey, arrived for a whirlwind visit. Half the media were still waiting for the police to truck them into the area when he announced an increase in the reward from $100,000 to $500,000. 'It is a horrifying story as it continues to unfold and provides more and more concern, particularly to my constituents in the local community here,'

Mr Fahey said. He promised Small all the resources he needed and then he was gone.

Meanwhile, back at the morgue, Dr Bradhurst was just beginning his examination of the seventh body. It was clearly a large male. Clearly Gabor, although that wasn't yet official. There was a triangular gag of stiff and crumbling cloth over his mouth, cowboy-style, tied at the back with a reef knot. That was interesting. The gag on Walters had a simple over-under-pull knot. Underneath, was another gag inside his mouth. It was later found to be either a small apron or small girl's dress. His zipper, too, was down. His hyoid bone was fractured, which indicated forceful pressure on the neck such as strangulation or a hard kick. This added one more dimension of horror to Bradhurst's mind, another form of torture in the growing arsenal of the killer or killers.

There were six bullet entry holes in the skull, and a number of fractures to the skull and upper jaw. Like Caroline Clarke, these were consistent with shattering caused by the explosive force of the bullets. There were no other bony injuries; no defensive wounds. The cause of death was given as gunshot wounds to the head associated with gagging and strangulation.

Bradhurst saw the steady escalation of injuries. The first murders had contained a brutal blunt object attack on Deborah Everist, but were consistently violent stabbing frenzies. Then, in the last two scenes, shooting and decapitation had come into it. It was an intriguing progression.

Gerard Dutton was at the post-mortem, examining the firearms evidence. Of the six shots in the head, three came from the left rear and three from the rear base of the skull. There was one exit hole on the right side. After Bradhurst sawed off the top of the skull, they pulled out four .22 bullets. So one other bullet must have exited somehow. Perhaps through the same exit hole. A fifth bullet was found among the bones in the upper body, so it was possible a seventh shot had been fired, but it was possible this bullet was one that exited his head. Maggot infestation has been known to transport spent bullets short distances within a body. It was a remote possibility.

The investigators needed to know straightaway if the same weapon killed Caroline Clarke. As Dutton put each bullet under the macroscope, he was extremely disappointed at what he saw. All five were damaged from impact with bone, but the four from the head were totally devoid of markings and were completely coated in a scaly substance. In the two years that had passed since Neugebauer's disappearance, chemical reactions between the bullets and decaying brain tissue had wiped every single mark clean. He removed the scaly matter by ultrasonic cleaning, but still nothing. Not even the most basic rifling characteristics. The fifth bullet was flattened and twisted beyond hope of meaningful analysis. All he had was five lumps of .22 calibre lead, but he could tell by an impressed dimple in their bases that they were made by Winchester, Australia. He rang the Winchester plant in Geelong, Victoria, and was told the dimple related to the amount of the metallic element, antimony, in the lead. These bullets had less antimony, so were softer. They were for hunting. The softer alloy assisted the bullet to expand upon striking flesh.

Dutton later aligned the six entry holes in Gabor's skull with the exit hole and found that the exit hole was definitely caused by two of the bullets exiting the same hole. Since Neugebauer's skull was resting on its right side when found, if he was shot in that position, the two bullets would have been found in the soil underneath him. A .22 would possess little velocity after going through a skull. They dug down 30 centimetres and mechanically sifted the soil, but found nothing. A large area surrounding Gabor's remains was searched by a metal detector and by sight, but no fired cartridge cases, nor the missing bullets, were found. Gabor had been shot somewhere else.

THIRTY-EIGHT

November 1993

FIFTY METRES

Back in Germany, the Neugebauers were again rung by Frank Zeller from the *Telegraph Mirror*. 'They have found them,' he said. 'It is not confirmed, but there is a very big probability it is them.'

Anke Neugebauer wept as she told him of the agitation in her son's voice in his last call home from Sydney. 'Gabor never usually sounded scared, but this time he did. Maybe he already knew his murderer, maybe it was someone he met at Kings Cross or was travelling or sharing petrol with. I just don't know. This person must be sick. Only a sick person could do something like this.'

The phone rang again several hours later. Manfred answered. It was Bob Godden. He said it was not confirmed yet, but the body was probably Gabor. Manfred had already been warned by the reporter so the shock was diluted. He knew, however, that this was important. He started recording the conversation on a micro tape-recorder.

'I'll let you know,' said Godden, 'we haven't told the newspapers yet – we'll do that some time later . . .'

Manfred gave a calm, 'Yes.'

'. . . But Gabor was shot six times in the head.'

The father exhaled like he'd been hit in the guts.

'Okay?' Godden asked.

'Yes. I understand.'

'Six times in the head,' repeated the policeman, maybe a bit casually, but then you have to be straight with people. 'And he had a broken bone in the neck, which is the hyoid bone, as if some attempt was made to strangle him.' Manfred made a feeble noise. 'That's the post-mortem report, Manfred, I'm sorry to tell you this, but we have to notify you people first, the relatives, before we tell anybody else. Okay?'

'Yes.'

Manfred had, since the reporter's call, been wondering what he could do now to help find the killer. He had made up a list. 'Let me ask some questions,' he said to Godden in a slightly broken but calm voice. The lump in his throat would have burst, but for the business at hand. 'Have you found a photo camera? A Pentax T?'

'We haven't found any camera.'

'He had a Pentax T camera. An electric hairclipper. Type Famex...'

'An electric hairclipper. Yeah.'

'Type Famex: foxtrot, alpha, mike, echo, X... X-ray... and a knife, a long knife for camping for example, and boots.'

'Do you know what brand knife?'

'No. Only the manufacture at Solingen, a famous town for knives in Germany... Sierra, Oscar, Lima, India, November...' And so the sad inventory continued for some minutes. Godden taking notes. Manfred wanted the mystery call he received back in Australia checked out. The one who said he saw the couple in Bali and who didn't want Manfred to contact police, but lived down near where the bodies were found. 'It may be nothing but we must use every trace,' said Manfred. 'Another question of my wife: how far did Anja and Gabor lay, ummm, apart from each other?'

'Fifty metres.'

'What was the reason of Anja's death, the same?'

'We don't know yet,' said Godden, knowing she had been decapitated.

'Did you receive the teeth files?'

'The German television crew arrived today and we have the dental charts.'

'Have you any imagination when the bones will be free for burial?'

'I'll find out tomorrow. What time is it in Germany now?'

'It's now a quarter past seven in the morning. It's a very good time.'

'I'll call you tomorrow at the same time.'

'Thank you very much.'

'Okay, Manfred. I'll ring you tomorrow. Bye bye.'

When Godden called back, he told Manfred: 'If the press ask you, Manfred, how many times Gabor had been shot, would you just say several times. We don't want them to know how many times . . . Anything else you want to know?'

'What is now your position? Do you think it was one man or more?'

'We are not too sure.'

'Can one man do? It's not so easy because my son was rather tall and very strong. But a very peaceful boy, but if he had to defend himself he would have struggled very hard. I think one man couldn't have overcome him.'

'We're not too sure because we're still looking at the other cases, the other bodies and we're trying to determine whether or not they may have been bound up. At this stage we just don't know.'

'Now I remember his last call. I think he was under very strong tension. But he couldn't explain it, and I'm really not sure if he was already during that time he rang us under foreign supervision. Not under his own command . . . as with somebody behind him giving him an allowance to ring us a last time. His last words to us [about] leaving this country had been a hint and then the telephone line broke.'

'Yeah.'

'We wondered because when he rang us from Cairns he seemed very happy to be in Australia.'

Godden rang back a few hours later. Manfred was at the university. Anke took the call. Her English was not so good, so Godden mouthed every word slowly and roundly. 'The doctor has had a look at the teeth and it is Gabor.'

'It's Gabor,' Anke repeated, her voice falling in quiet resignation.

'I'm terribly sorry,' he said, softer than he had been with Manfred.

'I can't understand it. I can't understand it.'

Other calls came in to the Neugebauer house. Some from police and officials who dealt with the couple in Australia. The recorder was switched on and the grief and the awkward expressions of condolence for Anke struggled across the language barrier and onto magnetic tape, permanent reminders of that awful frozen time.

'Is there anything I can do for you?' There wasn't. Through the sobs she told a policewoman she would come to Sydney alone. 'I didn't know how to bring Gabor back, in a coffin or a urn and therefore I must go to Sydney and maybe I will bring him back in a urn because I can take it with me.'

'Yes, that sounds easier.'

'But I have some fear then he must burn too . . .'

'You must try not to think like that. I know it's very difficult.'

Anke made the long flight to Australia to bring her son home. She had not seen him since she farewelled him at Bonn Railway Station some seven months before he headed to Australia.

She insisted on seeing his remains in the morgue. She brought them back to Germany along with Anja's and Simone Schmidl's ashes. Anja's identification was later confirmed by DNA analysis of tissue compared to DNA from her parents' blood.

All the while, searchers were still hard at work in the forest, shoulder to shoulder and down on their knees combing the area around the grave sites for more evidence. Out in Area A as the line moved forward through the low hard scrub at an excruciatingly slow pace, about 60 metres from the bodies towards where Anja's pink jeans had been, they found a bone that turned out to be a human finger. More ominously, there was a tangled mess of cable ties, sash cord, electrical tape and a brown leather strap. Some sort of bondage device. The tape formed two wrist restraints, like handcuffs, and the strap was a metre-long leash.

Nearby were signs of a struggle: a metal detector turned up a silver necklace. A minute search of Area A over the next few days turned up ninety more fired .22 cartridge cases. Forty-seven were 'Winners' with a crescent firing pin. The rest were Eley brand, fired by an obviously different weapon. Another empty cardboard box was found. It was in very poor condition, but was identified as having held Eley .22 subsonic bullets. A manufacturer's lot number was still faintly embossed into the flap. They were all rushed to Dutton.

The Eley cases were still important because it meant someone had been shooting close to the two Germans' graves; perhaps the murderer or an accomplice. Dutton sat down at the macroscope to examine the bullets and, bingo! The first Winchester case he looked at bore the distinctive chamber marks of the Clarke murder weapon. All the other distinctive features had been corroded away so their unique detail couldn't be examined, but he could see that the crescent-shaped firing pin was the same. All forty-seven Winchester cases checked out.

It could now be shown that the Clarke murder weapon had been within 165 metres of two other victims. Surely no coincidence. And, even though the bullets found in Neugebauer's skull were too badly corroded for meaningful comparison, there was nothing about them which excluded their being fired from the Clarke gun.

University tests were done with a scanning electron microscope to show that the bullets from both guns had been fired at around the same time. This was crucially important. There was almost certainly another gun involved so if, say, the offender had ditched the actual murder weapon, he might have kept the other gun (probably an Anschutz) which was now linked circumstantially to the murders.

The way Small and the investigators looked at it was that the killer was getting more comfortable, spending more time at the scene. The bodies were found 165 metres away from Anja's jeans and the ammunition in Area A. Halfway between the two scenes was a third where jewellery and a bondage device were found. Certainly, Gabor wasn't killed where he was found, and Anja probably wasn't, either. The investigators didn't know whether they had been dragged, dead, from Area A or marched across and killed where the leash was found. Regardless, it indicated a lot more time spent with the bodies close to a track. More risk.

By the second week of November, 280 searchers were at work. Divided into seven teams of forty, they were mostly given the task of 'proofreading' the corridors already searched – just in case. They were all equipped with long-handled, single-pronged rakes to help move debris. The new teams were shown explicit photographs of the four crime scenes so they knew what to look for.

The command post had grown from two small caravans to a military-style camp. Large tents had been erected for kitchens and shade. A big open log fire burned constantly. There was a mobile communications vehicle with digital phones to prevent media from using radio scanners to eavesdrop.

The search teams came and went at different times – often arriving clinging to the sides of packed Land Rovers – for their barbecue lunch of sausages and salad or sandwiches prepared by SES volunteers. It was a huge logistical exercise. The searchers stayed at the Goulburn Police Academy and each morning were paraded, then bussed to the command post where Superintendent Fred Brame would brief the team leaders who then briefed their teams. The day ended around 4 p.m. when they were debriefed and returned to the academy.

One search team caught a whiff of something rotten, the smell of death. They slowly headed shoulder to shoulder towards it and, as it grew more fetid, the line was brought to a halt and all officers were ordered down on their hands and knees as if grovelling towards the putrid odour. For almost a day they continued crawling, closer and stronger all the time, sifting the dirt with their hands as they inched forward, everyone fearing they were about to find another corpse. Finally they were upon it, a rotting dingo that had been shot.

The cadaver dogs arrived back and were met with some scepticism after having seemingly failed the first time. But on this first day back, they were deployed close to the Schmidl murder scene and almost immediately one of the labradors became frantic and dragged its handler to the spot from where her body had been removed days earlier. The cynics who witnessed it became devotees of the dogs after that. But still they couldn't find Anja Habschied's head.

The two young dog handlers became the envy of all the single officers there. They seemed to have no difficulty socialising with local females when they walked into a bar wearing their green wind jackets covered in police badges.

'When I get home, I'm gunna buy me a black labrador,' quipped one officer. They were starting to feel like monks, they didn't go home for weeks and then it was only for Saturday, returning Sunday night.

Two days after the official reward was posted, the Sydney *Sunday Telegraph* came out with its own. 'We offer $200,000. Help solve these murders.' The paper said that the combined reward – $700,000 – was Australia's largest. 'Someone out there must have some information . . . we hope readers can help police solve these frightening murders . . . police will treat all information confidentially . . . To obtain the reward, the information must be given to police on or before February 7, 1994, at which date the reward will lapse. The allocation of the reward will be at the sole and unchallenged discretion of the Commissioner of Police.'

All the publicity was generating plenty of assistance from the public. Too much to handle through the normal phone system. A toll-free hotline began at 5 p.m. on 9 November. By 7 p.m. it had taken 900 calls.

In its first twenty-four hours it took 5119. There were people dobbing in eccentric neighbours, violent ex-husbands and small-time crims. Sons gave up fathers. Fathers gave up sons, or sons-in-law who weren't treating their daughters so good. They were all listed as 'persons of interest'. Many people had the finger pointed at them more than once, like the German immigrant who lived alone on a small farm near Berrima. He kept to himself most of the time and owned a white kombi van. He was well and truly put through the wringer by police.

Some calls were shared around for a laugh. 'You must go out to the forest on the blue moon. The moon will come down from the sky and turn into an emu. Follow the emu. It will lead you to the killer.' There was another: 'I was talking to my dead mother the other night and she told me . . .' One woman claimed to see an aura around the photographs of the victims. 'Joanne Walters' soul is troubled,' she said. 'She will never rest until he is caught.' And another said helpfully that: 'The killer lives in a white house in a straight line from the Belanglo forest.' One man claiming to be a phrenologist offered to read the lumps on the heads of any suspects brought in for questioning.

Newspapers received their share of tips too. Memorably, one call received at the *Telegraph Mirror* switch was an off-the-wall screamer who didn't take kindly to reporters quoting psychologists describing the killer as no genius and a lunatic. 'Fuckin' gunna cut their dicks off . . . cut them slow, root them . . . you tell 'em when I get 'em.' It was all passed on to the task force.

All such reports had to be logged, no matter how absurd they seemed. For history had shown one thing with serial killer investigations: the vital clue would be in there somewhere, it would just be a matter of recognising it. Indeed, buried in that first day's calls was one from a woman who said her boyfriend, Marko Koskinen, worked at Readymix (CSR) with a guy who had a property down near Belanglo. He was a gun nut who was into four-wheel drives. His name was Ivan Milat. It was, of itself, a pretty meaningless snippet, among thousands just like it. But it was the third lead with the Milat name in it. Similarly, another caller that day was the woman who had picked up Paul Onions by the side of the highway, Joanne Berry. She rang in with her little story on the off-chance it might be of assistance.

Each call was logged on the computer and a hard copy given to Bob Godden and one to the head of intelligence, Bob Benson. They would then give priority to each call to be investigated. Nothing was thrown away. As all the information came flooding in over the next few days, Rod Lynch had to revise his estimate that it would take three years to go through it all. More like four. The number of officers manning the phones varied up to about ten. That was sufficient for most parts of the day, but there was usually a flood of calls just after the news. Calls would back up then, and even Lynch and Small would take down running sheets, as would Kevin Daley from the Media Unit. Late at night they were overstaffed. The pressure was well and truly on. Each disappearance had to be reviewed, every witness spoken to again, the victims' movements retraced as if they had disappeared yesterday. Compounding the difficulties was the fact that all the cases had been handled by different police. SouthWest Region Homicide had Clarke/Walters, Northern Region Homicide had Everist/Gibson. The Federal Police had Neugebauer/Habschied and the Victorians had Schmidl.

With the bodies found, the Darwin sightings of Neugebauer/Habschied could be ruled out. Sightings of Schmidl in Albury seemed unlikely. Detectives were still not happy with the British girls having been dropped off at Bulli Tops. Steve McLennan thought the women had got it wrong no matter how well-intentioned they were. Ray and Jill Walters still put a lot of faith in the two women; perhaps, he thought, they wanted something to hold on to.

Paul Onions' Australian mate, Bruce Hawker, rang him from Brisbane. Onions was out playing football, but Hawker eventually got hold of him. 'This is no bullshit, they're digging up all these bodies,' he told Onions. 'You'd better report what happened to you.' Onions had been reading about the bodies and the words Bowral and Liverpool in the stories. It was too much coincidence. He had been on the verge of reporting his attack, but Hawker's call prompted him to act.

He went to the local police who told him straight off to call the Australian High Commission which, in turn, gave him the hotline number in Australia. He rang it on 13 November 1993. The policeman on the phone seemed to play it down a bit. Onions went through his story. He gave Constable Nicholson's name which he had written down six weeks after the attack because she very kindly phoned to see if he was all right. She at least followed it up, unlike any detective.

The officer at the other end ran him through the story again, and that was it. Didn't even say they'd be back in touch. Onions felt like he'd done his bit, though, and so when nobody called back in the next few days, he presumed his information was of no use. He tried to put it out of his mind.

When the bodies of the three Germans had turned up, the information given by Lynn Butler suddenly had a lot more resonance. Detective Brett Coman was keen to follow it, but there was always so much to do. He made contact with Lynn again, trying to get a more formal statement from her and her husband, but she put him off. Christmas was coming and she was very busy. She then tried to find him again, but couldn't get through. And, like Onions, she presumed the information was of no use. Coman would later put it down to inexperience in homicide investigations that he didn't push harder to get more time away from other inquiries to do the Milats. But there were fresh leads coming in hourly and it was a juggling act.

While Gerard Dutton was fast becoming quite an expert on the Ruger 10/22, he had to pay a visit to the man who knew more about them and their quirks than perhaps anybody. Detective Superintendent Ian Prior, head of the AFP Ballistics and Firearms Branch, was the man in charge of finding the Colin Winchester murder weapon.

Prior gave Dutton the test-firing results from 550 Ruger 10/22s which the Feds had tracked down. For the next three days, Dutton sat at the macroscope and compared them to the Belanglo exhibits. So although Dutton didn't find any matches, he was fast gaining a good understanding of the weapon and the wide variety of marks it could leave on bullets and cartridge cases.

The science of forensic identification is built on the premise that no two things can be made identical but, while sitting there examining the 550 test firings, Dutton was amazed by the incredible variance between the firing pin impressions. Few of the 550 cartridge cases required any sort of careful analysis. Most could be eliminated in seconds. Those from 10/22s made after 1982 could be dismissed by the naked eye because of the narrower firing pin.

Over the next few months he would examine about 700 different 10/22s, and only saw six burr marks similar to two on the murder weapon – and never both marks on the same gun. He noted that the two test-fired rifles which came closest had a 120 prefix on the serial number. But some other weapons with 120 prefixes were totally different.

Over time, he would spend countless hours staring into the macroscope at every millimetre of the murder cartridge cases. He likened it to getting to know the face of a good friend. Over the coming months as he examined hundreds of test-fired cartridge cases, he felt like he was looking for that friend among the faces in a crowd. But every face was a stranger. Sometimes he thought he saw it, then looked closer and realised it was someone else. He knew when the face did show, he'd recognise it instantly.

The search in Belanglo was scaled down on 17 November. Over the next few days, all the equipment, tents and personnel disappeared leaving only silence and the odd piece of crime-scene tape dangling from trampled bushes. On the same day, the former police minister, Ted Pickering, was in demolition mode, intent on bringing down the edifice of corruption he knew existed within his old department. Towards the end of a wide-ranging speech in parliament, Pickering diverted his attention to Clive Small. 'It would be of interest to note that, following the Blackburn debacle, in which [the Commissioner] Mr Lauer appeared prominently, Mr Lauer did his level best to destroy the career of police officer Superintendent Clive Small.' Pickering said that Lauer had told him Small was a 'Black Knight'. 'It was only because of my very high regard for, personal knowledge of, and my personal protection for Mr Small, that this police officer's career was saved from Mr Lauer's quite improper attack on his integrity. As a result, we have him out there now working, and doing a fantastic job.'

So public an airing of the force's dirty linen only served to increase the pressure on all the investigators.

THIRTY-NINE
December 1993–January 1994

DELIVERANCE

On Saturday, 4 December, two distressed sixteen-year-old girls came into a service station restaurant on the Hume Highway at Yass. 'There's a man out there. He's the backpacker murderer. He has a gun and a knife and tied us up. He only let us come in here because we promised we wouldn't say anything.'

The police rushed there and arrested the fifty-year-old man. A knife, straps and bandages were found in his vehicle but no pistol as the girls alleged. He had picked them up hitchhiking on the Princes Highway at Batemans Bay on the South Coast at 6 p.m., offering to drive them across to the Hume Highway. He told them he knew a short cut and drove along a number of remote bush tracks before stopping his Ford F100 panel van and producing a large knife which he held to the face of one of the girls before tying them both up with bandages and straps. He blindfolded one girl and raped her. He then pitched a tent in the bush before untying and undressing the girls.

During the night he produced a revolver and asked one of them to shoot him, saying he had 'done bad things'. The terrified girl refused. Next morning, Sunday, he drove them to Yass where he stopped at the service station. The task force had him in their sights for most of December, but the itinerant gold prospector, David Bracken had an alibi. He was jailed for four-and-a-half years for sexual intercourse without consent, abduction and carnal knowledge.

It only went to demonstrate how many sickos were out there. The detectives already knew that. People like Bracken were popping up all over the place, coming strongly into the frame and slowly being eliminated or downgraded. They'd be discussed each morning when the inspectors would meet with the senior sergeants and sergeants for a briefing on the previous day's progress and what they proposed to do that day. There wasn't any set pattern to it all. The team leaders were appraised of new information, new 'persons of interest', POIs. New tasks were divvyed up in alphabetical order. One team would deal with subjects and suspects ranging from A to C, another from D to G and so on.

At the end of the day, detectives would come in and write up their reports which were submitted to either Bob Benson or Bob Godden for their appraisal, and then a decision made on whether further inquiries were needed. They'd put 'job: interview so and so', or 'no further action'. The report with its recommendations would be passed to the analysts for processing. It was not uncommon for field investigators to not know the bigger picture, only their own piece of the jigsaw.

In early December, Royce Gorman was sent to the Winchester factory in Geelong with the ammunition box found at the Neugebauer/Habschied scene. There, he learned that the box came from a batch of more than 300,000 bullets made during one shift. They were distributed to fifty-five different gun shops, half of them in New South Wales. Chances were, the killer bought more than just his ammo there. Apart from the actual crime scenes, these fifty-five shops were the closest investigators had come to the trail of the murderer, so Small and Lynch made an operational decision to drag just about every single investigator off what they were doing for a fortnight early in December and have them working on all the New South Wales gun shops.

Steve Leach, whose team was already on the gun, was given the job of going to the Horsley Park Gun Shop in Sydney's west. It was probably the biggest gun shop in the country and had bought the great bulk of the ammunition produced on the crucial shift. The shop was a sight to behold, lined with trophy heads of bears and deer and exotic Asian cats. Everything you needed to kill was on sale here.

Leach demanded to see all the records of the owner, Peter Abela, and together they went through his invoices and books. Abela was helpful enough. It wasn't a legal requirement for gun shops to record the sale of ammunition so the crucial link could not be made to the forest bullets, but Leach took down the names and details of all the purchasers of Ruger 10/22s and Anschutz rifles. It was hoped that by linking up names of the shop's customers to other information on the database, they might be able to start firming up suspects they already had. It was a better lead than chasing all 55,000 Rugers, but there was no real sense in Leach's mind of being close to the killer. As it turned out, some interesting purchases in Abela's books were made in the names of Jock Pittaway and Norman Chong, even though Abela knew the purchaser as 'Ivan'. But those names weren't next to a Ruger or Anschutz sale. As it would turn out, Mr Abela's paperwork was somewhat sloppy.

Around Christmas it was becoming clear that the computers weren't handling the job properly. The Task Force Investigation Management System, TIMS, had been set up for the Clarke/Walters investigation and now that everything was growing in size and complexity, it wasn't handling it. There wasn't enough flexibility. All the information on white kombi vans was spread over several different areas of the computer, but it was difficult to then take it out and compare it to information from other parts of the database, like the growing number of entries for Ruger owners.

Data had to flow through all these areas. With no end in sight to the investigation, it was decided to start all over again and introduce a newer, more flexible system which could also link in systems outside the police service's. It meant masses of information had to be re-entered and so the entry of new data was delayed by weeks but, in making the decision, Small and Lynch reasoned that it was better to get it over with now because the investigation might go on for years.

The decision annoyed some investigators who wanted information immediately. But the bosses reasoned that the murders happened so long ago, an extra day or week or month wasn't going to make much difference. It wasn't like a normal murder investigation where hours can be crucial.

Senior analyst for the task force, Detective Senior Constable Shaun Gagan, and his team of eight were given the unenviable task of reading, categorising, prioritising and inputting all the information from the phone-in. At least 2000 people had been named as the killer or someone who knew something about the murders. The mountain still had to be climbed and Gagan's lot got into it. Early in December they were still reviewing and assessing the information by hand, waiting for the new computer to get up and running. By mid-December there were 10,000 running sheets to be processed. Gagan couldn't help laughing when he read the name on the running sheet from a man who rang from England.

'Paul Onions . . . Hey, imagine having a name like Onions,' he said to Detective Constable Paul Martin beside him. The two analysts had a chuckle. Then Gagan began to read the information. It looked pretty good so he 'actioned' it for the attention of investigators, and threw it in with all the other good leads.

A few weeks later Martin came across a similar story. 'This must relate to that one of yours, Shaun,' Martin said, passing him the running sheet on Joanne Berry. Again, the report was given a kick along and handed up to the head of intelligence Bob Benson. The two officers went back to work.

In the very early days of the task force, Small and Lynch had put a request out for all stations between Liverpool and Goulburn to scour their records looking for old cases going back to 1970 involving hitchhikers between the ages of sixteen and thirty-five. They didn't want to define the parameters so tightly as to rule good stuff out, nor did they want everything.

They asked for an Australia-wide net to be thrown over all old missing persons and unsolved murder cases that might fit the bill. They found sixteen murders and forty-three missing persons cases matching the general hitchhiking criteria. Over time, the task force managed to locate some of the missing and to help interstate police put names to some of their long-unidentified bodies.

Among the unsolved murder cases were two street kids hitching from Adelaide. The bodies of John Ronald Lee, fourteen, and Fiona Burns, fifteen, were found dumped in bushland at a truck rest area at Kaniva, just inside the Victorian border on 18 October 1990. The two were lying about 50 metres apart. The boy had died from a knife wound to the chest, the girl from multiple stab wounds.

Intriguingly, two missing persons, Michelle Pope, eighteen, and her boyfriend Stephen Lapthorne, twenty-one, vanished one night in 1978 driving in Lapthorne's lime green Bedford van from Berowra to Asquith, quite close to Galston Gorge where James Gibson's backpack and camera were found. The couple was never found, though it was established that in the forty-eight hours following their disappearance a similar vehicle was seen in the Southern Highlands town of Goulburn.

Then there were the teenagers who had gone missing from the Newcastle/Central Coast region of New South Wales. There was Leanne Beth Goodall, twenty-one, an aspiring artist who vanished after leaving a hotel in Newcastle on 30 December 1978, heading for her parents' home in Belmont. She had been the first in an alarming spate of disappearances in the region. Dental nurse Robyn Hickie, seventeen, was last seen standing at a bus stop opposite her parents' home at Belmont North at dusk on 7 April 1979. Two weeks later Amanda Robinson, fourteen, vanished without trace from the nearby town of Swansea as she walked from a bus stop to her home around midnight after attending a school dance. But they didn't fit the pattern.

There were many more like them. Faces that would never age in the Missing Persons Bureau archives.

Because eighteen months had passed without another known murder, there was speculation within the task force that the killer had moved on. The nature of Belanglo suggested the killer was not a tourist, but detectives wondered if Belanglo wasn't the only dumping ground. They looked at the United States and saw a lot of highly mobile killers dumping bodies and moving on, with the police always one step and three states behind.

Tasmanian police had tried to establish if there was a link with the disappearance there of German backpacker Nancy Grunwaldt, in March 1993. With no known tourists having gone missing in New South Wales during 1993, they were worried the killer had found a new hunting ground.

In the first days of the New Year, ten extra detectives came on the task force, bringing it up to its full strength of thirty-seven investigators and analysts. Among the newcomers were Detective Senior Constables David McCloskey and Paul Gordon. They hadn't been there long when Royce Gorman handed Gordon a file. 'Have a look at this. I've tried to get Mr Small to have a look and he isn't that interested.'[108] It was Brett Coman's file on the Milats. Coman was going on leave.

Gorman had been keen to have someone look into this family for a while but, like everyone, was frustrated by all the other work that had to be done. So he wanted the two new bods, Gordon and McCloskey, to get straight into it.

Gordon was thrilled to be with the task force and working for Clive Small whose legend preceded him. Gordon had done his time around Darlinghurst and Kings Cross and had been the last detective put on at the old homicide squad in 1987, before it was disbanded when then-Commissioner Avery tried to shake up the force. Gordon looked inside the Milat file: three separate leads on one family. Interesting. There was Richard Milat's alleged comment about the Germans, there was Alex Milat's strange statement, and there was a third lead from the woman whose boyfriend worked with Ivan Milat. That wasn't so exciting. There were huge piles of those sorts of tips. Gorman instructed him to find out who the family was, what their form was like and, if he could, when they were working.

Lynn Butler hadn't heard from the task force for months since her chat with Brett Coman and Ewhen Hreszczuk in October. She was thinking that her husband's suspicions about 'Paul Miller' must have been mistaken. Then Paul Gordon phoned her at work and came straight over. She told him about Des' call on 11 October. 'He won't be happy with me puttin' him in like this. He'll go off his head.'

'Don't you worry about him. I'll fix it.'

Gordon and McCloskey interviewed Butler a few days later. Towards the end, Gordon said: 'Your wife's done the right thing... Don't blame her for doing it.' Butler didn't mind talking to the cops after all. He knew he had to do it, but he was still concerned for his safety.

'Are you frightened?' asked Gordon.

'If I had one of those things you've got strapped to your ankle I might feel a bit more secure,' he said, pointing at the detective's pistol.

Gordon and McCloskey came around to Paul Douglas' place a few days later as bushfires blazed all around Sydney and a smoky haze hung all about. Ash was falling at Bondi Beach. It was a strange time to be in Sydney, much stranger for Douglas, being involved in a murder mystery. He was a nervous person at the best of times and Gordon could see it.

'If you're going to give evidence, you know that you've got to get used to this.'

Douglas told them all about 'Miller' and, while he may not have been showing much on the outside, Gordon was feeling more and more confident about Richard Milat. The detective made a few enquiries at Readymix (CSR) about Ivan Milat on 12 January. All he was told by the boss were stories about what a hard worker and good bloke Ivan was. All he heard about Richard was how crazy he was. He asked both their respective workplaces for records of when they were working. Richard had seemed the natural suspect but when the timesheets arrived, they showed that Richard was in the clear for the Gibson and Everist murders. He worked from 6 a.m. to 2.30 p.m.

Then he got word on Ivan. He was off work on every single important date. Gordon's hard-on for the Milats was one among several leads that looked okay. But right from the beginning he felt like he was getting a negative vibe from those above him. He knew he had a soul mate in Royce Gorman, but otherwise he felt like he wasn't getting much interest from his superiors.

For psychiatrist Dr Rod Milton, the discovery of more bodies forced him to have another look at his profile of the killers. The task force gave him a lot of information on the five new murders. The beefed-up investigation had fantastic graphics produced in a spiral-bound book detailing the incidents and the evidence. There were videotapes of the scenes too, but Milton always found them far less revealing than photographs because of the narrower field. He studied all the photos and at the end of it felt no need to vary his original report. There was nothing in the following five murder scenes to alter his two-killer scenario. The stabber and the shooter were, he thought, probably different people.

But Clive Small wanted the psychiatrist to join a group he was forming. With no suspect emerging from the pack, Small had two problems. The most important was how to make sense of the million pieces of information the task force already held, and how to make way for that to double in coming months. The second was how to deal with the people of the Southern Highlands as he prepared to start a large-scale random door knock. What questions to ask? What to look for?

Small had the idea of getting a round table of people from different disciplines together to come at the problems from fresh directions. Milton was a logical choice. Small invited the Dean of anthropology at Sydney University, Dr Richard Basham, to come in. Basham had helped police working with Asian crime. Small already knew he could work with the engaging American who had studied at Berkeley University in experimental and clinical psychology in the 1960s. Basham thought his speciality – psychological anthropology – added a distinctive socio-cultural slant to the group.

Milton wasn't sure about Basham's expertise in interpreting some of the physical evidence, but respected his creative analysis. Basham, similarly, was generally a bit wary of psychiatrists, worrying that maybe they didn't get out enough, but he knew enough about Milton's incredible depth of experience to know he was invaluable to the secret little team. There were two computer experts. One of them, Bob Young, was a trained sociologist who now specialised in research methodology, particularly in areas where there were large amounts of messy data, just like a police investigation.

The group was nominally put together in December, but didn't meet with Small until late January 1994.

Despite the serious agenda there was an air of informality when they met, often with a six-pack of beer to break the ice.

The policeman presented them with his plan for what was, essentially, a house-to-house door knock of the Southern Highlands. Basham, for one, didn't favour it. He worried about the expenditure of resources, but also of individual energy. The police would become exhausted. He'd seen other investigations where the weight of time and information seemed to cause a feeling that the case would never be solved. He didn't know it, but the local detectives at Bowral were already feeling isolated from the investigation since it had moved back to the city. They felt like they were just doing the menial chores for the big city police – locating and checking the Rugers in the district. And there was already too much information coming from the hotline.

Basham suggested it might be better to start off interviewing school teachers, asking them about any kids they had taught who tortured animals, or tied up other kids, or lit fires: the classic kind of loner or bully behaviour which could alert them to a problem. Another chance was that if they could get better results out of the DNA from the hair in Joanne Walters' hand, they could contemplate DNA testing every family from Parramatta to Goulburn. Mitochondrial DNA runs through the female line so they'd only have to test grandmothers. Link the granny to the hair and you'd be inside the killer's family.

Small had given Basham a briefing on the details of the crime to get him up to speed. He mentioned that they had a guy with an apparently photographic memory. 'He is the sort of person who can pass by a sign and say: "Did you see the twenty-five shotgun pellet holes in that stop sign?" And if you stop and go back and count them, there's twenty-five.'

'Clive, I don't believe the guy's got a photographic memory,' Basham told him. 'If a guy tells me that there's twenty-five pellet holes in a stop sign, my first response would be that he put them there.'

Small went on to tell him about Alex Milat's statement.

As Small briefed the whole group, describing the manner of the killings, one thing that stuck in the anthropologist's mind was the separation of victims. It could be explained away by a perpetrator being embarrassed to perform his fantasy in front of the other victim, or to maintain control. However, it was much more plausible to explain it all if two perpetrators were there.

Basham said to Small, just as Milton had done to Godden a year earlier: 'I would suspect brothers, particularly if you are talking about crimes of this magnitude.' But the most striking feature was Anja Habschied's decapitation. As Basham saw it, a dominant male was making a statement to a subordinate. '"I'm the crazy mother around here." Then you make some kind of glib statement, you know . . . "Well, that should shut her up." It is black humour. It is domination over the victim *and* the subordinate. The murderer is giving all kinds of signs of a need for dominance in his relationships. It's something that comes from someone who was beaten by his father. A situation where a kid has felt a capricious authority figure dominating his life when he was younger.'

When Small told Basham a 'homemade' silencer had probably been used, Basham responded without reflection: 'Well, he must own a motorcycle.' The logic being that they were talking about a guy who lived in a fantasy world and the fantasy worlds which came to mind were that of the outlaw-cowboy-biker kind. Basham thought that this was where an anthropologist was useful because people live out the images society reflects upon them – what they pick up on the TV, video or from friends. If someone had gone to the trouble of making a silencer, it just seemed to him they'd have that outlaw, one-per-center image in their heads.

He thought they probably didn't live in an isolated spot, not totally isolated, because they took the victims to an isolated spot. He thought they could enjoy themselves much more if they could do it on their own property. He thought of *Deliverance*. It came to Basham from personal experience. He grew up in north Georgia where the book and movie were set. He knew the type. He knew people from those days now in jail for murder. He imagined a group of brothers roaming the woods, butchering animals, shooting targets.

When he mentioned the movie to Small at the group's first meeting in late January, Small said, 'We've got a family that fits what you're describing'. Small told him about the Milats, even though he didn't name them, and Basham replied: 'Clive, that's exactly the kind of family I'm talking about. You've really got to watch them.' Basham thought he saw a certain sparkle in Small's eye, an enthusiasm. If Small was giving Paul Gordon the impression he wasn't interested in the Milats, he was giving a different impression to the anthropologist.

There were plenty of other potential suspects – more precisely, POIs. It frightened Basham that there were so many out there on the margins of society seemingly capable of committing these crimes. Real shockers. He saw all the files. All had to be considered. With a couple of million people out there, it was to be expected that a few would have fantasies down the road to serial killerdom. Underwear sniffers, peeping Toms, stalkers, rapists. It was just a matter of what stage they were at.

The task force knew little about Ivan Milat's past at this time. Just that most of the brothers, although not Alex, had criminal records. There was no real reason to focus on them, but then again, they were scoring on virtually every point that Basham and Milton had come up with.

The group had a profile brainstorming session where Milton and Basham and the computer guys all threw around ideas. There was no point in saying the offender might ride a motorbike and belong to a gun club unless the computer guys had ways of getting that information into a database to cross-match names. It was around this time that Small and Lynch started to firm on the idea that the killer came from a corridor roughly between Parramatta in Sydney's west and Goulburn. The academics agreed with the premise. Could they get electoral rolls or telephone directories for cross-matching? Sociologist Bob Young who specialised in research methodology saw that police forces all over the world were facing the same problems as clunky, inaccessible mainframe computers gave way to personal computers. It was only from the late eighties that PCs had become powerful enough to put a database on and they still couldn't completely replace the system of the old guy with the filing cabinets who'd remember a thirty-year-old case, but they were very good for checking vast amounts of data, like car registrations. This type of investigation was all about cross-referencing databases, and continually adding small probabilities together. They had set up a computer system for the information on the 55,000 Rugers. They knew every single serial number, but hardly had any names and addresses next to them. That would all have to be found out and added. And as the Ruger database grew, they had to be able to cross-reference that with databases of vehicle owners, and electoral rolls, and subscribers to gun magazines. The computers in 1994 had some of that capability but not all.

As the last three bodies had turned up, Bruce Pryor felt pleased with what he'd done in finding Deborah Everist's body. He may have been subjected to trying times, but he knew in his heart he'd done the right thing. He had brought the terrible business to a head, but he still felt very much the focus of attention. He became fearful, paranoid almost, about what the police might be up to. He was certain he was being followed and his phone tapped.

Fiona was getting frustrated with him, too. After the search was called off, he had started going back to the forest. 'You're attracting attention. Leave it alone,' she told him, but he didn't care.

He started keeping diaries. He copied all his statements and every scrap of relevant paper and gave the copies to friends. He was under the impression that he was only a couple of wrong words away from being locked up. Then on Monday, 31 January, he was busy around the house when two men appeared in the backyard about 2 p.m. A big guy, looked six foot four, filled the door.

It was Paul Gordon. Pryor only had his socks on. He felt vulnerable. They weren't overtly aggressive, but he felt a strong undercurrent ran through every word. They didn't want coffee as they sat at the dining room table and told him to speak slowly because this was a formal interview, they'd be taking notes.

As the interview progressed, the questions – as before – got closer and closer to the point. 'How often do you use the Hume Highway between Liverpool and Bowral?' asked Gordon.

'I don't know.'

They asked him where he was at the time of the disappearances. He did his best to try to remember, but it was damn near impossible. Gordon had to put it to him. 'Were you responsible for the deaths of . . .' and he ran through the list.

They were there for two hours. Pryor was getting pissed off. He thought they were brutal the way they elicited information; the way they walked in, walked all over him and walked out again. They left him totally dumbfounded. 'Why come and bother me now after all this time?' he wondered. 'What are you missing?'

He was unaware that Gordon didn't think for one minute that Pryor was the killer – the Milats were already firm favourites in his mind, despite the lack of evidence – but he had to go through the motions. Even if it wasn't the Milats, Gordon reasoned that Pryor came from the wrong end of the equation. If it was committed by a local, Gordon would have expected some of the victims to have disappeared from the area, or that some victims were heading north to Sydney. But they all had the common denominator of heading away from town in the morning. They had been picked up by someone leaving home, not returning home.

FORTY

February–March 1994

THE HIGHWAY REVISITED

Paul Gordon wanted to work full-time on the Milats, but there were other pressing areas that needed to be looked at. Through early 1994, a barmaid from a Liverpool pub seemed to be the best lead yet. She said she'd overheard some soldiers talking about shooting people in a forest. She knew she heard it before she went to hospital for an operation and so they were able to place it right at the time of one of the murders. The job fell to Gordon to do and he wasn't that pleased. The army was very co-operative and he did the best he could to go through lists of soldiers' movements and those suspected of unusual behaviour. But his heart wasn't in it.

He couldn't figure out why more people weren't pro-Milat. He thought maybe Bob Godden and Royce Gorman were, but still they were throwing a lot of resources at the soldiers. It wasn't even that the army had activities down Belanglo way at the time, it was more to do with the strength of the barmaid's recollection. The fact she could place the time so definitely, and that the soldiers were talking about it before any bodies had been found.

But if that were the criteria, surely Douglas and Butler's evidence from Boral was even more compelling. And what if the soldiers were just talking about war games? Nevertheless, the soldiers were it. They took up a large slab of early 1994, as he also plugged away at the Milats.

Richard was clear because he had an alibi for Everist and Gibson, but Ivan was looking good – being off work on the day of every offence. His workmates were telling Gordon interesting stories about the guy, too. Gordon wanted to go in and interview the Milats because he didn't think he could take it any further. But his team leader, Royce Gorman, told him not to.

Gordon had already plodded through the long criminal histories of the Milats, noting their crimes – petty and not so petty – but there was absolutely nothing to indicate anything that could be construed as being part of the typical progression towards being a serial killer. He wanted to see things like peeping-Tom offences, minor sexual assaults and, ultimately, rape. But they were coming up clean of those.

Clive Small and Rod Lynch claim that someone else had told them Ivan Milat had serious form, and that when Gordon came back saying Ivan was clean, he was told in no uncertain terms: 'You are wrong. Go back and do it again.' Small said Gordon had failed to go through any old microfiche records.

Gordon maintains that he went through the microfiche on all the Milats except Ivan and later realised his mistake himself and went back to it. Whatever, there in the archives at Parramatta, among Ivan's car thefts, safe breaking and armed robbery acquittal, was the gem he was looking for. Details were scarce. Just that he'd been acquitted of a 1971 rape at Goulburn. But that was enough to get the big moon-faced copper excited.

He returned to the office at 3.40 p.m. and started working up a draft request for four listening devices – three in Milat's house and one in his car: 'Due to the information at hand, Ivan Milat must be considered a prime suspect for the murders of the seven backpackers.' He recommended 'greater priority be given to the investigation into Ivan Milat'.

He went into Small's office that afternoon. 'I think Ivan Milat is the killer,' he declared.

Small looked at him. 'Carry on and see if you can find any reason why he can't be the killer.'

Gordon couldn't believe what he was hearing. He was pissed off. He thought his boss could have at least added: '. . . and if it is him, what can we do to prove it?' Small went through the draft report correcting spelling mistakes as he went, according to Gordon. Rod Lynch was there, too. Lynch went off at Gordon because he hadn't gone back to the District Court's Criminal Registry for the full details of the rape case. In the context, Lynch wasn't particularly angry. He just saw it as his role in the reporting structure to identify such problems – he'd already had to get up Gordon for his sloppy paperwork – but to Gordon, it amplified his feeling of isolation from the hierarchy.

The office was set out in an L shape with Small and Rod Lynch's desks at the apex. Bob Benson and Bob Godden were nearby with Steve McLennan and Royce Gorman in the next row. Gordon was sitting behind two secretaries beyond a partition. He wasn't one of the inner circle. That hadn't worried him at first, but as he came to think that they weren't taking him seriously, he felt increasingly alone.

Next day, Gordon's partner Dave McCloskey contacted the District Court Criminal Registry trying to get a look at Ivan's rape case file. He went out to the archive at Parramatta rather than wait for it to be brought to the city.

McCloskey rang Gordon from Parramatta around midday and told him casually that he had found the file.

'What's it say?'

'Ivan picked up two girls hitchhiking from Liverpool to Melbourne and raped one of them near Goulburn,' said McCloskey, deadpan. 'He had two knives and rope.'

'Bullshit.' Gordon thought McCloskey was geeing him up. He was way too relaxed. This was too good to be true. When McCloskey insisted he was not having a lend of him, Gordon drove straight out to the archives and met McCloskey in the car park. McCloskey handed him the file and he flicked through it. Each page was gold. The making of a killer.

'It's fuckin' Ivan Milat,' Gordon said softly, smiling.

They went and celebrated with a good lunch at a local Chinese restaurant before returning to town with the file. Gordon was more certain than ever they had their man. 'It's Ivan Milat,' he declared to Small upon his return. There was no doubt in his mind that the Milats were the way to go, but he couldn't help feeling his boss wasn't interested.

Small's reasoning was sound, even if his people management skills were not. His greatest successes had been fixing other coppers' cock-ups which had started with an ill-founded certainty of someone's guilt – tunnel vision. And with all the political pressures swirling around with ex-police minister 'Torpedo' Ted Pickering on the rampage, this investigation wasn't going to fall into the same holes. It would be no witch-hunt. Of that, Small was certain. His function wasn't to get a conviction for the backpacker murders, it was to convict the backpacker murderer or murderers.

Small and Lynch saw their job as looking at all evidence in a negative sense. Their theoretical starting point had everybody in the country as a possible suspect, and they were working in from there, eliminating as many as they could. Of all the POIs who had looked stronger than the Milats, many were never going to be able to clear themselves. But one by one, most were falling down. As had all the Milats, bar Ivan. He kept getting stronger and stronger. Top 100. Top 50. Top 10.

Rod Lynch tried not to get excited when he saw the rape record. As far as he was concerned, emotions cloud the judgement, but he felt it was progress. Not conclusive, but another factor for consideration in his allocation of resources and the direction of the investigation. From now on, Royce Gorman's crew of Gordon, McCloskey and Coman would work largely on the Milats. He had the dogs sitting off Milat's place the next day.

Gordon, however, couldn't help thinking everyone was so terrified of tunnel vision they had the opposite – 360 degree vision – and couldn't, or wouldn't, focus on anything. Just a few words of encouragement would have been so welcome, rather than just the spelling mistakes. Small wasn't interested in listening devices until Gordon had done more work to clear Milat. If he couldn't clear him, well, then they'd bump him up the list of priorities. Gordon was peeved about the listening devices, but the rules are that before a telephone intercept or listening device can be installed, the senior officers have to swear to a judge that they've exhausted normal investigative procedures without a result. Gordon was resentful all the same. If he did clear Milat, no one need ever hear the tapes. If he couldn't clear him, they'd have a greater wealth of knowledge about who they were dealing with – if not the actual clincher.

Small and Lynch tried to get everyone in together once a week for a meeting – instant coffee, no doughnuts – where they could share their progress. As far as Lynch was concerned, the staff had to be kept motivated by giving out the signals that all avenues of enquiry were as important as the others. Otherwise, people on the less important avenues would start to wonder why the hell they bothered. Other enquiries had to go on in case the prime suspects were eliminated or to guard against the possibility that somewhere down the track a defence lawyer might point out that suspects B, C and D had not been eliminated and didn't they seem more like the real killer?

A full profile was done on the family. They drew up a family tree. A photo of Ivan was obtained from his passport application. The ownership records of their cars and houses and work records were obtained. They found the allegations his ex-wife Karen made against him about burning down the garage and owning guns.

Gordon called up a detective who'd handled the 1971 rape case who couldn't remember anything much of Milat, but he told Gordon all about some other low-life he'd locked up once, and thought was a good suspect now.

Had the task force installed listening devices, some interesting conversation would have been heard around February/March. Ivan rang Wally to ask if he could store some stuff in the little alcove under his bathroom. Ivan told him that the cops had been around at work asking about a threaded barrel and if they came looking for it, they'd find some other guns that weren't legal. At least that's what Wally would later say.

Wally went and got Richard from his caravan nearby and they drove the 45 kilometres up to Ivan's place in Wally's one-tonner. He backed it into the driveway and they started loading gear from the garage. Some of it was up in the ceiling through a manhole.[109] So they parked the truck under the manhole to pass it all down. There was a fair load of ammunition – 20,000 to 30,000 rounds – and with all the guns and other gear, the truck was about a quarter to a third filled. They covered it with a tarp and Wally drove home with Ivan, Richard following in Ivan's work truck. They unloaded it all into an alcove under Wally's place. Wally put a padlock on the door and hardly gave the gear another thought until three months later when a blue backpack in amongst the guns would land him in all sorts of strife.

Around this time, Ivan started visiting a lot of long-lost friends. He turned up unannounced at the Southern Highlands home of former RTA workmate Ross Jackson, on the red Harley-Davidson with Chalinder on the back. In the short time they were there, Ivan raised the subject of the backpacker murders. Sort of casual like.

'Have there been lots of cops around with the murders?' Ivan asked.

Jackson hadn't been on the list of Milat's workmates to check out. He hadn't seen any cops in that part of the woods.

'Do you meet lots of backpackers in your work?' Ivan asked, before turning the subject to guns and what type Jackson used in his new job at Australian Protective Services. Then they said their goodbyes and roared off.

Chris Masters had worked away at his story through the early part of the year. He was very conscious of the burden of approaching such a story without exploiting the horror; determinedly not making entertainment out of misery. He recreated each disappearance in the hope of jogging someone's memory. He interviewed Clive Small who told him there were no red-hot suspects as he stood in front of a whiteboard with the words AIR/MILAT written in large letters behind him.

Masters didn't know what 'Milat' meant but presumed it was a name. He gave Small a special viewing of the tape so that if there was any information that wasn't meant to get out, he could say so. Small just didn't notice the words, and the show aired on 7 March. Alex Milat was watching and complained to the ABC and the task force the next day, so the ABC pixelated the name out in the repeat showing that day.

Paul Gordon was furious about the slip-up, but another part of the story also had him spitting chips. Masters had interviewed a woman, Therese, who'd been attacked while hitchhiking with a friend in the seventies. It fitted neatly with Gordon's hitchhiker hypothesis and so he was pissed off that no one had told him about the pair.

The truth was, nobody else had attached any significance to it. Therese's friend, Mary, had rung the task force on 1 November, the day that Simone Schmidl's body was found, but couldn't get through, so she rang her local police who patched her through to Bowral where she spoke to Detective Sergeant Tony Roberts. She'd been called back once or twice but nothing had happened. Masters came across the story because Therese now worked in television and he had picked it up on the grapevine.

Gordon rang them and was embarrassed about the task force not having got back to them sooner. 'Sorry, we haven't forgotten about you. We've been really busy.' Mary told him the story.

It was Sunday, mid-afternoon in early July about 1977. The two nineteen-year-old university students were hitching back to Canberra after a fabulous party in the inner-Sydney suburb of Redfern. Two days earlier they had decided on the spur of the moment to come up with a bunch of uni friends.

The girls had to be back for work first thing Monday morning. They couldn't afford the train so they set out, desperately hungover, to hitch. It was the done thing. Everybody they knew without a car did it. A succession of lifts got them from Oxford Street, Paddington, to the old Hume Highway near Camden on Sydney's outer south-western fringe, where the urban sprawl had yet to take hold. They were standing on a cold miserable bridge in a light drizzle as cars wizzed by. It seemed like they had been there for ages. They were willing cars to stop, wondering if they'd make Canberra by nightfall.

Therese didn't get a good look at the quietly-spoken guy who rescued them. She jumped into the back seat of the sedan leaving Mary to the front. Both thought it was a greyish Toyota with a little handle to wind open the triangular window vents. It was very neat. They told the man they were headed for Canberra and he said he'd take them. He was heading further south to go camping and shooting with a brother on the New South Wales/Victorian border. When they introduced themselves by their first names, he didn't say his. Both were grateful for the lift and felt obliged to chat, but he didn't talk much. When he did, it was all gloom and doom. He seemed preoccupied with death, shooting, bombs or massacres.

'Isn't it a horrible world,' he said. 'All of these people are dying in wars or starving in other countries.'

Mary got the odd look at the guy from the passenger seat. He appeared to be in his late twenties or early thirties – an old man in her eyes. He was clean shaven with straight dark hair and an average build. His eyes and cheek bones made her think he might have been Yugoslavian. Having grown up in the South-Coast steel city of Wollongong, she knew what Yugoslavian workers looked like.

There were still a few hours of daylight left when they reached Mittagong, in the Southern Highlands where he drove into a garage. As he filled the tank, Mary told Therese she was worried about their good Samaritan. She thought he was weird. But, then, maybe she was just imagining it.

They couldn't afford to put in for petrol so, with the little change they had, Therese bought a packet of Ginger Nut biscuits. Both girls hadn't eaten that day and all three could share them, she thought. The man was back in the car when she returned. 'Here, this is to thank you for driving us to Canberra,' she said.

He took the biscuits with no acknowledgment and placed them on the dash, much to Therese's disappointment. She thought it was rude. Hunger was getting to her. They continued along the Hume towards Berrima, but a few kilometres out of Mittagong the guy turned right. The sign said: WOMBEYAN CAVES.

Mary tried to keep cool and hide the concern in her voice. 'Where are you going? This isn't the highway.'

'It's okay, it's okay,' he said.

'What are you doing?'

'It's okay. I go shooting around here with my brother, I know my way around.' It was a back way to Canberra, he said.

'You've got to be joking.'

'It's a short cut. Relax, it's a scenic drive. Much more pleasant.'

He was right about the scenery. The narrow bitumen road cut through pastures where kangaroos and wallabies grazed in small groups among the cattle. After about six kilometres the road turned to dirt, and began to wind around the side of a mountain. They came to a narrow tunnel blasted through a sandstone ridge. Barely out the other side, the Samaritan swung the car left down a track and soon stopped.

'I've got to go. Nature calls,' he declared, getting out. He opened the boot and seemed to be there forever.

'Mary, I think he's gone to get a gun,' said Therese in a petrified whisper. 'What'll we do?' They made a plan. If anything happened, one of them would shout 'Run!' and they'd both bolt.

He walked to the front of the car and opened the bonnet and stood looking at the engine, then got back behind the wheel. He just casually reached over and took hold of Mary's folded arms. 'Okay, girls, who's first?' he asked, like it was a right. 'Which one of you wants it first. I've given you a lift . . .'[110]

Mary suddenly smashed him in the nose. 'Run, Therese. RUN!' Therese was out the door before she knew, bolting down the steep track to nowhere, Mary by her side. They heard a man's screams behind them, either in pain or pursuit.

'Hit the ditch,' Mary shouted as they approached a mound. They jumped and began rolling down through the scrub. When Therese finally stopped, Mary was nowhere to be seen. All was dead quiet. Then she heard the car start and the vehicle come slowly down the track. He was looking for her. She was being hunted.

Covered in dirt, she lay in the scrub, amid the damp soil and dead leaves listening for his next move. She crawled behind some bushes, gripped by animal fear. Time stood still. All her senses were acutely focused by the terror. She could hear insects crawling over leaves; ants and crickets moving on the ground. She feared they would give her position away. Her heart was pounding too loud. She tried not to breathe lest he hear that too. She had to find Mary without being found herself. She continued on all fours, occasionally daring to whisper: 'Mary'. Then she realised that her clothes – jeans, black high-heeled boots and a bright-blue woollen top – made her somewhat vulnerable.

'This is my last hour,' she told herself. Searching through her pencil case she found a small, metal nailfile. It became a weapon. She gripped it tight.

Mary's senses, equally focused, heard her name on the breeze and they found each other. Mary clutched a rock for protection. They lay in the scrub too frightened to move, listening as the would-be attacker slowly cruised back and forth along the track, stopping now and then, occasionally revving the engine. It went on and on. Time changed somehow. When it went quiet, they'd get up and walk. If a car came along they'd run and hide. They heard him screaming and carrying on, swearing in the distance, their eardrums bursting from the sound of their own hearts.

Finally he left. They were about 30 kilometres from the Hume Highway, though they didn't know the distance, just that a long walk lay before them. They were still hiding from cars, but finally around dusk a young couple came along and the girls flagged them down. They were taken back to the couple's cottage and given tea as they recounted the ordeal.

The husband had to drive a load of hay into Mittagong and offered to take them to the police station. Both girls were grateful, but shunned the offer. Mary had escaped a worse encounter once before and Therese was fearful of the shame it would bring her Vietnamese parents.

The girls just wanted to get back to Canberra quickly, so they went back to the highway and once again stood in the cold with their fingers out, looking filthy. A station wagon pulled up with two young women and a guy. They were hippies. Cool. Mary and Therese lay on a mattress in the back and smoked joints all the way home. They put the encounter behind them. It was just part of growing up in the seventies. A downer.

For Paul Gordon, the story's significance lay partly in the location of the attack, only about 20 kilometres from Belanglo. But it was also on the Wombeyan Caves road where, nine years later, Wally and Richard Milat would buy their property. When he showed the two women a series of mug shots, they were hesitant. It had been a long time, after all. Therese said she'd been in the back seat, but she'd watched his eyes intently in the rear-vision mirror. Going on that, she chose two of the pictures. One was Ivan Milat. Gordon wrote in his notes that she thought Ivan's eyebrows and the shape of his face were, 'at first glance, most similar. Triggered some memory.'

Mary, interestingly, selected Richard Milat but when she later saw a picture of Wally on the television she thought he looked more like her attacker.[111] Their ID evidence was too old to be of much use. Richard would certainly have been in the clear because he was only twenty-one at the time of the attack. Too young to fit the girls' description. Wally was twenty-five.

A few days later, Paul Gordon interviewed the new owner of Milat's old Nissan Patrol, David Gill. Milat had sold it two months after the bodies of Clarke and Walters were found. Gill showed Gordon an unused bullet he found underneath the driver's seat shortly after he bought it. It was a Winchester 'Winner', consistent with the Clarke bullets and the same as the boxes found in Area A.

FORTY-ONE

April 1994

OUT OF THE BAG

Paul Gordon kept wondering what he had to do to convince Clive Small to put more resources on the Milats. Surveillance of Ivan had only gone for two weeks and stopped on 8 March. He'd been back to the computer a few times, putting in key words like hitchhiker, four-wheel drive, Liverpool and they didn't bring up anything of interest. He and another officer had spent a lot of time trying to get some crime report that might be linked to Ivan Milat. They had typed in 'silver four-wheel drive' in the hope that maybe there'd been a report of some attack or some oddity. But the machine came up with nothing. They weren't the only ones to grumble about the system which just wasn't coming up to scratch. It was meant to spit names out at them and link common features, but they hadn't seen it do anything useful.

They wanted to go through old intelligence reports to see if they could link incidents to Milat or his vehicles. A lot of data still had not been loaded. With no faith in the technology, Gordon and others gave up on the computer and started wading through all the hard copy running sheets that were sitting around in boxes. It was dull and tedious. Then, on 13 April, a piece of paper grabbed Gordon's attention. It was from an Englishman named Paul Onions. He'd phoned the hotline exactly five months earlier, on 13 November.

I was in Australia from 12/1989 to 06/1990. In 01/1990 I was travelling from Sydney to Melbourne. I caught a train to Liverpool and started to hitch a ride. A white Toyota Landcruiser 4 wheel drive with woolly seat covers stopped and I got in. It was being driven by a man in his early 40s who was fit looking, about 5'10" tall. He had a Merv Hughes moustache with black hair which had flecks of grey in it.'

Onions went on to briefly describe the attack and being taken to Bowral Police Station. But those first sentences had pushed all the right buttons. The car, the moustache, the locations. It all fitted. Gordon was jubilant. As he'd later say: 'I was lucky. The harder I worked the luckier I got.'

While the task force would eventually have got around to Onions, it was fortuitous that Gordon pulled him up with Milat clearly in mind because his information would have remained useless without a firm suspect. And it was only now that the shit hit the fan with Small. He was angry that not only had nothing been done to investigate the attack in 1990, but Onions' original statement had been lost. Fortunately, Onions had named Constable Janet Nicholson, who had made her own cursory enquiries with the RTA with no success. She had kept her police notebook which had more details – including that the person calling himself 'Bill' was a divorced roadworker of Yugoslav descent.

It turned out that Constable Nicholson had tried to investigate the attack. The loss of Onions' statement and the inaction by Bowral police led to a senior officer being paraded and counselled; and to much speculation as to what might have been avoided. Gordon later checked Richard and Ivan's work records on the date of the Onions attack. Richard was working that day until 2.30 p.m. Ivan was not. Ivan's work records also showed he had knowledge of the Galston Gorge area where James Gibson's backpack and camera were found. He had worked on the Dural roundabout between 12 and 19 December 1989, taking Christmas holiday leave on 21 December. The couple vanished on 30 December. It was a tenuous link, but still placed him in the zone. Gordon had another attempt at convincing Small of the need for listening devices. He began his application: 'I suspect that the indictable offences of murder, attempted murder, armed robbery, abduction and assault have been committed by Ivan Robert Milat and I believe that for the purposes of investigating these offences and of enabling evidence to be obtained concerning the commission of these offences and identifying the offender the use of listening devices is necessary.'

He ran through the crimes that had been committed and linked them to Onions and the 1971 rape victim. He noted that Margaret had been tied up, and that Onions bolted when he saw ropes. While none of the murder victims had been found bound, there was evidence indicating some may have been tied up prior to their murders, he wrote:

'During the trip from Liverpool the offender stated his name was "Bill", he worked for the RTA, he was divorced, he was going to visit friends in Canberra, he was of Yugoslav origin. He was described by the victim as being 5/10–6/0 tall, solid build, dark complexion, black hair, "Merv Hughes" moustache. The vehicle has been described by the victim and an independent witness as being a white or silver Nissan or Toyota 4-wheel-drive, possibly two door.

'Inquiries reveal that Ivan Milat between 1987 and 1992 was the driver of a 1987 Nissan Patrol 4-wheel-drive two-door wagon, silver in colour with a white canopy, registered number OPO-172. This vehicle was purchased and registered in the name of William Allan Milat, Ivan Milat's brother. At the time of the purchase it was paid for by a bank cheque drawn on the funds from the account of Ivan Milat. Birth records reveal that Ivan Milat's father Stiphan [sic] Milat is a native of Yugoslavia. At the time of this offence Ivan Milat was employed by the RTA Central Asphalt Depot, Unwin Street, Rose Hill, as a ganger (foreman) for roadworking machinery. He was married in 1984 and separated from his wife in 1987. They were divorced in 1989. His former wife has stated that Ivan Milat possessed a revolver in 1987. This information was corroborated by his stepson from that former marriage. Ivan Milat has been positively confirmed as having been employed under the name of and using the name William (Bill) Milat between September, 1988 and 1989. A passport photograph lodged in 1989 shows Ivan Milat as having dark brown-black hair and a Merv Hughes moustache. Police records show that he is 178cm (5'10") tall, solid build, fair complexion.'

He detailed the evidence from Boral about Richard and the Germans. He detailed Alex's statement and how implausible it was.

'When taken with the other information concerning Ivan Milat this statement of Alexander Milat raises serious concerns about the motives of Alexander Milat and the probative value of the information.

'It is proposed that three listening devices will be installed in a residence at 22 Cinnabar Street, Eagle Vale . . . It is proposed to place a listening device

into a motor vehicle registered number QBY 388 a 1992 Holden Rodeo 4 wheel drive wagon . . . It is proposed to attach a tracking device in or on vehicle QBY 388 at the a [sic] listening device is installed.'

Gordon thought he was a shoo-in this time, but was again told by Small to take it away and correct the spelling.[112] Alongside the paragraph about Alex's strange statement of sighting the British girls in the forest, Small, according to Gordon, drew a line down the side of the paragraph and wrote: 'Where does this take us? We're not seeking a listening device for Alex, and in the context of this application I have difficulty seeing where it takes us with Ivan!'

Gordon thought it was patently obvious. If Alex had made a mischievous claim, maybe he knew something more about it, and maybe he was the one who Ivan might be talking to on the phone.

He tried to put the case to Small.

But Small wouldn't have it. They argued. Small got angry: 'I'm telling you it's not going in.'

His tone shocked Gordon. He'd had this idea that all input was welcomed in homicide investigations. Gordon corrected the spelling then resubmitted the application, but heard nothing more about it.

The way Small and Rod Lynch saw it, it wasn't a matter of saying 'we want a telephone intercept or an LD'. You had to swear to a judge that normal investigative procedures had failed to come up with a result and they just couldn't get that through to Gordon.

For all his negativity about his bosses, the Milats were being taken more seriously now. As he cast his net wider in his investigation of the family, probably too wide, Gordon had to increasingly gamble on who he could and couldn't talk to. He could talk to no one and learn nothing, or he could get out and take a few risks.

Gordon and another detective turned up on Wally's ex-wife Maureen's front door on Sunday morning, 21 April. She was getting ready to go to work. 'We want to talk to you about the Milats.'

'Oh, what have they done now?' she asked, as she led them into the kitchen.

Gordon didn't say, but she thought maybe there'd been an armed robbery or something. He seemed most interested in Ivan.

'You're asking me about the wrong guy here,' she told Gordon. 'He's a nice guy. Anyway, what do you want with him?'

'Well, have you heard about the Belanglo murders?'

She couldn't fathom it at all. There were other people who she could imagine doing it. But not Ivan. No way.[113]

She got to nattering away and when she mentioned the time Ivan told her he killed someone, the investigators got a bit excited, so she had to play it down. 'It was nothing really. I was a kid. I'm sure he was joking.'

She hunted around for photographs. All the shots of Wally in her album had his face poked out by the point of a dart. She found the shot of her and Ivan in front of his car. The policemen noted it was dated 9 January, 1990, eleven days before Simone Schmidl disappeared.

When they came back to Sydney, Paul Gordon dismissed any involvement by Wally. Being nasty to your wife didn't make you a serial killer. There was a big difference. Gordon's scenario was that Ivan was learning how to do it in 1971 and had gone up a grade. There were still coppers saying that someone else was there with him, but Gordon was firm on the one-killer scenario. 'He's learnt how to rape and he's learnt how to get away with it and he's got lucky,' he'd argue. 'He's got fuckin' lucky. The big difference between a killer and a serial killer is fuckin' luck. Usually someone does it once and gets caught.'

Gordon thought that Ivan's workmate Tony Sara was a good risk, so he had interviewed him while up the coast doing Maureen. They arrived on his doorstep at Ulong in the north coast mountains unannounced. He was about to go fishing.

'We're from Task Force Air investigating the Belanglo State Forest murders.'

Sara looked at them dumbfounded.

'It's about Ivan Milat.'

He was stunned. He told them what he knew. Sara had been working at the RTA for six months when Milat had arrived back there from Boral. They worked together with Noel Wild on the profiler. Sara, a Kiwi, was Ivan's leading hand. Milat looked after him. He was big hearted.

Almost as soon as they met, Ivan asked: 'What's your hobby?'

'I'm into motorbikes and I've got a jeep.'

'Okay, well my hobby's guns. I'm into guns.' Sara told them he seemed really kosher, a Neighbourhood Watch kind of guy. The only time he'd lose it was if they put him in a room with a smoker on an away job. He was always on Sara's back about his smoking. This wasn't such good news for the coppers. The six cigarette butts at the Clarke murder indicated a smoker was the killer.

Sara had lived at Lidcombe, near Milat, so would visit him socially from time to time. Milat was initially stand-offish, but relaxed over a few months and started telling him stories about things he'd heard and things other people had done. He told the stories in third person, like when he spoke of cutting up safes, he'd say 'You'd be surprised how strong a man can be when a safe's fallen off the back of his truck and he's in a panic . . .' When he talked about being flown to Grafton Prison handcuffed to a copper, Sara thought he was kidding. It was only after this visit from the cops that he realised Milat was talking about himself and the stories were true. He just couldn't remember the specifics. Every time they went past a forest, he'd be saying, 'Jock [Pittaway] and I been huntin' in there' or 'got a few goats in here'.

Sara told the coppers about the time they were driving south past Belanglo in the Navara ute when Ivan said: 'You'd be surprised what's in there.' Sara thought he was just on one of his hunting reminiscences. 'What, snakes and kangaroos?' he asked. Milat didn't answer and Sara didn't push it. They had travelled that route on a number of occasions, he told the cops. It could have been Monday, 27 April 1992 – the day Sara was photographed in the cabin of the truck. He'd kept the picture and marked it with the date and the caption: 'Yass bound'.

Between jobs, they often went to the Horsley Park Gun Shop and Ivan would buy a stack of SKK ammo. Ivan was interested in a shotgun – nine-shot, pump action, all grey carbon fibre, weighing nothing. Awesome. Sara hadn't seen anything like it before. The staff seemed to know him.

As far as Sara knew, he had seventeen guns in his arsenal. Once he showed him a .38 pistol which he reckoned was used by the RTA for payroll security. He carried a blue bag everywhere. Sara picked it up a few times. 'Look out for me bag,' Ivan told him. 'And respect it.' Sara did. He never dared open it. It was bloody heavy.

'How many guns you got in here, Ivan?' he'd say, having a laugh. 'This thing's that heavy you must have a couple of shooters in there.'

No answer from the mystery-man Ivan.

*

Gordon didn't ask Sara to keep the visit quiet and, like many of his mates, Sara got straight on the blower to Ivan. 'I've been approached by two detectives who wanted to talk to me about you and the Belanglo murders.'

To Sara's amazement, Ivan just shut off. He began talking about work. There was no surprise in his voice. Sara felt later that maybe the police had a game plan; using him as bait to get Ivan talking through bugged phones. But much to Paul Gordon's frustration, that wasn't the case. And much to Small and Lynch's frustration, Gordon was going around identifying himself everywhere.

After Don Borthwick took his redundancy payout in mid-1992 and left to start up his own asphalt-laying business, he would from time to time run into his old mates at jointly contracted jobs. One day he bumped into Ivan who asked him to come over and help lay a driveway at his new house in Eagle Vale.

'Just supply the hot mix and the grog, mate, and we'll be there.'

Wally and Bodge were there helping, too. Wally almost made Borthwick sick when he popped his eye out, put it down on the driveway and spoke to it: 'Is that level enough?' It was soon after this that Borthwick got his first inkling that something was up. He was supervising a project one morning when his mobile phone rang. The man at the end of the line introduced himself as a detective attached to Task Force Air.

'We would like to come and interview you as part of our enquiries into the backpacker murders,' the officer said.

'What?'

'I'll explain when we see you.'

He arranged for the officer to conduct the interview at his office, Borthwick and Pengilly Asphalt Pty Ltd in St Clair. Said it was a routine enquiry. Ivan was one of many people they were looking at. They asked what he was like; how much control Borthwick had over his movements at the RTA. They asked about his work attendance. They were pretty casual. Borthwick thought it was all bullshit. Not Ivan. He didn't tell them what he was thinking, but he made it clear from his tone that they had the wrong bloke. Fifteen years working with someone, you get to know them, and Borthwick knew Ivan wouldn't be tied up in something like this.

About two days later, they ran into each other on a night job at

Gordon shopping centre. Borthwick couldn't keep mum about it. It was so far-fetched. 'Come over and have a yak, mate, when you get the chance,' he said.

Ivan finished up on the profiler about 1 a.m. and wandered over.

'The cops have been around asking questions about ya,' Borthwick told him.

'About the backpackers?'

'Yeah.'

'It's all over the yard at Readymix,' Milat told him. 'They been talkin' to management. They're trying to pin this on me, Donny. They've got nothing on me. They're putting a lot of time in for nothin'.'

'Geez, I hope so.'

Milat gave him that big grin of his. 'Nah, I've got nothin' to worry about, mate. I've done nothin'.' Borthwick was amazed at the coolness, the complete lack of concern.

'Why you?' he asked.

'I don't know what they're on about, mate. I'm fine . . . They tried to get me once for these bank robberies we did, too . . . We used to go and waste all the money on molls and get the best hotel rooms for the night . . . They must still be trying to get me.'

Mick Milat had already told Borthwick he'd been in on some robberies, but this was the first he'd heard about it from Ivan. 'We let Mick drive,' Ivan said, 'and he couldn't drive for shit.'

There were rumours going around the road building game that the Independent Commission Against Corruption was looking into the RTA and its contractors so the boys were real sensitive about being watched. One night, working down at Rockdale, they noticed a woman. Everyone reckoned she was a plain-clothes cop.

One of the boys said, 'Ivan, that car's been there all night, they've got to be coppers.'

'Yeah, ah huh, they're watching me. They're keeping an eye on me.'

Noel Wild, who had driven the prime mover which pulled Ivan's profiler, had left the RTA and was working for an oil company. He got a call in the truck from Paul Gordon who wanted to have a talk. Wild thought it was a mate of his from Queensland having a go at him. Didn't seem like a cop.

'No, I'm Paul Gordon from Task Force Air.' Wild had never heard of it. 'We're investigating the backpacker murders,' Gordon explained.

'Look if you're fair dinkum, I'm going to Castrol out at Guildford. I should be there about quarter past, half past two. I'll meet you out there.'

Wild still thought it was a joke. He got there late and Gordon jumped up into the rig and started asking about the knives and guns. Wild told him how Ivan saw himself as some soldier-of-fortune type. 'How did you get onto him?' Wild asked.

'We've been checking him out for a while. He's one of many that we're interested in.'

Wild mentioned, by the way, that Ivan had brought one gun in. 'We were standing alongside Duck Creek where we worked, and he fired a shot into the creek with the silencer. It was .22.' That got the copper excited. He wanted to know where he'd fired it exactly. They might be able to link him to the scene. But Wild could only give a general direction.

Wild had mixed feelings about Ivan. A lot of blokes were frightened of him, of his reputation. But Wild never saw him actually threaten anybody, except a couple of times in the truck someone would cut them off and he'd lean out and abuse Christ out of 'em, then sit back in and laugh about it.

Wild didn't keep in touch with him after leaving the RTA, but Ivan rang him once to tell him Rolf Breitkopf died. 'We just come back from his funeral.'

'Thanks for telling me.'

'You left and I never had a chance to ring you.'

'Oh, well. You still going with that Cylinder?'

'Yeah.'

'You should come up for a barbecue one night.'

'Yeah, all right.'

So they made a date months down the track and it just happened to be shortly after the cops visited that Ivan and Chalinder came over. Seven or eight people were there.

They sat down under the pergola and somehow the subject got on to the backpacker case so Wild couldn't help bringing it up: 'The police have been to see me about you and your guns.'

'Oh, well, they haven't been to see me,' Ivan said with his way of pulling his chin into his chest and shrugging his shoulders with hands turned out.

Somebody else mentioned a few more things about the case, but Ivan never said boo. Chalinder was sitting right opposite. Noel and his wife thought she would have heard, but she never said anything either. She was always very quiet. She was more interested in the garden and the plants around the pergola.

Ivan had never been demonstrative with Chalinder. He'd never told her he loved her but, around the end of the previous year, as all the bodies started turning up, the relationship seemed to her to become a little more intense. He talked about unconditional love and how you had to accept someone and trust them. He didn't go into any great depth. That was just him.

FORTY-TWO

Early May 1994

ONIONS

Paul Onions hadn't heard from any police since he called the hotline five-and-a-half months earlier. Then, out of the blue, Detective Stuart Wilkins rang at the end of April. Said they wanted him in Australia yesterday. They'd pay him for his time off work. They'd look after him.

Onions' boss was good about it and gave him the time (but it would take the New South Wales Government a year to pay up). He'd never told his parents about the incident in Australia and it was left to his brother Simon to burst in on them. 'You know that big case in Australia where those girls got killed, well Bunny's the main witness.' They were stunned.

Paul was on a plane within a week. Sitting there, at 30,000 feet with too much time to think, he thought a lot. He started to feel a bit used. The police hadn't done anything about his attack when he first reported it, then they sat on his tip-off all this time. Now he was expected to jump for them at a moment's notice.

Slowly, a worse thought dawned. He realised he didn't really know who the hell he was meeting at the other end. The bastard, 'Bill', had stolen his backpack with all his personal belongings, including his address and telephone number. Maybe Bill was setting him up for an ambush; waiting for him at the airport. He told himself to stop being stupid, just like he had done sitting in Bill's car four years previously.

He touched down on 2 May and was greeted by a surly immigration official: 'How long you here for?'

'Just two weeks.'

'Why would you come all this way for just two weeks?' the man with the stamp wanted to know. 'Nobody comes to Australia for two weeks.'

'I'm here on business. There's a Mr Wilkins here waiting for me.' The official didn't seem to believe him.

'Look, mate, I don't want to be here,' said Onions, as bothered as you can be after a twenty-four-hour flight with the thought in the back of your mind that a killer might be waiting for you just through the door.

He thought they were going to kick him out until the immigration officer got on the radio to verify there was a Mr Wilkins there. He eventually got through and Wilkins introduced himself and another officer.

'Pleased to meet you, mate, but, like I'm not going nowhere till you show me your badges.' They both fumbled around like two clumsy geezers as they pulled their eagle badges out. Onions had a good laugh. They put him into a hotel and gave him a day to get over the flight.

On 4 May, Wilkins and Detective Graeme Pickering took him for a drive. They told him they were on the Hume Highway at Liverpool, let him get his bearings, then gave him no more help as they drove south. They were under instructions to tell him nothing. To be distant. They couldn't be seen to be influencing an important witness. That was why Lynch didn't give Onions to the team that had been working on Milat. It would help quarantine his evidence, but it made the little pom uncomfortable.

He quickly pointed out the newsagency where he'd been picked up by 'Bill'. They got on the freeway and drove towards the Southern Highlands. 'We went through a town,' he told them.

'You can't go through a town. There are no towns on this part of the road,' said Wilkins.

'There was, like. There was some traffic lights and then a fork in the road.' Onions had no doubt about it because he remembered sitting at the lights when Bill's mood really swung around. The police later checked and realised that the Mittagong bypass hadn't gone through in January 1990.

Travelling south along the highway, jet lag was kicking in, but he had no trouble recognising the location of the attack. Adrenalin focused the mind. He ran through the events of the day: the tapes and the gun and the rope; about where he ran; where he flagged down the van. No one told him, but they were 800 metres from the Belanglo turn-off. Onions was looking good as a witness, but the next day would be the test.

Bob Godden and Stuart Wilkins brought him in to the Hat Factory to show him a videotape of thirteen men with moustaches. He was scared. He knew they hadn't brought him all this way for nothing. Here he was, Paul Onions from Willenhall, stuck in a tiny room with these huge coppers and a poxy video. Yet, what he was about to say might go a long way to putting one of these guys away for life. He knew that. He didn't want to stuff up. The cops continued to be stand-offish. He felt very alone – a pawn in a much bigger game.

There were those in the task force who had wanted to bring Ivan in for a line-up because an ID in a physical line-up is that much stronger evidence in court, and there was nothing better than someone refusing to be in a line-up. It looked bad in front of a jury and you could still get a picture ID. But Small and Lynch were more cautious and wanted a strong case on paper before they made any move on this Milat. So here they were.

'Just go through them slowly. See if you have any reaction to any of them,' said Godden. 'You can look at the video as many times as you like, for as long as you feel you want to,' said Wilkins. 'The photographs are numbered one to thirteen. So if the person that assaulted you is one of the persons depicted on that video you may nominate the number. Do you understand that?'

'Yeah, no worries.' Onions went slowly, looking carefully at each photo. The pressure was unbearable. He was hating every second of it. Four years had gone by. That was a long time to remember someone you knew for just over an hour. He reached the fourth photo. It was the first that caused a stir in him. He felt disturbed. He paused on it, then went through the rest. Number six had the right mo but the colour was too light. Number seven was a bit similar. He had the same Merv Hughes moustache. Number nine had the right moustache, but not enough grey in it, and his hair was too short. Too intimidating.

'Can I see number four and number seven again?' Godden gave him the remote.

'Yeah, take as much time as you like,' said Wilkins. Onions went through it all again, then rewound and did it again, quicker this time, until he got to number four.

'That's him, Stu, number four. He's identical to the face I see that approached me at the newsagency. He's got the same moustache and face. That's him.'

'Are you sure?'

'Yeah.'

They had a cup of coffee and Onions asked to go back to see the video again. The detectives' hearts sank, fearing he was about to change his mind, or maybe soften his line to a well-it-looks-like-him type answer that wouldn't carry as much weight to a jury. They went back up and again he stopped at number four. 'That's him. He's got the same strong facial features.' Wilkins got him to sign the video. He didn't know it yet, but number four's name was Ivan Milat.

His job was pretty much done. He returned home and tried to get back to his life. One thing he noticed was that the mystery illnesses he was suffering seemed to disappear. Word filtered out around the task force pretty quickly that the English backpacker identified Milat. The mood was hotting up. It gave Small the opportunity to arrest Milat and charge him with assault, armed robbery and maybe attempted murder, but there was no evidence to directly link him to the bodies. No jury could convict him of murder on the grounds that Onions had been attacked 800 metres from the Belanglo turn-off. Then again, there was nothing to clear him of the murders. He had the vehicle, the weapons and the time.

Small had swung back to the one-killer theory and the possibility that members of his family suspected as much as the police. He reasoned Milat had acted alone in the 1971 rape incident where he tied two women up and had rope and knives. His ex-wife Karen had said Ivan left her for a brief period in the late 1970s, a time when Therese and Mary claimed they escaped attack from a man resembling Milat on the Wombeyan Caves road. Now Onions had fingered Ivan, and again it was a lone attacker with a gun and ropes. But, if they raided his house with a lot of publicity and found nothing, it would look like another police wild goose chase. It was the sort of thing that could set his career back years. But if they didn't move straightaway, it just increased Milat's chances of ditching any remaining evidence. The opportunity would be lost forever.

Within days Small had decided to go in and arrest Milat and see what they could find. Who could tell? He might even confess. It was Small's call. Lynch had been wary, wondering if maybe they should let him run for a week or two longer, put phone taps on and see what turned up. Small was up for promotion and, if he got it, would not be with the task force much longer. He pushed for the raid to be Sunday, 22 May or 29 May. Sunday was preferred because of Milat's erratic working hours. The plan was to arrest him, search his house and simultaneously search the houses of Richard, Walter, Bill and his mother, who he was living with at the time of the offences. They'd also search the block down at Wombeyan and Alex's place in Queensland.

An arrest of this sort was a huge operation to organise. The orders had to be drawn up, warrants applied for, staff seconded, their transport and accommodation organised. Secrecy was essential, so most of the 300 involved would not be told what the job was. There'd been no heavy surveillance on Milat since 8 March, but it was being stepped up now, on 13 May. One team of 'dogs' was sitting in a van on a hill with a perfect view of the back of Milat's home. The constant presence of builders and Telecom repairmen was noticed by neighbours. Some guessed they might be undercover cops doing an operation against burglaries in the area.

The search warrants were a tricky business because they had to state what items were being searched for. A list of items like clothing, jewellery, camping equipment, cameras, airline tickets, passports, credit cards, cigarette packets was drawn up. The annexure to the warrant ran for several pages.

It was too much to expect that the murder weapon would be found, especially since they suspected that Milat knew they were onto him, but maybe they'd come up with a revolver matching Onions' description or even the other weapon used in Area A near the Neugebauer/Habschied scene. Ammunition matching that found in the forest or the distinctive silencer would be useful and they also might find insulating tape, sash cords and cable ties like those found in the leash at the Neugebauer/Habschied scene.

They knew that just a few items would be enough to create a strong circumstantial link to the murders. If they found nothing, the Milat brief would be dead. Then again, the history of serial killer investigations showed that half the time, when confronted by police, the perpetrator caved in and confessed all. They wanted to be caught.

Richard Milat dropped in on Bodge's old girlfriend Toppy and her boyfriend Scott Urquhart for a coffee around late April. 'The cops are watching Ivan's place,' Dick told them. He said they had a lookout placed on the grassy hill 400 metres behind. He said they'd already been to Wally's and tried to get him on the backpacker murders and now they were on to Ivan's place.

Milat knew he was in the police sights, but life continued as though his freedom was a given. He'd been looking at buying a Land Rover Discovery for a month or two. He'd turned up at Asquith and Johnstone in Parramatta on his Harley-Davidson. The salesman, Chris Hewitt, liked him. Found him easy to chat with. He gave Ivan a test-drive, but Hewitt was slow to get back to him with a trade-in price on the Holden Rodeo.

Impatient, Ivan and Chalinder headed over to Purnell Motors at Arncliffe on Sunday 15 May, where Milat, in his Harley T-shirt, almost broke salesman Trevor Taylor's hand when they shook. It wasn't a yuppie power shake, just a good old-fashioned handshake and a half. The couple was very specific. A three-door, V8, 3.9 litre, automatic Land Rover Discovery – 1995 series – which was going for around $50,000. They didn't want another test-drive. All they wanted was a price with a trade-in.

Taylor explained that he'd have to order something with those specifications and the car they'd get probably hadn't rolled off the production line in Britain yet. They'd have to wait three to six months. No problems. Milat seemed an agreeable sort of fellow. Taylor was struck by how clean Milat's car was. A lot of people detail their cars before bringing them in to sell, but he could tell this one was always kept like that. Little things like the pristine accelerator pedal and the inside door jamb free of any muck made it easier for Taylor to give a price on the spot. Within two hours, Milat had paid a deposit and signed a contract – 'William Milat'. Since Ivan had the choice of car, Chalinder got the choice of colour. A typical Land Rover-buying family routine, Taylor knew. She chose Epsom Green; more black with a hint of green running through it.

But life wasn't so completely normal for him. Old friends and people he hadn't seen for years started to find him on their doorsteps. He turned up one night at the doorstep of an old neighbour from Blackett, Chris Thompson, who used to get Karen's groceries when she was having the breakdown. Ivan was working on the Penrith expressway and he just lobbed out of the blue. They'd never mixed socially before and he'd never visited them. Thompson was asleep so his wife answered the door. 'I just had some time off,' Milat said. Thompson, like a lot of people at the time, wondered what he was doing.

On 16 May, detectives Donald and McCloskey went to interview Ivan's ex-wife, Karen, now thirty-five, remarried and separated again with another young child. Jason was almost eighteen. She was living in the Hunter Valley, still scared of her brutal ex. She was on the pension and had no phone. She gave her name as Karen Merle Milat even though she had changed it when she remarried.

They showed her the passport photo which Onions had identified and she confirmed it was her former husband, though she'd never known him to have a passport. The photograph was taken in August 1989, shortly after the divorce.

Karen ran through their history as a couple. She corroborated important little details from Onions' statement – that he had Yugoslav ancestry and spoke with an Australian accent. That he kept tapes in his car and knew the Liverpool area. She ran through the cars Ivan had owned. They asked her about guns.

'Ivan was gun crazy. He shot at his brother Alex's place at Buxton, his brother Wally's at Wombeyan Caves and also in the Belanglo State Forest. He would clean his guns all the time. He would have target practice at the back of our house with a slug gun.' She told them about the revolver and the ex-Armaguard pistol which he carried everywhere in the football sock. She described one rifle as 'the type you load the bullets by pulling something on the gun up and back and then putting them in. It was about 18 inches long . . . He also had a ten-inch-bladed knife. The knife was a folding one which was very expensive.'

She described the time they drove into Belanglo State Forest and Ivan shot the two kangaroos. This was a vital link in the circumstantial chain. If he tried to deny he'd ever been in the forest, it'd be another mark against him. She told them he had raped her at the time they first met and anally raped her when they were married.

Clive Small was promoted to chief superintendent in command of the St George Sutherland district on 17 May but he remained in charge of the task force. Next day, phone taps were applied for. As far as Paul Gordon was concerned, it was too little too late. The raid was due in five days, and the intercepts would not be in place until Friday, 20 May, two days before the arrest. He wanted to know why, when he wanted the phone taps, they had to wait until all normal investigative procedures were exhausted, but now, just when those normal investigative procedures had apparently succeeded, it was okay to apply. Small's argument was that they hadn't succeeded. They'd only got up an armed robbery case. They were after murder.

Small had gone to Dr Richard Basham and Dr Rod Milton – for reassurance about the raids as much as anything.

'Do you think the souvenirs will be there? This is really a bit of a punt,' he'd said.

He showed them the bits and pieces that had been gathered about the Milat family and the statements from Ivan's ex-wife. Milton was very taken with the wife's description of his 'obsessionality' and control, and the elements of sadistic behaviour. The shooting of the kangaroo. The coffee table incident where he shattered it and wouldn't let her clean it up. The way he delighted in seeing her suffer, and having the power to make her suffer. It was so like the Clarke crime scene that he had examined – the shooter, he thought. 'You have to hate people to sit there and fire one shot after another into some poor girl's head.'

The police also wanted to know if it was possible that one of his brothers could have been involved and, if so, which brother would be likely. They gave Milton some details. He looked at their criminal convictions and the odd bit of character evidence and he certainly wouldn't have said it was impossible, but that was all that he could say. Milton made some guesses based on the information. He was quite free in calling them guesses, because nothing was certain in his business. Milton thought of Milat as cold and impotent; needing to be cruel in order to make himself feel that he was worth something. He had no feeling for the sufferings of others. None at all. Evil.

The psychiatrist thought the most likely thing to have set him on the course was the feeling of powerlessness in a large family. There's often not a lot of affection to go around in a large family, he thought. For a large family to work, it needs well-balanced parents who can not only show affection, but also impose order, because kids were capable of doing dreadful things to one another. If parents let the kids work it out for themselves, they generally didn't. Kids get bullied, just the same as in boarding schools without supervision. 'There can be all sorts of abuses and terrible feelings of impotence.' Worse so in the institutions where Milat had been in his teens. Even without sexual attacks, the feelings of impotence could flourish with simple physical bullying.

People from these families could often deal with other people very well, either becoming bullies or dealing with bullying effectively, but in this case it looked like he ended up so impotent that he had to go and kill animals and people, and rape, to be somebody. Milton thought it very curious about the affair with his older brother's wife... nothing like getting your own back.

Milton didn't see him as a psychopath. He certainly had psychopathic traits, but he was organised. He was basically just a criminal. 'He got money when he needed it by working or taking it off others. He got sex when he wanted it, in his own fashion.' He had the strong narcissistic element – body building, dyeing the hair. An 'intense egoism'. It might fit that his rejection by women preceding the 1971 attack and again when the murders began in 1989 could be what psychiatrists call a 'narcissistic wound' followed by the need to get angry with someone else. Whatever, it was power.

Milton was firmly of the belief that the killer was likely to keep trophies of the murders, like snapshots, to enhance the memories. This was some assistance to Small, who had the weight of the world on his shoulders.

When Small told Richard Basham about Onions, the timing of the attack made the anthropologist reappraise his analysis of the number of killers. Onions was attacked less than a month after Gibson and Everist, then there was a gap of almost exactly a year until Simone Schmidl was murdered. The Everist and Gibson scene was consistent with one man being the killer. Onions was attacked by one man. Then the Schmidl attack showed the same knife frenzy. But the time lapse indicated he was spooked by the Onions screw up.

He did the Schmidl murder, a lone female, but he felt like he needed help if he was going to get pairs. So, reasoned Basham, he brought in the shooter. It was perhaps a brother, he thought. While he was more positive now about there being two killers in the later crimes, he was still open to the possibility of there being only one. A mood change, maybe brought on by drugs, might explain the differences, but he didn't really believe it.

Two people was neater.

But that was all by the by at this time for Small. They only had evidence against Ivan. Onions was their excuse to arrest him, and Onions was attacked by only one man.

The day before Milat was to be hit, Bob Benson and Stuart Wilkins and Detective Tony Roberts flew to Queensland to visit Alex Milat at

Woombye, an hour's drive north of Brisbane. Roberts had been included as a way of breaking the ice; before joining the cops he'd worked as a miner in a colliery with Alex.

'We just want to ask you some questions about your statement,' they had said politely over the phone. They arrived in a hire car about 10 a.m. The statement was their excuse, but they had a bigger agenda. Firstly, by getting in close to the family, they hoped to put the cat among the pigeons, maybe get the bugged phone ringing and maybe force Ivan to ditch evidence while the 'dogs' looked on. Secondly, there was a belief among several investigators that Alex, in making his bizarre statement about seeing two cars in Belanglo had in fact been secretly trying to point them in the right direction. Even if he hadn't, he certainly achieved that end. They hoped that maybe now he'd give them more pointers.

After going through a few preliminaries, Benson asked about bullets and backpacks. 'Have you got anything of that nature?'

'Yeah, I got plenty of bullets. Come and have a look.' Alex gave them a few hundred rounds. His wife Joan said they had a backpack down the back shed. Then, out of the blue, she said something about serial killers keeping mementos. She read all kinds of books about these sorts of cases. The coppers looked at each other funny.

Alex took them down to the shed and unlocked it. He didn't trust 'em there alone. He showed them a Salewa backpack.

'Where did you get it?' Wilkins asked Joan.

'Ivan gave it to me,' she said.

As soon as they saw it, Alex heard Wilkins say: 'We got him.'

If they had a search warrant, Alex never worried about it. If they wanted to have a look they would, he thought, with his experience of police going back to the sixties.

Joan explained that Ivan gave her the pack before they moved to Queensland, telling her it had belonged to a friend who was leaving for New Zealand. Alex and Joan watched as Benson took a mobile phone up to the top corner of the property, the only spot where mobiles worked. 'We've got Simone Schmidl's backpack. I'm sure of it,' they heard him say.

Before leaving, Benson asked Alex if he objected to giving a sample of saliva and hair. He gave it to them on the spot. Earlier, Joan gleefully thought they were in line for the reward. Now, watching Alex chew on some cotton wool for the cops made her scared they were going to charge him.

The pack was a huge breakthrough. It was the first hard evidence linking Ivan Milat to a murder. With the raids due the next day, it gave everyone a great sense of relief that they were on the right track. Even Rod Lynch allowed himself to get a little excited. They now just had to wait to see what the morning would hold.

Meanwhile, Royce Gorman, Mark Feeney and Brett Coman had gone to Bargo to see Bill Milat, but he wasn't there. His daughter Debbie told them he was staying at a caravan park at Lake Tabourie on the South Coast. After they left, Debbie called Ivan to tell him the police were asking questions about a silver four-wheel drive, but he brushed her off calmly saying there was nothing to worry about – same as he had with all his workmates. The investigators drove the 140 kilometres straight to Lake Tabourie. They told Bill they were investigating a car accident.

'You're kidding,' he said, knowing that three detectives from Sydney was a bit rich.

'Was it fatal?' Carol asked. 'A hit and run?'

Gorman said something about an armed hold-up, and that they wanted to know why Ivan's vehicle was registered in Bill's name. Bill explained that rego and insurance were cheaper if you lived in the bush.

At 2 a.m. next day, with the raids just four hours away, police monitoring the listening devices heard Bill phoning Ivan to tell him that the police had been around asking questions. Ivan didn't sound too concerned, but they already knew their target – codenamed Yugo – was a character who could play his cards close.

He must have been tired. He'd worked a twenty-four-hour shift, starting at 6 p.m. Friday going through to Saturday. The surveillance guys watched him leave the job to go pick up Chalinder around 2.15 p.m. Saturday. She had then sat in the car waiting for him for four hours. At the end of the shift the couple went and got takeaway and went home. Just another dreary day.

FORTY-THREE
22 May 1994

AIR I

Negotiator Wayne Gordon (no relation to Paul) first heard about the operation like a lot of other police. He was called on Friday afternoon and told to be at Campbelltown Police Station at 2 a.m., Sunday.

'What's it in relation to?' he asked the head of the State Protection Group (SPG), Superintendent Norm Hazzard.

'I can't tell you. Just go out there on Sunday morning and you'll know then. It's high profile . . . special arrest.'

The SPG were the hard heads of the New South Wales police – the sharp end of the spear when it came to resolving sieges and hostage situations. Since a number of arrests had gone infamously wrong in the early nineties because police barged into houses with guns loaded, it had become standard procedure for negotiators to be used on all jobs like this. If negotiations failed, they still had their battering rams.

Gordon was to be the primary negotiator in a team of four. When they turned up in their special ops four-wheel drive, the car park at Campbelltown Police Station was near empty, giving them no hint of what was up. As they stepped into a briefing room on the first floor, Gordon, a homicide detective himself, saw Clive Small and Steve Leach talking and he knew instantly that something was going down with the backpackers. Small was calm but buoyant as he briefed the negotiators. They were about to arrest a 'person of interest' who might be able to assist with the task force's enquiries, he said. Gordon was given Milat's profile to read.

During the next hour, the large room which was to be the central command post began to fill with more officers. There were twenty-one detectives and search police, twenty-one heavily armed members of the SPG assault team, plus general duties police and two police dogs. About fifty in all. Paramedics from the Ambulance Service Special Casualty Access Team (SCAT) had also been mustered for the operation codenamed 'Air I'. Similar teams were gathering in Queensland and Goulburn.

The Campbelltown team, part of the 'north' group, was to do the main raid on Milat's Eagle Vale home. After securing it and leaving it to the searchers, the group would move to Chalinder Hughes' house nearby, and then Milat's mother's place at Guildford.

No one had slept much, but they didn't need much for such a big job. Cops get used to running on adrenalin. And as Clive Small and Rod Lynch gave the main briefing to the assembled officers, there was plenty to go around. Those close to the investigation didn't need telling that the whole case rested on the next few hours. Simone Schmidl's backpack would not be enough. There could be trouble, too. Small briefed them on the phone call from Milat's brother, Bill. Ivan could be prepared for a siege.

At the end of the briefing, Wayne Gordon telephoned psychiatrist Rod Milton who the negotiators used as an on-call adviser. The two were well known to each other. Milton had worked with negotiators for more than ten years. He'd attended plenty of sieges in person, the most memorable being at the Hyatt Kingsgate Hotel where, if the amount of explosives wired to the building had been detonated, he and all the police would have gone up with it.

Milton thought Milat would be straightforward. The guy might be violent when he chose to be, but if someone had the jump on him, he'd be fairly tame. His advice to the detective was to be authoritative, not to back away or let Milat get control of the conversation.

When Gordon emerged from the police station, the car park was crammed with vehicles. At 6.15 a.m., with dawn breaking, the SPG led the convoy out to Milat's house five kilometres away. The ambulance SCAT team brought up the rear.

Everyone waited nervously while Wayne Gordon, a solid trunk of a man with dark curly hair and a moustache, picked up his mobile. At 6.36 a.m., he dialled 820 7500.

A male voice come on: 'Hello.'

'Mr Ivan Milat, is it?'

'No.'

'Is Mr Ivan Milat there?'

'No, he's not here at the moment.'

'Is that the premises at 22 Cinnabar Street, Eagle Vale?'

'Yep.'

'Mate, Detective Sergeant Gordon's my name.'

'Yep.'

'I'm a negotiator with the State Protection Group.'

'Mmm.'

'Now, police are around those premises; they're in possession of a search warrant to search those premises in relation to an armed robbery matter.'

'No joke?'

'Now I want you to, ah, to come outside for the safety of, ah, yourself and whoever's in the house with you. Now what I want you to do is to come out the front door. I want you to turn left, go through the front gate. I want you to walk with your arms out, exposed from your body . . .'

'Mmm.'

'You'll be then met by some State Protection Group police who'll be dressed in black. They will be armed and I want you then, at their direction, to lay face down on the ground.'

'Okie doke.'

'And when you leave, leave the front door open. And can you tell me who else is in the house with you?'

'Just me girlfriend.'

'Righto, mate, well you come out the door now.'

'Rightio, I'll just . . . let me put me pants on.'

'Yep, my word.'

'Thank you.'

'Thanks, mate.'

Gordon hung up.

Chalinder Hughes heard Ivan swearing. She was wondering what the hell was going on. He came back to her in bed. 'I think you better get dressed, love.' She had no idea what was going on. She approached him as he came out of the toilet wanting to know what was happening, but he wouldn't explain.[114]

The seconds ticked by and no one came out. The negotiating team had opened all the doors on their Land Cruiser parked around the corner so that everyone could hear the conversation, learn his demeanour, and offer advice if needed. Still no one came. One minute and fifteen seconds after hanging up, Gordon was told to dial the house again.

A female voice answered: 'Hello.'

'Hello. Is that Miss Hughes, is it?'

'Yes.'

'Yes, Miss Hughes, it's Detective Sergeant Gordon speaking. I just spoke with a gentleman, ah, a short time ago.'

'Yeah.'

Chalinder couldn't believe it when told what was going on. She couldn't accept what they were saying. It was surely a horrible mistake. She told him to hold on and he heard her saying to Milat: 'He wants us to leave the premises both one at a time.'

'Hold on, you'd better speak to him,' she said.

Gordon restated his command to Milat.

'Hang on, hang on,' Milat replied. 'Well, what you're tellin', you know, like, I, I just assumed you were someone from work ringin' up.'

'No, mate, I'm from the police. It's no joke, this is real.'

'Why didn't you knock on the bloody door or something?'

'Because I'm ringing you now for, ah, it's for safety of all people concerned. Now it is our procedure that we ring and contact the persons inside the dwelling to inform them that we are from the police. The matter is serious. The premises are contained by our police and the State Protection Group. We have a search warrant to search the premises relating to an armed robbery matter.'

Milat laughed: 'Oh.'

'Now I want you to come . . .'

'Hey, I'm just looking out the window, I can't see anybody . . .'

'Well, I can assure you . . .'

'I just . . . assumed that, that you, that you, that you, you know, I thought you were just ringin' up . . .'

'No. I am telling you once again . . .'

'That you want us to walk out lookin' like an idiot or something.'
'No.'
'Well, that's who I thought it was.'
'Well, I'm telling you once again it is no joke, no prank. I am from the police, my name is Detective Sergeant Gordon . . .'
'Well, that doesn't mean anything to me.'
'. . . and I'm asking you once again – I beg your pardon?'
'That doesn't mean a thing. You're tellin' me, right. I, I . . .' Just as Rod Milton had predicted, Milat was trying to take control of the conversation.
'Well, what I'm doing, I'm telling you to come outside the premises.'
'Well, I'll put me head out the door and I'll just, you know, but I just thought it was . . .'
'It is not a joke and I'm asking you to leave the premises, go through the front gate, turn left . . .'
'We haven't got a gate. So, so you mustn't be too bloody far wrong.'
'I haven't seen the premises. I'm out here from the negotiating point of view. It is no joke. I'm asking you to leave the premises and walk to your left from the front of your premises with your arms outstretched where you'll be met by police from the State Protection Group. Do you understand that?'

Milat continued to play dumb and Gordon continued repeating his instructions. 'Now for your, your safety and the protection of the police, can you, ah, just, ah, have your arms outstretched from your body?'
'Oh, I, I'll have no shirt on if you want me to.'
'That's fine, if you just walk down the street with your pants on and, ah, no shirt that's okay.'

Milat laughed.
'It's not a joke,' Gordon had to remind him. 'And can you just leave the phone open and, ah, I'll be able to speak with your girlfriend . . . And then she can come out likewise.'
'I think we'll just walk out together. I'm not real keen on this.'
'Well, walk out then . . .'
'Rightio.'

They hung up.

SPG officer Senior Constable Ray Duncan was positioned with Senior Constable Peter Forbutt on the front left corner of the house. Heavily armed and armoured, Duncan had earlier tried to look in the garage, but there was fabric covering the window. He was close enough to hear the phone ringing. And, after the second call, he heard a door opening inside the garage. About thirty seconds later, a car door opened and closed. Ten seconds later, he heard the same noise.

Word was passed down that Milat might be about to make a run for it. The search teams waiting around the corner moved their vehicles to block the road, and they nervously waited some more. If Milat got as far as them, it meant he had got past a team of six SPG officers armed with Heckler-Koch submachine-guns and shotguns, waiting at the only entrance to Cinnabar Street.

Three minutes after hanging up, there was still no sign of the front door opening, so Gordon was told to call again. Chalinder answered and told Gordon they were coming out. 'He's just trying to find the keys; he always loses them in the morning.'

'All right then . . . I'll tell, ah, the police to expect you out very shortly.'

'Okay.'

'Thank you very much.'

'Bye.'

Milat came out the door in his old checked shirt with his hands out in front. He couldn't see anybody. He turned right rather than left and was greeted by the sight of Duncan and Forbutt dressed all in black – boots, overalls, ballistic vests, baseball caps.

'Shit!'

He was staring down the barrel of Duncan's shiny black Remington shotgun and Forbutt's black Heckler-Koch submachine. Now they were talking his language.

'Turn to your left,' shouted Forbutt. 'Get down. Get down. Face down.'

Milat went down on the grass and was handcuffed with flexicuffs, a thicker version of the cable ties he used in the forest. The irony was probably lost on him, as six men in black rushed past him into the house with their guns raised, the lead man carrying a shield, all shouting their drilled instructions as they secured one room at a time. Steve Leach had taken charge of the arrest after Royce Gorman called in sick. Leach and Paul Gordon had been selected to make the pinch. They approached the house from around the corner to see Milat's face in the lawn. Chalinder was on the other side of the yard.

'I am Detective Sergeant Leach and this is Detective Sergeant Gordon . . . We will wait here until your premises are cleared by other police . . .'

'Okay.'

'Are you Ivan Milat?'

'Yes.'

They showed him the search warrant and explained the object of the search. (Milat denies being shown the warrant.) 'We are making enquiries in relation to an armed robbery upon an English backpacker named Onions on the 25th of January 1990.' They told him his rights. 'Do you understand that?'

'I understand that but I don't know what you're talking about.' (This is Leach and Gordon's version. Milat denies being warned until hours later. It is not a legal requirement to be read 'your rights' in Australia. In New South Wales, it is a police commissioner's instruction.)

'I will also be asking further questions in relation to your knowledge of the deaths of seven backpackers whose bodies were found in the Belanglo State Forest. You don't have to answer . . . as anything you say may be used in evidence against you. Do you understand that?' (Again, Milat denies being served this warning.)

'I don't know what you are talking about.' It was immediately clear to Leach that Milat wasn't going to be helpful. If it had looked like he was going to talk, Leach would have taken him straight back to the station for an interview, but now he thought it best to keep him there so that if anything was found, he could be confronted by it immediately. They'd been told they'd find bits of memorabilia of 'his own sick little nature' there. Maybe he'd slip up or cave in when confronted with evidence. The SPG assault team declared the house secure and the searchers moved in. Leach and Gordon entered the house with Milat now in metal handcuffs behind his back.

The search team had no idea whether it would take hours or days. The plan was to do one room at a time while Milat was still there, then do it again more thoroughly after he was taken away.

'Which is your room?' asked Leach. Milat, with his hands still cuffed behind his back, and an officer holding him from behind, walked them to the last room down the hall. Leach got him to show them each room and what it was used for.

The police version was that they then put Milat on the lounge. He claimed he was forced to kneel on the floor, his hands still cuffed, a detective standing over him with his hand on Milat's head.

It wasn't long before Leach was called into Milat's room. They'd found a postcard. It began: 'Hi Bill'. Leach confronted Milat: 'Have you ever been known by the name of Bill?' he asked, knowing that Onions' attacker called himself Bill.

'No,' replied Milat.

'What about this?' Leach showed him the card. Milat said he needed glasses to read it. He looked at the card. 'It must have been a mistake.'

It was from Jock Pittaway, addressed to Ivan at Campbell Hill Road, and dated 22 April 1992, just days after Clarke and Walters disappeared. In it, Pittaway asked if he was going to come over to New Zealand. 'If you do, I will see a guy about deer shooting.' The searchers also found some New Zealand dollars and Indonesian rupiah in his room. 'Where did you get this money from?' asked Leach, knowing that Simone Schmidl had been to New Zealand, just prior to disappearing.

'I've been to New Zealand, haven't I.'

'When?'

'A long time ago.'

'Who else lives in this house?'

'Just Shirley. She's my sister. It's her house.'

'Have you got any firearms in this house?'

'No.'

'Do you own any firearms?'

'No.'

'I have been told that you own hand guns and rifles.'

'I don't own any. Tell whoever told you that to come and give them to you.'

A bullet that had just been found in his bedroom was stuck under his nose: 'You said you don't have any firearms here. What are these?'

'I used to go shooting at my brother's place at Buxton.'

'Which brother?'

'Alex, but he went to Queensland earlier this year.'

Leach offered him coffee. (Milat claims to have still had handcuffs behind his back and that Leach offered him the cup facetiously.) Gordon got him a cup and his cuffs were put at the front of his body so he could drink.

They again told him they were investigating the armed robbery. 'Mr Onions has identified you as being the person responsible for committing this offence. Do you understand that?'

'No, I don't.'

'Do you understand what I just said to you?'

'Yes, but it wasn't me.' He denied knowing anything about the murders.

'Have you ever been to the Belanglo State Forest?' asked Leach.

'I know where it is. I have driven up a dirt track which goes past it.'

'When was that?'

'A long time ago.'

'How long ago?'

'In the mid-eighties.'

'Do you own a Ruger 10/22?'

'I told you before, I don't own any weapons.'

'Have you ever had in your possession a Ruger 10/22?'

'No.'

'Whose firearms do you use?'

'I used to borrow my brother Alex's.'

'What motor vehicle have you owned for the last six years?'

'None.'

'Who owns the vehicle in the garage?'

'It's me brother's.'

'Which brother?'

'You blokes know.'

The search team of Andy Grosse, Detective Constable Steve Blackmore, Detective Senior Constable Peter O'Connor and ballistics expert Gerard Dutton had gone into the unremarkable four-bedroom, single-storey brick house just after 7 a.m. The initial search for anything obvious came up with nothing, so they launched into a more detailed examination.

By 8 a.m., they had found nothing but the postcard, the bullet and the currency. As each minute went by without result, the fear that the operation might fail began to grow. They moved to the garage. There was a manhole in the roof and Peter O'Connor went up. He saw nothing obvious up there apart from a box of Christmas decorations, so started making his way slowly across the ceiling, removing insulation batts as he went. He'd been at it for about half an hour and was several rafters away from the manhole when he saw something down in one of the external walls. It was about a metre down, resting on a nogging – the horizontal piece of wood between the supports.

O'Connor's arm wasn't long enough to reach it, so he went back down the ladder and searched around until he came up with a stick about a metre long. Back up there, on his knees, shining a torch down, he could see it was a plastic shopping bag. He manoeuvred the stick into the handles and pulled it up. Peering inside, among some rags, there was what looked like part of a gun's trigger, and other gun parts. He wasn't really a gun sort of person, so he didn't know exactly what he had. He called the others up.

As Dutton looked in the bag, he could barely have been more excited if O'Connor had held the meaning of life. He recognised in an instant it was a complete breech bolt assembly, a complete trigger assembly and a Ram-line magazine from a Ruger 10/22. He knew this could be big. Surely no one would go to such lengths to hide the parts unless they were worth hiding.

Dutton went at the breech bolt with a magnifying glass. Bingo! The firing pin was crescent shaped and, yes, there were two small burrs on the bolt face, exactly where he hoped they'd be. His old friend was coming home. He couldn't wait to get at it with the macroscope.

They called Leach into the garage, and he then called out for Gordon to bring Milat in from the lounge. Leach held up the gun parts as they came in. 'What's this?'

'Looks like something out of a gun,' Milat answered.

'Have you ever seen it before?'

'No.'

'This was located in your ceiling. Have you any idea how it got there?'

'None.'

'Who's been in your ceiling?'

'You blokes and the builders,' he said defiantly.

They returned him to the family room.

O'Connor went back to the wall cavity. There was something else underneath where the bag had been. It was black and solid, but he couldn't pick it up with the stick. He called up Dutton and they tried to figure out how to get it up, but as they prodded it around, he knocked it off the nogging to the rung below – completely out of reach. O'Connor went back up the ladder and returned the plastic bag to where it had been so Andy Grosse could photograph it, all the while trying to figure out how to get this black object out of the wall cavity.

In the garage shelving, Peter O'Connor found a blue Salewa nylon bag that looked like a sleeping bag cover. That was interesting of itself, but inside was a silver, homemade gun silencer. Also in the bag was a green Vau De Hogan tent bag with tent and fly. It later proved to be Simone Schmidl's. Wrapped around it was a Compact-O-Mat band identical to the one found wrapped around her skull.

Leach was called back to the garage. Grosse showed him the tent bag. They called Milat back into the garage and showed him the camping gear. 'Who owns this?'

'I don't know,' Milat answered.

'Have you ever seen it before?'

'No.'

The bag had been found on the back wall of the garage in clear view of anyone using the place.

Back in the living room, Leach was shown a green army jacket with the name Preston written on the inside in black Texta. 'Who owns this coat?'

'I suppose it's me.'

Leach held up a number of boxes of ammunition found in the pockets. 'Whose bullets are they?'

'I would have been using them when I was at Alex's place.'

Leach then told Milat they were going to Campbelltown Police Station for further interviews. The decision to leave the house was Leach's. They had six hours at their disposal to talk to him and charge him. They'd found enough items of interest. Leach wanted to start processing him. Regardless of what had been found that morning, they were always going to charge him with the Onions matter.

'Before we go, are you sure you have no firearms located in these premises?'

'I told you I have not got any.'

'As well as the pieces of firearm I showed you earlier, there is a further piece in the wall cavity and we have got to get it out.'

'You get it out the best way you can.'

About 9.30 a.m., Gordon and Leach led Milat across his yard with a jacket draped over his head to hide him from the gathered cameras. He was put in the back of a police car with Gordon and Leach on either side. Bookends. He wasn't going anywhere. Two surveillance cops who'd been watching the house for a week from the hill 400 metres away cracked a bottle of champagne as they looked on.

When Leach and Gordon got him to the station, they sat down and wrote out the above version of events. They had not videotaped the arrest, nor taken contemporaneous notes. It was a quiet sort of time. People weren't gawking.

About 11 a.m., they began interviewing Milat on the ERIWSP – electronically recorded interview with suspected person – a wide-angled video camera with three simultaneous back-up audio tapes.

Milat's reactions had remained constant throughout the morning. Even as the gear started turning up, he remained cocky. He gave smart answers like the one about 'you blokes and the builders' being the only ones up in the roof. But when they got him on video, his demeanour changed. Suddenly he didn't understand anything. His hearing was bad. Leach could see his cunning.

The interview began with Leach asking: 'You told me just earlier that you are a little deaf... So if I speak up a little louder, will that assist?'

'I imagine it would,' said Milat with a quiet defiance.

There followed a convoluted explanation of what was going on, to which Milat played infuriatingly dumb.

'At a later time, you'll be given a copy of the videotape if you require it, if your legal representative wishes to view the video. Do you understand that?'

'What, I've got to say yes to everything you say or what?'

'Well, if you understand it the answer would be yes. If you don't understand it just tell me and I'll explain it again.'

'Yeah, well I'm just not sure what you, when you finish a question, if you want to say . . . so don't know whether to say anything to you or not.'

'Well, I would like you to answer the question as I put it to you so that I know that you do understand what I've spoken to you about. Do you understand me now?'

'Well . . . Have I got any choice in the matter? . . . I don't think I should be talkin' to youse at all.'

'Well, if you don't wish to talk to us, you can say that from the outset.'

'Well, I don't wish to talk to ya.'

Leach kept talking. 'This morning, I showed you some . . . trigger apparatus, a firing pin and ammunition holder . . .'

'You showed me some items . . .'

'You don't wish to comment on how they got in your ceiling?'

'I wouldn't have a clue. I presume youse had 'em.' He was stroppy, perhaps truculent, but certainly not fearful. Leach asked about the green tent from the garage.

'I've never seen it before.'

At the end of the four-minute interview, the station sergeant came in. 'Had they threatened you to make this interview?' he asked.

'Well, we didn't have an interview.'

'Have you any complaints about the manner in which you have been interviewed today?'

'No.'

Milat declined to sign the seals on the master audio tape.

At 11.10 a.m. they began interviewing him about the murders. This time, Leach gave him a warning about remaining silent. 'Do you understand that?'

'About what?' he asked dimly.

The conversation continued. Milat remained difficult: 'I told you I wanted nothing to do with it.'

'Do you agree that I also told you our conversation would be recorded on video and audio tape. Did you agree at the conclusion of the interview, you would be given a copy for your legal representative?'

'What about the legal bloke you talk about?'

'Do you agree that whilst at your house we had a conversation with you?'

'Basically youse are doing the talking.'

'You agree we showed you certain items located at the premises which included a tent and also some rifle parts?'

'You showed me things. I don't know where you got them from.'

'Our conversation has been recorded in Detective Gordon's notebook,' he said. 'Would you care for him to read out the conversation between yourself and myself so you can say if it is a true and accurate record of our conversation about . . .'

'About what?'

'About the conversation.'

'We never really had a conversation . . . I basically said nothing.' Milat continued much the same . . . 'I don't care what you do. I don't know what you are talking about . . . You are going to do it anyway.'

'Would you like to hear the conversation we say happened at your house?'

'We never had a conversation.'

Gordon turned to page 41 of his notes and started reading. Milat only interrupted when he was told he had been given coffee early on. 'I had handcuffs behind my back.'

After Gordon finished reading his notes, Milat said: 'I don't remember half the stuff . . . I never seen him write down nothin'.'

'We told you he wrote it down when we got back here. What part don't you recall?' asked Leach.

'We never really had a conversation . . .'

'Did we speak together at the house?'

'Very rarely.'

'Is there anything further you can tell us about the enquiries on the Belanglo forest murders?'

'I don't know nothin' about 'em. I haven't got a clue. I been saying that all along . . . I said I didn't do it . . . You can say anything anyway.'

'In relation to what?'

'Anything. How do I know where you got it from . . . All I know, I was kneeling on my knees with my hands behind my back and you were showing me stuff . . . You took me in there. That one with the plastic bag, whatever it was, he seemed to be laughing. I presumed it was his own stuff.'

The interview finished at 11.30 a.m.

The station sergeant asked again if he had any complaints and Milat mentioned that Gordon's notes were taken after leaving the house.

He was taken to the charge room, and he never spoke to the police again.

Solicitor John Marsden had come a long way since he helped Ivan beat the rape charge back in 1974. He now had eight offices spread through the western suburbs and city. He'd been head of the Council for Civil Liberties and, because of his reputation for hounding dishonest police, he was a member of the New South Wales Police Board. He'd been 'out' for years already, but most of his clients probably didn't understand the significance of the rainbow sticker at the entrance to his office.

He was putting on a barbecue for the Gay and Lesbian Mardi Gras board of directors at his palatial Campbelltown home, after yet another successful parade some three months earlier. The guests had all been hearing about the arrest on their car radios on the long drive from the Darlinghurst and Leichhardt ghettos to the deep south-west. It was the talk of the function.

Then the phone call came: 'Ivan Milat wants you,' said one of Marsden's assistants. 'He's been arrested for the Belanglo murders.'

'Shit!' said the solicitor.

Marsden apologised to his guests and jumped in the Rolls-Royce to drive to the local police station. As he closed the car door behind him, it dawned on him . . . 'Fuuuck! 1971. Shit! Sutton Forest. Not dissimilar. Why hasn't that crossed your mind before?' And he was wondering if the police knew he was Milat's solicitor in 1971. Surely they must. And here he was on the Police Board, being given updates by Commissioner Lauer on the running of the investigation. The board normally wouldn't have anything to do with operational matters, but since this was such a high-profile case affecting the image of the force, it was kept broadly informed. And Marsden was wondering if it had crossed Mr Lauer's mind that he was potentially compromising the lawyer, knowing full well he'd be representing Milat if it came to trial. But Marsden dismissed the thought. The briefings were too bland to be of consequence. Lauer certainly did, however, want him off the board. That was no secret.

Marsden parked the Roller and walked to the police station with his mind racing. As he went through the doors, one of the first people he came across was Clive Small, a man with whom he'd had some vicious clashes. Marsden had at first strongly opposed Small's promotion.

The Police Board's main function was to vet senior promotions, ostensibly so that the commissioner did not have absolute power over the force. People had been in Marsden's ear saying that Small was a dictator, that he was arrogant, had no humanity, was this and that. Marsden had read something he'd written where he quoted Attila the Hun and, as a civil libertarian, it had stuck in his throat somewhat. 'Who is this stupid cop?' he'd wondered. Marsden at that time didn't know about Justice Lee's comments, following the Blackburn affair. The board was kept in the dark as much as possible to stop them meddling in the commissioner's affairs, he would later conclude. So Marsden gave him a rough time in his interviews for promotion. Marsden was a man capable of turning on the spleen, but Small gave as much back. In the end, Marsden gave Small his vote for the job of St George Sutherland District Commander. But Small wouldn't have known that, and wouldn't have known that Marsden now thought of him as one of the best, straightest cops around. The solicitor came to realise his informant may have been right on some points but was basically a POPO – passed over and pissed off. So as they looked at each other in the foyer of the Campbelltown Police Station, there was an obvious tension.

Marsden came straight out with it: 'Superintendent, if you feel compromised because I have roughed you up on the Police Board, and you would rather me not be doing it, I have a leading partner from my office with me, he can take over the matter.'

'You have to do your job and I have to do mine,' said Small. And that was that. Marsden was taken down to see his client in the cells and the police left them alone. Milat was as relaxed and calm as Marsden remembered him. He told Marsden he didn't do it.

A hole had meanwhile been cut in Milat's lounge room wall to pull out the mystery object. It was a rotary magazine for a Ruger. The search continued elsewhere. In the bedroom, they found a current driver's licence in the name of Michael Gordon Milat with a photo of Ivan Milat in it. Inside a black bag with a Triple M radio station logo was a Wirtgen instruction manual for the machine Ivan used at work; three shooting magazines; a pay slip; a small raincoat; a jar of Nescafe; a Wirtgen cap; a tape measure; a plastic bag with three padlocks; scraps of orange skin and a foot-long Bowie knife.

Someone found a thin copy of *Bituminous Surfacing, Volume 2 1982*. Inside it was a thinner Ruger instruction manual. In a drawer was a bayonet painted green and brown camouflage. Nearby was a box of spent cartridge cases and some gun cleaning equipment. In a photo album on the coffee table was a picture of a Harley-Davidson with a revolver in a holster, it looked like a Colt .45 – suitable to carry visible copper-tipped bullets as per Onions' statement. There were four pictures of 'Cowboy Ivan' posing with a Winchester 30/30 repeater rifle. Another less striking photo was, however, to be the most important. (Days after the arrest, analysts noticed that in a picture of Chalinder posing innocently by the ocean, she was wearing a green and white Benetton top identical to that owned by Caroline Clarke. It was later found to be of a type not sold in Australia. The top itself, however, was never found.) There was a pair of well-worn Hytest boots as issued by Readymix and a paintball mask with 'IM' and 'Texas' written on it, with the address, 55 Campbell Hill Road. The search moved to Shirley's room where two sleeping bags were found in a walk-in wardrobe. One, a Salewa brand bag was later identified as having belonged to Simone Schmidl and the other was identified by Timothy Everist as similar to the one his sister Deborah borrowed from him.

Resuming the search in the garage, they found some black electrical tape at the front of the shelves with cotton sash cord. There was also a green and white cotton pillow case (later identified as having come from Campbell Hill Road) with a stain on it. Inside were five more cotton sash cords. They started pulling the sash cords out and photographing them. The third piece had a stain on it which looked like blood.

They found four black plastic cable ties with a 'G' stamped on them matching a black plastic tie found at the Neugebauer/Habschied scene which had 'G3' stamped near the locking device.

They pulled a bag marked CAD PAC 5 (Central Asphalt Depot) off the shelf. In it was the plastic butt of a rifle stock (later shown to be a Ruger 10/22), a strap with a metal buckle and some papers on a clipboard – the papers were addressed to Milat, thus linking him with the rifle stock.

In the hallway cupboard, O'Connor found a new pair of Hytest boots the same as in the bedroom. Inside one, however, was a Ruger receiver wrapped in plastic. (The receiver houses the bolt assembly, with the barrel's chamber attached to one end.) Its serial number had a 120 prefix which Dutton instantly recognised as the number which most commonly corresponded to the distinctive upward curve in the crescent-shaped firing pin. It was painted camouflage, the same as the trigger mechanism found in the wall cavity and also matching the camouflage on the paintball mask, the magazine and the bayonet. One of the colours was consistent with a jar of model paint which had already been found. All this was unknown to the searchers at the time. A lot of the things found didn't seem important at the time. It was only after painstaking work by the physical evidence guys in coming weeks that the modelling paints linked Ivan directly to guns including one that was about to be found at Wally's place.

The boot was in the size which Readymix had registered as Milat's size. There was also a black and white photocopied map of the Southern Highlands – including Belanglo – a map of Newcastle and one of Wollongong. O'Connor was going through one of Milat's model aeroplane kits when he found a telescopic sight and a green water bottle which had been scratched as though to rub something out. The word 'Simi' was later seen by subjecting the bottle to a range of different lights.

In the laundry, Gerard Dutton noticed a piece of plastic under the washing machine. The machine was lifted and the plastic pulled out. Inside was a pistol, a pistol holder, a bullet pouch, cartridges and a gun magazine. There were bullets in the pouch and the gun was loaded. It was a Browning 7.65 self-loading pistol (later identified as one of two pistols stolen from the Water Board in the 1972 to 1974 period when Milat worked there while on the run.)

In the kitchen pantry, up on the top shelves, was some camping and cooking equipment later identified as Simone Schmidl's. On the kitchen bench was a police radio scanner, switched on. It was painted camouflage and had 'I Milat' written on it with his driver's licence number, 9780LLNew South Wales.

An Olympus 'Trip S' camera, same as Caroline Clarke's, was sitting in a kitchen drawer. Shirley, meanwhile, had turned up and the camera was shown to her, but she was unco-operative. It was later found to be from a batch sold only in England. In a spare bedroom was a .22 calibre fired cartridge case – with a crescent shaped firing pin impression. Also found were five boxes of Eley subsonic cartridges, which were later shown to have the same manufacturer's lot number as the box found in the forest near the Neugebauer/Habschied scene. This meant they had all been manufactured on the same shift on 23 March 1979.

In a cardboard box on top of the bed they found copper-tipped bullets suitable for a Colt .45 which was a possible match with the gun described by Onions and seen in the photograph with the Harley.

In the living room was found a book – *Select Fire 10/22* – which explained how to convert a 10/22 to a machine-gun. One of Milat's fingerprints was later found on it. Over the next three days, everything in the house was looked in, under or behind. The Joint Technical Support Group brought flexible cameras as thin as pencils to look inside wall cavities.

At the time of the search, the camping gear and the guns had not been properly identified. The barrel, stock and cocking lever assembly of the Ruger 10/22 had not been found, and so while the investigators were hopeful, everything would rest on the identification of these items over coming weeks.

Meanwhile, reporters were busy canvassing the neighbours. Sandra Harvey from the *Herald* spoke to Joe Maric next door who described Milat as 'a really nice bloke'. 'What struck Mr Maric,' she wrote, 'was how tirelessly the man worked – washing his car, mowing his manicured lawn or tending the landscaped garden. He was also very tidy. "Everything he did was meticulous".'

Bob Godden had 210 men, two police dogs and two cadaver dogs to handle the searches assigned to the 'South' group – the homes of Richard, Wally, and Bill. As the North group had headed to Eagle Vale at dawn, Godden's group set off in convoy from the police academy at Goulburn up the Hume, past Belanglo, to their targets. They hit Wally's and Richard's places at Hilltop first. Richard's one-hectare property had two caravans and some sheds roughly linked together like a large humpy. He and his de facto, Liz Smith, were planning to build a house there, but were making do for now. Inside a cupboard, searchers pulled out a hessian bag, and a pile of camping equipment fell to the ground: a green and orange tent; a blue tent (later identified as the one given to the British girls by Steve Wright); a Karrimat bedroll (later identified as Caroline Clarke's) and two sleeping bags (later identified as Clarke's and Walters's). Asked later who it belonged to, he said that he didn't know.[115]

In his old Datsun – registered in his mother's name – they found blue and yellow Telecom rope similar to that found in Area A near the bodies of Habschied and Neugebauer. They found three rifles, a shotgun, a pistol and a crossbow. Then they found a driver's licence and Medicare card in the name Paul Thomas Miller. Out in the yard was evidence of a fire in which there were burnt buckles consistent with belonging to a backpack. They also found marijuana and later that day he was charged with firearm, drug and property offences.

When they hit Wally's place nearby, Detective Senior Constable Andy Waterman was so pumped up he forgot where he was. 'Are you Walter Milat?' he asked.

'Yes.'

'I am Detective Senior Constable Waterman and this is Detective Constable Wilkins. We are from the North Shore Murder Task Force.' Whoops, wrong murders. The searchers hit pay-dirt, however, when they went into the little alcove under the house. They found rifles, shotguns, a sawn off .22, three prohibited Chinese military assault weapons, and two .22 Ruger rifles – among others. There were hunting knives, two bayonets, two machetes and a complete set of twenty-one boning and skinning knives. There was a silencer, two crossbows, a quiver full of arrows. All up, they found twenty-four weapons and about a quarter tonne of ammunition. Police couldn't get over the arsenal. But, most importantly, there was a small blue High Sierra knapsack which belonged to Simone Schmidl and six packs of Winchester 'Winner' .22 ammunition with the same batch number as that found in the shooting gallery near the Neugebauer/Habschied scene. There were twelve boxes of Eley ammunition with identical batch numbers to the one found at Ivan's and the one found in the forest, dated to 23 March 1979. There was also an Anschutz .22 with its barrel threaded to fit a silencer – it was very likely the weapon that had been fired in Area A with the Ruger 10/22.

They also found 400 g of pot. That's 14 ounces, and could have landed him with a supply charge.

Wally later claimed that the searchers threatened him and his new wife that their children would be taken away from them if they didn't co-operate.

Up in Queensland, searchers were hopeful after having been given Simone Schmidl's backpack the day before by Alex Milat. They found ammunition with the same serial numbers on the packets as those found in Area A near the Neugebauer/Habschied crime scene and the same as those found at Wally's and Ivan's places. The Milat boys bought in bulk.

The biggest team of all, about sixty searchers, was targeting the 'Big Block' at Wombeyan and, later, Alex's former home at Buxton where they were to bring in a mechanical sifter to recover every bullet ever fired into the mound in his private rifle range. Wombeyan was bitterly cold in the mid-May westerlies on top of 'Milat's Mountain'. Most searchers were afforded billets in cheap motels in Mittagong, but for those who had the night watch at base camp, they could have sworn snow was falling. A week into the search, a ferocious gale swept over the peak, flattening tents. The sleepless coppers spent the night desperately trying to prevent the communications caravan from being blown off the cliff.

Detectives Gorman, Feeney and Coman had to go back to Lake Tabourie to search Bill and Carol's caravan. There was always a chance that, being away from home, they might have camping equipment with them. It meant they had to quickly organise a warrant over the phone because their warrants only covered the house at Bargo. It was cold and wet on the South Coast. Bill and Carol, still unaware what was going on at Eagle Vale, greeted them cordially enough. They said they were from Task Force Air, investigating the backpacker murders.

'What are you looking for?' Carol asked formally.

Coman handed her a list of property.

'Is this the property of the backpackers?' she asked.

'Yes.'

She looked at it, sat down and burst into tears.

Bill and Carol were told to go for a walk. They sensed that the mood had changed since the day before. The police moved into the caravan and started pulling things to bits.

Up at their home in Bargo their daughter Debbie would claim, like Wally and Lisa, that she was being threatened with having her son Michael taken away. When asked if there were any firearms in the house, she told police there was one in a cabinet in her brother Christopher's bedroom, where they found a .44 magnum Ruger carbine, plus a crossbow, sheathed knife, two rolls of electrical cord and five tins of ammunition.

They took away Debbie's collection of books. Some, like one on cannibalism, *The Last Taboo*, and one called *Open Season*, about a man in Alaska who picked up prostitutes and flew them to a remote area and hunted them down, were falling apart and covered in fingerprint dye when she got them back months later, such was the interest in linking them to Milat.

Over at 55 Campbell Hill Road, Mrs Milat was being difficult. She absolutely refused to open a padlocked locker in the back of the house. Detectives forced it and discovered a few guns and a rifle bolt wrapped in a shirt.

They found some dope plants growing in the backyard and put them in paper bags.

'What's this?' one of the detectives wanted to know.

'A brown paper bag,' Bodge replied.

'How long you been growing it?'

'Hey, Mum,' he yelled out, 'how long we been growing brown paper bags?'

Despite his brain injury and his debilitated speech, if you had a flat tyre, he was the sort of guy who'd tell you it wasn't so bad, only the bottom part was flat.[116]

More seriously, the searchers found a long curved sword in his room. It immediately made the detectives think of Anja Habschied's decapitation, although it was quite blunt. Out in the garage, they found a yellow shirt and a blue 'Next' brand shirt that would prove to be one of the most crucial pieces of evidence for the course of Milat's coming trial. They didn't know it yet, but the shirt was Paul Onions'. Its presence in the garage was the key factor in the young Englishman being allowed to testify at the trial because it so strongly substantiated his identification evidence.

Over coming days, anthropologist Richard Basham was fascinated to see what souvenirs Milat had kept. He was intrigued by the police stories of the way Milat had been shocked by the early morning phone call and had apparently spent some time hiding his souvenirs. Basham sensed that Milat didn't expect an arrest. He felt that he knew the law was so weighted in his favour that the cops were powerless. He hadn't counted on the Englishman that got away. Basham speculated that he would have wiped the incident from his memory.

A lot of people who knew that Milat knew the cops were on to him would simply not believe the police evidence against Ivan. They knew he was no fool. He wouldn't keep all that shit. But Basham and Milton knew that those people did not realise how important all this stuff was to him. When it emerged how Chalinder had worn Caroline Clarke's top, they saw it as a way for Milat to relive the whole experience. When he had sex with his girlfriend, he could think about having sex with his victim. Most people can't put themselves into that mindset so they don't understand.

PART THREE

FORTY-FOUR

May–June 1994

REVELATIONS

The news bursts out via radio and television. There are no names mentioned, but when the reports say that a man has been arrested at Eagle Vale, and properties are being searched in Guildford, Bargo, Hilltop and in Queensland, people who know the Milats have a uniformly uncanny feeling that they know who it is. Some recognise the posture of the man under the jacket; some just know.

His workmate, Don Borthwick, is typical. He spots the manicured garden straightaway and the white Readymix Pantec truck out the front. 'It's Ivan, they've got Ivan,' he yells to his wife. It hits him harder than a punch to the head. Can't believe it. If this is true, he'd never be able to trust friendship again.

About the only people associated with the case who can't understand what's going down are Richard's former workmates from Boral, Paul Douglas and Des Butler. Des and his wife Lynn are sitting at home watching the news when they spot Paul Gordon walking the guy across the yard, but they can tell it isn't 'Paul Miller' under the jacket. It is only the next day that the name Milat is made public. Paul Douglas rings Butler: 'Hey Christ, what's happening here? It's not Miller. It's his brother.' Then as gear is found at Richard's place, they expect he'll be arrested at any moment.

That day, Monday, Milat appears in front of a packed Campbelltown Court charged with the Onions robbery and with using a revolver with intent to commit an indictable offence. He enters no plea and his solicitor, Jim Marsden (standing in for his brother John), urges the magistrate to ignore two words: 'Belanglo' and 'backpacker'. They are, however, hard to overlook.

It isn't difficult to piece together that so many officers have been used to arrest the man and search so many properties, that it can hardly be some incidental matter uncovered during the course of the main murder investigation.

On the same day, Royce Gorman and Brett Coman go back to Bargo to interview Bill Milat. During a formal record of interview, Bill produces a photo album: 'This is a photo of Ivan's car.' The album shows the date as Easter '92, a time that the coppers know corresponds to the British girls' disappearance. But an earlier date has clearly been crossed out of the album. Both coppers think maybe Bill and Carol are trying to create an alibi for Ivan. Carol tells them she'd made the change ages ago, that she'd just put it in wrongly and that if she'd wanted to make up an alibi she would have done a much better job of it. When they take the album back to the station they realise the 1991 date is also written on the back of the photo. More crucially, hidden in the photo are the lambs wool seat covers that Onions had spoken of.

That morning, Phil Polglase buys a newspaper which starts messing with his head. His wife Gail is driving him up the coast to visit his sister and parents at Nambucca Heads. The arrest is all over the *Telegraph Mirror*. It doesn't name the suspect, but there is a map showing the properties being searched. It gives Phil a terrible feeling.

'I think I know who this is,' he tells Gail. 'I know . . . I know this guy. I know who done this.'

'Oh, sure.'

'I do! I know who done this.'

When they get to his sister's place, his mother hears a newsflash which she thinks says they've charged someone called Myla, or Meela.

'No, that's Milat. Ivan Milat's done this!' he shouts at the radio. 'The Milats. This is the Milats. I know them well.' Then he's just, like, 'Wowww!' Totally spun out.

He puts the paper on the table and shows his parents. 'Look at this. That's Ivan's place and, look, this is Dick's, I think that's Wally's . . .' To him, it confirms his fears that all that shit he heard when he stayed at the Milat place a few years earlier was all for real, and shit, shit, shit! He runs out on the balcony and just sort of loses it for a while. The more he thinks about it, the more blown away he is. He'd thought they were up to no good, but he'd never connected it to the backpacker murders until this.

Phil and Gail only stay up there for a few hours because they have to pick their five kids up from school. On the way back he tells Gail he might have some information to help the police.

'Wake up to yourself, Phillip,' she says, tired of his goings on. 'What could you possibly know?'

He doesn't go into it.

Phil has to go to Taree to deposit $80 to cover some cheques Gail had overdrawn, so she drops him at Johns River and he hitchhikes the last 30 kilometres into town. He stays overnight at his friend Eddie McDonald's house in Purfleet, the Aboriginal settlement on the wrong side of the Manning River from Taree. Phil gets on with all the black guys. He is a blond-haired honorary Koori. Even at thirty-nine he's still running around playing footy with them for South Taree, the only whitefeller on the team of thirteen. Captain/coach. He reports his knowledge of the Milats to the local police but knows it is a waste of time because he's had a few run-ins with them.

Phil leaves the station and goes home, but he knows in his gut he has to do more about the murders. He has Gail drop him on the highway. He doesn't tell her what he's doing because he knows she won't approve. Phil is always up and going places without saying anything, so it's nothing unusual. A friend sees him hitching on the road and takes him to Purfleet where he has to collect $60 that Eddie McDonald owes him so he can afford to buy a train ticket to Sydney.

Another mate from Johns River, Reg Galati, who is working in Sydney, picks him up at West Ryde station and takes him back to his parents' home.

He tells them what he knows about the Milats. It's bugging him – whether to do the right thing, or just walk away for the sake of Gail and the kids. He is scared of the Milats.

'Phil, if you fucking do, mate, just tell 'em what you know and leave it at that. Don't let the cops drag you in,' Reg tells him.

But old Joe Galati who's worked hard and kept his head down all his life tells Phil he's crazy. 'Phil, best not to say nothing to nobody about this. You know, just keep it to yourself what you know and don't say nothing to nobody. Don't go to the police, just shut up. Otherwise you're going to bring yourself a lot of trauma.'

Joe drives Phil to Eastwood Railway Station to put him on a train home before he does anything stupid. Phil thanks him and just walks straight through the subway under the tracks and out the other side into Eastwood Police Station. The officers there call the task force straightaway. Analyst Mick Rochester takes the call, but Brett Coman is listening in and gets the gist of it. Rochester informs the bosses still based down at Campbelltown and Coman pushes to follow it up. He's still kicking himself for not pushing harder on the Milats in the very early days of the task force. He and Royce Gorman head straight out to Eastwood.

One of the first things Polglase says in his statement to them is: 'I do not want any of my personal details released to anybody because I fear for my family under the circumstances.' He launches into how he knew the Milats and how he came to be at their place in the days after Christmas 1989. The cops know the importance of the date, and know they could be on to something. Everist and Gibson disappeared on 30 December. Polglase's dates are wobbly. He was in a car accident a few years earlier and it's hard pinning things down. He thinks that the time he stayed at the Milats' around New Year's Eve 1989 was the time Ivan came back with a bloody knife. He is sure it was just before New Year's Eve because he remembers Richard talking about a party he was going to. He recounts that incident to the police and how Bodge ran him around next day and told him about Ivan doing bad things. He also remembers Bodge mentioning once that he'd seen Ivan and Richard returning home with a rifle and a knife covered in blood.[117]

Then Polglase isn't so sure. The uncertainty leaves the cops a bit dubious about him, but they can see he does have a close knowledge of the family. He says he kept away from the Milats after that night and had only seen David once since, at Easter 1993.

Royce Gorman asks: 'Have you read or heard in the press or has anybody told you the dates that any of these people went missing in the forest?'

'The only thing I know is that these things happened between 1989 and 1992. I don't know any of the dates.'

He talks about a kombi van as though he thinks it is still the suspect's vehicle. He'd seen one around the Milats' place years earlier. Ivan was driving a blue Toyota Hilux four-wheel drive dual cab with mag wheels, he says.

'As far as I could see over the years Richard was the only person who was close to Ivan and I would say he idolised him in a sense. Richard did look up to Ivan and that was one of the reasons I was concerned about Richard.' He remembers Richard explaining once that: 'Ivan could cut your head off with one blow'.[118]

The interview ends. Gorman and Coman know they have something. Next day at 8.30 a.m., they pick Phil up and bring him in to go over some points and check him out. He does a lot of explaining about how he came to be at the Milats'. He adds to the conversation he had with Ivan when Ivan came back from hunting. 'After he told me "that's human blood I stabbed a bloke with it", he then said, "I stabbed him through the spine".'

'Is there some reason why you didn't tell me that conversation yesterday?' Gorman asks.

'Yes there is, when I was hitchhiking from Mooreland to Taree I was picked up by Colleen [a friend]. I mentioned to her that I had information in relation to these incidents and that I knew Ivan Milat. She told me that victims had been stabbed firstly in the spine. She said that after that, he had the victims powerless and could do as he wanted with them. I felt that her telling me this may compromise any evidence I gave.'

It is a long interview. Goes for hours. Polglase finishes up by saying, 'I want you to know that I had nothing to do with these things. I have told you everything I know because this is very serious. People are dead and that's not good.'

Polglase returns home badly shaken up. He is a worried man.

The derros who catch the winter sun in the little triangle of grass outside the Hat Factory are as happy as the rest of Sydney to see a result in the case. They are yelling out to the detectives as they get out of their cars in the morning: 'Hey, sarge, don't forget to beat him one for us.'

Milat has been remanded in custody until the following Tuesday, so police have eight days to work up a case to charge him with murder. If they don't, there is a possibility he'll get bail. So they begin a feverish week of identifying as much of the gear and guns as possible and linking them to the murders.

Clive Small had won his promotion on 17 May. There were those who thought at the time that he had hurried the arrest of Milat along in order to see it out before he left the task force. The view was that the listening devices should have been allowed to run a little longer but, as all the gear turns up, Small is proved right. Speed was essential in stopping Milat getting rid of evidence. They could have listened in for six months without him giving anything away and in the meantime they would have had to continue working on all the other suspects.

As the search of Milat's house winds down three days after the arrest, Lynch and Small consider that since they've found so much equipment on the premises, Milat has not gone to elaborate lengths to hide anything. If they had found nothing inside they might have dug up the yard. But they decide against it and so miss a pistol which Milat had buried there.

On 24 May detectives return to interview Karen Milat. Among a range of details, she tells them how he used to always stop at Lombardo's to buy Hubba Bubba bubble gum and a newspaper on the way down to Alex's. Bingo, that links him to the Onions pick-up point. The case is continually closing around him.

Paul Gordon had felt on the outer before. He'd earlier been 'officially counselled' by Rod Lynch over some matter. Then he'd come in for two days on his days off to see the raids through and then suffered the indignity of having his overtime claim rejected. He was told to change Saturday's entry from ten hours to eight before it would be signed. He thought he was part of a team, but to have such a petty rejection was quite unbelievable. Gordon is a bit of an instinctive player. He works hard, but his paperwork is sloppy. Royce Gorman had taken him aside a few times to tell him to get his running sheets in order. It sets him at odds with Small and Lynch who are both extremely meticulous. The only senior officer to tell him he did a good job is Bob Godden, and he really appreciates that.

In the days after the arrest, Gordon gets a phone call from Martin Warneminde from the *Sun-Herald* asking about his role in the investigation. It feels to Gordon like a small vindication. Warneminde knows the basic story already. Gordon might correct a few points. He knows that the ban on talking to the media still holds, so he listens to what the reporter puts to him, and politely declines to make any further comment. The reporter then puts it to him that he cracked the case almost single-handedly.

'I was just lucky,' the big copper says, bidding the reporter goodbye and expecting that his name won't be used.

The story comes out a few days later, beginning: 'A lone investigation by a young detective has led police to believe the Belanglo Forest backpacker murders could be linked to a rape case more than twenty years ago.' The story gives Gordon the credit for cracking the case and links it to the 1971 attack on Margaret and Greta, although neither woman is named. It also quotes Gordon saying he was 'just lucky'.

The story is problematic. Firstly, while Milat wasn't named as the 1971 attacker, the inference is there and the story also implies that he is the murder suspect. Since he is due in court two days later, Small fears it might allow the defence to use it as an example of how Milat could not possibly receive a fair trial. Small was still annoyed about Gordon's earlier upfront manner in checking out Ivan with direct approaches to workmates, openly telling them he was investigating the backpacker murders. The use of the words 'lone investigator' also gets up the noses of a lot of detectives.

Next day, Clive Small calls Gordon into his office and drags him over the coals. Really gives him the third degree. Small accuses him of not being a team player. Gordon takes it standing up, but feels like fainting as Small tells him to pack his bags. 'You're off the task force.' His promising career is in tatters. As Gordon turns to leave, Small's last, angry comment is: 'Now I can't do what I want to do.'

Gordon doesn't know what he means by that, but it sticks in his head.

What Small means is that he wanted to buy time. They have rooms full of seized exhibits that he wants completely analysed before he charges Milat with murder. Small feels now that he's going to have to rush it. That makes him angry, but Small would later maintain that Gordon was not sacked for talking to the media, but because he was 'less than truthful when asked about it'.

Small calls a meeting of the task force as Gordon waits just outside, tears in his eyes. Small explains to everyone that because of the comments, he has been forced to charge Ivan with the murders earlier than he wanted.

There are those in the room who took the newspaper story as a kick in the teeth, like they didn't deserve any credit. They see it that Gordon was handed the Milat file in January and everything else just fell into place.

There are others who feel sorry for him. Whatever the case, there is a consensus – Gordon included – that he should have known better.

Milat is charged with the murders next day, Tuesday, 31 May. Senior Crown Prosecutor Ian Lloyd QC makes public for the first time some of the brutal details of the murders and outlines some of the victims' alleged possessions found in the house. Milat is now clean-cut and well dressed. John Marsden, as expected, attacks 'Sunday's media' and asks the press to give his client a fair go.

Two days later, the task force is formally congratulated by the commissioner at police headquarters, but Gordon is missing. About thirty officers adjourn to the Hyde Park Plaza Hotel for celebratory drinks. They walk in on journalists Les Kennedy and Mark Jones. Clive Small and Bob Godden pull Kennedy aside and ask if the media is blueing over details of the planned raids being leaked to some outlets and not others.

Godden reveals that Paul Gordon has been sacked for his slip-up. 'It's cost the career of a good young police officer.'

FORTY-FIVE
Mid to late 1994

FATHER DEAREST

When Toppy Ambrose went around to Campbell Hill Road in her old Datsun to take Mrs Milat shopping about two days after the arrest, she sensed a feeling of disbelief among the family. Bodge was playing his Sega game. His oldest sister Olga – who'd changed her name to Diane – was there.

'Wouldn't it be strange if it really was Mac,' said Diane. Mac was always so calm and hard to rile. There'd be plenty of other people they would have thought more capable of it than him.

Margaret Milat had diabetes bad. She had high blood pressure and her heart and lungs were crook. Everything was shot. She had every reason to be cranky, but she didn't seem any more so than usual. She kept hauling herself out of bed to make Bodge's tea. It was like Bodge needing her kept her going.

It was easy for Toppy and Scott Urquhart to believe in Mac's innocence because – aside from the fact he was a good bloke – they knew that he'd known he was being watched for at least a month before the arrest. So to come out and claim he had all this gear on him and the gun parts was ridiculous. Mac was no dill. It smelt like a load up to them.

Lynise Milat had been on the lounge watching telly when she saw the backpacker suspect being led out of the house with a coat over his head and she just knew it was Ivan. She didn't even know he lived at Eagle Vale. It was the body shape, really, that gave it away. She rang her mother, Marilyn. 'They've got Ivan.'

'I'll ring Gran's and call you back,' said Marilyn, hanging up.

When she called back, she was crying. 'Yep, they've got him. It's him.'[119]

Lynise was still the only Milat who didn't know Ivan was her natural father. About six months earlier, her sister Charlene told her she was Ivan's but, when she'd finally confronted her mother over it, Marilyn just straight out denied it. Her answer seemed so rehearsed, though, and Charlene had said so many things, that Lynise didn't believe her. So she pushed a bit.

'You know, Mum, I'm not gunna judge you or anything. I'd just hate to think that you would know something this important and go to your grave and not tell me.'

'No, no, no. It's the truth.' Marilyn was adamant.

'Okay, fair enough.' Lynise left it at that.

The suspicions, though, ate away at her, growing all the time, and now she was being told the guy who might be her father could be locked up for life. She cried, angry with everything and everybody. 'I might've finally found my real father and I'm never going to get a chance to know the person. They're going to take him away.' What he had done to these people didn't enter the picture. Just: 'Okay, now it's going to get difficult for me.'

She still didn't know if Ivan really was her father. The last thing she wanted to do was to go to Dad – Boris – because she knew how much the whole thing had hurt him, and she was still frightened of him. But everything was different now. She was panicked and had nowhere else to go. It amazed her that she plucked up the courage to call him – and, that when she did, he was calm about it.

This moment of truth with Lynise was one Boris had dreaded all his life. He still regarded her as his own, but it was time to cut through the bullshit. 'I think there are a few things you ought to know,' he said quickly. 'I'm coming round to see you.'

Standing out near her front fence, he gave Lynise the story, again staying calm the whole time. So different from the dad of her childhood.

'Be careful,' he warned, 'because, you know, naturally Ivan's going to want to latch on to some sort of family blood at a time like this, and he'll take you down with him emotionally.'

She nodded, but she wasn't listening. She was angry at her mum.

'Why didn't anyone tell me?' she asked Boris.

'I don't know how you didn't know, because when we'd argue, I'd say all sorts of things about Ivan . . . then I'd think, "Oh, she's in the other room", and really regret it.'

But Lynise thought that was bullshit because when he was angry, he didn't care what came out. She must have just been too young to understand. She remembered them fighting about some uncle all the time. Next thing she'd be out of bed flying down the stairs trying to get Dad off Mum. That was all she remembered.

Two months after the arrest, Lynise rang Boris again. 'Dad, I know you won't be able to handle this, but I want to get to know Ivan.'

'Why?'

'I want to know why I was so unhappy growing up.'

'I didn't know you were unhappy growing up! Geez, we toured Australia for three months every year. I gave you a bike at five. You had everything you wanted.'

But Lynise was going through a stage where – even though her newfound father was accused of being a mass murderer – she was just so happy to have him. It was like: 'Oh good, now I can have the real dad I always wanted.' This would be a cure-all for all the trouble in her life. She was acting like an eight-year-old, she'd later realise, but at this point she needed that feeling.[120]

Marilyn had, meanwhile, started visiting her old boyfriend in jail. He'd never shown sufficient commitment on the outside, but now she had all he could give. He wasn't going anywhere.

Lynise went with her on a visit, nervous as anything, and Marilyn asked him: 'Are you innocent? Did you, or didn't you?'

He looked back at her with a pained expression. 'Well, no, you know.'

Lynise had to say her bit: 'Well, that's what I'm *not* here for, you know, so . . .'

'Aren't you?'

'No . . . It won't make any difference to me whether you're innocent or guilty. That's not what this is about for me.' She was looking for something deeper within herself. The subject of whose daughter she was came up and Lynise asked him would he have a blood test.

'Yeah, that'd be fine,' he said. 'I'll help you out if I can.' But Marilyn was carrying on, a blubbering mess. She made some snide remark, like: 'Don't worry, I'm not going to sue you for back maintenance.'[121] Ivan went off at her, and Marilyn played the drama queen.

Lynise went with her mother for more visits but they never seemed to go anywhere. In half an hour behind a perspex wall, there wasn't much you could achieve with the three of them there. Lynise felt that her mum got all the time. All the attention. So she bit the bullet. 'I'm a big girl now. I'll see him by myself.' She wanted to know why she grew up the way she did, suffered the way she did. It affected her still with her own son. She wouldn't let anyone mind him. She had to go to separation classes to get used to being away from him. She was always frightened of people hurting him, because if her parents could do what they did to her, what could an unrelated person do to him? Marilyn told her she was never physically beaten as a child, but Lynise's memory had Dad taking to them with the strap, for no apparent reason. She had become a problem kid, getting into trouble from her early teens, but she stayed at home until she was eighteen to help Mum against Dad. Dad was drinking by then, which he hadn't used to do, and one day he was smacking Marilyn in the mouth. Lynise went into their bedroom screaming. 'For God sake, stop it! You are so pathetic. Are you listening? Are you listening?' Boris went right off. Kicked her door and told her to get out, and so she did. And all the while, Lynise felt responsible but didn't know why.

She wanted answers and reasoned that if Ivan was guilty, he was going to cop the punishment, so there was no need for her to worry. Regardless of the coming trial, he was still the father she never had. The only time it ever got to her was when her partner, Paul, had asked her: 'How would you feel if it was me and you tied up?' That hit home, but generally she felt the same as the rest of the Milats: Ivan was family. Paul couldn't handle it and ended up leaving her and his son when she insisted on continuing to see Ivan. She just had to do it.

Lynise turned up for a visit one day and Chalinder was there. It was the only time they'd met, and Lynise was pissed off because she'd come all that way and now she'd have to share the visit. Afterwards, Chalinder advised her to put Ivan behind her, to get on with her life. Lynise fumed. 'Well, if you'd lived it the way I've lived it, you wouldn't be telling me to leave it alone. If anybody's got any rights to him, it's bloody well me.'

Lynise noticed that Ivan acted weird in front of Chalinder. He'd always seemed nice and polite, with that way of saying things without saying them that the family seemed to share. Now he was acting the jock, the dude. 'You're bullshit,' Lynise was thinking. It was another person in there. She was angry, but realised it was for Chalinder's benefit.

It seemed like Ivan was happy to see her alone. Happy to see anybody. But her earlier joy at finding a father began to sour. She found herself berating him. 'Why did you let me grow up like this? Didn't you know what it was like? Didn't you care?' She was angry for herself and for her mother. Why hadn't he come in on his Charger and taken them away?

Over time she grew up. Realised, like, maybe he just didn't care for her. That's what Marilyn said. Marilyn claimed he only ever cared for *her*. Lynise became realistic and began to think that maybe she didn't care for him so much, either.

Marilyn said to Lynise that Ivan had something unconscious against his mother because she was the first person he rang when he was arrested.

'Well, maybe that's natural enough,' said Lynise. 'She's always the one they've all fallen back on, you know, one way or another.'

'No, there's something that, you know, he's doing something to punish her. Maybe it's because she used to let him get minded by [a certain older woman].' Marilyn said the woman molested him when he was young and had an ongoing sexual relationship through his teens.

FORTY-SIX

Mid to late 1994

THE GUN

Gerard Dutton spent three days searching Milat's house, itching to examine all the firearms evidence which was off being fingerprinted. He got to it on the morning of 25 May. The Ruger parts were still number one priority. He knew he had three chances of connecting Milat to the murders. There was the fired cartridge case found in the bedroom. The silencer was a good chance of a positive match with the bullets from Clarke's body – if he could duplicate the unique gouges in test-firing. Then there was the bolt found in the wall, which he'd have to fit to another 10/22 body to test-fire.

He started with the fired cartridge from the bedroom, and put it in the macroscope. It looked good at first, but as he examined every millimetre of it, and as the hours went by, he became disheartened. A positive ID has to be based on features so unique that no other firearm in existence could duplicate them. Dutton thought that this case had been fired by the murder weapon, but it was in good condition compared to the corroded murder cases. An important factor was that he couldn't say what time had passed between the firing of all the cartridges. Characteristics left by a gun change as the gun ages and suffers wear and tear. The identifying features he was looking for on the bedroom case had not duplicated very well. A build-up of grease and dirt on the bolt face may have prevented transferral of marks to the case head. More importantly, the chamber marks were non-existent. So he was 99 per cent sure, but that wasn't good enough. It hurt to say, but it was no match.

He tried the silencer next. He could see just from looking through it that one of the washers was misaligned, but he had to duplicate the gouges if he was to prove it was the silencer used to kill Caroline Clarke.

Without the barrel, however, he had no idea how the silencer was orientated in relation to the muzzle. Also, the nut attached to the silencer was an unusual size. The inner diameter of the nut was more than the outer diameter of the muzzle of a 10/22. If this was the silencer he was after, the murder rifle must have been heavily modified.

He modified a 10/22 from the firearms reference library and attached the silencer, rotating it 45 degrees with each test. Some of the eight shots produced a scrape mark from the crooked baffle, but they weren't the same as the exhibit bullets. Dutton had doubted it was the 'murder' silencer to begin with because it looked so homemade. He now eliminated it definitely. Strike two.

His last chance was the breech bolt. He dismantled a Ruger 10/22 from the firearms reference library, and put the suspect mechanism in. He test fired this new weapon several times into the water recovery tank, which makes sure the bullets are marked by nothing but the firearm in question. He sat down at the comparison macroscope feeling exhilarated and tense. This was the moment he was going to make or break the backpacker murder case. Despite all the other evidence, the task force needed this. He placed one of the test-fired cases on one 'stage' of the macroscope and one of the Clarke cases on the other. He adjusted the light sources, so the right amount of light and shadow played across the nooks and crannies of the cases. He took a deep breath, bit the bullet, and put his eyes up to the binocular eyepiece.

It looked good. The long-lost friend? He changed the magnification – times 13, times 34, times 80 – homing in on all the familiar features, his excitement growing with each one. This was the friend. With each magnification, the certainty grew. Everything was so familiar in this city of strangers. Of the millions of Ruger 10/22 breech bolts ever manufactured, this was the one used to kill Caroline Clarke. 'You bloody ripper!' Dutton was in ballistics nirvana. A state of bliss he couldn't describe.

This now presented a weird set of connections between the Cinnabar Street breech bolt and the forest. The breech bolt was definitely linked to the Clarke murder. He couldn't link it directly to the cartridge cases found near the Neugebauer scene because they were too badly corroded, but he had already linked the Neugebauer cases to the Clarke cases by the chamber marks. The chamber which caused the marks, however, being part of the barrel, was never located. So even though it wasn't directly linked, it could be shown that the weapon was at both scenes. It was quite extraordinary. He'd never seen a link like it before. All this was racing through his head as a colleague at the Ballistics Unit examined the cases and confirmed the positive ID.

So, at 4.30 p.m. on 25 May 1994, he called the task force and asked to be put straight through to Clive Small with the news. Small was ecstatic. The noose was tightening. Dutton's job was far from over. Police were collecting all fired cartridge cases and bullets from Richard and Wally's property at Wombeyan and from Alex's old place at Buxton. If the murder weapon had been used there, they wanted to know because Ivan Milat could most certainly be linked to those properties. Dutton's jaw dropped when detectives brought in ten large tin tubes, 22 centimetres tall by 18 centimetres diameter, full of spent bullets and cases. And then they told him that was from just one property, Alex's, which had a shooting range. Someone calculated that the tins held about 14,000 .22 calibre fired cartridge cases and 41 kilograms of spent bullets – somewhere between 10,000 and 20,000 bullets. There were also thousands of cases of other calibres.

'Which ones came from the murder weapon?' the detectives asked.

Thousands more were coming in from Wally's and Richard's properties at Wombeyan and Hilltop. They all needed to be examined. Dutton was daunted by such a slog after his brilliant high. This was the downside of the job, but it was made easier by colleagues who helped do a preliminary sort, separating cases and bullets into a .22 calibre pile, then segregating cases with a crescent firing pin impression. It was dull and laborious, but eventually they had it down to 1500 cases fired by a 10/22, and about 500 .22 calibre bullets. Each had to be checked individually. He only needed one case or one bullet to match in order to connect Milat just that bit more closely with the murder weapon. Sure, the bolt was found in his house, but there were no fingerprints on it, and nothing to directly prove it was his.

One by one, he went at them and one by one all 500 bullets were found to be too damaged or corroded. Many of the bullets showed that they had been fired by a rifle with the correct number of right twists in the barrel, but that wasn't nearly enough for a positive identification. He did, however, find some cartridge cases in good condition and he identified four from Alex's old place at Buxton as having been fired using the Cinnabar Street breech bolt assembly – the murder weapon. He stopped looking because that was enough. No matter what Ivan might say, the prosecution now had a link between the murder and the Milats.

Meanwhile, Bob Goetz, senior forensic biologist at the Division of Analytical Laboratories, Lidcombe, had been given a pile of gear by Andy Grosse whose preliminary tests had found possible bloodstaining on almost 100 items. He gave them all to Goetz for more detailed analysis on 23 June.

There were tents, sleeping bags, bits of clothing, various lengths of rope, backpacks, a green water bottle, a sharpening stone, blankets, sheets, a sword in a scabbard and a Cobra knife, all of which had tested positive to the police's preliminary Sangur tests. The thing that first caught Goetz's eye was an orange backpack which was covered in a reddened brown stain that cried out blood. He mixed a brown substance called otolidine with clear peroxide, then scraped off a piece of the stain. Sure enough, it turned the solution blue. This was blood. He got very excited that he was onto something. When there's plenty of blood, as in this case, it is usual to do an 'ouchterlony test', whereby he put some sample blood in an agar gel on a glass slide and surrounded it with different animal antibodies, including human, and if the blood creates a line on the slide with any of the antibodies, that's the species the blood belongs to. And this one lined up squarely against the kangaroo.

After that, there were lots of little brown spots on the other items which had to be gone through, but they were all too old to bring out a reaction. The older blood gets, the more the red fades out, and dulls. He was subjecting the darker bits of clothing to extremely bright lights trying to find stains to test, but to no avail.

The only other thing he got a reaction out of was a section of stained white rope which had been found in Milat's garage. The rope, referred to by the police as sash cord, was like that which pulls the weight in old double-hung windows. It was 1.5 metres long. There were areas of bloodstaining along the length. He cut two sections out. One for the species test – it was human – and the other was frozen until blood samples from all the parents arrived.

When the blood arrived, months later, he had to do a reverse paternity test. Normally, paternity tests establish what DNA the child has received from the mother and, therefore, what's left has been received from the father. Then you see what DNA the father has to see if he really is the father. In a reverse paternity, you start with the parents and look to see what type of children they could produce.

Everybody has some DNA called vWA. They call them junk DNA because they don't seem to do much in the human body. Ian Clarke had fifteen copies on one chromosome and sixteen on the other chromosome. He was a 15,16. Jacquie had eighteen on both chromosomes so she was an 18,18. A child of theirs could only be a 15,18 or a 16,18. The blood on the rope was a 16,18.

There were fourteen separate DNA tests like this done in England and Australia. Goetz concluded that the blood on the rope was 792,000 times more likely to come from a child of the Clarkes than any other parents taken at random from the population.

Things didn't go so well with the vaginal swabs taken from Clarke and Walters two years previously. Unbeknownst to the investigators, they were given to a scientist who'd never done that sort of test before. He tested them a number of times and got different results each time. It was later shown that his samples, his equipment and his chemicals used in testing were contaminated, but it did appear that there was DNA foreign to Clarke and Walters in there. Whose, will never be known.

Similarly with the hairs taken from Joanne Walters' hand, an inexperienced scientist was used. In his first test he found four female hairs, three male and two inconclusive.

Upon retesting the male hairs, two tested as female and the third got no result. An experienced forensic scientist was brought in to fix up the mess and, of the eleven hairs he tested, two were Joanne's, three were too badly deteriorated for a result and six appeared to be from someone else – not Ivan Milat and not Caroline Clarke. The scientist concluded there was still a reasonable possibility the hairs were Joanne's.

Investigators had been around to the personnel department at Boral and called all Richard's old workmates off the production line, one at a time, to talk to them. Des Butler and Paul Douglas were amazed that other people who, in their opinion, knew as much about 'Miller' as they did, all told the cops nothing. They had a combination of a bizarre loyalty to their former workmate and, more importantly, a hatred of police. The only other colleague to give more information was Steve Scott.

He just remembered when the bodies were found at Belanglo 'Miller' saying: 'You could pick up anybody on that road and you'd never find them again. You'd never find out who did it either.'[122]

Paul Douglas had named Nick Collins, Richard's dealer, and about five others as people who knew more. There was no doubt about it in

Douglas' mind because Miller had always talked in front of everybody and they were all listening. But one after the other, they all denied that they knew anything.

Collins had left Boral and gone to live in Queensland, but the sunny dream hadn't matched the reality, so he came back to Sydney in January 1994. The first time the police came knocking on his door, he and a few mates were getting ready to go fishing in a hired boat. They'd had a few bongs when the doorbell rang. Stoned people don't like policemen at their door. It wouldn't have been the best environment for an interview, even if he'd wanted to speak. But a range of factors were weighing on his mind telling him to keep his mouth shut. He was scared for his wife and two children but, more than anything, he hated the cops from things he'd seen as a young bloke. Here they were, a few years ago, taking what he was sure was a bribe to get him off the drug bust at work and now the mongrels were trying to get him to put his life on the line *and* dob in a mate. No way. He'd always been taught not to be a dog. Of course it was different when you were dealing with crimes like this, but – all factors combined – he couldn't bring himself to have anything to do with it.

Over coming months, detectives would come around and stand out the front of his place, 'come out you dirty little druggie'. It didn't make him want to co-operate, but he felt the strain of it all.[123]

Richard continued visiting him after the arrest, but he'd never talk indoors. He was scared that Collins' house was bugged. He'd have a cone or two and – unusual for him – not say a word until he was outside. Sometimes he'd call from the BP Service Station down the road and Collins would have to go see him in a nearby paddock. Richard would bludge a cigarette even though he clearly had a packet on him. He'd take the packet and look inside it for a bug.

On 16 June 1994, Justice Beaumont allowed phone taps be put on Richard's caravan at Hilltop. He was living in two caravans connected by a common annexe and the phone was in the Viscount van. Given that his fears of police scrutiny were not unfounded, it was not surprising that the taps obtained no useful information. But Task Force Air had not finished with Richard yet.

A month after the arrest, Senior Crown Prosecutor Ian Lloyd QC was gearing up to counter what he expected would be a strong bail application with a hard piece of evidence uncovered at Ivan's Eagle Vale home. It was standing room only in the court. Milat appeared agitated from the moment he entered the room and sat in the dock, managing a smile to his sister Shirley in the tiny public gallery. Marsden approached Milat as he was led into the dock by five guards and handed him a document which Milat threw straight back at him shouting: 'Just get away.'

Marsden told the magistrate, 'I no longer appear for Mr Milat in these proceedings. I have been told he no longer wants me to represent him. He has chosen to represent himself.'

The magistrate asked Milat if he wanted to reconsider.

'No, today I'll look after meself. I don't want Mr Marsden to represent me and I don't want him to talk to the media.'

During the hearing, Lloyd said more than 1000 items had been recovered from Milat's home and various properties. He mentioned that Milat had once absconded while on bail awaiting rape charges and that they had found the name 'Simi' – Simone Schmidl's nickname – on a water bottle.

Milat blew up. 'I'm innocent. I'm stuck in jail and they don't have one iota of proof . . . they're making them up as they go along . . . I'm astonished by what he said. The world now thinks I'm a rapist. He didn't say I haven't been found guilty of any of them and he comes up with some water bottles. When are they going to give me some evidence? We want some honest evidence.'

The task force were heartened to see him lose his cool. Certainly, Milat had forgotten advice he once gave to his workmate Terry Palmer that John Marsden could 'get you off murder'.

There were people in Sydney who remembered Marsden's involvement in getting Milat off the 1971 rape matter and there were also rumours about the New South Wales premier John Fahey, who had worked for Marsden. In fact Fahey wasn't working on the case and he wasn't working for Marsden. It is difficult to know what was thought to be wrong. Neither man was particularly prominent at the time and the transcript showed there was no need to pull strings. Certainly the Labor Opposition was fishing around for possibly damaging information about the premier, but none was forthcoming and the matter was left to live only around the dinner tables of Sydney.

After the sacking, the speculation turned to a theory that Marsden had urged Ivan to plead guilty. Marsden admits that he might have said something along the lines of: 'The evidence is very strong. Think of your mother. If you have done it, tell me so we can look at diminished responsibility because no one who is fully sane could do this.'

Milat told Marsden he was not guilty and was going to defend the case. Marsden agreed. He thought that since the case was entirely circumstantial, it was eminently winnable.

There were, however, other lawyers and other prisoners circling around Milat getting in his ear. Giving him advice. Marsden named two high-profile criminal solicitors as visiting Milat to solicit for business – a highly irregular practice. It was the highest-profile case in Australia for years and it looked very winnable at that time. Everybody wanted a piece of the publicity.

The Milat family says that Marsden was dropped because he was on the Police Board and, therefore, too closely aligned with the establishment. Milat wanted someone to attack that establishment. He obviously missed the point that Marsden was on the board precisely because he had always been so anti-establishment.

Milat thought he'd never get a fair go from a New South Welshman. He appointed Andrew Boe, a confident young solicitor from Queensland. The irony was that Boe would later decline to attack the veracity of much of the police evidence and would instead attack Milat's family as the main means of defence. He certainly never claimed that Milat had been loaded up, as many of those solicitors knocking on the jail door would have done as a matter of routine.

Richard and Wally retained John Marsden for the defence of their gun and drug charges some weeks later. Marsden explained to Magistrate Peter Ashton their fascination with guns and the hardship placed on their families arising from the arrest of Ivan. 'Both have been fairly law-abiding citizens of recent times,' he said. Magistrate Ashton pointed out that he took a dim view of unlawful pistols. 'It is very hard to have them for a lawful reason. There are matters involving silencers which again I take a fairly sinister view of in the absence of some other explanation.'

Marsden said he, like the magistrate, could not understand how a person could be obsessed with guns. But, 'obviously Mr Richard Milat likes guns, obviously they like to play with them and obviously, Your Worship, they consider them as items of pleasure when they go out and shoot feral animals. I find that rather odd, but because I or you or anyone else finds it odd, I don't think that we can therefore judge them on that.'

Ashton said the possession of such an arsenal concerned him 'and probably should give every other person in this room, probably the whole state of New South Wales concern, because firearms are designed only for one thing, that is usually to kill. They cause a lot of trouble and this state is trying very hard to regulate their use and possession.'

But Richard got lucky. Ashton put him on a good-behaviour bond.

'Be warned . . . it would not pay to be found in possession of any firearms,' he said. He fined him $300 plus $46 court costs for possession of the 'Paul Miller' driver's licence and $200 plus $46 costs for possession of cannabis.

A month later, Walter Milat fronted court with his wife Lisa for support. He pleaded guilty to the firearms and drug charges and was fined $2700, placed on a $2000 three-year good-behaviour bond and ordered to pay $230 court costs.

Steve Leach went back to Ivan's ex-wife Karen on 30 June to see if she could show them around. She was still very nervous about the whole thing; still scared of Ivan and what he might do to her family, and had been placed in witness protection. She had a friend, Robyn, along for support. Leach felt sorry for Karen. She was such an obviously lovely person caught up in all this madness.

They took her to Liverpool and she pointed out Lombardo's. They went south and she pointed out the forest that 'Ivan and I went to that he called Belanglo State Forest'. She pointed out that the entrance was different now because of the freeway. That was good corroboration. She told them about Ivan shooting the two kangaroos there.

After that, they went back to the ballistics section where she identified some, but not all, of the guns found at Cinnabar Street as Ivan's. She did, however, tell them he always had a pistol with him whenever he drove any distance from home. 'Even to the pictures or his mother's house. He would wrap it in a brown and white sock, or a rag, and put it under the driver's seat. Other times he would put it down his right sock into his boot. If he was wearing shorts which he did a lot he would keep it under the car seat.' She told them about the only time they went camping in the twelve years they were together and took blankets with them because they had no sleeping bags. It was an important detail.

FORTY-SEVEN

Late 1994

WIRED

Phil Polglase married young, and moved his childhood sweetheart, Gail, away from all the crap around Guildford in 1975. They moved up the coast to Harrington. Happiest years of their lives before she got pregnant and they came back to Sydney. They moved away again in 1979 but they kept in touch with the Milats and other friends. Bodge came up to visit them a few times, and Phil always visited them when he was in town.

Phil and Gail bought a little five-acre property in the deep green foothills of the Great Dividing Range near Taree. Gail kept popping the kids out and became more and more the self-confessed country bumpkin, but Phil kept all his rough edges. He wasn't a big one for commitment and there was never enough building work around, so he'd go away for long stretches working. He left her a couple of times, too, always coming back until there was another job and another kid on the way.

In November 1988, Phil and Gail, expecting again, came down to Sydney and were visiting Gail's old friend Billie Marie Thomson and her husband Joe Marukic at Camden on the far south-western outskirts of Sydney when a dog bit Gail. She went into labour and had the baby prematurely. Billie Marie and Joe knew Phil needed work so they asked him to build their house for them. He agreed. He took Gail home and returned in January.

Marukic and Billie Marie were good friends with Richard Milat too, so Phil saw a fair bit of him. Bodge came over to labour for him some days too. When he did, they'd often go back to Guildford and have a game of pool at the pub. Bodge didn't drink after his accident, just smoked pot.

Polglase partly finished the job in September 1989, and went home to Gail, then returned just after Christmas with two ton of timber to build two great entrance doors.

He was staying in his caravan on site when Richard came around and drank a bit of scotch with him and asked him to do some work on his mother's house at Guildford. So Phil spent a couple of days there. He fixed a few things and turned the bathroom door around so they could get to Bodge if he had a fit. Phil first met Ivan while putting a door on his bedroom, right at the end of the year when the bodies were being pulled from the rubble of the Newcastle earthquake.

Polglase eventually realised that his first statement to the cops claiming that he'd seen Ivan with the bloody knife around New Year's Eve 1989 was wrong. It had happened Easter '92. The second time he met Ivan.

Now, here Phil was two years later telling his wife, Gail, how he believed there were more murdered bodies out there still and that he had to do his bit to stop there being any more.[124] She saw it as his big righteous thing.

But Gail never wanted to talk about it. She hated him bringing it up. Wished he'd never got involved. She was scared for the kids, but Phil, for all his faults, had a sense of what was right and what was really wrong. He was always for the underdog. Got into a lot of fights because of it.

Gail was sick of the police ringing. They were always checking things on the phone, coming up to go over statements; making new statements. They were putting the pressure on. Gail heard Phil arguing with them on the phone. He'd be yelling and swearing, and then hang up. They'd ring back, or he'd call . . . and they'd start yelling at each other again. But all the while she was getting the impression they were growing to like each other.

The task force offered to set him up in a new town with a new identity, but Gail wasn't moving the kids. She wanted to keep living the way they'd always lived. She knew Phil would go crazy cooped up in protection, unable to go to the pub when he wanted, or to jump on his horse to visit his mates. So she refused to go. And Phil wasn't moving without the family. He felt he had to stay now to protect them.

Despite his love of beer and bongs, Phil could run all day. He was always the fittest bloke in his rugby league teams and, even as he got into his late thirties, his trainer, Kevin Burgess, would be trying to drag him off because of some injury and he'd just outright refuse to leave the field. He'd just go and go. Always talking; geeing up the boys. Unstoppable.

His best mate, Greg Shine, a New Zealander who owned the local garage, played too. They'd jump on their horses and ride to the Wingham pub, 16 kilometres across the mountains, or sometimes to the pub at Harrington, or right into Taree.

Shine's kids idolised the guy. Phil had five of his own, but he was always borrowing more – bringing Aboriginal kids to his place for a spell. He was a nomad, a gypsy who knew someone everywhere he went and seemed almost larger than life. But he got in a blue with a copper in the late eighties, and it got to the point where he could hardly walk around Taree without some hassle. It was almost natural that he gravitated more and more to his blackfeller mates over the river at what they still called 'the mission' at Purfleet. He loved 'em. They loved him. They were all outsiders.

When Phil told Greg Shine how he was involved in the Milat case, 'Shiney' told him: 'You're full of shit.' But they sat down, drank a carton of grog together and he just kept raving and raving and the more intense he got, the more Shine started to think his mate could be for real. He told Shine that some of the backpackers' gear which police had found in raids on the Milat places had been there when he worked on the place at Guildford. He said he'd found a whole lot of gear stuffed behind a wall or something: backpacks; a couple of German passports. They were pulling the wall out, throwing the gear down on the bed. He remembered seeing a yellow belt. German passports. 'One of them was of a girl.'[125]

It was starting to turn into a major drama but Phil was still running around wild, drinking and living his old freewheeling ways. His motto had always been 'Don't be scared'. Used to say it all the time – on the footy field, blueing in the pub or about life in general. But Shine could see fear in his friend.

The cops came and put him on a plane to Sydney and interrogated him for another few days. When he came back he was virtually on the verge of a breakdown. He was staying with Shiney and he'd be ringing Gail, screaming and carrying on. The police were putting him under intense scrutiny. He was horrified. When they took blood and hair samples he knew he was under suspicion.

One of the things that Phil's friends knew about him was what a maniac he was on the piss. One of his party tricks was pulling out his pubes and flicking them at you. Now he was panicking because he said he done this once at the Milats' place and that they kept a hair and might have put it on one of the corpses.

He told Reg Galati that Richard's missus asked him for a lock of his blond hair for one of her dolls and he gave it to her and maybe Ivan could have planted that.

He said to Gail once: 'Do you think I'm guilty?'

'Well, you're really starting to sound like you are.'

'You! You think I'd do something like that?'

'Look, Phil, that's how you seem. You seem to know a lot.' He looked deeply hurt. 'What do you expect people to think?' she asked.

Though suspicious of his motives, Polglase's sudden appearance and allegations came as a revelation to detectives. For the first time they had someone who claimed to be close to members of the Milat family and willing to help. If the theory of another hand in the killings was to be proved correct, then Polglase might prove the means to establish if any persons within the clan were involved or harboured suspicions or knowledge of the killings. Given earlier information from Richard's former workmates at Boral about his braggings, Dick seemed a natural first target, even if Polglase was closer to Bodge as a mate.

Polglase wanted out. He changed his mind. He couldn't handle the pressure. But he was already in way deep. Detectives Royce Gorman and Brett Coman were coming up to Taree for a week to talk to everyone who knew him and check him right out. He knew that the only way out was to make sure his story didn't stack up. He found Kevin Burgess – his old football trainer who'd got him the job at the Easter Show in '92 – in the pub at Old Bar.

'So you've come back to finish the house have ya, Phil,' said Burgess as Polglase came through the door, referring to the almost-finished house Polglase built him.

'Nah, nah, mate, I need a big favour off ya. Remember that time at the show in 1992 where I went missing for a few days?'

'Yeah.'

'I just want you to say that I was with ya every night in Sydney, see.'

'But you weren't.'

'Well, would you just say I was? The police are going to want to come and see you and you'll be able to tell 'em I was with you every night.'

'Eh, wait a minute. I can't say that because you wasn't, you know.'

'Mate, you gotta, otherwise I'm in deep shit.'

Burgess was in a tight situation. He never gave Phil a definite yes or no. It was one thing to tell a fib for a mate and another to ask him to lie when there was serious trouble.

The police turned up soon after in a flash new car. They showed their ID and told him it was serious: don't tell any lies.

'Was Phillip there every night of the show?'

Burgess couldn't do it. 'No. Two nights he was missing.' He was wondering what the hell was going on with Phil. What had he done? The cops told him bits and pieces and he knew then that he had done the right thing.

Even despite his attempt to discredit himself, Gorman and Coman found themselves liking Phil. The more they checked him out, the more he stacked up, even though there were still flaws in his dates. At least they had the Easter weekend 1992 pinned down, thanks to Kevin Burgess and some other friends from Guildford who he'd visited. Phil was in it good and proper now. The only way out was to take it all the way through.

On 29 July, the Supreme Court granted warrants for listening devices to record conversations between Richard Milat and Phillip Polglase. But Phil told the cops it would look too suss if he just rang Richard out of the blue because they weren't such good mates. He suggested he ring Bodge who was a better mate.

Five days later Polglase went to Bass Hill Police Station where two bugs were fitted to him and one to an undercover cop. Phil wasn't too happy about having the cop along, but they said that was how it had to be. They went to 55 Campbell Hill Road about 1.30 p.m. The undercover guy stayed in the car while Polglase went in and talked to Bodge for an hour and twenty-five minutes. He felt really bad about doing it because he liked Bodge and he liked Mrs Milat. He managed to vaguely set up a meeting with Richard and called him up a few days later. Richard was suss all along.

'Right now, right now they'd be takin' pictures of us,' he said.
'Would they?'
'Yeah. You're talking on a bugged phone. You rang a few times lookin' for me. Wouldn't be surprised if they're sittin' over in the fuckin' house over here. That they've been here since six o'clock this morning.'
'Yeah?'
'No worries.'
'Well, that's why I didn't wanna talk to you on the phone.'

They arranged to meet at the Crossroads Hotel, Casula, on 6 August. Phil went to Liverpool Police Station beforehand and they again fitted him up with two listening devices under a big heavy coat. Phil wasn't a coat kind of guy, but they insisted. He and Tim Sierlis, a detective with undercover experience, drove there in an old car, arriving at 11.09 a.m. The pub, set between a freeway and a paddock, was more car park than hotel. There were ten television sets around the white walls competing for space with Pub Tab betting sheets and loud signs for four dollar steak sandwiches. It was the haunt of a mixture of bikies and printed-shirt ordinary guys. But definitely not a coat kind of place. Phil introduced Richard to his 'mate'. It all just looked so suss as far as Phil was concerned. He sensed from the beginning that it was going to be a fiasco, but he kept on with it. The undercover guy left them alone as they speared off and sat outside.

Phil started talking about the night he'd stayed over and Ivan came home with the bloody knife. Richard told him to keep quiet about it.

'Well, that's right too,' said Polglase. 'Well, see like that night I fuckin', I fuckin' I was workin' at the show, right? I'm workin' at the show. If they check me out where did I stay that night?'

'Best bet is just to say nothin', completely nothin',' said Richard. 'I mostly caused myself a lotta shit sayin' nothing but . . .'[126]

'So what Dick, like, way I look at it, they fuckin', they got this evidence here and they convict Mac? And what 'appens if I'm fuckin' there that night? I'm an accessory aren't I?'

'For what?'
'After the fact.'
'Nah. Overpanicking, Phil. No need to worry. No need to worry.'
'Well, ya don't reckon they can get onto that?'

'Yeah, but they'll arrest me before you.'

The conversation drifted and Polglase brought it back, mentioning that he was shown backpacks and a passport. Richard told him not to talk about it.

'Yeah, but Dick, that morning Mac got the fuckin' . . . he showed me backpacks and that passport, y'know like. What the fuck here? What do I say about that? I don't tell nothin'.'

'Just say nothing.'

'Just tell them "I've seen nothing, absolutely nothing."'

'Never seen nothing, never had anything, never had anything.'

Richard kept on telling him to say nothing: 'If you know anything, ya gunna be a police witness.'

'Oh, fuck that.'

'No, it's not, that's what it comes down to if you know anything.'

'Well, see like . . .'

'Your best bet's to know nothin'.'

The conversation moved on for a while and Polglase was increasingly feeling Richard was onto him,[127] but he kept on. 'I thought if they grab me, right? . . . and they say "where did you stay at Easter?", like . . . They can go back to the company where I [was] workin' every day . . . at the Showground for fuckin' three weeks and I had a blue with me fuckin' mate that I was with that day. I said "fuck ya mate" and I went out, and I went out to Granville, met Bodge and . . . I went and stayed at ya mum's place. It sorts me out, what if they say fuckin', "and what happened then?" y'know?'

'. . . But you just don't know nothing. Ya ask "are you arrestin' me officer?" And when he says "no", well just tell him, "fuck off. Ya may as well just fuck off. I'm not talkin' to ya".'

'Yeah, see Dick, what happens if they . . . find out I stayed at the house?'

'They can't do that. How can they do that unless you go up and admit to it?'

The tapes rolled and more crap spewed forth. Another ten pages of transcript would go by before Richard spoke of people being killed: 'Yeah, if you're mental. What gets me is . . . I've never heard of a serial killers don't fuckin' stop. They don't stop. There'll be heaps more bodies. You just take, just take me if you decide today, when this cunt comes out in his four-wheel drive we'll get him today. We'll just go and shoot him, rape him, whatever we wanna fuckin' do to the fucking prick, burn his car keep that car ourselves and drive round in it for six months. What, well, what'd you think in one month's time we're a bit sick of this, let's get another one . . . Where are we gunna stop? Only when we get caught. Ya not gunna stop two years before. We're not gunna stop because we think the police'll be hot on our trail. Once ya get that sort've fuckin' thing in ya, I figure it's just like havin' a beer. When are ya gunna stop? When the pub closes, or do we buy takeaway to take home in case we're thirsty . . .' There was a pause. It all sounded so surreal. His use of the word 'we' was fascinating, but for the police listening in, it was no good. He hadn't said anything incriminating. Just enough to keep them wondering.

Another eleven pages of transcript went by before it got interesting again. Richard: 'When it comes near the end, then that's time for me to start worrying.'

'Why's that?'

'Cause they can't come along and charge me with accessory before or after the fact until he's been proven guilty of a crime.'

'Right.'

'So no good. Can't come and arrest me today, say, "You knew that he was doin' that, he did this or he did that".'

'Yeah, but you didn't know he was doin' it.'

'Cause he hasn't been proven guilty.'

'That's right, yeah.'

Another fifteen pages in, Polglase asked about all the gear: 'Where'd ya get it from?'

'What?'

'The stuff that they took from your place?'

'All over the place. Like they take, they took this backpack saying it was theirs. I went an' bought 'em. I pinched some other hot stuff down in the city.' He paused . . . 'Off these people that we knew. Ah, presumably off this dead cunt, this bloke died. Um, I went and bought heaps of it, you just picking this stuff up. Ya taking the backpacks home and . . . er, your brother gives you this. Y'know I'm not sayin' nothin'. I'm . . .'

'In that, in that case ya can say ya fuckin' found the things, couldn't ya?'

'Well, I don't need to say anything. I just don't need to. I don't need to say anything. There's no way in the world they can come along and say that backpack. You can say it, you can say anything ya fuckin' want, but that doesn't mean it's true.'

Polglase could sense that Richard was getting more and more suspicious with him always going back to the subject.

Richard: 'To me it sounds like ya musta been sayin' somethin' already, has ya?'

'I talked to fuckin' Terry Ambrose, and he told me what he thought. And I told him fuckin' nothing. Told 'im nothin', I fuckin' . . .'

'Ya ask me the same questions as the police asked me.'

'Who did?'

'You did.'

'Did I?'

'Yep.'

'Fuck me dead.' Polglase paused and the police listening in could feel the tension. 'Maybe I shoulda been a fuckin' copper.' He was handling it beautifully. 'Fuck me drunk. They're on one side of the fence, Dick.'

'It makes the same sense, questions ya askin' me as they're askin' me.'

'Yeah, exactly.'

The tapes rolled and the crap flowed. They'd been going for more than an hour. A few beers in, the police heard Richard tell Polglase that the cops could be listening in from the van parked over there. He seemed to think they could have long range directional microphones. Little did he know that the van he pointed at contained members of the SPG carrying submachine-guns.

'So I'm a lunatic.' He paused. 'I'm not worried about, I don't worry if they come'n arrest me for fuckin' killin' all these backpackers too. I realise you just arrest me, charge me and bang I'm gone. There is very little defence for me, sayin' where I was, where I was at. But I'm not worried about them comin' and arrestin' me, what's the good of worryin'?'

Towards the end, page 70 of the transcript, Richard mentions Gabor Neugebauer and his injuries and Paul Onions and his size even though, at this time, that was known only to investigators and the offender.

Polglase: 'Yeah, well if ya fuckin', that's what it looks like I reckon anyway. I don't reckon one bloke . . . had done all that. Fuck me dead, that's stupid.'

'Well, that's what we're worried about. That's . . .' He paused. '. . . One of these fuckin' big German cunts, he's supposed to be about six foot four, 18, 19 stone. Here he is a broken jaw, broken arm, broken fuckin' back. What, one bloke do all this to 'im?' He paused, 'And if you can do that to him well how can some skinny fuckin' pommy backpacker get away from him. Ya say that he's firing shots at him in the fuckin' middle of the freeway, well why didn't ya just shoot 'em fuckin' dead. Drive up, pick him up. No people on the freeway. Who's gunna see something? Who's gunna know that I did. I seen that bloke shoot 'im? Didn't see nothin' would ya even if you actually seen who pulled the trigger. Bang ya shot in the head with a gun, you fall on the ground, don't ya? I pull back up next to you in the car, pick ya up, throw ya in there.'

It was tantalising, but it wasn't good enough. They needed more. They took the tape away and went through it, hoping something directly incriminating would jump out of the babble at them, but the only crime that he was perhaps incriminating himself on was attempting to pervert the course of justice with his exhortations to say nothing.

Phil was upset with himself too, thinking that maybe he should have pushed harder. That he'd missed his big chance.

Richard left the pub in no doubt that Phil was working for the cops. He went back and told his old friends Joe Marukic and Billie Marie Thomson – the people whose house Phil had worked on back in 1989 – how Phil kept on coming back to the murders again and again and how he had some git looked just like a cop with him. The couple found themselves in an awkward situation because they both liked Phil and they both liked Richard. They hadn't known Ivan as well, but they didn't have a lot of difficulty believing in his innocence because he was such a good bloke and, more importantly for Joe, he knew how capable cops were of making things up. Joe was a successful businessman, but he'd seen them tell so many lies when he was a kid getting into trouble. Why wouldn't they do the same now?

Phil went back to Taree a scared man. He knew Richard knew. He knew Richard knew where he lived. He was freaked out. Really upset. He was going on to Gail about how the cops were stupid. 'Here I am walking in with this guy acting like he's me mate, and I've got this big coat on. They think Richard's stupid or something . . . They gave me a set of questions to ask and Richard was just laughing at me. He smelt it and it was just blown from the word go . . . If they had a let me do it my way, it would have been better, but they wouldn't let me.'

But the more he talked to Gail, the more she didn't want to listen. He'd got the family in enough trouble as it was and she didn't need this. She needed him out working trying to save the property which was in hock to the lawyers – Stacks of Taree – who were fighting his compo battle for the car crash and who were going to end up with everything.

The more he told Gail, the more she cut it from her mind. She just closed her mind.

'You're not backing me up,' he complained. 'Where's your support?'

'Like, Phil, you're really getting into them dangerous people and so I just don't want to know,' she said, walking away, shaking her head. He'd follow her. He needed to talk.

He was all alone. She'd feel bad about it later, but she was a mother hen at heart and she just worried about her kids.

The happy-go-lucky Phil disappeared. He was scared, nervy. Shiney saw him in the street at Taree and he was white as a sheet. He said he was going to be the main witness in the case. Hell, he was scared. 'They're gunna get me before I get to court. And if they don't get me they'll get m'family.'

Shiney got him to move the family up to his place further up in the hills for a while. Phil came to think he was being followed. Gail'd ring up and say there's a car down the road, and he'd be yelling at her to get out. A couple of times people did come asking around for him, said they were really good mates of his, but the locals told them nothing. If they were such good mates why didn't they call?

Phil started marking escape routes in his mind wherever he went; planning to run across paddocks and over fences where he knew no one could catch him. He said to Reg Galati: 'Frank, [they both called each other Frank, it confused everybody] if I get killed, find out who done it, for fuck's sake.'

He was sure some other people knew as much as he did about the case, but they denied it all. He tried to get them to come forward to back him up. No way, man, no way were they getting involved. With good reason, thought Gail. That's why she kept telling Phil, 'You're the idiot. You've got the five kids and you're taking the risk.'

*

Bob Godden went to Europe to link the exhibits from the raids to the victims. It was shown, for example, that Simone Schmidl's tent was not sold in Australia and the salesman who sold her the sleeping bag and backpack remembered selling them to her. There was the tent swapped by Steven Wright for Joanne Walters' old tent. There were photos of Caroline Clarke's Benetton top to run by her friends and family.

On 1 September, police went to Chalinder Hughes' place with a search warrant looking for the top. Detective Sergeant Stuart Wilkins showed her the photo of her wearing it, but she refused to talk to him about it. Shirley, who had moved in with her after the arrest, was advising her, and everyone, not to talk to the cops. They didn't find the top, but the evidence was slowly mounting.

Five months after his arrest, Milat's committal hearing began at the late-Victorian Campbelltown Court House. The Crown had more than 310 witnesses of whom Milat's defence indicated it would test more than 200 in the dock. Forty witnesses were to be called from overseas.

An upstairs gallery was set aside to accommodate between sixty to eighty reporters. Paul Onions, living away from it all, didn't realise what a big case it was. 'The interest in the case blew my mind really. I shit myself,' he'd say later. 'I thought I could just walk into court and do my bit and that would be it. I knew it was big, like, but Geez.'

Now twenty-eight, he took the stand looking dapper in a light green double-breasted suit and green tie. His name had been suppressed in the preliminary court proceedings and he tried to have that continued, but Milat's barrister Cate Holmes wanted the order lifted. 'It is in the defence's interest that anybody who knows his name or knows anything about this case, comes forward. I would submit that the order be lifted.'

Magistrate Michael Price agreed and Onions' name and his dramatic story became public domain. As he told it, he was intensely aware of Milat's eyes bearing down upon him from only a few metres away.

Sitting over on the side of the court, detective Steve McLennan was watching Milat stare down every witness from the dock. The way his eyes followed them in and wouldn't leave. The only witness who he didn't face up to was his ex-wife Karen. She walked in and Milat's head went straight down, his chin to his chest, and stayed there as she detailed his love of guns and their visits to Belanglo.

Much of the committal was spent in the painstaking task of linking

Milat to all the equipment and the guns, slowly building the circumstantial case into a solid block of cohesive, damning detail. When Dr Bradhurst took the stand, however, a cat was thrown among the pigeons when Ian Lloyd QC asked him whether there could have been more than one killer.

'I would tend to think it more likely that more than one person was involved,' said the doctor. 'On the other hand, it is also my opinion it would still be possible for one to have caused the deaths if that person had been able to incapacitate one of the two at the time, before dealing with the other.' Bradhurst was surprised his comment caused such a stir in the court and in the papers next day. Being so close to it all, he'd just presumed that everybody would have been thinking that way.

The committal had been going a month when Ivan suddenly sacked his barrister Cate Holmes. Boe brought in another Brisbane advocate, Terry Martin. But Magistrate Price had refused him leave to appear because of the arcane rules about interstate advocacy. When Boe sought an adjournment for a few days to sort the defence team out, Price refused, so Boe withdrew. Left without a lawyer, Milat suddenly found himself being invited up to the bar table to defend himself.

'I can't defend myself,' said Milat. 'You're really crushing me... You've got all these charges on me and now you expect me to defend myself. I had a good legal team, especially after I got rid of John Marsden. I was quite happy here... I'm a road worker. Don't you read the newspapers. I'm not a solicitor.'[128]

He asked for an adjournment and when that was refused said, 'You may as well send me back down to the cells. I can't defend myself. I'm getting framed here for seven murders.'

Boe was soon back to defend Ivan and then Martin was cleared to appear.

As the committal had approached, Phil Polglase became increasingly nervy. Around mid-November he rang his mother and said: 'Don't be surprised if I'm not dead soon.'

She was too shocked to say anything.

He was absolutely certain someone was following him. And somebody was. Around the same time, he noticed a car tailing him to 'the mission' at Purfleet, where whitefellers stood out like dog's balls. Phil's mates stopped the car and chased the guy. Police later grabbed him only to discover he was a private investigator checking out Polglase's accident insurance claim.

Polglase visited the Shines on Friday, 25 November. He and Sandra Shine mostly just gossiped away. He didn't talk about the case or his fears so much. That was more men's business. He just told her: 'Sandy, I've told you "don't be scared", but I'm scared.'

'Why?' she asked.

He didn't want to go into it and neither did she, really. They went back to gossiping.

For all his fears, he was in a top mood on Saturday, 26 November. He had no money as usual, so his mate Reg Galati put ten bucks worth of juice in his car. They went to take a look at North Brother Mountain because it was the only place in the area Phil hadn't been. He was running around like a blue-arse fly – back to Reg's place at Johns River then down to the Coopernook pub for a few schooners of Tooheys New. It was the first time an acquaintance of his, Richard Gorton, had seen him in months. He was happy as Larry. Same old 'Polly'. Gorton knew him as a wild man. Saw him eat a seven-ounce glass once. The only thing he told Gorton about the shit going down was, 'What I know would really surprise you.' He left around nightfall and went back to Reg Galati's place where he and a mate, 'Tiny', had showers in preparation for heading to Port Macquarie to see Phil's brother Mick play in a band. But Tiny was pissed as anything and Reg convinced him not to go out. That left just Phil the gladiator to soldier on.

The gig was empty. Phil was virtually the only person at the bowling club to see Driftwood – two guitars, a sax and drum machine playing John Lennon–Neil Young sort of stuff. The two brothers then went to a nightclub and left around 4 a.m. They stopped at The Oak milk bar in Port Macquarie for a munch-out on sausage rolls and meat pies. As they headed home, Phil apparently dropped a pie at a roundabout and Mick would later say he ran into the back of Phil's car in his four-wheel drive. It left a dent in Phil's bumper. Then they drove off again into the night.

Gail Polglase was woken by Mick knocking at her door around 5 a.m., Sunday. He was in shock, not making much sense. Said Phil had been in a car accident. 'I think he's dead. I couldn't find a pulse.'

She was stunned. 'You left him?'

'Yeah.'

She couldn't understand why he'd do that, but she wasn't getting much out of him, other than it happened near the Johns River Bridge. She rang Reg Galati who lived close by. 'Phil's been in an accident. Mick gibbered on something about he didn't know if he was dead or alive when he left.' Galati jumped out of bed and sped the few hundred metres from his place to the bridge. The cops were already there as he pushed his way through to the half-crumpled Passat. Other cars crept by in a single lane, gawking.

Phil looked like he was asleep. Reg grabbed his mate's hand. It was cold, but his head was still warm. 'You fucking idiot. How the fuckin' hell d'you end up like this, Frank?' There were no marks on him, not a scratch on his face. He looked just like he used to when he slept on Reg's lounge and it'd take half an hour to wake him. Reg had his own little service in the car right there. He didn't want to see his mate in a box and, later, wouldn't go to the funeral.

Galati identified the body so Gail wouldn't have to see him.

He then had the job of ringing Gail. 'He is dead. He's gone.'

Later that day, Reg and his brother Mick Galati, with their sharp Mediterranean features and broad Australian accents, both qualified mechanics, went out to the scene to try and make sense of what happened. They were suss about it from the beginning and Reg couldn't help remembering how he'd promised Frank that if he died, he'd find out who done it.

What was certain was that as the road took a gentle left curve on the approach to the bridge, Phil's car had gone over to the left of the road and into the gravel. His car came out of the gravel and went right at about 45 degrees across the road, colliding with an oncoming Commodore, which wouldn't have seen him until he was about 75 metres away, owing to the curve and the low crest. The distance from his marks in the gravel to point of collision was about ten metres, as measured along the white markings put there by the accident investigation police. Phil's car stayed in the middle of the road and the north-bound driver ended up ten metres to the north.

And so the speculation began. Asleep at the wheel? Hit the gravel and over-corrected? Suicide by motor car? Phil had no money and couldn't afford to drink, so drunkenness wouldn't have been a factor.

Certainly, the rumours flew about the district that his death was no accident; that he was pushed off the road by a big black or red car. Mick Polglase told them he was driving ahead and when he noticed Phil wasn't behind him, he went back to see where he was and a red Falcon with a bullbar came flying past heading south. But the Galatis didn't think much of that story. Phil was in the Passat which could move along and it wasn't like Phil to follow anybody if he could help it, and Mick was only in the old Nissan four-wheel drive.[129]

They saw the dent in Phil's rear bumper bar. Reg knew it hadn't been there earlier when he put the petrol in. But Mick Polglase told them about the incident at the roundabout in Port Macquarie and that seemed to explain that. As far as suicide went, Reg Galati couldn't forget Phil's words. 'They'll have to kill me before I die, Frank,' he used to say.

'Five fuckin' kids, mate, and some cops were saying it was deliberate,' recalled Galati. 'Bullshit. I knew Frank, mate, and he'd never say die that bloke.'

The police investigators knew the importance of the case and it was gone into thoroughly. They found no suspicious circumstances.

For Mick Galati's money, however, it seemed like a third car was involved. Rammed him on the left and pushed him out into the middle of the road.

As in life, Phil was always running on empty. Reg calculated that with the ten dollars of petrol he put in Phil's car he would have run out right around the spot where the accident happened. They checked out the car a day or two later and the tank was empty, with no sign that it had ruptured in the crash. The gravel marks looked like he'd just pulled into the side of the road. If you'd run out of petrol it would have been a place where you could cruise to a halt. They speculated he was sitting there, maybe asleep with no foot on the brake, when he was rammed.

Richard Milat had been with Joe Marukic and Billie Marie Thomson all day Saturday and was around at their place on the Sunday afternoon when they heard the news that Phil Polglase was dead.

'Good,' he said, or words to that effect. He had no sympathy. Billie Marie was shocked by his indifference, but Polglase had tried to have the cops pin the murders on him, so she could kind of understand it.

*

With Phil gone, Gail's troubles with the lawyers, Stacks, continued and she faced losing the property. She sold some of the cows, except one in calf, but she couldn't bring herself to sell Phil's horse or his tools. She regretted now all the times Phil tried to talk to her about the case and she didn't want to know. She wished she'd been there to give him more support. Maybe it would have been different. Maybe she'd have appreciated more the extent of his heroism. Now he was dead and she hardly knew why.

Polglase's death knocked the wind out of the sails of those within the task force who thought Richard was involved. The task force was now divided by two views. The prevailing one came to be that Ivan had acted alone. He had tried to abduct Paul Onions alone, so that was his MO. These people didn't change. Cautious types like Rod Lynch, now in charge of the task force, had been very keen on the Polglase line of enquiry but had wavered as time went on. He wouldn't have used any of his evidence until they could do more work to stand it up. Some of it sounded real good, whereas other bits, particularly his chronology, seemed wrong.

There was the alternative view that Polglase was telling the truth and his memory was just a bit faulty but with more time it could have been stood up. This group – essentially pro-Richard as a suspect – argued that if MOs didn't change, why did the killer only start to shoot victims towards the end of the spree, well after the Onions attack. Both the anthropologist Basham and the psychiatrist Milton saw that as indicative of two people. They thought about Area A near the Neugebauer/Habschied scene. There were about 100 rounds fired off by two guns. Had one man fired fifty from one gun then fifty from the other, or were two people firing at once?

The pro-Richard faction had several points to work with. They had him talking at Boral about murders before they'd found the bodies. They had Polglase claiming to have seen a Salewa backpack with an internal frame. This corresponded to Simone Schmidl's pack, the one given to Joan and Alex by Ivan. They had Richard telling Polglase to keep his mouth shut.

When Richard's property was searched on the morning of the arrest, Richard only had property belonging to the British girls who were probably murdered the night Polglase said he stayed at the Milats.

They'd also found a red hairbrush in his green Datsun and had evidence that the first time Richard's girlfriend Liz saw it was when she came out of hospital, drying out, around mid-March 1993. She brushed her hair with it and, in the words of the police, her 'recollections were fortified' by her suspicions that he was having an affair. It looked so feminine. It was stamped with the word 'England' and both Clarke's parents identified the brush as similar to one owned by Caroline.

In his statement the day after the arrest, Richard had said that two or three weeks after moving all the gear from Ivan's to Wally's he went to his mother's home and picked up a cupboard containing the camping equipment. He admitted everything in there was his, except the camping gear. But his mother in her statement claimed that was Richard's cupboard for his exclusive use and, to her knowledge, Ivan did not use it. And his youngest brother Paul told police that Richard had camping gear in a cupboard at their mother's place.

The 'pro-Richard' faction to some extent wanted to score a goal for Rod Lynch, the man who'd taken over the task force almost immediately after Ivan Milat's arrest. If anything, they'd worked harder after the arrest trying to get the brief together, than they had before it. They saw Lynch as the direction behind it all, yet he was getting none of the credit.

The task force had shrunk to a core of about a dozen officers and, even though Polglase had passed on, they pushed the investigation further. A brief of evidence against Richard Milat was prepared and submitted to the Director of Public Prosecutions. The police suggested that at the very least they should be looking at a charge of attempting to pervert the course of justice or accessory after the fact. The evidence they had was well short of a murder brief that could stand up in court. Because he was dead, the rules of evidence would exclude all Polglase's statements as hearsay. The only evidence of Polglase's that a common law court might allow – depending on which judge you drew – would be the listening device evidence from the pub and, out of context, it wouldn't have been very persuasive to a jury.

Even Clive Small, publicly very strong on the one-killer theory, says he can't prove that either. 'The Milat family is a very complex family and it is quite obvious from things that they've said. If you take Alex. Alex Milat was quite happy, if you read his statement, to see a group of men taking a woman bound into the bush probably to rape her and he's not too worried about it. That's what comes out of his statement.

That was a bit of fun for boys, or something like that. So what I'm saying is the Milat family really appeared to tolerate a whole range of behaviour from its family members and other people that I would suggest are not normally tolerated. And I have got no doubt that members of the family were fully aware that Ivan was off the rails again, committing some sort of very serious crime. Whether they knew he was actually committing murders or whether they thought he was just raping women, I don't know. The fact is he is turning up with equipment out of the blue giving it to other members of the family . . . and there are no questions asked about where it is coming from, there is a sort of arrangement like that.'

Milat was committed to stand trial for the seven murders and the attempted murder of Onions. The trial was set down for 19 June 1995, just six months away. But the case was to be delayed for almost a year because the defence team was demanding more money from Legal Aid. They had the support of the trial judge, Justice David Hunt, but in the end that wasn't enough. Boe and Martin had to settle for the $2000 a day offered by the Legal Aid Commission. There were plenty of lawyers who would have done it for less, but as Justice Hunt told the commission: 'Some, I say with respect, I would not have appearing for me if I was up for an offence under the Dog Act . . . I have seen them in operation.'

FORTY-EIGHT

1995

JENOLAN STATE FOREST

Bob Benson had gone up to re-interview Alex, who was always full of suggestions for the coppers, but when he mentioned that there were lots of strange deaths around the Southern Highlands, it stayed in the copper's mind. 'Have you checked out any unsolved murders in the Jenolan State Forest?' The detectives didn't know what he was on about. He didn't elaborate any further. That was Alex. Benson continued with his interview but made a note to check it out.

Then Gary Miller and Steve McLennan found a file which had sat largely unopened for almost seven years.

At noon on Thursday, 21 January 1988, Mr Sajner Milos and his family were looking for a delicious type of wild mushroom just off a fire trail in the forest, 20 kilometres from Jenolan Caves. They had ventured only a short distance from their four-wheel drive when they stumbled upon the partially-clad decomposing remains of a man. Bushes and branches covered the body. It was just a skeletal upper torso with a badly decomposed lower half, clad in cut-down blue jeans, Parramatta rugby league socks and running shoes.

Two weeks passed before police learned the identity of the victim: Peter David Letcher, an eighteen-year-old unemployed sawmill worker from the central-western New South Wales town of Bathurst. Unsure of a motive, investigators followed a theory that the murder might have been drug related due to Letcher's marijuana use. A number of large marijuana plantations had been detected and destroyed in surrounding bushland. Letcher had travelled to Sydney to propose marriage to his teenage sweetheart, Leeann Caldwell, fifteen, who had moved from Bathurst to Busby, near Liverpool. She told him she wasn't ready to settle down.

Letcher left Busby on either 13 or 14 November 1987. He planned to catch a train home to Bathurst, but had changed his mind and decided to hitchhike the 160 kilometres over the Blue Mountains along the Great Western Highway. Detectives also established that he had obtained one brief lift from a man on a motorbike in the Liverpool area.

The things that jumped out at McLennan and Miller as they read the old file were the way he was shot five times in the back of the head with a .22, as if he had been held up for target practice, and the way his shirt had been wrapped around his head as a blindfold. He was shot through the material exactly as Caroline Clarke had been. The body was found face down in a hole created by a tree falling over and the roots coming out with it. About a metre deep, 1.5 metres wide, it was a ready-made grave, covered with sticks and leaf litter. The only difference between this and the backpacker murders was that it was in a pine plantation not native forest.

Letcher's body had only been there a few months, but it was the height of summer and there was very little left of his torso. Wild pigs and the summer heat had seen most of it decayed and scattered. There was no evidence of stab wounds but it was inconclusive because half his body was never found. The bullets, similarly, were eaten away by the corrosive reactions of the decay.

McLennan and Miller again checked Milat's record and found that, while Letcher probably disappeared on the Friday, Ivan started work on the Jenolan Caves road the following Monday. They learned from the co-workers that it was possible Milat could have gone up on the Sunday night to get an early start Monday.

These facts, compared to the MO at Belanglo, were too close to be mere coincidence, they thought. Although Jenolan Caves lay 80 kilometres north-west of Belanglo on the other side of the Great Dividing Range, his former wife Karen had also mentioned four-wheel driving in the area in 1983 and 1984 but, unlike most weekend visitors to the area, Ivan never took his family to the spectacular limestone caves. Karen left him nine months before Letcher was murdered.

The task force found Leeann Caldwell and her mother and the fellow who'd given Letcher a lift on the motorbike but none of them could shed any new light on the case. The kid had grown up dirt poor and in death was consigned a pauper's funeral. The only hope they had now of doing something for him was to find a shell to link him to one of Milat's firearms.

While not doubting the integrity of the first examination of the crime scene, Rod Lynch determined that a wider search of the area would be carried out in case the killer had fired on his victim from further away or left some other clue. They would also dig and sift the soil in the event that shells may have become trampled and buried.

They were all geared up for a large-scale search, but were twice rained out. Then the new Crown Prosecutor, Mark Tedeschi QC, didn't want them to go. He was nervous that it might give the defence ammunition that the trial was being prejudiced by the publicity.

They'd also looked at Ivan for the murder of Dianne Pennacchio, found in the Tallaganda State Forest, but his work records showed he would have had to drive for four hours after finishing his shift, abduct the woman and murder her, then drive another four hours to be on time to resume his next shift. He was capable of achieving such as feat, but it seemed unlikely.

In late February, Milat was hard pressed for cash and so he and Shirley were forced to put the house at 22 Cinnabar Street up for sale. The asking price was $189,950. In one advertisement placed by the real estate agent the house was featured under the heading: 'So Much Splendor'.

It stated: 'Immaculately presented home with the best of everything. Features four spacious bedrooms. Built-ins, ensuite and walk-in wardrobe to main. Formal lounge, formal dining. Huge timber kitchen with walk-in pantry, family room, internal access to LU garage. Landscaped yard. Make your day.'

The whole family was under intense pressure. Around this time, Ivan's sister-in-law, Carol Milat, was woken one night in February, about 12.30 a.m. 'Do you hear that?' she asked her husband, Bill.

'It's just your imagination,' he told her.

'I heard someone walking up the path, Bill. There's someone out there.'

'If there was someone there, the dog'd bark.'

Next morning, she opened the drapes and saw it straightaway. She went absolutely berserk. She propelled herself backwards away from the object so hard that her back hit the wall on the other side of the room, screaming: 'Police! Police! Police!' Neighbours heard her and thought it was actually a siren, before realising it was Carol. The next-door neighbour had to break the security lock on the front door to get in. He found her doubled over on the kitchen floor screaming.

'What's happening? What's happening?'

She tried to tell him but couldn't.

'Can you point?'

She tried, and after a while he got the idea and went over to the window and looked into the backyard. He went out and came back holding a human skull.

'It's not real. It's not real.' He shook her. 'It's not real. It's made out of concrete.' She slowly came to her senses, in shock, embarrassed. She'd piddled herself and somehow ripped a toe nail off in the frenzy. Carol rang Mark Feeney at Task Force Air and tried to tell him what happened, but she still hadn't regained control. He kept saying, 'I can't understand you.'

Carol felt like the incident had almost put her in a mental hospital. She'd strained all the muscles from her legs to lower abdomen. She couldn't talk for a week from all the screaming, and would go on to suffer an irrational fear every time she opened the blinds. She'd keep her doors locked at all times from now on.

FORTY-NINE

1996

TRIAL

Half the people in the public gallery have notepads. Some are students clocking up assignment time. Others have their own obscure reasons. As Milat comes in each day, the curious and the newcomers stand and peer over the semi-circular balcony to get a look at him, exhibit one. The best spot in the house is the front right corner, above the jury, where any citizen can see the exhibits as they're handed up, and all his reactions. You have to get there very early to get that seat. If you're late, you have to queue in the street until someone leaves before they'll let another person up through the metal detector. No bags allowed.

There is a skylight above, its sunlight boosted by fluorescent tubes, just as the words of witnesses and lawyers are amped up through invisible speakers in the walls which are gilded in mock gold leaf. If it wasn't so historic it'd be tacky. But this is wig and gown territory – the 101-year-old St James Road Supreme Court. The barristers wear black robes. The judge, Justice David Hunt, presides in red robes, and a bigger wig. His attendance each day is heralded by a black-frocked usher knocking on the door with a staff. But for the accents, it could be England, and Justice Hunt's intonation would just about qualify him for the Old Bailey. He swivels around in his big chair – 'business class' says one writer – presiding over it all with a dignified amiability.[130]

The eight men in the jury always file in first, followed by the four women.

The original Crown Prosecutor, Ian Lloyd QC, has taken up a job in Cambodia, helping to build a legal system there as the country grapples with a new constitution. His replacement, Mark Tedeschi QC, is a less flamboyant, but equally methodical character.

Tedeschi wants to make one thing clear to the jury. It doesn't matter, for the purposes of the trial, if Milat was alone or with an accomplice. The Crown can't prove it one way or the other. 'If there was another person or persons in the forest, the Crown says the accused and that person were acting together in causing those deaths.' He's just as guilty either way. The murders were for Ivan Milat's psychological gratification, 'killings for killings' sake', Tedeschi says.

Paul Onions is the first witness up. As cool as he looks as he struts into court, flanked by policemen much larger than himself, and surrounded by cameras, he is one scared puppy. He knows he's got it right, but the fear of wrongly putting a man away for life eats away at his confidence. Sitting in the dock, Onions is well aware of Milat's gaze; the grin always on the verge of breaking out. And the lips. There is something about the lips. When asked if he could see his attacker in the room, Milat had met Onions' gaze in what seemed like a long moment.

'Yes, it's the guy there,' Onions had gestured towards him.

He can't help but wonder what Milat really knows; about the gear that Milat stole off him and the other backpackers. He wonders if Milat read the letters from his girlfriend. He feels like it is a battle between him and defence counsel Terry Martin. He can feel Martin sizing him up, as he sizes up Martin. He keeps waiting for the barrister to start monstering him. He knows that if Martin can put cracks in his evidence, the flaws might start appearing in the whole case. He keeps waiting, and as the cross-examination drags on, he wonders why Martin isn't going the heavy.

There are times when it looks to be coming; when they talk about his ID of Milat on the video. His identification doesn't seem as strong, now, as it had at the committal.

'Mr Onions,' says Martin, 'I am suggesting to you that your identification of number four is mistaken, you understand? I am not calling you a liar by any stretch of the imagination, I am simply suggesting to you that you are mistaken in your identification. Do you agree with me or not?'

'For what reason? What mistake?'

'I am suggesting you made a mistake. That is all.'

'I find it hard to determine if I made a mistake. I am just looking at something that's the image I saw.'

'That is the image you saw?'

'Yeah.'

'And that is what you recall and you can't say anything more than that?'

'Yes. I was only there working on what image I see.'

'I'm sorry?'

'I was only working on what I could see. You understand.'

'You did your best?'

'Correct.'

The hellfire never comes. Martin, aware that Onions would have sympathy from the jurors only gently attacks the Englishman's original claim that his attacker was six foot tall and in his thirties. Milat was five foot eight and forty-five. Even when it is later shown that Onions was wrong in claiming that Milat's Nissan Patrol had chrome trim around the wheels and a spare tyre fitted to the back, the attack is blunt. It could open his evidence to intense scrutiny because Milat had both the spare tyre and the chrome trim fitted after Onions was attacked. So had he been told what to say by police? Onions explained the tyre away by saying he had a similar four-wheel drive on Fraser Island after the attack. It had a spare tyre on the back, so it confused him. Martin isn't interested in pursuing that angle. He has a different plan. Onions feels like he's got out easy, and the only answer he can come up with is that Martin knows that he isn't lying – that Milat is guilty – so the barrister had gone easier than he might otherwise have done. That's what Onions thinks anyway.[131]

Patricia Everist is the first of the parents to give evidence because Deborah and James disappeared first. The whole courtroom scene doesn't seem real to her. After each of the parents gives evidence they are allowed to sit in the public gallery where they have reserved seats on the impossibly hard benches directly above Milat. A perspex panel in front of them stops anything being dropped over the rail. Sitting up in the gallery, Patricia Everist wants to lash out, wants to scream. 'You have taken away from us something that can never be given back. You have deprived someone of the greatest gift they can ever have – life.' It is the first time [in her life] she has faced evil. But she just sits there.

Manfred Neugebauer is struck by the way Milat doesn't appear evil. He can't reconcile the image of the beast that killed his son with this ordinary man in front of him. 'If he is the one, it must be proved, because he looks so much like a normal citizen,' reasoned the good burgher. The coming months of evidence will change him. Sure enough, he grows to dislike Milat intensely. He is still able to entertain doubts. There are times when his confidence in Milat's guilt wavers. Onions' identification of the spare tyre, for example. But it is so outweighed by the points against Milat, these doubts subside, as they do for just about everyone who spends time in the court.

As the days blur into months, images remain: Simone Schmidl's father leaving the witness stand, shaking his clenched right fist down by his side and whispering something – a German expletive say those who are close – as he passes less than a metre from Milat; Joanne Walters' mother, Jill, being led, hunched, shaking and sobbing to the stand, and being excused almost immediately by Justice Hunt owing to her obvious frailty; the old woman in the gallery who doesn't mind letting it be known that the female victims brought it on themselves, 'hanging around all those blokes', before she is ushered out; the cold, hard steel of a sword shown to Dr Bradhurst who thinks such a weapon could have decapitated Anja Habschied; the tedium of stuffy afternoons with benches creaking while hundreds of photographs are painstakingly explained into evidence; Bill Milat beating up a photographer outside court after Carol copped a hard time from Tedeschi over the photo of Mac with the dates changed. That image gets beamed around the world. Of 356 exhibits tendered, none conveyed the horror of the victims' last moments more so than the navy blue T-shirt Joanne Walters had been wearing when attacked. Displayed on large white cardboard backing, it bore a multitude of cuts front and back. This brought a dramatic hush over the courtroom, the silence broken only by Mrs Walters weeping from the gallery.

The most illuminating days, however, are often those allocated to legal argument when the jury is absent and the court empty of all but one or two reporters who pop in every now and then. It is during these sessions that it first becomes obvious what the defence – Ivan – is planning to do.

In open court, it seeps out only slowly. Terry Martin asks Wally about his age, forty-four, his height, five foot three, and his claim that he didn't have a moustache in January 1990 when Onions was attacked. He admits he did have access to a revolver in January 1990 – a 3/57 Magnum, with a four-and-a-half-inch barrel. Martin establishes that he worked for the DMR twelve years earlier, and was divorced. He had access to rope. He wore sunglasses, and he knew where Lombardo's was.

Martin: 'Did you attack a backpacker by the name of Onions in January 1990?'

'No.'

'Mr Milat, a number of items were taken from your house including machetes?'

'Yes.'

'Were any axes taken?'

'I don't know.'

'Did you have any axes at your house at the time of the police raid?'

'Yeah.'

'And also a large number of knives were seized, is that right?'

'Yeah.'

'Some twenty-one knives, is that right?'

'I'm not sure how many, but there were quite a few there.'

'Were they butcher knives?'

'They were all sorts of knives.'

Wally then admits that he sold a .45 calibre pistol which Shirley had dug out of the backyard on Ivan's instructions from jail.

Martin: 'What do you say to the suggestion that you killed persons found in the Belanglo State Forest?'

'I didn't.'

'What do you say to the suggestion that you had some part to play in that?'

'I had no part in it.'

As it turns out, much of the trial is shadow boxing. The defence isn't engaging. For example, in order to show motive, the prosecution had geared up to demonstrate that the brutality of the attacks was such that killing the person was the prime objective, as opposed to, say, a robbery where the victim is murdered so they can't identify the culprit. Tedeschi has to show the jury that the act of killing and the pleasure gained from that, is the motive for these murders. And, of course, the jury would be suitably horrified by the evidence and would look across at Milat and wonder at the enormity of it all.

But before the brutality evidence is heard, the judge stops play: 'Mr Milat, on the evidence adduced at the committal proceedings and on the advice of your counsel, do you admit the following matters of fact which are not within your personal knowledge and the conclusions therefrom, that the only reasonable inference to be drawn is that the force used on each of the victims in counts one and two and four to eight was unusual and unnecessary and vastly more than was necessary to kill?'

'Yes, sir,' says Milat, effectively shielding the jury from much of the horror.

Similarly, he later admits that gear found at his house and at Richard's and Wally's is most likely the property of the missing backpackers. Only he has no idea how it got there. This stops the jury from having to look at the mountain of evidence against him, piece by piece. This way, it looks bad, but it is all over quickly. But he won't admit to Caroline Clarke's camera. There is no definitive ID on it, and it had contained an undeveloped roll of photos taken around his house, so it could show that the camera had not just been mysteriously put there.

And, daily, from a modern courtroom over the road, at the Police Royal Commission, come reports of police loading up suspects, fabricating confessions, stealing money, receiving corrupt payments. The first detective to investigate the Clarke/Walters disappearance, Neville Scullion, is one of the star villains, having rolled over and admitted his corruption after being confronted by overwhelming evidence.

If ever a jury was going to believe a claim that an accused has been framed it is now. On the day that Peter O'Connor gives evidence of searching the house and finding, among other things, the Ruger parts in the ceiling, the cynical are expecting a long afternoon of I-put-it-to-you-officer-that-you-placed-that-item-there type questioning, but it never comes, and O'Connor is out of the box in a short time. Martin is dancing around the ring, not swinging. Such a defence would go against his main counter punch, which he is saving for the final round.

His thrust is, however, becoming clear. With Wally in the stand, he puts it to the brother that he planted guns at Ivan's on the day that he and Richard took the guns away from Ivan's place.

'Did you put anything else in the house?' asks Martin.

'Like what?'

'Like gun parts in the cavity of the wall up in the ceiling of the house?'

'No.'

'What about a receiver to a Ruger 10/22? What do you say to the suggestion you placed a receiver to a Ruger 10/22 rifle in the hall cupboard of that house?'

'No, that's wrong too.'

'Did you place it in one of Ivan Milat's boots in the hall cupboard?'

'No.'

Martin needs Wally to have a motive for doing all this, so he suggests it was resentment dating back to Wally's suspicions that Ivan was having an affair with his ex-wife Maureen. Wally replies that he held no bitterness towards Ivan. He has never really thought about it. Doesn't worry him. That's it for motives.

Crown Prosecutor Mark Tedeschi, well aware of the looming defence tactic to shift blame towards the brothers, cuts to the chase early when Richard comes up in the dock sporting a moustache, unlike his clean-shaven appearance at his gun charge matters. 'Are you in any way responsible for the deaths of any of the seven backpackers whose bodies were found in the Belanglo State Forest?' he asks.

'No, I had nothing to do with the deaths.'

'Were you ever present in the Belanglo State Forest with any person who caused the death of any of the seven backpackers?'

'No.'

'Have you ever fired a Ruger 10/22 rifle in the Belanglo State Forest?'

'No.' And on it goes. Had he fired an Anschutz there? Had he stabbed anyone there? Did he know who did? No. No. No.

Having already ruthlessly shown Wally up as a liar on the ownership of a Ruger 10/22 – not the murder weapon – Tedeschi goes on to undermine any credibility Richard might have.

He reminds Richard of the day detectives asked him about the blue Sierra day pack found at his caravan.

'Why did you tell Detective Pickering that you did not recognise it?' Tedeschi asks.

'I don't know.'

'Were you lying to him?'

'Yes.'

'Deliberately?'

'Not deliberately.'

'You agreed that you lied to Detective Pickering?'
'Yes.'
'Have you agreed that you have lied to the court? Is that right?'
'About my statement, saying that to Mr Pickering, yes.'
'Yes, well, are you a person who lies all the time?'
'No.'
'Would you lie to protect yourself?'
'Possibly.'
'Would you lie to protect your mother?'
'I don't know.'
'Would you lie to protect a member of your family generally?'
'Possibly.'
'Well, would you lie about a matter that was very serious?'
'Possibly.'
'Would you lie about a matter that was trivial?'
'Possibly.'
'Would you lie in fact about anything?'
'I'm not sure.'
'Is it possible that you would lie about anything?'
'Anything is possible.'
'Have you deliberately come to court to try and give your evidence in a way which is designed with the aim in mind of trying to assist your brother Ivan Milat?'
'No.'
'Is that a lie?'
'No.'
'Have you told any other lies?'
'Not as far as I know.'
'Is it possible that you have told some other lies?'
'I couldn't be sure. That's why I have said in all my other answers, I'm not sure.'

Terry Martin uses his cross-examination to establish that Richard knew the layout of 22 Cinnabar Street. Richard says he didn't have a key but could probably have got access to the place, except that he could never remember the alarm code.

'1, 2, 3, 4,' says Martin, helpfully. 'Does that ring a bell?'

'Not to me.'

This is all designed to show that Richard could have got into the house to plant all the gear on his brother. A motive for that, however, is never proffered. Then Martin gets down to the serious business of making out that Richard, not Ivan, attacked Paul Onions. 'What height are you please?'

'Not quite sure, five foot ten, something like that.'

'What age are you?'

'I am forty now.'

'You are forty now, so in January 1990 you would have been in your mid-thirties?'

'Yes.'

'In January 1990 would you have had a thick moustache going down the side of your mouth?'

'I couldn't be sure.'

'You may have had, or may not?'

'Yeah, I couldn't be sure.'

'In January 1990 you had access to a revolver is that correct?'

'Yes.'

'Your father was Yugoslav?'

'Yes.'

'Did you have access to a silver or silvery-coloured four-wheel drive, apart from Ivan Milat's, in January 1990?'

Not as far as he knows, but he admits he could have hired one. He admits he wore shorts.

'Are you a racist, Mr Milat?'

'Not as far as I am concerned.'

'Look at it this way, do you think that there are too many Asians coming to Australia?'

'Yes,' Richard says, explaining that he's held that belief for a long time.

'Did you express that belief to any person or persons?'

'I don't think so.'

'You just kept it to yourself?'

'I could have mentioned it to somebody.'

'Did you mention it to a Mr Paul Onions an English backpacker who was attacked along the Hume Highway on the 25th of January, 1990?'

'No.'

'What do you say to the suggestion that you attacked Paul Onions along the Hume Highway after picking him up at Lombardo's shopping centre at Casula?'

'It weren't me.'

Richard agrees that he had different beards and moustaches at different times.

'Why have you always done that?' Martin asks.

'Just like why do some people have short hair and other people have longer hair? Just what you feel like.'

'What about the colour of your hair? What do you say to the suggestion that you made your hair lighter and darker?'

'No, I don't agree with that suggestion.'

'During that period at Boral?'

'Only once. It was before I went to Boral.'

'What do you say to the suggestion you killed the persons whose bodies were found in the Belanglo State Forest?'

'I would say that's a lie.'

'Or any of them?'

'That's a lie.'

'What do you say to the suggestion that you planted items in Ivan Milat's house?'

'I would say I never did.'

'You never did it? What do you say to the suggestion you planted Ruger gun parts in a cavity in the ceiling of Ivan Milat's house?'

'I never did it.'

Martin then goes on to Richard's rantings at Boral. 'Did you ever say to Des Butler words to the effect, "I know who killed the Germans"?'

'Not as far as I know.'

'Well, Mr Milat, please think about it. Did you ever say words like that to Des Butler?'

'Not as far as I know.'

'Why should there be any doubt? You either know whether you said it, or did not, don't you?'

'I don't know what happened years ago. I can't remember everything.'

'Can you conceive of any reason why you might say to Des Butler, "I know who killed the Germans"?'

'No, I can't see no reason why I would say that.'

Martin asks if he recalls saying that stabbing a woman is like cutting a loaf of bread.

'No, I don't remember saying that.'
'Did you say anything like that?'
'Not as far as I know.'
'Well, is that a thought that you do in fact have?'
'No, I never had that thought.'

After twelve weeks building a damning circumstantial case, the prosecution rests, having called 145 witnesses. At 12.45 p.m. on 17 June, the first of six witnesses for the defence is Ivan Milat. It's a surprise move. Most in the gallery have presumed he would hide behind a 'statement from the dock' whereby he can address the jury without being cross-examined. But he backs his ability to stand up to what will likely be days of cross-examination from Tedeschi.

In front of a court packed with anticipation, Milat, his deep voice resonating through the microphone, calmly and clearly answers questions from Martin. He denies being the killer; was in no way involved in their deaths; had no knowledge of the crimes. Dressed neatly in his court uniform – navy suit and/or navy jumper – that he wore each day, Milat listens attentively to the questions. He's never been to Belanglo, never owned a Ruger 10/22. He agrees, however, that he had used the name Bill in 1988. 'I was going through a divorce and my wife was sort of taking me to the cleaners, so I quit my job with the DMR and went and worked under another name,' he says.

Why did he move all the gear to Wally's place?

'I had heard the police were making enquiries about some of my guns and that is the main reason and also for better security. I knew if they came to my place, if they searched the place, they would see I had some illegal type rifles there.'

He has no idea where Chalinder got the Benetton top from. He doesn't know where any of the gear came from. Someone must have planted it. He thought Caroline Clarke's camera was Shirley's. He says he asked Richard who owned Simone Schmidl's backpack, 'and he said "nobody really owned it" and I said, "can I have it?"' Ivan says he then gave it to Alex's wife, Joan, before they headed up to Queensland.

After all the anticipation, his answers quickly become tedious and predictable. The following day, during the first of three days cross-examination, Tedeschi explores the theme of Ivan having been loaded up with all this gear in separate places at different times.

'They are amazing coincidences, Mr Milat,' says Tedeschi.

'Oh, well, yes I suppose so.'

Milat says he isn't suggesting police planted anything, but someone had planted the Ruger parts in his wall and in his boot. Someone planted Simone Schmidl's water bottle in his cupboard, her cooking set in his pantry and her tent in his garage. (Indeed, for police to have planted Simone Schmidl's backpack, they would have had to have done it before her body was found in order for Ivan to give it to Joan, and they would have had to plant Caroline Clarke's Benetton top in 1992 for it to be photographed on Chalinder.)

The shadow boxing and the tactical retreats continue. The police had gone to great lengths to prove Milat owned the boot found at Campbell Hill Road in which a camouflaged Ruger receiver had been hidden. Tedeschi had spent a lot of time getting it all into evidence. Then Milat takes the stand and admits it is his.

Extend the opponent; pull back; counter attack.

Tedeschi asks how the Indonesian currency got into his bedroom drawers.

'Are you mystified by it?' asks Milat. 'Because I am.'

Milat says he knows nothing about Schmidl's blue day pack found at Wally's place.

'You didn't take this from Simone Schmidl?' Tedeschi asks.

'I didn't take it from anyone.' He says someone must have planted two of his gun magazines in the pack, plus cartridges which matched the ones from his place. 'Obviously, somebody is trying to make me look real bad,' he offers by way of explanation.

Milat agrees that his burglar alarm had never gone off when he was out, and that, yes, the person who planted the parts must have known the code. It is sheer coincidence, though, that the parts were painted camouflage colours which, he agrees, he painted on his belongings.

The book on converting the Ruger to fully automatic was just 'interesting reading, that was all it was. I liked reading about them things'. The Browning pistol found under his washing machine was his, he says, but he had not seen it since he split with Karen in 1987. (That is, when police could last link it to him.) Shown his paintball face mask, he says he did not engrave a skull and crossbones and the initials IM on it.

'Did you hear any suspicious engraving noises at night?' Tedeschi asks, raising a chuckle.

'No,' replies Milat.

The next day it is more of the same. Tedeschi runs through Onions' description of his attacker – grey flecks in his sidelevers, Australian accent, dark hair, strong, used the name Bill, worked on the roads, divorced, had family from Yugoslavia, Merv Hughes moustache, white or silver Nissan two-door four-wheel drive with bullbar and running board, lambs-wool seat covers kept clean and cassettes between the front seats.

'Do you know of any other person in this world who has all of those features that I just mentioned, including features of your car?' Tedeschi asks.

'No,' Milat says.

Moving on to the gun buried in the bucket in the backyard – which Milat had already admitting asking Shirley to dispose of – Tedeschi asks: 'You had been charged with serious offences and your brother and sister were prepared to assist you to get rid of a firearm buried in your back garden?'

'Yes.'

Milat admits telling his niece's boyfriend, a security guard, that he would not mind a set of handcuffs. 'They just seemed to be interesting that's all . . . I didn't really expect him to get me a set.'

'You were interested in getting handcuffs to tie people up.'

'No.'

And on it goes.

The defence wraps up its case several days later after showing the jury blown-up photos of cricketer Merv Hughes and Ivan Milat. In the photos, Milat is wearing a Batman cap and earmuffs and his moustache is thinner and straighter than the cricketer's. He had earlier tried to deny even having a Merv Hughes at the time of Onions' disappearance, but one of his workmates found the photo and could link it to the job they were doing – thirteen days before Onions was attacked.

*

When, towards the end of the trial, Paul Onions starts hearing that the defence is saying it was Wally or Richard who might have been the murderers, he is horrified. If someone met him or his brother Simon, then had to identify them six years down the track, it'd be easy to mix them up. He knows the police are being harangued by the defence for not showing him a mug shot of Richard in the video when he first identified Ivan. He wishes they had. But he can't understand why the defence doesn't just call him now and get him to have a look at Richard. He is putting Ivan away for life, fucking hell, if they are identical lookalikes he doesn't want to be responsible for that. Why don't they bring Richard in and get this cleared up?

He doesn't realise that the defence can't risk that because Richard and Ivan don't look much alike at all. If he gives an emphatic 'no' to Richard and Wally, the whole defence case will fall down. All Martin has to do is create doubt, not prove innocence.

And Martin knows that a prosecution witness who has been looking at pictures of Milat for two years and has seen him so often in the witness box would now never concede having made such an error.

Onions doesn't realise any of this, so the stress of the enormous responsibility just sits on him. It's the weight of the world.

When the closing addresses begin in the trial's fifteenth week, Tedeschi tells the jury not to be seduced by the defence throwing Richard and Wally in to the spotlight. Anticipating the defence line to follow, he asks why Milat would keep all the incriminating evidence found at his house when he knew police were making inquiries about him.

'Well, ladies and gentlemen, the answer is this. This accused never dreamt that there would be a blitz, a blitzkrieg that took place on 22 May 1994 . . . Ladies and gentlemen, this is a man who had the utter arrogance to fire a shot during an attempted abduction of Mr Onions on the Hume Highway with cars whizzing by . . . that was the level of his confidence, that he was prepared to do that and he got away with it, nothing happened, nobody came knocking at his door a few days later. Indeed, the very abduction of the backpackers, taking them in a vehicle along a road where, for all he knew, forestry officers might come along during the time that the backpackers must have been alive in the forest. There was always the possibility that someone would drive along these dirt fire trails, come upon them. So, the incredible arrogance and the unbelievable self-confidence that the murderer had is exactly the kind of arrogance and self-confidence that led the accused to believe that no one was going to come to his house and come straight in and search it.'

Tedeschi says that 'the evidence strongly suggests a very real possibility of more than one person being responsible for at least some of the deceased backpackers'. Talking about the leash found near the Neugebauer/Habschied scene, he reminds them that it was made up of four pieces – cable ties, sash cord, electrical tape and a brown leather strap – all of which were matched to very similar items in Milat's garage. 'There would be very few, if any, garages in New South Wales that have all four items that can be linked in the way these items can be linked to the accused's garage . . . It is almost as though the accused left a fingerprint in the forest.'

His final address spills over into the next day which he uses to attack the defence's failure to call Ivan's sister Shirley Soire who might have been able to shed some light on all the possessions found in the house they shared.

'This is the Shirley Soire who has been good enough to bring witnesses to court, like her brother Walter,' he says. 'She was good enough to bring them to court, but not good enough to come through those double doors, go to the witness box and take the oath to tell the truth, the whole truth and nothing but the truth.' He points out that she might have been able to help them with Caroline Clarke's Benetton top and camera, Schmidl's cooking set found in her kitchen, and Schmidl's tent in her garage.

Tedeschi's address blows over into a third day. He concedes that the Crown does not deny Milat may not have been alone at the killings 'and we say it is possible, if there was someone else, that it was some member of his family'.

And so it is left to Terry Martin to rise and save the case; to tell the jury why all this is not enough to convict his client. He starts safely enough, reminding the jurors his client is 'facing the worst possible charges imaginable in Australian history' and that they have the worst job in the country.

'Need I remind you,' he says, 'it is a fundamental submission that whoever has planted the gear on Ivan Milat is, or is involved with, a serial killer ... Do you think a person capable of that behaviour would do anything to avoid conviction? Do you really want an explanation beyond that?'

Martin is through pulling back: 'There can be absolutely no doubt that whoever committed all eight offences must be within the Milat family or very, very closely associated to it. Blind Freddy can see that. There can be absolutely no doubt.' His speech grows in vigour. 'Who has committed these eight offences? The question is, do you have a reasonable doubt that it was Ivan Milat as opposed to someone else in the family? Well, that is the starting point. It has to be ...' There. Crunch. It is out. 'Whichever way you look at it, it is absolutely irrefutable that whoever has committed these eight offences must be either within the Milat family or so very closely associated with it, it does not much matter. The question is, who is it within the Milat family?' There is no more beating about the bush. The murderer is family. Blood. Ivan as good as says so himself. He must have approved this defence; must have initiated it. He could force his counsel to withdraw it at any time. Could sack them again. The family had no idea Ivan's lawyer was about to turn the blow torch on to Wally and Richard, yet they accept it.

Martin had already intimated in cross-examination that the killer was maybe Richard or Wally, but here he is saying it isn't my client, and it isn't likely to be anyone outside the family ... Add it up ... Similarly, he argues that whoever introduced himself to Onions as Bill, the divorced road worker, must have done so to put the blame on Ivan. So again, by extension, he's saying one of the Milat boys has done this to Ivan on purpose. The same brother has planted all the gear on Ivan in early 1994. (This scenario, perhaps, forgets Ivan giving Simone Schmidl's backpack to Alex and Joan more than a year earlier.) Was it Wally, smarting over a possible affair between his ex-wife Maureen and Ivan?

Martin attacks the police for not showing a picture of Richard Milat in the video from which Onions identified Ivan, but as was later pointed out by the Court of Criminal Appeal, he also criticises them for not including more men with Merv Hughes moustaches, and there is no known photo of Richard with a Merv Hughes.

Martin also points out that Richard was much closer to two significant points in Onions' description of his attacker: thirty-five-years-old and six foot tall. Richard was five foot ten and thirty-three in January

1990. He is more overtly anti-Asian than Ivan. Assuming he had a beard at the time, he could have shaved it down to a Merv Hughes.

He was rostered to work on the day of the Onions attack, but Martin argues that Richard could have got off early because of the de facto hour-on-hour-off system at Boral and been there to pick Onions up around 1 p.m. He could have got hold of one of the four-wheel drives that he fixed for workmates, or he could have stolen one. And as for Richard's comments about stabbing a woman being like slicing bread, he asks the jury: 'Is it not highly suggestive that Richard Milat is the killer? ... Why would anyone say anything as hideous as that in a joking fashion? ... Why is his face not on the video? Members of the jury, it could not be, could it, that Mr Onions has noted a family resemblance in Ivan Milat and that has triggered a memory. It could not be, could it, that Richard Milat was Mr Onions' attacker? Could it?'

And he tells the jury if they have a reasonable doubt that Ivan attacked Onions, then they must find him not guilty of all the murders.

He goes on to the spare tyre which both Onions and Berry said they saw. 'They didn't get it wrong. The vehicle that was used by the attacker had the back wheel on the back of it. There could not be any other explanation for two witnesses both saying the same thing.'

On the sixty-fourth day of the trial, a juror receives an anonymous phone call from a man who simply says: 'If you find my ... Look out, if you find him guilty, you're dead.' Hunt discharges the juror before he has contact with other jurors, avoiding having to abort the trial. It is found that the call came from Queensland.[132]

Hunt begins his summation on a Thursday and wraps it up the following Wednesday, 24 July. Amongst it all, he tells the jury that common sense suggests there was more than one killer, particularly since six of the victims were in pairs, but they the jury have to ask whether the reasonable possibility that Richard was involved excludes proof beyond reasonable doubt that Ivan was there too. He suggests they concentrate on the evidence that directly links Milat to the killings – the bloody sash cord, the Ruger parts and him getting a bullet hole in his car door fixed a week after Neugebauer and Habschied disappeared.

He sends the jury out to consider its verdict at 2.42 p.m., 24 July. The jury room is barely able to hold them all plus the 331 exhibits. 'I hope that I do not insult your intelligence,' says Hunt, 'when I point out that you have amongst those exhibits a considerable number of firearms and a considerable amount of ammunition, both of which are no doubt in reasonable working order. Please do not put any cartridges into any weapons, or try any experiments, as accidents can easily happen.'

There is nothing for it now, but to wait. Reporters loitering around the building quickly organise a sweep on when the jury will return. Most of the twenty or so entries go for a deliberation of between a few hours and two days. They wait and gossip and hypothesise around the court through the crisp blue July days. And one by one their bets on the jury's return blow out, as 5 p.m. Wednesday, 5 p.m. Thursday and 5 p.m. Friday roll by. A tiny doubt starts to creep into their collective mind.

The Milat family, counting on a not guilty verdict, plan to bring Ivan home for dinner at Bill and Carol's then whisk him off to a series of friends' places until it all blows over. Detectives are still confident of a conviction, but the jury is always an unknown. Steve McLennan tells Les Kennedy with a degree of sorrow in his voice: 'I don't know if I could face the relatives if he got off, I just couldn't face them.'

Saturday comes. Kieren Perkins is about to swim the 1500 metres final at the Atlanta Olympics when news that the jury is back comes down to the street. Everybody rushes inside for the verdict.

FIFTY

1996

THE PACK

Shirley had come around to Bill and Carol Milat's place in January 1996 with a pile of photos and a very worried look on her face. Three weeks earlier, Bill and Carol had put on a big Christmas party with an air castle for the kids, and everybody had a great time despite the weight hanging over the family. Shirley brought out the happy snaps, and they were all having a good giggle when she hit them for more cash. Ivan needed it for his defence, she said.

'We can't pay,' Bill told her. 'We don't have the money.'

But Shirley begged. Balled her eyes out. Their daughter Debbie walked out of the room in disgust, thinking Shirley was putting it on.

'He's going to be locked away for life if we don't get that money.[133] He's going to die in jail.'

Bill thought about it for a few moments, then said: 'We'll do it.' Carol couldn't believe what she was hearing. In twenty-three years of marriage, they had never once argued about money, but Carol blew up after Shirley left that night. A frugal, sensible couple, they had lived within their means and had saved and built a nice home. They were comfortable. Generally, when they talked about buying something on credit, they'd asked themselves if they really needed it. The answer was usually no.

Bill went to the bank next day, Monday, 16 January, to mortgage the house. Their credit was good and they had a $40,000 cheque for Ivan's legal fighting fund.

On their next visit to jail, Mac almost fell off his chair when they told him how much they'd borrowed.[134] Shirley had told Ivan they'd only borrowed $20,000.

Shirley said she'd pay the money back within six months, but they hadn't seen any of it by that time. They were struggling with the repayments and interest was accruing and they were desperate for money so, when a young filmmaker, Luke Bracken, was introduced to them by Wally's ex, Maureen, they were happy to listen to his offer.

He was also an old friend of John Marsden's, too, so they trusted him. Bracken wanted to make a documentary using footage from Bill and Carol's home videos. One showed Carol's fortieth birthday two months before Mac's arrest, another was taken while they were camping; all sitting around singing a jingle from a Toyota ad and jumping up in the air. It was really silly and Carol felt a bit stupid letting anyone see it, but they needed the money.

Bracken had approached the country's top-rating current affairs show, '60 Minutes', sounding out a deal. The producers were interested, but knew it wouldn't be acceptable to pay any member of the Milat family for their story. The producers agreed, however, to pay Bracken generously if he could deliver the Milats to an interview.

Bracken told Bill and Carol: 'We can't accept money through '60 Minutes', but I'm going to do a story with the videos and take that to England with me. Then you'll get payment through England.'[135]

'Okay.'

To their minds, they weren't defending a serial killer, they were helping a brother, but they were still unsure whether to do the interview. Carol asked Ivan what he thought. 'Do what you think is morally right,' he said. 'And if you can get any money out of it, do it.'

Still, they were undecided. Bracken was coming down night after night as the trial dragged on: 'Think of your mother-in-law,' he'd tell Carol. 'She's elderly. She needs her name cleared. You've got to do it for her.' They'd had a lot of reporters asking for interviews saying all sorts of similar stuff, but she believed Luke.

When the jury was out, Bill and Carol finally agreed to the interview and, right at the last minute, Richard agreed to be in it too. He babbled his way through and generally looked bad. They never got paid and Bracken received a considerable sum for teeing them up, but he could not interest anyone in his doco. Bill and Carol felt betrayed.

There were other elements to the story which '60 Minutes' needed. The 1971 'rape' victim Margaret was offered $20,000 by the

Channel Nine flagship,[136] but she didn't take it. She resented her friend Greta being paid a considerable sum by Channel Seven for its special on the case. She claimed it was $50,000 obtained through an agent.

Channel Nine's upmarket current affairs show, 'Sunday', had got in with Andrew Boe for a story from the defence perspective. The reporter Helen Dalley and producer Peter Hiscock didn't cover the trial, so they were probably the only journos on the case who weren't confident of Milat's guilt, which gave them a fresh eye.

Paul Gordon was just waiting there to be done. He'd left the force, disillusioned, a year after Small sacked him, his career in ruins. It took a few phone calls to find him selling investment units in Queensland but, when they did, he was nervous about talking. In their first meeting, he didn't say much. But his disillusionment with the way the investigation had gone, and Clive Small's management, was obvious. He didn't want money. That helped convince them he was genuine.

It would have been easy to portray him as the hero who nabbed the Milats and then was hard done by, but he didn't want that either, he told them. He wanted it to go further, to seriously analyse the investigation and see where the flaws were. First he wanted them to check out his credibility. 'I'm not corrupt. I haven't been up before the Royal Commission. You come back and tell me what you find out.' He came up clean.

Still, theirs was shaping as a story against the mainstream. Here was a copper saying the task force was flawed and there were serious mistakes made by the leadership, when all about them were lauding the team as heroes. It wasn't easy to accept. Where was the evidence? They had to sell it to their own boss for a start.

The friends of Gordon told them there'd been other complaints about Small, his management style, his ego. At the same time, the reporters heard from their news colleagues that various police were bad-mouthing Gordon – that he was a disgruntled bum whose allegations didn't stand up. Dalley found it interesting the way so many of the media followed the accepted line.

There was also an expectation that they were going to run some pro-Milat story because they were co-operating a bit too closely with the defence, but the more they got into the Gordon angle the more their story drifted away from Boe. They explored how the computer system was hopeless and how Small had been so slow to give the go ahead for phone taps and got in some experienced ex-cops from outside New South Wales to say so. Like every other news organisation they faced a brick wall in getting any official comment from the task force. Police claimed the silence was based on legal advice. Which, if it were the case, meant they had been acting irresponsibly in just about every other newsworthy case that ever went through a court. It is exceedingly common for police to talk in detail about cases on the understanding that nothing is published until after the verdict. In this case, they could neither claim credit for their good work, nor defend allegations of bad work.

Dalley and Hiscock lucked out with every hour the jury stayed out. When the verdict came back on Saturday, it put them in the box seat.

The *Daily Telegraph* was geared to publish ten pages on Milat, including a scoop on the secret bugging of Richard through Phil Polglase. By mid-afternoon on Friday, the *Telegraph* and *Herald* teams were despairing that the jury would come back on Saturday. Anything but Saturday. It meant the Sunday press would steal their thunder.

All that was missing from the *Telegraph*'s coverage was comment from Richard Milat about Polglase and defence claims that another Milat was the murderer. The task of fronting him fell to deputy chief-of-staff Mark Morri. As a police reporter for the old *Daily Mirror*, 'Moz' had covered the 1990 disappearance of Gibson and Everist. He was a veteran of many a hard 'knock' but nobody was too sure how Richard would react to the Polglase allegations. The *Telegraph* hired a corporate security guard – an ex-commando – to accompany him. The first address they knocked was Bill Milat's at Bargo.

Early winter's darkness had set in when they arrived to find voices coming from the garage. Morri called out and as the garage door opened, his minder told him to keep out of the light. Bill came out with Richard who was holding a hammer. The two brothers were working on a car inside. Morri introduced himself and stepped into the light. Then he dropped Richard's meeting with Polglase on him and the fact it was bugged. Richard said he knew Polglase, but he didn't know what the heck Morri was on about. Bill stood behind telling him: 'Don't say anything, don't say anything.' Morri didn't realise they had an arrangement with '60 Minutes'.

At 10.56 a.m. on Saturday, 27 July, the remaining eleven jurors file into the court for the last time. It is a tense moment as Milat stands. The foreman is asked how the jury find on the charge of the wilful murder of Deborah Everist. The foreman, a slim middle-aged man who has taken meticulous notes throughout the entire case, answers: 'Guilty.' There is a collective sigh. Milat, his hand gripping the rail of the dock, doesn't flinch. A few people clap, then a hush falls, broken only by a woman's soft sobbing from above. The Clarkes, the Walters, Peggy Gibson and Patricia Everist are there with detectives who couldn't get seats downstairs. As the seven remaining charges are read and seven more guilty verdicts come down, the sobbing above grows louder.

Sitting up the back, members of Task Force Air stretch out hands to each other in congratulations. Detective Andy Waterman, who helped catalogue the huge brief, closes his eyes and bows his head as a two-and-a-half-year chapter in his life comes to an end. Big boofy cops have tears in their eyes. Steve Leach's bearded chin trembles. Rod Lynch, sitting next to Bob Godden and Clive Small, pulls a handkerchief from his pocket and wipes his eyes.

Ivan Milat's knuckles grow whiter on the rail.

'Does the accused have anything to say?' asks Hunt.

'I'm not guilty of it. That's all I have to say.'

Hunt begins his sentencing. 'The case against the prisoner at the conclusion of the evidence and the addresses was, in my view, an overwhelming one. Although his legal representatives displayed a tactical ability of a high order, and conducted his defence in a skilful and responsible manner, in my view the jury's verdicts were, in the end, inevitable. I agree entirely with those verdicts. Any other, in my view, would have flown in the face of reality.' He commends the police for their painstaking efforts and begins to go back over the murders.

'The jury's verdicts mean that the prisoner was involved, either alone or in company, in a criminal enterprise to pick them up and then to murder them all. In my view, it is inevitable that the prisoner was not alone in that criminal enterprise, but I do not take that fact into account either in aggravation or mitigation when considering what sentences should be imposed . . .

'Each of the victims were attacked savagely and cruelly, with force which was unusual and vastly more than was necessary to cause death, and for some form of psychological gratification.' Justice Hunt's voice wavers slightly: 'These seven young persons were at the threshold of their lives, with everything to look forward to – to travel, career, happiness, love, family, and even old age.'

He composes himself and continues. 'Whatever the actual causes of their death may have been, it is clear that they were subjected to behaviour which, for callous indifference to suffering and complete disregard for humanity, is almost beyond belief.'

'Ivan Robert Marko Milat, on the third count [the attack on Paul Onions] I sentence you to a fixed term of penal servitude for six years. On each of the remaining counts, I sentence you to penal servitude for the term of your natural life . . . take the prisoner out please.'

Reporters rush outside. 'Guilty to all seven,' one shouts to waiting photographers and television crews. 'It's gold to Kieren Perkins,' they shout back, having watched the swimmer win gold on a portable television.

The parents are ushered to a room upstairs above the jury room for a final press conference. The verdicts had come as an immense relief to all, though Mr Clarke and Mr Walters agree with Justice Hunt that Ivan has not acted alone. 'We have still got the awful prospect that somebody is still on the streets,' says Mr Clarke.

'They have taken out the larger part of the cancer but there is still some left,' says Mr Walters. They are full of admiration for the depth of the police work, but now have to resume their lives. 'We have to wipe the slate clean and start again,' says Ian Clarke. 'We're not going to let Milat stop that. He will not get away with it. We have a responsibility to our other children.'

But Patricia Everist is equally representative in saying that, 'it has certainly changed my life forever'.

Paul Gordon had been hovering around the court in the days leading up to the verdict. He is like a lost soul, unable to join his former comrades in their triumph at the nearby New South Wales Leagues Club where they are hosting a light lunch and a few farewell drinks for the families. His dumping on perceived inadequacies in the investigation is set to go to air the next day.

The absence of Ivan's family from the court is conspicuous. If he had any friends or relatives there, no one put their hand up. The *Sunday Telegraph*'s Warren Owens, elated that the big story has fallen on a Saturday, manages to get a line from Chalinder Hughes. The verdicts are one of the biggest miscarriages of justice ever, she says. Bill Milat still reckons Ivan is a 'good bloke . . . helpful and friendly'. Margaret Milat is naturally distressed at the verdict against her son, and doesn't agree with it, but says: 'If he's done it, and the verdict is correct, then he should pay the price and serve his penalty.' Richard tells Owens he has no fears about defence council suggestions that he, and not Ivan, is the backpacker killer. 'I don't reckon they'll arrest me. If they thought it was me, they'd have me now, wouldn't they?'

It is almost lunchtime, Sunday, when Ivan Milat arrives at Maitland Maximum Security Prison in the Hunter Valley, north-west of Sydney, with a handful of other inmates. News of his pending arrival has swept through the jail where the majority of inmates are regarded as intractables and half the population is protected from the other half.

Milat's group is lining up as a prelude to reception – showers, the issuing of blankets and cell allocation – when a prisoner named 'Spook', all pumped up from weight training, asks the new arrivals: 'Which one's Milat?'

No one says a word, they just glance quickly towards Ivan. In a flash a solid punch connects to Ivan's jaw, and two more to the head. He goes down. 'Welcome to Maitland, you cunt.'

Alister McMillan from the *Telegraph* and Greg Bearup from the *Herald* find themselves at Richard's caravan on Tuesday after the *Telegraph* breaks the story that morning of the unsuccessful police bugging operation on Richard. Wally's keeping them occupied as they hear Richard call out: 'Just tell 'em to piss off.' Then they hear Richard make off on his trail bike through the bush out the back. Wally chats to both Bearup and McMillan. 'Look mate, if they wanted to arrest Richard they would have done it a long time ago,' he reiterates. Wally says Richard only knew Polglase to talk to. He says in his brother's defence, 'If it was my brother [Ivan] well they've stopped a maniac, haven't they. But I don't think it was him. It certainly wasn't Richard. If it was Ivan, well he deserves everything he gets.'

He says his family gave evidence to the police that damaged Ivan's case because they too wanted the killer caught.

Richard Milat becomes hot news and many nervous reporters are sent to his caravan to ask if he did it. He has cameras on his tail for days as he does the rounds of friends' places, gauging their reaction to him after being virtually called a murderer in court. He pops in on Toppy Ambrose and Scott Urquhart. 'Dick, how ya goin'? You want a cup of coffee?'

'Nuh, I just thought I'd say hello. I'll be going . . . Channel Seven'll be here in a minute. They're following me.' He sits by the window and looks out. 'Ah, no I will have that cup.' A news car has pulled up outside. 'The truck'll be here shortly, it couldn't keep up with me.' He takes his coffee over to another chair where he can't be seen from outside and tells his friends, vaguely: 'Wait about two weeks and the shit will hit the fan. It's not over yet.'

Toppy's daughter comes screaming out. 'Quick there's somebody at me window!'

'That'll be them.' He drinks his coffee that quick it must burn his mouth, and then he's off, before the camera crew can unpack and before the guy can scramble back over the fence. Apparently they've been playing this game for days.

Channel Seven sends some money George Milat's way. That's what he claims. He doesn't like Ivan much, anyway, so why shouldn't he pocket a few thousand to fire off his old musket for the camera. Seven say he only got a case of Victorian Bitter beer. But the one that Seven is really angling for is the love child, Lynise. They've offered her and her mother, Marilyn, $12,000 between them to talk to Neil Mercer on 'Today Tonight'. Lynise tells them to go away. 'I'm not going to bring this sort of attention on myself for a stinking $6000.' She asks Ivan about it on one of her visits and he tells her: 'If you're ever going to talk, don't give it away.'

The station continues to talk to Marilyn and the offer keeps rising but, for some reason, Mercer wants the love child more than the lover. Marilyn rings Lynise and tells her the offer has been upped to $25,000. Lynise is tempted, but there is a lot of tension between mother and daughter. Lynise is still going through the break-up with her boyfriend Paul and she believes that her mother is encouraging him to go for custody of their child. She moves house and Anita Jacoby, a researcher for 'Today Tonight', finds her.

'What would it take?' asks Jacoby.

'It'll take $30,000. I'd be stupid in my position to do it for less.'[137]

The money comes through but it is a two-interview deal. One with 'Today Tonight' and one with the magazine, *Woman's Day*. Both sharing the cost. Her mother has been squeezed out of the deal. Marilyn gets nothing.

The magazine rushes the story into print. *I'M IVAN MILAT'S LOVE CHILD* and Channel Seven treats it similarly.

Ten days after the verdict, Steve Leach and Brett Coman are heading to Dubbo, 400 kilometres north-west of Sydney, to raid a property belonging to Ivan Milat's nephew, Henry 'Hank' Shipsey. His mother Olga [changed to Diane] is Ivan's oldest sister. Someone had phoned in saying that Ivan had supplied Shipsey with guns, and another informant claimed that he was around at Shipsey's place having a few bongs and Shipsey showed him a skull. It was immediately linked to the missing skull of Anja Habschied.

They search his property, with its forbidding 'savage dogs, enter at own risk' sign, but the only heads they find are a large ceramic skull and a substantial quantity of marijuana hidden in a tree stump in a paddock.

On the same bitterly cold day, the task force heads up to Jenolan State Forest to have another look at the Letcher crime scene in a cleared forestry paddock 20 kilometres east of Oberon. They are armed with metal detectors and archaeological sifting machines. It starts snowing the first morning and will snow every day they're there. Nothing is found.

After his humiliating arrival at Maitland Jail, Milat settles right in. He is allowed two visitors a month. Chalinder Hughes, Shirley Soire, Marilyn Milat and Lynise Milat are his regulars.

Among the sixty other inmates of 'A Wing' is George Savvas, a forty-seven-year-old former council alderman who owes his wealth to heroin and cocaine. Savvas had escaped from Goulburn Maximum Security in 1996 by simply donning a blond wig, sunglasses and a change of clothes and walking out during visiting hours. More than eight months later he was recaptured dining out with two women in a Japanese restaurant in Sydney. Facing twenty more years imprisonment does not suit the entrepreneur. He needs to get out no matter what the cost or who he has to enlist.

Ivan Milat is one of three recruited for the job. Maybe he figures the hunt for Milat will draw heat off him. Savvas has organised a team to wait outside the prison to aid the getaway. The plot is audacious and desperate. The plan is to overpower two guards in a storeroom near the north-western wall of the prison, then to tie three small ladders together to scale a seven-metre wall in a spot just out of sight of security cameras. The two inmates who would accompany Savvas and Milat are to use blankets and their bodies to flatten three tiers of razor wire, allowing the others to clamber over them safely. Savvas picks Saturday, 17 May, 1997, for the escape.

Yet Savvas' talk of escape has caught the ears of the Independent Commission Against Corruption (ICAC) which is investigating the possibility that corrupt prison officers were involved in his earlier escape. In an operation codenamed Bengal, ICAC investigators and teams of police and the prison riot squad lay in wait throughout the morning. Somehow, Savvas' cohorts on the outside learn a trap has been set and get a message to Savvas via a visitor. The escape hour comes and goes. Two hours later prison officials inform Savvas and Milat that their plot has been sprung. That night, Ivan is transferred to Goulburn Jail's high-security segregation wing. Savvas is placed in a segregation cell. Guards tell him he is facing thirty years of constant surveillance; his telephone calls recorded and monitored; his mail opened and read. At 8.25 a.m. the following day, as Corrective Services are trumpeting the foiling of the escape to media outlets, Savvas is found hanging from a noose made from a bed sheet tied to a security grille.

The media arrive that morning to hear prisoners calling out: 'Murderers! Murderers!' An inquest finds Savvas took his own life despite the rumours flowing through the prison. At the time of publication, neither Ivan, nor any of the alleged conspirators have ever been charged over the escape.

EPILOGUE

It is Good Friday, 1992, and we – Les Kennedy and Mark Whittaker – are finishing our first book, *Granny Killer: The Story of John Glover*, in a little beach town called Manyana. Tomorrow, Caroline Clarke and Joanne Walters will leave Kings Cross for some vague destination. Tomorrow, they will be dead and we'll be enjoying an Easter break.

Over the following months, we speculate about them and other missing hitchhikers, convinced there is another serial killer at work, and perhaps another book – but then again, we could just have serial killers on the brain. The story unfolds and Les covers it for the *Daily Telegraph Mirror*, later the *Daily Telegraph*. Mark's last news story on the case, for *The Australian*, is headed, 'Police rule out mass graves near backpackers' bodies', published a few days after Clarke and Walters were found. He wonders who's more embarrassed about that one.

Les spends a few weeks at Bowral when the next batch of bodies turns up. Gets hammered by the cops for revealing how the bodies were found with the sticks and the fireplaces. The story goes around the world and proves right in the end. Didn't stop them lying that it was incorrect. They have their reasons.

The cops catch Milat and we want to go searching for the soul of this guy. He hasn't come from nowhere. All the old questions are there: What makes him tick? Is he mad or bad? Are serial killers worth the worry? From the beginning, there is plenty of doubt that we can answer any of them.

Our first point of contact with a Milat is when Les goes to knock Wally on a moonless night in June 1994 after *Who* magazine ran a controversial, sub judice photo of Ivan on its cover. Wally, quoted in the article by our mate Craig Henderson, isn't there. A car pulls in, and someone mistakes Les for Wally in the blackness. It is Boris. He doesn't display any animosity to his brother, at first: 'I don't really know the true story, I never talked to the boys, and the fact is that I grew up with Ivan and I knocked around the streets with Ivan . . . and I never seen him misbehave at all. But there again, nobody's going to believe me. Like the police come the other day. They are trying to do a profile on Ivan, but all we can do is close up, because the fact of the matter is, the last six, seven or eight big cases, they have all been turned around and the government has been sued because they have all made mistakes.'

The brothers come up again and again in his conversation. All good, clean-living boys. 'Go and talk to Alex. Alex has got a lot more to say about all this thing than us . . . You never know, I might have something to say. I'm coming down here to say plenty at the courthouse. Everything they are, I am. And nobody has even pointed the finger at me. Nobody has even come to my place, you know.'

But Boris never fronts at court and he moves house with no forwarding address. He'd said enough, however, to make us realise the key to this business was the family. Within a day or two, an elderly woman rings Les: 'You've been talking to one of my sons,' the woman says, annoyed.

Beg pardon?

'Been talking to one of my sons, Boris.' The penny drops. 'I want you to leave him alone, he's upset over what's happened and hasn't seen his brothers for years, he doesn't know anything about Ivan. Leave him alone.'

Les persists. He only wants to know who Ivan is – what everyone is asking – is he capable of doing such things? Who is he?

'He's a good boy . . . he lived here when all these things are supposed to have happened. I used to wash his clothes. If anyone knows Ivan it's me.' She agrees to be interviewed, just so long as he doesn't talk to Boris. Les interviews her once for the *Telegraph* and we go back again for more detail for the book.

We go to 55 Campbell Hill Road and Bodge, with his slurred, post-accident speech, shows us in. He demonstrates how he can bend his arm back around himself because there is no bone from the shoulder to the elbow since a second accident.

Margaret is sitting in a light blue nightie. She should be flat on her back. Doctors orders. She has a slipped disk. But she's slumped in a big recliner chair. A poster of the Pope hangs on the wall with pictures of various grandchildren around the room. Through an open door, in her apricot bedroom, a picture of Jesus hangs above the bed with matching Virgin Mary and Last Supper on the other walls.

'I have to go to church on Sunday,' she says. 'Doesn't matter what happens.'

Mrs Milat tells us she's had a dream twice in the last few days. Ivan, dressed all in white, is hanging by the neck from the door separating the two small rooms. That's all. The dream seems to concern her more than the fact he's been accused of seven murders. It is more real to her.

She talks. She remembers meeting her husband Steve on a day like this – grey and rainy. Doesn't remember what he wore. She thought she hit him bad and was so worried she turned around and went home and had to have a cuppa. The only point that we later find any evidence to contradict her on is her claim that Ivan and Marilyn never had an affair. 'She would talk to everybody. Boris was jealous but nothing was going on with them and he is still the same today. Hasn't changed a bit.' Boris is the outsider. Ivan does no wrong. She seems a nice old lady. You've got to pity her.

We spend a few weekends driving up to Newcastle trying to find Karen, and at petrol stations all the way up, 'Missing' posters for a newly abducted schoolgirl are constant reminders that the sickness is still around.

We knock on a lot of doors, follow a few leads and eventually we find Karen, but Witness Protection moves her on almost immediately. We really pity her. She still lives in hiding, fearful of Ivan's reach. Police considered prosecuting Ivan over the arson attack on her mother's car and garage, but because of her mother's frail health and the fear of Ivan, she did not wish to proceed. Nor will action be taken over Ivan swindling her out of her share of the Blackett home.

In February 1995, we are just leaving the house of the old schoolfriend we called 'Collar' in this book. He asks us if we know why Ivan turned into a killer. Something has been weighing on his mind. 'Now I remember,' he says, suddenly, in a loud voice. 'It was because of his father. His father. No, no I don't want to remember that, you've made me remember. I don't want to remember that. Go, go.'

We never find out what he means.

In April 1995 Mark is in Brisbane and so decides to call in on Alex up at Woombye, an hour and a bit north. He finds the number in the phone book and rings from a nearby booth.

'How much is it worth to me,' are Alex's first words. 'There are that many people going on about it, I'm not saying a word without some cash. We've had people out here and they all say so much crap. They are gunna do this and that, and they just say what the police tell them. In a few years time when it comes out and you find that my brother is innocent and the cops are lying, you can write another friggin' book.' He hangs up without allowing another word to be said.

Mark rings back, unusually angry: 'You say you want to help your brother and complain that nobody's telling your side of the story and you won't say a word without money. What do you expect?'

He talks about his sighting of the two car loads of people going into Belanglo. 'The only reason I rang the bastards was I was going to Queensland and I'd seen they offered half a million. "Yeah I'll have a cut off that." Until then they didn't have a clue or whatever. This statement I made to them, I showed it to a Victorian cop, he said "If you have got any relations who ever served time they will bust him because it makes it look like you are covering him." . . . They said Ivan was off work every day one of them got killed. If a body has been lying for sixty-five months in the forest how can you tell when it's been killed within a month. Every day he wasn't at work, one of these girls died. Ninety-five per cent of the population was off work. It was a Saturday.'

And on it goes. Mark arranges to meet him the next day, out in the hinterland behind the Sunshine Coast. On entering the house Alex gets straight down to business. 'What can you do for me?'

There is no money being paid to anyone. Mark can only promise to tell the truth – a line which is a truism but also somewhat manipulative, the truth being always subjective. It seems to satisfy Alex and he demonstrates how the family can continue to believe in Ivan. He makes point after point that is later contradicted by the evidence. He plucks these 'facts' from a vast array of sources.

Mark copies his statement by hand. It takes about an hour, while Alex plays with his grandchildren. When finished, Alex asks, 'What do you reckon?'

'There is a lot of detail there,' Mark replies with awkward diplomacy. 'You must have a good memory.'

'Yeah, I do. My recall is very good. I remember all the odd things. I think I told them too much. One of them also had three earrings in the nose and in the left ear. I remembered that too but didn't tell them. You can't fit in everything.' He says the cops told him he saw too much for that period of time. 'But I was up above them looking down. You see a lot.'

Mark keeps waiting for him to say the obvious: 'Well, wouldn't you remember if you saw a girl gagged in a car full of shotgun-wielding weirdos.' But the line never comes. Of course, that raises the equally difficult issue of why on earth he never reported it at the time, a question he answers in the statement: 'I was of the opinion that it was just some young blokes taking some girls into the forest to have a good time.' Les has also made a similar journey for the *Telegraph Mirror*. Both of us are greeted as familiar faces.

John Powch and John Preston, cohorts in the 1971 armed robberies, don't return our letters to them in jail. Powchie has spent about a year on the outside since he went down in 1971. He was second-in-charge of a major heroin ring and got twenty-five more years. Should be out early next century.

The next month, Mark is in England talking to Ian and Jacquie Clarke. Spends six hours with them at their lovely country home with their beautiful labradors. He's astonished at the Clarkes' friendliness and their strength in adversity. The Clarkes are southerners and never intended staying in Northumbria, 16 kilometres from Hadrians Wall, but they are staying.

'Well, Caroline's up here,' explains Ian. 'We couldn't leave her. You know she's buried at the church here?' Jacquie and he booked grave sites next to hers with its view over rolling green fields. Several times Mark has had to hold back tears. They buy him dinner despite his protestations. He owes them so much.

Next day, the Walters decline to talk.

The trial comes and goes. Patricia Everist had been putting everything off until it was over. She had the death of her husband and Deborah's disappearance to worry about. Six and a half years of hell. Now it is over. An ex-neighbour, Dianne, turns up unannounced and starts cleaning up her yard in the rain as the interview continues warm and dry in front of the heater. It reminds Mark there are so many good people. So many sad ones, too.

'What do you say,' she begins the interview. She talks of Deborah fondly. There are long pauses. 'I'm afraid I'm not being very helpful. I don't know what to tell you . . . You know, whatever she was like, and she had a brilliant future ahead of her, it wouldn't have mattered if she was the dumbest kid in the world, he took her life and he had no right to do that. It's quite incidental, really, what they're like. Clever or bright or plain or awkward, they had a right to live.'

Words fail Mark. He finds refuge in her pile of newspaper clippings.

He asks her to talk about the missing years. She talks quietly of the fluctuating moods between hope and despair. 'You'd go to bed and you'd lie there and you'd imagine everything possible except you never imagined anything like this.' There is a long silence, maybe thirty seconds. 'It was a very nothing time very difficult to know . . .' Her voice is trailing off barely audible . . . Then louder: 'I used to say the worst thing was not knowing. Sometimes I wish I didn't.'

Mark says his goodbyes. It is a short interview. Maybe an hour and ten. The grief is too intense. Too sad. He's run out of anything to say. It put tears in his eyes writing this a year later.

Les spends tens of hours on the phone to Margaret who had 'sex without much choice' with Ivan in 1971. He had tracked her down for the *Telegraph Mirror* and conducted two face-to-face interviews. She's forgiven Ivan. She sounds more dirty on Greta for taking money for appearing on television. She talks about how she has written to him and visited him in jail with his sister-in-law, Carol.

'I do give him the benefit of the doubt that he might not be guilty and I'm just incredibly sad that he was in that situation. It's not as though I don't think the crimes are very bad, but I felt very sorry for him . . . He seemed extremely happy to see me. As I said he sees me as a friend. Everybody in the visitors room was looking at him like he was famous. He smiles at everyone. And you know he's genuinely very nice.' That sort of thing.

Les got up her for that.

Margaret is a complex person. A gentle soul. Willing to help in any way. The sort of person who really couldn't kill a fly. She is willing to forgive those who've wronged her in her past. And all too willing to forgive Ivan who's wronged so many others. It is a genuine belief in the goodness of people.

We find Marilyn in a caravan park on the Central Coast. She isn't home. We ring her later that day on a mobile phone from a car in the middle of a thunderstorm and she doesn't want to meet us, but she's happy to talk on the phone. And so begins another extraordinary telephone relationship between Les and her. She was still in love with the man despite everything. 'There are things I'd like to tell you but I can't.'

Marilyn is torn between belief in his guilt and dreams that he will one day marry her. She says that he's even received a stream of letters from an 'obsessed woman' claiming to have borne him a child.

One thing Marilyn and Clive Small agree on is that he went off the rails when his women left him. Marilyn can't help blaming herself.

We are in the front bar of the Albion Hotel where Paul Douglas and Lynn and Des Butler first got together and decided to call the police about Richard Milat. Douglas seems a naturally nervous kind of bloke, but he hasn't really relaxed since the day Des called the police. When people talk about reward money, they've got to remember that these people needed guts to make that call which was the first to bring the Milats into the frame. Douglas can't see why people like Nick Collins and others who knew things about Richard didn't come forward. He's copped a hard time at work over it

'My life is on the line. It's okay till after the appeal goes through, then if they don't arrest Richard, I'll be out of this place. I'll leave Australia altogether. Des feels the same. Our lives have been threatened. You know his brothers and all of that . . . He knows where I work. He knows where I live, what car I drive. He can do anything at any time. So you know why people are hesitant to give information to police. Which doesn't make it right.'

When we find Richard's former workmate, Nick Collins, he is friendly and affable. He says he knows stuff and it looks like he wants to get it off his chest, but he just can't say. There is a constant feeling that he is saying: 'If you knew what I knew.'

He says he was scared for his kids and his wife. He hates the cops from things he'd seen as a young bloke. He'd always been taught not to be a dog. There are Christmas decorations through his house and some amazing displays along the street. It is like a David Lynch movie, with picket fences and dark underbellies. Up close, his fears don't seem so unreasonable.

'He told us all things,' says Collins. 'There's a hell of a lot I have not told anyone.'

Boris had told Les that Lynise was really Ivan's, on the condition we not approach her, but when she sells her story, we are up to see her in a flash. An attractive blonde with a small frame, she has a scar from a road accident that runs up from the left corner of her mouth almost to her nose. She has Ivan's eyes. She seems tired. She's battling to bring up her five-year-old son Adrian by herself. He's running around the house thinking of new ways to grab attention from the adults sitting around the dining table. She has the air of a survivor, tough. As she talks we wonder just how tough.

'And so I shafted Mum,' she tells us. 'You know, that sounds really cold to you people, but if you knew the situation . . . What really pissed me was when it was down to twelve-and-a-half thousand each. It was twelve and a half for you and twelve-and-a-half for me, you know, she couldn't give me thirteen, she's got a house and a car and a property, you know what I mean. She's just a tight-fisted bitch and I thought, what goes around comes around. You're getting yours. I didn't do anything nasty or anything. I just took what I could. She's written letters to Dad telling him to sort me. She's written letters to Ivan to tell him to disown me. She's getting Paul [the ex] to give me a hard time.'

We resume our hunt for Boris in the belief that a brother who hates Ivan might be more interesting than Alex. Lynise mentions that he lived in a small town up the coast, Mannering Park. We head up there and fluke on to a mixed business/petrol station, where a girl tells us she doesn't like him much because he owes $28 for some diesel he got on credit. He left town ages ago but his ex-wife, the second, still lived around the corner somewhere. We knock on doors at random and find her. She says he has a new name and gives us his last address at Dora Creek. That proves to be a vacant lot, but a white-haired old lady next door tells us he actually lived two houses up and moved to another town. Boris had married again, but left the new wife, Helen, the third, then followed her to this other town (which we've promised Boris to keep secret). The old lady didn't like him either. He owed her $35.

We find two addresses for Boris in this new town. A woman in hot pink bicycle shorts comes to the gate and denies knowledge of Boris.

There is a 'Beware of the savage dog' sign on the padlocked, shoulder-high fence. We find him fifteen minutes later at another premises where the woman in pink shorts is talking to him. She scurries inside at the sight of us. Boris approaches with a funny nervous-yet-polite anger. His hands are trembling like he's got Parkinson's. He demands to know how we found him, but before we can give our rehearsed (misleading) story, he says it doesn't matter. 'I'm not talking. I don't think there's anything I can tell ya. I could tell you a thousand things.'

Then, without any pressure, he suddenly changes his mind. 'Come on up the back,' he gestures towards a white Holden ute with balding mag tyres and we stand around the bonnet in the fading light.

He has been running from his family, he says. 'They call me a drunk and say all sorts of bad things about me, like I used to beat up my wife, but it's not true. I don't drink or smoke any more. I speak to my mum and still know what's going on.'

When asked if he still thinks Ivan is innocent, Boris is defensive, but adds darkly: 'All my brothers are capable of extreme violence, extreme violence, given the right time and place, individually.'

It annoyed him that Lynise had claimed he was in jail when she was conceived. It was Ivan who was, in fact, jailed nine months and two weeks before her birth, but Boris maintains he hadn't gone near his wife for months. 'I was in jail for one weekend when I was twenty.'

He begins to relax and his trembling ceases.

'The things I can tell you are worse than what Ivan's meant to have done.' He starts talking about how he followed Ivan's movements. 'Everywhere he's worked, people have disappeared. I know where he's been.'

Then he poses a question: 'Do you think he's done it?'

We think he has.

'If Ivan's done these murders, I reckon he's done a hell of a lot more.'

How many? we ask.

'. . . um . . . twenty-eight!'

His attention shifts. There is so much he wants to say about growing up with Ivan. The word 'lawlessness' crops up again and again. So does 'buzz'. He freely admits his own rages and paranoia, but says: 'I don't do that any more.'

He digresses and talks about what good blokes the brothers are, then about trips away, about someone they knew who 'rattled cars'. They'd look for a couple parking, pull up and, 'throw the guy out and screw the arse off the sheila . . . I find that hard to say cause I think rape is a terrible thing. What I mean to say is raping someone you don't know or don't know very well. I think it's different if you are raping your wife.'

He says he's been told Ivan has talked about killing himself. 'I know this much. He doesn't want to spend the rest of his life in jail.'

Right at the end, Boris says: 'If I wanted to frame him I could have. I was working next door to his place at the time and the boys did all his gyprocking. I could have helped the defence and I could have harmed the defence, but I kept me mouth shut.' We leave, pretty stunned. Over time, the things he told us that could be checked out, seem to check out, but so much is just his word. There is something about him though that made us believe most of what he said.

We are driving up the coast and there is a palpable sense of anger and conspiracy in the air when we come to Taree to talk to Phil Polglase's wife and mates. The hellos are easy; Les had been before and broken the story about the undercover operation. Now everyone wants to talk. His missus faces losing their property. The solicitors look like they are going to get it all and she and her five kids aged between four and fifteen don't know where they will go.

Two days later we are at South West Rocks on the New South Wales North Coast, talking to Wally's ex, Maureen. She has spoken publicly because she wants the world to know that Ivan was a nice guy. Her photo album has Wally's head obliterated by pin pricks in all the shoddy 1970s prints in which he appears.

We move on up to Nanango central Queensland, where Mick Milat moved during the eighties. It's a town well away from those parts usually chosen by southerners looking for the Queensland idyll. It is gnarly Queensland; this-country-could-be-great-if-it-wasn't-for-the-socialists-in-Canberra Queensland. Visitors to Nanango are greeted by a billboard erected by local Christian businessmen: REPENT AND TURN TO GOD That Your Sins Be Blotted Out Through Our LORD JESUS CHRIST. (Acts 3:19)

Old properties have been cut up and sold to the poor townies with dreams of running a few chooks. 'Blockies', they call them. We find Mick on one of the blocks out of town. The day we arrive, in the beautiful warmth of an October afternoon, plumes of white smoke cut the blue sky as farmers burn off.

Mick comes out of his fibro place barefoot in T-shirt and grey shorts to meet our woozy Japanese hatchback. His hair is long at the back, short and a little balding at the front. An animal cut, straight out of Guildford. He is Ivan, but rougher. He has the big Merv Hughes, the 'Yugo box head', a leathery complexion and a little pot belly. He looks suspicious as he walks towards us. His wife, the widow of his brother Alex's son, Darin, is standing behind him at the door, watching her man. We introduce ourselves.

'Okay, get off the property,' he says, turning his back. We are silent, thinking what to say. Les is just opening his mouth, 'but . . .' when Mick turns and growls. 'I don't mean tomorrow. Get off the property, now.' The last word oozes aggression, as his finger guides us to the gate, 50 metres behind.

We shit ourselves and get out quick smart, but head the wrong way out of the gate so we have to drive past the place again. Then a silver sedan we think we'd seen at Mick's place pops up behind and we're certain we are being followed. We have the little rental chugging along at 150 kmh, but it's probably all our imaginations.

We go into these and other interviews with Milat family members carrying negative, preconceived ideas. With the exception of Michael and Richard (who tells us to fuck off, via an intermediary) we always come away liking them more than we expected, feeling some of their frustrations. We hardly understand them better, we don't always know whether we can believe what some of them say, but we somehow think they're okay. Their friends seem like good people, too. Most of them have worked hard and done well in life.

The microscope has been passed over the Milats, however, and they haven't always looked good, but it is not fair to blame them for the sins of a brother . . . Thanks to his defence lawyers, however, it's pretty easy to do. A shadow hangs over them all.

Mark goes back to Europe after the trial. Manfred Neugebauer picks him up at the Bonn Railway Station. Manfred insists that Mark stay with him and Anke. No correspondence. They put him in a room right next to Gabor's old room. Anke uses it now to make her jewellery. Pictures of Gabor are all around.

Anke's parents wanted to spread Gabor's ashes at sea, but he was buried in the village cemetery down the road. Each night one or both of them walk there to light a candle at his grave, as is the local custom. They return in the morning to put it out.

Manfred takes Mark on a bicycle ride around town, and on a tour of the spectacular terraced vineyards of the Aar Valley where they taste the sweet wine and talk of German history and about the case and about life in the military. Mark stays two nights and they seem disappointed when he says he has to leave. Such good people. He's crying again, writing this.

Then, in England, Paul Onions takes him up the local for a few pints of lager. They're in Willenhall, West Midlands. It used to be a town, but it's more a western suburb of Birmingham now. It seems a bizarre coincidence that the 'Granny Killer' John Glover spent much of his early life here, and in neighbouring Wolverhampton and Wednesbury. He and Les were here in February 1992, while Joanne and Caroline were picking grapes at Capogrecos.

The thing about Onions is, he's a really good bloke. Thoroughly likeable. He doesn't want the reward. 'It was just too important for the reward. After what happened to me, you can see that the reward don't mean a shit.'

All people seem to want to talk to him about is the reward. He can't get it through to them that something so profound had happened to him, and something far more evil had happened to the others, it would be defiling their memory if he took the money. He got a few quid from '60 Minutes' and he's got his life to get on with and that's enough for him.

He's come out of it with a more relaxed view of life. There isn't much to worry about when you've been through all that. He's saying that talking to someone who wants to know the full story has been very therapeutic. As I tell him bits and pieces we've picked up on our way, it becomes clear that he doesn't know much about the case at all. The police kept him insulated and we're opening up new chapters, he says, over a cup of tea back at his mum's place after closing time. Like us, he refers to Milat with the familiar 'Ivan'. It sounds unnerving coming from him.

He can't contemplate the atrocities that he so narrowly avoided. He spent the whole trial so scared of saying the wrong thing, he couldn't afford to dwell on the murders. 'I wanted to know what was going to happen to me that day . . . I mean that girl, they never found her head, did they?'

It's so hard to reconcile that this friendly bloke could so easily be one of these disembodied names who we feel we know so well from only blurred photographs and the recollections of loved ones; that we could be talking to, say, Caroline or Gabor or Deborah as 'the one that got away'. Walking ghosts. They'd all be about twenty-eight as this is being written. Pleasant people only a little younger than ourselves with life stretching out before them.

The Belanglo sign has became a target for souvenir hunters and people can still be seen having their photo taken next to it.

We never got any closer to the soul of the guy. We never found if he was mad or bad. Sure, he had a tough upbringing, but so do thousands and thousands of good honest people. It's some conspiracy of genes and experience. We didn't want to blame it on the dehumanising effects of Grafton Jail in the sixties, but yesterday another graduate of that evil place, Earl Heatley, was sentenced to die in jail for another brutal murder. One of Heatley's former workmates, Chris Lau, was just telling us what a good bloke he was. Carried ten broken fingers given to him by the Grafton warders. He told people how they did it with a hammer, one finger at a time. Then again, he was a callous murderer before he went there.

And we've spent so many thousands of hours writing a book about someone we don't like and in all the often delirious hours of work and going to the pub and holding down regular jobs, we've long ago stopped talking to each other and three sons have been born, Oliver, Marcus and Charlie, and all the original questions still reverberate, some answered, some more unclear than before.

You search for meaning to it all, but it won't come. It's as though there can never be any good come from all this.

POSTSCRIPT

Clive Small was promoted in 1997 to Assistant Commissioner of the Crime Agencies, created in the anti-corruption reformation of the New South Wales Police Service. In January 2001 he left Crime Agencies to command the Greater Hume Police Region. Rod Lynch was his deputy at Crime Agencies, but retired in 1999 as Superintendent. In September 1997 both men received commendations for their leadership and management skills with Task Force Air. A third commendation was awarded to Detective Senior Constable Andy Waterman for his professionalism in preparing the brief of evidence.

In 1999, at the instigation of Rod Lynch, Small presented Task Force Air detectives with certificates of appreciation for their efforts. One task force officer was forced to leave the service after gambling away cash from a social fund.

On 21 June 1995, Ivan's nephew, Christopher Milat, was found guilty of possessing an unlicensed firearm and was fined $700.

On 7 November 1996, William Milat pleaded guilty to maliciously damaging two cameras and assaulting *Daily Telegraph* photographer Warren Clarke after leaving the court on 27 March, 1996, the day Carol was accused of fabricating an alibi for Ivan. The magistrate did not record a conviction, but ordered him to pay $2000 of the $3300 camera damage bill.

On 19 December 1996, Ivan's sister, Shirley Soire, pleaded guilty in Campbelltown Local Court to a charge of possessing an unlicensed .45 calibre pistol. She was fined $1000.

On 17 January 1997, Ivan's nephew, Henry Shipsey, was found guilty in Dubbo Court of possessing a prohibited drug. He was fined $1400.

On 24 March 1997, Ivan's daughter, Lynise Eileen Milat, thirty-two, was charged in Gosford Local Court with possessing a .25 calibre semi-automatic Bayard pistol, a prohibited switchblade, stealing a knife and possession of cannabis. She had been initially charged with breaking into the Long Jetty home of her former de facto Paul Gould on 12 December 1996, during which she took four photograph albums and personal documents. Detectives found the pistol and switchblade in her bedroom. Her solicitor told the court the break-in was the result of a bitter break-up. She pleaded guilty and was fined $400 and placed on a $1000, three-year good-behaviour bond.

Karen Milat and her son, Jason, disappeared into the witness protection program after giving evidence against Ivan. There were rumoured sightings of Ivan's stepson in the Campbelltown area, but nothing concrete. Then, on 1 September, 1999, a thin, gaunt-looking Jason pleaded guilty in the Burnie Magistrates Court in Tasmania to a charge of attempted robbery with a knife. Local reporter, Fran Voss, said he looked lost, starving and confused. He still couldn't shake the Milat name, appearing as Jason Ivan Milat on the court register. If his mum was there to lend support no-one noted her presence.

Jason had been living in East Devonport when on 20 July, 1999, four days before his 23rd birthday, he walked in to the local milkbar, Walker's Family Store, and produced a pocket knife. He was quickly overpowered and disarmed by Mr Alan Walker, who sprayed him in the face with a can of mace. Jason had first pleaded not guilty. Magistrate Tim Hill placed Jason on suicide watch while he awaited sentencing in the Burnie Supreme Court. On 2 November, 1999, Justice Ewan Crawford sentenced him to 12 months imprisonment with a seven month suspended sentence on condition he enter into a two-year good behavior bond and seek medical treatment and counselling.

Boris Stanley Milat's bid to seek public anonymity were dashed on 26 May, 2000, when he faced Cessnock Local Court in the NSW Hunter Vally charged with breaching two Apprehended Domestic Violence Orders (ADVO).

He had moved from where we last saw him and was living in a defacto relationship with Ms Helen Smith and her son in Ellalong. The 57-year-old self-employed brick cleaner sobbed throughout the hearing. His lawyer Robert Littlewood played on the shame felt by Boris for being akin to a serial killer and his hard family upbringing. Magistrate Alan Ralton was told Boris changed his name to Steven Stanley Miller by deed poll in 1994 after his brother's arrest for the backpacker murders. The court heard he was raised in a household where everyone was expected to work long hours on their father's acreage and that Dad was a strong disciplinarian who encouraged the brothers to practice with guns. Mr Ralton was told Boris and his siblings were often left alone for long periods and fought regularly with each other.

Police initiated the ADVOs against Boris to protect Ms Smith after he assaulted her during an argument at their home on 19 December, 1999, causing bruising and redness to her face. He had breached the order twice by approaching her. A pre-sentence report said Boris was a happy and helpful man who had done substantial charity work in his life. Mr Littlewood said Boris had not consumed alcohol for five months and had completed an anger-management course. The couple had reconciled. Boris got 100 hours community service, was fined $750, and placed on 18 months good behavior with an order not to approach Ms Smith after consuming alcohol.

Alex Milat has become active in the gun lobby opposed to federal and state gun laws introduced in the wake of the 1996 Port Arthur massacre in Tasmania. In February 1998, he announced that he planned to stand as an Independent for election to the Queensland Parliament. His ticket would be a pro-gun, pro-knife carrying, against all Aboriginal handouts, against political correctness. Alex told the *Courier-Mail* he believed everyone should be given a .303 bolt action rifle to protect Australia. He said that even though he would have to overcome the stigma of being the brother of Ivan Milat, he had plenty of supporters.

Richard Milat has finished building his house in Vera Street, Hill Top. He is ever wary of media and police. He was last understood to have been working at Eastern Creek raceway in track maintenance.

Wally Milat lost much business following Ivan's arrest, but has slowly recouped it. In the lengthy period between Ivan's arrest and conviction he was caught shoplifting in Bowral.

Marilyn still visits Ivan. Chalinder Hughes continues to see him but less regularly. Her love interest has gone.

Since the publication of the book in 1998, none of the $200,000 reward offered by the *Sunday Telegraph* had been paid. Initially, Paul Onions said he would not apply for the $500,000 reward offered by the New South Wales Government, but after Ivan lost his appeal in 1998, he said he would seek some money to give to the families of the victims.

Mrs Joanne Berry, Paul Douglas, Des and Lyn Butler, and Marko Koskinen, whose information were key links in the chain which put police on Milat's trail, were eligible for both rewards. In 1999, some monies were paid but the Police Service kept secret the recipients and amounts. However, Paul Douglas and Des Butler benefitted to the tune of $30,000 each, while Lyn Butler got nothing. Des wasn't happy with his lot. The efforts of Philip Polglase in going undercover for police go unrewarded.

Despite the overwhelming Crown case against Ivan Milat, he continues to profess his innocence through the formation of supporters who have dubbed their lobby group the F.I.R.M. – Friends of Ivan Robert Milat.

He remains in the Goulburn Jail extreme security unit where he has limited contact with inmates and visits are strictly supervised. The limits were imposed after warders allegedly found part of a hacksaw blade in a packet of Arrowroot biscuits in Ivan's cell during a search on 8 January, 1999. Two days earlier two other high-risk prisoners were removed from the block amid allegations of an escape plot.

The belief that Ivan Milat killed more than those found at Belanglo and that a second secret killing field exists on the coast somewhere north of Sydney persists among police. In March 1998, Task Force Fenwick, led by Detective Inspector Wayne Gordon, began a two-year reinvestigation in to the disappearances and suspected murders of 12 teenage girls and women and three males from the Central Coast, Newcastle and northern Sydney areas spanning 15 years from 1978.

Three couples were among the missing, one couple were hitching from Sydney to northern NSW. Most of the cases involved people hitching, waiting to catch buses or walking to their homes when they vanished. Ivan featured heavily in the inquiries, in particular his stays at the Golden Eagle Hotel at Gateshead in 1978 and 1979 and other north coast motels while away on road-work trips.

Among the cases where Ivan Milat is suspected are the disappearance of Leanne Goodall, 20, on 30 September, 1978 while travelling from Newcastle to her parent's home at Belmont; Robyn Hickie, 18, who disappeared while waiting for a bus opposite her parent's home on the Pacific Highway at Belmont North on April 7, 1979, and Amanda Robinson, 14, who vanished after catching a bus home to Swansea from a dance at St Mary's High at Gateshead – opposite the Gold Eagle Hotel – on 20 April, 1979.

Ivan has never given an interview, but often trumpets his innocence through letters distributed by supporters to select media outlets.

One of his few permitted contacts is a clerk at the prison library who furnishes him with legal texts which he reads, ever hopeful of learning the law to launch a new appeal.

He conducts occasional hunger strikes during which he takes water and tea. In early 2001, he swallowed razor blades in an alleged escape plan. Ivan is back in a fitness regime of one-handed pushups – 200 at a time, apparently.

He has never commented publicly about this book.

Ivan's regular quote to prison guards is: 'I'll be out of here before I die.'

We are greatly indebted to many people without whom this book could never have been written. Aside from the hundreds of people interviewed we would like to give special thanks to others who gave generously of their time and expertise, in particular: Jan Nelson, Vicki Cook, Marcus Clinton, Paul Blackmore, Dean Sewell, Steve Barrett, Morgan Ogg, Robert Wainwright, Jennifer Ezzy, Brendan James, Eamonn Fitzpatrick, Wayne Miller, Anne Connolly, Lisa Powers, Janet Fife-Yeomans, Cindy Wockner, Jenny Curtin, Mark Jones, Lisa Williams and the *Australasian Police Journal*, David Lotty, Task Force Air officers Clive Small, Rod Lynch, Paul Gordon, Bob Godden, the New South Wales Police Media Unit – in particular, Kevin Daley, Bill McClerg, Craig Regan, Lisa Breeze, Mark Hargraves, Tracy Arthur. The News Ltd and Fairfax libraries. Lurline Campbell, John Knight, Col Alan, David Armstrong, Campbell Reid, James Hall, Candy Baker, Steve Fosbery, Murray Waldren, John Lyons, Anthony Schofield, Lisa Green, Sarah Harris, Helen Dalley, Peter Hiscock, Steve Warnock, Trish Croaker, Scott Willis, David Mott, Tamsin Growney in London, Louise Cassar and Darren Goodsir, Dave Kennedy for German translations and interviews with Mr Schmidl, Betty Card for her evocative descriptions of Moorebank, Steven Barlow at the Land Titles Office. Medical consultant Dr John Rooney, Richard Blackburn, David Callan, Kimbal Cook, Stephen Gibbs, Marianne Carey and the NSW Fire Brigade.

Their are many more who remain anonymous. They include friends of the Milat family, and indeed members of the Milat family to whom we are indebted for their openness. There are also many investigators attached to Task Force Air – who we could not name, due recently to a standing order on secrecy with the case until Milat's appeal was complete. We apologise to those who also suffered in the editing cuts.

END NOTES

1. Interview Alex Milat 4/10/96
2. Interviews Alex Milat 20/12/95, Boris Milat 6/6/94
3. Interview Alex Milat 20/12/95
4. Interview Margaret Milat 15/9/94
5. Interview Margaret Milat 15/9/94
6. Interview Alex Milat 4/10/96
7. Interview Margaret Milat 2/95
8. Interview Boris Milat 24/2/97
9. Interviews Boris Milat 24/2/97, 1/3/97
10. Interviews Margaret Milat, 2/95, Lynise Milat 31/8/96, Marilyn Milat 9/2/97, Boris Milat 24/2/97
11. Christopher Keating *On The Frontier: A Social History of Liverpool*; Hale and Iremonger
12. Interview Betty Card 3/8/96
13. Interview Alex Milat 20/12/95
14. Interview Boris Milat 24/2/97
15. Interview David Armstrong 22/12/94
16. Interview William Milat 12/10/96
17. Interview Boris Milat 6/12/96
18. Interviews Peter Cantarella 4/10/96, Boris Milat 6/12/96
19. Interview Peter Cantarella 4/10/96
20. Interview Peter Cantarella 4/10/96
21. Interview Peter Cantarella 4/10/96
22. Interview Peter Cantarella 4/10/96, William Milat 12/10/96, Boris Milat 6/12/96
23. Interview Margaret Milat 15/9/94
24. Interview Boris Milat 6/12/96
25. Interview Lynise Milat 31/8/96
26. Interviews Marilyn Milat 7/9/96, 6/10/96, 10/10/96, 2/12/96
27. Interview Peter Cantarella 4/10/96
28. Interview Boris Milat 25/9/96
29. Interview Boris Milat 25/9/96
30. Interview Boris Milat 25/9/96
31. Interview Boris Milat 6/12/96
32. Interviews Boris Milat 6/12/96, John Parsons 17/11/96
33. Interview Boris Milat 6/12/96
34. Interview John Parsons 22/9/96
35. Interview Boris Milat 25/9/96
36. John and Jenny Parsons 22/9/96
37. Interviews Boris Milat 24/2/97, Marilyn Milat 26/2/97
38. Interviews Boris Milat 24/2/97, Marilyn Milat 26/2/97
39. Interview Boris Milat 24/2/97
40. Interview Marilyn Milat 28/2/97
41. Interview Boris Milat 24/2/97

42. Interviews Boris Milat 6/12/95, 24/2/97, Lynise Milat 31/8/96
43. Interview Marilyn Milat 28/2/97
44. Statement Sgt Andrew Graham Anderson 15/7/65, Sydney District Court Records
45. Interview George Milat 6/6/95
46. Interview Boris Milat 24/2/97
47. Interview Marilyn Milat 26/2/97
48. Interview Boris Milat 1/3/97
49. Interview Boris Milat 6/12/96
50. Interview Marilyn Milat 28/2/97
51. Sydney Court of Quarter Sessions 13/10/67
52. Interview Alex Milat 4/10/96
53. Interview Boris Milat 6/12/96
54. Interview Boris Milat 25/9/96
55. Interview Margaret Milat 15/9/94
56. Interview Boris Milat 6/12/96
57. Interview Boris Milat 6/12/96
58. Interview Marilyn Milat 2/12/96
59. Interview Margaret 4/98
60. Interview William Milat 12/10/96
61. Bob Bradbury and Wilf Tunstall's evidence at committal hearing 14/10/71
62. Interview 'Eve Carey' 4/8/96
63. Interview John Marsden 28/11/96
64. Interview David Preston 7/9/96
65. Interview John Marsden 28/11/96
66. Interview Maureen Murray 28/9/96
67. Interviews David Preston 7/9/96, Bill Milat 12/10/96
68. Interview Kimbal Cook 19/9/96
69. Interview Yvonne Carroll 27/9/96
70. Interview Maureen Murray 28/9/96
71. Interview George Milat 6/6/96
72. Interview Noel Manning 5/5/95
73. Interview Noel Manning 5/5/95
74. Interview Boris Milat 6/12/96
75. Interviews George Milat 6/6/96, Scott Urquhart 19/9/96
76. Interview Maureen Murray 28/9/96
77. Interview Maureen Murray. The policeman's statement twice says that he was invited into the house
78. Interviews Scott Urquhart, Danielle Ambrose 19/9/96
79. Interviews Noel Wild 1/12/96, Don Borthwick 5/12/96
80. Interview Margaret Milat 15/9/94
81. Interview Jeff Cinconze 9/96
82. Interview Cathy Beattie 17/8/94
83. Evidence of Ivan Milat, *R v Ivan Milat* Supreme Court 1996
84. Interview Boris Milat 24/2/97
85. Interview Des Butler 25/9/96
86. Evidence of Paul Douglas, *R v Ivan Milat* Supreme Court 1996
87. Evidence of Paul Douglas, *R v Ivan Milat* Supreme Court 1996

88. Evidence of Des Butler, *R v Ivan Milat* Supreme Court 1996
89. Phillip Polglase's statement to police 25/5/94
90. Royal Commission into Police Corruption, evidence of Detective Senior Constable Tim Kelly 27/6/95
91. Royal Commission into Police Corruption, evidence of Detective Sergeant Neville Scullion
92. Royal Commission into Police Corruption, evidence. Scullion claimed he and other detectives only kept $200 each
93. *Who Weekly* interview 5/8/96
94. Gerard Dutton as yet unpublished article written for *Australian Police Journal*
95. Gerard Dutton ibid
96. Evidence of Paul Douglas, *R v Ivan Milat* Supreme Court 1996
97. Phillip Polglase's statement to police 25/5/94
98. Interview Bruce Prior 12/10/96
99. Interview Bruce Prior 12/10/96
100. Interview Bruce Prior 12/10/96
101. Ted Pickering speech to parliament 17/11/94
102. Interview Paul Douglas 16/11/96
103. Interview Des Butler 29/9/96. Except where stated otherwise, all information on pp. 327–9 taken from evidence of Paul Douglas and Des Butler, *R v Ivan Milat* Supreme Court 1996
104. Alex Milat statement to police used in Ivan Milat's pre-committal bail hearing at the central local court
105. Interview Bruce Prior 12/10/96
106. Interview Bruce Prior 12/10/96
107. Neil Mercer, *Fate: Inside the Backpacker Murders Investigation*; Random House; 1997
108. Interview Paul Gordon 30/9/96
109. Evidence from Walter Milat *R v Ivan Milat* Supreme Court 1996
110. Interviews Therese 26/6/96, Mary 4/8/96
111. Interviews Mary 4/8/96, Paul Gordon 30/9/96, Neil Mercer, *Fate* ibid
112. Interviews Paul Gordon 30/9/96, Clive Small 8/5/98
113. Interview Maureen Murray 28/9/96
114. Neil Mercer, *Fate* ibid
115. Police evidence, *R v Ivan Milat* Supreme Court 1996
116. Interview Scott Urquhart 19/9/96
117. Phillip Polglase's statement to police 25/5/94
118. Phillip Polglase's statement to police 25/5/94
119. Interview Lynise Milat 31/8/96
120. Interview Lynise Milat 31/8/96
121. Interview Lynise Milat 31/8/96
122. Evidence Steve Scott, Ivan Milat's committal hearing
123. Interview 'Nick Collins' 3/12/96
124. Interview Gail Polglase 24/4/96
125. Interview Greg Shine 27/9/96
126. Police affidavit to Supreme Court 6/9/95
127. Interview Reg Galati 27/9/96
128. From transcript, Ivan Milat's committal hearing

129. Interviews Mick and Reg Galati 26/9/96, 27/9/96
130. Except where stated otherwise, all information in this chapter direct from court transcripts in the matter *R v Ivan Milat* Supreme Court 1996
131. Interview Paul Onions 22/12/96
132. Information included in Justice Hunt's mid-trial judgements, issued day of jury release
133. Interview Carol Milat 10/12/96
134. Interview Carol Milat 10/12/96
135. Interview Carol Milat 10/12/96
136. Interview Margaret 4/98
137. Interview Lynise Milat 31/8/96

INDEX

Abela, Peter 363–4
Adam, Detective Mick 340
Adriaansen, Anneke 200
'Air' (Eyre) Task Force formed 330
    Air I 405–27
Ambrose, 'Toppy' 149–51, 301, 302, 398, 439, 501
Amy, Paul 202
Anderson, Andrew 56–7
Andrea, Detective Anne Marie 311
Ashton, Peter 451–2
Ashwood, Detective Mick 311
Avery, Commissioner John 321, 366
Ayres, Bill 332–5, 336

Baker, Gill 222, 223, 224
Barnes, Gay 195
Barrett, Steve 200
Basham, Dr Richard 368, 369, 370–1, 401, 402, 426–7, 469
Bearup, Greg 500–1
Beattie, Cathy and Lyndon 167, 169–70, 177, 178
Belanglo Forest 285
    Area A 339–47, 355–7
    bodies found 267–84, 294–7, 303–17, 339–47
    first settled 182
    Ivan shooting in 161–2, 400, 452
    search scaled down 361
Benson, Detective Bob 330, 358, 363, 365, 376, 402–4, 472
Berry, Joanne 195–6, 358, 365, 519
Big Block 166, 425
Bilby, Alan 258
Bilias, Detective Angelo 330
Bishop, Russell 243
Blackmore, Detective Constable Steve 413
Boe, Andrew 451, 465, 471, 496, 497
Borthwick, Don 143, 146, 153, 176, 263, 390–1, 431
Bowral Pistol Club 270, 288, 312, 332, 336

Bracken, David 362
Bracken, Luke 495
Bradbury, Detective Sergeant Bob 104, 105–6
Bradhurst, Dr Peter
    autopsies 270–1, 272–4, 276–8, 314–15, 350–1
    at committal 465
    at murder sites 269, 313, 343, 348–9
    as witness 479
Brame, Superintendent Fred 356–7
Breitkopf, Anne-Marie 163–4, 165
Breitkopf, Rolf 164
Brennan Detective 52, 60
Brown, Barbara 164, 165
Bucton, Detective Constable Keith 60
Burge, Nicola 290
Burgess, Kevin 249–50, 251, 455, 456–7
Burke, Andrew 315
Burns, Fiona 365
Burns, Susan 260–1, 266, 290
Butcher, Peter 201
Butler, Des 246–7, 285–6, 327–9, 330, 367, 374, 431, 448, 485, 511, 519
Butler, Lynn 328, 329–30, 338, 360, 367, 511, 519

Caldwell, Keith 267, 307
Caldwell, Leann 472–3
Campbell, Detective 52
Cantarella, Carmel 33, 35–6
Cantarella, Peter 33, 38, 40
Capogreco, Vince 238, 239
Card, Betty 20, 21, 22, 24, 43, 77
Card, Chris 20
Card, Enid 20
Carroll, Senior Constable David 312
Casata, Jim 35
Casey, Pat 118–19

527

Childs, Archie 39–40, 74–5
Childs, Marilyn *see* Milat, Marilyn
Chong, Norman 364
Cinconze, Jeff 169, 170
Clarke family 447–8, 509
  at funeral 291
  looking for Caroline 256–7, 264–5, 320–1
  told about murder 271–2, 276
  at trial 498, 499
Clarke, Caroline 359
  autopsy 276–8
  background 222–6, 238–41, 243
  found 269–71
  memorial service 290–1
  murder 294–5, 296, 297, 401, 473
  sleeping bag 423
  striped top 421, 427, 464
  tent 240, 423
Clarke, Neville 234–7, 242
Clarke, Ric 202
'Collar' 28, 29, 32
Collins, Diana 217
Collins, Nick 212–14, 215, 216–18, 244–5, 285, 448, 449, 511–12
Coman, Detective Brett 330, 337–8, 360, 366, 377, 404, 425, 432, 434, 435, 456, 457, 502
Connell, Graham 75–6, 78
Cook, Kimbal 121–4
Cooke, Bill 69–70
Corbett, Philip 257–60

Daley, Kevin 359
Dalley, Helen 496–7
Dellsperger, Wendy 199
Dent, Margaret 254–5
Donald, Detective 399–400
Donnolley, Constable Jason 276, 279
Douglas, Jean 98
Douglas, Paul 215, 216, 218, 246, 285, 327–9, 367, 374, 431, 448, 511, 519
Dowton, Detective Bill 304, 307, 336–7
Drake, Glenn 258, 260
Duck family 138, 139
  fire 173, 204

Duck, Jason 143, 144, 148, 157, 158, 166, 204, 400
Duck, Karen *see* Milat, Karen
Duncan, Senior Constable Ray 410
Dutton, Gerard 276–83, 344, 348, 350–1, 355, 360–1, 413, 414, 422, 444–6
Dyer, Craig 287

Edwards, Tania 273
El Hallak, Samir 232
Eldridge, Joan 89, 135
Everist family 185–6, 187, 329, 509–10
  searching 189, 198–200, 202, 302–3
  told about murder 317–18
  at trial 478, 498, 499
Everist, Deborah
  autopsy 316
  background 184, 185–8
  body found 303–17
  murder 195, 350
  sleeping bag 421
Eyre ('Air') Task Force formed 330
  Air I 405–27

Fagan, Dora 98–9
Feeney, Mark 404, 425, 475
Fielder, Constable Allen 90
Forbutt, Senior Constable Peter 410
Foster, Paul 250
Fox, Alan 200

Gagan, Detective Senior Constable Shaun 364–5
Galati, Joe 433–4
Galati, Reg 433, 456, 463, 466, 467, 468
Gibson family 184, 186, 187
  searching 189–90, 198–200, 202, 302–3
  told of murder 313
  at trial 498
Gibson, James
  autopsy 314–15
  background 184–8

backpack found 199–201, 365
body found 303–15
murder 195
Gill, David 383
Godden, Detective Inspector Bob 274–5, 278, 280, 283, 288, 293–4, 299–300, 305, 318, 320, 330, 336, 352–4, 358, 363, 374, 376, 396, 423, 436, 438, 464, 498
Goetz, Bob 447–8
Goldie, Detective Sergeant John 279, 309, 310, 313, 316, 340, 343
Goldthorpe, Noel 223–4
Goodall, Leanne Beth 365–6
Gooley, Pat 100–1
Gordon, Detective Senior Constable Paul 366–8, 371, 372, 373, 374–6, 377, 378, 379, 383, 384–8, 390–2, 400, 411, 413, 416, 418, 436–8, 496, 499–500
Gordon, Detective Sergeant Wayne 405–10
Gorman, Royce 338, 363, 366, 368, 374–5, 376, 404, 411, 425, 432, 434, 435, 436, 456, 457
Gough, Senior Constable Roger 269
Gould, Paul 174, 518
Grafton Maximum Security Prison 64–6, 74, 78
Greta, hitchhiker 85–92, 496, 510
rape trial 134–6
Griffiths, Dr Chris 313, 342, 346–7
Grosse, Senior Constable Andrew 267–8, 269, 270–1, 276–7, 294–5, 309–10, 313, 314, 345, 413, 447
Grunwaldt, Nancy 366

Habschied family
searching 233–7, 241–3, 251–5, 258
Habschied, Anja 344, 355, 356, 357, 359, 370, 479
autopsy 348
background 228, 229–31
found 345–9, 353
Hammond, Detective Sergeant Kevin 332, 336
Harris, Bill *see* Milat, Ivan

Harris, Sarah 258
Hawker, Bruce 198, 359
Hemming, Alex 69, 70
Hilton, Professor John 275
Hiscock, Peter 496, 497
Hitchcock, Ben 224
Holmes, Cate 464, 465
Honeyman, Myrna 260–1, 266, 290
Hreszczuk, Detective Ewhen 330, 367
Hughes, Chalinder 262–3, 264, 301–2, 378, 392–3, 399, 404, 407–8, 410, 411, 442–3, 500, 502, 519
wears Clarke's striped top 421, 427, 464
Hunt, Justice David 471, 476, 492–3, 498–9

Inglese, Senior Constable Steve 316

Jackson, Ross 378–9
Jacoby, Anita 502
Jenolan State Forest 472–4
Jensen, Dr Deborah 225
Jensen, Jean 225, 237, 255–6, 257, 258, 259
Jensen, Nicholas 225
Johnson, Trevor 287

Keeley, Constable Nerida 121–2
Keeling, Detective Barry 200
Kennedy, Les 315, 493
Klaason family 242, 243
Koskinen, Marko 358, 519

Lambert, Lynn 72–3, 77, 111, 114–15
Lapthorne, Stephen 200, 365
Lauer, Commissioner Tony 321, 322, 323, 341, 361, 419
Leach, Detective Steve 330, 363–4, 405, 411, 412, 413, 414, 415–16, 417–18, 452, 498, 502
Lee, John Ronald 365
Lee, Justice 323
Lendrum, Chief Superintendent Dick 104
Lennon, Paul 76

Letcher, Peter David 472–4, 502
Liestins, George 67–8
Lloyd QC, Ian 449–50, 465, 476
Lombardo, Cosmo 76, 144, 248, 436, 452
Lovell, Detective Peter 308–9
Lynch, Detective Inspector Rod 324–5, 359, 363, 364, 365, 375–6, 377, 387, 390, 395, 404, 406, 436, 469, 470, 474, 498, 518

Mangan, Steve 200
Manning, Noel 126
Marcon, Sergeant 262
Margaret (hitchhiker) 85–92, 496, 510
   rape trial 126–34
Maric, Joe 423
Marita 184, 185, 187, 202
Marsden, Jim 431
Marsden, John 431, 438, 495
   asked for by Ivan 419–20
   rape trial 126–36
   represents Mick and John Preston 78, 107, 109–10
   represents Wally 148
   sacked by Ivan 450–1
Martin, Detective Constable Paul 365
Martin, Terry 465, 471, 477, 479–80, 481, 483–6, 489, 490–2
Marukic, Joe 453, 462, 468
Mary (hitchhiker) 379–83
Masters, Chris 341–2, 379
May, Chief Inspector Bob 325, 342
McCloskey, Detective Senior Constable David 366, 376, 377, 399–400
McLennan, Detective Sergeant Steve 269, 271, 274–5, 280, 283–4, 293–4, 299, 311, 320, 376, 464, 472, 473, 493
McMillan, Alister 500–1
Mercer, Neil 501–2
Milat, Alex 38, 40, 124, 507–9, 519
   and backpack 301, 403
   and cars 24
   childhood 12, 14, 15, 16, 18, 21, 22, 24

dreams 82
and guns 14, 17, 24, 144, 165
juvenile crime 25
marries Joan 32
moves to Queensland 301
place searched 425
questioned 402–4, 472
statements 332–8, 369, 386–7, 470–1
as suspect 379, 403
work 31, 56
Milat, Bill (William) 474, 497, 518
   beaten up 37, 38, 40
   caravan searched 425
   and cars 40, 73
   childhood 16, 22, 27, 30
   crime 37–8, 52, 57–9
   girlfriend 77
   goes straight 59
   married 116
   money for Ivan 494
   questioned 404, 432
   at trial 479
Milat, Boris ('Bull') 37, 38, 58–9, 505–6, 512–14
   and cars 25, 42
   childhood 13, 18, 21, 22
   crime 25, 29, 45, 46–8
   drinking 173
   and guns 17, 31, 45
   health 18
   and Lynise 55, 440–1, 442
   meets Marilyn 39–40
   work 50–1, 56
Milat, Carol (née Pritchard) 123, 474–5
   married 116
   money for Ivan 494, 495
   questioned 404, 432,
   as witness 479
Milat, Charlene 42, 174, 440
Milat, Christopher 518
Milat, David ('Bodge') 73, 390, 439, 457–8, 506
   accident 426, 453, 454
   childhood 30
   Ivan doing 'something bad' 251, 434

Qantas hoax 120–4
    and Toppy 149, 150–1
Milat, Debbie 425–6, 494
Milat, George 70, 123, 149, 157, 501
    accident 82, 83
    and cars 73
    childhood 22, 53
    crime 66
Milat, Ivan Robert Marko
    and alcohol 144, 145
    aliases 117–18, 364, 412
    arrest 405–27
    and backpack 301, 403–4
    bail hearing 449–50
    Belanglo Forest, shooting in
        161–2, 400, 452
    body building 66, 117, 126, 145,
        157, 165
    at Boral 217
    bullet hole in car 232–3
    buys house 156–7
    and cars 42, 80–1, 87, 148–9,
        171, 175, 399, 423
    charged with murders 438
    childhood 14, 21, 22, 25, 26,
        27–8, 29, 30, 31, 443
    cleanliness obsession 87, 145,
        148–9, 157–8, 159, 168, 175,
        399, 423
    committal hearing 464–5, 471
    cruelty to animals 162, 175
    and death of father 161–3
    and Duck fire 173, 204
    girlfriends 71, 80
    Glen Innes Forestry Prison Camp
        66
    Grafton Maximum Security
        Prison 64–6, 74, 78
    and guns 31, 35, 40, 45–6, 144,
        148, 158, 159, 162, 165,
        166–7, 175, 177, 217, 219,
        231, 389, 400
    'head on a stick' 150
    and hitchhikers 85–92, 107, 144,
        397
    juvenile crime 29–30, 31, 34–40,
        41, 45
    and knives 150, 158, 163, 175, 176

Maitland Maximum Security
    Prison 500, 502, 503
marriage 160–1
Neighbourhood Watch 159
in New Zealand 115
and Preston gang 99–103, 105–8
rape trial 126–36
and Richardson murder 124
road work 143, 144–5, 152–3,
    176, 178
and sister's death 83, 87
suicide attempts 107, 109
talks about killings 81, 126, 250
theft 46–7, 49–50, 52, 57–8, 59
torching cars 67
trial 476–93, 498
truck driving 138, 143
with Water Board 59, 422
Milat, Jack 9–10
Milat, Joan 32, 82, 124
    given backpack 301, 403
Milat, Karen (née Duck) 138–9, 148,
    378, 507
    Amway sales 163–4
    at committal 464
    ill treatment by Ivan 157–8, 159,
        164–5, 167
    Jason born 143
    marriage 160–1
    move to Blackett 156–7
    questioned 399–400, 436, 452
    sees change in Ivan 161–3
    walks out 168–9, 473
Milat, Lisa 166, 204, 452
Milat, Lynise 174–5, 205, 518
    offer for story 501–2
    parentage 54–5, 56, 79, 137,
        512
Milat, Margaret Elizabeth (née
    Piddlesden) 140, 141, 231
    axe incident 15–16
    health 37–8, 40–1, 42, 116,
        124–5, 439, 506–7
    house searched 426
    and innocence of sons 28, 30, 38,
        40, 41, 44, 53, 59, 60, 61–2,
        75, 107, 136, 500
    motherhood 12–26, 28, 30

Milat, Margaret Maria 23, 50, 73
    killed 82, 83
Milat, Marilyn (née Childs) 510–11
    and Ivan 40, 50–1, 53, 54–6, 63, 64, 67–9, 74–5, 79, 81, 84, 124–5, 137, 173, 174–6, 204, 205, 519
    Ivan's arrest 439–40
    offer for story 501–2
    pregnant 40, 53
    remarried 205
    split with Boris 174
Milat, Mary 13, 33
Milat, Maureen (née Parsons) 72–4, 77, 124, 146–7, 148, 495, 514
    and Ivan 79–80, 81, 111, 141–3, 203–5
    marriage 112, 115, 116
    pregnant 114–16
    questioned 387–8
    separation from Wally 153–5, 157, 203
Milat, Michael 17, 38, 52, 69–70, 126, 391, 514–15
    assault 75–6, 77–8, 226
    and cars 97
    married to Sherie 204
    in Preston gang 92–103, 105–8
    trial 109–10, 112, 113
Milat, Patsy 149
Milat, Paul Thomas 41, 50, 73
Milat, Pelly 10, 11
Milat, Richard James 26, 118, 378, 398, 495, 519
    at Boral 212–18, 285–6
    comment about Germans 247, 367
    has crossbow 246
    and guns 246, 451–2
    and Liz 302
    marijuana 161, 244–6
    Onions suspect 385
    Paul Miller alias 244–7
    and Polglase 287, 434–5, 453–4, 468
    property searched 423–4, 446
    retains Marsden 451
    talks about killings 218, 247, 285, 327–8, 367

theft 146–7, 156
    Wombeyan Caves road property 166–7, 216
Milat, Robert 115, 116, 141, 142, 154, 155, 204, 205
Milat, Sherie 204
Milat, Steven
    death 161
    drinking 17–18, 24, 34, 156
    labouring 11–16, 23–4
    market gardening 16–23
    Moorebank 19–26
    politics 10, 20, 138
    punishment by 18, 21–2, 23, 24, 28, 42, 53, 59–60
    Rossmore 16–18
    and television 31, 60, 151
Milat, Susan 141, 142, 154, 155, 204, 205
Milat, Wally 22, 73, 77, 141–2, 203, 500–1
    accident 166, 390
    accused 479–80, 481–2
    goes straight 148
    and guns 148, 154–5, 158, 216, 451–2
    and marijuana 216, 217
    married 115, 116
    in prison 114, 115–16
    retains Marsden 451
    on roads 155–6
    search of property 423, 424, 446
    separation from Maureen 153–5, 157, 203
    theft 146–8, 519
    Wombeyan Caves road property 166–7, 216
Milat's Mountain 166, 425
Miller, Detective Gary 311, 472, 473
Miller, Paul *see* Milat, Richard
Miller's Mountain 216, 285
Milos, Sajner 472
Milton, Dr Rod 293–9, 368–9, 371, 401–2, 406, 409, 427, 469
Mohr, Marie 290–1
Morri, Mark 497–8
Muller, Jeanette 207, 208

Murphy, Detective Stephen 308–9, 310, 318–19
Murphy, Doris 207, 208
Murphy, Kristine 206, 207

Needham, Mark 123, 139
Neugebauer family 515–16
    searching 233–7, 241–4, 251–5, 303
    told of murder 352–5
    at trial 478–9
Neugebauer, Gabor 359, 461–2
    autopsy 350–1
    background 226, 227–31
    found 345–9
Newall, Detective 52
Nicholson, Constable Janet 196, 359, 385
Nicola, Katrina and Peter 99
Noble, Detective Sergeant Tony 260, 271
Norman, Hilda 157–8, 162–3, 167–8, 178
'Novak, Stephen' 147–8

O'Brien, Justice Jack 126–36
O'Connor, Detective Senior Constable Peter 413, 414, 415, 422, 481
O'Keefe, Detective Mick 269
O'Malley, Peter and Rita 242
Onda, Naoka 243, 261
Onions, Paul ('Bunny') 358, 461, 516–7
    attack on 190–8, 402
    at committal hearing 464
    reaction to experience 201–2, 289–90
    and reward 516, 519
    shirt found 426
    tells story 359–60, 365, 384–5, 394–7, 432, 436
    at trial 477–8, 479, 489
Original Backpackers Hostel, Sydney 221, 235–6

Palmer, Terry 145, 152, 153, 162, 163, 168–9, 172, 173, 176, 263, 264, 450

Parsons, Jenny 160, 161, 262–3
Parsons, Johnny 42, 49–50, 51, 52, 53, 262–3
Parsons, Maureen *see* Milat, Maureen
Pember, Eileen 92–5
Pember, Eric 33, 92, 114
Pember, John 92–5, 97, 101–2, 107, 113, 114
Pennacchio, Dianne 283–4, 474
Pfanner, Bill 286
Pickering, Detective Graeme 395
Piddlesden, Lillian 10, 14, 16, 18, 24, 161
Piddlesden, Margaret Elizabeth *see* Milat, Margaret Elizabeth
Piddlesden, Stanley Gordon 10–11, 12, 16
Piddlesden, Shirley ('Big Shirl') 24
Pittaway, Jock 364, 412
Polglase, Gail 432, 433, 453–6, 462, 463, 466–7, 469, 514
Polglase, Mick 466, 467, 468
Polglase, Phil 118, 124
    and committal 465–6
    dead 466–8
    and Ivan's knife 250
    questioned 455
    statement 432–5
    wired 457–61, 497, 519
Pope, Michelle 200, 365
Post, Geoff 117–18, 124
Powch, John 98–103, 104–6, 112, 113, 114, 126, 509
Preston gang 92–108, 113
Preston, Dave 75, 92, 96, 108, 114
Preston, Johnny 75, 77–8, 92–103, 106–8, 112, 113, 114, 226, 509
Price, Michael 464
Prior, Detective Superintendent Ian 360
Pritchard, Carol *see* Milat, Carol
Pryor, Bruce 303–10, 315, 318–19, 336–7, 372–3
Purcell, Detective Senior Constable Leo 70, 71

Rayner, Detective Sergeant Dennis 90, 91

Reid, Pauline 220–1, 248, 259–60
Rich, Harry 122
Richardson, Bronwyn 124
Roberts, Detective Sergeant Tony 379, 402–4
Roberts, Senior Constable Suzanne 269
Rochester, Mick 434
Roulis, George and Tina 102–3
Rullis, Senior Constable Martin 340

Sara, Tony 388–9
Savvas, George 503
Schiels, Senior Constable Roger 316
Schmidl family
　searching 209–11
　told of murder 342–3
　at trial 479
Schmidl, Simone 261, 355, 359, 402, 412
　autopsy 344–5
　background 205–8
　backpack 301, 403–4, 424
　found 339–44
　sleeping bag 421
　tent 415
　water bottle 207, 422
Schuster, Cindy 209
Scott, Steve 245–6, 448
Scullion, Detective Sergeant Neville 259, 261, 268, 481
Shine, Greg 455, 463, 466
Shipsey, Henry ('Hank') 23, 502, 518
Shipsey, Olga (née Milat, aka Diane) 82, 502
　childhood 12, 15, 16, 18, 21, 22–3
　and Ivan's arrest 439
Siely, Keith 267, 307
Sierlis, Tim 458
Sing, Alan 258
Sissons, Katherine 186, 187, 188, 189
Sisterson, Dennis 248
Small, Superintendent Clive 321–6, 336, 338, 340–1, 342, 344, 347, 349, 356, 361, 363, 364, 365, 366, 368, 369, 370–1, 375–7, 379, 384, 387, 390, 397, 400–1, 402, 405, 406, 419–20, 435–6, 437, 446, 470, 496, 497, 498, 511, 518
Smee, Norman 23, 31
Smith, Detective Keith 269
Smith, Liz 217–18, 246, 302, 423
Soire, Gerhard 50, 203–4
Soire, Shirley (née Milat) 155, 422, 480, 502, 518
　builds house with Ivan 264, 412, 474
　and Chalinder 262, 464
　childhood 14
　divorced 203–4
　marriage 50
　money for Ivan 494–5
　at trial 450, 490
　work 33–4
Springett, John 307–8, 310, 315

Tanner QC, Leon 127–36
Tedeschi QC, Mark 474, 476–7, 479, 480, 482, 486–8, 489–90
Therese (hitchhiker) 379–83
Thompson, Chris 167, 399
Thomson, Billie Marie 453, 462, 468
Tomasello, Ernie 57–8
Trichter, Sergeant Jeffrey 339–40
Tsimiklis, Janice 224, 225
Tunnicliffe, Nina 224, 248
Tunstall, Detective 104, 105

Urquhart, Scott 124, 139, 140, 149, 150, 301, 398, 439, 501

Wallace, Jeanette 209
Walters family 280
　searching 255–6, 257, 259, 261, 264–6, 287, 359
　told of murder 272, 276, 278–9
　at trial 479, 498, 499
Walters, Joanne 359, 369
　autopsy 272–4
　background 220–2, 224–5, 237–8, 239–41, 243
　found 267–9
　memorial service 290–1
　murder 295, 296, 297

sleeping bag 423
T-shirt 268, 479
Ward, David 138
Ward, Sharon 138
Waterman, Detective Senior Constable Andy 330, 424, 498, 518
Wharton, Simon 224–5, 260
Wild, Noel 165, 219, 233, 264, 388, 391–3

Wilkins, Detective Stuart 330, 394–6, 402–4, 424, 464
Wilson, Mark 187, 188
Wilson, Stephanie 187–8
Winter, Paul 61
Worley, Detective Senior Constable Ian 112
Wright, Steve 240, 248–9, 423

Young, Bob 369, 371